FOR REFERENCE

Do Not Take From This Room

American River College Library
4700 College Oak Drive
Sacramento, CA 95841

COMEDY

COMEDY

A Geographic and Historical Guide

VOLUME II

Edited by Maurice Charney

PRAEGER

Westport, Connecticut
London

Library of Congress Cataloging-in-Publication Data

Comedy : a geographic and historical guide / edited by Maurice Charney.
    v. cm.
    Includes bibliographical references and index.
    Contents: Academic humor / Paul Schlueter—African American comedians / Frank J. Miles—African American humor / John W. Lowe—African film comedy / Carina Yervasi—American drama since 1975 / Richard Brucher—American film / Leo Charney—American Jewish humor / James D. Bloom—American literature in the nineteenth century / Susan Welsh—American political cartoons and comics / Kalman Goldstein—Animation / Kirsten Thompson—Arthurian romance / Andrew Welsh—Black comedy / Benjamin Nathan Schachtman—British contemporary comedy / David Hawkes—Canadian comedy / Gerald Lynch—Children's humor / Kathryn Douglas—Commedia dell' arte / Frances K. Barasch—English comedy, Elizabethan and Jacobean / Naomi Conn Liebler—English comedy, restoration and Augustan / John Richetti—English comedy, Victorian / Heather L. Braun—Farce / Norman R. Shapiro—French contemporary comedy / Alyson Waters—French drama in the 17th century / Philip Koch—German comedy / Bettina Brandt—Greek comedy / Mary C. English—Irish comedy / James M. Cahalan—Irony / Don L. F. Nilsen and Alleen Pace Nilsen—Italian comedy / Nina da Vinci Nichols—Middle English comedy, Andrew Welsh—Native American trickster tales / Arnold Krupat—The philosophy of humor / Adrian Bardon—Queer comedy / Ken Feil—Roman comedy / Maurice Charney—The romantic period / William Galperin—Satire / Harry Keyishian—Shakespeare's comedies and romances / Margaret Mikesell—Spanish comedy / Nina Gerassi-Navarro and Raquel Medina-Bañón—Stand up comedy / Lawrence E. Mintz—Television sitcoms / Leo Charney.
    ISBN 0–313–32706–8 ((set) : alk. paper)—ISBN 0–313–32714–9 ((vol. 1) : alk. paper)—ISBN 0–313–32715–7 ((vol. 2) : alk. paper) 1. Wit and humor—History and criticism. 2. Comedy—History and criticism. I. Charney, Maurice.
PN6147.C565 2005
809'.7—dc22   2005008410

British Library Cataloguing in Publication Data is available.

Copyright © 2005 by Maurice Charney

All rights reserved. No portion of this book may be reproduced, by any process or technique, without the express written consent of the publisher.

Library of Congress Catalog Card Number: 2005008410
ISBN: 0–313–32706–8 (set)
    0–313–32714–9 (vol. I)
    0–313–32715–7 (vol. II)

First published in 2005

Praeger Publishers, 88 Post Road West, Westport CT 06881
An imprint of Greenwood Publishing Group, Inc.
www.praeger.com

Printed in the United States of America

The paper used in this book complies with the Permanent Paper Standard issued by the National Information Standards Organization (Z39.48–1984).

10 9 8 7 6 5 4 3 2 1

Contents

	Introduction	1

VOLUME I

1.	Academic Humor *Paul Schlueter*	9
2.	African American Comedians *Frank J. Miles*	24
3.	African American Humor *John W. Lowe*	34
4.	African Film *Carina Yervasi*	48
5.	American Drama since 1975 *Richard Brucher*	62
6.	American Film *Leo Charney*	78
7.	American Jewish Humor *James D. Bloom*	93
8.	American Literature in the Nineteenth Century *Susan Welsh*	106
9.	American Political Cartoons and Comics *Kalman Goldstein*	121

10.	Animation *Kirsten Thompson*	135
11.	Arthurian Romance *Andrew Welsh*	153
12.	Black Comedy *Benjamin Nathan Schachtman*	167
13.	British Contemporary Comedy *David Hawkes*	185
14.	Canadian Comedy *Gerald Lynch*	199
15.	Children's Humor *Kathryn Douglas*	214
16.	*Commedia dell'Arte* *Frances K. Barasch*	233
17.	English Comedy, Elizabethan and Jacobean *Naomi Conn Liebler*	248
18.	English Comedy, Restoration and Augustan *John Richetti*	263
19.	English Comedy, Victorian *Heather L. Braun*	280
20.	Farce *Norman R. Shapiro*	296
21.	French Contemporary Comedy *Alyson Waters*	314

VOLUME II

22.	French Drama in the Seventeenth Century *Philip Koch*	331
23.	German Comedy *Bettina Brandt*	350
24.	Greek Comedy *Mary C. English*	363
25.	Irish Comedy *James M. Cahalan*	380

26.	Irony *Don L. F. Nilsen and Alleen Pace Nilsen*	394
27.	Italian Comedy *Nina daVinci Nichols*	410
28.	Middle English Comedy *Andrew Welsh*	429
29.	Native American Trickster Tales *Arnold Krupat*	447
30.	The Philosophy of Humor *Adrian Bardon*	462
31.	Queer Comedy *Ken Feil*	477
32.	Roman Comedy *Maurice Charney*	493
33.	The Romantic Period *William Galperin*	512
34.	Satire *Harry Keyishian*	528
35.	Shakespeare's Comedies and Romances *Margaret Mikesell*	542
36.	Spanish Comedy *Nina Gerassi-Navarro and Raquel Medina-Bañón*	560
37.	Stand-Up Comedy *Lawrence E. Mintz*	575
38.	Television Sitcoms *Leo Charney*	586
Glossary		601
Index		649
About the Editor and Contributors		657

22

French Drama in the Seventeenth Century

Philip Koch

When, in the last two decades of the fifteenth century, Charles VIII and then Louis XII sent royal armies over the Alps into Italy, these kings of France surely had no idea of the durable consequences they were setting in motion. These were not a permanent expansion of national borders, for whatever Italian territories Charles and Louis managed to retain after initial successes were irretrievably lost in the reigns (1515–1559) of their Valois successors, Francis I and Henri II. No, the deep, the lasting effects of the Italian campaigns were nothing less than a cultural revolution better known as the French Renaissance. Simply put, instead of conquering, France was *conquered* by what it found in that envied land, and enthusiastically set about emulating it. It was in imitation of Italian palazzi that many of the fabled châteaux along the Loire River (e.g., Chambord) and elsewhere (e.g., Fontainebleau) were built, often with the assistance of Italian artists such as Francesco Primaticcio. Indeed, the greatest of them all, Leonardo da Vinci, was not only lured to France by Francis I; he died there (in Francis' arms, according to legend) and lies buried in some still undiscovered French grave. What is true for architecture is also true for everything from style of clothing to behavior, the latter best illustrated by the effect of Baldesar Castiglione's *Libro del cortegiano* (*Book of the Courtier*). First published in 1528 it was translated into French but nine years later (in 1537) and quickly, permanently affected the manners of nobles and cultured bourgeois well into the seventeenth century and beyond.

Although the preceding instances clearly suggest a preponderant influence of Italy on France, they shed small light on the specific nature of that influence. In short, what makes it the *R*enaissance, what was being *re*born, *re*awakened, *re*discovered in fifteenth- and sixteenth-century Italy, then shared by it with the rest of Europe, France included? The answer, as we all know, is a new, deeper awareness of and respect for Greek and Roman antiquity. However, that awareness, that respect did not result in a slavish copying of ancient models but rather in their adaptation to contemporary needs and values. Literature provides an insight into this adaptive process, and no genre more sharply than vernacular comedy, which arose in the first years of the sixteenth century through writers such as Ludovico Ariosto. At the very beginning of his first comedy, *La Cassaria* (*The Strong-Box*, 1508), does not Ariosto's prologue proudly declaim: "A new kind of comedy I present to you full / Of multiple artifices that neither Roman / Nor Greek tongues ever recited on stage"? And Ariosto's "multiple artifices" do, in fact, create a complex plot that would have been inconceivable for Plautus and Terence, from whom this Renaissance Italian author borrowed extensively. The starting point is traditionally "ancient" (i.e., two young men, Erofilo and Caridoro, enamored of two slave girls whose owner, Lucrano, requires for them a price much higher than the lovers can pay), but the happy ending—and comedies *must* have happy endings—is prepared by so many subterfuges, including transfers from hand to hand of the title's strong-box, that not one but two clever servants, Volpino and Fulcio (rather than the slave one would expect in Greco-Roman comedies), are necessary to carry them off successfully.

Ariosto's *Cassaria* should thus make it abundantly obvious that originality did not have the same meaning for the Renaissance—and the seventeenth century—as it does for us. What was original then included the *new* way writers mixed preexisting stock elements (in this case, the initial situation of the lovers plus the slave trader) into complications of their own invention. Another example is Niccolò Machiavelli's justly famous *La Mandragola* (*The Mandrake*), composed about 1518, which illustrates a somewhat different combination of new and old. Here, the author's original plot, reminiscent of the lusty Italian novella from Boccaccio on, pits the young lover Callimaco, eager to bed pretty young Monna Lucrezia, against her dimwitted, old husband Messer Nicia. Need one add that Callimaco gains his desired ends thanks to a trick, involving the mandrake plant, that is carried out by Callimaco and his associates, Ligurio and Fra Timoteo? Despite appearances, there are classical aspects to this play as well: prologue and epilogue, the five acts that contemporary theory maintained were obligatory in "regular" theater, and the presence of the ubiquitous classical parasite, Ligurio in this instance. *La Mandragola* prompts an additional remark. Fra (Brother!) Timoteo, so essential to Lucrezia's seduction, is a man of the cloth and in that capacity represents Machiavelli's satiric commentary on social corruption of his day. These kinds of Renaissance Italian comedy, always set in a contemporary world inhabited by types familiar to the audience, would seem to take particular delight in dealing with flaws in society and, even more, with brazen sexuality. Not so another variety of Italian comedy, the *favola boscareccia,* or pastoral, which firmly rejects the two foci of raw sex and society.

The pastoral, too, is normally, though not always, set in sixteenth-century Italy. Torquato Tasso's *Aminta* (1573) takes place in the country near Ferrara; Battista Guarini's tragicomedy *Il Pastor fido* (*The Faithful Shepherd*, 1589) in ancient Arcadia. In either case, the setting is really a timeless, idealized world of elegant shepherds and sheperdesses who seem to have no cares beyond hunting, lamenting, and lovemaking. Herein lies the nucleus of an even greater difference from the previous types of comedies. In the works of Ariosto, Machiavelli, and their emulators, on the one hand, love is reduced to carnal satisfactions offered to clever males who overcome the external obstacles represented by blocking characters (e.g., unscrupulous slave traders, old husbands), and in such contests the woman passively accepts being the prize. In pastoral, on the other hand, she is an equal and at first reluctant partner who must ultimately give her consent to male pursuit for there to be a happy ending. In brief, this kind of comedy has the potential of being highly psychological (i.e., the obstacles to contentment exist *within* the protagonists rather than deriving from an external blocking force, and the ensuing anguish can be depicted with ever-increasing intensity right up to the resolution), although sixteenth-century usage tended to make the plays descriptive, static, and elegiac, in imitation of their ancient lyric models like Hesiod and Theocritus.

Despite important differences, the varieties of Italian plays discussed to this point do have one thing in common: they belong to a general category frequently labeled "scripted comedy," precisely because they were written down—as opposed to an *improvised* comedy universally known as *commedia dell'arte*. *Commedia* improvisation is not synonymous with uncontrolled spontaneity, however, for, though they will certainly differ from one performance to the next, such plays remain faithful to carefully detailed outlines or scenarios, collections of which are still preserved today. What the scenarios reveal is a free recourse to all three types of scripted comedy: winning the girl of one's desires, stealing another's wife, and pastoral flight/pursuit. The peculiar originality of *commedia* lies in the introduction into the basic plot of numerous coarse skits, or *lazzi*, that could be verbal (one of the many Italian dialects, puns, malapropisms), physical (slapstick, pratfalls, general acrobatics), or both. A successful *commedia* production was, therefore, an ensemble effort that depended on professional actors for whom playing the role they were assigned would be second nature, a requirement that in turn explains why *commedia* actors and actresses concentrated on one part during their careers. The roles fall into three general categories: old or grotesque men (e.g., Pantalone, Doctor Graziano, the braggart Capitano) who might serve as rivals, inadequate elderly husbands, or parents refusing to approve their children's marriages; the young lovers male and female (all sorts of appealing names); male servants who help the young lovers adeptly (e.g., Crispino, Scappino) or bunglingly (e.g., Arlecchino, Pulcinella) together with a clever, equally helpful soubrette with names such as Colombina. Why actors to fill these parts suddenly appeared at this juncture remains an insoluble mystery, but beginning roughly in the mid-sixteenth century there is clear evidence of their activity in Italy, where they formed temporary companies traveling the peninsula and later sallying forth into foreign lands—among them France some time after 1570.

The French Renaissance, thus, had the examples both of printed plays and live performances on which to base a national comedy, yet the results were slow in coming and somewhat disappointing in number. As late as 1549, Joachim Du Bellay's famous literary manifesto, *The Defense and Illustration of the French Language*, makes two points of interest to us here: following Greek, Latin, *and* Italian models is the only way to lift French literature out of its current medieval mediocrity; to date, France has produced no comedy (or tragedy). And indeed, another three years passed before the first comic exemplar: Etienne Jodelle's *L'Eugène*, which out-Machiavellis Machiavelli. Eugène, the title character, is a churchman who is lusting for Guillaume's wife, Alix, and who decides furthermore to offer his sister to the soldier Florimond as a way out of personal danger. Despite the apparent success of *L'Eugène*, between 1552 and 1574 no more than ten French comedies were written, from 1575 to 1588 perhaps three times that number saw the light of day, and, subsequently, there were none at all until well into the next century. Reasons for this meager production are not hard to find.

In addition to stageworthy works, three more requirements must be met: actors to play the parts, an audience to be enchanted, and boards on which to stride. None of these was fully developed in sixteenth-century France. National actors were all amateurs (as they were in Italy originally), students for the most part, and audiences in limited numbers assembled on irregular and special occasions, such as academic exercises or courtly celebrations. In view of the infrequency and unpredictability of theatrical spectacles, not to mention the select public they drew, it is understandable that intimate venues (e.g., a university space, a ballroom or dining room in a royal or a noble palace) would be preferable to—and less costly than—a formal theater, though one did exist in Paris, in a building called the Hôtel de Bourgogne. There is one final reason for the paucity of comedy in the French Renaissance, a historical one that reinforces the other three. After the untimely death of Henri II in 1559, a period of civil war in France began, made all the more bloody and cruel for its religious nature. The protracted struggle between French Huguenots and Catholics would not end until the final coronation in 1594 of Henri IV, the first of the Bourbon monarchs. In the horrors of this brutal conflict there was little time or taste for the distractions of theater.

With the return of peace and economic reconstruction came as well a new fervor for dramatic art, and all the pieces that were wanting in the previous periods somehow fell into place. Just as inexplicably as in Italy some fifty years earlier, suddenly French-speaking acting troupes arose that began touring the country, and the Hôtel de Bourgogne in turn began renting its stage to them when they passed through Paris because there was now an audience regular enough to make its use financially attractive. In the 1620s, a troupe settled into more or less permanent residence at the Hôtel and was soon confronted by a second one on a rival stage, the Théâtre du Marais. The repertoire of these professional French actors did not include comedies at first; the public seemed to demand gory tragedies and tragicomedies fraught with perils for hero and heroine, a leftover of the earlier internecine wars, no doubt. But comedy would revive at last and with some vigor during the same 1620s, in particular after 1624, when Cardinal Richelieu becomes Louis XIII's prime minister in a resurgent national government and when there came of age a new generation of playwrights, foremost among whom is Pierre Corneille (1606–1684).

Although Corneille is best known as a tragic poet, except for his second play, the wild, exuberant tragicomedy *Clitandre* (1630), his remaining five early works are all comedies: *Mélite* (1629), *La Veuve* (The Widow, 1631 or 1633), *La Galerie du Palais* (The Palais Arcades, between 1631 and 1634), *La Suivante* (The Lady-in-Waiting, 1634) and *La Place Royale* (1634). By the 1644–1645 theatrical season, there would be three more, Corneille's last, interspersed in his ever-growing tragic production: *L'Illusion comique* (*The Comic Illusion*, 1636), *Le Menteur* (*The Liar*, 1642 or 1643), and *La Suite du Menteur* (The Continuation [Return?] of the Liar, 1643, 1644, or 1645). All eight comedies were well received by the contemporary public, so much so that, in the *Discours*, or critical introduction, to volume 1 of the three-volume collective edition of his plays in 1660, Corneille was moved to reflect on the reasons for their success, particularly in the case of the first two by a fledgling writer. "The novelty of a very pleasing kind of comedy, and that had not till then appeared in the theater" is the only explanation, he writes (1:71. All English translations in this chapter are the author's). While we may accept Corneille's remark on the newness of his comedies at face value, we will get no closer to understanding the precise nature of this "*nouveauté*" unless we turn to the plays themselves, initially to the first three as a group.

When, in an early scene of *Mélite*, Eraste, the long attentive but unsuccessful suitor of Mélite, introduces his friend Tircis to his beloved, the inevitable occurs: the two new acquaintants fall immediately in love, and the jealous Eraste vows vengeance. Revenge will consist of convincing the lover of Tircis' sister, through forged letters, that Mélite is deeply smitten with the charms of this fickle character, appropriately named Philandre. Informed falsely of Mélite's "infidelity," Tircis exits to die of grief while our heroine faints *dead* away on hearing of her lover's resolve, and Eraste goes literally mad with remorse. Eraste's madness in turn reveals the truth to the lovers, who are quite alive, and the play ends with promises of marriage between (1) Tircis and Mélite and (2) Tircis' sister and the now chastened Eraste. As for Philandre, he loses everything, but, after all, he deserves his punishment, does not he? A rather similar situation obtains in *La Veuve*. Philiste, as persistant as *Mélite*'s Eraste, has been courting the widow Clarice for some time but with greater prospects of success. Philiste and Clarice love each other, but he is too timid to declare his affection openly, for she is much wealthier than he. There is also a second couple, Alcidon and Philiste's sister (yes, another sister), but this is only a pseudocouple. Alcidon really has designs on Clarice, and, when he is convinced he cannot win her, he resolves to abduct her and does so. Fortunately for all concerned, he enlists the assistance of a friend, Célidan, who is clever enough to penetrate the spurious motives alleged by Alcidon for the kidnapping, and he returns Clarice to her lover. As his reward, Célidan will receive the hand of Philiste's sister, for whom he had been yearning all along. No surprise: Alcidon will be odd man out, once more for good, moral reasons.

Though the outcome will be the same (conjugal bliss foretold), the plot is structured rather differently in *La Galerie du Palais*. As Corneille himself observed in the *Examen*, or critical evaluation, appended to the play (as to all the others in the three-volume 1660 edition of his theater): "[Unlike that of the first two comedies] the fifth act [here] . . . results in two marriages without leaving anyone disappointed" (*Théâtre* 1: 239). In other words, rather than five, there will be only four people in love: Célidée, whose affection for Lysandre has been approved by her father at the play's outset, and Hippolyte, whose beauty catches the eye of Dorimont while they are shopping in the Arcades of the Palais. Comic tension in this initial pairing, which will also be the final one, derives from the affection Hippolyte secretly harbors for Lysandre, her best friend's galant, and from the tricks she invents, with the help of servants, to disunite the two lovers. At first successful, her efforts will ultimately fail, and a chastened Hippolyte will accept the hand of Dorimont.

This rapid (and superficial) examination of Corneille's first three comedies should make abundantly clear what creates their basic originality: they derive from the *pastoral* tradition. Like their inspiration, these three plays, and those that follow, deal *exclusively* with love's effects on young adults without the intervention of an older, blocking generation that constituted the frame for Renaissance nonbucolic comedies. These effects of love can be highly emotional. Pastorals, Cornelian comedies too, contain many intense duets between lovers or those who would be: scenes of harmony, pleading, grief at separation, sorrow of rejection, disdain, and mockery, to which Corneille adds charming scenes of coy declaration between young people who have just met. As in pastorals, his plays also choose for protagonists normally between three and five principal characters who seem to have nothing better to do than to talk of and experience love. Yet there are significant differences between the pastoral model and Corneille's use thereof. Rather than in an atemporal, idealized pastoral golden age, Corneille chose to set his comedies squarely in contemporary France. The Arcades of the Palais de Justice, for example, linked the courthouse to the Sainte Chapelle and, during the seventeenth century, also provided a home to many small shops, such as the ones that allowed

Dorimont to glimpse Hippolyte for the first time. The Place Royale was another landmark of the day where elegant people would stroll, one that still exists today under the name of the Place des Vosges. Even when Corneille does not use place names for titles, constant allusions to cities (Paris, where most of the plays take place, Bordeaux, Lyon), sections (the Marais), promenades (the Tuileries), and buildings (the Hôtel de Bourgogne) anchor his works in the real world.

There is a similar realism in the protagonists, for, as Corneille notes in his address to the "Gentle Reader" of *La Veuve*: "Comedy is but a portrait of our acts and our words, and the perfection of portraits resides in their resemblance. On this principle, I try to put in the mouths of my characters only what in their place would likely say those whom my actors represent and to have the latter speak like well-bred people [*honnêtes gens*]" (*Théâtre* 1: 154). These *honnêtes gens*, male and female, who correspond to the pastoral shepherds and shepherdesses, are clearly recognizable as people of their time, though hardly commoners. They belong rather to a well educated, witty, rich, but idle society, as evidenced by the brilliant conversation to which they devote their time. Given the propensity of the men to draw their swords in defense of their honor, "gay blades" in the strictest sense, everything points, further, to their membership in the warrior class of French nobility. Now we understand better perhaps why, according to Corneille, an *honnête homme* may not steal like a highwayman nor kill in cold blood, though it is quite excusable to do in a rival in the heat of passion (the *Discours* to vol. 2, 1660 edition)! Further insight into contemporary morality is offered by the continued recourse to trickery by both men and women in the comedies to win the affections of the beloved. After all, "*en fait d'amour la fraude est légitime*" ("in matters of love deception is legitimate"), opines contented Mélite at the end of her play (*Théâtre* 1: 76).

Clearly, the concept of love in the early seventeenth century is not quite ours in the twenty-first. Youth can still subscribe to the underpinning of that concept, a neo-Platonism first introduced by the fifteenth-century Italian humanist Marsilio Ficino, as aptly summarized by Isabelle in *L'Illusion comique*: "[Heaven] unites here below through a mutual attraction / The souls that its decrees have up above destined for each other" (*Théâtre* 1: 529). Such a theory explains why two rather imprecise terms are frequently used by the enamored characters to justify their affections: the *je ne sais quoi* (the "certain something") that absolutely defies definition and *le mérite* ("merit") by which promise of superior skill or performance thereof neutralizes limited discrepancies in social position. The reason Philiste is so timid in courting Widow Clarice is his relative poverty compared with her wealth. Indeed, the latter would seem to be a factor of her mérite in his eyes (just as his je ne sais quoi and assiduousness add to his appeal for her). A material consideration of this kind does not debase Philiste's feelings—by the standards of the day at least—for there is another aspect to falling in love. Reason must consent *freely* to the emotion before it can take hold, or as Corneille wrote in the dedicatory letter of *La Place Royale*, "The love of a gentleman [*honnête homme*] must be always willed [*volontaire*]" (*Théâtre* 1: 383). Nor, hard as it may be for the modern reader to conceive, does this self-determined love lack feeling and intensity for the characters involved. In any case, it is simply a pastime, a passionate *game* to engage idle, youthful minds until the serious, practical business of life (marriage, family, career) take over. Seen from this perspective Cornelian comedy assumes its underlying function of provoking a gentle, perhaps even wistful smile.

There is, moreover, in these love comedies a less charming side that Corneille made no effort to hide: their tendency to sacrifice the second female lead, sister or friend, by forcing her to marry whoever makes the happy ending possible for the principals. This "sacrifical expedient" helps explain why the *seconda amorosa* invariably appears as frivolous and coquettish: it is apparently a defense mechanism to assuage the disappointment of imposed unions. Listen to this excerpt from the plaintive monologue in *La Veuve* of "light-hearted" Doris, Philiste's sister, reflecting on selection of a husband: "[Oh,] cruel servitude! strange tyranny! / All freedom of choice is denied me! / . . . However, we are talking about the rest of my life, / And I dare not consult ever so slightly my own wishes" (*Théâtre* 1: 216). For that matter, Doris' mother, too, will allude briefly elsewhere in the play to her own forced separation from the man she loved in her youth. (Can their own often imposed marriages add credibility to the facility with which Cornelian parents approve the love unions of their offspring?) In addition to the subdued social criticism implied in these secondary figures, the first three comedies reveal an aesthetic weakness in the plays: the inherent interchangeability of all the lovers, male in particular. They are so bland and similar, for the most part, that no telling reason exists to justify one's success and another's failure. In his remaining comedies, Corneille is patently seeking a way out of dull predictability.

The next play, *La Suivante*, innovates, in fact, by manipulating the pastoral plot. We are dealing again with five love leads, three men and two women, but in a new configuration. Though the *prima amorosa*, Daphnis, in appearance has only one suitor, she has actually two more (for a total of *three*): Florame and Théante, who feign to court Daphnis' lady-in-waiting, Amarante, only to gain access to her mistress. (Amarante thus has none!) What is more, Florame, Théante, and Amarante are each aware of the subterfuges of the other two and propose to outwit them. Trickery, *la fraude*, is therefore everywhere but, in a sense, nowhere, because of an agreement between Daphnis' father and Florame, the only one Daphnis really loves. In exchange for Daphnis' hand, Florame barters away his sister, who has aroused the lust of the old man. (*Seven* love leads now?) Since this deal remains a secret, Amarante and Théante keep up their own deceptive but baseless lies, with the result that everyone is confused by conflicting assertions about the state of affairs and no one discovers the operative truth until almost the end of act 5, where the secret understanding is finally revealed to all. Thus can the happy ending occur for Daphnis and Florame as well as for her father and the invisible sister of Florame, but for no one else in this sparkling example of a fast-paced, supercharged comedy of errors.

With *La Place Royale*, we move from error to character study in the person of Alidor. Though passionately loved by sweet, constant Angélique, he is unhappy because their attachment is stronger than his free will, his *honnête* ideal of "liberty within love's chains" (*Théâtre* 1: 393). Given this tension and his comic inability to act on his principles of freedom, Alidor opts to make Angélique leave him for his friend Cléandre, who has just confessed his love for her. Alidor will attain his objective by means of an intentionally intercepted, false love letter he will pretend to write another woman. Since the plan backfires (Angélique agrees to marry a third candidate for her hand), Alidor woos her once again, and they agree to commit the seventeenth-century crime of elopement. In fact, Alidor plans to let Cléandre carry out the act, but, in a magnificent "night act," Cléandre abducts the wrong woman, whom he will eventually marry, the only wedding in this skewed pastoral. Disabused and contrite, Angélique will enter a convent, while Alidor gloats that no one will get the woman he loved and left—a strange pastoral, indeed, that stretches the genre to the limit.

The last two comedies composed by Corneille deal with a character as unusual as Alidor: Dorante the liar, suggested respectively to Corneille by two Spanish plays: Juan Ruiz de Alarcón y Mendoza's *La verdad sospechosa* (Truth Uncertain) and Lope Félix de Vega Carpio's *Amar sin saber a quien* (Loving without Knowing Who). In the first, *Le Menteur*, a young Dorante, just returned to Paris from law school, falls in love with Clarice, wrongly identified as her friend Lucrèce, an error that creates the crux of the play. Will Dorante become engaged to the real Clarice as his father desires? Will he thus become the rival of his friend Alcippe? What will happen when he learns the truth about the mistaken identities? These are merely some of the questions that challenge Dorante's resourcefulness, his penchant for prevarication, before the amazed eyes of his valet Cliton—and the audience's. Indeed, Dorante's talent is so "heroic" that, unlike Alarcon's ultimate punishment of this sinner, Corneille rewards the young man by having him fall in love at the end with the true Lucrèce he must marry, while Alcippe gains the hand of Clarice in another even-numbered pastoral.

Alas, Dorante's new rectitude is short-lived; *La Suite du Menteur* reveals that he abandoned his fiancée Lucrèce and Paris when he realized that he was too young to be bound in marriage (shades of Alidor!). Now older and more mature, he finds himself in Lyon and once more obliged to lie, this time to protect the life of an unknown *honnête homme*, a more honorable, or at least venial, application of his special talent. When the indebted gentleman urges his sister, Mélisse, to befriend Dorante, she pushes her "duty" to the point of becoming his beloved. The working out of this reciprocal affection occupies most of the first four acts and is rather unusual for a pastoral. There are no rivals to speak of, just a growing attraction between the lovers, a situation strangely approaching what will make Marivaux famous in the next century—down to the use of the *double registre*, in the present case, an embryonic courtship between the servants Cliton and Lyse mimicking their masters'. But all this will change in act 5 when a struggle between love and duty arises with the tardy interjection of Philiste, a newly revealed rival to whom Dorante owes a moral debt. Despite the anguish, everything will work out happily—after Philiste's "generous" renunciation of all claim to Mélisse's hand, an ending reminiscent of Auguste's unexpected clemency in Corneille's *Cinna* (1640). Obviously, our playwright could no longer be fully satisfied with a comic vision.

There were already traces of the tragic muse in the Angélique of *La Place Royale*; its presence is even clearer in *L'Illusion comique* that Corneille called "*un étrange monstre*" ("a strange monster") in the dedicatory letter to this play (*Théâtre* 1: 502). Though it is an exaggeration to call it "monstrous," *L'Illusion* is definitely strange (in the sense of unusual): "The first act is only a prologue; the three successive ones form an imperfect comedy, the final one is a tragedy: and all that sewn together makes up a comedy." Corneille's description is quite accurate in this further passage of the dedicatory letter, except for his remarks on act 1, which are incomplete. It is certainly a prologue introducing the magician Alcandre and Clindor's father, Pridamant, whom Alcandre promises to show what has happened to Clindor since the father's severity chased him from home ten years before. However, since Alcandre and Pridamant reappear at the end of each subsequent act (plus the beginning of act 5) to comment on the events witnessed, they serve, more accurately, as a frame to the rest of the play. What they witness in acts 2–4 is, as Corneille observed, a comedy, a basically pastoral one in which Clindor competes successfully against two rivals (three on one again) for the affections of Isabelle. One of them, Capitano Matamore, is inconsequential. He is there only to provoke laughter at his preposterous vainglory; the other, favored by Isabelle's father, will be eliminated when Clindor slays him in the heat of passion. Sentenced to death, Clindor will escape from prison thanks to Isabelle's maid, who seduces the jailor.

With the flight of the two women, Clindor, and the jailor, act 4 ends, and, when act 5 begins, we seem to see events that followed their escape. Now in fabled England(!), Clindor has won the trust of the prince and become a person of rank, as has his wife Isabelle. Alas, Clindor has not abandoned his philandering ways (in the "comic" middle three acts, he had been flirting with Isabelle's maid) and is murdered by the jealous prince, just as Isabelle's love has convinced Clindor to change. Though old Pridamant is understandably distraught at his son's untimely end, Alcandre appears unconcerned, and when Pridamant utters a discreet reproach, the magician reveals what he had inadvertently (?) failed to make clear: Clindor and his associates have never been to England; in fact, they are living in Paris, where they became actors. What Pridamant saw in act 5 was simply the tragedy Clindor's troupe is performing at the moment, and *L'Illusion* ends with Alcandre's eloquent defense of contemporary theater. Thus, what Pridamant and the audience with him have witnessed is a tragic play *within* a comic play of which Alcandre is the director, all *within* a strange monster of which Corneille is the author. It would truly be difficult to find a work more infused with the spirit of the baroque than *L'Illusion comique*, and one is free to wonder what Corneille's baroque mind, so fond of *la fraude*, would have invented still if a new mindset had not gradually imposed itself in the course of Louis XIV's reign (1643–1715): French classicism, most admirably illustrated by Molière.

Except for a common interest in dramatic art and a generally congenial acquaintance (so congenial that, pressed for time, Molière could persuade Corneille to flesh out practically all of the last four acts of *Psyché*, his 1671 rendition of the Psyche-Eros legend), these two playwrights show more differences than similarities. It is not so much a question of age, though, sixteen years his senior, Corneille did belong to an earlier generation than Jean-Baptiste Poquelin (1622–1673), alias Molière, and outlived him by eleven years; rather, major divergences appear in their relationship to the theater. To begin with, Corneille was a financially comfortable man of letters composing plays in the tranquillity of his study. On the contrary, Poquelin was directly involved in the stage from his twenty-first year, when he joined a short-lived, unsuccessful Paris troupe, the Illustre Théâtre (1643–1645), first as an actor and soon, it would seem, as its director—while acquiring, with equal speed, the still unexplained stage name of Molière. After the financial collapse of the Illustre Théâtre, for Molière and some loyal colleagues there began a period of seasoning and wandering in southern France that lasted until a triumphal return to Paris (1658) when Molière and friends succeed in pleasing the king. His pleasure was so great that Molière's troupe received Louis XIV's approval to share the stage of the Palais-Royal alternately with a company of Italian actors to whom Molière ever referred as his "good friends." Yes, in addition to the Hôtel de Bourgogne and the Marais, Paris could boast, from midcentury on, a third officially sanctioned company, but of *commedia* actors improvising in Italian, to which was joined a fourth that would, in 1665, receive the royal privilege of calling itself La troupe du Roi.

Once the soon-to-be King's Troupe settled in Paris, Molière added to his roles of actor and director that of playwright, for all of his plays were written between 1659 and 1673, except for the two (perhaps four) he composed during his years of wandering. In this compositional domain, we again find differences between our two authors. Where Corneille experimented in all current genres (comedy, tragicomedy, tragedy, and machine plays), Molière restricted himself to comedy alone—if we may discount his signal failure in the realm of "serious" theater: *Dom Garcie de Navarre* (1661). And these comedies come in all sizes: one-acters, presented at the end of a performance as a kind of light-hearted encore; three acts, in the *commedia* manner; and five acts, the requisite length of "regular" French plays, the only kind for Corneille. Moliéresque plays also display a wider range in comic mode. Though most of them fit the external-obstacle pattern pitting young lovers against blocking types (rarely, however, for the favors of a married woman as in *Tartuffe* and *Amphitryon*), we also find both the occasional coarse farce and a goodly number of pastorals written primarily as court entertainments in the earlier style of languishing shepherds and maids. In all his plays, Molière assumed but once the lover's role: as Dom Garcie de Navarre, a failure that may have convinced him to abandon not only serious plays but also romantic leads. At any rate, there is no further example of his playing a part other than that of the adjuvant servant or the blocking object of ridicule.

There is one more important comparison to be drawn between the two authors, this time in relation to the number of plays written and the time required to write them. Their total production is basically the same (thirty-two for Corneille; thirty-two, perhaps thirty-four, in the case of Molière), but here the convergence ends. It took Corneille forty-five years to complete his theatrical canon (1629–1674); for Molière, a mere fourteen were required (1659–1673)—if we exclude the two (or four) plays he brought with him from the provinces. Thus, where Corneille strikes us as having proceeded at a leisurely, reflective pace, Molière must have lived constantly under the gun (think of *Psyché*, more Corneille's than his)—as the many signs of haste in his plays amply attest. Even in a day when using someone else's plot as a springboard for one's own was not considered a lack of originality, the frequence of Molière's debt to predecessors (Latin, Italian, Spanish, or French) is striking. Nor would he hesitate, for lack of anything better, to present a series of discrete scenes held together by the flimsiest of motives (e.g., *Les Fâcheux* of 1661, where comic spoilsports, or *fâcheux*, one after another simply delay Eraste's rendezvous with his beloved). And when his plots reached the denouement, Molière was not above offering most contrived resolutions: far-fetched recognition scenes or a deus ex machina. Aside from Molière's admissions of pressure (e.g., the five days acknowledged to concoct *and* stage in 1665 *L'Amour médecin* [*Love's the Best Doctor*]), the clearest proof of haste is the prose of so many of his plays, for the age's convention expected substantial plays to be in verse. All of Corneille's were; Molière did not always have time to rhyme.

Perhaps the most serious consequence of Molière's harried creativity is the absence of a fully developed personal aesthetic (similar to Corneille's *Discours*) that might help in a selection of his plays, for space limitations make choice a necessity. Fortunately, Molière did leave enough scattered remarks for us to piece together a coherent comic theory. In the dedication of *Les Fâcheux*, his very first royal entertainment, he speaks, for example, of his delight in contributing to Louis XIV's amusement, *divertissement*. It is possible to extend the concept of amusing (*divertir*) beyond the king to audiences in general and maintain that entertainment looms large in most of Molière's plays, where it often bears a striking resemblance to the *lazzi* of his good Italian friends: pratfalls, slaps, regional dialects, the French tongue rent by foreign speakers, simply funny sounds. (Curiously, Corneille's first *Discours* similarly makes *divertir*, or its equivalent, *plaire*, the primary goal of comedy, though surely not on such a low level.) By 1663, however, a broader comic theory suggests itself when a character of *L'Impromptu de Versailles* (The Versailles Impromptu) asserts that "the object of comedy is to represent in general all the faults [*défauts*] of man, and principally of man in our century" (1: 564). This new attitude crystallizes even further in the first petition to the king concerning *Tartuffe* (1664): "The duty of Comedy [is] to improve [*corriger*] man while entertaining [*divertissant*] him" (1: 686). Molière here assumes the posture, so typical in French classicism, of *moraliste*, or writer interested in describing socially good and bad behavior. It is the comedies of this Molière, his "major" ones, that thus form the object of the ensuing analyses—with the clear understanding that there are also many other excellent comedies that are "merely" amusing, entertaining, and that Molière continued to write these as well right up to the end of his career—and life. These major comedies, eight in number, require two final remarks: (1) their plots oscillate between the love conflicts and the special social "fault" of the blocking character, and (2) Molière always took the latter part, except for *Dom Juan*, where he reverted to the servant role he assumed in the "minor" plays.

The social *défaut* to which Molière turns first, in *L'Ecole des femmes* (*The School for Wives*) of 1662, is the traditional fear of being cuckolded, as personified by Arnolphe, a wealthy, old bourgeois of forty-two. This fear prompts Arnolphe not only to mock all the cuckolds he knows but also to raise an indigent child, Agnès, in total ignorance so that he may marry an innocent who, he boasts, can but "Pray God, love me, sew and spin". Nature, however, is stronger than Arnolphe's best-laid plans, for during his latest absence Agnès met and fell in love with young Horace, as she sweetly confesses to a horrified Arnolphe, who resolves to be on his guard. His plans are abetted by favorable chance: Horace is the son of one of Arnolphe's old friends, and on this basis Horace reveals his secret plottings to his unsuspecting rival. Horace's regularly foiled attempts to contact Agnès constitute the comedy's *lazzi*-laden action, which might have culminated in Arnolphe's ultimate victory were it not for one of Molière's patented contrived denouements. Agnès is not the poor peasant's daughter Arnolphe believed her to be, but the offspring of a gentleman newly returned from abroad with a fortune who had—again by chance—already made arrangements for Agnès to wed Horace.

Hypocrisy becomes the next object of Molière's attention in *Tartuffe*, which took him five years of struggle to perform (1664–1669), for the hypocrisy chosen was a particularly sensitive one at the time: religious mummery represented, in the final version (there were at least two earlier ones), by the lay spiritual adviser Tartuffe. Tartuffe is not, however, the blocking character; he is, rather, the corrupting influence on the latter, Orgon, who is so taken in by Tartuffe's unctuousness that he disowns his son, makes Tartuffe his sole heir, and betroths his unwilling daughter, Mariane, to this evil man. Since Mariane has a more acceptable suitor and rival, *Tartuffe* qualifies as an obstacle play. Indeed, it does so on another, purely Renaissance, ground as well: Tartuffe lusts for Orgon's second, presumably young wife Elmire, who skilfully leads Tartuffe into an open confession of his hypocritical prurience while Orgon hides under the table (a *lazzo*, if ever there was one). Orgon's blindness, a prominent motif, is now ended, but, since Tartuffe, recently made Orgon's sole heir, also holds compromising documents of his benefactor, catastrophe would ensue without the intervention of Louis XIV, a supreme, all-seeing deus ex machina, who forgives Orgon and has scoundrelly Tartuffe arrested. This ending is also Molière's gesture of gratitude to the king by whose authority the comedy was ultimately staged in 1669.

While striving to win permission for *Tartuffe*, Molière wrote his most problematic work, *Dom Juan* (1665)—problematic because it is absolutely devoid of unity and clear purpose. At best, it could be described as a suite of fragments, in the manner of *Les Fâcheux*, that form a kind of *Rake's Progress*, particularly since both William Hogarth and Molière were dealing with the corruption of a libertine, though there is no progress in Molière's case—until the end, that is. The first four acts reveal *coexisting* aspects of Dom Juan's character: in act 1, the unfaithful husband; the busy seducer in act 2; the humane and noble freethinker in act 3; the man-about-town in act 4 who will not pay debts and mocks his father. Then, in act 5, occurs a sudden transformation of Dom Juan, who will unflinchingly meet his eternal damnation at the hands of the Commander's statue. It is this late and seemingly arbitrary transformation that gives the play its probable meaning, for in act 5 Dom Juan becomes a religious hypocrite, thereby enjoying a fashionable vice. Molière appears to be aiming at the pious persecutors of *Tartuffe* by showing that no significant difference exists between them and freethinkers, an amalgamation that may leave modern readers uneasy who find much to admire in the Dom Juan of the first four acts—and Molière might have, too, if questioned off the record. Serious problems of interpretation these, but Dom Juan's fearful, abject servant Sganarelle (Molière's part) was there to entertain and deflect critical judgment.

In an odd way, *Le Misanthrope* (1666) forms a trilogy with the two preceding plays in that it studies the extreme opposite of hypocrisy: absolute sincerity, the vice from which misanthropic Alceste suffers. He cannot abide masking truth by politeness, and he is at war with society for its compromises. This conflict is worked out in a plot almost as unsubstantial as *Dom Juan*'s—unless one views it as a skewed pastoral. Alceste loves the young coquette Célimène, and he selects this day to make her announce to which man she is really attracted: Alceste or one of his three rivals: Oronte, a courtier with unjustified poetic pretensions, plus Acaste and Clitandre, foppish marquises (three vehicles for social satire). Once it is revealed that Célimène ridicules all of them behind their backs, the three rivals depart self-righteously. Only Alceste remains, but when Célimène declines to join him in fleeing Parisian society, he too stalks off, thereby leaving what we might call the second love leads, Philinte and Eliante, as the sole (pastorally) happy couple left on stage.

By its antifeminist bias, Molière's penultimate play, *Les Femmes savantes* (*The Learned Ladies*, 1672) is today probably even more difficult to appreciate in its historical context than *Dom Juan*; yet there is no question, this time, of the author's point of view. The full-blown salon activity of the classical age had pushed women's intellectual expectations to the point of considering the distaff rôle as beneath their dignity, thus provoking Molière's outburst. In fact, the satirical focus of the play is precisely a salon, presided over by Philaminte, one of her daughters, and her sister-in-law, as well as the fatuous literary circle these three attract. The wrong-headed female influence goes even further, for Philaminte completely dominates her henpecked husband, Chrysale (a circumstance vaguely reminiscent of Tartuffe's control of Orgon) to the extent of insisting on the marriage of her other daughter, Henriette, to the salon's star Trissotin (*tri* in French meaning "thrice" and *sot*, "foolish"). Since Henriette already has a more personable suitor, one approved by timid Chrysale, *Les Femmes savantes* easily qualifies as a conflict play, one enhanced by a battle of the sexes. It is doubtful the "good" side would have won without a subterfuge, invented by Chrysale's brother, proving Trissotin was interested only in the family's money. And we do not know if Chrysale will ever free himself of Philaminte's domination.

In addition to the "unnatural" pretensions of women, Molière was also troubled by contemporary movement in the social order resulting from the growing influence of new wealth. Was not love of money becoming too important? *L'Avare* (*The Miser*, 1668) was at least a partial response to his question. Harpagon, the Miser, is overly fascinated by the acquisition *and* retention of wealth, as Molière shows in discrete episode after episode: Harpagon refusing to spend money on clothing and receptions, Harpagon the heartless usurer, Harpagon on the verge of madness when his buried treasure is stolen. However, the most surprising is sixty-year-old Harpagon in love, but a necessary Harpagon for there to be a love conflict: between father and son, for Mariane, just as there will be a conflict between young Valère, disguised as a servant of Harpagon to be near his daughter, and elderly Anselme, chosen by Harpagon for her. Two contrived events bring about the happy ending of this primarily social satire: the theft of Harpagon's strongbox by his son's servant (plus the ensuing extortion), the discovery that Mariane and Valère are really Anselme's children.

An even lighter, equally fragmented treatment is used in *Le Bourgeois gentilhomme* (*The Would-Be Gentleman*, 1670) to comment on the social mobility that money expects to buy. Hence the paradox, more clearly expressed in the French title: a member of the prosperous middle class, M. Jourdain (a *bourgeois*), who would become a noble (a *gentilhomme*). It simply cannot be done, and as a consequence M. Jourdain will be pitilessly victimized by every other character in the comedy, from the various teachers who try vainly (and abjectly) to educate him to his wife and serving maid, who constantly ridicule him. Why, even the young lover, Cléonte, easily gets the better of Jourdain, who will accept only a noble son-in-law—by pretending, in a meaningless "Turkish" gibberish, to be the son of the Grand Turk eager to marry the bourgeois' daughter once the father undergoes a (fabricated) Turkish initiation that will confer on him the "noble" title of *Mamamouchi*. It is the outlandish spoof of this *Cérémonie Turque* that constitutes the high point and raison d'être of the play, a grand royal entertainment.

Molière's last play, *Le Malade imaginaire* (*The Imaginary Invalid*, 1673) was intended as another entertainment for the king though never performed at court by the author. This time, the comic butt, Argan, will suffer from a double défaut: the hypchondria of the title and domination by a scheming second wife, Béline, who ingratiates herself even more by coddling her "sick" husband (in effect, a female Tartuffe). Scholastic, bookish medicine, the only kind known then in France, thus becomes the focus of Molière's ridicule, to the point that pompous, vapid *Dr*. Thomas Diafoirus, recent university graduate, is chosen by Argan to marry his older daughter, already in love with a more eligible rival. Both pressures on the *malade imaginaire* will simply melt away at the end when (1) pretending to be dead, Argan discovers how repulsed Béline really is by her foul-smelling, well-purged "invalid" husband, and (2) he becomes his own doctor in a final musical-comedy ceremony that bestows the medical degree on him after a satirical oral exam in macaronic Latin. This light-hearted denouement, which presumably will also allow the daughter to marry whom she would, bears with it an exceptional irony: during the ceremony in the fourth performance (February 17, 1673), Molière-Argan, far from an imaginary invalid himself, was stricken by an attack of his recurrent pulmonary illness; he died several hours later. Thus was the world deprived prematurely of further comic inventions from this brilliant mind.

To return to an earlier observation, precisely how did Molière expect his social comedies to "improve [*corriger*] man"? Surely, the mere identification and portrayal of certain human défauts in the plays, whether the main or incidental focus, are part of the answer—but only part. These comedies contain one or more calm, rather marginal characters, called *raisonneurs*, who witness, comment on, and, in the best of cases, gently participate in the events of the play. The consummate examples of this type are Eliante and, especially, Philinte of *Le Misanthrope*, the only characters to attain the rewards of love, while the most questionable case has to be Sganarelle, whose cowardice and inarticulateness increase the ambiguity of *Dom Juan*. Whatever the degree of participation, their primary function is to criticize the attitudes of the misguided blocking characters by means of sententious remarks, *sententiae*, reflecting the age's common wisdom. First of these beliefs is the importance of nature, whether curing sickness or reserving true love for the young only. More striking is the concept of the golden mean, of moderation, expressed insistently by one raisonneur after the other: Chrysalde in *L'Ecole des femmes*—"In this as in all [other matters] one must avoid extremes"; Philinte in *Le Misanthrope*—"Perfect reason avoids all extremes"; and so on and so forth. The significance of this Moliéresque leitmotif is that it epitomizes the French classical version of the self-restrained honnête homme—as contrasted with Corneille's earlier version, where a rationally sanctioned impetuosity triumphs.

Guided by the raisonneurs, not to mention the palpable folly of the warped characters, Molière's spectators become honnêtes, moderate, simply by laughing at the plays' targets. As Molière noted with extraordinary insight in his preface to *Tartuffe*: "An outstanding way to undermine [human] vices is to expose them to the mockery of everyone.... People are quite willing to be bad but not ridiculous" (1: 682–83). If the audience is "improved" (*corrigé*) in this manner, the same cannot be said of the characters Molière singles out for ridicule. Far from being changed for the better, they are at the denouement exactly what they were at the outset. Indeed, they remain forever so firmly locked, by Molière's genius, into the types he designed them to illustrate that, by a stylistic process called antonomasia, their names become synonyms of their character flaws. Such might be the case for "Don Juan" to mean a philanderer, but can this figurative use be definitely ascribed to Molière when, to name but one, Mozart's *Don Giovanni* is in contention? Other examples are less problematic and have long functioned as a kind of cultured shorthand in the French language. Pride of place belongs to Tartuffe (hypocrite) who can also boast an abstract noun for hypocrisy: *la tartufferie*. He is closely followed by Alceste (uncompromising truthfulness), Arnolphe (brutish love), Harpagon (unbridled avarice), Célimène (coquetry), Philaminte (female pretentiousness), and so forth. Antonomasia has even affected sympathetic characters such as Agnès (innocence with natural strength of character), perhaps Philinte (whose "golden" reasonableness you are free to like *or* dislike). We may say, however, even more about the power of Molière.

At the end of the justly unsuccessful *Dom Garcie de Navarre* (1661), a play dealing with the repetitive fits of jealousy Dom Garcie displays if his beloved merely looks at another man, the gentle woman forgives him for the nth time with these strangely prophetic words: "I see, Prince, I see that a certain indulgence is owed / To the faults [*défauts*] toward which Heaven's influence inclines [us]" (1: 341). Her words appear strangely prophetic in that they foreshadow the indulgence Molière himself often demonstrates toward the grotesque butts of his mockery by suddenly revealing unsuspected complexity of character. (This indulgence is less apparent in *Le Bourgeois gentilhomme* and *Le Malade imaginaire*, royal entertainments where psychological depth was not expected, than in the six other plays.) The difficulty experienced in interpreting Dom Juan's behavior immediately comes to mind, but there are other, clearer examples.

For one, Arnophe (*L'Ecole des femmes*) claims he will marry a girl he arrogantly thinks he has made into little more than a Helot, but, confronted finally with an emancipated Agnès, he desperately offers to allow her the freedom to behave *any* way she wants, if only she consents to marry him. His love for her is deeper than he had imagined, and as she abandons him for Horace, Arnophe's parting word is a simple "Oh!" to which only the most accomplished actor can do justice. Two more examples, Alceste and Célimène, come from *Le Misanthrope*. His défaut is peculiar; it is an excess (i.e., beyond the golden mean), but it is an excess of what is good! Even the two models of moderation, Eliante and Philinte, have affection for and admire him. Ambiguity could not be greater. It exists in his relation to Célimène as well. This man, the epitome of sincerity, loves a coquette, the antithesis of what he values, and at the denouement, when her insincerity has been proven by letters she wrote, he alone forgives her provided she will leave with him. Célimène declines, but in the process displays a similarly unsuspected complexity of character when she explains: "Solitude [on your country estate] is frightening to a twenty-year old" (2: 109). Stripped bare now of all coquettish bravado, Célimène suddenly appears as a vulnerable, insecure girl who needs the flattering attention of men to assure her of her worth. It is not uncommon for great comic authors to capture the spirit of their age (witness Corneille), but few are they who, like Molière, can rise to the heights of such indulgent humanity.

It must be obvious that Corneille and Molière did not exist in a literary vacuum, that they were surrounded—and succeeded—by many gifted comic authors about whom something must be said. If we turn first to Corneille's generation, when it all began, it is surely no surprise to learn that the pastoral model reigned supreme. Not only were the successes of the Italian *Aminta* and *Pastor fido* fresh in the young playwrights' minds; they had, as well, constantly before their eyes a voluminous, best-selling French novel of the day to inspire them: Honoré d'Urfé's *Astrée* (five parts, 1607–1627) relating the *mis*adventures of shepherd Céladon and shepherdess Astrée (along with innumerable others) in their endlessly frustrated attempts to reunite. No doubt of filiation to the *Astrée* exists in the case of *Les Bergeries* (The Shepherds' Life, 1619–1625?) by Racan (Honorat de Bueil, Marquis de, 1589–1670), for both works are set in a pseudopagan Gaul, presumably in the same fifth century c.e., though in different parts of that fictitiously bucolic land. Both works underline, furthermore, the inherent limitations of the unmixed pastoral mode by embellishing it. After all, how many original psychological (internal) motives can there be justifying initial antagonism between lovers that will resolve itself eventually into perfect bliss? Racan's solution is both external and double in his five-protagonist comedy: (1) introduce a *fraude*, or treachery, that will also eliminate the villain from the happy ending (as Corneille would do), and (2) continue postponing the remaining lovers' potential happiness by repeated reference to an ambiguous oracle whose true, joyful meaning becomes clear only at the denouement—in the best baroque tradition.

Another credible dramatic tension lay in contaminating the pastoral with swashbuckling, novelistic adventures (e.g., sword fights, magic, royalty, pirates), in the manner of *Astrée*. In fact, Jean de Mairet (1604–1686) was so carried away by this blending he described the subtitles of two of his plays (one of which, the 1630 *Silvanire*, he admits derives from *Astrée*) as "*pastoral* tragi-comedies" (emphasis added). In other cases, the contamination is so integrated that, even if the play is called a comedy, the genre distinction is often blurred—as in the "comic" *Belle Alphrède* (Beautiful Alfreda, 1636) by Jean Rotrou (1609–1650), arguably the century's fourth greatest playwright after Corneille, Racine, and Molière. In this dizzyingly paced baroque work, the audience is transported (1) to the Barbary Coast, where a *pregnant* Alphrède, disguised as a valiant swordsman to further her secret pursuit of a faithless lover, vanquishes the local Arab pirates after her shipwreck, and (2) to storied London, where she succeeds in regaining her man's tender affections. Thus can Rotrou offer, in separate locales, a tragicomedy and a pastoral, truly a "strange monster" in a vein similar to Corneille's *Illusion comique* of the same year.

The scene of the preceding comedies, whether ancient Gaul, North Africa, or England is hardly recognizable. These locations are simply exotic pretexts for events that do not relate to a specific place—or time, for that matter. Such is not the case for an unusual play by Jean de Mairet, a true and brilliant comedy called *Les Galanteries du duc d'Ossonne* (The Duke d'Osuna's Dalliances, 1632) dealing with a real person, recently deceased (1624), who was, from 1616 to 1620, Spanish viceroy of Naples, where the play unfolds. More to the point, the *Galanteries* is a pastoral turned inside out. Instead of languishing for their beloved, the duke and his three companions are interested only in temporary, sensual pleasures to satisfy which these four would not hesitate to betray one another. Such hanky-panky might be tolerated in Naples, but certainly not in the Paris and environs to which a modernized, domesticated pastoral migrated in the 1630s. In addition to Corneille's comedies, we have the pleasant example of *Les Vendanges de Suresne* (Grape Harvesting in Suresnes, 1633 or 1634) by Pierre Du Ryer (1605–1658), where wealthy Dorimène is finally allowed to marry her preferred but impoverished suitor (after he acquires a good inheritance) and to reject a rival for whom she cares not at all. Realistic touches, such as the bourgeois preoccupation with money or summering in suburban Suresnes by the well-heeled, add to the special charm of *Les Vendanges*.

With the 1640s and 1650s another contaminating fount for the pastoral mode developed with a new vogue for Spanish sources, of which Corneille's *Menteur* and *Suite du Menteur* are merely the most memorable examples. Beyond the 1630 derring-do, this Hispanic influence adds a generally more focalized reliance on foreign setting (Spain), intensity of passion, a stringent honor code, serenades—and a hapless comic servant called the *gracioso*, a new trend most strikingly represented by Paul Scarron (1610–1660). Though the passionate love plot is present in Scarron's comedies, it is overwhelmed by constant gracioso shenanigans, witness his *Dom Japhet d'Arménie* (1651 or 1652). Here the principal character is Dom Japhet, a mad court jester convinced of his (nonexistent) noble origins who is mocked and victimized by the rest of the cast as he tries unsuccessfully to supplant a more suitable rival for possession (literally) of the fair maid. By his presence Japhet introduces a literary parody of the play's love element, a kind of parody the French call *burlesque* for which Scarron is justly famous.

Parody and burlesque can also be vehicles of a social satire one rarely finds in the love-oriented comedies of the 1630s and 1640s, except perhaps for *Les Visionnaires* (The Dreamers, 1637) of Jean Desmarets de Saint-Sorlin (1595?–1676) and *Le Pédant joué* (The Pedant Fooled, 1645 or 1646) by Savinien de Cyrano de Bergerac (1619–1655). Both plays mock current intellectual excesses, *Les Visionnaires* taking aim at foibles like erudite poetry or an all-consuming infatuation with theater, *Le Pédant* obviously excoriating pedantry. In such plays, the love plot matters little, be it pastoral or external-obstacle; the primary objective is to hold up the chosen social vice to ridicule. No one did this better than Jean Racine (1639–1699) in *Les Plaideurs* (*The Litigants*, 1668), which derides mercilessly those French who would bring even minor disputes to trial and the judges who preside over them. Racine was so successful because, perfectly fluent in Greek, he was intimately familiar with Aristophanes, whose *Wasps*, with its trial of a dog for stealing a cheese, is the starting point of Racine's hilarious satire—but only the starting point. Besides the Aristophanic dog trial (riotously expanded by Racine) and the house arrest of the senile, monomaniacal judge by his son, Racine introduced two unforgettable litigants, as mad as the old jurist, and a minor love plot with external obstacle, additions made to further his original, never executed plan to offer the play to the Comédiens Italiens (thus their three-act structure). This work is so arresting (for its mirthful poetry, too) one wonders what Racine might have accomplished had he turned again from his powerful tragic muse to that of comedy. Of course, he did not, and besides, he was treading on the ground of social comedy that Molière had already made his own.

Comedy in the 1660s belonged to Molière, who dwarfed all competition, this Molière who, though surely not alone responsible for setting the dramatic action in contemporary France, can yet take major credit for widening the focus of comic analysis beyond the tribulations of young galants and their loves. Indeed, after his disappearance in 1673, he continued to exert incalculable influence not only on his immediate successors but also on the subsequent course of Parisian theater history. Not long after his death, what remained of Molière's troupe was joined, by royal decree, with the Théâtre du Marais (1673), and only seven years later Louis XIV further satisfied his absolutist centralizing impulses by ordering the fusion of that troupe with the Hôtel de Bourgogne to form the Comédie Française. As of 1680, then, there were but two theaters in Paris: the Comédie Italienne, which began, curiously, to perform plays in French at about the same time, and the Comédie Française, which to this day continues alternately to be called *La Maison de Molière* (Molière's House). More to the point, however, is the undeniable effect he had on comedy as a genre. During the eleven-year period 1689–1700, three times as many comedies (one-, three-, and five-act works combined) were produced in Paris as tragedies, an astounding growth. Further, unlike the "nobler" tragic genre, comedies tended now to be in prose, with the notable exception of the late ones by Jean-François Regnard (1655–1709). Using prose, as mentioned earlier, was a compromise to which hard-pressed Molière frequently resorted, a compromise his late-century disciples eagerly aped—not to mention his indifference to carefully crafted plots. We find, as well, that many of these comic authors resembled Molière in being simultaneously actors, foremost among them the prolific Florent Carton, sieur Dancourt (1661–1725), who penned some sixty-seven titles, for the most part casually assembled one-act works referred to as *dancourades*.

Whatever their length, quite striking in these end-of-century comedies are the constancy with which they make France, particularly Paris, the locus of action and, above all, the effort to create a social typology—in imitation of the master. How often do we find in the titles the categorizing definite article *le, la, l', les* (think of <u>Le</u> *Misanthrope*, <u>Les</u> *Femmes savantes* by Molière): <u>La</u> *Veuve à la mode* (*The Fashionable Widow*, 1677), by Jean Donneau de Visé (1638?–1710); <u>L'</u> *Homme à bonne fortune* (*The Ladies' Man*, 1686), by another actor-playwright, Michel Baron (1653–1729); <u>Le</u> *Chevalier à la mode* (*The Man of Fashion*, 1687), by Dancourt and the obscure M. de Sainctyon (?–

1723); *Le Joueur* (*The Gamester*, 1696), by Regnard. There is, however, another kind of social comedy in which Molière did not indulge and that may, therefore, be considered an original contribution of these late writers: takeoffs on current events, especially juicy scandals. Such is *La Devineresse* (The Fortune-Teller, 1679) by Pierre Corneille's much younger brother Thomas (1625–1709) and Donneau de Visé (1638?–1710), an unmasking of sham magical practices vaguely prompted by *l'affaire des poisons*, a horrible case of poisonings, love potions, abortions, and black masses involving some of the most illustrious French nobility. Such are, as well, so many slap-dash, cleverly dialogued *dancourades*: *La Désolation des joueuses* (The Lady Gamblers' Sorrow, 1687), based on a recent royal ordinance forbidding certain popular card games, and *L'Eté des coquettes* (The Coquettes' Summer, 1690), dealing with the lengths to which frivolous ladies must go to amuse themselves in the summertime while "real" men are supposedly away at war.

There is yet a greater innovation than topicality in the plays of the post-Molière era; the very intent of comedy was transformed. Over and over we are struck now by the cynicism, the moral indifference in all these works. In *Le Chevalier à la mode*, for example, a down-and-out chevalier has been courting three women at the same time in the hope of making a financially suitable marriage, but unmasked by two of them, he settles on the third *provisionally*, as the play's last words (his) make quite clear: "Let's continue to flatter her till I happen on better fortune" (*Théâtre XVIIe* 3:424). In *Le Joueur*, we have a kind of pastoral in that Valère is torn between love for Angélique and an almost personified gambling. Convinced at last that Valère will never change, she leaves him for a more responsible man (the even-numbered pattern), while Valère tranquilly accepts his fate with the final remark: "Well, well, let's console ourselves, Hector [his valet]; and some day / Gambling will compensate me for love's losses" (*Théâtre XVIIe* 3:811). These two heroes(?) are not only unchanged and unrepentant; they go unpunished. Others will be *rewarded* for their knavery—as in Regnard's last and very best comedy, *Le Légataire universel* (The Sole Heir, 1708), where penniless Eraste must have his dying bachelor uncle name him sole heir to win the girl he claims at least to love. To succeed, he must eliminate the other relatives and even find a way to forge his uncle's will when the latter appears to have expired prematurely. (He has not, and therein lies a further complication.) Nevertheless, the outcome will be most felicitous for Eraste, thanks largely to the help of his alert, inventive adjuvants at swindling, Crispin and Lisette, in this cleverest of external-obstacle plays with its dialogic pyrotechnics.

We should not dig too deep under the surface brilliance of *Le Légataire*, however, for the only moral bedrock we will find is Lisette's *sententia*, "We must by our wit create our own destiny" (*Théâtre XVIIe* 3:916). What a far cry, in all these late comedies, from Molière's wish to improve (*corriger*) as well as amuse (*divertir*)! There *is* no improvement, only amusement—in the form of a sardonic smile, at that. Post-Molière comedy reflects a collapse of confidence, a moral crisis, we can relate to the historical situation of the country. Beginning approximately in 1680, an aging Louis XIV launched France into religious repressions, a stifling of dissent, and costly, catastrophic wars that resulted in military defeats, heavy taxation, and social disruptions as a new financier class began to arise. The ensuing decline in national stature and self-esteem provoked a contained disillusionment to which these late comedies bear clear witness, and the atmosphere continued to deteriorate up to the end of the Sun King's reign in 1715. *Le Légataire* is hardly the only theatrical example of the ambient cynicism between 1700 and 1715. In the regency (1715–1723) that followed, prospects for France brightened once more, and a new eighteenth-century spirit, the Enlightenment, began to stir that would quickly lead a revitalized French comedy in directions unknown to the age of Corneille and Molière.

REFERENCES AND FURTHER READINGS

Calder, Andrew. *Molière: The Theory and Practice of Comedy*. London: Athlone, 1993.

Corneille, Pierre. "Discours." In *Théâtre complet*. Ed. Pierre Lièvre and Roger Caillois. Vol. 1, 60–136. Paris: Gallimard, 1950.

———. *Théâtre complet*. Ed. Maurice Rat. 3 vols. Paris: Garnier, n.d.

Gaines, James F., ed. *The Molière Encyclopedia*. Westport, CT: Greenwood, 2002.

Hollier, Denis, gen. ed. *A New History of French Literature*. Cambridge, MA: Harvard UP, 1989.

Jeffery, Brian. *French Renaissance Comedy, 1552–1630*. Oxford, UK: Clarendon, 1969.

Knutson, Harold C. *Molière: An Archetypal Approach*. Toronto: Toronto UP, 1976.

Mallinson, G. Jonathan. *The Comedies of Corneille: Experiments in the Comic*. Manchester, UK: Manchester UP, 1984.

Molière [Jean-Baptiste Poquelin]. *Oeuvres complètes*. Ed. Maurice Rat. 2 vols. Paris: Gallimard, 1956.

Sypher, Wylie. *Four Stages of Renaissance Style: Transformations in Art and Literature, 1400–1700*. New York: Doubleday, 1955.

Théâtre du XVIIe siècle. Ed. Jacques Scherer, Jacques Truchet, and André Blanc. 3 vols. Paris: Gallimard, 1975–1992.

23

German Comedy

Bettina Brandt

What we find funny, comical, or hilarious depends on where we come from, in which country (even which region of a country) we grew up, and what language(s) we speak. There is, of course, a certain communality in what cultures consider comical (loss of bodily control and indecency, veiled insults, small misfortunes like those provided by the banana skin rank high on that list), but a significant part of the comical and the comedy remains specific to a culture and is, therefore, almost untranslatable.

There is, in other words, a direct but complex relationship between nationality and sense of humor. What we see as comical or funny does not only depend on us as unique individuals; on the contrary, it largely depends on our identity as part of a larger social group. For instance, what solicits the highest respect from one group (religious rituals or nationalist celebrations are favorites here) can be seen as comical by those who look at it from the outside, who are embedded in a similarly social but crucially different structure of their own group.

Also, what makes us laugh does not only depend on belonging to a certain social class or culture; it is quite directly related to our own place in history. What a particular society finds comical, at a certain time, is an accurate reflection of its (changing) social norms. Over the centuries, Germans have tended to identify themselves with the tragic and tragedy rather than with comedy and the comical, so much so in fact that the "tragic German" or the "humorless German" almost became the national character type. The connection between humor and Germany and the Germans was, for the longest time, quite literally a joke that was eagerly exploited, especially in the international marketplace. The 2003 summer advertisements of the biggest low-cost airline in North Rhine Westfalia, called Germanwings, read, for instance, "Nice to Munich, 19 Euros. No, it can't be a joke since it is German." What is remarkable about this advertisement is not that the precarious link between Germany and the comical is reiterated one more time, but that this is purposefully done by a new, young, and trendy German company to underline the seriousness of its business in a humorous manner. This Germanwings ad is also significant because it is illustrative of broader change that has been occurring in Germany since reunification.

Germans, who in the first part of the twentieth century had a thriving cabaret scene and a long history of producing excellent satirical magazines, finally seem able to make fun of themselves again. John Morreal argues that "throughout history, opposition to comedy and laughter has been strongest in societies which emphasize physical restraint, decorum and conformity.... The more authoritarian the regime, the greater the suppression of comedy. Hitler even set up 'joke courts' to punish those who made fun of his regime—one Berlin cabaret comic was executed for naming his horse Adolf." The author seems to suggest one explanation why the relationship between Germany and comedy and the comical has only recently changed. In the early twenty-first century, German film and television comedies (multicultural), stand-up comedians, local cabaret, satirical magazines, and funny fictional texts are, once again, flourishing in postreunification Germany. Let's hope that, this time, the genre is here to stay.

Komödie, or *Lustspiel* as it is often called in German, has never been a major genre within German literary history, and as a consequence, German comedy has suffered a bad reputation and received relatively little attention. One of the reasons for its undervalued position might be directly linked to the early theories that were written about the genre. From its beginnings, German writings on comedy and the comical largely followed Aristotle's (348–322 B.C.E.) negative assessment of the genre. As early as 1624, for instance, Martin Opitz (1597–1639), who attempted to rescue baroque literature that was written in German from its parochial status and to connect it to the larger Western European literature of his time, rejected comedy as an example of bad taste. In his *Buch von der deutschen Poetery* (Book about German Poetics) he condemned the genre, arguing that it focused on the portrayal of "schlechte personen," or "bad characters."

Fatally influential for the low profile of German comedy over the next 200 years were the writings of Johann Christoph Gottsched (1700–1766), the most prominent author of the German Enlightenment before Gotthold Ephraim Lessing (1729–1781). Although the German word *Lustspiel* had been coined as early as 1536, it was Gottsched who successfully replaced the adapted loanword *Komödie* with the word *Lustspiel* in his *Versuch einer kritischen Dichtkunst* (Attempt at a Critical Poetics, 1730) which gave the word *Lustspiel* its place in the German theater world. Attempting to raise the level of German theater by following French classicist theater, Gottsched submitted comedy to the rules of tragedy and the authority of reason.

In tune with an overall European trend, German theories of comedy were more homogeneous than theories about tragedy. Never taken quite seriously because that position was already occupied by German drama, German comedy has always been closely intertwined with tragedy—and seldom to its advantage. In the German-speaking world both tragedy and comedy were subject to the *Ständeklausel*, an absolutist class rule of Renaissance and baroque poetics that spelled out that tragedy as a genre was reserved for the fate of kings, dukes, and other persons of high rank whereas bourgeois characters, and their weaknesses, were the subject of comedies because, as was argued at the time, their lives lacked dignity and importance for the tragic genre. Originally formulated by Horace (*Ars poetica*) and still in effect during the time of Gottsched, it is not until the slow rise and the eventual establishment of the German bourgeoisie that this poetic rule was finally abandoned. The plays of Lessing are most important in this respect. As comedy as a genre developed to include a realistic representation of bourgeois life and its culture, the perspective on the comic was increasingly internalized. This new type of comedy provoked a quieter, more philosophical response from the theater-goers; they laughed about the comically deviant characters but tended to identify with the idealized, virtuous, bourgeois characters.

Due to the lack of a unified German nation state and a missing established cultural life, the *Lustspiel* as a genre did not gain importance in Germany until the late seventeenth century. The early attempts of the medieval nun Hrosvith von Gandersheim (935–973) and the humanist comedies of Johannes Reuchlin (1455–1522) and Jakob Wimpheling (1450–1528) lack distinctiveness and remain without following. From 1592 onward, adapted Elizabethan dramas were performed in the German-speaking countries. Small touring companies of the Englische Komödianten, who spoke at first in English but from the early seventeenth century onwards increasingly in German, were popular. W. E. Yates notes in his survey of this early tradition of German comedy that the first part to be played in German was that of the comic figure (15). As the result of the upheavals of the Reformation and the disaster of the Thirty Years' War (1618–1648), Yates explains, these channel crossings soon came to an end, and throughout the remainder of the seventeenth century theater troupes started to include more and more German-speaking actors. It was actor-dramatist Josef Anton Stranitzky (1676–1726), known as the first Viennese *Hanswurst* (a German-speaking harlequin type), who adopted this English kind of drama, with its elements of comedy and spectacle, for his own purposes. By 1711 his Teutsche Komödianten (German Comedians) were installed in Vienna (by then a major center for touring troupes) in the newly built Theater nächst dem Kärtnerthor. (In tune with the ideas of the German Enlightenment Gottsched, working together with Caroline Neuber, would ban the figure of the *Hanswurst* from the German stage again some years later.) In the seventeenth century, the comedies of Andreas Gryphius (1616–1664), especially *Absurda Comica: Oder Herr Peter Squentz* (1658) and *Horribilicribifax* (1663), are worth mentioning.

German classicism did not have a great affinity for the genre of comedy and mostly limited itself to imitating Italian and French theater. Neither Johann Wolfgang von Goethe nor Friedrich von Schiller was a great comedy writer though they contributed to the literary and philosophical theories on the genre of comedy, and Lessing was the major comedy innovator in Germany during the eighteenth century. The first and in many ways still the classic German *Lustspiel* is Lessing's five-act play *Minna von Barnhelm oder das Soldatenglück* (Minna von Barnhelm, or the Soldier's Happiness, 1767), which premiered at the Nationaltheater in Hamburg in 1767. Written a few years after *Miss Sara Simpson* (1755), a so-called *bürgerliches Trauerspiel* ("bourgeois drama") in which Lessing rejected the rules of French tragedy and created a sensitive portrait of a bourgeois family, *Minna von Barnhelm* is the first German play to portray aristocratic characters in a comedy. His *Emilia Galotti* (1772) is the first play in which the aristocracy and the new bourgeoisie meet in a tragic confrontation. Lessing's work is a staple on the contemporary German stage. The comedies of August von Kotzebue (1761–1819), a popular playwright who drew large crowds in his time, never came near the level of sophistication of Lessing's plays, and today his comedies are seldom performed. For the rising middle classes of the German Enlightenment, the use of comedy became part of a deliberate program of consciousness-raising and is indicative of the way in which the literary is informed by social norms and concerns.

The German Romantics gave considerable significance to the comic genre through their writings and theories but did not make a lasting impact on the genre. Hoping to fundamentally reconcile the philosophical and material contradictions of existence, German Romantics found in the comic precisely those virtues (ambiguity, incongruity, and contrast) that they saw as intrinsic to their own conception of art and life. As a mode of being that supplements the intellectual insight of the Enlightenment with the vital forces of nature and emotion, romanticism reintroduced the comic and the comical as part of a natural human disposition. From Friedrich Schlegel via Gottfried Friedrich Hegel and Adam Müller to Joseph Freiherr von Eichendorff, the German Romantics, following Lessing, rejected Gottsched's strict ideas and celebrated comedy, laughter, and humor as a means of renewing the German theater tradition. Influential in this respect were the comedies of Aristophanes, which Aristotle, on whom Gottsched had based his evaluation of the comic genre, had ignored and which Schlegel discovered for the German Romantics. Emphasizing an idealized Greek comedy, the German authors started producing their own comedies; Ludwig Tieck (1773–1853) and A. W. Schlegel wrote *Fastnachtspiele* ("Shrovetide plays") looking for inspiration in the earlier medieval German comedies of this type. Tieck, inspired by Aristophanes, also wrote two popular experimental literary comedies: *Der gestiefelte Kater* (*Puss in Boots,* 1797) and *Prinz Zerbino* (1799). German Romantics were also important translators of Shakespeare's comedies. Clemens Brentano (1778–1842) created with his *Ponce de Leon* (1801) a successful satirical comedy that thrived on ironic wordplay.

Four comedies of the nineteenth century that are still regularly staged are Heinrich von Kleist's *Der zerbrochene Krug* (*The Broken Jug*, 1808); Christian Grabbe's *Scherz, Satire, Ironie und tiefere Bedeutung* (Satire, Irony and Deeper Meaning, 1822), Georg Büchner's *Leonce und Lena* (1836), and Franz Grillparzer's *Weh dem, der lügt* (Woe to the Liar, 1838). Kleist and Büchner are particularly important for the history of German comedy.

The role of Adam, the eloquent village judge in Kleist's *The Broken Jug* is one of the most prominent and one of the most coveted roles in German theater. Simultaneously persecutor and offender, Adam, like the first man, is almost a tragic character. He desires Eve whose "jug" has been broken (the play is heavily symbolic not only as far as the names are concerned but also in regard to the objects that structure it), and he uses, to no avail, all his wit to avoid incriminating himself. Widely considered the comic counterpart to *Oedipus*, this clever comedy is still a classic favorite on the German stage.

Büchner's *Leonce and Lena*, written in 1836 but not performed until sixty years later, was inspired by Brentano's *Ponce de Leon* and "constitutes an early example away from the playful atmosphere of the Romantic comedy towards and ironic reflection on the impotence of the aesthete" (Pye 134). In the play Büchner (1813–1837), who had turned to literature after failing to start a revolution in his native Hessen, criticized the higher strata of society. He ridiculed the German system of small states and the romantic vagaries and pessimism of his younger contemporaries. For the characters in *Leonce and Lena* life is deprived of any meaning, and there is but one relief: withdrawal from the world. Comedy as a genre grew in popularity as the human condition was increasingly understood as made of more and more inconsistencies and incongruities that seem to eliminate any rational interpretation. Grillparzer, who was the official playwright of the famous Burgtheater, was politically and poetically conservative, and in most every respect Büchner's opposite. After *Weh dem, der lügt*, a play that investigates the question of whether the end justifies the means, was hissed by the Viennese public; he withdrew from the stage and lived in the strictest seclusion.

Büchner and Grillparzer each wrote one comedy (neither author is famous for his contribution to the genre), but the most successful comic dramatists at that time came from Vienna and the Viennese popular stage. Ferdinand Jakob Raimund (1790–1836) and Johann Nepomuk Eduard Ambrosius Nestroy (1801–1862) are important in this respect. Raimund's plays are typical examples of romantic magical comedies with fairy stories, moral allegories and deus ex machina happy endings; *Der Alpenkönig und der Menschenfeind* (1828, The King of the Alps and the Misanthrope), *Das Mädchen aus der Feenwelt oder der Bauer als Millionär* (1826, The Girl from Fairyland, or the Farmer as Millionaire) and *Der Verschwender* (1834, The Dissipator) are still occasionally staged. In contrast to Raimund's interest in romantic and magical fantasies, Nestroy emphasized parody and criticism even though his comedies were written under the strict censorship of his time. His interest in wordplay was legendary, often blending Viennese dialect with his figure's failed attempt at educated speech. Among his most important plays are a number of burlesque comedies, a genre called *Posse* in German, which he adapted to carry social criticism and biting satire. Nestroy also satirized some of Grillparzer's plays.

Worth mentioning, though rarely performed today, are the socially critical period plays of Karl Ferdinand Gutzkow (1811–1878), the comedies of Eduard von Bauernfeld (1802–1890) and Julius Benedix (1811–1873), *Die Journalisten* (The Journalists, 1854) of Gustav Freytag (1816–1895), and the popular comedies of Ludwig Anzengruber (1839–1889), whom the naturalists admired, especially his *Die Kreuzelschreiber* (The Illiterates), in which Anzengruber's affinity with a literature that both delights and instructs are best expressed.

John Osborne explains that "Comedy was not a field in which the Naturalists—either German or European—were particularly productive, nor was it one in which they particularly excelled" (132). German naturalists, like most of their fellow German nineteenth-century authors, tended to favor the novella and tragedies, but their social-critical stance and their desire to engage literature in the problems of their age drew them to a particular kind of comedy, the satirical comedy. Gerhart Hauptmann (1862–1946), Germany's strongest naturalist voice, first wrote several tragedies before turning his attention to his first comedy, *Kollege Crampton* (Colleague Crampton) in 1892, at which point naturalism was past its prime. The unifying element of Hauptmann's dramatic work is his sympathetic concern for human suffering; his characters are generally passive victims of social and other elementary forces. His plays, the early ones especially, are still frequently performed. German naturalists exploited the comic possibilities inherent in automatonlike human behavior, but their comic characters pale beside the great sympathetic figures of naturalist tragic literature such as the bigoted old Hilse of *Die Weber* (The Silesian Weavers, 1892), the self-flagellating Fuhrmann Henschel from the play with the same title, 1899, or the pathetic Henriette John of *Die Ratten* (The Rats, 1911). Hauptmann's comedy *Der Biberpelz* (The Beaver Coat, 1893), written in a rich Berlin dialect, centers on a cunning female thief and her successful confrontation with pompous Prussian officials and has a sequel in the tragiccomic *Der rote Hahn* (The Red Rooster, 1901). Both are comedies of situation: the outwitting of the slow and foolish by the quick and nimble. German naturalist comedy, and *Kollege Crampton* and *Der Biberpelz* in particular, tend be seen as conservative as they lean "towards the preservation of the existing social order, by smiling on the weaknesses of those who come to terms with it. This kind of humor emerges in the later stages of Naturalism, along with an increase in tolerance to other means by which the individual can come to terms with a hostile world" (Osborne 140).

German impressionism produced the comedies of Arthur Schnitzler (1862–1931) and Hugo von Hofmannsthal (1874–1929). Hofmannsthal, internationally famous for his collaboration with the German composer Richard Strauss, created a complex and lighthearted modernist comedy in 1921 when he wrote *Der Schwierige* (The Difficult Man), a play in which he analyzed a sophisticated mind inhibited by the weight of social tradition. Together with Max Reinhardt, he founded the Salzburg Festival, which has regularly staged performances of his plays. Arthur Schnitzler, who received extensive medical training and was very interested in psychology, a fact that influenced his writing a great deal, is mostly known today for his novellas *Fräulein Else* (1924) and *Leutnant Gustl* (1901) and his play *Der Reigen* (The Round, 1900). In his works he depicted the decadence of pre-1914 Vienna. His comedies, though not as successful as the rest of his work today, include *Der grüne Kakadu* (1899) and *Anatol* (1893).

German expressionism brought about grotesque satirical forms of comedy in the works of Carl Sternheim (1878–1942). Sternheim, like his contemporary Frank Wedekind, attacked the middle class, but unlike Wedekind, he did not lend himself to explicit moralizing and contented himself with satire pure and simple. He was the only German playwrights of his time who concentrated almost exclusively on comedy. He saw himself in the role of a "modern Molière" and, like his ancestor, aimed at holding up a mirror to the ruling classes of his age: the German bourgeoisie at the brink of World War I. This he did in a cycle of comedies written in the years immediately preceding 1914 to which he gave the general title *Aus dem bürgerlichen Heldenleben* (From the Bourgeois Hero's Life). Three of these comedies, *Die Hose* (The Pants) of 1911, *Der Snob* written three years later, and *1913* (written in 1915), trace the rise of a bourgeois family through three generations. The playwright's most striking tool to reveal bourgeois mentality is his artificially contrived language; far removed from everyday speech, it exposes the triteness of bourgeois values.

The writings of German philosopher Friedrich Nietzsche (1844–1900) have been largely credited for the eventual positive evaluation of laughter and humor in the German world. His distinction in *Die Geburt der Tragödie aus dem Geist der Musik* (*The Birth of Tragedy out of the Spirit of Music*, 1872), between the Apollonian and Dionysian elements of art, was of considerable consequence. The view spread that classical art could not only be serene but also ecstatic, and that the origins of Greek drama sprang from the orgiastic intoxication of Dionysian religious mysteries.

During the Weimar Republic, German cabaret was a great outlet for comic relief during an increasingly disastrous economical situation. In 1923–1924, at the height of German inflation, there were about 100 cabarets in Berlin alone and about 200 in all of Germany. In the first few years of the newly founded republic, very few cabarets dared to present a literary or political program. There was, however, a close collaboration between the cabaretists and the journalists of the Weimar Republic, especially those working for the liberal paper *Die Weltbühne,* who wrote for the cabaret stage. Kurt Tucholsky (1890–1933) is probably the best known of these outside of Germany. He wrote under various pseudonyms such as Peter Panther, Theobald Tiger, Ignaz Wrobel, and Kaspar Hauser and attacked nationalism, militarism, organized religion, and the blindness of justice. Tucholsky collaborated in a number of cabaret shows, including *Bite Please* and *Madame Revue*.

Karl Valentin (Valentin Ludwig Fey, 1882–1948), whom Bertholt Brecht (1898–1956) greatly admired, was "probably the greatest clown Germany ever produced" and perhaps the most beloved person on the Weimar stage (Senelick 30). Valentin began his career in the Munich beer gardens of the 1900s singing in the tradition of Bavarian folk songs, but his material went over equally well with the elegant cabarets of the 1920s and 1930s. Valentin, who worked together with Liesl Karlstadt (Elisabeth Wellano, 1892–1961) from 1911 onward, placed most of his satires in proletarian or petit bourgeois settings. He was less of a political satirist and more of a Dadaist, protesting everything rather than exposing specific political behaviors. Like Charlie Chaplin, he reached a broad and diverse audience, who laughed at his sketches, songs, and monologues in which he toyed with language. Another voice of that time, Adolf Gondrell (1902–1954), began as a character comedian, worked as a master of ceremonies at Munich's cabaret Simplizissimus, bought the cabaret Simpl in 1929 and soon became the most important master of ceremonies outside of Berlin. He also directed some of Valentin's routines.

The most versatile and enduring of Berlin songwriters was Friedrich Hollaender (1896–1976), who became the house composer and the conductor for the literary and political cabaret Schall und Rauch (Sound and Smoke), which operated from 1919 to 1925. There he wrote some of cabaret's greatest hits, including "Jonny, wenn du Geburtstag hast" (well known in English from Marlene Dietrich's rendition "Johnny"). Taking charge of the Munich Bonbonniere in 1925 he turned the ordinary glamor revue into a far more political entertainment. He is well known for having written scores for Frank Wedekind and Max Reinhardt and having written the popular songs of the film *Blue Angel* in 1931.

A unique voice in the Berlin cabaret was that of Werner Finck (1902–1978), who started out as a master of ceremonies at the Katakombe. The Catacomb cabaret had been founded in 1929 by Finck and other young actors as a competition to the KadeKo, or Kabarett der Komiker (Comic's Cabaret), a large restaurant, more music hall than cabaret, whose performers dressed formally on stage. In the Catacomb, where Hans Eisler, who worked with Brecht, played the piano, performers wore casual clothes, especially baggy pants. Finck's strength was his puns, wordplay, and unfinished sentences. As the fascist regime tightened its grip, Finck became more and more outspoken, ridiculing Adolf Hitler and the Nazi salute on stage. In March 1935, Finck was sent to Esterwegen concentration camp.

German cabaret has its origins in the nineteenth century. Its precursors can be found in printed media like the satirical journals with their Enlightenment intentions: a mix of entertainment and arts; a combination of poetry, journalism, and politics. The direct model for the German cabaret was the *cabaret artistique* of the Parisian Montmartre scene, in particular the famous cabaret Le Chat Noir, which Rodolphe Salis had founded in 1881. The original cabaret, Schall und Rauch (1901–1902), for instance, operated in the spirit of the original Montmartre cabarets. Politically democratic and leaning toward the left, the cabaret addressed and questioned the increasingly more visible militaristic and nationalist tendencies in the German empire. It took on the establishment until the spring of 1921, when the cabaret took a turn toward apolitical entertainment. In 1925 the cabaret ceased to exist and was turned into a dance bar. The Cabaret Größenwahn (Cabaret Megalomania), which opened in 1920, and the cabaret Wilde Bühne (The Untamed Stage), in which Brecht, in early 1922, sang two songs, "The Ballad of the Murderer Apfelböck" and "The Legend of the Dead Soldier" (that provoked a riot) were attempts to continue in the tradition of the Schall und Rauch political-literary cabaret. The Berlin cabaret Der blaue Vogel (The Blue Bird), which had been founded by Russian emigrant I. E. Duvan-Tortsov, a former Moscow Art Theater actor, is worth mentioning as well.

Proletarian agitprop cabarets and revues took on the Nazis and their leader and actually hoped to change German society. Erwin Piscator and Felix Gasbarra are important in this respect and initiated the phenomenon when, in 1924, they staged the *Revue Roter Rummel* (Red Rumpus Revue) for the German Communist Party on the eve of the November national elections. Between 1926 and 1933 there were nearly 200 agitprop groups working in Germany, almost all of them on the political left. "The most famous of these troupes were the *Red Rats* (*Rote Ratten*) of Dresden, a socialist group founded in 1926; the *Red Blacksmiths* (*Rote Schmiede*) of Halle, founded in 1928; and the *Red Megaphone* (*Rote Sprachrohr*) of Berlin, also founded in 1928" (Senelick 239).

In Switzerland, where many artists of war-torn Europe had fled, the founding of the Cabaret Voltaire in the Spiegelgasse in Zurich in 1916 led to the birth of the Dada movement. Hugo Ball, a writer, theater manager, and pianist; Emmy Hennings, a cabaret singer; Richard Huelsenbeck, a medical student; Marcel Janko, a Romanian architect and painter, and his fellow countryman and poet Tristan Tzara; plus Hans Arp and Yvon Goll were founding members who experimented with performance techniques that provoked artistic and political scandals. Two decades later, in December 1933, the Cabaret Cornichon (Pickled Gherkin) was opened by Walter Lesch and Otto Weissert. Combining the folk tradition of the Basel *Fastnacht* (Shrovetide) with political allegory, the performers spoke in Swiss dialect. Songs like Max Werner Lenz's "Man without a Passport" from 1935, which criticized the lack of support for refugees from the Nazi regime, are still relevant today.

Satire magazines were important in the second part of the nineteenth century and the first part of the twentieth century as well. *Kladderatsch*, a Berlin satirical newspaper founded by David Kalisch (1820–1872), was published weekly between 1848 and 1944. In the course of its history, the newspaper changed from a liberal democratic opposition newspaper to a nationalist one. *Simpliccismus*, founded by Albert Langen (1869–1909) and published in Munich, appeared on a weekly basis between 1896 and 1944. Its political content and its high-quality texts and drawings plus its frequent run-ins with the censors, made the journal, named after one of the first novels to be published in the German language by Hans Jakob Christoffel von Grimmelshausen (1622–1676), the most important and most renowned magazine of the German Empire. Further examples of satirical magazines are *Der wahre Jakob* (The Way to Do It), the satire magazine of the German Social Democrats, established in 1900, *Frankfurter Lantern* and the *Fliegende Blätter* (The Flying Leaves, or Flying Pages).

In German theater history of the early twentieth century four names are prominent: Carl Zuckmayer (1890–1971), Brecht, Friedrich Dürrenmatt (1921–1990), and Max Frisch (1911–1991). In the 1920s Carl Zuckmayer started his career and became popular, especially thanks to his comedy *Der fröhliche Weinberg* (The Merry Vineyard, 1925), which marked the end of German Expressionism. His most popular works are the comedy *Der Hauptmann von Köpenick* (The Captain of Köpenick, 1931) and *The Devil's General* (1946), a drama about a Nazi general and the German resistance. The *Weinberg* and the *Hauptmann* are among the most frequently performed comedies on the German stage. *Der fröhliche Weinberg* was a great success in Berlin, but the comedy aroused fierce protest in the provinces, where the nationalist opposition, already raising its head, was stung by the caricature of a reactionary student. Written throughout in the broad Rhenisch dialect of Zuckmayer's native region, the comedy consists of a succession of drinking bouts, riotous tavern brawls, and love-making. With the *Weinberg*, Zuckmayer struck the keynote of his work, although he later expanded its range to include tragedy and history. *Der Hauptmann von Köpenick,* ironically subtitled "A German Fairytale," is based on a real life incident about a shoemaker in 1906 who masquerades as a Prussian officer and turns the political system upside down. It was one of the last critical comedies before Hitler seized power and Zuckmayer left Germany and fled into exile to the United States. The play was adapted as a film by Helmut Kautner in 1956 with Heinz Rühman in the role of the captain.

The theories of Bertholt Brecht, the most influential German in modern European theater, have something in common with both Gottsched and the German Romantics. Like the former, he envisioned a didactic form of theater, and like the latter he turned to the *Lustspiel* as a fertile ground for innovation. But whereas Gottsched had attempted to purify the *Lustspiel* by applying the rules of tragedy to comedy to mold it into a pedagogical form, Brecht turned the tables and applied the rules of comedy to tragedy. Brecht's comedy *Mann ist Mann* (1927, Man Is Man) is the first of his plays to introduce "songs," which are, for the most part, incorporated in his first collection of poetry *Die Hauspostille* (Book of Family Prayers, 1927). Despite its exotic setting in British India, *Mann ist Mann* was obviously an attack on the revival of militarism in Germany at the time, and Brecht fled the Third Reich soon thereafter. His comedy *Puntilla und sein Knecht Matti* (1940, Puntilla and His Valet Matti) was written in exile. Comedies occupy a unique place in the work of the poet and playwright whose signature is epic and ideological theater. One of the features of Brecht's dramatic work is its absurdist character. For Brecht, the Marxist, absurdity is a feature of an outmoded political system that is comic when viewed from the perspective of a socialist future. Brecht makes frequent use of a Marxist dialectical relationship between the perspective of society as comic and its portrayal by comic means. Thus, the comic in Brecht's work functions as a means to alienate our perceptions of our historical materialist reality while exposing that which, from a bourgeois point of view, does not usually appear as comic, but which from the perspective of socialism is quite absurd indeed (Pye 144).

The Swiss writer Friedrich Dürrenmatt, alongside his compatriot Frisch, is perhaps the most frequently cited mid-twentieth-century comedy writer in the German language. Dürrenmatt's work, characterized by a love for the paradoxical and written during the cold war, follows a more liberal political line than Brecht's. He was a writer "torn between the dual legacy of metaphysical and political comedy, whose heterogenous style bears the hallmark of hesitation between the two models" (Pye 146). The way in which Dürrenmatt dealt with both the legacy of Brecht and that of late romanticism and expressionism is significant for the understanding of the direction in which attitudes to comedy have progressed. Gillian Pye, in an extensive study, argues that Dürrenmatt incorporates the difficult position into which comedy sees itself maneuvered. Dürrenmatt does not see the world as a fundamentally absurd place but he also does not directly engage with the world in the manner of Brecht. For Dürrenmatt the world has become a fundamentally paradoxical place and he focuses on the human aspect to this paradox, which he does not so much see as a product of specific Marxist historical-materialist circumstances than as a part of a basic human situation. As Pye explains:

The "worst possible turn" events can take is when they become "comic"—when they attain a pinnacle of incongruity and absurdity, distorted from the familiar, exposing great contradictions which lie beneath the surface of our existence. Whilst such incongruities . . . may clearly have been created by humans (such as the atomic threat in *The Physicists*) they are nevertheless incalculable and, as such, Dürrenmatt undermines the potential of the rational to correct them. (146)

For Dürrenmatt "the worst possible turn of events" is not, as it was for Brecht, the result of false logic; rather, this twist happens as a result of chance. "The hero does not fall, he stumbles; and that over which he stumbles is something ridiculous, even laughable" (Pye 146–47).

Max Frisch (1911–1991), like Dürrenmatt, convinced that comedy had remained the only appropriate tool to understand the world after World War II, created comedies about the problems of his age as well. In his lighthearted but serious comedy *Don Juan oder die Liebe zur Geometrie* (Don Juan, or the Love of Geometry, 1953), the dramatist plays with the literary tradition of the Don Juan motive, turning for inspiration especially to those earlier texts (of Tirso de Molina) in which the erotic drive of the seducer is not yet critically questioned and where the motive of metaphysical revenge has not yet been secularized. In Frisch's comedy, Don Juan is reinvented as a smart, somewhat melancholic cynic who is annoyed and disgusted with the world and longs for the clear, pure self-sufficiency of geometrical figures and mathematical abstractions. In this successful critical comedy, Frisch the architect and writer reflects upon the situation of the modern intellectual.

Comedy and the comical are not necessarily intertwined. As we have seen, since the eighteenth century there have been a number of German *Lustpiele* that were not at all funny or even dealt with tragic matters. In the twentieth century, after two world wars and the following cold war, comedy and tragedy even became, to a certain extent, hard to clearly separate. The comical itself has always also been a part of life and not just of literature. As the second half of the twentieth century progressed the comical in the German-speaking world developed a broader base again and permeated more of society than before.

In the mid-1980s, the *Erlebnisgesellschaft* ("events society") reared its head and the word *Spasskultur* ("fun culture") was coined to suggest that a hedonistic playfulness had emerged in German culture. In other words, *Spasskultur* self-consciously breaks the identification between German culture and the tragic. Contemporary German *Spasskultur* can be seen in film, where comedies are dominant; in literature; and even in a revival of cabaret.

About two decades after the first *Gastarbeiter* ("guest workers," or non–permanent residents) had come to Germany and the country was slowly becoming a multicultural society with several million foreign workers in its midst, we saw the beginnings of a new type of political cabaret: German-Turkish cabaret. Some of the best cabaret performers of today can be found in this corner. In 1985, Muhsin Omurca (1959–; winner of the German Cabaret Prize of 1998) and Şinasi Dikmen (1945–), both from the city of Ulm, created the first *Gastarbeiter-Kabarett* (literally, "guest-workers cabaret") called Knobi-Bonbon cabaret (Garlic Bonbon), which was dissolved in 1997. Omurca and Dikmen took on the relationship between Turks and Germans as well as Germany's attitude toward its recent historical past. In 1998 Dikmen, together with Ayşe Aktay, opened a new cabaret in Frankfurt, the Kabarett Änderungsschneiderei (Cabaret Tailors Alterations), or KÄS ("cheese"). Omurca went solo in 1997 with a show called *Diary of a Skinhead in Istanbul*. Sedat Pamuk (1952–), from the city of Freiburg, is also worth mentioning. In his comedy act *Gastarbeits-Los* ("Fate of the Guest Worker"), he addressed the topic of unemployment. Creating a new invented word out of a wordplay on the term *gastarbeiter*, (as the workers from Turkey, Italy, Greece, the former Yugoslavia, and other countries were officially called, reflecting a German immigration policy that saw them as "temporary additions" to West German society rather than as the immigrants they had become in the meantime) and the words *"arbeitslos"* ("unemployed") and *"Los"* (which can mean both "lottery ticket" and "fate"), Pamuk exposes cliché after cliché.

Cabaret made its way back into Berlin as well; from Die Stachelschweine (The Porcupines) and Die Wühlmäuse (The Voles) to Distel (The Thistle), the cabaret scene was varied and funny. In Leipzig Die Pfeffermühle (The Peppermill) attracts crowds.

In the realm of literature, two novels, Dietrich Schwanitz' *Der Campus* (The Campus) and Thomas Brussig's *Helden wie wir* (*Heroes Like Us*), both written in 1995, were successful comical texts that were quickly adapted for the screen (*Der Campus* was filmed in 1998 and *Helden wie wir* in 1999). In *Helden wie wir*, Brussig's second novel, told in the form of an interview with a *New York Times* reporter, the clueless antihero, Klaus Uhltzscht, who helped tear down the Berlin Wall with the help of his oversized penis, defeats communism and helps to reunify Germany through this act. According to Stephan Brockmann, *Helden wie wir* and *Der Campus* made fun of "hypermoralism," both in the former East and in the former West, "a lack of democracy and a lack of humor," and "the unhealthy obsession with the German past" (43).

Recently, comedy and the comical have made their way into the German television networks. One successful program called *RTL Samstag Nacht* (RTL Saturday Night), hosted by Wigald Boning, is a German adaptation of *Saturday Night Live* and combines both stand-up routines and sketches. The host, wearing outrageous and shocking clothing, takes a critical stance toward German national identity. Harold Schmidt, another popular television performer, is a former stand-up comedian whose programs mimic the format of David Letterman's *The Late Show*. Schmidt's comedy, unlike Boning's brand of humor, has been described "as degrading humor, ridicule, and thinly veiled aggression toward ethnic minorities in Germany" (Gamarra 338). Also tapping into the recent surge of popular demand for comedy is Guildo Horn, who was renowned for his pop vocals during the 1960s and 1970s; his retro concerts still draw huge crowds today. Horn has a lowbrow sensibility that is mirrored in the so-called trash mentality. As Edward A. Gamarra argues, "While it seemed that the structure and format of the most popular comedy shows are lifted directly from the most popular American programs, the subject matter and the content seems [*sic*] specific to the German condition" (338).

The early 1990s have been called the Golden Age of German Comedy, and humor plays indeed a crucial role in German film of that decade. Traditional German film scholarship either neglected or dismissed any serious analysis of the film comedy as a genre. Sometimes Siegfried Kracauer and his groundbreaking study *From Caligari to Hitler: A Psychological History of the German Film* are blamed for this. Focusing on films from 1918 to 1933, Kracauer argued that Germans were inherently incapable of having a sense of humor, and that this lack of humor explained the lack of film comedies. Best at making films about the dark side of life, they produced the great cinema of shadows, monsters, and murders. As the book was published in 1947, one can hardly criticize Kracauer for his pessimistic outlook on the German nation and its inhabitants.

The New German Cinema of the 1970s and 1980s (dominated by directors such as Werner Herzog, Hans Jürgen Syberberg, Rainer Werner Maria Fassbinder, Volker Schlöndorf, Margaretha von Trotta, and Helma Sanders-Brahms) featured difficult and serious films that were sometimes well received abroad while remaining relatively unpopular at home. Turning toward the history of their parents, these directors dealt in their works with *Vergangenheitsbewältigung* (a coming to terms with the German past) and, as Anton Kaes demonstrates in his film study *From Hitler to Heimat: The Return of History as Film*, reified history through cinema. Many films of the New German Cinema are explorations of the past that serve as a cinematic catharsis for the generation they represent.

By avoiding difficult themes and turning to comedy, a genre well established in Hollywood and successfully exported to Germany, filmmakers of the 1990s found a niche for themselves in German film. No longer rejecting entertainment and amusement per se, German directors started to build stories around these comic axes. Starting with Doris Dörrie's *Men* (1985), German cinema turned toward the humorous. *Men* became a surprise hit, at home and abroad, and initiated the trend toward romantic comedies (known as relationship comedies, or *Beziehungskomödien*), which meanwhile have become the standard in new German comedy (Coury 360). These early films were followed by a flurry of comedies a few years later; from Detlev Buck's *Wir können auch anders* (We Could Rapidly Change Our Tune, 1993) to Sönke Wortmann's big hit *Der bewegte Mann* (The Moved Man, 1994), Helmut Dietl's *Rossini oder die mörderische Frage, wer mit wem schlief* (Rossini, or the Fatal Question, Who Slept with Whom, 1996), and Wolfgang Becker's *Das Leben ist eine Baustelle* (Life Is a Construction Site, 1997) and *Goodbye, Lenin* (2003). They all were commercial successes and all feature some type of happy endings. Helmut Dietl's *Rossini*, a social satire, or "*Melodramödie*," as the director himself calls it, introducing a new German word that mixes *melodrama* and *comedy*, was perhaps the greatest box office hit. The film even gave birth to a new expression: "*Die Rossini-Deutschen*" ("The Rossini Germans"). Based loosely on the actual Munich film scene, the film was winner of German film prizes for best film and best director of 1997. Brockmann explains that "*Rossini* is a comedy that achieves much of its humor by making fun of tragedy and seriousness. As Dietl notes, the film depicts events that are both 'schön und schrecklich' [beautiful and awful] not consecutively but at one and the same time, so that what is funny is also sad, and vice versa" (44).

Contemporary German comedy has been greatly influenced by the United States. Film director and writer Dörrie (1955–), to just give one example, studied drama and film at the University of the Pacific in Stockton, California, and then at the New School for Social Research in New York. The new American cinema, particularly Martin Scorsese, John Cassavettes, and Bob Rafelson, is a lasting influence on her work. Not all critics, however, view this new trend in Germany—or in Europe in general—as desirable. Critics and cineastes also criticize the general tendency to create market-driven and audience-oriented films at the expense of visual aesthetics.

Asking why exactly German culture took a turn toward the more light-hearted, Brockmann, like some other critics, suggests that "if the devotion to tragedy had been part of Germany's *Sonderweg*, the current devotion to comedy can be seen as a declaration that the special path is over and that Germany has become a nation just like other nations" (48). Others, making use of Sigmund Freud's insight into humor and wit (as expressed in his *Jokes and Their Relation to the Unconscious*), argue that the newly developed or, rather, (re)discovered sense of humor Germans exhibit in their words and comedies is "a developmental stage in which they are learning to observe themselves more compassionately and less critically" (Gamarra 338). Freud suggested that there was a basic resemblance between jokes and dreams in that both are essentially outsmarting our inhibitions. Humor, according to Freud, can then be seen as the release of inhibition, and, we would add here, on both the personal and the national level.

The success of the new German comedies has been poignantly summarized: "Germans are funny, but in a manner particular to that nation-state, that language, that cultural system. Translation does not guarantee that all people can communicate all ideas at all times" (Gamarra 339).

REFERENCES AND FURTHER READINGS

Brockmann, Stephan M. "The Politics of German Comedy." *German Studies Review* 23 (2000): 33–51.

Brussig, Thomas. *Heroes Like Us*. New York: Farrar, Straus and Giroux, 1997.

Coury, David. "From Aesthetics to Commercialism: Narration and the New German Comedy." *Seminar: A Journal of Germanic Studies* 33 (1997): 355–73.

DuBruck, Edelgard E. *Aspects of Fifteenth-Century Society in the German Carneval Comedies*. Lewiston, ME: Edwin Mellen, 1993.

Freud, Sigmund. *Jokes and Their Relation to the Unconscious*. 1905. Trans. James Strachey. New York: Norton, 1960.

Gamarra, Edward A. "German Comedy, Part 1: The Problem of American Scholarship." *JPCS: Journal for the Psychoanalysis of Culture and Society* 6 (2001): 142–45.

———. "German Comedy, Part II: How Germans View Their Own Humor." *JPCS: Journal for the Psychoanalysis of Culture and Society* 6 (2001): 337–40.

Kaes, Anton. *From Hitler to Heimat: The Return of History as Film*. Cambridge, MA: Harvard UP, 1989.

Kracauer, Siegfried. *From Caligari to Hitler: A Psychological History of the German Film*. 1947. Princeton, NJ: Princeton UP, 1974.

McKenzie, John R. P. *Social Comedy in Austria and Germany 1890–1933*. New York: Peter Lang, 1992.

Morreal, John. "Comedy." *Routledge Encyclopedia of Philosophy*. Ed. E. Craig. London: Routledge. 17 Oct. 2003. <http://www.rep.routledge.com/article/MO15SECT1>.

Osborne, John. *The Naturalist Drama in Germany*. Manchester, UK: Manchester UP, 1971.

Pye, Gillian. *Approaches to Comedy in German Drama*. Lewiston, ME: Edwin Mellen, 2002.

Senelick, Laurence. *Cabaret Performance*. Vol. 2 of *Europe 1920–1940: Sketches, Songs, Monologues, Memoirs*. Baltimore: Johns Hopkins UP, 1993.

Van Cleve, John Walter. *Harlequin Besieged: The Reception of Comedy in Germany during the Early Enlightenment*. New York: Peter Lang, 1980.

Yates, W. E. *Nestroy: Satire and Parody in Viennese Popular Comedy*. Cambridge, UK: Cambridge UP, 1972.

24

Greek Comedy

Mary C. English

Greek comedy began to flourish at the beginning of the fifth century B.C.E. in the city-state of Athens, where playwrights staged ninety-minute productions as part of contests held at annual dramatic festivals. Although these plays eventually developed into the situational comedy that inspired modern television sitcoms and the romantic films of the top Hollywood studios, comedy in Athens was fiercely satirical, highly attuned to the social, political, and cultural events of the moment, and, by our contemporary standards, vulgar because of its scatological and sexual humor. In fact, the comedies performed at these festivals are often compared to the skits of *Saturday Night Live*, to the nightly monologues of Jay Leno or David Letterman, or to such animated sitcoms as *The Simpsons* and *South Park*. But whereas these modern venues provide opportunities for the American public to laugh about the problems that beset their communities from the privacy of their living rooms, Greek comedy provided a public forum for the city-state to examine the concerns of its citizenry and to expose the folly of its most prominent members.

The organization of the dramatic festivals at Athens compelled spectators to consider comedy's relation to tragedy. For the most part, Greek tragedies focused on the extreme problems facing characters from the mythological past; audience members could then contemplate the most troubling aspects of the human condition by considering the lives of figures far removed from them by time and social status. The average Athenian watching Sophocles' *Oedipus Tyrannus* would probably not find himself trapped by a destiny that compelled him to kill his father, assume the kingship of Thebes, marry his mother, and beget children by her; however, the play would force him to consider the questions of free will and predetermined fate from a safe and distant perspective. By contrast, Greek comedy focused on the social and political questions most germane to contemporary Athenian life; by combining this type of critical civic analysis with comic spectacle and slapstick humor, the playwrights allowed the audience members to purge themselves of the problems they confronted on a daily basis and to use the performance as a springboard for further reflection and debate.

Because Greek comedy rarely dealt directly with universal questions and focused rather on matters specific to the fifth-century city-state of Athens, modern readers often find the plays difficult to understand. Translators of ancient Greek complicate matters even further by updating the jokes, by transferring the plots to contemporary settings, and by interpreting the original scripts through modern lenses. Unfortunately, very few directors have staged Greek comedy successfully. Hopefully, this chapter can entice students of comedy and theater practitioners to reexamine the plays that survive from this period and to launch new productions that more accurately capture the spirit of the Greek comic playwrights.

ORIGINS OF GREEK COMEDY

It seems more than fitting that dramatic performances in Athens were associated with the god Dionysus, the deity often described as presiding over wine, women, and song. However, he can also be considered as a god of shifting identities because almost all of the stories involving Dionysus and his followers detail what happens to individuals when they explore the outer limits of their personalities, either in altered states of intoxication (whether induced by wine or by passion) or in the art of mimesis, where people assume roles and imitate the behavior of others. Thus, in some respects, drama is a definitive form of worship for Dionysus: actors don masks and perform the lives of characters so different from themselves in order to bring to life, at least temporarily, a fiction that can ignite the imaginations of the audience members.

More specifically, Greek comic playwrights built their commentary on fifth-century society around the predemocratic institution of the *komos* (hence, the Greek word *komoidia*, which literally means the "song of the *komos*"). A band of revelers, typically representing some sort of organized group, gathered in the streets of the city and aired their views about current events and influential members of the community. Along with their criticism, the crowd danced and sang, participated in other types of folk entertainment, and competed against rival groups. Depending upon the composition of the komos, these performances were often seen as forms of political expression where rival groups could explore conflicting ideologies within an environment distinct from the civic arena. Ideally, then, the revelry of the komos became an opportunity to debate issues of concern to the citizenry before such matters became overwhelming societal problems. Thus, from its initial origins in Western culture, comedy served not just dramatic but also social aims.

Scholars have long debated exactly how the institution of the *komos* blended with the dramatic festivals in Athens to produce the genre *old comedy*. We know from the "insult poetry" of authors such as Archilochus and Hipponax that artists in the northern and eastern Aegean were using iambic verses to express through humor dissatisfaction with their contemporaries as early as the sixth century B.C.E. In Athens, this type of poetry factored into the celebration of the Eleusinian Mysteries and might have become part of the choral rituals honoring Dionysus. This type of formal poetic expression somehow combined with the revelries of the *komos* and the already flourishing genres of tragedy and choral performance to produce the first comic scripts. Greek comedies as we know them today were not officially entered into the City Dionysia, the major dramatic festival at Athens, until 486 B.C.E., although tragedies had been performed there for several decades. Given the political upheaval in Athens at the end of the sixth century that resulted in democratic reforms and the abolishment of tyranny, the introduction of comedy to the City Dionysia can perhaps be seen as another "democratic" innovation that gave voice to popular concerns and further limited the power of the elite. From 486 to 388 B.C.E., over 600 comedies, written by approximately fifty different playwrights, were performed in Athens.

THE DRAMATIC FESTIVALS AT ATHENS

Although we can certainly draw many connections between ancient and modern comic performance, the conditions under which Greek comedy thrived were strikingly different from our theatrical settings. The dramatic festivals at Athens were unique combinations of artistic, religious, civic, and political events that were organized for public benefit. The most important of them was the City Dionysia, a five-day festival held sometime during March or April in the Theater of Dionysus, an open-air structure located on the southern slope of the Acropolis. This celebration attracted a national audience and provided Athens with the opportunity to showcase to non-Athenians the performances of its best producers, playwrights, actors, choral singers, and dancers. After a series of prefestival sacrifices and religious processions in honor of Dionysus, the most powerful elected officials in Athens inaugurated the City Dionysia by offering libations to the god of the theater. Among the other opening ceremonies was a procession of war orphans who appeared in traditional hoplite gear given to them at the expense of the city and who assumed seats of honor in the theater for the duration of the festival. Also, delegates from the communities who were subject to Athens presented their monetary tributes to the city as well as squadrons of soldiers to serve in the army. Thus, before the plays themselves began, Athens performed its own drama for the festival attendees in which the personal sacrifices of individual families were juxtaposed against the tangible rewards of a militarily aggressive state. Especially when Athens' power peaked during the years of the Peloponnesian War, this tension between one's responsibility to family and one's obligation to the community, so effectively presented in the opening ceremonies of the City Dionysia, became the dominant focus of both Greek tragedy and comedy.

In 440 B.C.E., the Athenians started the Lenaea festival, a more local dramatic competition for the residents of Athens held in January or February. At first, the Lenaea was probably celebrated in a theater different from the one that housed the City Dionysia, but by the fourth century the performances were definitely transferred to the Theater of Dionysus. It is interesting that comedy, a genre that in Athens openly debated political and civic issues of crucial concern to the citizenry, dominated this festival where few foreign visitors populated the audience. Perhaps Athens was reluctant to air its greatest concerns before the delegates from the subject states and chose rather to promote the civic dialogue that comedy generated at an event that was organized primarily for the home community.

City officials presided over the organization of both of these festivals: the *archon eponymos* for the City Dionysia, and the *archon basileus* for the Lenaea. The playwrights interested in entering the competitions applied to the appropriate magistrate and the winners each received a chorus. For the City Dionysia, the archon eponymos selected three tragedians and five comic playwrights (although the number might have been reduced to three during the years of the Peloponnesian War); for the Lenaea, the archon basileus designated two tragedians and five comic playwrights. At the City Dionysia, the tragedians would each write a trilogy and a satyr-play while each comic poet focused on only one production. At the Lenaea, the tragedians were limited to two plays apiece, and comic poets again concentrated on one script. After the archon assigned the choruses, he handed over the major financial responsibilities for each playwright to a *choregos*, who would sponsor the training of the chorus and provide the costumes, props, and masks for this group. The *choregoi* were part of the liturgy system in Athens whereby wealthy citizens were required to fund some sort of public activity, whether it was a chorus for one of the major festivals or the maintenance of one of Athens' great warships. Thus, Athens valued sponsorship of the performing arts as much as the financing of military campaigns and so worked into its system of taxation a public obligation to fund large-scale theatrical events.

Crowds of well over 15,000 spectators gathered for the events at the Theater of Dionysus, and the boisterous audience of poor and rich alike assembled in the outdoor seating probably made the festivals seem more like modern sporting events than refined evenings at New York or London theaters. Exactly which members of the community attended the productions is a matter for debate, although many scholars believe that not only male citizens but also women and slaves filled the seats at the Theater of Dionysus. Each member of the audience paid a two-obol admission fee for a day at the festival, a somewhat steep price considering that the average laborer earned about six obols for a day's work. As in modern theaters, the most prominent people were allotted seats in the first rows, and these included such dignitaries as the judges of the competitions and the high priest of Dionysus.

The performance space in the Theater of Dionysus consisted primarily of a dance floor called the orchestra, where the chorus unveiled their numbers. Although it is tempting to conclude from fourth-century remains that the orchestra was circular (as it typically appears in modern reconstructions of Greek theaters), some earlier archaeological evidence indicates that in the fifth century this space was more rectangular. In the middle of the orchestra was a stage altar that served as a visual reminder that the theater doubled as a religious sanctuary. This altar was probably no more than a modest collection of stones or, at most, a small brick or stone-cut construction that in no way impeded the dramatic action. Passages to the left and right of the orchestra through which performers entered and exited the dramatic space (i.e. the wings) were called *eisodoi* or *parodoi*. Behind the orchestra there was a building referred to as the *skene*, one side of which served as the backdrop for the action of the script and offered doors through which actors could enter. The inside of the building probably contained dressing rooms and storage areas for stage properties and other equipment. Immediately in front of the skene was a raised platform with steps leading down to the orchestra. This platform offered a second performance space. In the fourth century, when the chorus became a less integrated part of the dramatic script, the platform of the skene was probably restricted to the actors while the orchestra remained solely the performing space of the chorus.

The Theater of Dionysus also featured two major pieces of theatrical equipment. A platform on wheels, called the *ekkyklema*, could be rolled out of the central door of the *skene* and provided yet another performing space for the production. This feature was especially attractive to playwrights who needed to stage a tableau or a single scene at a setting distinct from the main action. Equally impressive was the theatrical crane or *mekhane* (similar to our cherry-pickers, only decorated) that allowed actors to appear above the regular performance space. The mekhane was often used when deities appeared to intervene in the lives of mortals, or when characters needed to escape the setting of the play by fantastic means. We have no reason to believe that the Greeks did not embellish their performances with all sorts of special effects, as ancient sources testify to stage devices that could replicate the sound of thunder and produce fake lightning.

All roles in the comedy were performed by male actors who wore masks, costumes padded generously at the stomachs and the rumps, and large comic *phalloi* made from leather that dangled below their short tunics. Typically, three or four professionals shared all the major parts, although the producer could add as many mute actors as he wished. The comic choruses consisted of twenty-four young citizen males who came from the local Athenian neighborhoods and who were selected for participation in the dramatic festivals not just because of their talent, but also because civic duty obligated them to serve the city in this capacity. Because choral performance featured so heavily in all of the competitions at the dramatic festivals, it is likely that a good portion of the audience, perhaps even a majority, at one time or another sang and danced in a chorus. This combination of professional actors and amateur choruses created an interesting dynamic in the plays. The exchanges between the two groups could be seen as a dialogue between the fiction of the play and the reality of the chorus or between individuals and the community. Thus, we observe again that Athens valued drama, and in particular comedy, as a powerful civic vehicle that reflected, explored, and challenged the values of democracy.

ARISTOPHANES: COMIC POET AND CIVIC CRITIC

Aristophanes, perhaps the most influential Greek comic dramatist, was born sometime early in the 440s B.C.E. and belonged to the city deme of Cydathenaeum, a community that also produced Cleon, the leading popular politician of the 420s B.C.E. and a source of constant animosity to his neighbor the playwright. Little else is known about Aristophanes' personal life aside from his work in the theater. His comedies are the only ones that survive intact from fifth-century Athens, although we do possess numerous fragments of the plays written by his rivals. Thus, our concept of Athenian comedy is shaped largely from interpreting his plays and appreciating his approach to dramatizing the concerns of his community. When Aristophanes first entered his work into the competitions at the dramatic festivals, Athens was dedicated to the ideals of democracy as well as to the power of empire. The city had just entered into a civil war with Sparta and her allies in the Peloponnese. What ensued was a thirty-year struggle that ended with the surrender of Athens in 404. At the same time, Socrates and other progressive thinkers were becoming increasingly popular amongst the young men of the city as the birth of philosophy radically changed the scope of Athenian education. This situation pitted the elders of the city, who associated themselves with the ideals they believed won Athens her victories against the Persian Empire, against their younger counterparts, whose imperial aggressiveness was embodied in the attitude and disposition of such upstarts as Alcibiades. Aristophanes used comedy to vent his frustrations, and probably those of countless Athenians, at these situations and to explore the possible solutions to these civic and political issues, however farfetched or outlandish they might have appeared.

Although Aristophanes wrote over forty-four comedies, only eleven of them survive intact. Nevertheless, we can draw some conclusions about his early career from the fragments of his first two plays. In 427 B.C.E., Aristophanes entered *Banqueters* into the comic competition at one of the festivals (exactly which one is unknown) under the name of Callistratus, his official producer or *didaskalos*, and the comedy finished in second place. In this play, a father from the rural countryside of Attica sends his two sons to the city to be educated. The Virtuous Son runs back to the farm at the first whiff of the temptations of urban life while the Corrupted Son indulges in the novelties of the city, becomes an aggressive orator, and assumes an effeminate appearance. Needless to say, the father is very upset. The Corrupted Son now thinks that his father is antiquated and borrows the vocabulary of Athens' rising intellectuals, including the sophistically trained Alcibiades, to challenge his family's conservative ways. Aristophanes uses the hyperbolized disputes in this family to illustrate the conflict in fifth-century Athens between the traditional system of Athenian education, which valued the study of great poets such as Homer and required young men to engage in rigorous athletic training, and the sophistic teaching of great thinkers such as Socrates, which many perceived as a corrupting influence on the young and a great threat to the stability of the city. This idea became a theme to which Aristophanes returned many times in his career.

The following year, Aristophanes, again through the assistance of Callistratus, staged his *Babylonians* at the City Dionysia and earned his first victory. It is unclear from the surviving fragments exactly how the plot unfolded. Apparently, there were two main issues debated in the play: the behavior of the foreign ambassadors to Athens who manipulated their audiences with flattering speeches; and the democratic posturing of the cities that sponsored these envoys. Somehow within this framework, Aristophanes staged a harsh satire of the politician Cleon and other leading officials of the city. Cleon charged Aristophanes before the Council with slandering Athens in the presence of foreigners. Although the Council dismissed the charges against the playwright, the feud between the two contenders continued steadily for the next several years as Aristophanes launched one virulent attack after another against Cleon.

At the Lenaea of 425 B.C.E., Aristophanes garnered another first-place victory for his production of *Acharnians*. In this play, the comic hero Dicaeopolis (Greek for "Just Citizen") arrives at the Athenian Assembly, grows disgusted at the gullibility of his fellow citizens and their inability to achieve reconciliation with the Spartans, and arranges a private treaty with the enemy so that his family can enjoy the luxuries of peace. Dicaeopolis stages his own celebration of the Rural Dionysia, a neighborly festival that Athenians held within their own local communities. Dicaeopolis' festival no doubt recalled for his audience members the happy times before the war when neighbors came together to drink wine, feast, play games, and laugh. However, the celebration comes to an abrupt end when a chorus of angry old men from Acharnae appears on the scene and hurls stones at Dicaeopolis and his family. Acharnae was a city north of Athens that had suffered terribly in the opening months of the war when its farmland was devastated in the Spartan raids. Acharnae put tremendous pressure on Athens to retaliate, and the elders of the city would have been justifiably upset to hear that Dicaeopolis would rather negotiate with the enemy than continue to settle the score. In order to win their approval, Dicaeopolis borrows costumes and props from the tragic playwright Euripides and stages a parody of his *Telephos*, where the main character appears in pitiable garb to earn the sympathy of his audience. After his successful appeal, Dicaeopolis opens his own marketplace where merchants from enemy states can enjoy free trade. Among other traders comes a Megarian who has dressed his daughters in pig costumes, a clearly sexual overture, so that he can sell them for an attractive price at the market.

What follows is perhaps Aristophanes' most controversial scene, where a father so desperate for food prostitutes his young daughters. The play ends with a contest between Dicaeopolis and the general Lamachus where Dicaeopolis carefully packs his picnic hamper with sumptuous banquet items while his rival stuffs his knapsack with the rations for an extended military campaign. By the end of the play, the luxuries of peace have defeated the commodities of war, and Dicaeopolis is leading the audience in a triumphant exit song. *Acharnians* is the model Aristophanic comedy: it features a comic hero of working-class origins who cannot seem to reconcile the rhetoric of the politicians with hardships facing his family; it showcases the hero's fantastic plan to overcome this discrepancy; and it ends with the comic rejuvenation of the hero through excessive banqueting and celebratory indulgences. We also see, especially in the scene with Euripides, that Aristophanes has established a dialogue with tragedy and enjoys staging parodies of famous tragic scenes that caught the audience's attention at earlier festivals.

In 424 B.C.E., Aristophanes continued to explore facets of contemporary politics when he produced the first comedy under his own name at the Lenaea festival and earned yet another first-place victory. *Knights* is an allegorical play where the master of the house, Demos (Greek for "Athenian People") has recently acquired a new household slave by the name of Paphlagon. As the comedy unfolds, we discover that Paphlagon is a loosely disguised caricature of Cleon, the demagogue that Aristophanes lampooned several years earlier in his *Babylonians*. When the other slaves in Demos' house grow weary under the oppressive reign of this steward, they decide to find someone equally slick and roguish to contend with their tormenter's underhand tactics. Amidst the rabble at the Athenian agora, they locate their man, a Sausage Seller who reputedly stuffs his sausages with dog and ass meat. In a series of contests, this lowly merchant exposes Paphlagon's tricks, strips him of his stewardship, and secures for himself the favor of Demos. Here again, Aristophanes draws attention to the gullibility of the Athenian people who fall prey to the tricks of slippery politicians like Cleon, who ignore the needs of the city and can be replaced only by individuals who surpass them in dishonest tactics. Even though this satire of Cleon did not prevent him from winning an important election in the weeks after Lenaea, Cleon again indicted Aristophanes, and this time the charges did not disappear so easily. Because public opinion did not vociferously support Aristophanes' comic attack, he was forced to offer a public apology to Cleon, however insincere.

At the City Dionysia of 423 B.C.E., Aristophanes presented *Clouds*, a comedy much like *Banqueters* in that it explored the danger of words and the threat of sophistry. It became arguably Aristophanes' most infamous play because of its satirical portrayal of Socrates. Despite its ambitious plot, it finished last in the comic competition. This defeat stirred in Aristophanes disgust for public opinion because he had hoped to impress his audience with a new approach to comedy. Unfortunately, we do not possess the original script of the play that prompted such a reaction from its author. We have only an unfinished copy that reflects Aristophanes' attempt to revise his beloved failure. Despite its initial reception, however, Aristophanes' *Clouds* had so great an impact on public opinion that in his *Apology* Plato singled it out as a prime source of popular animus against Socrates. In the play, Strepsiades, a country farmer married to an urban wife, decides to send his wastrel son Pheidippides to Socrates' Thinkery in order to learn how to make a wrong argument sound right. Strepsiades hopes to use this new knowledge to develop a way of evading his creditors. When Pheidippides refuses to attend the Thinkery, Strepsiades decides to enroll himself. When he arrives at Socrates' school, he finds the pupils running around naked because they gave their expensive clothes to Socrates as part of their tuition. They are studying what Strepsiades considers absurd topics, but he still decides to subject himself to the teachings of the great philosopher. Socrates grows increasingly frustrated with Strepsiades' ignorance, although he manages to impart enough knowledge that Strepsiades impresses his son upon his return home. Pheidippides begs his father to attend the Thinkery, and there he learns his lessons so well that he easily helps his father chase off the creditors. However, Pheidippides has mastered the sneaky ways of Socrates almost too zealously. He now uses Thinkery logic to declare that it is right for sons to beat their fathers, and, more shocking, their mothers as well. Strepsiades is so disgusted at the treacherous implications of Socrates' teachings that he gathers the necessary equipment and sets fire to the Thinkery. Although in places *Clouds* resembled the scripts that helped Aristophanes secure victories at the dramatic festivals of the 420s, it departed from the stock burlesque scenes and hyperbolic celebrations of these productions and focused instead on a more intellectual approach to comedy that obviously failed to appeal to the popular demands of the audience.

Aristophanes returned to this conflict between the generations in his *Wasps*, a play performed at the Lenaea of 422 B.C.E., where he seems to have entered a second comedy *Proagon* (a satire on the festival event that allowed playwrights to present a "sneak preview" of their productions) into the program under the name of Philonides. *Proagon* finished first in the competition, and *Wasps* earned second place. Aristophanes was obviously determined to revive his reputation after the failure of *Clouds* at the City Dionysia of the year before. The action of *Wasps* takes place at the house of Bdelycleon (Greek for "Loathe-cleon"), a wealthy young man whose elderly father Philocleon (Greek for "Love-cleon") lives with him. Philocleon is obsessed with sitting on Athenian juries and casting the deciding vote in important cases. He constantly sneaks out of the house and meets other old men preoccupied with the same obsession. Bdelycleon convinces his father that he could stage mock trials at home and enjoy all the conveniences of domestic life as he renders his verdicts. After father and son set up this bogus court, Bdelycleon presents a trial where one household dog charges another with pilfering a hunk of Sicilian cheese and devouring it. Actors dressed in dog costumes appear as the prosecution and the defense, and life-size utensils from the kitchen serve as witnesses. The trial serves an allegorical purpose as well. The defendant, here named Labes (Greek for "Snatcher"), is a caricature of the Athenian general Laches, who was accused of using his expedition to Sicily as a means of personal gain, and the prosecutor then becomes a satire of Cleon, who publicly denounced Laches for his actions. Although Philocleon is determined to convict Labes for stealing the cheese, Bdelycleon tricks him into acquitting the dog. Philocleon is so disgusted with himself that he swears never to hear cases again. Instead, he decides to attend an "intellectual" drinking party with his son. Philocleon indulges in every excess at the party, and, by the end of the play, his completely rejuvenated self is leading the celebratory dance that ends many comedies from this period. *Wasps*, much like *Acharnians* and *Knights*, champions a comic hero who defies social norms and achieves the sort of exultant rebirth that most hardworking individuals only imagine.

The next year, Athens was surprisingly optimistic at the time of the City Dionysia. Negotiations for a peace treaty with the Spartans were well underway. In fact, immediately after the festival, the Athenians adopted the Peace of Nicias and, at least temporarily, thought the civil war that had plagued them for a decade was finally coming to an end. Amidst these settlement discussions, Aristophanes composed *Peace*, a play that finished in second place at the City Dionysia of 421 B.C.E. The comic hero Trygaeus, much like Dicaeopolis in *Acharnians*, decides to achieve peace on his own terms. He flies to Mount Olympus on a giant dung-beetle, a clever parody of Euripides' *Bellerophon*, so that he can consult with Zeus about the situation on earth. When he arrives there, he finds that the gods have abandoned Olympus and left the mortals in the hands of War, who has fittingly imprisoned the goddess Peace in a cave. Trygaeus and chorus eventually rescue Peace and her attendants Opora (Greek for "Vintage") and Theoria (Greek for "Holiday") and begin to plan celebrations in honor of Peace's restoration. While Trygaeus is making the preparations for the upcoming sacrifice and the banquet, various intruders, such as an Arms Dealer, a Helmet Maker, and a Spear Maker, interrupt him and complain that Peace will ruin their livelihood. Trygaeus, however, is not deterred and stages an exuberant celebration of Peace in the final scene, which includes his marriage to Peace's attendant Opora. Most likley, Aristophanes had a glimmer of hope when he composed *Peace* that the negotiations over the Peace of Nicias would result in a successful, albeit fleeting, truce with the Spartan opposition. The comedy and the celebrations become all the more poignant when we consider that the hero Trygaeus represented the desires and frustrations of the average Athenian during the first phase of the Peloponnesian War and that, when the treaty disintegrated and hostilities resumed, their disappointments were probably all the more acute.

In the next decade, Athens not only defended itself and its allies against Spartan campaigns but also, at the urging of young statesmen like Alcibiades, developed plans for a large-scale expedition to Sicily that city officials hoped would result in the island becoming a subject state to the Athenian Empire. Many conservative politicians, with the peace-keeping Nicias as their spokesman, worried that Athens' aggressiveness in sending these troops to Sicily would result in defeat (as it eventually did) and betray what they perceived was an alarming increase in Athens' greed and lust for power. When Aristophanes entered *Birds* into the comic competition at the City Dionysia of 414 B.C.E., many people still believed that Athens would emerge triumphant from the Sicilian expedition and the continued conflicts with Sparta. *Birds* is one of Aristophanes' most ambitious scripts, and it has prompted a host of interpretations that raise more questions than answers. In the comedy, two men, Peisetaerus and Euelpides, flee Athens in search of a new community. They meet up with some birds and, with them, establish a comically utopian city called Cloudcuckooville that, because of its location in the sky, conveniently separates mortals from immortals. Because Peisetaerus' plan prevents the gods from receiving their sacrificial offerings, he in effect starves them into recognizing his leadership and allowing him to marry the princess Basileia in honor of his sovereign power. Scholars have debated whether the city that Peisetaerus creates is really a second Athens or a state in opposition to it. Whatever the case, *Birds* exemplifies the utopian quality of old comedy, where the hero is able to act out "ideal" solutions to the problems that overwhelm him in reality and, by extension, he empowers the audience to imagine that they too can achieve the same results.

When Aristophanes staged his *Lysistrata* at the Lenaea of 411 B.C.E., Athens had already suffered terrible defeat in the Sicilian expedition and had only begun to recuperate from its losses. In order to prevent complete devastation, Athens elected a board of ten officials (*Probouloi*) to expedite decisions and bypass the debates in the Assembly. Many Athenians reacted negatively to this diminishment in their democratic liberties. It is no surprise then that, amid the political and financial instability of 411, Aristophanes decided to voice his concerns through a female voice. If critics took offense at Aristophanes' advice, he could always dismiss their reaction by emphasizing the improbability of women like Lysistrata's ever gaining control of the city. In the play, the comic heroine Lysistrata summons the women of Greece, both Athenian and Spartan, and together they plot to put an end to the Peloponnesian War after almost twenty years of civil strife. Lysistrata compels the younger women to refuse their husbands sex while she persuades the older women to take over the Athenian treasury on the Acropolis. Although many of the women weaken under Lysistrata's strict regulations, their plan eventually works and the men of Athens allow Lysistrata to arrange a peace treaty. She leads onstage a beautiful dancing girl and uses her body as map to illustrate the terms of the negotiations. In *Lysistrata*, Aristophanes once again stages a challenge to the leaders of Athens to engineer an end to the hostilities with Sparta and implement an appropriate peace treaty before the community suffers further hardship. Even today, *Lysistrata* has a certain resonance with audiences, and the play has seen numerous revivals in recent years, including a series of productions staged in March 2003 throughout the United States to protest President George W. Bush's decision to invade Iraq.

As the City Dionysia of 411 B.C.E. approached, conditions in Athens had grown even more volatile, and the anxiety of its citizens perhaps compelled Aristophanes to enter his *Thesmophoriazusae* into the comic competition, the only one of his surviving plays that is completely apolitical. The tragedian Euripides has just learned that the women of Athens have decided to plot his destruction when they gather, without the men of the city, for the Thesmophoria, a three-day festival in honor of Demeter. Apparently, they are disgusted at his portrayal of women and believe that he must suffer accordingly so that other playwrights (and audience members) do not adopt his misogynistic attitudes. Euripides convinces one of his in-laws to disguise himself as a woman and infiltrate the festival, and the two of them borrow the necessary accoutrements from the tragic poet Agathon. However, despite his clever costume, the women spot the spy, strip his dress off, expose his comic phallus, and hold him prisoner. Euripides is then forced to rescue his relative, and he uses tactics and stage properties from his own plays to achieve the rescue. *Thesmophoriazusae* is a clever satire of the state of gender relations in late fifth-century Athens, where a man's status in the community depended upon the respectability of his household. Aristophanes pokes fun at male phobias about female propriety, anxieties that Euripides brought to life on the tragic stage in such characters as Medea and Phaedra.

Almost a decade later, Aristophanes was still creating comedies that explored the genre's relationship to tragedy. At the Lenaea festival of 405 B.C.E., Aristophanes produced *Frogs* under the name of his coproducer Philonides. Dionysus, depressed at the tedium of contemporary tragedy, decides to venture down to Hades so that he can rescue one of the great tragedians and restore Greek drama to what it once was. In order to gain easy admission to Hades, Dionysus borrows a disguise from his half-brother Heracles, who, as part of his Twelve Labors, spent some time in the Underworld. Although the Heraclean costume causes Dionysus more harm than good, he eventually convinces Pluto to allow him to judge a contest between Aeschylus and Euripides. The tragedian with the most influential verses can return to the land of the living and compose plays that will benefit Athens. Although he finds it difficult to select a winner, Dionysus awards the prize to Aeschylus because he believes that this playwright will offer the most cogent advice to the city. Soon after the production of this play, Aristophanes was recognized in the Assembly and awarded a celebratory olive garland for the advice that he gave the city in *Frogs*. As a further honor, Athens allowed the comedy to be performed a second time, a mark of distinction granted to few other poets.

Athens surrendered to Sparta in 404 B.C.E., and the hostilities of the previous thirty years were brought to a conclusion, however unsatisfying it might have been for the Athenian populace. Aristophanes survived the political turmoil that ensued and even became a member of the city's Council in 390 or thereabouts. At the same time, he composed his *Ecclesiazusae*, another play in which the women of Athens, led by the comic heroine Praxagora, take control of the city. Here, they disguise themselves as men, infiltrate the Assembly, and establish a communist government where citizens will enjoy the benefits of collective property. The second half of the play demonstrates through comic exaggeration the limits of such a plan. In one scene, a good citizen is lining up his household items so that he can hand them over to Praxagora for redistribution. A dissident comes along and suggests that the good citizen keep his most valuable possessions in case democracy is restored. Even more absurd is the suggestion that sex should be distributed equally among the citizens of the city. According to one of Praxagora's decrees, a young man must sleep with a few older women before he can enjoy the pleasures of a young, attractive lover. Despite the obvious flaws in the plan, the play ends with Praxagora leading the city in a triumphant celebration of the new regime. Aristophanes' *Ecclesiazusae* is one of the earliest texts, comic or otherwise, that debates the merits and drawbacks of communism. Plato's *Republic*, published only a few years later, also discusses similar ideas about collective property and the role of women in government and confirms that such notions were prevalent in Athens at the outset of the fourth century B.C.E.

Economic issues continued to interest Aristophanes at the end of his career. In 388 B.C.E., he is believed to have won first prize at one of the dramatic festivals for his production of *Wealth*. He competed against four other comic poets who staged mythological burlesques, evidence that comedy had undergone significant changes since Aristophanes composed *Banqueters* in 427. At the outset of *Wealth*, an older Athenian, Chremylus, and his trusty slave Carion are returning from the oracle at Delphi where Apollo has instructed Chremylus to take charge of the first person he meets upon leaving the shrine. This individual turns out to be Wealth, a blind old man whose lack of sight prevents him from properly evaluating individuals before he endows them with the benefits of a prosperous lifestyle. Chremylus vows to help restore Wealth's vision, and he engineers a successful plan whereby he and Carion take Wealth to a shrine of Asclepius and allow the god of healing to implement a remedy. Despite the outcries of the character Poverty, once Wealth regains his vision, he begins to reward the virtuous and punish the wicked, and by the end of the play even the Olympian gods surrender to his supremacy. Although *Wealth* has received little attention from modern scholars of comedy, it was the most popular Aristophanic script circulating in the Middle Ages, perhaps because Christian scholars, and subsequent generations of translators and editors, preferred to read a play relatively devoid of the bawdy humor and sexual innuendoes that dominated Aristophanes' other works. In contrast, *Wealth* can easily fit into the Christian canon of the Middle Ages, where good individuals receive rewards for their upright behavior.

Aristophanes' son Araros produced his last two plays, *Cocalus* and *Aeolosicon*. Both of these mythological burlesques were considered definite precursors of middle comedy. *Cocalus* won first prize at the City Dionysia of 387 B.C.E., and, as *Vita Aristophanis* (the ancient biography of Aristophanes) testifies, it showcased elements of comedy that Menander imitated. *Aiolosicon* featured the sort of cook that became a stock character of middle and new comedy. By the end of his career, then, Aristophanes had greatly transformed his approach to comedy. No longer did he focus on the satire of social and political issues or create appealing comic heroes who championed the concerns of the average Athenian and invented hyperbolic solutions to these problems. He and his fellow playwrights seemed to focus instead on retelling the mythological stories of the tragic stage with a comic twist, an approach that would eventually lead to the domestic farces of Menander. No doubt, we can see the roots of modern comedy in the plays of Aristophanes: the comic timing of standard slapstick routines, ridiculous disguises, cheap sexual jokes, and exaggerated norms. More importantly, Aristophanes proves the social value of comedy and links our preoccupations with those of the Athenians.

ARISTOPHANES' RIVALS

Although our primary evidence for the form and content of old comedy comes from the surviving plays of Aristophanes, we possess thousands of fragments from his contemporary playwrights that help shape our knowledge of the genre. In his *Poetics*, Aristotle records that Chionides was one of the earliest comic playwrights, and he is widely regarded as the first official victor at the comic competitions of the City Dionysia. However, after the initial surge of comic poets in the 480s B.C.E., the genre seems to have suffered from a lack of innovation and satiric wit in the 470s and 460s. Magnes was the most prominent playwright in this period and earned a total of eleven victories at the City Dionysia, a record that was not surpassed in the history of old comedy. However, Aristophanes implies that the quality of Magnes' comedy was not very high.

In the 450s B.C.E., Cratinus, the next major comic playwright, and his contemporaries began to revive old comedy with fresh routines and a return to the political satire that so defined the earlier plays of this period. Perhaps these innovations drew their inspiration from the comedies produced on the island of Sicily that were popularized by the comic poet Epicharmus (fl. c. 500–465 B.C.E.). These plays seemed to focus on current issues of interest to the local population and often staged utopian solutions to common problems. The exact relationship between comedy in Athens and Sicily is unclear, although the Athenian poets who thrived at the end of the fifth century seem to owe a debt to the comic tradition that developed independently on this island.

Aristophanes certainly credits Cratinus (fl. c. 453–423 B.C.E.) as being his most formidable predecessor and the fiercest competitor of his early career. In 430, just after the initial outbreak of the Peloponnesian War, Cratinus staged his *Dionysalexandros*, one of our most complete fragmentary comedies. It draws its plot from the mythological tale of the Judgment of Paris in which the Trojan prince Paris, when asked to select the loveliest of Greek goddesses, chooses Aphrodite because she promises to reward him with the most beautiful mortal woman, Helen, the queen of Sparta. Cratinus alters the myth by having Dionysus disguise himself as Paris so that he can judge the contest and benefit from any sexual enticements the goddesses might offer to secure his vote. Dionysus too awards the prize to Aphrodite and eagerly lures Helen away from her home in Sparta. When the couple arrives back in Troy, the true Paris stumbles upon the pair and demands that Dionysus return Helen to her Greek husband. Helen begs Paris not to surrender her to the Greeks, who will no doubt be angry at her adulterous ways, and Paris eventually agrees to marry her. Somewhere within this mythological burlesque, Cratinus made the disguised Dionysus serve as a caricature of Pericles, the leading Athenian statesman whom public opinion accused of initiating the events that led to the Peloponnesian War. However, Cratinus' most interesting play was not this mythological burlesque but a semiautobiographical comedy, *Wine Flask*, that won the comic competition at the City Dionysia of 423, the same festival where Aristophanes' *Clouds* finished in last place. In *Wine Flask*, the poet himself served as the protagonist. His wife Comoidia (Greek for "Comedy") is seeking a divorce from Cratinus on the grounds of neglect and mistreatment, most likely because he is smitten with Drunkenness. If the fragments are any indication of the quality of the play, it is no wonder that Aristophanes' *Clouds*, with its wordy jokes and bleak ending, failed to impress the festival audience.

A number of other playwrights frequented the festivals as Cratinus' career drew to a close and Aristophanes replaced him as the most notorious comic voice in Athens. Crates (fl. c. 450–430 B.C.E.) composed comedies that featured banquets and symposia instead of references to contemporary individuals. Celebratory scenes of this sort certainly became stock features of old comedy at the end of the fifth century and contributed to the tradition of featuring a cook or mad chef in middle and new comedy. Crates was also credited with creating more universal plots and moving the genre away from ad hominem attacks. His *Animals*, for example, imagined what would happen if humans were forced to stop consuming animals as food. At the same time, Pherecrates (fl. 437–after 415) generated "courtesan comedies" in which prostitutes starred as the leading characters, and he was considered an obvious forerunner of later Greek playwrights who favored love themes as opposed to political satire. He also staged such utopian comedies as *Agrioi* (Wild Men), where men leave "civilized" urban life to live a more "primitive" existence, and *Metalles* (Miners), which portrayed the Underworld as full of luxuries and abundance.

Just before Aristophanes began to enter his plays into the comic competitions, Eupolis (fl. 429–412 B.C.E.) launched his career and soon became one of Aristophanes' fiercest rivals. He won seven first-place victories from his seventeen entries at the festivals. At the Lenaea of 421, he staged his *Maricas*, a satire of the demagogue Hyperbolus that resembled Aristophanes' caricature of Cleon in *Knights*, although Eupolis dared to take Aristophanes' humor one step further and included jokes about Hyperbolus' mother. Two of Eupolis' other plays were clear forerunners of Aristophanes' *Frogs*. His *Demes*, performed somewhere between 418 and 406, featured illustrious Athenians of the past who were summoned from Hades to offer advice. In *Taxiarchs*, Eupolis depicted Dionysus aboard a boat in a scene where Phormion instructed the god of theater on military and naval training just as Charon taught Dionysus to row in *Frogs*. Ameipsias (fl. 423–c. 395) also premiered a few years after Eupolis and Aristophanes. Although few of his plays survive even in fragments, we know that at least two of Ameipsias' comedies defeated Aristophanes' masterpieces. His *Connus* placed second at the City Dionysia of 423, where Cratinus' *Wine Flask* won and Aristophanes' *Clouds* lost. Connus was Socrates' music teacher; Socrates himself had a role; and the chorus featured a band of sophists. In 414 Ameipsias' *Comastae* robbed Aristophanes' *Birds* of a victory at the City Dionysia.

Later in his career, Aristophanes' most formidable competitor was Plato Comicus (fl. 422–c. 380 B.C.E.), who secured his first victory at the City Dionysia around 410. Throughout his career, he composed both political satires and mythological burlesques. Several other comic playwrights also challenged Aristophanes' reputation: Strattis (fl. c. 410–c. 385), who appeared to focus on tragic parody in plays such as *Medea*, *Philoctetes*, and *Phoenissae*; Archippus (fl. 403–400), whose utopian comedy *Fishes* resembled the plot of Aristophanes' *Birds* except that this time the characters forged their alliance with aquatic creatures; and Philiscus (fl. c. 400–380), who produced several plays that featured comic versions of the birth legends of the Olympian deities. When Aristophanes withdrew from the theater, comedy had no doubt undergone significant transformation; what began as the civic and political dialogue of the komos, where rival groups used humor and satire to air their frustrations with the city, had developed into a flourishing profession.

THE TRANSITION TO MIDDLE COMEDY

The next major phase in the history of Greek comedy, aptly termed *middle comedy*, began at the death or retirement of Aristophanes (c. 385 B.C.E.) and lasted until the premier of Menander's first comedies (c. 321 B.C.E.), although most scholars agree that these dates are an artificial construct generated to facilitate discussion of Greek comedy's evolution. Many factors contributed to the shift away from the political satire that so defined old comedy. There seems to have been a series of legislative acts designed to curtail the voice of the comic poet and limit the scope of his satire. A popular mythology even developed around these decrees. Scholars of antiquity began to identify Eupolis' death as an instigating factor in the shift from old to middle comedy. Although the truth of the account is, at best, only plausible, Alcibiades reportedly threw Eupolis overboard en route to the Sicilian expedition because he was vexed at Eupolis' satire of him. Apparently, after this incident, comic poets started to worry about the ramifications of their attacks on leading individuals and gradually changed their comedy. Also, at the beginning of the fourth century B.C.E., the institution of the choregos did not appear as financially sound as it had been at the height of Athenian democracy. Most important, however, dramatic poets wanted to market their plays outside of Athens, and topical comedy was naturally hard to sell to foreign audiences. A combination of these issues prompted Athenian playwrights to abandon the traditional approach to Greek comedy that provided a public forum for a comic look at the foibles that plagued the city and to turn instead to mythological burlesques or domestic farces that featured such stock characters as "the young man in love," "the cook," "the parasite," "the wily slave," and "the difficult old man."

Unfortunately, the surviving fragments of middle comedy do not allow scholars to construct detailed portraits of the playwrights who thrived during this period. Comic poets such as Anaxandrides (fl. c. 385–348), Antiphanes (fl. c. 387–306), Eubulus (fl. c. 375–c. 335), and Alexis (fl. c. 350–c. 275) composed plays that featured banquet scenes and the preparations for such feasts; provided comic commentary on social institutions such as marriage or on workaday experiences such as trips to the marketplace; and offered philosophical, yet lighthearted, observations about life in general. One playwright, Timocles (fl. c. 345–c. 315), seems to have continued in the tradition of Aristophanes by creating satires of such leading political figures as Demosthenes. Almost all of these dramatists generated vast numbers of plays, clearly more than could have been performed at the annual dramatic festivals. These statistics betray the tendency of these playwrights to market their material outside of Athens and indicate a shift in the persona of the comic poet. No longer is his role civically defined by his participation in the competitions and democratic ceremonies of the Lenaea and the City Dionysia; his loyalties have now moved to more professional aims and to assuring the wider circulation of his scripts.

MENANDER AND NEW COMEDY

Born between 343 and 341 B.C.E., Menander composed over 108 comedies, many of which were probably produced outside Athens, although, unlike many of his contemporaries, he did not choose to seek artistic patronage abroad. Although he was not that popular a playwright during his own lifetime, he was considered the most noteworthy poet of new comedy in later generations. Menander inherited a tradition of comedy that had been apolitical for at least thirty or forty years. Athenians were now conflicted as to whether they should support the regimes of Macedon that succeeded Alexander, or pursue independence. Given this instability in the city at the end of the fourth century, it is no wonder that Menander chose to focus on the humor of domestic situations and relegate to the past the vituperative satire of Aristophanes. Menander's success developed from his ability to mold the stock characters of middle comedy into more individualized and compelling figures with sympathetic and distinctive traits. A student of both the comic playwright Alexis and the philosopher Theophrastus, Menander took care to bring his characters to life and to carry Greek comedy one step further toward realism.

The plays of new comedy were all but lost to modern scholars until the end of the nineteenth century, when fragments of Menander's plays were discovered amid the papers at St. Catherine's monastery at Mount Sinai. By the beginning of the twentieth century, several important papyrus finds and the publication of an important medieval codex greatly changed our impression of Menander, which had previously depended upon the Roman adaptations of his plays. Thus the field of new comedy has been radically transformed in the past century. The importance of these discoveries is heightened by the fact that we possess only one other identifiable fragment from this period—a monologue of a "mad chef" from a comedy by Straton (fl. 302). We do know that Diphilus (fl. c. 320–c. 285) and Philemon (fl. 327–c. 263) were contemporaries of Menander, but scholars cannot attribute any comic fragments to these authors.

Whereas Aristophanes relied very little upon plot structure to achieve his comic agenda, Menander based the humor and richness of his productions on the intricacies of his narrative. It is unfortunate that only his *Dyskolos* (*The Grouchy Old Man*) survived in entirety. It was performed at the Lenaea of 316 B.C.E. Just as in Menander's other plays, the action was divided into five discrete acts, separated from one another by choral interludes that had nothing to do with the progression of the story. Doors on skene represented the houses of the two families in question. At the outset, we meet the curmudgeon Cnemon, who embodies all the qualities of a misanthrope and constantly expresses his disgust with humanity. He lives next door to his stepson Gorgias and Gorgias' mother. Cnemon's beautiful daughter resides with him. Sostratus, a handsome young man visiting the countryside, spots the daughter at a well and falls madly in love with her. He appeals to Gorgias for help in securing the girl's hand in marriage. Gorgias suggests that Sostratus impress his stepfather by zealously performing chores on the farm. Meanwhile, Cnemon falls down his family's well. Thankfully, Gorgias is able to rescue him. Cnemon is so overwhelmed with gratitude that he officially adopts Gorgias and appoints him guardian of his daughter. Gorgias awards her to Sostratus, whose father agrees to consider Gorgias as his son-in-law. At the end of the play, Cnemon is carried off to the wedding celebration, somewhat more resigned to casting aside a few of his misanthropic ways. Here we see one of the standard stories of new comedy, where the action revolves around schemes to unite two hapless lovers. Although the audience expects the story to end happily with some sort of wedding celebration, they derive pleasure from watching young men like Sostratus undergo trials and tribulations in order to win his bride.

A few years later, in 313 or 312, Menander staged *Perikeiromene* (*Shorn*), a play based on the exposure of a child, a storyline that the playwrights of new comedy pilfered from the tragic stage. In the fifth century B.C.E., Sophocles in *Tyro* and Euripides in *Ion* popularized this type of dramatic narrative. In *Shorn* the tale unravels not in a mythological context but in a Corinthian town. A soldier, Polemon, returns home from a military campaign only to find his mistress, Glycera, embracing the neighbor, Moschion. He immediately concludes that the couple is having an affair, cuts off all of Glycera's hair, and expels her from the house. Glycera and Moschion are not lovers but siblings. Apparently, their father, Pataecus, exposed the children, who were in turn adopted and then separated. Glycera eventually learns the truth about her parentage, but she never tells Moschion. Polemon confides in his friend Pataecus that he is miserable without Glycera. Pataecus visits Glycera on Polemon's behalf and recognizes that Glycera's possessions belonged to his wife. The truth about the siblings is revealed, and Polemon and Glycera are reunited. The exposure of infants, although not nearly as common in Greece as the plays of Menander seem to indicate, provided a convenient construct for all sorts of comic misunderstandings and allowed unlikely relationships to spring up between the characters in the drama.

In other plays, the action of the comedy revolved around a young man's rape of a local girl. Although this situation startles most modern readers, fourth-century audiences would have sympathized more with a respectable girl being robbed of her innocence than with one who succumbed to the powers of seduction. In *The Samian Woman*, Demeas has taken a Samian prostitute named Chrysis as his consort. His son Moschion is the father of a baby that Niceratus' daughter Plangon bore after Moschion raped her. Demeas and Niceratus do not yet know about their children's situation, and Chrysis tries to help the couple by taking care of the baby. Demeas and Niceratus, still ignorant of the rape, plan a wedding to unite the households. When Demeas learns about the child, he mistakenly concludes that Chrysis has betrayed him by having an affair with his son. Demeas throws Chrysis out of the house, and, in order to rectify things, Moschion admits to his actions. Demeas and Chrysis reunite, and Niceratus, albeit reluctantly given the rape, agrees to betroth his Plangon to Moschion. Although like *The Grouchy Old Man* in that it too features the thwarted union of two young lovers, the plot of *The Samian Woman* is driven not by the unrequited love of the couple but by their shame and embarrassment.

Roman playwrights of the third and second centuries B.C.E. championed new comedy and closely modeled their productions on the scripts of Menander and his contemporaries. We know for certain that Plautus based his *Aulularia*, *Bacchides*, *Cistellaria*, and *Stichus* on close interpretations of Menander's plays, and that Terence altered Menander's style and adjusted his plots to fit the comedy of his *Adelphoe*, *Andria*, *Eunuchus*, and *Heautontimorumenos*. Later generations of dramatists, from Shakespeare to the creators of modern sitcoms, used the comic misunderstandings and thwarted love affairs of these narratives as source material for their romantic comedies and domestic farces. Although there seems to be no connection between the new comedy approach and the biting satire and civic criticism of Aristophanes and his rivals, old and new comedy both reflect the preoccupations of their audience. Fifth-century Athenians viewed comedy as a vehicle through which they could air their frustrations at the political and social issues that overwhelmed them in their daily lives. Their Roman descendants chose to use comedy as a means of examining the disappointments and dissatisfactions of the home front. Despite this shift in priorities, the power of comedy remained consistent: it allowed the audience to laugh at their problems, whether public or private, and enjoy a momentary release from their anxieties.

REFERENCES AND FURTHER READINGS

Dover, K. J. *Aristophanic Comedy*. Berkeley: U of California P, 1972.

Harvey, David, and John Wilkins, eds. *The Rivals of Aristophanes: Studies in Athenian Old Comedy*. London: Gerald Duckworth, 2000.

Henderson, Jeffrey J., trans. and ed. *Aristophanes*. 4 vols. Cambridge, MA: Harvard UP, 1998–2002.

Hunter, R. L. *The New Comedy of Greece and Rome*. Cambridge, UK: Cambridge UP, 1985.

MacDowell, Douglas M. *Aristophanes and Athens: An Introduction to the Plays*. Oxford, UK: Oxford UP, 1995.

Silk, M. S. *Aristophanes and the Definition of Comedy*. Oxford, UK: Oxford UP, 2000.

Sommerstein, Alan H. *Greek Drama and Dramatists*. New York: Routledge, 2000.

Webster, T.B.L. *An Introduction to Menander*. Manchester, UK: Manchester UP, 1974.

25

Irish Comedy

James M. Cahalan

Consider the following comic samples from five widely different sources—a recent joke, the world's most famous satire, a history play by Shakespeare, the most celebrated Irish novel, and a contemporary film based on a novel by another very popular Dublin author:

1. What's the definition of Irish Alzheimer's disease? That's where you forget everything except the grudges.
2. In "A Modest Proposal" (1729), Dublin bishop Jonathan Swift argued that Irish overpopulation and starvation could both be greatly ameliorated via the simple mechanism of selling the babies of the poor to be eaten by other Irish people such as landlords "who, as they have already devoured most of the parents, seem to have the best title to the children" (2146).
3. In *Henry V* (1600) Shakespeare sent MacMorris, a bumbling Irishman, onto the stage to ask belligerently and drunkenly, "What ish my nation? Ish a villain, and a bastard, and a knave, and a rascal? What ish my nation? Who talks of my nation?" (act 3, sc. 2, 724).
4. In *Ulysses* (1922), James Joyce revised Shakespeare's scene by having his modern Cyclops, the anti-Semitic, super-Gaelic "Citizen," hurl the same question at his comic Odysseus, the Jewish ad salesman Leopold Bloom, in Barney Kiernan's pub:

    —What is your nation if I may ask? says the citizen.
    —Ireland, says Bloom. I was born here. Ireland.
    The citizen said nothing only cleared the spit out of his gullet and, gob, he spat a Red bank oyster out of him right in the corner. (272)

5. In *The Commitments* (1991), members of Dublin's white soul band of that name appropriate James Brown's slogan, exclaiming on the big screen, "I'm black, and I'm proud!" Band leader Jimmy Rabbitte explains more graphically in Roddy Doyle's original novel (1987): "The Irish are the niggers of Europe, lads" (9).

As diverse as they are, what do these various examples have in common? They all take Ireland's long colonial history, along with prejudice both against and amidst Irishmen, as the butt of jokes, satire, and comedy. Like Jewish and African American peoples, the Irish boast long, exceptionally rich comic traditions, and much of their comedy offers not only comic relief but also defense mechanisms against and comic intensification of the centuries-old oppression of their island. This is true whether the comedy is multifaceted, as created by native Irish writers such as Joyce and Roddy Doyle, or stereotyping from outside Ireland, as in Shakespeare's stage Irishman (despite Eugene O'Neill's father's belief that Shakespeare was an Irishman).

Much as W. H. Auden wrote about the country's greatest poet, William Butler Yeats, that "mad Ireland hurt you into poetry" (2398), it is paradoxical that Ireland's tragic history provoked much of its comedy. Some decidedly unfunny background is necessary here. Before 1600 Ireland existed largely as a series of disparate little kingdoms, each controlled by a different Gaelic chieftain, beyond the "Pale" surrounding Dublin that was controlled more directly by the representatives of the English crown. During the 1590s Ulstermen Red Hugh O'Donnell and Hugh O'Neill joined forces in order to maintain control over their northern regions, and they waged a campaign that spread across Ireland to the south—culminating at Kinsale, County Cork, in 1601, where the chieftains and their Spanish allies were defeated by the English. O'Donnell and other so-called earls subsequently fled the country, and the English annexed their lands, according to the ongoing pattern of Irish history whereby native resistance was repeatedly met with an increasingly severe colonial backlash. In the 1640s, as a further example, the uprising of Leinsterman Rory O'More was followed by the brutal invasion in 1649 of the forces of Oliver Cromwell, which began with the extermination of 3,000 men, women, and children in Drogheda and continued with an eight-month campaign of terror that broke the backbone of remaining native opposition. "To hell or to Connaught" was the slogan after 1649, as Catholic farmers in the fertile midlands were forced to leave their lands and move to the rocky highlands of the west coast. English, Scottish, and Anglo-Irish Protestant landlords were given their lands, with Scottish plantation most extensive in the north, creating the circumstances for the Ulster "Troubles" that continue to this day.

In 1689–1690 the rival kings, Catholic James II and Protestant William of Orange, fought out their disagreements on Irish soil in such key sites as the city of Derry and the Boyne River valley, with James' forces defeated at the battles of the Boyne and Aughrim in 1690. An anti-Catholic Penal Age ensued, and the Siege of Derry and "Remember the Boyne" remain the touchstones of twenty-first-century Protestant hardliners. Outlawing Catholicism meant criminalizing the vast majority of Ireland's population. It was in the depths of the Penal Age that Swift published his hilarious, biting "Modest Proposal." This Anglo-Irish dean of St. Patrick's Cathedral could be scornful of his Catholic, Gaelic countrymen, but he was also representative of a privileged Protestant class that came to see that its interests were not well served by English imperialism. The most enlightened Protestant leaders increasingly identified themselves with a growing sense of Irish nationalism, and they had the money and the political power to do something about it. A Dublin "Patriot Parliament" (1782–1800), led by such Protestant politicians as Henry Grattan and Henry Flood, demonstrated the advantages of Irish Home Rule. More radical Protestant nationalists led short-lived rebellions against English rule in 1798 in counties Mayo, Wexford, and Antrim. The result of 1798 was the 1800 Act of Union, which abolished the Patriot Parliament and fully annexed Ireland under direct rule from London. In the 1820s Daniel O'Connell, the most popular Catholic leader in Irish history, organized massive rallies against the

Penal Code and won Catholic Emancipation in 1828, though it was partial, with only middle- and upper-class Catholics given the vote.

Then a virus struck the potato crop that Irish peasants everywhere had come to depend on for a living; the island's population, squeezed onto small and poor farmlands that they could only rent, had burgeoned to 8 million by the early nineteenth century. During the Great Hunger of 1845–1851, more than a million people died and more than a million others were forced to emigrate. It took the country a half century to recover; by 1900 Ireland's population was about 4 million, half what it had been a century earlier, and it remains highly unusual if not unique among nations in that even today the population of the whole island—now about 5 million—is much lower than it was two centuries ago. Reforming land acts were passed in the late nineteenth century, and the word "boycott" was coined by the Land League, which waged a nonviolent campaign in 1880 against a land agent, Captain Charles Boycott. The cause of Irish nationalism was set back in 1890–1891 by the eventual defeat and death of the Protestant leader of the Irish Parliamentary Party, Charles Stewart Parnell, the century's second great Irish leader, widely called the "uncrowned king of Ireland."

Only in the twentieth century did decisive change come to Ireland. After the one-week Easter Rising in April 1916, led by nationalist Patrick Pearse and his Irish Volunteers and by socialist James Connolly and his Irish Citizen Army, yet another English backlash consisted of the summary execution of Pearse, Connolly, and thirteen other leaders. This time, though, Irish people produced their own, bigger backlash. George Bernard Shaw acerbically and accurately quipped that by executing the Rising's leaders, the English canonized them. As people read the accounts of the executions—which included descriptions of how Connolly, wounded during the fighting, was brought before the firing squad in a wheelchair, with gangrene in his legs—apathy was replaced by outrage. A Sinn Féin ("ourselves alone") movement established a Dublin Dáil (parliament), and the subsequent Anglo-Irish War of 1919–1920 resulted in the infamous yet pivotal treaty of 1921 that divided the island between a twenty-six-county Free State, which became the completely independent Republic of Ireland in 1948, and Northern Ireland, consisting of the only six counties with Protestant majorities, where solutions to never-ending Troubles are still being sought today.

All of this grim history provides the context in which Irish people required comedy for therapy and survival. Irish history has also been itself the subject of pointed yet witty tales. Take, for example, the two historical figures in Irish history about whom more folktales were collected, within the world's single largest national folklore archives, than anyone else: Oliver Cromwell and Daniel O'Connell. These two involve stark contrasts. Remembered partly in English history as a political reformer, in Irish history Cromwell was, in harshly objective rather than moral terms, the most successful Protestant, English leader ever to deal with Ireland: he wiped out Catholic opposition in eight months. In contrast, O'Connell may have been the most popular Irish Catholic leader ever, but his career ended in defeat. Not only did he become unpopular after 1843, but he died in despair in "Black '47," in the middle of the Famine.

However, the many folktales about Cromwell and O'Connell subvert the actual trajectories of their careers and reverse their positions in terms of success and failure. In the traditional stories, Cromwell always loses and O'Connell always wins—in telling and entertaining, often macabre ways. In truth Cromwell died in bed in London at the age of fifty-nine, but in Irish folktales he "is generally said to have killed himself either by cutting his own throat or casting his body against a spear" (Ó Súilleabháin 481).

Various stories have him dying in Ireland, with his corpse then rejected by the Irish soil and the coffin found back aboveground each morning. He is then cast into the sea and drifts like a boat around the Irish coast, trying in vain to land somewhere, but is rejected everywhere; finally he sinks to the bottom of the Irish sea, which explains why its waters remain so turbulent even today. The "curse of Cromwell"—sometimes still invoked by Irish parents who tell their children that if they disobey, "Cromwell will come and get you"—is thus reversed, exacted on Cromwell himself in bizarre forms of revenge.

As for O'Connell, his disgrace and demise during 1843–1847 are nowhere to be found in Irish folktales. Instead, he is a trickster figure who always outsmarts his opponents. O'Connell did in fact become a successful lawyer and outstanding orator—features of his career that storytellers readily embellished. As with Cromwell, the power of wishful, revengeful thinking is readily apparent in these stories. For example, "O'Connell Wears His Hat in Parliament" tells of an Englishman who swore that he would shoot himself if O'Connell ever sat in Parliament. Then O'Connell was not only elected, but insisted on not removing his hat in Parliament, excusing himself with the claim that he had a bad headache for which he needed the hat. After three days of this ruse, O'Connell proclaimed to the House that "Whatever passes three days in Parliament becomes law," so that he could keep his hat on while everyone else was bareheaded, while he also complained that there was a "perjurer" in the House. "The man who had sworn to shoot himself heard the remark, and he went out into the yard and shot himself" (O'Sullivan 233).

Like African Americans, Irishmen were depicted as gorillas in cartoons, in English magazines such as *Punch*. In stories such as this one—which hinges on not only the magnificence of O'Connell as trickster, but also the literal-minded idiocy of his English opponent—Irish storytellers exacted their comic revenge. The *Punch* cartoonists and their like made fun of Irishmen from an *out*side, racist perspective; this story about O'Connell is told from the Irish *in*side. It literally explodes the Englishman, who, like Cromwell, is pushed back outside Ireland, and who, like Cromwell, commits suicide—a more moral, if macabre, form of revenge than if either were shot dead by O'Connell or another Irishman.

The *outside* and the *inside* of Irish comedy also involve the clash—but also the fusion, in the best modern Irish writing—of two very different languages: English and Irish Gaelic. The classic English of Shakespeare and Swift is worlds apart from the Gaelic of the teller of the story about O'Connell's hat, Seán Mac Criomhthain (as translated by Sean O'Sullivan). Yet it was the thesis of Vivian Mercier's book *The Irish Comic Tradition* (1962), the single most important study of Irish comedy, that "an unbroken comic tradition may be traced in Irish literature from approximately the ninth century down to the present day" (vii). In his groundbreaking work, Mercier links not only writers in both languages, but also the literatures of modern and ancient Ireland, emphasizing the "archaic" obsession of much modern Irish writing (Cahalan, "Mercier's Irish Comic Tradition" 142–43). During the nineteenth century the percentage of Gaelic speakers declined from about 50 percent in 1800 to about 10 percent in 1900, with the major Irish-speaking, or Gaeltacht, areas limited to parts of Counties Donegal, Galway, and Clare (including the Aran Islands), and Kerry, and west Cork. However, Douglas Hyde founded the Gaelic League in 1893, Irish was revived if not restored, and even more importantly for modern literature, writers such as Hyde, John Millington Synge, and Lady Augusta Gregory invented new forms of "Irish English," based directly on Gaelic as well as on the versions of English spoken throughout Ireland. Much of their best writing was comic, as in Synge's *The Playboy of the Western World* (1907) and Gregory's *Spreading the News* (1904).

Mercier points out that the wildest, most innovative modern work, Joyce's *Finnegans Wake* (1939), was founded on the oldest of forms, the pun (80)—beginning with its often mispunctuated title, which refers not only to the alcoholic song "Finnegan's Wake" but also to the awakening of many Finnegans. Mercier argues that even though Swift knew no Irish, "he fits perfectly into the Gaelic tradition" (188), and he included whole sections devoted to "Similarities between Swift and the Gaelic Satirists" and "The Influence of Swift on Gaelic Satire." Many Irish writers would get into trouble with the harsh censorship imposed beginning in the late 1920s by the ironically named Irish Free State. Even perfectly innocent books such as Eric Cross' *The Tailor and Ansty* (1942), about the wonderful County Cork storyteller Tailor Tim Buckley, were banned. Frank O'Connor accurately declares in his preface to that book that reading the Senate debate that led to its banning was "like a long, slow swim through a sewage bed" (8). In *The Unfortunate Fursey* (1946) and *The Return of Fursey* (1948), Mervyn Wall cleverly avoided censorship by setting these fantastic satires in medieval times and omitting any reference to sex. He included a censor who finds the Old Testament "in general tendency indecent" (the catch-phrase of the Irish censors) and who has two independently moving eyes—one to read a text in general and one just to focus on the "dirty" words.

Even before the "Free" State, a socially and sexually reactionary Irish nationalism had warmed up by provoking riots in 1907 over Synge's *The Playboy of the Western World* (now regarded as perhaps the greatest Irish play ever written). Synge's masterpiece told of a young man at first harbored and lionized by a village after he claims that he killed his father. Dublin nationalists were scandalized by Christy Mahon's reference to "shifts" (slips) late in the play when he proclaims that he loves Pegeen Mike so much that he would be indifferent if he were offered "a drift of chosen females, standing in their shifts itself" (54). Apparently this mention of women's undergarments was regarded as even more shocking than Gaelic Ireland's embrace of a supposed murderer. But the irony is that Synge was inspired by ancient Gaelic narratives about Cúchulain, the epic hero who had already been turned into a national hero by Standish O'Grady, Yeats, and Gregory. "Cúchulain was permitted the vision of thirty naked virgins in the native manuscript and in Lady Gregory's version," points out Declan Kiberd, who became Mercier's successor as the leading scholar of Irish literature in both languages. "Synge had clad his maidens demurely in 'shifts' to appease the prudish members of the Abbey audience," but "the latter-day disciples of Cúchulain could not tolerate the vision of a peasant boy, whose fury was soothed (if only in his imagination) by females standing in shifts" (119).

Cúchulain's naked virgins constituted only a relatively mild sample of the old Gaelic tradition, which was often much racier in its comic manifestations, as in this short verse cited by Mercier and translated by modern short-story comic master Frank O'Connor: "There's a girl in these parts— / A remarkable thing! / But the force of her farts / Is like stones from a sling" (109). Similarly, Queen Medb (Maeve), Cúchulain's great epic compatriot, was known to urinate so forcefully that she washed away entire mountains. Such outrageous descriptions readily inspired the modern mock-epic narratives of Joyce and Flann O'Brien, as in Joyce's introduction of his Cyclops in *Ulysses*:

From shoulder to shoulder he measured several ells and his rocklike mountainous knees were covered, as was likewise the rest of his body wherever visible, with a strong growth of tawny prickly hair in hue and toughness similar to the mountain gorse (*Ulex Europeus*). The widewinged nostrils, from which bristles of the same tawny hue projected, were of such capaciousness that within their cavernous obscurity the fieldlark might easily have lodged her nest. (243)

In *At Swim-Two-Birds* (1939), O'Brien's similarly exuberant descriptions were still more thoroughly rooted in old Gaelic narratives informing his celebration of his version of Finn MacCool, the other chief hero of the old sagas. O'Brien, who held an M.A. in Celtic Studies from University College, Dublin, assures us that Finn's thighs were "as thick as a horse's belly, narrowing to a calf as thick as the belly of a foal. Three fifties of fosterlings could engage with handball against the wideness of his backside, which was large enough to halt the march of men through a mountain-pass" (10).

Mercier delineates several major types of comedy that run through both Gaelic and Anglo-Irish writing: fantasy, the macabre and grotesque, wit and wordplay, satire, and parody. All of these types lie at the heart of much of the modern Irish literature best known to most readers. Yet Mercier did not attempt to cover all of the types of Irish comedy; he admitted, for example, that he had drafted another chapter on stage-Irish plays, but then left it out because there were no Gaelic plays and thus continuity could not be shown (viii). Therefore, Maureen Waters' *The Comic Irishman* (1984) is a valuable complement to Mercier's book, as she devotes herself to the character types of "The Rustic Clown or Fool," "The Rogue," "The Stage Irishman," and "The Comic Hero" in Anglo-Irish writing. Whereas Mercier's comic types are all native or "inside" in origin, the stage Irishman was more "outside," hankering back to Shakespeare's MacMorris. Stage-Irish comedy was indeed dependent on the gulf between England and Ireland, and much of it was created by Irishmen in England, including the Anglo-Irish playwrights William Congreve, George Farquhar, Richard Brinsley Sheridan, Dion Boucicault, Oscar Wilde, and George Bernard Shaw. Some medieval settlers in Ireland had become "more Irish than the Irish themselves," but Wilde and Shaw became more English than the English themselves. Perhaps the most perfect example of this phenomenon is Wilde's masterpiece *The Importance of Being Earnest* (1895). Intimately acquainted with upper-crust English society, yet always examining it from the perspective of a Dubliner who spent his first two decades in Ireland, Wilde outrageously parodied English societal customs and language, creating a world so perfectly balanced as to be deliciously ludicrous. English society exacted its infamous revenge on Wilde shortly after the great success of this play, not only because of his homosexuality but also, one feels, because of his Irishness.

Boucicault, a Dubliner descended from French Huguenots who had become more Irish than the Irish themselves, created the most influential stage Irishmen on London and New York stages in his nineteenth-century plays *The Colleen Bawn* (1860), *Arrah-na-Pogue* (1864), and *The Shaughraun* (1875). Each starred a clever Irish trickster, witty with words, who outsmarts his foes rather like Daniel O'Connell in the folktales. Boucicault was even more influential than his Irish contemporaries in fiction, Lover and Lever, two writers who, though often joined together because of that catchy phrase formed by their surnames, were actually quite different: Samuel Lover turned Irish peasants into cartoon-style buffoons in such novels as *Handy Andy* (1842), whereas

Charles Lever much more adroitly lampooned his own Anglo-Irish upper class in many side-splitting, better novels, such as *Charles O'Malley, the Irish Dragoon* (1841).

Boucicault's fingerprints remained evident in the writings of such twentieth-century Irish masters as O'Brien and Sean O'Casey. O'Brien lifted the name of one of Boucicault's tricksters, Myles na Gcopaleen ("Myles of the little horses"), when writing his great Gaelic satiric novel *An Béal Bocht* (The Poor Mouth, 1941) and his satiric columns in *The Irish Times* for many years. As for O'Casey, who rivals or perhaps even outstrips Synge as the greatest playwright of Dublin's Abbey Theatre and beyond, he grew up imbibing Shakespeare and Boucicault as his chief theatrical influences. *The Plough and the Stars* (1926), O'Casey's great exposé of the 1916 Easter Rising, provoked the second most notorious set of riots in the Abbey Theatre's history after Synge's *Playboy*. O'Casey naturalistically depicted the shop-looting that the play's piously nationalist audience wanted to forget in 1926, most particularly when he juxtaposed the blood-martyr rhetoric of Patrick Pearse against the realistic pub dialogue of working-class men with the significantly named prostitute Rosie Redmond.

Fluther Good, the play's proletarian, malaprop-mouthing Everyman, brings to mind both Falstaff, Shakespeare's wise fool, and Boucicault's stage-Irish Shaughraun. Fluther's favorite word is *derogatory*, which means almost anything for him. As for politics, he insists, "There's no reason to bring religion into it. I think we ought to have as great a regard for religion as we can, so as to keep it out of as many things as possible" (O'Casey, *Three Plays* 142–43). Like its predecessors in O'Casey's Dublin trilogy, *The Shadow of a Gunman* (1923) and *Juno and the Paycock* (1924), *The Plough and the Stars* was a very innovative play because it was a tragicomedy intermixing and fusing laughter and tears in portraying and responding to Irish history, and also because of its ensemble cast in which every character matters; each is a protagonist. In *The Shadow of a Gunman*, Seumas Shields offers a telling observation of which Oscar Wilde would have been proud: "That's the Irish People all over—they treat a joke as a serious thing and a serious thing as a joke" (*Three Plays* 84). And in *The Plough and the Stars*, O'Casey proved that he was willing to laugh even at himself. Before writing plays he had served as secretary to James Connolly's Citizen Army and was a hardline socialist who opposed that army's participation in the Easter Rising because he viewed nationalism as a betrayal of socialism, as he argued in his 1918 history of the Citizen Army. Yet perhaps the funniest character in *The Plough* is the character whose ideology parodies O'Casey's own views, the Young Covey. The Covey is hopelessly addicted to "Jenersky's *Thesis on th' Origin, Development, an' Consolidation of th' Evolutionary Idea of th' Proletariat*," spouting it even when Rosie Redmond comes on to him in the pub: "Comrade, I'll leave here tomorrow night for you a copy of Jenersky's *Thesis on th' Origin, Development, an' Consolidation of th' Evolutionary Idea of th' Proletariat*" (*Three Plays* 165).

Much as Waters' *The Comic Irishman* is a useful successor and complement to Mercier's *The Irish Comic Tradition* because it examines the stage-Irish tradition, so too is Theresa O'Connor's later collection of essays *The Comic Tradition in Irish Women Writers* (1996), in which the contributors developed further the work of such women writers as Maria Edgeworth, Lady Gregory, Somerville and Ross (Edith Somerville and Violet Martin), Molly Keane, Edna O'Brien, Julia O'Faolain, and Nuala Ní Dhomhnaill. Another useful book on the subject, published that same year, is Don L. F. Nilsen's *Humor in Irish Literature: A Reference Guide*.

Many important features of Irish comedy, and indeed Irish fiction and even other literatures, can be found rooted back in Edgeworth's classic novella *Castle Rackrent* (1800), the greatest Irish political satire after Swift's "Modest Proposal." Beginning with its mock-Gothic title (balanced by its mock-scholarly subtitle, *An Hibernian Tale; Taken from Facts, and from the Manners of the Irish Squires, before the Year 1782*), *Castle Rackrent* introduced several comic innovations: a colloquial and unreliable narrator; a "curious stancelessness" and "absence of plot," as Anthony Cronin (25) put it; and would-be erudite footnotes to go along with the subtitle. Joyce in *Finnegans Wake* and O'Brien in *The Third Policeman* would similarly incorporate frenzied footnotes. Edgeworth's narrator, Thady Quirk, a steward on the Rackrent estate, was inspired by the Irish-English speech of the Edgeworths' actual steward in County Longford.

From his first long-winded sentence, Thady rambles along in a highly ornamented style reminiscent of Irish folktales as well as ornamental styles in Irish traditional music and the Book of Kells:

My real name is Thady Quirk, though in the family I have always been known by no other than "Honest Thady," afterward, in the time of Sir Murtagh, deceased, I remember to hear them calling me "Old Thady," and now I've come to "Poor Thady," for I wear a long great-coat winter and summer, which is very handy, as I never put my arms into the sleeves; they are as good as new, though come Hollandtide next I've had it these seven years; it holds on by a single button round my neck, cloak fashion. (Edgeworth 1)

Edgeworth's still longer historical footnote on "great-coat" calls to mind Buck Mulligan's wisecrack early in Joyce's *Ulysses* about how the earnest Englishman Haines's book could have "five lines of text and ten pages of notes about the folk and the fishgods of Dundrum" (11). Indeed, *Ulysses* with its wildly demotic, oral styles could never have been imagined if Edgeworth had not set out such a course for the Irish novel over a century earlier. Each book sets up its comic premise in its title. Joyce's title is the only place where he states directly that his whole masterpiece is a parody of *The Odyssey*, as each of his well-known Homeric chapters is only numbered, not titled. Similarly, since Thady expresses only his highest admiration for each member of the Rackrent family throughout the whole book, only their very name as introduced in the title directly indicates their less than admirable "rack-rent" status.

Nor could Mark Twain's *Huckleberry Finn* have been penned if Edgeworth had not already let Thady Quirk rip, as her humble yet all-controlling narrator, as Twain would later do with Huck. Thady's diction is very different from Huck's, but his marvelous combination of seeming naiveté with hard-won wisdom are comparable. His masters' series of ridiculous flaws are made all the more funny because of the understated, admiring tone with which Thady recounts them. Each Rackrent lord has his specialty. Sir Patrick drinks himself to death. Sir Murtagh litigiously sues everyone and dies when he bursts a blood vessel in the midst of a legal argument. Sir Kit loves to duel and is thus shot dead. Only Sir Condy ("ever my great favourite" [*Castle Rackrent* 23]) is more versatile: he manages to drink, womanize, and politick altogether too much, each of these vices combining with his complete neglect of his estate, to bring about his downfall. Like Swift, Edgeworth has a serious point behind her satire—using the Rackrents to show exactly how *not* to be a good landlord—but as in the case of Swift, her comedy is what the reader remembers. Here, for example, is Thady's "praise" of Sir Murtagh:

> As for law, I believe no man, dead or alive, ever loved it so well as Sir Murtagh. He had once sixteen suits pending at a time.... He used to boast that he had a lawsuit for every letter in the alphabet.... He was a very learned man in the law, and had the character of it; but how it was I can't tell, these suits that he carried cost him a power of money: in the end he sold some hundreds a year of the family estate; but he was a very learned man in the law, and I know nothing of the matter, except having a great regard for the family. (7)

Critics have forever debated whether Thady is truly naive or secretly wiser; Edgeworth left professors guessing, which as Joyce knew is "the only way of insuring one's immorality" (qtd. in Ellmann 521). *Castle Rackrent* boasted many other, non-comic innovations—as the first Big House novel, the first regional novel, the first saga novel, and the first novel to fully adopt Ireland as its chief subject, if not the first Irish novel—but its comic imprint is perhaps most indelible.

Among Edgeworth's best comic successors were the cousins Edith Somerville and Violet Martin ("Somerville and Ross"), especially in their collections of "Irish R. M." stories published between 1899 and 1915. Somerville and Ross were much like Charles Lever in that these stories, often misunderstood as stage-Irish, actually made much fun of their own Anglo-Irish ascendancy, beginning with the R. M. (resident magistrate) himself, Major Yeates. The very first story, "Great Uncle McCarthy," sets the scene: Yeates moves into his rain-drenched Big House and soon believes that it is haunted, until he learns that the upstairs noises were really caused by a family of fox-poachers secretly squatting in his attic. Somerville and Ross's Anglo-Irish women are impressive comic characters. In "The Bosom of the McRorys," we learn of Bobby Bennett that "her dancing is a serious matter, with a Cromwellian quality to it, suggestive of jack boots and the march of great events" (*The Irish R. M.* 533). And old Mrs. Knox, modeled on Martin's mother, is unforgettably depicted in such late R. M. stories as "The Aussolas Martin Cat" and "The Finger of Mrs. Knox." As Yeates notes, Mrs. Knox "pervaded all spheres" or, as her admiring grandson Flurry Knox puts it, "There's no pie but my grandmother has a finger in it" (436). Mrs. Knox wanders about eccentrically "swathed in hundreds of shawls, in the act of hurling . . . tongs and some unseen object" (434), yet her voice is so commanding that Yeates feels that it "would have made me clean forty pig-sties had she desired me to do so" (63).

Though they made sure that their major's last name was spelled differently, there remains the chance that Somerville and Ross were playing a secret joke on Ireland's national poet, Yeats. The cousins preferred to collaborate closely and privately, refusing to write for Yeats' Abbey Theatre even after another cousin of Martin, Lady Gregory, invited her to do so (Cahalan, *Double Visions* 78–79). Gregory's work was much more like theirs than that of the more somber national poet. Her one-act play *Spreading the News*, for example, was a very popular folk comedy—rather like an Irish game of "telephone"—about the rapid-fire dissemination of a false rumor about a reputed murder committed by a man seen following someone with a pitchfork.

The Anglo-Irish Yeats remained mostly serious, but it seems a telling reflection of the native Irish comic spirit, as traced so extensively by Mercier, that its greatest fiction writer moved so steadily into comedy in the course of his career. *Ulysses* and *Finnegans Wake* are as deeply comic as Joyce's earlier *Dubliners* (1904) is tragic and *A Portrait of the Artist as a Young Man* (1916) is earnest and idealistic. *Ulysses* has been taken very seriously as the greatest modern novel in the English language, but it is also simply one of the funniest books ever written. Its overarching structure as a parody of the *Odyssey* is itself the stuff of fabulous humor, with Leopold Bloom as Odysseus, Molly Bloom as Penelope, and Stephen Dedalus as their "son," Telemachus. These characters' lives in the course of one day, June 16, 1904, are themselves amusing to think about as constituting a modern odyssey: Leopold cooks breakfast for Molly, visits the public baths, attends a funeral, goes about his work as a newspaper ad canvasser, eats lunch and dinner, visits a couple of pubs, continues a titillating correspondence, is sexually excited by a young woman at the beach, endures some anti-Semitism, worries about the affair Molly is having, meets the drunken Stephen at a party in a hospital, and finally rescues him from a whorehouse and a scrape in the street with an English soldier, taking him home to sober him up before he goes on his way. Before encountering Leopold, Stephen leaves the Martello tower in Sandymount where he has been staying with his eccentric cohort Buck Mulligan, teaches his morning class at a school in Dalkey, walks along Sandymount Strand, delivers a letter by his schoolmaster to the editor of Leopold's newspaper, and then drinks and carouses the rest of the day. Molly stays home all day, makes love in the late afternoon to the manager of her singing tour, and eventually lies in bed thinking until after Leopold comes home. The delightful Homeric parallels and parodies throughout *Ulysses* have been copiously traced by scholars—including, for example, Molly not only as Penelope but as Calypso, Nestor transformed into Stephen's bigoted schoolmaster, Proteus into language beside the Irish Sea, the Cyclops into a bad drunk, Nausicaa into a young woman who has read too many romances, Circe into a Dublin whorehouse madam, and so on.

Comedy is often two-dimensional: Roadrunner squashed flat on the highway. Perhaps no better example can be found of how comedy can be two-dimensional yet at the same time multidimensional and deep than the Cyclops chapter of *Ulysses*. It is two-dimensional in at least two ways, thus multiplying its rich humor. First, we have classical Greece versus dear, dirty Dublin, with Homer's fearsome, one-eyed monster recreated as the eye-patch-wearing, bigoted Citizen. Add to that the two opposite styles of this chapter: the working-class pub narrative versus mock-epic discourses modeled on nineteenth-century English translations of Homer. As Joyce in turn "translates" back and forth from one style to the other, the result is hysterical—as in this example, where the mock-epic description of the arrival of new characters at Barney Kiernan's pub is followed, and deflated, by the pub raconteur's Irish-English, Dublinese "translation":

And lo, as they quaffed their cup of joy, a godlike messenger came swiftly in, radiant as the eye of heaven, a comely youth and behind him there passed an elder of noble gait and countenance, bearing the sacred scrolls of law and with him his lady wife a dame of peerless lineage, fairest of her race.

Little Alf Bergan popped in round the door and hid behind Barney's snug, squeezed up with the laughing. And who was sitting up there in the corner that I hadn't seen snoring drunk blind to the world only Bob Doran. I didn't know what was up and Alf kept making signs out of the door. And begob what was it only that bloody old pantaloon Denis Breen in his bathslippers with two bloody big books tucked under his oxter and the wife hotfoot after him, unfortunate wretched woman, trotting like a poodle. I thought Alf would split. (245)

Joyce keeps us suspended in midair between these two styles for many pages, guffawing, until he finally merges them in this chapter's final sentence, describing how Bloom escapes the wrath of the Citizen by retreating quickly out of the pub and down the street: "And they beheld Him even Him, ben Bloom Elijah, amid clouds of angels ascend to the glory of the brightness at an angle of fortyfive degrees over Donohue's in Little Green street like a shot off a shovel" (283).

Another uproarious example of Joyce's two-dimensional comedy comes in the "Nausicaa" chapter, when the fireworks display visible above Sandymount Strand provides an objective correlative for Bloom's masturbatory encounter with Gerty McDowell. Just a small sample will have to suffice here, as the fireworks and the sex both come to their climaxes:

And then a rocket sprang and bang shot blind blank and O! then the Roman candle burst and it was like a sigh of O! and everyone cried O! O! in raptures and it gushed out of it a stream of rain gold hair threads and they shed and ah! they were all greeny dewy stars falling with golden O so lovely, O, soft, sweet, soft! (300)

Thus does Joyce make us laugh for over 600 pages.

Finnegans Wake is, yes, harder to read but, yes, just as funny. As much as the *Wake* borrows from many of the languages of the world in creating its own polyglot, the basic language of this book is nonetheless clearly a *spoken* one that goes back to the roots of Irish oral tradition. It is a kind of great blathering dream, world folktale, and Jungian myth composed in four cyclic books, with a father-type, a mother-type, and two brothers who are continually changing identities. A leading comic aspect of Joyce's final book is that he carries on a running joke with his "ideal reader suffering from an ideal insomnia" (120, lines 13–14), both teasing the reader and making fun of himself and his own text. At one point Joyce advises his reader, "Herenow chuck english and learn to pray plain. . . . Think in your stomach" (579.20–22). But he also admits about his own work, "What a mnice old mness it all mnakes!" (19.7–8). He makes fun of both male and female readers: "You is feeling like you was lost in the bush, boy?" (112.3), and "So sorry you lost him, poor lamb! Of course I know you are a viry vikid girl to go in the dreemplace" (527.4–6). And he collapses the traditional distinction between narrator and reader with his direct addresses in the first person linking narrator and reader: "We shall perhaps not so soon see" (32.2); "We seem to us (the real Us!) to be reading . . . in the sixth sealed chapter of the going forth by black" (62.25–26). Joyce admits in a footnote that both author and reader are "making it up as we go along" (268n2). He leaves it perhaps deliberately unclear whether he is talking about the reader or about himself (or both) when he remarks, "O, you were excruciated, in honour bound to the cross of your own cruelfiction!" (192.17–19)—and also when he calls his book an "Impassable tissue of improbable liyers!" (499.19) and asks, "What static babel is this, tell us?" (499.34).

Moreover, Joyce deconstructs the author/reader polarity completely by addressing not only his "dear reader," but the "gentle writer" himself: "I can tell you something more than that, drear writer" (*Wake* 476.20–21). Joyce muddies his waters even further by appearing to interrupt his own narrator: "So you were saying, boys? Anyhow he what?" (380.6). He confesses his own ignorance in another footnote: "I'm blest if I can see" (273n2). And "It's all deafman's duff to me, begob" (467.17–18). Concerning the murky crime that seems to lurk at the very center of the *Wake*, it is freely admitted that "little headway, if any, was made in solving the wasnottobe crime conundrum" (85.21–22). As for his readers, "They know how they believe that they believe that they know. Wherefore they wail" (470.11–12). What can we do with

Finnegans Wake except throw up our hands, question "the all-riddle of it?" (274.2–3), and read on? Confessing that he had begun reading the *Wake* unsuccessfully many different times, Flann O'Brien asked: "What would you think of a man who entered a restaurant, sat down, suddenly whipped up the tablecloth and blew his nose in it? . . . That is what Joyce did with our beloved tongue that Shakespeare and Milton spoke" (qtd. in Powell 59). O'Brien was himself joking here, in "Cruiskeen Lawn" (Little Full Jug), the brilliant and rollicking column that he wrote for the *Irish Times* for a quarter century, subsequently collected in such O'Brien anthologies as *The Best of Myles*. O'Brien, whose real name was Brian O'Nolan, was perhaps Joyce's closest rival as the comic madman of modern Irish fiction. His first novel, *At Swim-Two-Birds*, appeared the same year as the *Wake* and offered three separate beginnings: one about the folkloric character The Pooka; a second about one John Furriskey, who was born at the age of twenty-five; and a third about the epic Finn MacCool.

Like the *Wake*, O'Brien's work takes us into the furthest realms of fantasy and satire, equally so in his novels *An Béal Bocht* and *The Third Policeman*. In *An Béal Bocht* he returned to the roots of Gaelic satire by writing in Irish and developing frenzied parodies of such Gaelic autobiographies as Tomás O Criomhthain's *An Toileánach* (*The Islandman*). Typical of O'Brien's sense of humor is the speech of an obsessively Gaelic politician at a rain-drenched festival (as translated by Patrick C. Power):

—Gaels! he said, it delights my Gaelic heart to be here today speaking Gaelic with you at this Gaelic feis in the centre of the Gaeltacht. May I state that I am a Gael. I'm Gaelic front and back, above and below. Likewise, you are all truly Gaelic. We are all Gaelic Gaels of Gaelic lineage. He who is Gaelic, will be Gaelic evermore. I myself have spoken not a word except Gaelic since the day I was born—just like you—and every sentence I've ever uttered has been on the subject of Gaelic. (54)

Meanwhile, this book's unnamed protagonist and his "Gaelic" compatriots suffer through life in ignorance and poverty so complete as to be both perfect and ridiculous. Other visiting Gaelic politicians praised a neighbor "for his Gaelic poverty and stated that they never saw anyone who appeared so truly Gaelic. One of the gentlemen broke a little bottle of water which Sitric had, because, said he, it spoiled the effect" (86).

The protagonist of *The Third Policeman* is also unnamed and in the dark. He hatches a scheme with one John Divney to kill an old man for his money in order to finance his own research on the crackpot scientist and philosopher de Selby. He remains unaware of how this plot backfires on him, oblivious to his own demise because he is so lost in the deranged theories of de Selby, which are expounded in increasingly long footnotes (one running six pages) that deliberately derail the novel's main narrative. De Selby insisted, for example, "(a) that darkness was simply an accretion of 'black air' . . . and (b) that sleep was simply a succession of fainting-fits brought on by semi-asphyxiation due to (a)" (115n1). The protagonist gets lost not only in de Selby, but even in the disputes among de Selby scholars and their conflicting interpretations. O'Brien would have been pleased that his fictional scientist lived on in the popular mind, as, for example, in a spate of *Irish Times* letters to the editor in 1976 about de Selby.

Joyce's other main disciple was also his opposite: Samuel Beckett. Beckett himself noted the difference in a wise statement that was typically self-disparaging and funny: "The more Joyce knew the more he could. He's tending toward omniscience and omnipotence as an artist. I'm working with impotence, ignorance" (qtd. in Cohn 391). Just how deep comedy runs in the Irish psyche is underscored by its strong presence even in the writings of this Anglo-Irishman, self-exiled to Paris, writing by choice in French. Beckett is typically treated somberly as an existentialist and minimalist prophet, but he is also profoundly humorous. He also takes us back where I began—to the strong links between Irish comedy and the agonies of Irish history. As Nell says to Nagg in *Endgame*, where both are trapped in trash cans as emblems of old age, "Nothing is funnier than unhappiness. . . . Yes, it's the most comical thing in the world" (18).

Here Nell returns us to the roots of comedy in misfortune as therapeutically leavened with laughter—to the likes of Roadrunner, flattened in the highway, and to Cromwell, boiling in the Irish Sea in the revengeful Irish folktales about him. We laugh at Roadrunner much as the Irish storytellers got in the last laugh at Cromwell. Even more therapeutic than laughing *at*, however, is laughing *with*—making fun of oneself, in self-disparagement. And in this necessarily brief introduction to Irish comedy I will give Beckett the last word. When Clov complains to Hamm in *Endgame* that Hamm is badgering him—"You've asked me these questions millions of times"—Hamm replies, "I love the old questions. Ah the old questions, the old answers, there's nothing like them!" (38).

REFERENCES AND FURTHER READINGS

Auden, W. H. "In Memory of W. B. Yeats." 1940. *The Norton Anthology of English Literature.* Ed. M. H. Abrams et al. 4th ed. Vol. 1. New York: Norton, 1979. 2398–99.

Beckett, Samuel. *Endgame.* New York: Grove, 1958.

Cahalan, James M. *Double Visions: Women and Men in Modern and Contemporary Irish Fiction.* Syracuse, NY: Syracuse UP, 1999.

———. "Mercier's *Irish Comic Tradition* as a Touchstone of Irish Studies." *New Hibernia Review* 8.4 (Winter 2004): 139–45.

Cohn, Ruby. "Joyce and Beckett, Irish Cosmopolitans." *James Joyce Quarterly* 8 (1971): 385–91.

The Commitments. Dir. Alan Parker, Perf. Robert Arkins, Michael Aherne, Angeline Ball et al. Beacon Communications and Ardmore Studios, 1991.

Cronin, Anthony. *Heritage Now: Irish Literature in the English Language.* Dingle, County Kerry, Ire.: Brandon, 1982.

Cross, Eric. *The Tailor and Ansty.* 1942. Cork, Ire.: Mercier, 1999.

Doyle, Roddy. *The Commitments.* 1987. New York: Vintage, 1989.

Edgeworth, Maria. *Castle Rackrent: An Hibernian Tale; Taken from Facts, and from the Manners of the Irish Squires, before the Year 1782.* 1800. New York: Norton, 1965.

Ellmann, Richard. *James Joyce.* Rev. ed. New York: Oxford UP, 1982.

Gregory, Lady Augusta. *Selected Plays of Lady Gregory.* London: Colin Smythe, 1983.

Joyce, James. *Finnegans Wake.* 1939. New York: Viking, 1959.

———. *The Portable James Joyce.* Ed. Harry Levin. New York: Penguin, 1966.

———. *Ulysses.* 1922. Ed. Hans Walter Gabler. Corr. ed. New York: Vintage/Random, 1986.

Kiberd, Declan. *Synge and the Irish Language.* Totowa, NJ: Rowman and Littlefield, 1979.

Mercier, Vivian. *The Irish Comic Tradition.* London: Oxford UP, 1962.

Nilsen, Don L. F. *Humor in Irish Literature: A Reference Guide.* Westport, CT: Greenwood, 1996.

O'Brien, Flann [Brian O'Nolan]. *At Swim-Two-Birds*. 1939. New York: New American Library, 1976.

———. *The Best of Myles*, by Myles na gCopaleen [Brian O'Nolan]. 1968. London: Pan, 1977.

———. *The Dalkey Archive*. 1964. London: Pan, 1976.

———. *The Hard Life*. 1961. New York: Pantheon, 1962.

———. *The Poor Mouth*. Trans. Patrick C. Power. Trans. of *An Béal Bocht*, by Myles na gCopaleen. 1941. London: Pan, 1975.

———. *The Third Policeman*. 1967. London: Pan, 1974.

O'Casey, Sean. *Three Plays*. New York: St. Martin's, 1957.

O'Connor, Theresa, ed. *The Comic Tradition in Irish Women Writers*. Gainesville: UP of Florida, 1996.

Ó Súilleabháin, Seán. "Oliver Cromwell in Irish Oral Tradition." *Folklore Today: A Festschrift for Richard M. Dorson*. Ed. Linda Dégh, Henry Glassie, and Felix J. Oinas. Bloomington: Indiana U Research Center for Language and Semiotic Studies, 1976. 473–83.

O'Sullivan, Sean, ed. and trans. *Folktales of Ireland*. Chicago: U of Chicago P, 1966.

Powell, David. "An Annotated Bibliography of Myles na Gopaleen's (Flann O'Brien's) 'Cruiskeen Lawn' Commentaries on James Joyce." *James Joyce Quarterly* 9 (1971): 50–62.

Shakespeare, William. *Henry V*. 1600. *The Complete Plays and Poems of William Shakespeare*. Ed. William Allan Neilson and Charles Jarvis Hill. Cambridge, MA: Houghton Mifflin, 1942. 708–46.

Somerville, E. OE. [Edith], and Martin Ross [Violet Martin]. *The Irish R. M.* 1928. London: Sphere, 1989.

Swift, Jonathan. "A Modest Proposal for Preventing the Children of Poor People in Ireland from Being a Burden to Their Parents or Country, and for Making Them Beneficial to the Public." 1729. *The Norton Anthology of English Literature*. Ed. M. H. Abrams et al. 4th ed. Vol. 1. New York: Norton, 1979. 2144–51.

Synge, Jonathan. *The Playboy of the Western World*. 1907. New York: Dover, 1993.

Wall, Mervyn. *The Complete Fursey*. Dublin: Wolfhound, 1985.

Waters, Maureen. *The Comic Irishman*. Albany, NY: SUNY P, 1984.

26

Irony

Don L. F. Nilsen and Alleen Pace Nilsen

Irony is such a broad topic that we will present just a sampling here, chosen to illustrate the characteristics of irony that are manifested across various time periods and genres. English speakers inherited the word *irony* from the Greek *eiron*, which means "language dissembler."

In modern usage, *linguistic irony* commonly refers to speech incidents in which the intended meaning of the words is contrary to their literal interpretation or to the expected meaning. The ability to catch on to and appreciate linguistic irony comes fairly late in language acquisition. Unless speakers give clues with their body language, their tone of voice, and their facial expressions, children and unsophisticated adults may interpret ironic statements as either mistakes or lies. In contrast, sophisticated adults know that irony is a form of "lying" that gives itself away through elements of playfulness. When ironic statements are delivered in a deadpan style, they are all the funnier to the listeners who catch on.

People often refer in the same sentence to *humor* and *irony*. That the two words are used as a set like *bread and butter* or *salt and pepper* shows that in people's minds the two concepts belong to the same semantic area. They have something in common, but they are not exactly the same or people would not feel the need to use both words. Not all irony will make people laugh, or even smile, and not everything that people find funny falls into the category of irony. Both humor and irony contain exaggeration and distortion. With a joke, the distortion is resolved as the climax or the point of the joke. With irony, the distortion is sometimes, but not always, resolved. It is enough for the irony to just "be there," and if it is resolved the resolution comes from an unexpected angle so that the receivers of the message get a view that is aslant.

The terms *irony* and *satire* are also used together, but again there is a difference. While irony may be a part of satire, the creators of satire have a vision in mind. They want to point readers or listeners to what they think is a "better" vision of life. Northrop Frye says that a discourse is mostly irony when readers are not sure what the author's attitude is or what their own attitude is supposed to be. Satire is didactic and pushes readers to long for the good parts of a utopia and to be repelled by the bad parts of a dystopia. With irony, an author only draws attention to the paradoxes without attempting to pass judgments.

While this is a helpful distinction, it is also an overgeneralization because many authors and speakers include ironic statements as part of satire, sarcasm, and wit where its indirectness—its sideways slant—serves to soften the message. In general, irony deals with "edgy" topics, thereby leaving the listener or reader with something to think about. Bell-shaped curves are called "normal" curves because most human experiences and expectations cluster together in the center where things are similar. Irony, either in real life or in literature, comes from either, or both, of the flattened ends of a normal curve. Irony deals with the unusual, or the unexpected. There has to be a surprise to it, but at the same time that it breaks expectations, it has to stay close enough to the normal pattern that the observer (the reader or the listener) is led to appreciate the irony.

IRONY THROUGH LANGUAGE PLAY

Linguistic irony comes the closest to the definition of "language dissembler" because people purposely arrange their words, or the manner in which they say them, so as to communicate that a different meaning is intended. Speakers can use intonation, pitch, stress, and tone, along with body gestures and facial expressions, to communicate that what they are saying is not what they mean. This is especially true with slang, as when teenagers describe something they like as *bad!* or *phat!* or when adults roll their eyes and sarcastically say things like, "Oh, really?"

Paradoxical statements are a technique that works either in speech or writing. Clever people exert themselves to devise statements that highlight contradictions or unexpected shifts. Paradoxes are especially popular when old ideas and systems clash with new ways of thinking as reflected in this sampling of quotes arranged chronologically:

- "Sits he on ever so high a throne, a man still sits on his bottom." (Montaigne, 1500s)
- "We have just enough religion to make us hate, but not enough to make us love one another." (Jonathan Swift, 1700s)
- "I laugh so that I may not cry." (Pierre Augustin Caron de Beaumarchais, 1700s)
- "The English have a miraculous power of turning wine into water." (Oscar Wilde, 1800s)
- "When a feller says, 'It hain't th' money, but th' principle o' the thing,' it's the money." (Josh Billings, 1800s)
- "In Italy for thirty years under the Borgias they had warfare, terror, murder, bloodshed—they produced Michelangelo, Leonardo da Vinci and the Renaissance. In Switzerland they had brotherly love, five hundred years of democracy and peace and what did that produce . . . ? The cuckoo clock." (Orson Welles, 1900s)
- "All animals are equal, but some animals are more equal than others." (George Orwell, 1900s)
- "True terror is to wake up one morning and discover that your high school class is running the country." (Kurt Vonnegut, 1900s)
- "We have met the enemy and it is us." (Walt Kelly, 1900s)
- "I'd kill for a Nobel Peace Prize." (Steven Wright, 2000s)

Parodies are another kind of ironic statement because the parodist makes fun of the original through enlarging its characteristics, while at the same time paying tribute to the original by expecting readers to know it well enough to catch onto the parody. Some parodies target a whole genre, as did Mark Twain in his "War Prayer" (1923). After asking the Lord's help with such things as laying waste the enemy's "humble homes with a hurricane of fire," wringing "the hearts of their unoffending widows with unavailing grief," and turning their little children "to wander unfriended the wastes of their desolated land in rags and hunger and thirst," the prayer-giver closes his prayer, "in the spirit of love, of Him Who is the Source of Love, and Who is the ever-faithful refuge and friend of all that are sore beset and seek his aid."

In the 1970s, as the feminist movement began gaining a substantial audience, the makers of Virginia Slim cigarettes launched an advertising campaign with a parody of a fairy tale. A beautiful castle served as the background for a "Once-upon-a-time" story about a prince who went looking for a good wife to cook his meals, to clean the many rooms of the palace, and to bear him many sons who would carry on his noble name. The story ended, "And the prince lived happily ever after."

The gothic genre is so overstated and melodramatic that some critics argue that gothic novels are automatically parodies and therefore ironic. Whether or not this is true, such gothic novels as *Dracula* (1897) and *Frankenstein* (1818) are often parodied. Jane Austen's *Northanger Abbey* (1818) is both a gothic novel and a parody of the sentimentalism and "terror" of the gothic-novel genre. It is about a plain, ordinary, and tomboyish girl named Catherine Morland, who though coming from a commonplace family, feels she is destined to become a romantic heroine. Showing no aptitude for drawing or music or any of the other required accomplishments, this future seems unlikely. But at age fifteen, she considers herself in training, and when she visits Northanger Abbey, she finds a manuscript that she takes to be a cryptic record of secret crimes committed and suffered in the abbey. However, on closer examination, this manuscript turns out to be an inventory of linen needing to be washed.

Much of the ironic humor in Lewis Carroll's *Alice's Adventures in Wonderland* (1865) comes from parodies, as in the wonderful scene with the Mock Turtle and the Gryphon, who explain that their schoolmaster was called Tortoise "because he taught us." They studied "Laughing and Grief" (Latin and Greek) and "Reeling and Writing" (reading and writing), along with "the different branches of Arithmetic—Ambition, Distraction, Uglification and Derision." Extras were listed as "French, music, and washing" (meaning that there was an extra fee if the school did the students' laundry) as well as "Drawling, Stretching, and Fainting in Coils" (drawing, sketching, and painting in oils).

Carroll thumbed his nose at the grim message of G. W. Langford's popular poem warning parents of the high mortality rates for children:

> Speak gently to the little child!
> Its love be sure to gain;
> Teach it in accents soft and mild;
> It may not long remain.

Even though few of today's readers know the original poem, the parody is strong enough to stand on its own when the Duchess sings to a piglet wrapped in baby clothes:

> Speak roughly to your little boy,
> And beat him when he sneezes.
> He only does it to annoy
> Because he knows it teases.

In the movie *Zelig* (1983), Woody Allen parodied a documentary film and ironically had such real-world characters as Susan Sontag, Irving Howe, Saul Bellow, and Bruno Bettleheim appear as themselves. Allen's *Bananas* (1971) is also a parody of a documentary, this time about life in a banana republic. Allen had sports announcer Howard Cossell do a play-by-play announcement in the style of the *Wide World of Sports* of events as different as the consummation of a marriage and the assassination of a president.

Quentin Tarantino's 1994 film *Pulp Fiction* parodies the whole genre of pulp fiction with its sensationalism and violence. Early in the film, Mia tells a joke making light of death. Three tomatoes are walking along. The Pop Tomato and the Mom Tomato are in the front while the Baby Tomato lags behind. The Pop Tomato gets mad and squashes the Baby Tomato while exclaiming, "Ketchup!" Later in the film, Vince and Jules are caught in a stream of bullets, but not one hits them. In contrast, a single bullet fired accidentally when their car hits a bump results in the death of their hostage and their car being filled with blood and body tissue. The mess is so bad that the men drive to Tarantino's actual house and use his garden hose on the inside of the car as well as on themselves.

VISUAL IRONY

Art is in itself ironic in that moving objects are changed to permanent and nonmoving objects, while three-dimensional images must be painted onto two-dimensional canvases. But all great artists have the ability to use relative sizes, shadings, colors, and so forth to trick the spectator into perceiving some objects as close and others as far away. M. C. Escher went a bit further in his visual trickery by creating waterfalls that flow uphill, people who walk on walls and ceilings, hands drawing pictures of themselves, and objects leaving the paintings and entering the real world. He transformed triangles into birds, black-on-white into white-on-black, and ceilings and walls into floors. He made famous the kind of art called *trompe l'oeil*, which literally means "to deceive the eye." René Magritte played with linguistic irony when he painted a picture of a pipe and captioned it "Ceci n'est pas une pipe." Of course it was not a pipe; it was a picture of a pipe.

Medieval religious artists sometimes used figures of animals to caricature individuals or stereotypes as seen in some of England's best-known cathedrals. At St. Mary's in Beverly, two foxes in religious vestments hold pastoral staffs, while a goose peeps out from a hood. In the church of Budleigh in Devonshire (where Sir Walter Raleigh regularly attended and where his head is still buried), various incongruous and ironic devices are hewn into the pews, including a scissors, a man-of-war, and a cock holding a sheep by the tail. At Winchester, a boar plays a fiddle while a young pig dances. Probably the most famous incongruous piece of art is an imp carved in the rafters of Lincoln Cathedral. One explanation of such art pieces carved high in cathedrals is that the artisans were tricking the church fathers, who would not be brave enough to climb on the scaffolds to conduct up-close examinations.

Today, respected architects are hesitant to be playful with million-dollar buildings, although there are some exceptions. For example, the city fathers in Tempe, Arizona, wanted to be "different" and to communicate a spirit of free thinking and so had their city hall built in the shape of an upside-down pyramid. Tom Wolfe wrote that when Frank Lloyd Wright saw Jorn Utzon's plans for the Sydney Opera House, he exclaimed,

"The circus tent is not architecture." People are understandably braver with outdoor art, which is separated from something as permanent as a building; for example, the giant baseball bat that Claes Oldenburg created for the city of Chicago and the hundreds of pieces of sidewalk art that have become fashionable decorations in American cities and towns.

However, in towns that work hard to attract tourists, ironic architecture is perfectly acceptable as with the New York, New York hotel in Las Vegas, Nevada, which advertises itself as "The Greatest City in Las Vegas." It includes a casino made to look like Central Park and then crams in a silhouette of the Manhattan skyline and reproductions of Grant's Tomb, Ellis Island, the Statue of Liberty, and the Coney Island roller coaster. The WonderWorks building adjacent to the Orlando Convention Center in Florida is made to look as if a tornado had lifted up a large, white neoclassical building complete with its nearby street lights and palm trees, flipped it upside down, and planted it at an angle on top of a red brick warehouse. Inside the structure are restaurants and other entertainment centers.

IRONY IN REAL LIFE

Wayne Booth writes about observable irony (what philosopher Quintilian 2,000 years ago called *rei natura*), such as when a premature monsoon ruins an army's invasion or lightning strikes just as a preacher raises his arms to make a dramatic point about God.

News stories often report events or situations that the participants view as straightforward, but that reporters and readers view as ironic or funny. For example, a United Press International story told how eighty-seven-year-old Andrija Artukovic was sentenced to death by a Yugoslav court because during World War II he had ordered more than 1,000 Croatian deaths. However, a medical review determined that the man was in no condition to be executed, but "plans would resume if and when his health improved."

The largest Puerto Rican bank in New York City worries that English-speaking robbers might misunderstand a clerk's slowness to respond and begin shooting. Hence, they post the following sign:

> ATTENTION WOULD BE BANK ROBBERS
> THIS IS A SPANISH-SPEAKING BANK. IF YOU
> INTEND TO ROB US, PLEASE BE PATIENT FOR
> WE MIGHT NEED AN INTERPRETER.
> THANK YOU,
> THE MANAGEMENT

Today such stories are spread on the Internet, with many of them turning out to be urban legends or FOAF tales (told by a friend of a friend). Also spread through the Internet are people's discoveries of ironic signs like the one on a West Coast bridge that during World War II instructed drivers: "In Case of a Bombing Attack, Drive Directly Off the Bridge," and a sign posted on the steepest ski slope of the Snowbowl in Flagstaff, Arizona: "Out-of-Control Skiers Yield Right-of-Way."

Most spelling errors and awkwardly written sentences are just plain old mistakes, but when the result comes close to another meaning, irony can occur, as with such product names as Japanese Dew Dew dried apples and Brown Gross Foam hair mousse. Signs that international travelers have reported seeing include:

- "Flower & Bucket Maker" (a florist shop in Afghanistan)
- "The manager has personally passed all the water served here" (a hotel in Acapulco)
- "Barbarism" (a barber shop in Afghanistan)
- "Ladies are requested not to have children in the bar" (a hotel in Norway)
- "Swimming is forbidden in the absence of a savior" (a French Riviera beach)
- "Ladies may have a fit upstairs" (a Hong Kong tailor shop)

Former English teacher Richard Lederer put together students' errors for his 1987 book *Anguished English: An Anthology of Accidental Assaults upon Our Language*. He undoubtedly supplemented the students' errors with his own creativity. The best-known piece is "The World According to Student Bloopers," which contains this paragraph:

It was an age of great inventions and discoveries. Gutenberg invented the Bible. Another important invention was the circulation of blood. Sir Walter Raleigh is a historical figure because he invented cigarettes and started smoking. And Sir Francis Drake circumcised the world with a 100-foot clipper.

While ironic events occur in everybody's life, they often go unnoticed, which has caused people to ask a question similar to the one about a tree falling in a forest: Is there a sound even though no ears are in the vicinity to interpret the airwaves? The comparable question about irony is whether something is truly ironic before it is observed by someone clever enough to recognize the irony and to put it into some kind of a public presentation—a comedy routine, a story, a film, a joke, and so forth. For example, the United States was in such shock over the September 11 attacks on New York City's Twin Towers that it took a few days before people realized the irony of the attacks coming on *9–11*, the national telephone number for emergencies.

IRONY IN POPULAR ENTERTAINMENT

Many contemporary comedians—or their writers—are attuned to real-life ironies, which they point out to laughing readers or audiences. Jean Kerr got the title for the playful antihousekeeping book that was a 1957 best seller when she prepared a beautiful table and a perfect luncheon for a guest she wanted to impress. Before going out to pick up her guest, she gave her children thorough instructions that she thought covered every possible contingency. She was surprised to come home and find the table centerpiece to be nothing but a few bedraggled stems. She had not thought to tell her children, *Please Don't Eat the Daisies*.

Comedian Lily Tomlin tells how when she bought a wastebasket, the clerk put it in a paper bag so she could carry it home. But as soon as Tomlin got home, the first thing she did was to put the paper bag into the wastebasket. Tomlin also asks the ironic question, "How come when you talk to God you're praying, but when God talks to you you're schizophrenic?" (qtd. in Nilsen 168).

Author and radio star Garrison Keillor gets laughs whenever he mentions his fictional hometown, Lake Wobegon, "where all the women are strong, all the men are good-looking and all the children are above average." Educators refer to the *Lake Wobegon syndrome* to point out the absurdity of parents thinking that all their children are "above average." Although Keillor's Lake Wobegone syndrome has entered into the public's consciousness, the term is used mainly by educators and psychologists.

The Bates Motel, the scene of the gruesome murder in Alfred Hitchcock's 1960 film, *Psycho*, is also working its way into the public consciousness as an ironic allusion. A Bates Motel in Coeur d'Alene, Idaho, does a brisk tourist business selling I-Slept-at-the-Bates-Motel T-shirts. For Gary Larson's 2002 calendar, he drew a cartoon of four worms driving up to a seedy little *BAIT* Motel. At the 2003 Golden Globe Awards, when Jack Nicholson was honored as Best Actor for his part in *About Schmidt*, he got the biggest laugh of the evening when he leered at his costar, Kathy Bates, and alluded to the Bates Motel. In *About Schmidt*, Nicholson played the part of a house-guest on the night before his daughter was to marry the son of Bates' character. The joke is that she had tried to seduce him in her backyard hot tub.

A better-known ironic allusion that has come to be used by the public in general is the title of Joseph Heller's 1961 *Catch-22*. In Heller's antiwar novel, the character Yossarian can be excused from flying bombing missions only if he is declared insane. However, the fact that he is trying to get out of flying bombing missions proves his sanity, and he therefore has to keep flying. In the mid-1980s, Heller explained in a speech at Arizona State University that his naming of the paradox was a play on military customs where everything was given a name and a number. He liked the alliteration in "twenty-two," plus it was a high enough number to imply that Yossarian had already had to deal with numerous other tricks or catches.

The term *catch-22* is now included in dictionaries and is frequently used to refer to such situations as when authors cannot get their manuscripts read by publishers because they do not have an agent, but agents will not work with authors until they have had their work published. Young people cannot get jobs until they have experience, but they cannot get experience until they have a job. A few years ago, newspaper stories told about the state of Texas being caught in a catch-22 because of a law forbidding the execution of anyone insane. A prisoner on death row was refusing to take the medication that would keep him sane, thereby postponing indefinitely the date of his execution.

Scott Adams' *Dilbert* comic strip often highlights the ironies in modern life, as when a company buys its top executives laptop computers, and then worries about theft and so pays extra money to have them clamped permanently onto people's desks. In the 1990s, Adams was the first cartoonist to go online and invite readers to share their frustrating or ironic experiences with him. He receives hundreds of e-mail messages everyday, and manages to turn about one in 100 into a cartoon. While his subject matter is supposedly corporate America, he says he receives just as many e-mails from people who work in hospitals, the military, and religion. These are all hierarchical institutions, where the clashes between top-down and bottom-up decision-making often result in ironic situations.

Cartoonist Gary Larson, as shown by these examples taken from *The Far Side: Last Impressions* (his 2002 calendar), uses a wide range of techniques to create irony. A simple reversal is the basis for a panel showing a boat belonging to "Al's Glass-Bottom Tours." It has turned upside down and sunk, so that fish are now peering in at the frantic tourists. There is surprise in a four-panel joke showing a man stranded on an island under a single palm tree. In the third panel, when a space ship approaches, apparently on a collecting mission, the man is thrilled: "Thank God. I'm saved!" And sure enough, the ship opens its hatch and takes something in, but it takes the palm tree rather than the man. In a drawing showing a truck plunging through the guardrail on a mountain road and falling into the La Brea Tar Pits, the irony comes from linguistic coincidence because the truck is carrying "Mrs. Gibson's PRESERVES."

In more complex examples from the same calendar, Larson uses dramatic irony in which viewers can see things that the characters in the cartoon are ignoring. In an especially funny one, a line of cows is walking up a ramp into "Anderson's Meats." One cow coming from a different direction is met by, "Hey! You! . . . No cutting in!" In two cartoons featuring Native Americans, viewers have the advantage of history to help them understand the irony. Three Indians are waving good-bye to the Niña, the Pinta, and the Santa María, and one is asking, "Did you detect something a little ominous in the way they said, 'See you later'?" The other one shows the heads and shoulders of six Indian braves facing inward from the corners and the sides of the cartoon frame. The caption: "Custer's last view."

Perhaps the most interesting thing about these examples, which we chose from the last three months of the 2002 calendar year as particularly good illustrations of irony, is that they all deal with some aspect of death. The other interesting thing about them is the number of intertextual allusions they contain. People have to know things about the real world and the history of the world to understand the ironies, as in one cartoon printed over the caption "Inside a nuclear power plant." Three people are busy at various high-tech tasks, while one man walks past a door with a sign on the window: "Warning: Radioactive Area." The speaker is in front of a standing birdcage and in great alarm is yelling, "Aaaaaaa! Run everyone! The canary has *mutated*!" A close inspection shows that the canary has three eyes.

IRONY IN CHILDREN'S LITERATURE

Children's literature, as part of the popular culture, often serves as the grounding for ironic allusions because people remember from their childhood many of the same old folktales, nursery rhymes, and picture books. However, in what is a real-life irony, researchers are discovering that many children have met the parodied or ironic versions first on television or in popular movies, books, and games. For example, in the 1980s millions of children began talking about Michaelangelo, Donatello, Leonardo, and Raphael—not the famous Italian Renaissance painters but the animated Teenage Mutant Ninja Turtles, who, in 1987, had their own television show and in 1990 their own movie, along with comic books, clothing items, and computer games. Children who in 2003 loved the ocean setting of Pixar's animated movie *Finding Nemo* will probably sit up and take notice when they are old enough to get acquainted with Captain Nemo in Jules Verne's *Twenty Thousand Leagues Under the Sea* (1872).

It may be years, if ever, before children now reading the Lemony Snicket books, each of which can be described as "A Series of Unfortunate Events," will catch on to the ironic allusions behind many of the names in the books, which are popular with adults as well as children. The main characters are three orphans: Violet, Klaus, and Sunny Baudelaire. Violet's name is acknowledged to come from T. S. Eliot's poem "The Violet Hours." However, the names of her siblings are likely to suggest to knowledgeable adults the most famous murder case of the 1980s, when the aristocrat Claus von Bulow was accused, convicted, and then declared innocent of injecting Sunny, his wealthy, diabetic wife, with a deadly dose of insulin.

The only friends the Baudelaire orphans have are two other orphaned children, Isadora and Duncan Quagmire. Their given names are an apparent allusion to the American dancer Isadora Duncan (1877–1927), who became a tragic symbol of the "Roaring Twenties" when she was killed as a result of her long, elegant scarf getting tangled in the wheels of the convertible in which she was riding. Other names that fly by almost too fast to be recognized include that of a villain referred to as Coach Genghis; a school administrator named Nero, who plays very bad, late-night violin concerts; Dr. Georgina Orwell, an eye doctor and hypnotist who acts a lot like George Orwell's Big Brother, and the Ahab Memorial Hospital, where a character is sent after he loses his leg at the sawmill. By using these ironic names the author forces readers—at least those who have the information needed to understand the allusions—to ponder whether his whimsical exaggerations are really as exaggerated as they first appear.

We would not expect children to catch on to most of these allusions simply because they do not have the background knowledge, but their minds are able to appreciate irony at a surprisingly early age. When babies giggle playing peek-a-boo, they are laughing at the irony of someone being "gone" but still "there." Nursery rhymes, which are usually recited in calm and loving voices, ironically reconfirm children's suspicions about the world being a dangerous place:

> Hush-a-bye, baby, on the tree top,
> When the wind blows the cradle will rock;
> When the bough breaks the cradle will fall,
> Down will come baby, cradle, and all.

They also reconfirm children's exaggerated views of their mothers' overprotectiveness:

> Mother, may I go out to swim?
>   Yes, my darling daughter.
> Fold your clothes up neat and trim,
>   And don't go near the water.

The best-loved folktales include irony, as in "The Three Billy Goats Gruff," in which the first two little goats convince the troll under the bridge that he should wait to eat their big brother. But when the big brother comes, he is strong enough to knock the troll back into the water, where he belongs. In "The Three Bears," children choose age over species when they side with Baby Bear. They know it was wrong for Goldilocks to go uninvited into someone else's house, and especially to eat the strangers' breakfasts, try out their chairs, jump on their beds, and finally crawl into baby bear's bed and go to sleep. In "Little Red Riding Hood," they laugh at the irony of a wolf trying to impersonate a grandmother, and in "Jack and the Beanstalk," they love the irony of a boy's getting such a high return on what looked for all the world to be a foolish stock market trade. To young children accustomed to being their mothers' darlings, it does not seem at all unbelievable that the giant's wife would side with Jack over her husband.

Children undoubtedly love the rhythmic patterns of Dr. Seuss's books, but they also love the ironies in his stories. In *Yertle the Turtle* (1958), it is very satisfying when the humble little Yertle, who is at the bottom of the stack, gives a tiny little burp and causes the whole tower to topple. The king of all the turtles, whose idea it was that everyone let him stand on top of them so that he could survey all that he owned (really, only one mud puddle), ends upside down with his head and shoulders buried in the mud. In *Horton Hatches the Egg* (1940) it is ironic that when lazy Mayzie's baby is finally born, it looks as much like an elephant as a bird, and it is ironic that when *Gertrude McFuzz* (1958) finally manages to get more feathers than Lolla-Lee-Lou, she is too heavy to fly.

Barbara Robinson's popular read-aloud book *The Best Christmas Pageant Ever* (1972) is filled with irony. In it, the Herdmans, who are without a doubt the worst kids in town (they even smoke cigars and steal stuff from the Sunday School cabinet), show up to get parts in the church's annual Christmas pageant. Their fresh view of the events and the true empathy they feel for Mary and her baby bring new meaning to an old tradition.

Dramatic irony is the clue to the popularity of Peggy Rathman's 1996 award-winning *Officer Buckle and Gloria*. When Officer Buckle goes with his police dog, Gloria, to give safety lectures to schoolchildren, the dog stands behind him and performs tricks that make the audience laugh and cheer. Officer Buckle swells with pride over his newly acquired popularity until a TV news camera catches one of his (and Gloria's) performances and he is let in on the secret.

In James Marshall and Harry Allard's *Miss Nelson Is Missing* (1971), the readers are privy to a secret that the children in the school do not know. These children have the wonderfully pleasant Miss Nelson as their teacher, but they take advantage of her and misbehave and play tricks. So one week, Miss Nelson goes missing and her place is taken by the terrible witch, Miss Viola Swamp. After a week with Miss Swamp, the children are so relieved and happy when Miss Nelson comes back that they never again misbehave. On the last page, Miss Nelson is shown relaxing at home in her bedroom, where the closet door happens to be open. Clever readers spot the wig and the dress that Miss Nelson wore when she disguised herself as the terrible Miss Swamp.

The Harry Potter books are filled with both linguistic and observable ironies. It is ironic that Harry Potter is a boy with wondrous magical abilities, but the people who raise him are the extremely conservative and controlling Dursley family. J. K. Rowling cleverly uses ironic names to show that she is creating a parallel world that is *crosswise* or *diagonal* from the real world. The first magical place that Harry is taken is to Diagon Alley, where he buys his school supplies. Then he has to catch the Hogwarts Express on Track Nine-and-Three-Quarters at Kings Cross Station. Harry's godfather is Sirius Black, who animages into a great black dog and proves himself worthy of being named for the Dog Star in Canis Major. Lord Voldemort's name hints at his association with the Death Eaters, while the names of Harry's enemies (Draco, Crabbe, and Goyle) hint at their personalities through association with such words as *draconian*, *crabby*, and *gargoyle*.

During the 1970s, a major change occurred in the publishing world when publishers began producing ironic and even tragic books for teenagers. Northrop Frye has described a literary circle in which romance (cognate with spring) and comedy (cognate with summer) are in the upper half of the circle, while irony (cognate with fall) and tragedy (cognate with winter) are in the lower half. When Robert Cormier published his first young adult novel, *The Chocolate War* (1974), one of the reviews was printed with a black border around it and the heading, "Goodbye to Youthful Optimism." The point was that books for young people had nearly always had happy or at least hopeful endings, but Cormier's book, and many that have followed, were definitely in the lower, more pessimistic part of the literary circle. J. D. Salinger's *Catcher in the Rye* (1951) was such a book, but it was marketed to adults, with young people left to find it on their own.

Cormier's *I Am the Cheese* (1977) is a good illustration of the use of irony in sophisticated books for young adults. The title is an ironic allusion to the old nursery song and game "The Farmer in the Dell." The story is about a boy named Adam Farmer and his mother and father. As far as the boy knows, his father has always been an insurance agent, but actually the boy's father used to be a newspaper reporter. Because of secrets he uncovered, the family was placed in the government's witness protection program. When the boy is a young teenager, his family is involved in a terrible automobile accident, which Adam happens to survive. Readers soon realize that the accident was part of a plot to murder the family. The book opens after the accident. Adam is in an institution, apparently on heavy drugs. He is constantly being questioned by a man named Brint, who switches back and forth between being a psychiatrist and an evil interrogator. Brint is trying to find out what Adam knows and whether anyone else knows his family's history. To help readers catch onto the allusion, Cormier has Adam reminisce happily about how the Farmer family used to play the game "Farmer in the Dell." The book closes with the line "And the cheese stands alone." Cormier leaves it to his readers to remember the next-to-the-last line in the game, "The rat takes the cheese," which hints at the future of the doomed boy.

IRONY IN FILM

At the beginning of the twentieth century, when people first had the chance to pay money to see a "movie," much of what they saw was simple irony, as when a train appeared to be coming straight at the audience or a swimmer appeared to be going over a waterfall. In an ironic play on the naiveté of moviegoers, Edwin S. Porter in 1902 made a short film, *Uncle Josh at the Moving Picture Show*, which made fun of a country bumpkin who is so excited by a kissing scene in a movie that he tears down the screen.

The great actors of silent film—Ben Turpin, Charlie Chaplin, Buster Keaton, Harold Lloyd, and Harry Langdon—were often portrayed in ironic situations. Stan Laurel and Oliver Hardy teamed up in 1927 and were among the relatively few stars of silent film who were able to move on and succeed in the talkies. Their trademark was reciprocal violence. One of their most unforgettable films was the 1929 *Big Business*, in which they sell Christmas trees and happen to get the top of a tree caught in a prospective customer's door. When they ring the doorbell to ask the home owner to release their tree, he clips off the top. Laurel and Hardy respond by cutting off the man's tie. In the twenty-minute film, the business partners demolish the man's house brick by brick, while the man takes their delivery truck apart and reduces their load of trees to kindling.

The Marx Brothers were a bit more subtle in their creation of irony in the 1933 *Duck Soup*. Groucho and Harpo look very much alike, which adds to the irony of Harpo being a spy for Sylvania, while Groucho is the president of its enemy, Freedonia. The song "Hail Freedonia" is partly a parody of "Hail Britannia," but the words "Oh Freedonia, Oh don't you cry for me," are sung to the tune of "Oh Suzanna," and followed up by "All God's Chillen got guns." This is the film with the famous scene when Harpo and Groucho do the same actions on opposite sides of what appears to be a mirror, but the audience then gets to see that it was not a mirror at all, but only an empty frame standing between the brothers.

Terry Southern and Stanley Kubrick's 1964 film *Dr. Strangelove; or, How I Learned to Stop Worrying and Love the Bomb*, along with the 1965 film *The Loved One*, based on Evelyn Waugh's 1948 novel of the same name, and Terry Southern's 1969 film *The Magic Christian,* are filled with ironic incidents and statements. But because they have such clear targets (war, the funeral industry, and capitalism, respectively) they fit the definition of satire more than of irony. From the 1970s, the Monty Python skits and movies come closer to being pure ironies because while viewers walked away from these movies with much to think about—or at least to laugh about—the films fit into Frye's description of irony that leaves the audience unsure of what the author's attitude is or what their own attitude should be.

Monty Python and the Holy Grail (1975) plays with the idea of the romances, the wars, and the quests of the Middle Ages. The knights carry "the holy hand grenade of Antioch" in the "Arc of the Covenant." When asked how the weapon works, the knights advise the questioners to consult the "Book of Armaments" in the Bible. When King Arthur fights the Black Knight, he cuts off the knight's arms and both of his legs, but the Black Knight still taunts King Arthur and wants to continue the fight. Episodes feature not only Sir Lancelot and Sir Galahad the Chaste, but also Sir Robin the Not-So-Brave.

Monty Python's The Life of Brian (1979) features such characters as Nautius Maximus, Biggus Dickus, and Incontinentia Buttocks. It takes place in Bethlehem on a Saturday afternoon at teatime during the time of Christ. When Brian of Nazareth is asked if he is the Messiah, he says, "No," and the villagers respond "Only the *true* Messiah denies his divinity." When the Christians stone the Romans for blasphemy, asking what the Romans had ever done for them, the rhetorical question is answered with a list: aquaducts, sanitation, roads, irrigation, medicine, education, public baths, and peace. Playful language ironies include allusions to the Israelites as the "Red Sea pedestrians" and questions over whether myrrh is a *balm* or a *bomb*. When the Christians write graffiti on a palace wall in the form of "*Romans eunt Domus*" ("Romans go Home"), the Romans ignore the meaning and set about correcting the grammar. The song "You don't need to be followers. Yes, we're all individuals," is ironically sung by a large chorus, while the movie ends with Brian and several others hung on crosses, but happily singing, "Always look on the bright side of life."

As with this example, irony is a main technique used by the creators of *black humor*, which is also referred to as *dark humor*, *gallows humor*, *theater of the absurd*, and *film noir*. The creators of such material play with a fading line between reality and fantasy. In Southern's *The Magic Christian*, Guy Grand buys a huge newspaper and converts it entirely to readers' opinions. Is this a joke or simply a forerunner of today's talk radio and Internet chatrooms? Going back to the film *Pulp Fiction*, when Mia suffers a drug overdose, her rescuers use a Magic Marker to mark her chest for the adrenaline shot. This was a joke in the movie, but after some disastrous mistakes, some hospitals now actually use Magic Markers to keep from amputating the wrong body part.

IRONY IN LITERATURE

Critic Wayne C. Booth refers to irony in literature as *stable irony*, which he says is a linguistic phenomenon created by humans to be heard or read with some precision.

It allows readers to glimpse an author's most private and original thoughts. The Greeks, from whom English speakers inherited the word *irony*, were well acquainted with it. What could be more ironic than the story of King Midas, whose golden touch turned his food, his drink, and even his beloved daughter into cold, hard metal? Or the story of foolish young Arachne's being conceited enough to challenge Minerva to a weaving contest, and as a result being turned into a spider so that she and her descendants can go on weaving for all time? Narcissus loved himself so much that he tried to embrace his own reflection in a pool and drowned. Sisyphus is condemned to forever push a rolling rock up a hill, while Tantalus stands in water that he cannot drink and under hanging fruit that he cannot eat.

Sophocles (496?–406 B.C.E.), the great Greek playwright, created the ultimate ironic tragedy in his play *Oedipus the King*. The king is a wise and beloved ruler happy in his good fortune. He is married to a beautiful woman, Jocasta, who harbors the secret that years before she had sent her newborn son (Oedipus) away to be killed. Oedipus has his own secret, about killing an old man in a fit of youthful temper. Once it is revealed that the old man was his father and that Jocasta is his mother, Oedipus is a ruined man.

The story of Oedipus is a prime example of dramatic irony, in which the audience knows things that the characters on the stage do not. The mad scene in Shakespeare's *Hamlet* is another example. The audience knows that Hamlet only appears to be talking to himself; in reality he is "louding" for Polonius, who is observing the scene from the wings. Another bit of dramatic irony is when the king is totally unaware of how close Hamlet comes to killing him while he is praying. The stronger irony in this scene is Hamlet's respect for religious beliefs in the midst of murdering his stepfather. He still plans to kill the king, but at a time that would not send him to heaven because of being "in prayer."

Another way that authors create irony is through contrast. Shakespeare's Sonnet 130 is a good example, where the narrator describes his mistress's eyes as "nothing like the sun." He goes on to say that coral is more red than his mistress's lips, and that her breasts are "dun," her hair is wires, she has no roses in her cheeks, and her breath "reeks."

Contrasting characters are often used to set the scene for irony, as when in *The Pickwick Papers* (1836–1837), Charles Dickens pairs up the colorful and impudent Sam Weller with the innocent and benevolent Mr. Pickwick. J.R.R. Tolkien does something similar in *The Hobbit* (1938) and the Lord of the Rings trilogy (1954, 1955, and 1956) when he chooses two small, unadventurous, and peace-loving hobbits to protect the ring against all the powers of evil. C. S. Lewis relies on the ironic breaking of his reader's expectations all the way through *The Screwtape Letters* (1942). Screwtape is a senior bureaucrat in Hell, who writes letters to his nephew, Wormwood, telling him how to lead people to damnation. Screwtape refers to a "Lowerarchy" instead of a Hierarchy, and to "Our Father Below." He disparages joy and fun because they belong to God (the enemy), but he nevertheless believes that jokes and flippancy can be of some value, especially to the British, "who take their 'sense of humor' so seriously that a deficiency in this sense is almost the only deficiency at which they feel shame" (Lewis 59).

The gallows irony in Edgar Allan Poe's "The Cask of Amontillado" (1843) comes from the contrast between the fun of the carnival and the pleasant connotations of the wine cellar when contrasted with the ominous words. In the end, Fortunado, who is not so fortunate as his name would imply, is entombed alive in a dark wine cellar.

W. S. Porter (O. Henry) used plot development to create irony, as when, in his short story "The Gift of the Magi" (1906), a husband sells his treasured gold watch to buy combs for his wife's beautiful hair. At the same time, she has gone out and sold her hair to buy a gold chain for his watch. In another O. Henry story, "The Ransome of Red Chief" (1907), the gang that kidnaps a young boy finds that they have bitten off more than they can chew.

Such Gilbert and Sullivan comic operas as *H.M.S. Pinafore* (1878) and *The Mikado* (1885) get their comic ironies from laws that are as pointless as they are harsh. In *Pinafore*, social advancement is a mere matter of form. All a person needs to do to become the Ruler of the Queen's Navy is to polish up the handle on the big front door. In *The Mikado*, "The flowers that bloom in the spring . . . tra . . . la . . . have nothing to do with the case." In singing about her upcoming execution, Ko-Ko trivializes the grisly subject and makes it sound comic through alliteration and rhythm when she sings about "awaiting the sensation of a short, sharp shock/From a cheap and chippy chopper on a big black block!"

The irony in Flannery O'Connor's short stories—what she calls "Catholic grotesque"—comes from her belief that it is the sinner who is at the heart of Christianity, for no one knows as much about Christianity as does the sinner. In "A Good Man Is Hard to Find," a family is murdered by the not-so-good pair of escaped convicts they find, while in "Parker's Back," the protagonist gets back to his religious faith by having a giant picture of Jesus tattooed on his back.

Sometimes the irony comes through intertextuality and the knowledge that readers or listeners bring to the piece, as with Edward Albee's *Who's Afraid of Virginia Woolf?* (1962). The title scans like the line from the children's story, "Who's afraid of the big bad wolf?" while at the same time alluding to feminism and to Virginia Woolf's pointed criticisms of a patriarchal society. The protagonists are named George and Martha, as in George and Martha Washington, the first president and first lady of the United States. But in contrast to the middle-class values generally assumed to be the core on which the United States was founded, Albee's play ridicules motherhood, marriage, and middle-class values. The couple constructs and deconstructs a fantasized child, which they talk about to the young couple they are supposedly welcoming to the faculty of the college where George teaches. Nick (at age twenty-eight) and Honey (at age twenty-six) are themselves only a few years older than the fantasy child. Later in the play, George goes to the door and says he has received a telegram informing them that their son has died. After George reads the telegram, he symbolically eats it, so that not only was the son, but also the message about his death, totally constructed and deconstructed in plain sight of the audience.

While it is easy to see how authors achieve irony through creating characters that are the "opposite" of each other, they can also achieve irony through creating characters who are doppelgangers to each other, like Tweedledee and Tweedledum in Lewis Carroll's *Wonderland* and Harpo and Groucho Marx in the famous mirror-scene already mentioned from *Duck Soup*. Vladimir and Estragon in Samuel Beckett's *Waiting for Godot* (1952) are indistinguishable from each other. They are filled with angst as they talk about their discomfort, but this is undercut by the fact that they do nothing about it. They do not even get the rope they will need to carry out their threat of suicide. The audience does not know who Godot is, or who he represents, but they do know that Vladimir and Estragon will continue to wait.

The doppelgangers Rosencrantz and Guildenstern in Tom Stoppard's *Rosencrantz and Guildenstern Are Dead* (1966) are parodies of both Shakespeare's Rosencrantz and

Guildenstern and Beckett's Vladimir and Estragon. Stoppard's doppelgangers are nonentities, and, like Vladimir and Estragon, they are masters of the non sequitur and of philosophical, illogical reasoning and surrealistic and automatic reactions. Just as the Shakespearean audience is not able to distinguish between Rosencrantz and Guildenstern, the modern audience cannot distinguish between Stoppard's doppelgangers. They are so interchangeable that they even get their own names confused. When Stoppard has them interact with characters from *Hamlet*, they use actual lines from the Shakespeare play; however, when this interaction is finished they return to speaking in colloquial twentieth-century English. Their soliloquies make perfectly good sense, but not the kind of sense one would expect. Guildenstern talks about being dead and about being placed in a coffin. Then he asks Rosencrantz, if he were stuffed in a coffin whether he would prefer to be alive or dead, and answers his own question, "Naturally, you'd prefer to be alive. Life in a box is better than no life at all.... You could lie there thinking—well, at least I'm not dead!" (Stoppard 70–71).

In summary, irony is often associated with, and used to create, humor and satire. However, unlike humor it serves to make people think more than to make them laugh; and unlike satire, it does not strive to change people's opinions or to move them to take action. Linguistic irony includes various kinds of language play, as when people create a new kind of slang by reversing words to mean the opposite of their original meanings, or when they make paradoxical statements or create parodies. Visual irony is created by artists and architects with a sense of humor and incongruity combined with a desire to be different. Ironies that occur in real life are called "observable" irony. They are usually caused by accidents of nature—including human nature. Comedians, cartoonists, writers, and speakers often build their discourses around these kinds of ironies. They also use whatever other techniques they can think of to create various kinds of ironies (dramatic, tragic, comic, visual, and so forth) to add interest to art, film, drama, and literature written for both children and adults.

REFERENCES AND FURTHER READINGS

Alford, Steven E. *Irony and the Logic of the Romantic Imagination.* New York: Peter Lang, 1985.
Barbe, Katharina. *Irony in Context.* New York: John Benjamins, 1995.
Behler, Ernst. *Irony and the Discourse of Modernity.* Seattle, WA: U of Washington P, 1990.
Booth, Wayne C. *A Rhetoric of Irony.* Chicago: U of Chicago P, 1974.
Carroll, Lewis. *The Annotated Alice: "Alice's Adventures in Wonderland" and "Through the Look Glass."* Edited by Martin Gardner. Illus. by John Tenniel. New York: Wings Books/Random House, 1960.
Falletta, Nicholas. *The Paradoxicon.* New York: Wiley, 1983.
Frye, Northrop. *Anatomy of Criticism: Four Essays.* Princeton, NJ: Princeton UP, 1957.
Gilbert, William Schwenck, and Arthur Seymour Sullivan. *H.M.S. Pinafore.* London: Chappell, 1878.
———. *The Mikado.* London: Chappell, 1885.
Glicksberg, Charles L. *The Ironic Vision in Modern Literature.* The Hague: Martinus Nijhoff, 1969.
Good, Edwin M. *Irony in the Old Testament.* Sheffield, UK: Almond, 1981.
Green, D. H. *Irony in the Medieval Romance.* Cambridge, UK: Cambridge UP, 1981.
Gurewitch, Morton. *The Ironic Temper and the Comic Imagination.* Detroit, MI: Wayne State UP, 1994.

Handwerk, Gary J. *Irony and Ethics in Narrative: From Schlegel to Lacan.* New Haven, CT: Yale UP, 1985.

Holland, Glenn S. *Divine Irony.* Selinsgrove, PA: Susquehanna UP, 2004.

Larson, Gary. *The Farside Last Impressions: Off the Wall Calendar.* Kansas City, MO: Andrews McMeel, 2002.

Lederer, Richard. *Anguished English: An Anthology of Accidental Assaults upon Our Language.* New York: Delacorte P, 1987.

Lewis, C. S. *The Screwtape Letters.* London: Geoffrey Bles, 1942.

Lurie, Alison. *Don't Tell the Grown-Ups: Subversive Children's Literature.* Boston: Little, Brown, 1990.

Marx, Groucho, et al. *Duck Soup.* Hollywood, CA: Paramount Pictures, 1933.

McPhee, N. *The Book of Insults, Ancient and Modern.* New York: Penguin, 1978.

Muecke, Douglas Colin. *Irony and the Ironic.* New York: Methuen, 1980.

Nilsen, Alleen Pace, and Don L. F. Nilsen. *Encyclopedia of 20th-Century American Humor.* Westport, CT: Oryx P/Greenwood, 2000.

O'Connor, Flannery. *The Complete Stories,* New York: Farrar, Straus and Giroux, 1971.

Opie, Iona, and Peter Opie. *The Oxford Dictionary of Nursery Rhymes.* Oxford, UK: Oxford UP, 1951.

Schickel, Richard. "How Lucky Does He Feel?" *Time,* February 28, 2005, 62–65.

Southern, Terry. *The Magic Christian.* New York: Random House, 1960.

Stoppard, Tom. *Rosencrantz and Guildenstern Are Dead.* New York: Grove P, 1966.

Twain, Mark. *The War Prayer.* 1923. New York: Harper and Row/St. Crispin Press, 1951.

Wolfe, Tom. *From Bauhaus to Our House.* New York: Farrar, Straus and Giroux, 1981.

27

Italian Comedy

Nina daVinci Nichols

There is no such thing as Italian comedy, not to Italians. They think comedy *is* Italian. It took root in Rome sometime B.C.E.; flourished in the works of Plautus and Terence; survived adaptations in medieval school plays; was reborn in Renaissance satire of the fourteenth century, then revived in "learned" and literary drama. Thereafter it found popular form in the sixteenth century's *commedia dell'arte*, and inspired Goldoni's well-made plays in the eighteenth century. Some of this rich legacy reappeared in nineteenth-century street comedies throughout regional Italy, while its literary life entered into the theatrical experiments of Pirandello in the twentieth century. Fragments of classic comedy still appear in current performance pieces and film, especially Italian film. In a word, the history of comedy in the West parallels Italy's unique history as the site of continuous civilization. Admittedly, a historian might quibble over accuracy here since Italians use the term *commedia* to describe epic, spectacle, fantasy, pageant, song and dance, domestic saga—almost any form of theater other than tragedy, a dramatic relic they find somehow regrettable. When Dante ushered the Italians into heaven with his *Commedia*, they sent the tragic impulse northward to Germany and England with no sense of loss and no return ticket.

A glance at theater architecture underscores the point. All across Europe, elegant buildings copying Roman models offer irrefutable evidence that comedy was the ruling form of entertainment. The structures incorporate the fixed tectonic scene for comedies of the town square, or replicate the design of a street for the perspective stage. A theater floor was designed to illustrate the plays to be performed according to a pattern of colored squares that actors followed. Some fixed sets in sixteenth-century palaces advanced on Roman designs by calling for a deep perspective of two streets meeting in the distance on a painted flat. Intricate buildings pictured on each side of the street represented courts, residences, churches, towers: in short, a small city. Any play of Terence or Plautus might be performed on such a set, as were many Renaissance plays known now by name only.

From geographical perspectives too, the idea of an Italian comedy means little to a people who face "the problem of the language," meaning the absence of one standard Italian spoken by all. Film, where words are secondary, has tended to exploit regional dialects and styles, whereas literature and drama take the Tuscan language for the standard. For these reasons alone, comedy is a fragile flower that wilts on definition. A few added theories will bury it forever. As one wit put it, theories of laughter are no laughing matter. With that warning, I dispense with all explanation not strictly necessary for clarity and summarize a few antecedents of distinctly Italian traits.

First, in primitive forms whose echoes still linger, comedy was phallic and orgiastic, featuring a procession, a feast, a sacrifice. Anthropologists say these primitive actions expressed a triumph over death, a favorite trope that lived on in medieval plays. A young hero debated with the reigning monarch, who ultimately was killed to make way for youth and a new year. At similarly deep levels, comedy spawned the antic figure of the clown, the grinning fool who diverted the wrath of the gods from the anointed figure of the king. Sometimes he accomplished it simply with an outburst of laughter that shattered solemn occasions, sometimes by conjuring up mischievous devils. Always by his presence alone, the clown confirmed a sense that comedy was built on doubles: double occasions, double premises, double values, double views, the doubled character who was the fool. In Christian countries, he presented a ludicrous or reverse mirror image of the hero or ruler, a mortal and therefore but a fool. Fool was a victim of more clever persons who took pleasure in his humiliation.

Comedy is cruel. It releases aggression, and farce especially enacts hostilities only expressible in that form. At its most harmless, comedy involves an awareness of incongruities, absurdities, the ludicrous element in an otherwise unified whole: a grotesque, circus nose on a beautiful woman. Paradoxically, by indulging the inverse or aberrant, comedy points to a desire for rationality, of paramount important since comedy appeals to the intelligence, pure and simple. Still, precisely how a comic plot reaches that elusive order and how it triggers laughter, no two critics agree. Sigmund Freud thought anxiety caused laughter; Henri Bergson linked laughter to "anaesthesia of the heart" and a kind of automatism that blocked sentiment. Luigi Pirandello, thinking of comedy as humor, linked it to a perception of "the opposite," *il contrario*, in any experience or event. And still others see comedy as an explosion of relief after the brush with danger that arrives in everyday life. These same machineries reach into primitive levels of meaning too trenchant for most forms of light humor. Surprisingly, the more serious the work, the more readily its theatrical devices and psychological gambits evoke old, old levels of comic action.

If a distinction exists among Italian and other Western versions of comedy, it may well lie in the intersection of a few variables: (1) an Italian genius for self-staging; (2) delight in an intellectual response to experience; and (3) an attraction to, even admiration for, cleverness and trickery. Usually meaning deceit, yet not quite synonymous, "trickery" has been a staple of comedy at least since Plautus. Its nearest translation in Italian is *inganni*, which includes a high tolerance for the sort of double meanings referred to above. An *inganno* is a twist on a truth, or situation, or common understanding. At its most serious, the word refers to betrayal; on its lighter side, an *inganno* means a "ruse," or "scam," bordering on fraudulence and cheating. Whether a plot or a character, an *inganno* also implies delight in its own inventiveness, no matter how ludicrous. The con artists turned failed crooks in Mario Monicelli's film *I soliti ignoti* (1958; released as *Big Deal on Madonna Street*, 1960) cannot possibly succeed as jewel thieves. The comedy rises out of their tricky, un-self-conscious efforts to overcome obstacles as one thing after another goes wrong. Compare the prevailing sentiment and self-consciousness in a British caper comedy like the *The Lady Killers* (1951). The framing joke lies in bamboozling a dear, old, innocent landlady into putting up members of the mob as boarders, believing them to be concert musicians. Far from enjoying their duplicity, they squirm with guilt, and nobody has the heart to correct the landlady's impression.

Sometimes the nearly unsurmountable obstacles facing a comic hero hint at far more serious traits than trickery touching on the national identity. In Lina Wertmuller's film *Pasqualino settebellezze* (*Seven Beauties*, 1976), the hero-victim, the inmate of a Nazi labor camp, dreams of an outrageous scenario for escape that involves making love to his enormous, sadistic, battle-ax of an overseer. Physically he is small and unprepossessing; his sole asset is his manhood, if it is an asset. His face glows with inspiration as he hits on the idea. The situation showing German might and ideology as superior to Italian is familiar in post–World War II Italian film. The hero's trick, however, hinges on a common fantasy about male power: in gender relations and in the film's social reality, men dominate. Comedy's doubled point of view comes into play here. At first, the hero sees only his physical entrapment: the barbed-wire gates, the guard's club and whip, her masterful size. These nonetheless dwindle to nothing beside his imaginary priapic potentiality, the trick's basic expression of faith in the triumph of the individual male, no matter the odds. Any Italian male may overcome a state, including his own.

The film's German-Italian opposition also delivers a dose of class resentment, though it is not developed as such. The wealthy, the successful, the privileged need not resort to trickery to stay alive. To the contrary, from Roman times to the present, trickiness and cleverness characterize servants and underdogs. While they often appear in light comedy, their most congenial settings tend to be in satire, since it probes deceit and doubleness of all sorts in manners and morals. After all, cold as it is, satire appeals to an intellectual elite, real or imaginary, and constituted by the play. Put the other way around, satire flatters its audience by implying some desirable standard or conduct inconsistent with common facts. The game means to expose, mock, and eventually exorcise a foolish or vicious or simply different outsider, while the superior audience looks down on some poor devil to note, with Shakespeare's Puck, "what fools these mortals be." It follows that satirists never have been wholly popular: the great satirist Juvenal was exiled from Rome. Pure satire, in any case, would lose an audience faster than a lecturer on nuclear physics in a movie house. Satire is what closes on Saturday night.

Briefly, the form offers a rough equivalent in action to irony in speech. Since Renaissance comedy revived Roman forms, Niccolò Machiavelli's *Il Mandragola* (The Mandrake Root, 1518) suggests itself as a point of departure for a few critical comments, especially since he attacked corruption among the elite. Carlo Goldoni in the next century took misogyny for the subject of his satire and based his best-known plots on tricks over sex and money. Pirandello's satire initiated black comedy with his mordant jokes, his doubles, and sly philosophers, inspiring Theater of the Absurd. Eduardo De Filippo, not quite a contemporary, celebrated cleverness as a necessity among a depressed social class. Dario Fo retrieved the medieval Passion plays for popular responses to his parodies and performances. And finally, the great satirist Federico Fellini returned to the machineries of primitive comedy for its irrational focus, its sensual feasts and parades of grotesques. The works of these writers release an archaic self in moments when chaos nearly reigns, although an audience may remain unconscious of any such effect on them. As for comedy's happy endings and romantic couples, well—not in satire. The temporary resolution of a problem may be the happiest ending satire can manage, and sexual chicanery the closest it may come to romantic ideals.

THE LITERARY TRADITION

Still unmatched for its sharp bite, Machiavelli's *Mandragola* has been in continuous performance since its own day partly because of its timeless ridicule of sex, class, and duplicity. Two rich men in the framing plot wager that a third cannot seduce a chaste woman. That theme has been milked ever since society institutionalized marriage. To the Italian relish of trickery, the play adds a misanthropic worldview that banishes sentiment and responds intellectually to experience. Judging by this play, not all the aggressiveness of primitive comedy eroded away with time and sophisticated manners. The play's inner circle of aristocratic characters evoke a resemblance to the genuine, the innocent, the inadvertent rationalist—a sort of dope who speaks the truth—all of them Machiavelli's ingenious contributions to history's gallery of comic types. Essentially they are victims. The inner plot pivots on that third man, a "young lover" of low design who pursues the young wife of an impotent husband with the help of a salacious friar, a fool of a learned doctor, and the bed trick of substituting one partner for another in the dark. Shakespeare used it twice, in *Measure for Measure* and in *All's Well That Ends Well*. A fine dust of fraudulence, that doubled view of appearances referred to above, hangs over the acting out of these deceits.

All the play's scheming and manipulation advance the main theme of "horning," a peculiarly Italian preoccupation and to this day a nasty form of abuse. To call a man *cornuto* (cuckolded) may well instigate violence. Here the complaisant, impotent husband Nicia receives "procreative intervention" on his behalf by the younger man. The element that shocked Machiavelli's audience, beyond the explosive language, was the complicity of the pure-hearted wife. She is persuaded by her confessor and a discourse in nonsense Latin that the next man to sleep with her will die. Out of doubt and goodness, she agrees that this fate ought not to befall her husband and allows the unscrupulous young trickster Callimaco into her bed. Doubling, in other words, serves as both particular theatrical device and primitive action leading to death. And that is how the wicked Machiavelli pulled death up from the underpinnings of comedy and used it to motivate sexual pursuit in the main plot. The primitive contest between an older, reigning "king" and a challenger concludes as it must with the success of the younger man, in Machiavelli's view a wastrel, a cynic, a herald of corruption. Triumphing over death carries a price. Either the wife pays willingly for her own and her lover's joy, thus colluding in depravity, or Machiavelli damns her for her ignorance at being taken in by trickery.

The play also strikes a particularly Italian note in the sexual perfidy of the two representative men and their attitude toward chastity. It confirms their privileged status, since popular entertainments typically avoid debate about abstract issues. Probably more serious is the play's ridicule of religious piety, damning it as equivocal in a country where church and state are neither quite separate nor equal. An aristocratic audience may be worldly, even dismissive, about religious practice that remains sacrosanct among the working class. Machiavelli condemns the tricky friar, who after all has a reputation from medieval times of moral equivocation, born of his missionary walking among commoners. At best, Friar Timoteo represents a realist in his putatively spiritual profession, for anticlericalism plays a prominent role in Italy's comic tradition. Even the great Molière (properly, Jean-Baptiste Poquelin de Molière) satirized behaviors that undermined conventional images of piety, quite a different business than mocking the church. A priestly community ordinarily rose above serious moral criticism; but it hardly was exempted from satire after Machiavelli by either Shakespeare or Molière, both committed to puncturing a guise of holiness at the expense of virtue. *Tartuffe* (1664), after all, remains a quintessential expression of doubt about the relation of human dereliction to priests and priestliness. And then there is that devil of righteousness, the "Puritan" Malvolio in *Twelfth Night* (1602).

Keeping one satirical eye on social class, Goldoni transformed the standard subjects of sex and marriage into comedy of manners with his *Mirandolina* (1753). By also playing up the importance of money in courtship, he ridiculed a strain of materialism in his culture that he found deplorable. Uniquely for her time, the play's heroine is an innkeeper, no ingenue who needs a man to introduce her to the world and worldliness. Goldoni brings the violence of farce into the flirtatious teasing on the surface action, while puncturing the bubble of romance. Implicitly, as Mirandolina's suitors are aristocrats, a marquess and a count, Goldoni also advances the pattern of upper-class man pursuing lower-class woman. The hero-villain Ripafratta, a blue-blooded misogynist, falls in love with Mirandolina in spite of himself. He and a rival ply Mirandolina with jewels and gifts while she employs a trickster's brain to lead them on, despising them, all in the interests, she says, of demonstrating that women, unlike merchandise, cannot be bought with riches or flattery. Early in act 1, after the Marquess admits he would marry her if it came to that, she says in soliloquy:

God knows, if I'd married everyone who wanted me, there'd be a husband in every room by now. I'm lovely—and they love me.... They pay the bill, they propose, I send them packing. It's practically a daily occurrence. That oaf Ripafratta.... He hates women, does he? Why? What's wrong with him? Nothing I can't fix, at any rate! I like a challenge. It's a weakness of mine, you see: I have to make everyone adore me. I thrive on it. And the count? He'll have to look elsewhere. Money has its uses.... Besides, I've got a mission: to convince the doubters that women really are the best idea nature ever came up with.

Flouting conventional female passivity, Mirandolina expresses her hostility for men by word and deed. Comedy's ace in reserve, the antic death, pops right up into the main plot when she nearly tricks her suitor into a duel with his rivals. Then, having set up his murder, she rushes in at a last moment to stop the event and appear as his savior. The psychology is all the more interesting for being veiled. Mirandolina fails in her mission to deceive all suitors. Even after having been seduced by her wine and wiles, Ripafratta rushes away more than ever a confirmed woman-hater vowing to avoid women in the future. We gather that Goldoni's idea here is that a spoiled, rich man could hold little true appeal for a strong, clear-eyed, middle-class woman of character. Yet it also seems undeniable that Goldoni punished his heroine for her antipathy to men by withholding a lover. His stinging insights into the heroine's motives drove as well into the mens' policy of avoidance. Nor does Goldoni endorse the romantic notion that love alters character, usually understood to be for the better. The play might be a harbinger of complex investigations in our day into the secret agendas guiding love and marriage. Finally, perhaps, the tricky woman may have offered an uninvited look into Goldoni's own spirit.

Given the topical nature of comedy, even its purest forms immediately reflect social issues. Class remains in the satirical mix in the twentieth century since European societies remain far more stratified than Americans may know. In general, Italy's industrial north still mocks the agrarian south as socially regressive. Still, over the century, emphasis on class modulated as social mobility began to build momentum, whether as a daydream or as a reality. Fellini's *I Vitelloni* (roughly, Street Life, 1953) springs to mind as an outstanding illustration of social and economic instability after World War II. The film features alienated, young middle-class men without a direction or a future—more of this later.

At the same time, from literary perspectives, comedy's primitive elements of doubling and fake death grew all the more prominent in major works of the period: first, as surface topics of sex and money eroded and changed, and secondly as primitive elements were distilled and imported into absurdist and black comedy. In any event, fake death has a long theatrical history and adds an edge of anxiety to any work where it appears. The Italianate Shakespeare certainly drew on the theatrical jolt the theme delivers in *Romeo and Juliet* and, differently, in *Much Ado about Nothing*. Also exciting a kind of suppressed nervousness, doubling and doubles question identity on both the surface as well as the primitive level of action. Plautus, for instance, exploited the anxiety created by doubles with his *Menaechmi* (*The Brothers Menaechmus*, 192 B.C.E.), and Shakespeare again upped the ante on the topic by creating twin masters and twin servants with his *Comedy of Errors* (1592).

The revolutionary man of theater, Pirandello, played the fake death card several times for high stakes. Faking death, after all, teases fate and laughs sardonically at human limits. It is the ultimate trick of the clown who holds the center ring, a spectral character in Pirandello, who resembles himself. He almost disguised the theme in plays based on debates, where deep and surface levels coincide. In the farcical *Cosi e (se vi pare)* (*Right You Are If You Think You Are*, 1917), an entire town, from its provincial administrator to its dimwitted gossips and grotesques, generates a heated debate over the probable madness of neighbors Mme. Frola and her son-in-law, Sr. Ponza. The townspeople disagree about whether Ponza's wife is dead or alive. Humor is generously woven into the action, while the play's philosopher-fool, Laudisi, doubles for Pirandello and poses as *raisonneur*. Then, instead of debate ending in death as in primitive comic patterns, controversy between passionately ignorant townspeople and coolly rational Laudisi spirals down toward chaos, another kind of death.

As for trickiness and its delights, Pirandello never wrote a word that fell outside of his own definition of comedy in his essay *Umorismo* (*On Humor*, 1908). He defined humor as the form always containing a perception of its opposite, *il contrario,* a description as much as declaring that doubleness was his credo. An imp of the perverse sits at the top of his comic worlds, pulling the strings with a wry grimace passing for a smile. Usually his literary games begin incidentally and then drive straight up into the realm of pure ideas. Or, to change my metaphor to suit dramatic action, his works tend to begin with disarming simplicity and dive straight down to dissolution. The short play *L'Imbecile* (*The Imbecile*, 1922) draws on the tradition of a trick or practical joke that backfires. In Pirandelllo's hands, the device takes on a deeply menacing complexion, its plot no longer determined by deceit but by bitterness, anger, and despair.

Not to imply that the fake death or the ubiquitous doubling in Pirandello automatically generates humor and laughter; they, rather, carry a dry, unemotional valence apparent in his first major work, *Il fue Mattia Pascal* (*The Late Mattia Pascal*, 1904). A summary of the novel might go as follows:

One fine day at the turn of the century, a pleasant young librarian named Mattia Pascal longed for and so took another identity. First he declared himself dead. Cleverly, he saw to his own funeral, where his wife and family mourned his death in a manner suitable to the times, and assured himself that all appearances corresponded with his wishes. Then he left town. He adopted the name Adriano Meis, odd pun, and by happenstance fell in love with a woman named Adriana, alerting the reader to a certainty that problems were in the offing. One day years later, he decided he was not enjoying his new life as much as he had hoped and decided to return to his old one. He traveled back to his home town and introduced himself around, but no one remembered him, not even his wife. His family looked on him cordially as a stranger. The trickster was tricked; his joke came back like a boomerang to hit him in the head. With cool equanimity, Pirandello enlisted the element of triumphing over death while elaborating his abiding theme of what human identity might mean.

Three films have adapted the novel, the most recent with Marcello Mastroianni in the role of Pascal. None quite captures the novel's sense of doubling as a fearful symptom of psychic unease, though all three present the mirror as a diabolical instrument of mental disintegration. But doubling is ubiquitous in Pirandello. The actress Donata in *Trovarsi* (*To Find Oneself*, 1932) discovers that her very life depends upon doubling herself in the characters she plays. In a film based on the play, Donata experiences a terrifying glimpse of ego annihilation before a mirror. The theme seems at once harmless yet more exaggerated in *Il giuco delle parti* (*The Rules of the Game*, 1918), which situates the heroine's husband and lover in the dynamic tension of doubles. Other of Pirandello's doubles may arouse incidental laughter while more deeply stirring up black comedy. In *Pensaci Giacomino* (*Better Think Twice About It, Giacomino*, 1916), an older man offers to secretly support a young man's marriage to the woman he loves since he suspects that his age will inspire mockery if he offers himself as her suitor. Giacomino at once doubles himself and cancels out one identity. Another older man remains in the wings of a desirable young woman's love affairs in *Vestire gli ignudi* (*Naked*, 1922) With all the cruelty of farce, the world and former lovers crowd in to harass the heroine for fictionalizing her life in a newspaper story. Still, Pirandello's most significant experiment with doubling occurs in *Enrico Quarto* (*Henry IV*, 1922), where it leads inexorably to attempted murder. The hero deliberately lives out the role of the (putative) Emperor Henry, whose costume he wore to a party where he suffered a riding accident. A doctor, touchingly named Belcredi (literally, "wholly trustworthy"), tries to cure the hero's delusion that he lives in the stopped time of the accident; but oddly enough the hero resists the idea of a cure. In the end, he shoots the doctor, thus proving that he may indeed be insane. Doubles cannot coexist. So too, Pirandello understood masking on- or offstage as a privileged doubling that nevertheless led to kinds of madness, especially in the theater plays.

Fragments of the theme appear almost covertly in Pirandello's most celebrated play, *Sei personnagi in cerca d'autore* (*Six Characters in Search of an Author*, 1921). The Father and the Director engage in debate reminiscent of old king and new king in primitive comedy. Action proceeds on a rational, if excited, level of dialogue that also functions on a nearly buried level of subplot as a phallic contest: the men's controversy, after all, hinges on allusions to both the Father's possible incest with his stepdaughter, as well as to her separate sexual adventures as a streetwalker. Repetition of this material in the dialogue may be considered doubling of a rhetorical sort—not to discount Pirandello's typical probing and searching style as of primary significance. The play involves more obvious doubles in the action prior to the play, when the Father was replaced by the Mother's second husband, who fathered the (step)daughter and two other children. The implicit contest between doubled fathers results in the death at the play's end not of an old king, but of the second father's innocent children, a boy and girl, precisely as if punishment for a mysterious crime of fathers descends on the children. It's a very Ibsenesque theme. The boy shoots himself and the little girl drowns. The acts, shocking and nearly incomprehensible in performance, yield up their logic on the ritual level of plot.

In sum, Pirandello the high modernist, who redefined the very idea of theater, calls up primitive comedy with his grotesques, his bleak conceits and ironic jokes. He named his typical form "tragical farce," referring to dark symbolic meanings of action barely expressible in a modern world whose only values were farcical. Tragical also may allude to his belief, first to last, in life's mutability versus the fixed, and thus dead, forms of art—he played many variations on the theme. The metaphysics and the psychology he tinkered with implied an irrational focus on the world, ultimately dangerous as it might at any moment become permanent—as it does in *Enrico Quarto*. So too, Laudisi's laughter at the cacophony of provincial administrators and gossips debating about madness offers a chilly warning that the abyss of irrationality is opening before them. Ultimately, the farce in tragical farce dispenses with euphemism and thrives on passionate, even furious, argument unleavened by reason and so insusceptible to conclusions, or agreements, or conventional solutions. Put differently, literary forms of debate refined over centuries into drawing room comedy and comedy of manners degenerate in Pirandello's plays and grow ludicrous. Short of murder, debate ends only when a third element, or disposition, intervenes, like the appearance of a mysterious lady at the end of *Cosi e* (*Right You Are*, 1917). In superficially literary senses, Pirandello might be compared with his contemporary G.B.S. Shaw, another debater in drawing rooms, who nonetheless seems never to have set foot in ritual territories. Shaw's philosophical fools, doubles of himself, do not argue with god, reason, or a reigning king. Not even in his most metaphoric *Heartbreak House* (1918) do characters knowingly stand poised at the brim of chaos, whereas Pirandello tricks his characters into precisely such circumstances.

Eduardo de Filippo acted in several of Pirandello's plays and counted himself fortunate to have attracted the great man's interest. Apparently Pirandello agreed to collaborate with him on a play, *L'abito nuovo* (*The New Suit*, 1936), but died while it still was in its first phase of development. De Filippo was accused later of copying Pirandello in his own plays and rightly dismissed the charge as silly: no writer matched Pirandello either in literary, theatrical, or psychological power. De Filippo's unassailable contribution to the tradition is his comic masterpiece *Napoli milionaria* (A Neapolitan Millionaire), staged in 1945. He turns a spotlight on the Neapolitan working class, calling on a bag of tricks that had been forming from time immemorial since Naples had its own tradition of comedy. (The standard Italian clown is a Neapolitan dialect character.) Be that as it may, the play's characters are cunning, exuberant, wickedly hypertheatrical, and touched by the genius for what I called self-staging. In current terms, they "act out." Whereas the play begins in high farce, it slips into a style of realism that pervades both stage and film from the 1940s on.

Setting, therefore, is exemplary, in Naples during World War II, where the action concerns a big-hearted family inventing stratagems for survival. Police know that the family's house has been serving as a local transfer station for black-market goods, and they raid the place. At a signal saying they are at the door, Papa Gennaro Jovine leaps into bed and plays dead. Mama and family light candles at four corners of the bedstead and distribute themselves in attitudes of mourning. Two runners in the black market don wimples and begin intoning prayers. Solemnity reigns. While the canny arresting officer, who knows his ingenious townsfolk, waits for them to give up the game, an air raid begins; everyone scatters for shelters, leaving the officer and the corpse to play out the scene. The black-market goods—coffee, chocolate, olive oil—have been stuffed into the mattress, but not until the last possible moment does Gennaro return to life, at which point the savvy, patient officer agrees not to arrest him. The fake death brilliantly displaces meaning, for Gennaro and family will die—may as well be dead—without black-market goods. The gallows humor distances the audience from the characters' grim reality, as if it were indeed retrieving the archaic self that grins at danger.

Run-ins with the law offer ideal occasions for celebrating cleverness, and in the play's community, the law clearly is a polite suggestion. Act 2 takes place three years later when Gennaro has vanished and everyone believes he must indeed be dead, the victim of a stray bomb, or bullet, or other hazard of war. When he reappears unexpectedly, he finds that his wife and her lover have built a thriving business on earnings from the black-market goods under Gennaro's bed, a choice metaphor in the sly, nearly inaudible way of wit at its most cerebral. Gennaro sees the town's changed condition with clarity and disappointment. The highest asset of the class was cleverness that wrested triumph out of seemingly impossible odds of economic hardship. Improvisation and quick-wittedness had an immediate utility, gave trickery a positive name. Now the family as a stable unit has degenerated. The son steals cars; the daughter is out at night. Games with the law no longer spring up as life-saving strategies. A wartime morality based on petty deceit and double dealing—the very machinery of comedy—needs to be eradicated.

The key illustration of the theme occurs with the little girl Rituccia's dangerous illness and reveals the hopeless ignorance of the locals. The doctor, a traditional voice of reason, and usually summoned too late to cure any illness, since these backward people believe he brings death, calls for an expensive medicine. The wife now trained in buying and selling fails to move the dealer by her need for his medicine to save her daughter's life. So, far from being faked, death moves up from its place in a primitive underplot into the fictive everyday reality. De Filippo shows the regressiveness of these southerners evoking the very mordant consequences that formal satire implies. Ironically, life as is, normally the social scope of a comedy, cannot sustain the play's opening ebullience. To the degree that comedy always reflects a version of social reality, it grapples here with contradiction between a self and a group, the wife and the black marketers who appeared to operate on the same side.

While literary and popular comedy diverged throughout the century, many playwrights after World War II chose antiliterary modes. Mario Fratti for example, Italian born and living in the United States, rejected the well-made play as not only old-fashioned but ill suited to the topics of contemporary life. Fratti's early plays written in Italian in the 1960s were broader in scope than the many written in English, at last count numbering about fifty. *The Refrigerators* (1977) considered the comical impact of the new science of cryogenics; *Academy* (1977) imagined a hilarious school for gigolos. The recent plays, by comparison, are short, fast-paced statements of one problem with two or three characters. The titles of plays in a volume collecting works from the seventies to the nineties reflect his current focus: *Famiglia* (Family, 1995), *Amiche* (Friends, 1972), *Madri e Figlie* (*Mother and Children*, 1972 and 1975). Fratti's plot, typically a debate, builds to a final knockout punchline for theatrical effect. In some ways, the plays compare with the strategy of stand-up comedians, who use language solely for delivering jabs and swings en route to a joke. Fratti, in the introduction to *Amiche*, says his mission is to communicate what he sees happening around him, or what he believes to be people's hidden agendas. These, however, tend to be private rather than political or broadly social, since Fratti interests himself in personal relations. In effect, his plays ask: how is it that two persons sharing a common language cannot find common ground? Finally, however, the axis of conspiracy between Fratti and his audience pivots on cleverness, and a good trick is its own reward. To that degree, dialogue in his plays works to set up a surprise rather than to reveal social malaise or elicit primitive comedy.

There seems to have been no period in Italy when a work like the English folk play, for instance, blossomed into a literary comedy. It is entirely conceivable that King George and the Dragon skits performed along the byways of rural England in the fifteenth and sixteenth centuries helped create the climate for the virtual explosion of drama toward the close of the period, perhaps even for Shakespeare's historical kings. The reverse happened in Italy: Renaissance "learned" comedy filtered down into the general parodies of *commedia dell'arte,* and later on, unscripted playlets merged with regional and local puppet shows. These remained highly popular in Sicily, where the most successful company still operates with an ecumenical collection of *commedia* and classic fairy tale figures: the *Befana* (Fairy Godmother); *il Gigante* (the Giant), the *Arlecchino* (Harlequin), the *Magnifico* (a Prince or Ruler), as well as contemporary carabinieri and an ingenue. A dashing Casanova was an immensely well-known figure in the late eighteenth and early nineteenth centuries and may have inspired Goldoni's misogynist hero Ripafratta in *Mirandolina.* More significant as folk drama are the medieval Passion plays still performed around Easter time. They represent a separate, liturgical tradition, enacted by amateurs and studied by scholars as both performance art and theatrical show.

Dario Fo appropriated the medieval plays with his "slash and burn" approach to comedy. His interest as a left-wing socialist always pivots on the abuse of institutionalized power from political, to religious, to social. Yet he is more of a performer, a self-staging opportunist rather than a writer; his published satires read as outlines of action. While his *Mistero Buffo* (*Comic Mysteries*, 1974) undermines the church for what he sees as its repressiveness, he also sees the condemnation that often follows, by conservatives and liberals alike, as proof that Christian myth should be stripped of its mystery. One of his brief *Passion Plays* (1978–1983), called *The Fool Beneath the Cross, Laying a Wager*, travesties the chief event in the liturgical year and involves three "Crucifiers." The Fool helps to strip and then show off the naked Christ to the crowd for a few pennies. Next he joins soldiers nailing the body to the cross; he plays dice with the Crucifiers; he robs the hero of the Judas silver still in a pocket; and finally the Fool reverses himself and arranges with some others to save the hero. The hero, however, refuses to be released and the Fool rages with frustration: "The Son of God is mad!" (111).

The government removed Italy's most popular television show, *Canzonissima,* from the airwaves after Fo portrayed a twelfth-century pope who hung disagreeable monks by their tongues from the church doors. Such work may function as catharsis for its performer rather than for its audience. Gesture, movement, mime, music, pictures, most of them painted by himself, all figure into Fo's shows in a manner described by his translator, Ron Jenkins, as "untranslatable." In pieces based on familiar folk narratives—*The Birth of the Jongleur,* or *The Birth of the Villeyn*—Fo retells the story with shrieks, laughter, shouts, picture slides, and slapstick as well as a comic's assortment of asides and colloquies with the audience. According to Jenkins, his wild actions in performance sometimes originate in scenes from celebrated paintings by Hieronymus Bosch, Francisco Goya, and Giotto among others, which Fo reproduces in a commentary or a tableau. Fo plainly enjoys improvising, a legacy from his revivals of *commedia dell'arte*. He may incorporate a topic suggested by his audience first into performance and then into a written work. An economic crisis mentioned during a performance one night on one of his tours resulted in a long riff on the subject and, eventually, the angry play *"We Won't Pay, We Won't Pay"* (1974).

THE FILM TRADITION

Comedy's basic machinery of mistakes and disguises, its clowns and fools, its parades and excursions into the fantastical, all find their most innovative forms of expression nowadays in contemporary film. Given the huge range of Italian film since its rebirth in the 1940s, I refer to only two directors as touchstones, both known best for their fantasies tinged with satire: the Taviani brothers, Paolo and Vittorio, for their success with using spectacle and pageantry, and Federico Fellini, for his entrepreneurial advancement of the state of the art.

The Tavianis' Marxist agenda appears in all their films, sometimes overtly, as in the political story about the birth of the republic, *Allonsanfan* (a wordplay on "Allons enfants," 1973), and sometimes more indirectly, as in their fairy tale *Buon giorno, Babylonia* (*Good Morning, Babylon*, 1987). Positioned somewhere between comedy and epic is *Notte di San Lorenzo* (*Night of the Shooting Stars*, 1982), set in 1944. The small town of San Martino, expecting a bombardment by German fascists, enacts an exodus, while the camera closes in on individual stories. International audiences looking for polemics may be unaware that the Tavianis use simple images to politicize Italian history. Many encode Italy's indebtedness to and betrayal of communist principles in a disarmingly easy style or in seemingly incidental scenes. As the townsfolk of San Martino gather on the porch of the town's church, for example, the camera separates the priest from the community by adopting the point of view of the socialist, who will lead the group away from the priest's sanctuary. We might digress to notice the sharp contrast to Fellini's carefully constructed images, say in *8½* (1963), comprising a minor nightmare of the garish and the grotesque. Fellini's feasts and parades especially can slip into visions of excess and perversity. Even a sunny film like *Amarcord* (I Remember, 1974) suggests those primitive, irrational forces always ready to break through into everyday life. He exploited a carnivalesque style that became his trademark, a satiric view of the material world at once exuberant, playful, and sensuous, yet also potentially dangerous.

To return to the Tavianis' epic, *Notte*, at a moment when the two young émigrés are despondent about finding steady work, an elegant D. W. Griffith strolls past production tables on a movie set, points with his walking stick to a huge papier-mâché elephant the brothers have carved, and asks for eight of them. Presto, these Italian sculptors and stonecutters, who arrived in Hollywood without a sou, metamorphose into quick-witted, all-purpose designers and ace filmmakers. Using a remarkable system of communication involving winks, nods, gestures, whistles, and tricks—they know each other's minds inside out—they practically invent the making of motion pictures overnight as a game. Now, here is Italian cleverness put to wondrous significance. The brothers not only devise a new language sans words—visually hilarious—their secret, tongue-in-cheek clowning promotes the emergence of the most powerful industry in contemporary Western culture. The idea of transatlantic adventure works nicely too as a metaphor since they perfected their art in the old country and then recreated it as a skill in Hollywood on a gargantuan scale.

The film is fantasy about a fantasy that comes true. Film, in fact, was born as an industry in Turin, Italy, and in Hollywood, California, almost simultaneously, circa 1903. On both sides of the Atlantic, the camera both recorded and generated spectacle. In the Tavianis' nod to circus motifs in the film, eight elephants from one only begin to symbolize the grand scale of Griffith's visions, and the Italians were no more restrained, having chosen Turin in order to take advantage of the majestical Alpine landscape. They filmed with operatic impulses and in epical scope—works like *Cabiria* (1914) during the golden age of Italian film before World War I, and then after sound became predictable, *The Defeat of Hannibal* (1937). When they were not behind the cameras, Italians created the machineries and production systems they and Hollywood still use. *Good Morning, Babylon* is filled with nostalgia for that heyday, when clever improvising might solve a technical problem, or lead to a new film script, or discover a new filmmaker, the salient point.

But the title alone cues up the film's mild-mannered satire. Babylon, place of the proverbial female, remains a metaphor for sin, corruption, and prostitution. The brothers' art, nurtured by their father, and implicitly by generations of collective fathers, must metamorphose into commercial assembly-line production implied in Griffith's order for eight. Griffith himself appears all in white, a stunning fairy-tale model of elegance and success. He is the American father of a new culture and the brothers' new father. When they serve him, they too wear suits, win pretty, star-struck girlfriends who become wives for a pair of brothers in twin marriages. At the great wedding feast, at either end of a long table, the new father in white toasts the old father in black, who arrived from the old world to celebrate and to see for himself. Everyone is smiling. Differences between yesterday and this morning seem manageable, even desirable, one positive effect of weddings. Everyone radiates promise and confidence in the future. Except that the sons, of course, replace their father in America not as progenitors of high art, though not a word of this is spoken.

No longer are there moments in deep green woods when one brother (Vincent Spano) stands alone, silent, half smiling and crashing enormous cymbals. Their boom circles the landscape while reverberating inside his head, presumably summoning ideas, or images, or art itself into being. The other brother, equally solitary though less theatrically, toys with pouring water (or wine?) from one glass to another, also a conjuring act with sacramental overtones. America is a big land, with big space, plainly enough to accommodate the big elephant of imagination, yet it fails to appear. The new world, instead, brings forth real children and the death of one wife in labor. The magic ends; it was a version of the dying American dream. The bereaved brother rejects comfort and their lifelong partnership collapses, along with what remains of ideals about art. They next meet by happenstance on a battlefield in France during World War I. The golden age of Italian filmmaking ends.

Images are operatic, sometimes symbolic yet curiously vacant, their potential meanings not pursued. The doubles, pageants, and feasts mentioned above simply appear as in fairy tales without tight connection to story or plot. Doubled brothers seem to pun on success in Hollywood where more is twice as good as enough; or they might express a perfect fit of the brothers' natural gifts to the environment. The doubled fathers, however, suggest a less sanguine picture, even though their contest is not over a woman but over art: idealized in the old world for its rich legacy, utilized in the new without reference to history or continuity. Yet death pops up to part the brothers, maybe on cue as a result of their doubling, maybe not since the wife is barely distinguishable as a character until she dies. Images in fairy tales suit a rough psychological pattern. So, for instance, the entire film shifts gears from a fairy-tale sense of "good morning" to its ending in realistic warfare.

Looked at along simple Marxian lines, the film presents an allegory of Italy's perception in the last decades of the twentieth century. The brothers' naive idea of the film industry's basis in a commonality, an ideal community of artists, falls into disarray as they discover the industry's true organization and dependence upon Griffith, his money, and his drill sergeant of a production manager. The brothers themselves represent an ideal historical identity that turns out not to be transportable to the new world. In each of their films, the Tavianis' overriding concern with depicting the Italian body politic includes an awareness of discontinuities in the historical process. Geographical borders are very real cultural barriers.

Audiences may have credited the biographical more than the allegorical aspect of the film. Spectacular pictures in the Tavianis' other films also suggest a sweep of historical time while the camera follows individual experiences within the larger frame. The technique allows them to synthesize a macrohistory, as it is called, with a microhistory. Synthesis as a policy is reflected, too, in their love-hate relationship with neorealism, the "father" with whom they grew up. They keep neorealism's themes of the forties and post–World War II period but adopt folktale settings and sepia colorings. These lend a utopian look to a vision of the future. For example, the film *Night of the Shooting Stars,* important as a quasi-historical document, opens like a folktale: the camera looks out a window with billowing white curtains at a starry blue sky where a star shoots past. A female narrator recounts the liberation as the wish fulfillment of her little girl self. She tells of her town's flight from fascist occupation under the leadership of one Galvano Galvani (Omero Antonutti), the same strong actor who plays the father in *Good Morning Babylon*. Like another Moses, he marshals the townspeople to guide them out of the range of imminent bombardment, though not all wish to follow him. They pull in diverse directions, propose disparate solutions to their plight, until Galvani can impose his program on those people remaining and recreate them, so to speak, as a unified group. Some still refuse to join him: the baron and his wife in smart hat and veil, the local doctor, the priest whose cathedral sheltered them all on the first night of battery by enemy guns. Division is along class lines, after all. But to be on the road serves in this film, as in *Allonsanfan,* as a strong metaphor of an ideological progress toward a communist social policy and an undisclosed better place.

Fantasy ranks highest on a list of distinctively Italian elements of comedy high and low. The recurring subject of film-on-film, for instance, supplies fantasy that nearly overburdens the humor in *Cinema Paradiso* (1988). A man's memories of himself as a boy in a movie house projection booth couples once again, as in *Good Morning,* with nostalgia for film's beginnings. Similarly gentle sentiment is evoked by the mild-mannered fantasy *Il Postino* (1994). A simple postman learns to love poetry while delivering mail to a famous poet; he uses his new skill to woo a local beauty. Or to take an example of the fantastical with more subtle content, *Mediterraneo* (1991) presents lyrical pictures of five servicemen stranded for three years on a remote Aegean island in 1941. On one level, it's a Robinson Crusoe adventure. They must resort to ingeniousness and wit to invent a few simple utensils for their survival. Then, in a wry twist of plot, they discover after a year or so that they are not alone: the island's population, on the side distant from their cave, consists of children and old women, since all the men were deported by the Germans. The scenery is so pretty and the humor so lovely that the thinness of the plot matters little. Amusing episodes hinge on the deployment of types: a lieutenant who reads poetry; a youngster who surrenders his virginity to the local prostitute and marries her; the shy fellow who falls in love with the leader, a bluff man's man.

Mediterraneo's focus, in other words, remains on closeups of individual wish or fancy, pleasure or weariness, and so on. The message of the larger action, however, subverts the men's Italian-ness and the historical reality of the Italy they left behind in the war. Slowly, as the men shed military discipline and adopt local dress, they go native and begin to regress. A repeated phrase of good will during interaction with the Greeks is "one face, one race," blurring the identity of the people who sent them into combat. Their discontentment with Italian social and political life also is expressed in small ways that ultimately lead to the mens' disengagement from history, though only one of them directly mentions fascism. In the end, when they are rescued by snappy-looking British, the new young husband remains on the island, one man needs to be dragged off. In the final frames, two men return to the island years later and find another of their group already there performing homely tasks. Disillusionment with postwar Italy's mood and inertia could not be clearer.

As for that streak of cleverness in satires that seems quintessentially Italian, judging by films, nature herself made Italians clever. It can be implied simply by film's built-in *sine qua non* of doubleness, say, by a picture counterpointing words. Vittorio Gassman's handsome face in *Il Sorpasso* (*The Easy Life*, 1963) radiates a breathtaking arrogance, while the director in the composition of every frame tells that his hero is riding for a fall. Conspicuously, cleverness is the trait of clowns and fools busily staging themselves. It is exploited directly in the brilliant *I soliti ignoti* as both subject and attitude of the underclass toward authority. A gang who come together to pull off a jewel robbery automatically expect to outwit the law; it's a matter of every man's proud individualism and his self-esteem. Of course, the crooks are so attractive and such accomplished comics—Gassman and Mastroianni among them—no audience believes them to be hardened criminals. When the trick fails, as it must, these heroes become victims of their own imaginations—the role of the victim is opposite to that of the trickster, who has his own long history in film comedy. Alberto Sordi built a career on playing the victim with a rueful demeanor; so did Toto, the sad clown.

In a sly variant on the universal contest between father and son, *Alberto Express* (1992), with Alberto Sordi, a father tries to trick his son, nature's ideal victim, into paying for the cost of his daily keep from the day of his birth to his fifteenth year. The bill comes due on the day his own son is born. It's a family tradition, the diabolical father explains. An adding machine totting up charges in the millions with surreal insistence does as much psychological violence to the victim as the vengeful joke itself. The son flees while his wife is in labor and discovers only in a hallucinatory final scene of grandfathers and great-grandfathers that no son has ever paid the debt. By magical means, the assembled fathers dress him and free him from liability. He returns home triumphant as he has killed the father's hold on him. In the film's conservative psychology, Italy's sons may owe a debt to the past, but it remains uncollected. Indeed, the oedipal situation offers a new motive for son to kill the father, though the action never moves in that direction.

No amount of cleverness affects the plight of Nino Manfredi, the victim in *Pane e ciocolatto* (*Bread and Chocolate*, 1973). The film tells the grim tale of a man dislocated economically, socially, and so psychologically—the Marxian implications explain themselves. In a vein crossing fantasy with acute realism, the film pushes at the boundaries of definition as comedy. More accurately, it is a powerful "problem film," close to documentary in its focus on the quest of one, luckless Everyman for a job, possibly in rich Switzerland, for a place, a connection to give his life meaning in financially chaotic, postwar Italy. Solitary and unable to make a friend of man or woman, his initial displacement at the film's opening, when he loses his job, gradually becomes disillusionment and detachment. At his most desperate, he even tries chicken plucking with a group of grotesques, who play at resembling the animal and lead him to ask incredulously, "do you know me?" He ends up alienated from a country with no role for him. In this film like others straddling the subject matter of neorealism, elements of primitive comedy almost merge into the painful surface action. At one point in his efforts to adapt to any possible role, Manfredi dies his hair blond and doubles himself in a Germanic image. This calls down humiliations as grave as those he suffers in his own persona as an outcast.

Satire's comic victim is a far more robust creature. The film that fixed the high bar for the genre is of course *Divorzio, italiano* (*Divorce, Italian Style*, 1961). A victim of marriage, a rueful Mastroianni personifies the perfect balance of satire and humor in what may be the funniest film ever made. Italy is a Catholic country, after all, and divorce is as unattainable a goal as heaven for the ungodly. The idea of divorce inspires fantasies of escape as wild and implausible as marriage itself according to the director, Pietro Germi, who with this film basically created an intimate version of comedy of manners. It is not the social framework of marriage so much as its small daily humiliations that the camera sees with hilarious clarity. Germi reworked the theme in *Sedotto e abbandonato* (*Seduced and Abandoned*, 1964), where a Sicilian pursues the code of honor regarding an imagined sexual offense to his sister. Comic action actually centers on the imaginings of the girl's father, who lays out an elaborate scheme for the revenge of his daughter to the amazement of the court, where he expects retribution within the law.

Germi, like other Italian satirists, exploits regional and class biases as unspoken facts of everyday life. Italy to Italians remains a disunified country with forty-two dialect languages. But comedy's double view of the world needs to enlist broadly recognizable stereotypes and two suffice: traditionally, northerners as industrious members of the middle class, southerners as a species of grotesques: socially backward, intellectually regressive. Germi with the same mechanism also exaggerates Italy's north-south division in religious terms, since southern implies a rigid adherence to the Catholic code of conduct carried to extremes not only by the unlettered. Any film that wants international as well as national distribution nowadays probably guards against offense to conventional views. It means that popular and classical comedy take opposite attitudes toward grotesques and grotesquerie. Pirandello's farce pivots on grotesques; Fellini built a career on them; and Fo turns himself into a grotesque in performances. Again, satire is what closes on Saturday night.

In these territories of the satirical and the grotesque, Fellini stands as a monument to Italian film during its cultural primacy. His genius allowed him to alternate hilarious comic images with dreamy ones in *Amarcord* ("I remember," 1974) without either losing their respective power or poignancy. Not even he matched his most memorable pictures of, say, the entire townsfolk at sea in small craft in the middle of the night waiting for the passage of the great steamship, the *Rex*. Or the assortment of sex-crazed adolescent boys in a sentimental moment dancing with imaginary partners on the steps of the closed-up grand hotel. Fellini's garish caricatures, nevertheless, seem to sidestep cruelty: to cite at random, the vain, parasitic brother-in-law with his hairnet; the bean seller with a few black teeth in a grimace of a face; the ludicrous schoolteachers; the apoplectic father driven by his sons to the verge of mayhem; the fat midget emir draped in jewels and followed by thirty concubines. The power of the images must, I suspect, be related to their rise almost untransformed from primitive levels of the psyche. A procession of young uniformed school boys; contrasted with a funeral procession and brass band; contrasted again with staged processions of athletic youth; and again contrasted with the military carrying a huge replica of Mussolini's face made of flowers. The sense of him as the source of all blessings is ironically expressed by the fat boy's vision of il Duce marrying him to the girl he adores.

Fellini's parades escalate the tradition of the evening *passegiata* ("promenade"), when the townsfolk indulge in their gift for theatricality. The town's beauty, Gradisca, sashays through the square daily with her honor guard of less remarkable young women on either arm. But display, whether of the self marching along the seashore, or of nuns fluttering in their wimples, always hints at the threat of violence. It's the silk hat that evokes the snowball. It explodes in the square as military police fire round after round at the church bell tower, where someone unseen plays a gramophone recording of the "Internationale" while a platoon of fascisti march through. This is one of several incidents in the film directly expressing Fellini's political resistance. The town's lawyer, serving as the film's narrator and town guide addressing the audience directly, shrugs his shoulders helplessly when it comes to explaining the black shirts. The gesture also expresses part of the film's attitude toward ideology and revolution. That is to say, the film takes for granted Fellini's condemnation as implicit in his political engagement, especially in this film, whose deep subject is memory.

Collective memory is even more unreliable than personal recollection and likely romanticized, since it is institutionalized in the fictional national identity. Shortly after *Amarcord*, by the late seventies, film's critique of sociopolitical mores was ending and subjects became more personal. In this chronology, Fellini again provides a model. His late film *Cita delle donne* (*City of Women*, 1981) turns to his known obsession with women in a phantasmagorical, a surreal landscape of disconnected and discontinuous dream scenes telling the psychic life of one man. In horrendous fashion, women of all shapes and ages, in all locales victimize the hero, Mastroianni standing in for Fellini. Drugged teenage girls try to run him down, older ones race after him; ugly and mystifying images matter more individually than they do in any linear or cumulative sense. There is no plot and nothing is resolved, not time, place, narrative, or motive. The film is a pure distillation of images from a broken mind replete with doubles, deceits, and forms of death. The end of the film finds the hero in a boxing ring where his mother waits, talking to him as if taking up a broken-off conversation.

Finally, yes, there is Italian romantic comedy, only it rarely centers on the storied ups and downs of young love. The film *Zuppa di pesci* (*Fish Soup*, 1992) for instance, falls into the category, offering charming entertainment; it is not about anything much, pretty to look at, made by an assortment of international filmmakers, and meant for the mass market. In outline, it pictures a summer at the seashore with a filmmaker, played by Philip Noiret, and his good-looking family. He goes broke, apparently not for the first time, and bailiffs claim all the family's movable possessions, but they nevertheless improvise a wedding party for the eldest daughter the next day on the terrace of their lovely, rented villa. The younger teenage daughter is afflicted with regular fits of weeping, apparently over her inability to shed her virginity, while watching glamorous women pose and lick their lips on television. The film's content is negligible, and similar films are legion.

There can be no equivalent in the Italian film repertory to the madcap, mildly ironic adventure stories like, say, Preston Sturges' *Sullivan's Travels* (1941) or *The Lady Eve* (1941); and nothing like Ernst Lubitsch's glamorous blondes who frequented dream-like, all-white nightclubs that never were. American versions of the genre bloomed in the 1930s during the Depression, when extravagant beauties and places suggested high times ahead. The best writers and production teams were as much affected by the economic blight as people in other sectors of public life, and so more of them were available for superior work at cut rates. At the same historical moment, film was discovering its own limits, venturing outward from visual and spectacular experiments into domestic and intimate scripts, into verbal comedy and areas previously dominated by theater. Romantic comedies thereafter became part of Hollywood's stock in trade and continued to evolve as a favorite form.

Italian film, instead, reinvented itself in the late 1940s out of the country's nearly total financial post–World War II collapse. With no budget for scripts, or actors, or settings, cameras took to the streets and filmed what was there—to the industry's everlasting credit. The resulting mode, known as neorealism, and its looks, especially its black-and-white, grainy quality, became pervasive, even for certain comedies. A caper comedy of standard make like *Oro di Napoli* (*Gold of Naples*, 1955) keeps the neorealistic look of dark, empty streets, although such images add nothing to either the film's content or style. The film's sole asset is Anna Magnanni's face. The other circumstance governing romantic comedy is the Catholic establishment. To put it roughly, the industry's attitude toward romantic pursuit is in one sense a good deal more direct than its American versions, and in another sense more inhibited insofar as images of nudity and sexual activity are concerned. The chase may be more fantastical when capture is guaranteed. Even so, the equivalent love story, like our idea of romantic comedy, may lie somewhere between scripts about sex and fantasy. The couples in *Good Morning,*

Babylon, which is not a romantic comedy, nonetheless present an ideal set of airy characters for the genre: the women are young and sweet, the men young and handsome; their decorous flirtation leads directly to the altar.

Finally, a word about humorous and slapstick comedy, dominated recently by the work of Roberto Benigni. In fact, his most important film, *La vita e bella* (*Life Is Beautiful*, 1997), stakes out a claim to territory neither slapstick nor humorous, although remarkably enough it includes both. The film overlaps the categories of fantasy and black comedy in a hybrid mixture of laughter and tears—if, that is, comedy can be triggered by outrage. Since the script is based on the memory of childhood by a man, Giosue, telling his story in a voice-over, doubling in the film becomes exponential—in the character, in views shifting between past and present, in the instability of the teller at either time. In the key scene at the opening, the boy Giosue is being carried, intermittently asleep, by his father making his way through a foggy background. They are returning to the father's barracks after a Nazi dinner party and pass what seems to be a mass grave full of twisted corpses.

The scene establishes the narrator's place in the tradition of Holocaust testimony, an approach that calls for a constant elaboration and adaptation of history in order to make it available to a third generation. At the same time, the remembered history must be true in a medium with its own forms of distancing and representation. To protect his boy from the unalterable meaning of what they see, the father jokes and plays the antic, thus destabilizing the serious content of the scene forever in the boy's memory. He thus becomes the film's consciousness. The antics also incorporate comical business into the audience's awareness of doubleness. They recognize scenes from film documents of the century's most horrific events, and they are asked at the same time to displace their recognition into the comic spectacle that the boy's father creates out of unspeakable suffering. In other words, since Benigni as writer and performer invests himself in misrepresentation, the film constantly accommodates doubling on doubling, insisting with every frame on a metalevel of meaning. It challenges the audience to accept the clowning of the protagonist whose consciousness refers to the deeply tragic.

Benigni's autobiographical motives refer back to his own father's stories of his detention in a Nazi labor camp after the Italian armistice with the Allies in 1943. As the narrator, Benigni refers to his father directly: "He told us about it, as if to protect me and my sisters, he told it in an almost funny way—saying tragic, painful things but finally his way of telling them was really very particular. Sometimes we laughed at the stories he told." At the end of the film, the voice-over narration concludes: "This is the sacrifice that my father made. This was his gift for me." The man acknowledges the fairy-tale quality of his biographical account, while claiming that his story is true though not all details are accurate. Not all critics accepted Benigni's experiment as morally unassailable, much less accepted it as comedy.

REFERENCES AND FURTHER READINGS

Berthold, Margot. *A History of World Theater*. New York: Frederick Ungar, 1972.

Casty, Alan. *Development of the Film: An Interpretive History*. New York: Harcourt Brace Jovanovich, 1973.

Dalle Vacche, Angela. *The Body in the Mirror: The Shapes of History in Italian Cinema*. Princeton, NJ: Princeton UP, 1992.

Duckworth, George E. *The Nature of Roman Comedy: A Study in Popular Entertainment*. Princeton, NJ: Princeton UP, 1952.

Fo, Dario. *The Passion Plays*. In *Mistero Buffo*. Ed. Stuart Hood. Trans. Ed. Emery. London: Methuen, 1988.

———. *We Won't Pay, We Won't Pay*. Ed. Franca Rame. Trans. Ron Jenkins. New York: Theatre Communications Group, 1999.

Fratti, Mario. *Academy*. New York: Samuel French, 1987.

———. *The Refrigerators*. New York: Samuel French, 1987.

———. *Sister and Lovers* (two plays). Ed. Nina daVinci Nichols. Toronto: Guernica, 2001.

Goldoni, Carlos. *Mirandolina*. 1753. *Venetian Twins*. 1748. *Two Plays*. Trans. Ranjit Bolt. Bath, Eng.: Absolute, 1993.

Life Is Beautiful [*La vita e bella*]. Dir. Roberto Begnini and Giorgio Cantarini. Miramax, 1998.

Machiavelli, Nicolo. *Il mandragola* (*The Mandrake Root*). 1518. Trans. Anne and Henry Paolucci. Indianapolis, IN: Bobbs-Merrill, 1957.

———. *The Prince*. 1513. Trans. W. K. Marriott. Indianapolis, IN: Bobbs-Merrill, 1963.

Marcus, Millicent. *After Fellini: National Cinema in the Postmodern Age*. Baltimore, MD: Johns Hopkins UP, 2003.

Pirandello, Luigi. *On Humor*. (1908). Trans. Antonio Illiano. Chapel Hill: U of North Carolina P, 1960.

———. *Il fue Mattia Pascal*. 1909. Trans. William Weaver. New York: Doubleday, 1964.

Segal, Erich. *The Death of Comedy*. Cambridge, MA: Harvard UP, 2001.

Sypher, Wylie. *Comedy*. 2nd ed. Baltimore: Johns Hopkins UP, 1980.

28

Middle English Comedy

Andrew Welsh

The historical period in which literature was composed and written in Middle English runs from about A.D. 1100 to about 1450. All through the Middle English period literature in England was also being written in Latin and in French, and only gradually did English become the dominant medium of literary expression. That process was still underway in the fourteenth century, and even late in the century the poet John Gower hedged his bets by writing a major work in each of the three languages—one in Latin, one in French, and one in English. Geoffrey Chaucer, however, Gower's London contemporary, wrote exclusively in English, and by the time of his death in 1400 English was solidly established as the language of English literature, a position strongly buttressed by Chaucer's own works.

People living in the Middle English period laughed at much the same things we laugh at now, and probably at some other things we are no longer able to identify as funny: there may be humor in Middle English texts we simply cannot recognize. Still, to judge from the first major literary text in Middle English, *The Owl and the Nightingale*, we have no difficulty identifying and enjoying both high and low forms of Middle English comedy.

SATIRIC COMEDY: DEBATE, FABLE, AND FABLIAU

The Owl and the Nightingale, probably composed sometime between 1189 and 1216, is the earliest and best example in Middle English of the debate poem, a form that was widely put to use in both serious and trivial ways in the Middle Ages. A debate poem focuses on two speakers who take opposite sides to dispute a particular subject or range of subjects. Because the two speakers in *The Owl and the Nightingale* are birds, the poem also has elements of the beast fable, in which animals speak in human language and also think and behave suspiciously like humans. Both forms go back to classical literature and are traditionally didactic, meant to teach a lesson or to illustrate a moral meaning. It's significant that this poem appears to preserve none of the didactic intentions of traditional debate and fable; in good comedy, wit is more highly valued than moral instruction.

The Owl and the Nightingale is a fairly long work, composed in octosyllabic couplets and running to 1,794 lines. An unnamed narrator overhears two birds, the Owl and the Nightingale, debate a number of topics. Their extended dispute is always anchored in personal issues—which bird has the better song, lives a more proper life, or is more useful to man—but along the way it ranges into broader areas as well, such as the characteristics of jealousy and spite, the superiority of cleverness over strength, whether celebration and joy or penance and weeping are the essence of religion, questions of witchcraft and excommunication, of love and the nature of women, problems with adultery, the conditions of a good marriage, and the forms and tactics of debate itself. Although modern attempts to nail down a particular allegorical signification for the two contentious birds have not been very successful, it does seem possible to say in general terms that the Nightingale argues for the wisdom of youth (love songs, summer joys, pleasure, things that pass) and that the Owl represents the wisdom of age (prayers, winter consolations, thought, things that last).

The two debaters provoke in each other the quick thinking and sharply pointed language that lies at the heart of comic vitality. The debate form shows that cruelty and aggression, too, are essential to comedy. The Nightingale begins by heaping abuse on the Owl—on her song, her appearance, the food she eats, and the lack of toilet training demonstrated by her young chicks. (Both birds are female.) In the Owl's presence, the Nightingale complains, her own song fails: "Because of your wretched yodeling / I'd rather spit than sing!" (Treharne 381, lines 39–40). The Owl's body is too short, her head is too big, her eyes are oversize and black as coal, her beak is a crooked hook, and her song is only clacking. She eats frogs, snails, mice, and other foul creatures. Her nest is filthy and so are her children:

> You are loathly and unclean—
> I'm speaking about your nest,
> And also about your foul brood:
> You are bringing up a very filthy family.
> You know very well what they do in there:
> They befoul it up to the chin.
> They sit there as if they were blind.
>
> (p. 382, lines 91–97)

The Owl is furious—"she sat puffed up and swollen, / As if she had swallowed a frog" (p. 383, lines 145–46)—but, being an owl, she must wait until nightfall to reply. Several hundred lines later she pays back the Nightingale in kind, saying that the Nightingale dwells in the secluded hedges and thickets that people use for toilets:

> By a hedge and thick weeds,
> Where men go often for their need,
> There you approach, there you dwell,
> And you shun other clean places.
> When I fly at night after a mouse,
> I can find you at the privy;
> Among the weeds, among the nettles,

You sit and sing behind the seat.
That is where you'll most often be found,
Where men thrust out their behinds.

(p. 392, lines 587–96)

At the end of the poem the birds fly off to submit their dispute to a certain Master Nicholas of Guildford for judgment. The birds praise him in ways that suggest Master Nicholas is in fact the author of the poem. He seems to combine the good qualities of both birds with none of the bad. He used to be wild, the Owl says, and the Nightingale and her ways were dear to him, but now Master Nicholas has cooled down into a mature and sober way of life. His home is in an obscure village in Dorset—and that is "much shame to the bishops" (Treharne 415, line 1761), who would more often have the benefit of his wisdom if they would provide him with more sources of income. Those powerful men do wrong, the Owl says:

Who abandon the good man
That knows so many things,
Who provide him with income very erratically
And esteem him very casually.
They are kinder to their relatives,
And give incomes to little children!
Their own intelligence judges them in error,
To keep Master Nicholas still waiting!

(p. 415, lines 1771–78)

The hyperbolic praise given to Master Nicholas is a mixture of parody and comic complaint. It is at once his overblown advertisement for himself, a reproach put into the mouths (or beaks) of birds that his wisdom, judgment, and accomplishments have been carelessly ignored by his superiors and left to go begging, and a rueful recognition that, given the way the world runs these days, this short-sighted neglect of his sterling qualities is likely to continue. The poem ends before Master Nicholas is given an opportunity to display those qualities by judging the dispute of the birds and leaves him still awaiting the bountiful benefice or plump patronage he so confidently feels he deserves.

The Fox and the Wolf, a poem of 295 octosyllabic lines, is a clear example of a beast fable. It could have been written shortly after *The Owl and the Nightingale* or as much as a century later. The narrative is in two parts, a tale of Reynard the fox and Chaunticleer the rooster, and another of Reynard and Sigrim the wolf. Both tales were familiar episodes in Continental literature—earlier versions survive in the long Latin poem *Ysengrimus*, the French beast epic *Roman de Renart*, and the German cycle of tales *Reinhart Fuchs*—and continued to be retold in English for centuries afterward. (The first tale is the basis of Chaucer's *Nun's Priest's Tale*, and the second was still being told in the nineteenth century in the Uncle Remus stories of Joel Chandler Harris.) But *The Fox and the Wolf* is the first, and until Chaucer the only, beast fable to survive in Middle English.

Reducing a character to a single, and thus exaggerated, quality is a favorite device of comedy, and especially of the fable. Reynard is essentially an uncontrolled appetite on legs; hunger, thirst, and sexual desire lead him again and again into troubles and dangers that stronger superegos would manage to avoid. He sets out at the beginning of the poem unable to think of anything but his empty stomach:

> He would rather meet one hen
> Than half a hundred women.
>
> (Treharne 332, lines 7–8)

In the episode with Chaunticleer he appears to devour three hens in the blink of an eye (the poem is vague about this, they disappear so quickly), but then his thirst leads him to a well in the garden of a friary and into the second tale of the poem. To quench his thirst he rashly leaps into a bucket of water hanging from the well. But the bucket is on a pulley, and Reynard sinks with the bucket down to the bottom of the well. Sigrim the wolf happens to come to the well, and Reynard proceeds to convince him that he is in paradise at the bottom of the well and that the wolf would do well to join him there. There is food, there is drink, there is happiness without toil, he tells Sigrim, and the wolf may join him there as soon as he is shriven of his sins. The wolf, hungry and gullible, makes his confession to the fox and then jumps into a second bucket, which sinks into the well as it pulls Reynard in his bucket up to the surface.

The fox's description of paradise to the wolf parodies the language of medieval sermons and hymns describing the joys of heaven, and the wolf's confession is a burlesque of the Christian sacrament of Penance. When the wolf reaches the bottom of the well he finds not the paradise of abundant food he was expecting but a continuing penance:

> The wretch finds nothing beneath
> But cold water, and hunger binds him.
> To a cold feast he was invited;
> Frogs have kneaded his dough.
>
> (Treharne 337, lines 253–56)

Finally the friars discover Sigrim trapped in their well, pull him up, thrash him with pikes, staves, and stones, and set vicious dogs on him. In real life this would be sadistically cruel, but in the comic world of the fable it is the just reward for being a dolt. The quick-witted fox trots off unscathed. With his verbal dexterity and resourcefulness in tight spots, he is an ancient version of the modern confidence-man—shell-game master, escape artist, or smooth genius of the sting.

Dame Sirith, a poem of 450 lines composed sometime in the late thirteenth century, is the only example of a fabliau to survive in Middle English before Chaucer's tales. (By contrast, about 160 fabliau survive in French literature from the same period.) A fabliau is a tale about trickery or deception. Often it is a frankly bawdy tale centered on some kind of sexual deception, but even then trickery more than sex is the point of the tale. Dame Sirith is a go-between, an old woman who helps the clerk Wilekin to win the body (affections are not an issue) of Margery, the coy wife of a busy merchant. Dame Sirith feeds her dog pepper and mustard to make its eyes run, and then takes the dog to Margery and tells her that it is her own married daughter, forever weeping because she was transformed into a dog by a clerk whose love she had rejected. Margery, who earlier had rejected Wilekin's advances for the sake of virtue, now does an about-face for the sake of remaining a woman and warmly welcomes him into her bed. The tale passes no moral judgment on this situation: its concern is with the fun of the trick, and with the bawdy humor.

The play of language is an important part of the sexual humor in the story. At the beginning of the tale Wilekin ("Little Willie") racks his brains thinking of how he might get Margery "in ani cunnes wise" (Treharne 338, line 15). The more innocent meaning of the phrase is "in any sort of way," but given the context there is probably the subterranean sense of "in any cuntly fashion." He first goes himself to visit Margery, who welcomes him with words in which both innocent courtesy and sexual innuendo can be heard:

> If I may do anything
> That is pleasing to you,
> You might find me very generous.
>
> (p. 339, lines 32–34)

But when the clerk does tell her what he wants, she rejects him; she is a married woman, she says, and would never betray her husband, "neither on the bed nor on the floor" (p. 340, line 102). Still, the flirtatious play in her conversation suggests that Margery is not entirely innocent. At the end of the tale Dame Sirith leaves Margery and Wilekin to their "playing," and her last words of advice to Wilekin imply that he will have his hands full:

> And look that you till her,
> And stretch out her thighs.
> God give you much sorrow
> If you spare her
> While you are with her.
>
> (p. 348, lines 440–44)

Except perhaps for the dog, no one is hurt in this tale. The young couple have their vigorous pleasures, the old woman has a rich payment along with the triumph of her successful trick, and the busy merchant away at a fair doesn't know what he is missing.

Winner and Waster is a debate poem of 503 alliterative lines from about the middle of the fourteenth century. The poem lacks a formal ending, but it appears that we have most of this dispute between "Winner," who accumulates goods and riches, and "Waster," who freely spends them. The poem can also be seen as an elaboration of the fable of the grasshopper and the ant, though without that fable's puritanical moral. Yet another favorite form of medieval literature used by the poem is the dream vision, in which a narrator falls asleep and wanders in a dream through symbolic landscapes peopled with allegorical figures—such as Winner and Waster. As in *The Owl and the Nightingale*, neither disputant is judged to be the winner of the debate—in part because the unique manuscript of the poem breaks off before such a judgment can be given; in part because the king, who is to give the judgment, is himself both a "winner" and a "waster"; and in part because the opposing figures actually represent two interrelated principles that are necessary to any functioning economy. The king instead commands them to alternate their presence in his court and never to be both in his country at the same time.

This debate poem is not simply, or even primarily, a comic poem, but the exchanges between the two opponents display the familiar weapons of social satire: the exaggeration of an opponent's faults, the scathing disparagement of his morals, the contemptuous description of his physical body or way of life, and all the other barbed arrows of verbal abuse. Winner is described by Waster as a miser, a figure of avarice:

> When you have tossed and turned and stayed awake all night,
> And every person in the world who dwells with you,
> And have filled your wide houses full of wool sacks—
> The beams bend at the roof, so much bacon hangs there,
> And silver coins are stuffed under steel bonds—
> What would become of wealth if no spending should happen?
> Some would rot, some rust, and some would feed rats.
> Leave off cramming your chests, for the love of Christ of heaven!
> Let the people and the poor have a share of your silver!
>
> (Treharne 587, lines 248–56)

Winner, on the other hand, sees himself as teaching the principles of good government and as working toward the common good, showing lords how to save and not spend too much, how to live on only what is necessary. If there are poor people, he says, Waster himself has brought that about with his dissolute habits of consumption. He sells the woods on his ancestral land to pay for sumptuous feasts; he forgets to plant, to harvest, to store, to prepare for the coming winter:

> And you will go to the tavern, sit before the barrel,
> Every man ready with a bowl to blear your eyes,
> You order up whatever you would have and whatever your heart likes,
> Wife, widow, or wench dwelling around there.
> Then it's nothing but "Fill up" and "Fetch forth," to make you show your money,
> "Wee hee!" and "Climb up!" and many such words.
> But when the money is gone, the wine must be paid for;
> Then it happens that you must lay down pledges or sell your land.
>
> (p. 587, lines 277–84)

In passages such as these the medieval poet seems to anticipate the merry genre-scenes and proverbial themes of the great Dutch artist Pieter Brueghel the Elder, two centuries later.

LYRIC COMEDY: WINE, WOMEN, AND SONG

One of the great pleasures of medieval literature is the Middle English lyric tradition. The word *lyric* did not yet exist in English, but hundreds of short poems of various kinds, usually in stanza form and often intended to be sung with music, have survived in English from the twelfth through the fifteenth century. The majority are religious poems, praising Christ or the Virgin with devout words elevated in song. But many are not, and they praise instead the coming of spring or the beauty of a woman, or complain in courtly terms of the pain of love and of the aloof lady who causes it.

Yet others find less elevated human responses to religion and love, mocking the formal rituals of both.

A poem written originally in French by Charles d'Orléans (1394–1465) and then translated into Middle English is a full-blown parody, in the manner of *The Fox and the Wolf*, of the language of the confessional:

> My spiritual father, I confess myself
> First to God, and then to you,
> That at a window (do you know how?)
> I stole a kiss of great sweetness.
>
> (Robbins 183, no. 185)

Asking to be forgiven for the theft, the sinner solemnly swears to restore the stolen kiss. Another poem mocks those conventions of courtly love that say a lover will always be thinking of his lady, that for love of her he will lose both appetite and sleep and become pale and withdrawn, and that even if she rejects him he will faithfully continue to serve her and to hope for her favor. This rejected lover, however, feels differently:

> I am sorry for her sake,
>   I can eat and drink well;
> When I sleep I don't awaken,
>   I think so much about her.
>
> (Robbins 34, no. 37)

"The Complaint of Chaucer to His Purse," perhaps the last poem written by Geoffrey Chaucer, parodies the courtly lyric in a different way. This poem is an appeal to the newly declared king, Henry IV, for some funds. Chaucer's purse is presented as his "lady dear," and the poem complains that the lady has become "light," which causes the lover great sorrow:

> For which unto your mercy thus I cry:
> Be heavy again, or else I must die!
>
> (Benson 656)

The poem creates a rich pattern of comic wordplay by invoking courtly vocabulary and attitudes. A further irony lies in our knowledge that this parody of a lover's complaint was soon answered with a stipend of forty marks a year from the king, making it more successful than most of the poems it parodies.

The rhetorical "low style" of comedy enters the language of lyric in various ways. Sometimes it is simply by evoking the humor associated with bodily functions, as in the way male animals welcome the coming of spring in the famous thirteenth-century lyric "Sumer is icumen in": "The bullock jumps, the buck farts" (Brown 13, no. 6). A poem complaining about a noisy blacksmith shop recreates in colloquial and heavily alliterative language the banging and hammering that keeps the speaker awake:

> Black-smocked smiths, soiled with smoke,
> Drive me to death with the din of their dints!
> One never heard such noise by nights:

> What noise of the boys, and clattering of blows!
> The snub-nosed rascals cry "Coal! Coal!"
> And blow their bellows so that all their brains burst.
>
>   (Robbins 106, no. 118)

The voice in poems such as these exists at some distance from the idealistic tones of the more formal religious and courtly lyrics in Middle English.

That colloquial voice is heard again in poems describing the pleasures and pains of the alehouse, another enduring source of comedy. A plea to an alewife named Agnes Taylor to open her door creates a Falstaffian scene both plaintive and comic:

> Friend, though we are far into debt
> For your fine good wine, God knows,
> A short measure has a pint pot;
> I drank once; I would drink still.
>
>   (Robbins 5, no. 6)

Short measure or not, the effects of too many pint pots are predictable, as in another poem in which a stupefied tippler and his companions are trying to stay on their feet:

> D . . . drunken—
> Drunken, drunken, drunk—
>   . . . drunken is Tabart with wine,
> Hey . . . sister, Walter, Peter,
>   You all drank very deeply,
>   And I shall also.
>
>   (Robbins 106, no. 117)

In comedy, if not in life, the drinker is a source of good fun, a figure of careless freedom, associative wit, and hilarious pratfalls. In an early-fourteenth-century poem known as "The Man in the Moon" a medieval W.C. Fields stands outdoors conversing with the moon. The common people of medieval England saw the Man in the Moon as a complete human figure, a peasant with one foot set in front of the other and carrying on his fork a load of stolen brushwood. The poem's inebriated speaker puzzles over why the striding figure never takes another step. He imagines that a bailiff, or hayward, has taken a "pledge," perhaps meaning a fine, from the thief for the bundle of brushwood. With fuzzy generosity he concocts an elaborate scheme to help him. They will invite the bailiff to his home and give him strong drink. His wife will flirt with the bailiff, and when he gets drunk they will "borrow" the pledge back:

> We will ask the hayward home to our house
>   And put him extremely at ease,
> Drink to him affectionately with very good booze,
>   And our sweet goodwife shall sit by him.
> When he is drunk as a drowned mouse,
>   Then will we redeem the pledge from the bailiff.
>
>   (Brown 161, no. 89)

But the Man in the Moon ignores this excellent plan and remains fixed in the sky, while the exasperated drinker remains below, yelling at the moon.

Sex and the battle of the sexes are unfailing subjects for humor. A popular counterpart to the courtly complaint is the seduction poem, often told from the point of view of a woman looking back on the seduction warmly or ruefully. Unlike courtly lyrics, these poems do not shy away from saying, either directly or through vivid folk imagery, what it was all about:

> Forsooth, then Jack and I went to bed.
> He rode and he pranced, he did not want to stop:
> It was the merriest night I ever had.
>
> (Robbins 23, no. 28)

> Sir John is taken in my mouse trap;
> Fain would I have him both night and day.
>
> (Robbins 20, no. 26)

Love is seen as a slightly ridiculous pleasure, and even its natural outcome is seen with a wry humor: "Soon my womb began to swell / As great as a bell" (Robbins 25, no. 29); "Now my belt will not meet" (Robbins 18, no. 24).

A large number of Middle English lyrics get their laughs from traditional antifeminist humor. When many absurd and unnatural things happen, says one—when nettles bear red roses in winter, fish walk in forests and chase harts, wrens carry sacks to the mills, and so on—then you can put your trust in a woman (Robbins 114). Other poems warn young men, in terms still familiar to television situation comedies, against marrying a woman too quickly (nos. 39, 40, 41); against marrying an older woman, who is sure to become domineering (no. 43); against marrying a woman who will spend all that one earns (no. 44); and generally against marrying just about any woman one is likely to come across. One poem appears to praise women, claiming in ten quatrains that women are faithful, discreet, meek, peaceful, sincere, patient, sober, slow to anger, adverse to chatter and gossip, and careful with a husband's money. But following each quatrain is the Latin refrain line "Cuius contrarium verum est" ("The opposite of this is true," no. 38). This poem shows more clearly than most the source of much antifeminism in the Middle Ages. Women did not normally learn Latin, and the refrain line is a clerical in-joke intended to dupe women and to exult in a feeling of misogynistic superiority. Chaucer, who is discussed in the next section, uses the same form of joke in the "Nun's Priest's Tale" but puts it in the mouth of a pompous rooster.

Women are of course known to express corresponding opinions about men. We do not know the gender or anything else about the authors of most Middle English lyrics, but some of them do present sexual comedy from a woman's point of view. The old man who courts a young woman is a traditional butt of comedy and is likely to be treated harshly. One young woman, whose aged lover has proven impotent in bed, tells him to come to her window in the dark of night for a kiss. When he does, "She turned out her ass and that he kissed." The aged lover, realizing that he has been dismissed, observes:

> Indeed, lover, you do me wrong—
> Or else your breath is wonderfully strong.
>
> (Robbins 34, no. 36)

Chaucer uses the same fabliau motif in the "Miller's Tale."

The dismissed woman of another poem does not leave so mildly. The entire poem is a scathing letter to her former lover ("To my love true and able, / As the weathercock he is stable"). She describes him from top to bottom with lavish sarcasm—he is as handsome and fair as an owl, his manly face with its flat nose is like a hare's or a cat's, his clothes hang on him as on an old goose with a broken wing, his legs are bowed, his feet are crooked, and even his heels are ugly. Any woman, she says, would want such a sweet man, though the one who does had better beware:

> She that would once in a dark night
> Run for your love till she had caught a thorn,
> I wish her no more harm than to be hanged on the morn,
> Who has two good eyes and has chosen for herself such a mate,
> Or would once lift up her hole for your sake!
>
> (Robbins 219–20, no. 208)

Hell hath no fury like this, and probably no comedy like this either.

NARRATIVE COMEDY: CHAUCER

Geoffrey Chaucer (c. 1340–1400) was well known as a lyric poet in the century following his death, but for us he is above all a narrative poet, the storyteller of *The Canterbury Tales* (1387–1400). For most of his life Chaucer lived and worked in London, and for most of his life he was attached to the royal court, first as a page, then as a squire, courtier, civil servant, administrator, diplomat, and perhaps spy. Three kings in succession—Edward III, Richard II, and Henry IV—required and rewarded his services. A famous illumination in a fifteenth-century manuscript of *Troilus and Criseyde* (Corpus Christi College, Cambridge, MS 61), Chaucer's other major work, depicts him reciting to an audience of royalty and nobility—including Richard II, Queen Anne, and perhaps John of Gaunt—assembled in the garden of a royal palace. But however much the court honored his verse, it is likely that it was his other services that won him royal patronage throughout his adult life.

Chaucer's humor appears throughout his body of work, as we see if we look first at one of his early poems. *The Parlement of Foules* ("The Parliament of Birds," and punningly "The Parliament of Fools"), a poem of 699 lines in rhyme-royal stanzas from about 1377–1380, draws on several literary traditions: specific Latin, French, and Italian works have all contributed to the poem. As an allegorical dream-vision concerned with questions of love, it is directly in the French tradition of the *Roman de la rose*. But it is also a debate poem, an argument among birds representing various human types, and in that is very much in the English tradition of *The Owl and the Nightingale*, though it is difficult to say how much Chaucer knew of that tradition. The poem's narrator falls asleep and finds himself in a garden of love. All the birds of the earth have gathered there on St. Valentine's Day to choose their mates, driven and guided by the goddess Nature. The owl and the nightingale are there, along with eagles, falcons, swans, robins, parrots, starlings, peacocks, and every other kind of fowl. The birds are divided into four groups, which are generally understood to represent four classes of human society: birds of prey (the nobility), birds that eat worms and bugs (the bourgeois artisans), water fowl (merchants), and seed-eating fowl (farmers).

At Nature's behest the noble birds choose first, but three eagles delay the proceedings for most of the day while they debate in courtly terms which of them best loves a beautiful "formel" (female) eagle sitting on Nature's hand. Chaucer's gift for parody of literary styles, which will become one of his most distinctive comic techniques, is already evident in this section, as in the concluding stanza of the first eagle's speech:

> And since that none loves her so well as I,
> Though she never promised love to me,
> Then should she be mine through her mercy,
> For I can fasten no other bond on her.
> Nor never, for no sorrow, shall I cease
> To serve her, however far she may go;
> Say what you please, my story is finished.
>
> (Benson 391, lines 435–41)

The less aristocratic birds, eager to choose their own mates and frustrated by the delay, finally revolt. But when Nature hands over to them the judgment, they are unable to decide which eagle most deserves the formel, and the entire assembly falls apart in squabbling and insult. Finally, Nature lets the formel herself decide, and she chooses not to have any mate at all this year. Thus the aristocratic eagles must wait a year, but the other birds quickly choose their mates and fly off singing amorous songs.

Another consistent characteristic of Chaucer's humor evident in this early work is his self-effacing narrator, a figure who is naive, guileless, and at times clueless in ways the sophisticated and ironic author of the poem never is. The narrator of the *Parlement* says at the beginning that his feelings are so astonished and his thoughts so bewildered by the "terrifying joy" of love that he does not know whether he is awake or asleep. But he admits that all he really knows about love comes from books:

> For though I don't know Love from experience,
> Nor know how he pays people what they've earned,
> Yet I often happen to read in books
> About his wonderful deeds and of his cruel anger.
>
> (Benson 385, lines 8–11)

When the narrator falls into his dream, Scipio Africanus appears to him (from the book he has been reading) to guide him as far as the gate to the walled garden of love. Over the gate are two inscriptions, both describing the experience of love as it will be found within the garden: one promises fertility and happiness, the other sterility and sorrow. The dreamer stands perplexed and helpless, unable to decide whether to enter or to flee, until Africanus unceremoniously grabs him and shoves him through the gate. Don't worry, he tells the dreamer, those inscriptions are meant only for lovers, and you seem to have lost your taste for love. But even though you are dull, perhaps you'll see something you can write about! This figure, who sees so much and understands so little, is Chaucer's comic version of himself. He reappears as "Chaucer," one of the pilgrim storytellers in *The Canterbury Tales*, where he tells a story—a parody of a Middle English romance—so tedious that the Host, Harry Bailly, abruptly cuts him off: "Thy drasty rymyng is nat worth a toord!" (VII.930). His presence is a key element in

Chaucer's comedy, allowing the author to maintain his ironic distance from all that he narrates and leaving him free to observe anything and everything without the responsibility of passing judgment.

The Canterbury Tales is a "framed" collection of tales, like *The Thousand and One Nights* (which Chaucer would not have known), Giovanni Boccaccio's *Decameron* (which he may well have known), or his friend John Gower's *Confessio Amantis* (which was being written at about the same time). The narrators of the tales are all characters in another story, the frame-tale, which adds another level of irony to the tales. The "General Prologue" (as we call it, though Chaucer did not) sets up the frame-tale of a group of pilgrims who meet at the Tabard Inn in Southwark, across the Thames from London, and who set out together the next morning on horseback for the shrine of the martyr Thomas à Becket at Canterbury, a leisurely journey of three or four days. They agree to tell stories along the way to pass the time; the teller of the best tale will be treated by the rest to a supper on their return. Chaucer's original plan envisaged thirty storytelling pilgrims, counting himself, plus Harry Bailly, their Host at the Tabard Inn who decides to accompany them and to adjudicate their tales and conflicts. Each pilgrim was to tell 4 tales, 120 tales in all, but that proved to be too ambitious, and the collection was left unfinished at Chaucer's death. In the work we have there are 24 tales, 2 of them only fragmentary. The frame-tale, then, establishes a storytelling situation that is both secular and religious, the story of a game begun in a tavern and of a pilgrimage ending at the tomb of a saint. But most of the "General Prologue" is given to descriptions of the storytellers.

The pilgrims are both individuals and types. On one level the series of portraits, some of them quite elaborate, show us representatives of the various classes and professions of medieval society. Each pilgrim is the best example of his class: the Knight is a "true, perfect, noble knight" (I.72; Benson 24), the Doctor is the best physician to be found anywhere ("In all this world there was none like him," I.412; p. 30), the Plowman is "a true worker and a good one" (I.531; p. 32), and the Friar, as a member of a mendicant order, is "the best beggar in his house" (I.252; p. 27). On another level the pilgrims are also individuals. The Prioress speaks French (though with a local accent) and affects delicate table manners, which we could expect from a woman who is the head of an abbey and one of the more aristocratic members of the group. We could also expect a woman in a religious order to carry a rosary, which she does. But what are we to make of the golden ornament that hangs from it?

> A pair of beads, with green division-beads,
> And thereon hung a bright golden brooch,
> On which there was first engraved a crowned "A",
> And then *Amor vincit omnia*.
>
> (I.159–62)

"Love conquers all" could of course refer to Christ, but we cannot be sure what it means to her—perhaps she is not either.

Another pilgrim is the Monk. A typical monk lives a secluded life in a monastery, praying, and fasting, but the Prologue's Monk is "a lord full fat and in good condition" (I.200; Benson 26) who loves hunting, keeps horses and greyhounds for that purpose, and keeps a good table as well:

> Now certainly he was a fair prelate;
> He was not pale like a wasted-away ghost,
> A fat swan loved he best of any roast.
>
> (I.204–06)

By contrast, the Clerk of Oxford, who is a clerical student and devoted to philosophy, is thin ("hollow") and wears a threadbare cloak:

> For he had obtained no benefice for himself as yet,
> Nor was he so worldly as to have a job.
>
> (I.291–92)

The Wife of Bath has a successful cloth-making business, as the many scarves she wears on her head on Sunday testify (I.453–55). But her primary identity is "Wife," an occupation at which she has also been successful:

> She had married five husbands in church,
> Not counting other company in her youth—
> But there's no need to speak of that now.
>
> (I.460–62)

As types, the pilgrims are descended from the literature of medieval "estates satire," works fulminating against how the various classes, from kings to commoners, fail to live up to the ideals each should embody. As individuals, the pilgrims are products of Chaucer's keen observation of human character and behavior. His comic vision sees them with humor but not with malice, and he describes them with irony but not (as in *The Owl and the Nightingale*, say) with judgmental invective.

Not all the stories told by these pilgrims are comic. *The Canterbury Tales* mixes different genres of narrative and different modes of narration. The formal romance of the "Knight's Tale" is followed by the earthy fabliau of the "Miller's Tale," the lugubrious series of "tragedies" in the "Monk's Tale" by the brightly comic beast fable of the "Nun's Priest's Tale." Even in the serious tales Chaucer's gentle and humane sense of humor is never entirely absent. But the broadest humor is to be found in the fabliaux. Five finished tales in the collection are fabliaux: the "Miller's Tale," the "Reeve's Tale," the "Summoner's Tale," the "Merchant's Tale," and the "Shipman's Tale." A sixth tale, the "Cook's Tale," is only a fragment, but was headed in the same direction. All the fabliaux in *The Canterbury Tales* involve vulgar language and bawdy behavior: they are not courtly stories. The situations they deal with—a wife tricked into the wrong bed in a dark bedroom, an adulterous couple discovered fornicating in a pear tree, and so on—are all found as well in oral tradition in the type of folktale known to folklorists as a *Schwank*, a "merry tale," humorous jest, mocking anecdote, or dirty joke. But even the simplest of Chaucer's bawdy tales expands and deepens the artistic boundaries of the fabliau form well beyond those of a work such as *Dame Sirith*. That is particularly true of the "Miller's Tale," the gem of this group.

Wherever we look in the "Miller's Tale" we find Chaucer's humor at work—in the narrative structure, the fictional characters, and in the language itself. The tale combines three typical fabliau motifs into one story: "the Flood," "the misdirected kiss," and "the lover's burned rump." The characters are built on the comic stereotypes of the jealous old husband, the lusty young wife, the clever student, and the foppish suitor. Nicholas, an Oxford "clerk" (or student) who dabbles in astrology, boards with the carpenter John and his young wife Alison. He persuades John that the stars have predicted a second Flood about to engulf the earth. John, under Nicholas' direction, builds three large wooden tubs and hangs them from the high rafters of his house. On the evening the Flood is to arrive, Alison, Nicholas, and John climb up to the three tubs, where they are supposed to spend the night praying in chaste solitude until the waters come and carry them away. But John falls asleep in his tub, and Nicholas and Alison quietly climb down and go to bed to frolic. They are interrupted by Absolon, another admirer of Alison's, who comes to the window and asks for a kiss. The night is dark, and when Alison sticks out her rump Absolon kisses it. Realizing that he has been tricked ("For he knew well that a woman does not have a beard," I.3737), Absolon borrows a red-hot plow-coulter from a blacksmith's shop and comes to the window a second time. When he again asks for a kiss, Nicholas, thinking to repeat the trick, sticks out his own rump, and Absolon strikes home with the hot iron. Nicholas cries "Water!" and with that cry two more or less separate plots are suddenly joined and consummated, for it awakens John the carpenter, who believes that the Flood has come, cuts the rope holding his tub to the rafters, and falls to the floor, breaking his arm. At the end of the tale only Alison is unscarred.

Alison is beautiful, but as a way of indicating both her class and her realistic view of the world Chaucer describes her beauty with imagery drawn from farm and field. Her body is as slender and graceful as a weasel's and softer than sheep's wool; her singing is as loud and eager as a barn swallow's; she is as playful as a kid or calf and as skittish as a colt (I.3233–64). Nicholas the clerk is described as indeed clever, but finally he is too clever. His plan involving the stars, the Flood, the tubs, and all the rest is unnecessary in order to win Alison, who is already won; it is really to show that a clerk can outwit a carpenter. John the carpenter is old and rich, which is bad enough in a fabliau, and he is possessively jealous of his young wife. But he is also smug in his ignorance and slightly hypocritical. He preaches that one should not pry into God's secrets with books and astrology, that it is enough to know one's Creed. But he knows the biblical story of Noah only vaguely and forgets that story's covenant of the rainbow. Thus he is completely taken in by Nicholas' prophecy of a second Flood. Absolon the suitor lives in a small town but sees himself as a courtly lover out of medieval poetry. He is introduced as dancing, singing, and playing a "giterne" (cittern, a medieval form of guitar) like a courtier, but his aping of courtly manners is suddenly deflated when Chaucer adds:

> But truth to say, he was somewhat squeamish
> About farting, and dainty of speech.
>
> (I.3337–38)

He plans to serenade and to court Alison all through the night while her husband is away. But first he catches a few hours of sleep, and when he sets out he remembers to chew spices and licorice to sweeten his breath. Only Alison is free of the self-delusions that turn all the men into comic figures.

Chaucer's wordplay adds to the comic irony of the action and the characterization in the tale. Nicholas is called "hende Nicholas," an innocuous adjective meaning "gracious," "polite," or "gentle." But it can also mean "handy, clever with his hands," and it is used again just a few lines before the most outrageous rhyme in the poem:

> ... on a day this *hende* Nicholas
> Fell in with the young wife, carrying on and playing around,
> While her husband was at Osney,
> Since clerks are very subtle and clever [*queynte*];
> And secretly he caught her by the cunt [*queynte*].
>
> (I.3272–76)

The comedy of Nicholas' subtle and clever move is highlighted by the pun, by the *rime riche* (repeating the same word with a different meaning for a rhyme), and by a reader's sense that Chaucer just could not resist the temptation offered to him by the language.

The "*Nun's Priest's Tale*" is one of two beast fables in *The Canterbury Tales*. It uses the story of Reynard the fox and Chaunticleer the rooster mentioned earlier as the basis for the first part of *The Fox and the Wolf*. The story tells how Chaunticleer is tricked by the fox, who persuades him to crow with his eyes closed and seizes him when he does; the rooster in turn tricks the fox by coaxing him to mock his pursuers, and he escapes when the fox opens his mouth to do so. The moral for the rooster is "Keep your eyes open," and the moral for the fox is "Keep your mouth shut." But the fable morals are barely noticed, and the relatively simple plot is almost incidental to the tale. The heart of the tale, and the heart of the comedy, is verbal performance.

When Chaunticleer has a dream warning him of the fox, the hen Pertelote, his favorite wife (of seven), tells him that it is only indigestion and prescribes laxatives. Chaunticleer argues that dreams can be true, and the ensuing debate between a rooster and a hen covers broad areas of medieval thought: the theory of the four "humors" (blood, choler, phlegm, and black bile), which explained human physiology and illness; medieval plant lore, which was the basis of pharmacology; the theory of dreams, which organized dreams into categories according to their kinds of truth and usefulness for prognostication; and more. Chaunticleer in particular buttresses his arguments with citations from his wide reading in classical and medieval texts.

The elaborate debate between the two chickens may be intended to reflect the intellectual interests of the Nun's Priest, the fictional narrator of the tale. We do not learn much about him, other than that he is a hearty and well-formed man in the employ of a woman, the Prioress. Possibly the covert tones of a clerical misogyny, which we noticed earlier in other comic poems, also appear in Chaunticleer's argument. We hear the same kind of joke that mocks women in Latin when Chaunticleer says to his wife:

> For just as sure as *In principio*
> *Mulier est hominis confusio*—
> Madam, the meaning of this Latin is,
> "Woman is man's joy and all his happiness."
>
> (VII.3163–66)

The meaning of the Latin is "In the beginning / Woman is man's ruination," but putting it into the mouth of a rooster, especially this rooster, is a joke on the original joke.

As the story proceeds the Nun's Priest treats his listeners to further parody in wonderfully comic passages of mock-heroic and mock-scholastic style. The fox hidden in the henyard is compared in richly overblown language to notorious deceivers and traitors—Judas Iscariot from the gospels, Ganelon from the *Song of Roland*, and Sinon the Greek from Virgil's story of the Trojan horse. The narrator stops the action to consider profoundly philosophical issues of freedom and necessity in the situation. If Chaunticleer's dream truly predicts the future, is there any place for free will in the chicken's universe? When the fox seizes Chaunticleer and runs off with him, that entire universe explodes into pandemonium. The farmhands, yelling and blowing horns, pursue the fox, the dogs run after them barking loudly, the cow and her calf and even the hogs also run, frightened by the dogs:

> The ducks cried out as if someone wanted to kill them,
> The geese for fear flew over the trees;
> Out of the hive came the swarm of bees,
> So hideous was the noise—ah, God bless!
>
> (VII.3390–93)

Chaucer tells us in the "General Prologue" that Harry Bailly fed the pilgrims well on the night they met at the Tabard Inn. But it is the Nun's Priest who serves up for them a great feast of language in a tale that is one of the high points of comic literature in English.

The "Wife of Bath's Tale" is an Arthurian romance and not a comic tale, though it does have its moments of Chaucerian humor. The tale itself is overshadowed, however, by the narrator's lengthy preamble, the Wife of Bath's Prologue. The Wife harangues, shocks, and entertains the Canterbury pilgrims with her views on marriage and authority. She speaks from "experience," she says, and has no need of ecclesiastical "authority" to teach her about marriage. She vigorously defends her five successive marriages against clerical views that a woman should marry only once, and then she defends the institution of marriage itself against the Church's higher ideal of virginity. For what purpose were the "membres of generacion" ("members of generation," III.116) made, she asks, man's "sely instrument" ("poor little instrument," III.132) and her own "bele chose" ("lovely thing," 3.447)? Do not try to tell her that they were made simply to distinguish men from women and to purge urine, for experience has taught her otherwise.

As she narrates the history of her five marriages the Wife's central point emerges, and we are once again immersed in the comedy of the battle of the sexes. Women should have sovereignty in marriage, she argues. All her marriages were successful because in each one she managed in one way or another to gain the upper hand. The Wife vividly re-creates for the pilgrims how in her first three marriages she constantly attacked her husbands, who were all old and rich, falsely accusing them of accusing *her* of every fault attributed to women by traditional antifeminism—vanity, extravagant spending, a lascivious nature, lying and deceit, stubbornness and nagging—until they surrendered to her control over their wealth and lands, and control over her own freedom:

> And thus of one thing I boast,
> At the end I had the better of them in every way,
> By cunning, or force, or some other method,
> Such as continual grumbling and complaining.
>
> (III.403–6)

Her fourth husband was a reveler and had a mistress, until the Wife gave him a taste of his own medicine:

> . . . I showed others such a friendly manner
> That I made him fry in his own grease
> From anger and from true jealousy.
> By God! I was his purgatory on earth,
> For which I hope his soul is now in heaven!
>
> (III.486–90)

She made the mistake of falling in love with her fifth husband and of turning over to him the lands and wealth she had accumulated from her previous husbands. But soon he began to abuse her trust, and to make matters worse he would read to her in the evenings from a "book of wicked wives" (III.685), a collection of antifeminist tracts by various Church authorities. The Wife has no use for those clerical misogynists:

> The clerk, when he is old, and cannot do
> Venus's works worth his old shoe,
> Then he sits down, and writes in his dotage
> That women cannot stay faithful in marriage!
>
> (III.707–10)

Eventually she conquers this husband as well and forces him to throw his book into the fire. What is particularly interesting about the humor of the Wife of Bath's Prologue is that most of what she says is taken from those same antifeminist texts that she consigns to the flames. Somehow the Wife has succeeded in using the misogynists' own words against them and in turning their arguments upside down. That, too, is an old, and often very satisfying, technique of comedy.

The works of Chaucer would be a high point for humor in any period, and with them we close this view of Middle English comedy. In viewing a different literary period it would be natural to look first to the stage for comedy, but only at the end of the Middle English period did dramatic performances fully develop. Throughout the Middle Ages minstrels and mimes certainly performed at courts and fairs, and folk plays associated with religious and seasonal festivals would have occurred regularly as well, but very little documentary evidence of such performances or even of their existence has survived. In the fifteenth century, however, texts of complete plays and records of their performance began to appear. The plays, known as "mysteries" (plays on a scriptural or hagiographic subject) and "moralities" (dramatized allegories, such as *Everyman*), are essentially performed narratives, and some of them include comic genre-scenes or farces within a larger pattern of religious significance. The soldiers in the York play of the Crucifixion who are nailing Christ to the Cross complain in voices still familiar among laborers today about the inaccurate measurements made by the craftsmen who bored the holes in the Cross. The shrewish and railing wife of Noah in the play of the Flood embodies an antifeminist stereotype that the Wife of Bath would recognize. The sheep-stealing shepherds of the Wakefield *Second Shepherds' Play* unknowingly enact a farcical parody of the Nativity. But even that famous episode is subsumed under the larger religious vision of the play. It is in the Renaissance that English comedy comes into its own on stage.

REFERENCES AND FURTHER READINGS

The original Middle English texts for "Satiric Comedy" can be found in Treharne, for "Lyric Comedy" by poem number in Brown or in Robbins, and for "Narrative Comedy" in Benson's edition of Chaucer. Translations are by the author.

Brown, Carleton, ed. *English Lyrics of the Thirteenth Century*. Oxford, UK: Clarendon, 1932.

Charney, Maurice. *Comedy High and Low: An Introduction to the Experience of Comedy*. New York: Oxford UP, 1978.

Chaucer, Geoffrey. *The Riverside Chaucer*. Ed. Larry D. Benson. 3rd ed. Boston: Houghton Mifflin, 1987.

Jost, Jean E., ed. *Chaucer's Humor: Critical Essays*. New York: Garland, 1994.

Leonard, Frances McNeely. *Laughter in the Courts of Love: Comedy in Allegory, from Chaucer to Spenser*. Norman, OK: Pilgrim, 1981.

Muscatine, Charles. *Chaucer and the French Tradition*. Berkeley: U of California P, 1957.

Perfetti, Lisa. *Women and Laughter in Medieval Comic Literature*. Ann Arbor: U of Michigan P, 2003.

Robbins, Rossell Hope, ed. *Secular Lyrics of the Fourteenth and Fifteenth Centuries*. 2nd ed. Oxford, UK: Clarendon, 1955.

Ruggiers, Paul E., ed. *Versions of Medieval Comedy*. Norman: U of Oklahoma P, 1977.

Treharne, Elaine, ed. *Old and Middle English: An Anthology*. Oxford, UK: Blackwell, 2000.

29

Native American Trickster Tales

Arnold Krupat

The indigenous peoples of what is now the United States did not develop a form of alphabetic writing and so they communicated, stored, and transmitted information of every kind by means of a wide variety of genres or types of *oral performances*. A body of songs, chants, speeches, prayers, and, importantly, narratives or stories constituted for indigenous peoples what we refer to as religion, science, politics, philosophy, pedagogy, and esthetic expression or literature. A character who appears in a great many of these stories among all or most of America's indigenous tribal nations is the *trickster*. It has again and again been said in print that the term *trickster* first appeared in English in Daniel G. Brinton's *The Myths of the New World*, published in 1868, although Lewis Hyde, in a recent major study of the trickster, states that he has not been able to find the word in any one of the three editions of Brinton's book! Hyde suggests that it is in Franz Boas's (1898) introduction to James Teit's *Traditions of the Thompson River Indians* that the term actually first appears (Hyde 355).

In any case, since the late nineteenth century, the term *trickster* has been used to describe a character who is a wandering, bawdy, and gluttonous figure, usually male but able to alter his sex at will. Hyde has noted that "all the canonical tricksters operate in patriarchal mythologies" (80), and that in Native America, the few female tricksters to be found appear primarily among the Hopi and Tewa people of the Southwest who are matrilineal and matrilocal. But even there, as Hyde affirms, building upon a detailed study of the subject by Franchot Ballinger, most of the tricksters are still male. It is possible of course that a body of narratives with female tricksters existed, but if so, they have disappeared with hardly a trace.

Trickster, then is amoral, foolish, destructive, and a threat to order everywhere. As his name indicates, Trickster is one who dupes others in order to engage in obscene and taboo behavior, copulating, for example, with his daughter, daughter-in-law, or mother-in-law. In one set of stories, he fabricates female sexual organs to "marry" the son of a chief, while, in others, we find him sending his enormous penis (on occasion he carries it in a box) swimming across rivers in search of sexual adventure. He excretes and asks his shit for advice, or he may decide to perform oral sex on himself. Some stories have him setting fire to his anus as a punishment for not obeying his instructions to guard his food while he sleeps. He is selfish and often destructive; again and again, he does things every properly socialized Hochank or Hopi or Mohawk person should not do. Yet he usually emerges more or less unscathed by his actions, and his actions almost always provoke laughter. The trickster is an important comic character in traditional Native American oral narrative.

And yet we find that this indecent and obnoxious fellow in indigenous oral narrative traditions is also a powerful, godlike, creator-transformer who, in the long, long ago time of myth, when the earth was still "soft" and not yet fully formed, helped to give the world exactly the shape and order that humans would historically come to know. Stories about the trickster Wakjankaga among the Hochank or Winnebago were classed among the *waikan*, what-is-sacred, for Wakjankaga is not only the "Foolish One," but Kunuga, first son of Ma'una, the Earthmaker, sent to earth by his father to chastise or destroy monsters who would be harmful to the human beings who would soon people this earth. A tale from the Northwest coast published by Melville Jacobs has the title "Coyote Made Everything Good"—not the sort of thing the trickster, Coyote usually does, but something he certainly has the power to do. In other stories Trickster is the one who obtained fire for the people, accidentally or intentionally brought it about that humans would die, determined the proper number of fingers for human hands, and established the appropriate relations between hunters and the animals they would kill, between fishermen and the fish they would take for food. Trickster, then, is a character who does everything wrong, stumbling and bumbling, opportunistically and selfishly cheating and lying and fornicating, but he is also a character who prepares the world for the people who are coming, someone so powerful—indeed, sacred—that stories about him, for most Native peoples, are to be told only in the winter, when the earth is asleep, and snakes are not above ground.

Trickster, thus, is a boundary-breaker but also an important boundary-maker; a destroyer of order and an institutor of order. That a single story character could have this double nature, being at one and the same time what the anthropologist Paul Radin referred to as both "benefactor and buffoon" (124), has long been taken as a problem by Western commentators.

Trickster figures like those found in the oral traditions of Native America are by no means unknown to the premodern West (dating the modern period roughly from the eighteenth century and the spread of so-called Enlightenment values of secular rationality), although it is important in these regards to distinguish, so far as possible, tricksters from such parallel characters as the picaro, the clown, the jester or fool, and the confidence man. This distinction, as we will see later, is especially important when we come to the postmodern West (dating the postmodern roughly from perhaps the mid-1960s and the spread of a sense that Enlightenment values no longer pertained). An image on a wall of a cave among the Trois Frères in France is said to date back some 16,000–18,000 years, and contemporary scholars believe that it represents a shaman or a trickster, although it is extremely unlikely that we will ever know for sure. Hermes, for the ancient Greeks, was a thief in his youth, occasionally something of a clown, but also a god with powers beyond those of mortal men, very much the trickster. The Scandinavian Loki, like Hermes, is both thief and mischief maker yet also a god. Trickster has also been documented in many parts of Africa, where he is frequently figured as Anansi, the spider or known as Eshu-Elegba; in China, where he is the Monkey or

Monkey King; in the Hawaian islands, where he is Maui-of-a-thousand-tricks; and also in Tibet, Turkey, South Asia, and Polynesia. If not quite universal, trickster figures are most definitely widespread throughout the world.

As I have said, these "true" tricksters—such a characterization is inevitably oxymoronic!—need to be differentiated from premodern scoundrels of one sort or another such as Gargantua and Pantagruel in France, characters who act in ways we call "Rabelaisian," after the great author who wrote down some of their adventures, or indeed like sly Renard the Fox. The Germans also have a *Reineke Fuchs.* Their Till Eulenspiegel, along with some of the Italian folk originals of the Pinocchio figure and the Spanish figures Gil Blas and Lazarillo de Tormes, are more nearly picaros, clowns, and confidence men than actual tricksters. The Cherokee scholar and theologian Jace Weaver has recently suggested biblical parallels to Trickster. "The biblical figure that most closely resembles the Native tricksters," Weaver writes, "is Jacob," and he cites Genesis 25.19–37 as "a trickster cycle, as any Indian reader immediately recognizes" (248). This is the story in which Jacob, the younger son of the patriarch Isaac, persuades Esau, his older brother, to "sell" him his birthright for "bread and pottage of lentils" and later deceives or tricks his father into believing he is Esau in order to obtain Jacob's blessing. In time, Jacob is given the name Israel by God, promised that "kings shall come out of thy loins," and that the land God had given to Abraham and Isaac would be given to him and to his children (Gen. 36.10–12). Esau becomes Edom, and the thirty-sixth chapter of Genesis ends with a very lengthy list of "the generations of Esau the father of the Edomites in mount Seir" (36:9). Weaver gives a selective summary (the summary above is also highly selective), which he then compares to an intensely hybridized Anansi tale (Africa by way of the Miskito and Spanish of Nicaragua), but I cannot see many similarities between this Señor Anansi—who, like all tricksters, is sometimes animal, sometimes human, sometimes good, sometimes bad—and the biblical Jacob. I must also confess to doubting whether "any Indian reader" would, "immediately" or not, recognize Jacob's narrative as a "trickster cycle."

Weaver goes on to claim that "there are aspects of trickster evident in Jesus himself" (253), this time citing Luke 2.41–51 as not only illustrating "Jesus' messianic mission from an early age" but also as "a trickster story" (253). Weaver wishes to show that Hyde's observation that "trickster only comes to life in the complex terrain of polytheism" (Hyde 9–10, qtd. in Weaver 255) is unnecessarily restrictive. But it does seem overwhelmingly the case that all the major examples of tricksters *do* appear in polytheistic contexts and, moreover, that tricky or paradoxical behavior on the part of a patriarch or even of Christ is not best explained by thinking of them as tricksters. Jesus has godlike powers, to be sure, and he most certainly can work against the prevailing social order, but one simply cannot imagine him (or Jacob for that matter) changing shape or sex, or engaging in bawdy business, or other sorts of "dirt work," as Hyde calls it (pt. 3, "Dirt Work" 151), typical of tricksters.

Before going further, note that the trickster, as we have come to call him, has no such generic name among the various tribal nations themselves. Rather, these peoples each have very specific and concrete names for Trickster. In California, Oregon, the inland plateau, the Great Basin, the southern plains, and the Southwest, the trickster figure is most commonly called *Coyote.* In the Southeast, trickster is *Rabbit* or *Hare;* *Raven* or *Crow* in the Arctic and sub-Arctic; *Jay* or *Wolverine* in parts of Canada. Among the Lakota of the plains, whose people we call the Sioux, the trickster is *Iktomi* or *Ikto,* a word translated as "spider." Among the Hochank or Winnebago, as I have already noted, the trickster is named *Wakjankaga*, although *Wacdjungega, Hare*, is also a Hochank trickster. For the Anishinaabe or Chippewa, the trickster is *Nenabos* or *Manabozho* (also *Hare*), in a number of variant pronunciations and spellings. For the Gros Ventre of Montana *Nixant* is the trickster's name, as it is *Veeho* for the Cheyenne, *Sitconski* for the Assiniboine, *Istinike* for the Ponca, and *Napi* for the Blackfeet people. In the Northeast we also find a trickster known as *Gluskap* or *Gluskabe*. Among the Cree peoples of Canada, the trickster is known as *Wesucechak* or *Wisahketchahk*, anglicized to "Whiskey Jack."

Further examination of the oral literatures (some have called them "oratures") of Native American peoples turns up many other trickster or tricksterlike characters. Among the Modoc of California, for example, we find someone called *Tusasas* or *Joker*. Northern neighbors of the Modoc, the Klamath people tell tales in which *Skunk* sometimes acts the role of the trickster, but there are also stories told of *Mink* and his younger brother *Weasel* in which they also behave as tricksters. And there are yet other names for Native American tricksters. New England Algonquian-speaking nations have *Lox*, who seems to combine characteristics of the beaver, the badger, and the wolverine, along with a figure known as *Ableegumooch*, who appears to be *Rabbit* under another name. The Native American trickster is important to the history of comedy because, whatever other reactions traditional Native audiences may have had and continue to have to tales about him, we know for certain that they regularly laughed to hear of his adventures.

A great many of the names given here for trickster figures in Native North America are the names of animals. Is it then the case that we are to visualize characters called Coyote or Raven or Rabbit as the animals we know by those names? The answer, like so much else about the trickster, is a firm yes and no. For one thing, in the mythic age of long, long ago, the age in which the traditional trickster operates, the distinction between humans and animals (like so many other distinctions) was not nearly so great as we find it today. Paiute Coyote stories, for example, begin with the phrase *Sumu onosu nemeka nan quane ynas*, "Once long ago when we were all the same." Barre Toelken, a longtime student of Navajo Coyote tales, notes that the words used for Coyote's fingers and toes are the words in Navajo used for human fingers and toes, not the words used for the paws and feet of animals (Toelken and Scott). But this is not to say that the Navajo Coyote (and other trickster Coyotes) doesn't eat and run and behave the way *Canis latrans*, today's coyote, does. The point here would be that even for contemporary Navajo people, this difference makes no difference. Coyote is both animal and human, and there is no contradiction or "problem" in that fact. As the traditional, contemporary Northern Tutchone narrator Tommy McGinty put it in his "Story of Crow," "crow was both *human being* and *bird*, either way, back and forth" (Legros 33). It has also been suggested, a variation on the above, that

From the Indians' viewpoint a Myth Era actor who was named Skunk was really a human-like being possessed of a supernatural which was both a skunk and human-like. At a later precultural time [nearer in time, therefore, to historical time as we know it] he metamorphosed into a skunk, to remain a skunk for all eras to come. (Jacobs 6)

But this may be a Western attempt to mediate the simple—if not for us, surely for traditional Native peoples—fact that one being could be *both* a skunk *and* a human being "either way, back and forth." (Of course this one being is also at one and the same time a mischief-making scoundrel and a godlike transformer of the world, "either way, back and forth.")

An exception to some of this is the Lakota trickster, Iktomi. That word, I have noted, is translated as spider. But Ikto—short for Iktomi—does not ever seem to have had the actual form of a spider. Consultants told Dr. James R. Walker (who served as physician at the Pine Ridge Agency from 1896 to 1914) many different things about Ikto's appearance, that he was spider*like*, but also that he was human*like* although deformed, or else that he looked more nearly like a fat bug. This trickster, Iktomi, it should be said, although he most certainly does comic things, occasionally makes us laugh, and even sometimes (e.g., in the first of Ella Cara Deloria's *Dakota Tales* (1932), called "Ikto Conquers Iya, the Eater") acts for the benefit of the people, is for the most part very dangerous and a threat to the well-being of the individual and the community; as Julian Rice puts it, he is "a powerful enemy of human welfare" (*Lakota Storytelling* 83). Rice also quotes Rachel Ashley, a Dakota woman interviewed in 1977, as saying that the closest thing to the word for "witch," a very dangerous person, was probably Unkto, the Dakota form of Ikto (*Before the Great Spirit* 40). When it comes to characters like Wakjankaga or Gluskap, it is extremely difficult to specify in what form narrators and their audiences visualize them.

In general, for tricksters with animal names, it seems to be the case that Native narrators and audiences adjust their *view* of the character according to what the character *does*. Thus when McGinty's Crow encounters a beautiful woman and sets out to make love to her, we will probably imagine him as a man with the *power* or perhaps even the nature of a crow, but as a decidedly human-looking personage. Something similar is probably true for Mrs. Coyote, in a Hopi tale. Having dried her dead husband's penis and ground it into a powder, Mrs. Coyote, after putting her daughters to sleep, applies the powder to the appropriate anatomical spot, and then proceeds to make noises loud enough to wake the children. Human and animal, both ways, back and forth.

To offer some further sense of the things Coyote, in particular, does, we may look at the table of contents of William Bright's collection *A Coyote Reader*. Bright offers such categories as "Coyote the Glutton," "Coyote the Lecher," the thief, the cheat, the outlaw, the spoiler, the clown, the (horny) old man, and, too, the survivor. From Barbara Babcock's list of sixteen traits of the trickster, in an important essay of 1975, I will note only some few (others have to some extent already been indicated). Babcock writes that tricksters "exhibit an independence from and an ignoring of temporal and spatial boundaries"; that they "tend to inhabit crossroads, open public places, . . . and thresholds" (Hyde notes that *Hermes* once meant "he of the stone heap," [6] referring to the piles of stones travelers would leave at crossroads) and "have an enormous libido without procreative outcome" (162). (This is not to say that tricksters do not also sometimes appear as fathers—and, though much less often, mothers of sons and daughters.) Tricksters "have an ability to disperse and to disguise themselves . . . ," and "may be portrayed as both young and old, as perpetually young or perpetually aged" (Babcock 163).

The developmental psychologists David Abrams and Brian Sutton-Smith suggest that Trickster displays "oral behavior" (32), in terms of being preoccupied with food, but also, as we have noted, in performing oral sex on himself. We may also point, however, to a decidedly anal aspect of Trickster as well, that is, the fact—as noted above—that several stories find him blaming his anus and punishing it for not watching his food as he slept. In a number of other stories, too, Coyote ties or otherwise obstructs the anus of one or another small animal in order, later, to unplug it and have the resulting explosion kill yet other animals for food!

Abrams and Sutton-Smith further describe aspects of Trickster's orality as including the "narcissism" he demonstrates in his boastfulness and exhibitionism. Further, when he violate taboos, he seems to be ignorant of the effects or consequences of his behavior. He cares little for others and has little sensitivity toward the feelings of others. He is clumsy, falling over frequently and finding various parts of his body in conflict (e.g., his right arm may fight with his left), and he exhibits "variable behavior" in that "one never knows what he will do next" (Abrams and Sutton-Smith 32–34). This account obviously associates Trickster with early stages of childhood, ages five to seven, for the most part (and it should be said that Abrams and Sutton-Smith used Bugs Bunny as the example of a trickster in their study). But, as we have seen, the childish trickster in indigenous oral narratives is also a very powerful personage, not only capable of all that adults do but capable as well of things that only supernaturals or gods can do.

In regard to the meaning and function of these stories in the societies that grant them enormous importance and yet laugh at them at the same time, the opinion expressed by the majority of Western observers has, at least until recently, differed markedly from the opinion of indigenous people—traditional narrators, for the most part—who have been willing to speak in the abstract about them. I shall conclude this chapter by attending to some of what these Native narrators have had to say, after some further attention to Western consideration of the trickster.

As already noted, Western scholars, until fairly recently, began by attempting to resolve what they persistently took as the *problem* of trickster's double nature, what I referred to, with reference to Radin, as the fact that he is both "benefactor and buffoon" (124), lowlife and godlike. They have engaged this "problem" from perspectives that may be broadly grouped as *psychological, cultural*, and *philosophical*—although it will soon be apparent that it is not really possible to keep these perspectives distinct from one another, or from closely related perspectives (e.g., the social, the political, and so on).

Concluding that the "problem" of understanding trickster as both "benefactor and buffoon" was "basically a psychological one" (xxiv), Radin himself solicited a concluding essay for his publication of a cycle of Winnebago trickster stories called *The Trickster* (1956) from Carl Jung. Jung's "On the Psychology of the Trickster Figure" asserts that "Considering the crude primitivity of the trickster cycle [!], it would not be surprising if one saw in this myth simply the reflection of an earlier, rudimentary stage of consciousness, which is what the trickster *obviously seems to be*" (Radin 201, emphasis added). Jung is well aware that such an explanation "would certainly not meet with the approval of the Winnebagos" (200), but that doesn't in the least concern him. Jung believes that "Radin's trickster cycle . . . points back to a very much earlier stage of consciousness which existed before the birth of myth, when the Indian was still groping about in a similar mental darkness" (202). This utter dismissal of the point of view of the Native in regard to aspects of her own culture appears, today, not only ethically disreputable but epistemologically disastrous, the reductive imposition of a Western evolutionary perspective on very rich and variegated material.

A developmental perspective of a more Freudian sort (although it is a somewhat unorthodox and idiosyncratic Freudianism) appears in the work of Melville Jacobs. Commenting on a story called "Badger and Coyote Were Neighbors," which he published in his important volume *The Content and Style of an Oral Literature* (1959), Jacobs remarks that "The Coyote of this myth is to a degree consistent with the familiar Columbia River Valley composite of a *more or less entertaining narcissist* . . . and *an adult, mature, and deity-like* man" (30, emphasis added). Jacobs continues, "The structuring of such a personality in a plot which also has two parts—*the first Id-dominated, the second reality-oriented*—connects with the native conceptualization of genetic developments in the personality of a man" (30, emphasis added). He further comments that whenever Coyote "responds to a wholly internal stimulus or need, he is a bungler. When something entirely outside himself challenges, something much more important than himself, his responses are powerful, adult, even deity-like" (32). Apart from the fact that such an account ignores the fact that there are probably as many trickster tales that *do not* fit this pattern as *do*, it is hard to see why Native conceptualizations of human development would make mature manhood include "deity-like" responses. That Northwest Indians, like Native peoples elsewhere, see Coyote as a selfish bungler and also as godlike seems certain; that this double nature can be explained as a "transition" from the one to the other, from nearly the child to more nearly the superhuman, seems far less certain. Other psychological approaches to trickster tales are more or less consistent with those few mentioned here. Thus Rice writes of the Lakota trickster Iktomi that he "is an adolescent potentiality in each person for creation or destruction" (Before 55).

By this time, it should be clear that cultural perspectives on the function of trickster tales overlap considerably with psychological perspectives. Babcock's generalization that "psychological explanation" primarily involves concepts of "projection and sublimation" (180), for example, can serve as a bridge to the sociocultural. Thus Jacobs also believed that myth tales—this would include trickster stories—tended to treat particular points of stress or anxiety that *cultures* (not just individual persons) did not adequately resolve in their everyday social practice. He writes, for example, that "Feelings about older women [in Clackamas culture] were . . . mixed with respect and resentment, to a degree that *the mythology contains many projections of how they were actually regarded*" (12, emphasis added). More generally, he notes that "Clackamas literature cited only the supernaturals, not the public rites; *it thereby shows where Clackamas were unsure of themselves*, for *they did not need to project into myth* the ceremonials which a hamlet conducted with efficiency" (13, emphasis added). This seems sensible although at least potentially circular in its reasoning: had Jacobs determined from observation or from material *other* than that contained in Clackamas literature that Clackamas people were more than ordinarily conflicted in their feelings about older women? Or did he come to think this as a result of intuitions he had about the stories?

The French scholar Laura Makarius has generalized that "the contradictions involved [in trickster myths] are those that arise from the violation of taboos for the purpose of acquiring magical power for the group" (663). Once again, this surely may be true in some regards but it is hard to believe that it carries across the broad spectrum of trickster tales. From the time of his 1964 doctoral dissertation at least until 1993, Mac Linscott Ricketts developed the idea that tricksters operate as parodies of traditional shamanic figures, and by invoking laughter serve to blunt the fear and awe that might be felt toward those who claimed to have access with considerable supernatural power. This is to say that cultures with highly developed shamanic rituals would be likely to require highly developed bodies of trickster stories to keep their balance, as it were.

Reviewing scholarship on the trickster to 1975, Babcock listed six "propositions" that had been offered as explaining "what role or function this type of narrative [trickster narrative] plays in society" (179). The fifth of these, "the reflective-creative function," which Babcock calls "perhaps the most important" (180), also links psychological issues to cultural and sociopolitical issues, and to explain it, Babcock turns to Arthur Koestler's 1964 discussion of creative thought. Koestler speaks of what he calls the "bisociation of two matrixes" as "a pattern fundamental" to the act of creation (Koestler 35). What Koestler means by "bisociation" is the *"perceiving of a situation or idea . . . in two self-consistent but habitually incompatible frames of reference"* (emphasis in original). Koestler coined the term "bisociation," he explains, "in order to make a distinction between the routine skills of thinking on a single 'plane,' as it were, and the creative act which . . . always operates on more than one plane. The former may be called single-minded, the latter . . . double-minded . . ." (35–36). "In contrast to routine thinking," Koestler continues, "the creative act of thought is always 'double-minded', i.e., a transitory state of unstable equilibrium where the balance of both thought and emotion is disturbed" (36). The disturbance of routine or ordinary thinking that can provoke creative flexibility in individual understanding as it develops, as Koestler describes it, is very close to what Abrams and Sutton-Smith, in their discussion of trickster stories in relation to the play of children, call "adaptive potentiation" (46). Abrams and Sutton-Smith suggest that adaptive potentiation may also work at the sociocultural as well as the psychological level. Human societies, this is to say, may find it beneficial to explore, at least imaginatively in narrative, possibilities beyond what established conventions allow.

Hyde has developed this idea, pointing to the historical paradox "that the origins, liveliness, and durability of cultures require that there be space for figures whose function is to uncover and disrupt the very thing that cultures are based on" (9). Although cultures and societies obviously cannot sustain themselves if their boundaries are not respected most of the time, Hyde remarks that nonetheless sociocultural *"liveliness* depends on having those boundaries regularly disturbed" (13, emphasis added), as in a variety of carnivals, festivals of misrule, and the license accorded ritually to clowns and fools. Babcock observes that although the experience that individuals and societies may have of disturbing the boundaries in narrative or ritual may produce "an exhilarated sense of freedom from form in general" (181), to the point even of posing a threat to "established forms," still, that experience can also provide exactly the stimulus that social and cultural forms require creatively to adapt and change in culturally acceptable ways. These ideas accord quite well with what traditional narrators of trickster tales have had to say about them. Tales of the trickster push the mental and social envelope, as it were, testing, probing, and challenging limits and norms, yet in a manner that seems to have adaptively positive effects.

The philosophical perspective on the function of trickster tales may be subdivided into *logical* and *rhetorical* perspectives, although once more the reader should be aware of overlaps of all sorts. The logical perspective derives most prominently from the French anthropologist Claude Lévi-Strauss. In a 1955 essay called "The Structural Study of Myth," Lévi-Strauss first claims that, contrary to popular belief, myth and poetry are not at all similar but entirely different. This is because while poetry is always in some measure untranslatable—something important always gets lost in translation—myth is always fully translatable. No matter what culture it comes from, no matter what sort of story it tells, no matter what the exact words of the story or the gestures and tonalities of the narrator (Lévi-Strauss was not at all interested in the actual performance dimensions of oral stories), "the mythical value of the myth remains preserved, even through the worst translation" (174). This is because the sort of translation Lévi-Strauss thinks necessary to get at the "mythical value of the myth" is a translation from the concrete and particular details of the story itself into abstract categories (e.g., a pine or a cottonwood become "trees"; crows or whippoorwills become "birds"). Lévi-Strauss claims that *every* myth can be shown to work "from the awareness of oppositions toward their progressive mediation . . . two opposite terms with no intermediary always tend to be replaced by two equivalent terms which allow a third one as mediator" (188).

Turning to trickster stories (he had first done a structural analysis of the Oedipus myth), Lévi-Strauss asks the question, "Why is it that throughout North America [the part of trickster] is assigned practically everywhere to either coyote or raven?" (188). Lévi-Strauss answers that it is because both are carrion-eating animals, and carrion-eating animals can be logically classified as mediators between prey animals and herbivorous animals. Like the first, they eat animal food, but like the second, they do not kill what they eat. The problem for what Lévi-Strauss called "the primitive mind" (but he believes that all minds work this way) is something like, How can it be that some animals eat animal food while other animals do not eat animal food?

Of course, as we have seen, there are a great many more trickster figures than Coyote and Raven, and, too, coyote in empirical fact (as well as in the stories) is not usually a carrion-eater. But as Michael Carroll writes, this error makes no difference; for Carroll, Lévi-Strauss is correct to insist that myths function to express a logical, analytical, or, as I have called it, a philosophical dilemma in such a way "as to provide some sort of cognitive model that allows the individual to lose sight of the inherent contradiction that the dilemma entails" (307). It seems, then, that we are not dealing with social constraints, specific points of tension or unease in cultural life, or with human developmental stages, but with an invariant structure of the mind as it engages the world. This is not strictly the unconscious, as it has usually been understood, but more nearly what is hardwired in the brain, as we understand it today (both Lévi-Strauss and Carroll were writing before this latter analogy, if it is accurate, became possible). Worked upon by Western abstraction and analytic logic, trickster becomes not so much a character in a story as a cognitive model for the solution of a dilemma—albeit a dilemma of which neither the storyteller nor the audience has any conscious awareness.

Carroll himself sees trickster tales as mediating a different set of contradictions from Lévi-Strauss. For Carroll, the "inherent contradiction" that Trickster mediates is the desire to have unlimited sex (this seems a more likely "desire" for males than females, given the inevitable consequence of sex for women, i.e., pregnancy)—what Carroll calls "uncontrolled sexuality"—and the desire to live socially, to inhabit a "culture." The contradiction here resides in the fact that "the first would lead to the destruction of the second" (301). But apparently the tales cause us "to lose sight of the inherent contradiction that the dilemma entails" (307). Subsequent work along these lines has demonstrated both the possibilities—with enough ingenuity, the interpreter can posit all sorts of nonfalsifiable and nonverifiable yet *interesting* abstract pairs in any story—and the limitations of this method, chief of which, once again, is that it ignores entirely the culture-specific meanings of the stories' details (e.g., if one is thinking of the category *trees* there is no way to get at what the cottonwood or the pine *specifically* means to a given people).

Rhetorical accounts of trickster narratives are a subheading of the philosophical. Rhetoric, the art of persuasion in language, seems to have been formally "invented" in fifth-century B.C.E. Sicily by two men named Corax and Tisias, Greeks who accepted the patronage of the Sicilian tyrant Hiero I. Corax is said to have produced the first treatise on rhetoric; Tisias is said to have been the first paid teacher known to the West. These men, at a time when Greek alphabetic writing was beginning to challenge the oral transmission of knowledge in the Athens of Socrates (who did not write) and Plato (who did), elaborated the techniques and modes of persuasion with oratorical performance in mind. Rhetoric, as it developed further, described and catalogued a variety of technical figures some of which—metaphor, simile, anaphora (punning), irony—have become more or less familiar to students of literature and of comedy. The philosophical perspective on trickster tales that invokes rhetoric does so almost exclusively with reference to irony and the ironic.

In an important essay called "Multiple Levels of Religious Meanings in Culture: A New Look at Winnebago Sacred Texts" (1982), Lawrence Sullivan also considers Trickster's double nature as a problem to be solved. Sullivan's solution is to refer the contraries, oppositions, or contradictions in Trickster's behavior to the Western rhetorical trope of irony. "Irony," Sullivan writes,

binds widely separated opposites into a single figure so that contraries appear to belong together. In Trickster chaos and order, sacred and profane, farce and meaning, silence and song, food and waste, word and event, pretended ignorance and pretended cunning . . . [etc.] compose not only an ironic symbol but a symbol of irony.

Trickster's character and exploits embody the process of ironic imagination. . . . In him the double-sidedness of reality reveals itself. (238)

Sullivan's invocation of the ironic as a solution to an ongoing sense that Trickster's dichotomous nature is a problem to be solved seems to have felt "right" for its historical moment in much the same way as Lévi-Strauss' solution must have felt right for its historical moment. This is to say that in view of what Allan Ryan has called the "trickster shift"—the proliferation of subversive play and undercutting wit in a good deal of postmodernist, contemporary Native American visual art and literature—many have accepted the fact that the traditional, oral trickster must also be essentially and functionally ironic, and, moreover, that this irony is subversive of the prevailing order, ideologically revolutionary and liberating.

Such a view of the trickster would seem to animate Shane Phelan's suggestion that "Coyote stories can illuminate options for [contemporary] lesbian and feminist politics." Phelan explores "the ways in which Coyote can refresh lesbian and feminist politics by offering us a less stable understanding of identity and a looser and light—and therefore more empowering, interpretation of the political cosmos and human action" (13). Phelan is attempting to build on Donna Haraway's suggestion, in 1991, "to see feminist theory as a reinvented coyote discourse" (qtd. in Phelan 132). Although Phelan seems to be much more aware of the postmodern "coyote" than of traditional coyote tricksters, her particular interpretation, as conveyed in the quote just above, nonetheless comes close to what we have said about the culturally creative and adaptive possibilities of trickster figures in the oral narratives.

The foremost champion of the most extreme view of the postmodern, ironic, subversive, and revolutionary trickster is the Chippewa or Anisinaabe writer Gerald Vizenor. In a considerable number of important texts, Vizenor has said things like the following: "The Trickster is not a presence or a real person but a semiotic sign in a language game, a comic narrative that denies presence" (204). The many trickster characters in Vizenor's stories and novels are devoted to breaking down barriers, transgressing order, and avoiding closures of any kind. Vizenor's claims for the trickster go beyond Phelan's somewhat more modest claims (claims consistent with what we have found for the trickster of oral narrative) for trickster as possibly lightening, or destabilizing, overly narrow or rigid conventions. While there is no question that the contemporary postmodern trickster *is* ironic and subversive, offering to Native peoples (and others) what may be a powerful dramatization of the possibilities of what life beyond the constraints of colonialism (or sexism of a variety of kinds) might be like, the oral trickster, subversive as he often is, is not only subversive. Traditional oral tricksters, as we have seen, are *both* subversive *and* normative, boundary makers as well as boundary breakers, and "representational in the currently devalued sense," as Andrew Wiget has put it, "with a range of references restricted by historical, cultural, and social knowledge, and interpretable as dramatizations of accessible truths about beliefs and values" (478).

The extraordinary capacity of the traditional oral trickster both to subvert and yet also to affirm "truths about beliefs and values" is indeed a paradox, but it should not be taken as a problem. Trickster's behavior, as we have seen, requires the *"perceiving of a situation or idea . . . in two self-consistent but habitually incompatible frames of reference"* (Koestler 35), spurring creative thought. To return to Hyde's words, trickster stories remind us that the "liveliness and durability of cultures require that there be space for figures whose function is to uncover and disrupt the very things that cultures are based on" (9). This is why the telling of trickster tales is an important part of what I will call Native American philosophical thought and pedagogical practice.

This account of trickster thus far, it must be admitted, only confirms the fact that "few of the thousands of printed words explicating the various Native American trickster figures can be attributed directly to traditional storytellers" (Danker 505). In part, this is because the earliest recorders of trickster and other Native American oral narratives do not seem to have asked traditional storytellers what they themselves thought or understood about the stories. It is not clear what sorts of responses might have been forthcoming. Anthony Mattina has noted that "the lay members of these communities do not normally verbalize their abstractions of their literatures" (4–5). Nonetheless, over the years a small but important body of commentary from traditional storytellers has come into being, and this is absolutely indispensable for an understanding of the narratives from an indigenous point of view. One thing that has become clear is that the "problem" of trickster's double nature for Western commentators is decidedly *not* a problem for Native narrators and their audiences. Toelken writes that while to

the western mind this odd combination of sacred and secular, wise and foolish, in one character is perhaps a "tricky" idea, . . . in fact it makes palpable a fairly common concept among Native American tribes: good and evil, sacred and secular, smart and dumb are not mutually exclusive qualities, but are overlapping, interdependent aspects of each other. This is a much more complicated idea than trickery would account for . . . it represents a set of assumptions far more rare in western thought than [contemporary, Western] Trickster fans are likely to appreciate. (193)

But it is surely time to turn to Felix White Sr., a Hochank or Winnebago teller of trickster tales who worked with Kathleen Danker; to Hugh Yellowman, a Navajo, and George Wasson, of the Coquelle people, both of whom worked with Barre Toelken; to Louis Bird, a Swampy Cree narrator; to Harry Robinson, an Okanagan elder, who worked with Wendy Wickwire; to Tommy McGinty, a Northern Tutchone man who worked with Dominique Legros; and to some few other traditional storytellers. Their words make clear that those who have told and continue to tell the stories important to Native cultures are engaged in important philosophical and pedagogical work. Let us speculate that oral storytellers who narrate cosmological stories, for example, are local intellectuals engaged in thinking about the beginnings of the known world, teaching their audiences to understand better who they are now by understanding where they have come from, in what the West would call metaphysical or theological terms. In much the same way, those who tell tales about the people's culture heroes, we might guess, are people committed to thinking, by means of narrative, about the heroic or grander possibilities of human behavior.

It seems likely, therefore, that those who tell trickster tales are people fascinated by the kinds of paradoxes (they do not, to repeat, see these paradoxes as a problem) already noted—from Radin's "benefactor and buffoon" formula, to notions of boundary making/boundary breaking, and the curious fact that the ongoing health of a culture seems to require that it be able to tolerate a measure of cultural dis-ease. The tellers of trickster tales are thinkers committed to exploring the possibilities of *both/and* rather than *either/or* logics in the interest of the sort of creative change that is both new and traditional at once—nor is this phrase a paradox or contradiction.

Felix White Sr. narrated a series of Winnebago trickster tales—many of them concerning that same Wakjankaga who appeared in the lengthy cycle of tales earlier published by Radin—to Danker, who tape-recorded, transcribed, and, with White's participation, translated his narratives. Danker also posed questions to White about his stories. Regarding Trickster himself, White said, "The story character, he does so many unthought of things in there that it causes the listener to start thinking, 'Why does he do that?' It's a process of making somebody exercise his mind to think" (qtd. in Danker 522). This narrative mode of prodding the mind to think, Louis Bird observes, is something that "our ancestors must have been aware [of] . . . and therefore have tell [*sic*] stories to their young ones knowing that in the years to come, all these [stories] that they have told the young one will be useful once they have passed away" (263). When the children ask the question cited by White, "Why does he do that?" Bird notes that "whoever tells the story will not stop to explain—they will just keep on telling stories, which keep the children in suspense, sort of. The story keep in suspense and kept alive that way and the children always wanted to hear a bit more explanation to it. . . . That was traditional education system" (264).

Thinking about Tommy McGinty's recollections of the stories he heard and how they affected him, LeGros usefully recalls Walter Benjamin's classic essay "The Storyteller," in which Benjamin notes that "it is half the art of storytelling to keep a story free from explanation as one reproduces it" (qtd. in Legros 38–39). Like Bird, Vi Hilbert, a Lushootseed storyteller and educator, also recalls this aspect of the art of oral storytelling. Hilbert says, "While the stories were told to me in great detail, . . . the moral was never ever explained to me. I had to figure that out for myself. . . . It is my belief that most of our story tellers followed this practice" (qtd. in Ryan 6). As a troubled and difficult youth, McGinty was put in the care of an accomplished and respected older man named Copper Joe. As LeGros reports, "Old Copper Joe had answers in the form of stories for nearly every question the young Tommy asked and *he told unasked stories to make the eager little boy think and raise more questions*" (253, emphasis added).

When there was a nightlong storytelling session, as Mattina learned from his Colville consultant, Peter Seymour, youngsters might, after listening for some time, fall asleep, not yet able to comprehend "that the stories told by their elders contain principle by principle the secrets of how to be Colville—*what it means to have been preceded in life by Coyote*, by the other animals of their land, and by the birds of their sky, and by the fishes of their water" (16, emphasis added). As an elderly man, Harry Robinson recalled how, in his youth, his infirm and partially blind grandmother would call to him, " 'Come here!' And I sit here while she hold me. And she'd tell me stories, kinda slow. She wanted me to understand good. For all that time until I got to be big, she tell me stories" (Robinson 12). Other elders also passed on their stories. "I got enough people to tell me. That's why I know," Robinson says (12). Listening close, half-listening, questioning, or maybe even falling asleep, young and old find that the stories make you exercise your mind to think: trickster stories, as we shall see further, demanding perhaps more mental exercise than any others.

Certainly trickster, White observes, "was a person that had a mind of his own, and you might say that he could be disobedient" (qtd. in Danker 526). But that is certainly no reason not to tell the stories to children. To be sure, Hilbert's earlier comment had the qualifier that "the stories were told to me in great detail, *allowing for my delicate ears*" (qtd. in Ryan 6, emphasis added), and Bird says of the bawdy trickster story he tells that it would be told "mildly" if children were present: "The stories are very flexible that way" (264). These stories, told one way or another, as we have seen, are the basis of the child's education. As Hugh Yellowman replied in answer to Toelken's question, Why tell Coyote stories to children? "If my children hear [the stories], they will grow up to be good people; if they don't hear them, they will turn out to be bad" (Toelken and Scott 80). Children need to learn; adults need to have affirmed the truths and values of the culture they live daily, and Trickster's exploits teach—usually by negative example—what should and should not be done.

But, further, to return to a matter raised earlier, Trickster's exploits not only teach what should and should not be done, but also, beyond should and should not, they teach dramatically what it is *possible* to do. As Yellowman explained, "Through the stories everything is made possible. . . . If [Coyote] did not do all those things, then those things would not be possible in the world" (qtd. in Toelken and Scott 80). Something similar is expressed by White when he notes that Wakjankaga "goes through everything—everything a human can do *or has potential to do*" (qtd. in Danker 526, emphasis added). And Bird says of his Cree people that "They have told these stories [of Nanabush and Wiisaakechaahk] to cover every aspect of human nature." As noted earlier, those who specialize in telling trickster stories are interested in the *creative* possibilities of individual behavior, even to the point where such possibilities may threaten the serious business of culture and society. Those who hear the tales have the opportunity, in Hyde's words, imaginatively to "scout the territory" (12) of forbidden—although always *possible*—adventures. Or, as Toelken has written, the stories provide "culturally enjoyable correlatives to a body of thought so complicated and profound that vicarious experience in it through entertainment is one of the only access points available to most people" (Wasson and Toelken 193). These outrageous and very funny stories are engaged in very serious business among traditional Native peoples.

Trickster's creative possibilities continue to be invoked today, by lesbians and feminists, Native theologians and critics, and postmodern Indian writers and visual artists. For the most part, the Native American trickster figures that appear in contemporary art, literature, and critical theory are largely subversive ironists engaged in the formidable task of breaking the boundaries of colonial constraints. Although some of them have tribal relations and tribal memories, few, it seems, have yet felt able to begin affirming potentially life-giving boundaries. Perhaps this will happen in time. Meanwhile, trickster stories continue to be *told* locally in many places. Some of these have been recorded and transcribed to the printed page, thus to circulate beyond the local community. But a fair number—it is unlikely that one could establish such a number empirically—do *not* ever appear on the page to become generally available for appreciation and study. Nonetheless, a considerable body of trickster tales exists in print for the non-Native or, indeed, the Native person with no access to the continuing oral tradition to read, to learn from, and to enjoy. That enjoyment is sure to include rich comic laughter.

REFERENCES AND FURTHER READINGS

Abrams, David, and Brian Sutton-Smith. "The Development of the Trickster in Children's Narrative." *Journal of American Folklore* 90 (1977): 29–47.

Babcock, Barbara. " 'A Tolerated Margin of Mess': The Trickster and His Tales Reconsidered." *Critical Essays on Native American Literature*. 1975. Ed. Andrew Wiget. Boston: G. K. Hall, 1985. 153–84.

Ballinger, Franchot. "Coyote, He/She Was Going There: Sex and Gender in Native American Trickster Stories." *SAIL/Studies in American Indian Literatures* 12 (2000): 15–43.

Bird, Louis. "The Legend of Wissaakechaahk" and "Cannibal Exterminators." Ed. and introd. by Paul DePasquale. *Algonquian Spirit: Contemporary Translations of the Algonquian Literatures of North America*. Ed. Brian Swann. Lincoln: U of Nebraska P, 2005. 262–90.

Bright, William, ed. *A Coyote Reader*. Berkeley: U of California P, 1993.

Brinton, Daniel G. *The Myths of the New World*. 1868. Westport, CT: Greenwood, 1969.

Carroll, Michael. "Levi-Strauss, Freud and the Trickster: A New Perspective upon an Old Problem." *American Ethnologist* 8 (1981): 301–13.

Danker, Kathleen. "Because of This I Am Called the Foolish One: Felix White, Sr.'s, Interpretations of the Winnebago Trickster." *New Voices in Native American Literary Criticism*. Ed. Arnold Krupat. Washington, DC: Smithsonian Institution P, 1993. 505–28.

Deloria, Ella Cara. *Dakota Texts*. 1932. New York: AMS, 1974.

Evers, Larry, and Barre Toelken, eds. *Native American Oral Traditions: Collaboration and Interpretation*. Logan: Utah State UP, 2001.

Hyde, Lewis. *Trickster Makes This World: Mischief, Myth, and Art*. New York: Farrar, Straus and Giroux, 1998.

Hynes, William, and William Doty, eds. *Mythical Trickster Figures: Contours, Contexts, and Criticisms*. Tuscaloosa: U of Alabama P, 1993.

Jacobs, Melville. *The Content and Style of an Oral Literature: Clackamas Chinook Myths and Tales*. Chicago: U of Chicago P, 1959.

———. *The People Are Coming Soon: Analysis of Clackamas Chinook Myths and Tales*. Seattle: U of Washington P, 1960.

Koestler, Arthur. *The Act of Creation*. New York: Dell, 1964.

Legros, Dominique. *Tommy McGinty's Northern Tutchone Story of Crow: A First Nation Elder Recounts the Creation of the World*. Canadian Ethnology Service Paper 133. Hull, Quebec: Canadian Museum of Civilization, 1999.

Lévi-Strauss, Claude. "The Structural Study of Myth." 1955. *The Structuralists: From Marx to Lévi-Strauss*. Ed. Richard and Fernande de George. New York: Anchor, 1972. 169–94.

Makarius, Laura. "The Crime of Manabozho." *American Anthropologist* 75 (1973): 663–75.

Malotki, Ekkehart, and Michael Lomatuway'ma. *Hopi Coyote Tales: Istutuwutsi*. Lincoln: U of Nebraska P, 1984.

Mattina, Anthony. *The Golden Woman: The Colville Narrative of Peter Seymour*. Tucson: U of Arizona P, 1985.

Phelan, Shane. "Coyote Politics: Trickster Tales and Feminist Futures." *Hypatia: A Journal of Feminist Philosophy* 11 (1996): 130–44.

Radin, Paul. *The Trickster: A Study of American Indian Mythology*. Commentaries by Karl Kerenyi and C. G. Jung. New York: Schocken, 1956.

Ricketts, Mac Linscott. "The North American Indian Trickster." *History of Religions* 5 (1966): 327–50.

———. "North American Tricksters." *Encyclopedia of Religion*. Vol. 15. New York: Macmillan, 1987. 48–51.

———. "The Shaman and the Trickster." *Mythical Trickster Figures: Contours, Contexts, and Criticisms*. Ed. William Hynes and William Doty. Tuscaloosa: U of Alabama P, 1993. 87–105.

Rice, Julian. *Before the Great Spirit: The Many Faces of Sioux Spirituality*. Albuquerque: U of New Mexico P, 1998.

———. *Lakota Storytelling: Black Elk, Ella Deloria, and Frank Fools Crow*. New York: Peter Lang, 1988.

Robinson, Harry. *Write It on Your Heart: The Epic World of an Okanagan Storyteller*. Comp. and ed. Wendy Wickwire. Vancouver: Talonbooks/Theytus, 1989.

Ryan, Allan. *The Trickster Shift: Humour and Irony in Contemporary Native Art*. Vancouver: U of British Columbia P, 1999.

Sullivan, Lawrence. "Multiple Levels of Religious Meanings in Culture: A New Look at Winnebago Sacred Texts." *Canadian Journal of Native Studies* 2 (1982): 221–47.

Toelken, Barre, and Tacheeni Scott. "Poetic Retranslation and the 'Pretty Languages' of Yellowman." *Traditional American Indian Literatures: Texts and Interpretations*. Ed. Karl Kroeber. Lincoln: U of Nebraska P, 1981. 65–116.

Vizenor, Gerald. "Trickster Discourse: Comic Holotropes and Language Games." *Narrative Chance: Postmodern Discourse on Native American Indian Literatures*. Ed. Gerald Vizenor. Albuquerque: U of New Mexico P, 1989. 187–211.

Walker, James. *Lakota Belief and Ritual*. Ed. Raymond DeMallie and Elaine Jahner. Lincoln: U of Nebraska P, 1980.

Wasson, George, and Barre Toelken. "Coyote and the Strawberries: Cultural Drama and Cultural Collaboration." *Native American Oral Traditions: Collaboration and Interpretation*. Ed. Larry Evers and Barre Toelken. Logan: Utah State UP, 2001. 176–99.

Weaver, Jace. "Trickster: The Sacred Fool." *Other Words: American Indian Literature, Law, and Culture*. Norman: U of Oklahoma P, 2001. 246–57.

Wiget, Andrew. "Review of *Narrative Chance: Postmodern Discourse on Native American Indian Literatures*." *Modern Philology* (May 1991): 476–79.

30

The Philosophy of Humor

Adrian Bardon

Philosophy is an unusual field of study, in that it does not concern any particular subject matter (as do, for example, fields like biology or Russian literature), but rather consists in a kind of activity. Philosophy is the activity of reflective critical thought applied to fundamental concepts and systems of thought and behavior. Individual philosophers pursue this activity while drawing on distinctive views of human beings and the natural world, as well as certain beliefs about the nature of human beings, their ideas and values, their social existence, and the world. The primary goal of this activity is simply to gain a better understanding of us and the world around us. A life lived in engagement with this kind of activity is something the ancient Greek philosopher Plato called the "examined life." The idea that living such a life is valuable in itself is shared by all those with an interest in philosophy. It is natural, therefore, that so many great philosophers have taken an interest in a phenomenon so pervasive and distinctively human as humor.

It is often said that nothing ruins a joke so much as the attempt to explain it. Despite this danger, a number of well-known figures from the history of philosophy have proposed *theories of humor*. That is to say, they have offered explanations of the nature of humor and the causes of the particular sort of amusement associated with humor. (One can be "amused" in nonhumorous ways, as when *amused* is used to refer to the opposite of *bored*. Throughout this chapter, *amusement* will refer specifically to the amusement we experience in response to a situation or event we find humorous or comic.) *Humor* is a general term that (in its usual sense) refers either to something intended to cause amusement or to whatever quality makes something amusing. The (intended) presence of humorous content explains what makes a literary or theatrical presentation a comedy; humor is the quality that is the common element in farces, satires, absurdities, jokes, witticisms, and anything else that may be found to be amusing. Humor and laughter are universal to human cultures. But what *is* humor? What is it that humorous or comic events have in common that makes them humorous or comic? Major philosophers have offered a surprising diversity of theories of humor. In his *Arg-*

ument of *Laughter*, D. H. Monro sorted these individual theories into three categories, corresponding to three basic views about humor. Following some contemporary philosophers, I shall call these the superiority theory, the incongruity theory, and the relief theory.

HISTORICAL THEORIES OF HUMOR

The superiority theory is the theory that the humor we find in comedy and in life is based on ridicule, wherein we regard the object of amusement as inferior and/or ourselves as superior. A number of major philosophers have expressed a view like this one. In Plato's dialogue *Philebus*, Socrates (Plato's teacher, who frequently appears as a character in Plato's works) takes a negative view of comedy and amusement along these lines. (Excerpts of Plato's work on humor, as well as excerpts of work by many of the figures mentioned in this chapter, are collected and discussed in John Morreall's *The Philosophy of Laughter and Humor*.) He explains that the object of laughter in comedy is the "ridiculous." The ridiculous, more specifically, is the self-ignorance of others when they falsely believe that they possess wisdom. In other words, laughter results from a feeling of pleasure at seeing others suffer the misfortune of being deluded about their own wisdom. Socrates argues, however, that the soul experiences both "pleasure and pain" when amused by the ridiculous portrayed in comedy: one can feel pleasure and laugh when presented by such fools in comedy, but to feel pleasure at others' misfortunes is to feel malice, which he considers a "pain of the soul." The laughter and pleasure, then, that we experience when enjoying comedy is mixed with malice and pain.

Another important negative thesis about comedy is expressed by Plato in his most famous dialogue, the *Republic*. In this dialogue Plato (through Socrates again) describes the education of an ideal caretaker class—the "guardians"—for the ideal society. The most important criterion for being a guardian is that one be ruled by reason, and so be in control of one's base desires and emotions. When those who hold power in society are ruled by base desire and emotion, they will make bad decisions and be tempted to abuse power. Socrates describes amusement leading to laughter as an emotion that leads to other violent emotions and loss of control over oneself. Therefore he maintains that guardians should not be "lovers of laughter." In the ideal society, then, any story or theatrical portrayal of persons or gods as "overcome by laughter" should be suppressed. This will prevent the young from thinking that losing control of one's emotions is a good thing.

Plato's student Aristotle maintains a similar line about amusement and laughter. In his dissertation on drama, the *Poetics*, he describes comedy as "an imitation of people who are worse than the average." The ridiculous portrayed in comedy, he continues, is a kind of ugliness at which we laugh derisively. Like Plato, Aristotle thinks of the amusement of comedy as essentially derisive: when enjoying comedy, we laugh at ugliness (if that ugliness is not painful or destructive to us in the given context). But his assessment of such amusement appears to be similar to Plato's: amusement is the malicious or derisive enjoyment of others' shortcomings, and indicates a baseness of the soul.

Aristotle also agrees with Plato about the possible drawbacks of excessive indulgence in humor. In the *Nicomachean Ethics* he explains that the best life is lived when one is ruled by reason. He does consider "relaxation and amusement as a necessary element in life," but carrying humor to excess is vulgar and improper. "A joke is a kind of abuse," and only jokes that abuse what is itself improper (i.e., satirical humor directed at irrationality) gain Aristotle's acceptance. Humor not in service to reason is of negative value: one who enjoys humor excessively is a "slave" to it. Persons rather ought to be in control of themselves and guide their behavior by reason.

Plato and Aristotle, while disagreeing on some issues, agree that virtue and the best kind of life come from being ruled by reason rather than by emotion and desire. They also agree that to indulge excessively in the enjoyment of humor is to be carried away by emotion at the mistakes of others. This emotion may seem pleasant, but really involves a kind of slavishness to certain baser parts of oneself. As a result we lose the ability to exercise rational control over our behavior. Twentieth-century philosopher of humor Morreall calls this the "Irrationality Objection" to humor ("The Rejection of Humor in Western Thought"). But he responds that amusement does not usually lead to a loss of control, as violent emotions like anger or fear can. There may be some temporary physical loss of control associated with great amusement, but such amusement does not incline one to act in particular ways, other than to laugh and relax.

The philosopher often regarded as making the strongest statement of the superiority theory is the seventeenth-century English political philosopher Thomas Hobbes. He observes in *Human Nature* that those who laugh often are the same as those who are "greedy of applause from every thing they do well" (qtd. in Morreall, *Philosophy* 20). He sees laughter as arising from joy, primarily from the feeling of one's own achievement or the realization of one's own ability. The realization of one's own superiority can be sparked by the presentation of the failings of others; when others are seen to be grossly incapable, one's own self-image is enhanced by comparison. For this reason we become joyous and are moved to laugh at the infirmities and absurdities of others.

This picture of humor seems justified when we consider that many examples of comic characters are objects of ridicule. Consider Aristophanes' Socrates in *The Clouds*, Shakespeare's Falstaff, or the Three Stooges. Our amusement in response to these characters seems to derive from their high degrees of incompetence, villainy, and/or emotional immaturity.

Hobbes concludes that "the passion of laughter is nothing else but sudden glory arising from some sudden conception of some eminency in ourselves" (qtd. in Morreall, *Philosophy* 20). Like Plato and Aristotle, then, Hobbes thinks that amusement is found primarily in that which is inferior to us; he adds that the joy we find in such evidence of others' weaknesses derives from the assurance we thereby receive regarding our own relative superiority. Like Plato and Aristotle, his view of humor is negative: he characterizes the experience of amusement as base and, further, unlikely to be conducive to social unity.

Hobbes' view of the primary cause of amused laughter receives support from C. R. Gruner's speculation about the physiological origin of the phenomenon of laughter, *Understanding Laughter: The Workings of Wit and Humor*. As Jon Roeckelein explains in *The Psychology of Humor*, Gruner imagines that our early ancestors, after defeating an opponent in violent combat, would bare their teeth and pump their shoulders (as a dominance display), and chop up their breath into grunts (thereby facilitating a return to homeostasis after exertion). If this sort of behavior is the ancestral origin of laughter, it would not be surprising to find that the essential object of humor is the inferiority of others, and the source of joy a sense of one's own supremacy. There is, after all, a great deal more laughter in the locker room of the victorious team than in that of the losers.

A number of theorists, however, have noted a serious weakness of the superiority theory: there seem to be many experiences that might make us feel superior but are not amusing. Eighteenth-century Scottish philosopher and minister Francis Hutcheson observed, in *Reflections upon Laughter*, that witnessing someone in pain puts us in "greater danger of weeping than laughing." Human suffering and degradation, mishaps and accidents are often anything but amusing. Furthermore, it is debatable that Plato, Aristotle, and Hobbes are right that humor in comedy is always, or even primarily, directed at the negative traits of others. There are many instances of humor that have nothing to do with the follies of others. The presence of some perceived inferiority, then, seems neither necessary nor sufficient for humor. So it has seemed to many that superiority theorists have missed the main issue in amused laughter and are focusing instead on an incidental characteristic of some humorous situations.

Partly in response to the superiority theory, some philosophers have proposed a radically different account of the comic. According to this theory, humor is found primarily in an intellectual recognition of an absurd incongruity between conflicting ideas or experiences. The incongruity theory has been embraced in different forms by Hutcheson, Immanuel Kant, Arthur Schopenhauer, Søren Kierkegaard, and Luigi Pirandello.

In support of his critique of Hobbes, Hutcheson offers a number of examples of situations that, while humorous, give rise to no feelings of superiority in ourselves. We might find amusing, for example, the following fanciful explanation of a pistol's failure to fire:

> But Pallas came in shape of rust,
> And 'twixt the spring and hammer thrust
> Her Gorgon shield, and made the cock
> Stand stiff, as 'twere transformed to stock.

He notes that simply stating that the pistol was too rusty to fire would not have been particularly amusing, even though this plain statement would give as much a feeling of superiority over the foiled assassin as the colorful description above. So some other quality of this description must be responsible for its humorousness. Hutcheson adds that we can also be made merry by observing "some ingenuity in dogs and monkeys, which comes near to some of our own arts," yet he can find no account whereupon this sort of merriment derives from some conclusion regarding superiority or inferiority (qtd. in Morreall, *Philosophy* 27, 29).

He goes on to say that most situations in which others suffer mishap or inability to cope are not considered humorous. "The enormous crime or grievous calamity of another" does not usually give rise to mirth. He concludes that it is not the inferiority of others, or our perceived superiority, that we find comic. According to Hutcheson, amusement derives from the intellectual recognition of an incongruity: "the cause of laughter is the bringing together of images which have contrary additional ideas, as well as some resemblance in the principal idea" (qtd. in Morreall, *Laughter* 32, 37). An incongruity is some sort of unusual or unexpected juxtaposition of events, objects, or ideas. The "greatest part" of humor is founded on the contrast of ideas of grandeur, dignity, sanctity, and the like with the experience of meanness and baseness. What amuses is the incongruity, rather then any incidental degradation of the object of amusement. This is evident when we consider examples in which there is humor based on wordplay or creative imagery, with no evidence of human inferiority. Even when we are amused by human folly or mishap, the true object of humor is not the inferiority of the victim. We may laugh at seeing a person of great gravity and dignity take a fall, but our enjoyment (insofar as we find the situation *humorous*) derives not from a resulting sense of our own superiority, but from the contrast between the victim's demeanor and his or her situation. The humor that is occasionally found in human error derives not from our sense of others' inferiority, but rather from our high opinion of humans as possessing wisdom that separates them from the animals: this opinion provides the contrast when mistakes are made. The laughter of ridicule is just one subspecies of laughter (and a low one at that).

Empirical evidence gives a lot of support to the view that humor and comedy derive from incongruity. Contemporary British scientist and humor theorist Richard Wiseman has been studying the psychology of jokes (see Friend). His work has included collecting and studying tens of thousands of jokes, and has even extended to competitions for the best joke ever created. He describes the four joke themes or archetypes that keep recurring: "There seem to be only about four jokes that come up all the time: someone trying to look clever and taking a pratfall; husbands and wives not being loving; doctors being insensitive about imminent death; and God making a mistake" (Friend 79). What is striking about this list is that each joke archetype is based on an incongruity between expectation and reality.

But what is enjoyable about such contrasts? Hutcheson suggests that incongruity provides enjoyment because it distracts from negative emotions, but beyond that he says little about the reason why there is humor in incongruity. The great eighteenth-century Prussian philosopher Immanuel Kant (in *Critique of Judgment*) agrees with Hutcheson that humor derives from an intellectual recognition of incongruity, but adds a curious physiological theory as to why we have a pleasant reaction to that intellectual recognition. According to Kant, we laugh at absurdities not because the intellect itself finds pleasure in that which frustrates it, but because the intellect's attempt to reconcile an absurd conjunction of ideas causes a physical response that we find pleasant. Kant (as translated in Morreall, *Philosophy* 48–49) focuses on jests as paradigm cases of humor and explains the response to the punchline:

It is remarkable that in all such cases the jest must contain something that is capable of deceiving for a moment. Hence, when the illusion is dissipated, the mind turns back to try it once again, and thus through a rapidly alternating tension and relaxation it is jerked back and put into a state of oscillation . . . to this sudden transposition of the mind, now to one now to another standpoint in order to contemplate its object, may correspond an alternating tension and relaxation of the elastic portions of our intestines which communicates itself to the diaphragm (like that which ticklish people feel). In connection with this the lungs expel the air at rapidly succeeding intervals, and thus bring about a movement beneficial to health; which alone, and not what precedes it in the mind, is the proper cause of the gratification in a thought that at bottom represents nothing.

A disturbance in our gut mirrors our intellectual confusion when we are confronted with irresolvable absurdity; this, of course, is laughter. We gain a pleasant feeling not from the intellectual confusion itself but from the physical motion it causes (as we might from vigorous exercise, or a massage). This feeling is amusement.

A recent offering from a neuroscientist suggests an evolutionary explanation for laughter that would support the Incongruity Theory. V. S. Ramachandran has theorized that laughter developed to indicate spurious threats. One part of the brain detects some anomaly, while another processes it and (when no threat is present) communicates back a "no threat" signal associated with laughter: "The main purpose of laughter may be to allow the individual to alert others in the social group (usually kin) that the detected anomaly is trivial, nothing to worry about" (qtd. in Friend 82).

The nineteenth-century German philosopher Schopenhauer (in *The World as Will and Idea*) also embraces the idea that humor lies in incongruity and frustrated intellectual expectation; however, he has a quite different explanation for the pleasure derived from absurdities. It is his view that we have two ways of grasping things: through abstract concepts and through sense-perception. He finds that amusement derives from a perceived conflict between thought and perception. In particular, laughter is the expression of the realization of an incongruity between one's intellectual expectation and what is perceived by the senses to be the case. He cites as an example the following epitaph of a doctor: "Here lies he like a hero, and those he has slain lie around him." The humor in this case arises from an incongruity between one's conception of a doctor as a preserver of life and the evidence that this doctor was responsible for the reverse. There is another incongruity between the concept of a hero, as we understand it, and the reality of this case: someone fits the description of an epic hero like Achilles, Beowulf, or Roland (someone who finally succumbs, having slain many), but the attempt to apply the *concept* of a hero to this person is frustrated by other *perceived* facts of the situation (the person in question was a doctor and his patients the victims).

Schopenhauer's theory as to why incongruity is often found pleasant diverges from Kant's in an important respect. According to Kant, there is no pleasure to be found in the contradiction of intellectual expectation itself: only intellectual frustration could result, and frustration is not a pleasant state in itself. Schopenhauer argues that, on some subconscious level, we are resentful of our higher intellectual faculties, so we are pleased when they are frustrated: laughter is the expression of a kind of pleasure that derives from seeing thought frustrated by perception when expectation is contradicted by reality. Why would this be pleasurable? Sense-perception is the medium of the present moment and of "direct satisfaction." Thought is the medium of concern for the past and future, and so is the vehicle for conscience, caution, and fear. Thought often opposes the senses by denying them the gratification of our immediate desires. For this reason, we are secretly delighted to see our intellect get its comeuppance when the intellect's expectations are frustrated by reality. In this way Schopenhauer ingeniously finds a cause of pleasure in the experience of absurdity itself, rather than in the physiological reaction to that experience.

The incongruity theory, in any of the above forms, has been subject to certain objections. Twentieth-century philosopher George Santayana (in *The Sense of Beauty*) notes that we laugh in situations that don't involve incongruity: we laugh in victory, in sympathy with others, or just at being tickled. He concludes that absurdity or conceptual contradiction is not a necessary element in amusement. Is incongruity a sufficient condition of amusement? Nineteenth-century Scottish psychologist and philosopher Alexander Bain produces an impressive list in *The Emotions and the Will* of incongruities that are not amusing:

A decrepit man under a heavy burden, five loaves and two fishes among a multitude, and all unfitness and gross disproportion; an instrument out of tune, a fly in ointment, snow in May, Archimedes studying geometry in a siege, and all discordant things; a wolf in sheep's clothing, a breach of bargain, and falsehood in general; the multitude taking the law into their own hands, and everything in the nature of disorder; a corpse at a feast, parental cruelty, filial ingratitude, and whatever is unnatural; the entire catalogue of the vanities given by Solomon, are all incongruous, but they cause feelings of pain, anger, sadness, loathing, rather than mirth. (Qtd. in Morreall, *Philosophy* 108)

In *The Physiology of Humor*, nineteenth-century philosopher, social reformer, and biological theorist Herbert Spencer cites Bain as an influence in spurring his own theory of humor, the relief theory. This theory—the last of the three major historical theories of humor—was thus developed in response to the incongruity theory. The relief theory is the view that humorous laughter is a manifestation of the release of nervous excitement or emotional tension. In making his case, Spencer focuses on an account of the physiological basis for the phenomenon of laughter. He notes a wide variety of ways in which the body stores excess nervous energy and releases it through physical activity. When we feel intense pain, an affected limb may move involuntarily, as the face contorts and we may vocalize our anguish. Joy and fear also are manifested physically. He argues that, in a similar way, laughter is a physical manifestation of the release of nervous energy.

Spencer agrees that laughter often occurs in contexts involving some humiliation of others, or upon experiencing some absurd incongruity. But, he claims, what characterizes *all* situations resulting in laughter is the release of some nervousness or emotion. He discusses the reaction of a theater audience watching an absorbing dramatic play. A climax is reached, in which the sympathetic hero and heroine have achieved a reconciliation after a painful misunderstanding; at this moment a tame kid goat wanders onto the stage, walks up to the lovers, and sniffs them as they embrace. The audience roars with laughter. While the actors are, in a way, put out by the incident, and there is a certain incongruity in having the goat on stage, Spencer argues that the audience's response is inexplicable on the hypothesis that amusement arises from witnessing the humiliation of others, or from an escape from intellectual order. Rather, what has happened here has to do with the nervous energy that has been built up by the drama. The energy has been channeled into a buildup of emotion, but now the arrival of the goat has checked the movement of energy by suddenly taking the audience out of its immersion in the drama. The audience's emotional energy has nowhere to go, so it is released in muscular movements. The release of tension tends to be pleasurable, so this muscular release is pleasant. Humiliation or incongruity may be occasions for laughter, but the release of nervous energy is the cause both of laughter and of the pleasant feeling accompanying it which we call amusement.

Bain had claimed that laughter is release from the serious: life in general is fraught with tension, fear, and negative emotion. Contact with triviality or vulgarity gives moments of relief from the chronic strain, thereby causing pleasure. The outpouring of built-up tension, Spencer adds, is the explanation for the physical phenomenon of laughter that accompanies such relief.

Sigmund Freud, the famous father of psychoanalysis, argues for a thesis about humor similar to that of Spencer. In his essay "Humor," Freud distinguishes "humor" (joking) from "the comic" (the absurd situation): when we laugh at the comic we are releasing pent-up energy that was summoned in order to do some cognitive processing of the situation. When we recognize the absurdity, we realize that the energy summoned for the sake of understanding the situation is unnecessary, and so we release it in laughter. As for Spencer, the saving of energy is the direct cause of the pleasant feeling associated with the comic. For Freud, the pleasure associated with the comic comes from the saving of energy required for thought. The pleasure associated with humor, on the other hand, arises from a saving of psychic energy that otherwise would have been spent either in emotion or the repressing of emotion. He describes the origin of the pleasure caused when one man hears another tell a joke:

He sees the other person in a situation which leads him to anticipate that the victim will show signs of some affect: he will get angry, complain, manifest pain, fear, horror, possibly even despair. The person who is watching or listening is prepared to follow his lead, and to call up the same emotions. But his anticipations are deceived; the other man does not display any affect—he makes a joke. It is from the saving of expenditure in feeling that the hearer derives the humorous satisfaction. (Qtd. in Morreall, *Philosophy* 112)

The most interesting question for Freud, however, is why we come up with humor in the first place—why, in other words, there exists the "humorous attitude." Just as Bain claimed, the answer is that we make jokes to avoid or redirect negative feelings deriving from the harsh reality of life. Humor is attractive to us because it represents "the triumph of narcissism, the ego's victorious assertion of its own invulnerability. It refuses to be hurt by the arrows of reality or to be compelled to suffer. It insists that it is impervious to wounds dealt by the outside world, in fact, that these are merely occasions for affording it pleasure" (qtd. in Morreall, *Philosophy* 113). His extreme example of the generation of humor in order to deflect suffering is the comment on the part of the prisoner being led to the gallows on a Monday, who observes: "Well, this is a good beginning to the week." According to Freud's theory of the unconscious, the impulse to create humor derives from "the pleasure principle," the primitive psychic mechanism that directs us to avoid or repress negative feelings and pursue pleasure. Since life is full of opportunities for suffering, the impulse to make jokes out of fear, conflict, or unhappiness is universal. In other words, for Freud all humor is, to some extent, gallows humor.

Modern evolutionary theory might offer some support to the relief theory. If humor functions as a relief valve for excess energy or negative emotions, it might provide a significant survival advantage. Human beings are usually safer and more prosperous in stable communities than when isolated. Yet human beings also have a tendency to anger and aggression. The relief theory argues that humor lessens tension levels; if so, individuals with an appreciation for humor have an advantage over those who don't, in that it will be easier for them to maintain community membership (Lefcourt). As systems of mutual cooperation and coordination of activities, communities confer a survival advantage on their members. So a good sense of humor is survival enhancing. The theory of natural selection would then predict that such a trait is likely to be pervasive among human beings.

Humor also can enhance community cohesion by functioning as an invitation to social interaction (Lefcourt). It can enhance community by acting as a binding agent: playful engagement in humorous activities is pleasant; so individuals who engage in these mutually pleasant activities will associate social interaction with pleasure, and hence be encouraged to spend more time together with others in their group. As Lefcourt points out, Charles Darwin (in *The Expression of Emotions in Man and Animals*), in fact, viewed humor primarily as a form of social communication.

If we conclude that a tendency to enjoy humor and comedy is a binding force for a society, then group-selection theory also provides an evolutionary explanation for the persistence of humor in human society. Group-selection theory (a variation on natural selection theory) is the theory that natural selection functions at the level of communities. A more unified community is more likely to coordinate activities and prosper, so that community is more likely to survive and grow. If humor functions as a relief valve for negative emotions and makes communities more stable, group-selection theory would predict the persistence of humor as a social and cultural aspect of human communities. In conjunction with group-selection theory, the relief theory would imply that, over time, we should expect an increase in both the distribution and population of communities with a good collective sense of humor.

RECENT AND CONTEMPORARY THEORIES OF HUMOR

Some twentieth-century and contemporary philosophers have offered thought-provoking updates on the major historical theories of humor. Among the most compelling and influential are those of Henri Bergson, John Morreall, and Ted Cohen.

Bergson presents the superiority theory in a rather different light from that of his predecessors in his influential essay *Laughter: An Essay on the Meaning of the Comic*. Bergson focuses on the social function of laughter and comedy. He thinks that there is one characteristic that all comic situations have in common: people are found to be comic, or in a comic situation, when they experience a sudden downfall, caused by their own "mechanical inelasticity." By this term Bergson means a certain rigidity of thought or habit, which exposes one to errors of behavior or mishaps. Laughter, he argues, is a kind of corrective to ways of thinking and acting that are detrimental to the greater good: we laugh at "a certain rigidity of body, mind, and character that society would still like to get rid of in order to obtain from its members the greatest possible degree of elasticity and sociability." One example is a person running along a street who trips and falls. The fall, Bergson says, is the result of "absentmindedness and a kind of physical obstinacy." He adds that, similarly, victims of practical jokes are funny because they approach a situation with certain expectations that are not subsequently met; again, a kind of inflexibility or force of habit leads them to a mishap. He also observes that comedies often play off the automatism of persons in the grip of a particular emotion, like jealousy. Echoing Plato in the *Philebus*, Bergson claims that "a comic character is generally comic in proportion to his ignorance of himself." Think of the proverbial person who is walking around with (unbeknownst to him) toilet paper stuck to the bottom of his shoe. Or—more directly to Bergson's point—consider Molière's miser, Harpagon, who doesn't realize that his obsession with wealth has drawbacks for him and others. Why does mechanical inflexibility and self-ignorance make a person an object of laughter? Bergson's answer is that flexibility of mind is required to live a successful life, and society is threatened by people who lack the willingness to continually adapt to one another as members of a community. The derisive laughter of others is painful, and so serves as a spur to change one's attitude. In this way, "laughter pursues a utilitarian aim of general improvement."

Bergson's theory is often regarded as falling into the superiority theory category, in that he agrees that amusement and laughter are primarily derisive and usually are directed at people demonstrating a certain kind of inferiority. However, his view is rather more upbeat with regard to the practice of appreciating the comic, since for him laughter and derision actually serve a positive societal purpose. For this reason he does not devalue or reject humor and laughter as Plato, Aristotle, and Hobbes do.

Another interesting aspect of his theory is the representation of amusement as a *cognitive* state, rather than as an *emotional* state: he states specifically that "the comic will come into being, it appears, whenever a group of men concentrate their attention on one of their number, imposing silence on their emotions and calling into play nothing but their intelligence." This represents another significant break from other proponents of the superiority theory, who represent the response to the comic as an emotional state. By representing amusement as a cognitive state, Bergson's theory has this much in common with most versions of the incongruity theory.

The claim that humor has to do with the development of a certain *cognitive flexibility* is also central to John Morreall's theory of humor (see his essay "A New Theory of Laughter" in *The Philosophy of Laughter and Humor*), even though Morreall's theory is actually a development of the incongruity theory. He notes that superiority theories like those of Plato, Aristotle, and Hobbes can't handle many cases of amused laughter: babies laugh at peek-a-boo, and adults might laugh at a magic trick or upon unexpectedly running into an old friend. Puns and sight gags in which physical laws are apparently broken give rise to amused laughter without inciting any feelings of "sudden glory" or superiority. So evidence of others' inferiority is not at all necessary for amused laughter. While a certain flexibility of thought is necessary to handle all these absurd or surprising situations with good humor, these kinds of situations do not necessarily involve some mechanical attitude or inflexibility on the part of the object of laughter. Thus Bergson's theory seems to fall short in accounting for many cases of humor as well.

The various versions of the relief theory fare no better, according to Morreall. Consider the quip, "My car can stop on a dime—and leave a nickel change." There are no negative feelings to be suppressed here, and no buildup of nervous tension, emotion, or intellectual energy that requires release. Many instances of joking or humorous experiences are like this—especially one-liners, which can be effective even when they have no buildup at all. Moreover, to respond that we laugh in general to relieve our everyday pain and suffering is not too convincing in light of the fact that very young children do more laughing than anyone, even though they usually have the least tension to release. While laughter can result in some stress relief, one might argue that adults tend to laugh more when they are relaxed. This is fundamentally inconsistent with what would be predicted by Bain, Spencer, and the relief theory.

Morreall favors, with some small refinement, the theory that says that the cause of "humorous amusement" is incongruity. He claims that instances of humor tend to involve some "cognitive shift," or psychological reorientation. Just as several proponents of the incongruity theory describe, such shifts take place when some intellectual expectation is frustrated by reality, or upon some unexpected or absurd juxtaposition of ideas and experiences. To be amusing, the shift itself needs to take place in a context that is not somehow threatening or painful to the amused person. Morreall's theory is that humorous amusement is the enjoyment of a pleasant cognitive shift, though this amusement is often boosted by a simultaneous affective pleasure (i.e., a pleasure deriving from a positive emotion). As he suggests, one advantage of his theory is that it would explain why children are so prone to laughter: for children, almost everything is new and unexpected.

Morreall needs to answer three questions in order to make this theory plausible:

- Why are some incongruous situations not amusing?
- How should we account for the fact that we sometimes do laugh for other reasons, such as triumph or relief?
- What explains our disposition to feel pleasure upon experiencing cognitive shifts?

Many situations that require a cognitive shift are not amusing because they are accompanied by negative emotions. As Morreall says, "If I opened my bathroom door to find a pumpkin in the bathtub, for example, I would probably laugh. But if I found a cougar in the tub, I would not laugh" ("New Theory" 130). Both situations involve incongruity, but one would not find the second pleasant if it gave rise to fear. We might laugh at the latter situation, however, if it was presented in a film, since there is no danger to the audience, and no real danger to the actors. Bain noted that, for example, a "corpse at a feast" and "parental cruelty" involve incongruity, but give rise to negative feelings instead of amusement. But this is perfectly consistent, Morreall would say, with the notion that incongruity gives rise to pleasant cognitive shifts that can at the same time be quite drowned out by negative emotion. Even a corpse at a feast, or parental cruelty, can be humorous when presented in a nonthreatening light (such humor is sometimes referred to as "dark" or "black" humor): a corpse at a feast was a source of humor in *The Rocky Horror Picture Show*, and violence directed toward an abandoned child was the central theme of the *Home Alone* movies. These situations are presented without negative consequences for the viewer, and in each case the presentation is such that negative emotions (such as fear or pity) are not aroused.

Morreall is the first to agree that we may laugh out of triumph, and that we may laugh upon experiencing relief from powerful emotion. But it is a big jump, he says, to conclude that laughter just expresses derision or the release of nervous energy. Even when we laugh under such circumstances, the situation in question usually includes a sudden cognitive shift of some kind. Given that all instances of humor do seem to involve such a sudden intellectual reorientation, he thinks it is more plausible to say that humor is the enjoyment of the cognitive shift, which can be greatly enhanced by a pleasant affective shift. He offers as an example someone laughing upon seeing a character in a film accidentally lean against the lever of a slot machine and hit the jackpot; he observes that the laughter would likely be greatly enhanced if one were to do the same thing oneself. But in the latter case the laughter is merely enhanced by the accompanying feelings; the absurdity of accidentally achieving something so unlikely remains the real object of humorous amusement.

Another example of laughter is mean, barking, derisive laughter over the broken body of a beaten enemy (a paradigm case of laughter for Hobbes). Perhaps this should not be called "laughter" at all, but rather a vocalization similar to laughter, meant to communicate dominance. What about the laughter of relief or release? Laughter purely from relief (say, after finding out one is being released from prison) would appear to derive from a release of nervous tension of some kind, but it wouldn't really be directed at anything that is actually found humorous. So such laughter is not really related to *amusement*.

As to why the cognitive response to absurdity or incongruity might be pleasurable, Morreall has his own evolutionary account, "Funny Ha-Ha, Funny Strange, and Other Reactions to Incongruity." Understanding incongruity as "deviations from the way things are supposed to be" (*Philosophy* 190) Morreall argues that several responses to incongruity are survival enhancing. Negative emotion, like fear or distress, is an appropriate response to situations in which a sudden danger or pain disrupts the normal order of things. Without this response, we would be much more likely to succumb to threats to our continued existence. Puzzlement at the strange, or "reality assimilation," is an appropriate response to other nonthreatening, anomalous situations since it spurs us to orient ourselves in ways that are likely to help us pursue our goals more effectively. Our curiosity impels us to solve puzzles about our experience; this leads to a better understanding of the world around us, thereby putting us in a better position to satisfy our needs. In practice this impulsion is applied to many areas of life (and sometimes even can be dangerous), but its survival-enhancing effects are clear.

Both the negative affective response to dangerous or painful situations and the puzzled response to unfamiliar situations contribute to the resolution of anomalous situations, usually to our benefit. Morreall thinks that the amusement we often find in incongruity is explained by the benefits of anomaly-resolution: "The survival value of our seeking variety in our cognitive input is that it makes us curious, exploring creatures, and thus motivates us to know our environment better. Improved knowledge of our environment, of course, enhances our ability to cope with it and so to survive." So creatures who naturally take pleasure in trivial novelties, anomalies, and incongruities, and who thus crave varied, nonthreatening stimulation, have a survival advantage: they thereby will tend to be more adaptable in nontrivial anomalous circumstances that threaten survival or procreation. The young of many species of animals engage in play fighting and play hunting; this prepares them for more serious challenges ahead. The situation is much the same, according to Morreall, with regard to the appreciation of humor in human beings. Humor is explained by human beings' special conceptual abilities. The pursuit of humor represents a kind of play that contributes to conceptual flexibility. The feeling of enjoyment associated with this kind of play is amusement.

This explains why Morreall ("Rejection of Humor" 249–55) disputes the "Irrationality Objection" to humor associated with Plato and Aristotle. Not only does indulgence in humor not lead to irrational behavior, it actually helps sharpen our ability to respond to cognitively challenging situations. This would also explain why adults tend to demand more clever and subtle humor than children do: one needs humor of increasing subtlety and complexity in order to challenge one's cognitive flexibility, and humor can only be *funny* when it does this.

Morreall's view of the benefits (and the harmlessness) of a good sense of humor also explains his rejection of what he calls the "Irresponsibility Objection" to humor in Western thought ("Rejection of Humor"). He sees a strong line of thought in the Western tradition rejecting indulgence in humor as ethically objectionable. The ancients thought a tendency to indulge in humor is a negative characteristic because it is a nonserious attitude, which is not conducive to solving problems. When confronted with a problem, laughing at it is not going to contribute to solving it, and so indulgence in amusement might be thought to be irresponsible. As Morreall notes, the Judeo-Christian religious tradition rejects a nonserious, jocular attitude: the Bible says, "The fool lifts up his voice with laughter, but the wise man scarcely smiles a little" (Ecclesiastes 7:4). It is possible that the Christian rejection of humor arises from the ascetic and puritan elements of that tradition; these elements regard with antipathy any form of physical arousal. Morreall, however, considers humor harmless in most cases and beneficial to problem-solving abilities. Furthermore, the kind of arousal (in his view) essential to humor is cognitive, not physical.

This theory incorporates an important idea of Bergson's: namely, that humor has to do with the development of a kind of cognitive flexibility. Morreall claims, however, that the survival and relief theories focus on incidental benefits of the enjoyment of humorous situations. Sometimes there are personal emotional and social benefits of expressing superiority over others. The individual may receive an emotional boost, and may also gain in social status in some circumstances. There may be some benefit to society from the tendency to laugh at others' inflexibility. Laughter certainly can serve to relieve nervous tension as well. The tendency to enjoy humor can confer a survival advantage by checking anger and aggression and enhancing social communication. These advantages give the human tendency to laughter a boost; however, if Morreall is right, they represent occasional side-benefits of humor rather than the real explanation of it.

While Morreall's update of the incongruity theory is probably the most successful (or the least flawed) theory of humor to date, it still falls far short of giving a complete explanation of the phenomenon. As any struggling stand-up comedian knows, many cognitively incongruous statements and experiences, even though they do *not* give rise to negative emotions, are merely puzzling, confusing, nonsensical, or just not funny. Why are some incongruous experiences amusing and not others? A recent offering by philosopher of aesthetics Ted Cohen addresses this question ("Humor"). He agrees with the incongruity theory and adds his own view of why incongruity should be humorous: his is a kind of double-aspect theory that relates experiences of incongruity to feelings of power and to feelings of powerlessness. According to Cohen "anomalous" experiences (unexpected experiences of absurdly incongruous juxtapositions of events, things, or ideas) can be pleasant in two respects. Anomaly is pleasant when it provides a sense of power and freedom. It also can be pleasant when it inspires a mood of willing acceptance of one's own powerlessness. Amusement, according to Cohen, can represent either of these two kinds of pleasant response to incongruity.

When does humor give one a sense of power? Wordplay and wit, for example, provide a sense of having "the power to free oneself from the normal strictures of language." Other varieties of humor involve analogous declarations of independence: "More generally, the humor of anomaly regularly involves the placement and action of things—including people—in circumstances not regularly permitted by society or by nature. This is, perhaps, the humor of *freedom*. It is our freedom, at least in imagination, from the linguistic, social, cultural and natural constraints that are the inhibitions of our normal lives" (Cohen 380). In a certain respect this conception of humor echoes that of Schopenhauer, who argued that amusement is the rebellious pleasure of the perceptive, instinctive part of our psyche when the rational and controlling part of the psyche is frustrated by incongruous experience. While Schopenhauer claimed that humor is a rebellion against internal constraint, Cohen finds that humor can be a kind of rebellion against external constraints.

Cohen adds that there is another important kind of humor. When a situation is so extreme as to be incomprehensible, one can find a different humor in the resulting sense of powerlessness. One can experience "a mood of acceptance, of willing acknowledgement of those aspects of life that can be neither subdued nor fully comprehended" (380). His double-aspect theory of humor makes it both "the province of the powerful and of the powerless." It also explains why it is so hard to predict what is funny: while humor arises from incongruity, it can reflect a sense of either strength or weakness.

Cohen's theory that a large part of humor is essentially tied to a sense of freedom approaches very closely some of Morreall's comments: for Morreall, humor is *conceptually liberating* because it frees us from established ways of thinking. Further, humor for Morreall is *practically liberating*, in that it gives us a sense of distance from worldly concerns. He discusses the characteristic humor of Zen Buddhism and argues that its role is to foster a sense of disengagement—to "liberate ourselves from attachment" ("Rejection of Humor" 258–62).

Although Cohen's theory focuses on humor as a response to anomaly or incongruity, it could be extended to accommodate some themes of the superiority and relief theories. As Cohen notes, his view that the humorous response can derive from a feeling of power to free oneself from constraint is not too far from Hobbes' view that humor usually involves a feeling of power over another. The release of nervous tension could also result in a certain feeling of freedom from that tension; from this perspective, the relief theory also relates humor to a feeling of freedom.

Cohen's theory thus provides a thought-provoking twist on the incongruity theory of humor while partly incorporating aspects of the superiority and relief theories as well. If he is right that humor is tied essentially either to a feeling of freedom from external constraint or to a good-natured acceptance of powerlessness, then the humor of traditionally oppressed communities might be considered paradigm manifestations of humor. Jewish humor, for example, is widely considered a genre of humor unto itself and is associated with a religious and cultural tradition that has historically suffered a great deal of persecution. As an extreme example of humor in the face of powerlessness, consider the following example of World War II–era Jewish humor: "Two Jews meet in Warsaw and one of them is eating perfumed soap. The other asks: 'Moyshe, why are you eating soap with such a scent?' He answers: 'If they turn me into soap, I might as well smell nice' " (Ostrower). For a striking example of humor used literally in a rebellion against constraint, consider sociologist Anton Obrdlik's description of the resistance of native Czechoslovakians during the Nazi occupation in " 'Gallows Humor': A Sociological Phenomenon." Czechs began surreptitiously painting walls with jokes directed at the occupiers. Despite their attempts to erase the graffiti and suppress the practice, the Nazis were demoralized, while the Czechs experienced a significant boost in morale (Lefcourt). If Cohen is right, these are not just examples of humor but, indeed, examples of the employment of humor in its truest form.

Any theory of humor is bound to be general, since it must incorporate a wide variety of phenomena under one theory. There are still a number of situations involving *laughter* that are not captured by any theory described above, such as laughter at being tickled or the objectless laughter of a lunatic. But we don't tend to call these instances of laughter in response to *humor*. Only some of the theories discussed above seem general enough to explain our responses to many or most situations we commonly call "humorous." However, each of the theories is at least a thought-provoking contribution to our understanding of some puzzling and important human behavior.

There is still a lot of room for a better understanding of humor. It remains unclear whether any existing theory—or combination of theories—can adequately explain all instances of humor. Humor theory is an interdisciplinary field that demands contributions from cultural studies, history, sociology, psychology, neuroscience, and evolutionary biology, among others. The complexity of the problem makes philosophy an ideal locus for the study of humor. Philosophy is inherently interdisciplinary since it is by definition simply the activity of critical reflection on what we know and on the meanings of the concepts we use. Areas of applied philosophy (such as the philosophy of art or humor) function as environments in which theories can be nourished by ideas from different disciplines. Receptive to data of all kinds, philosophers critically examine and interpret what we learn in light of their particular reflections on some of the cognitive, emotional, and social aspects of being human.

REFERENCES AND FURTHER READINGS

Bain, Alexander. *The Emotions and the Will.* 3rd ed. London: Longmans and Green, 1875.

Bergson, Henri. *Laughter: An Essay on the Meaning of the Comic.* Trans. Cloudesley Brereton and Fred Rothwell. New York: Macmillan, 1911.

Cohen, Ted. "Humor." *The Routledge Companion to Aesthetics.* London: Routledge, 2001. 375–81.

Freud, Sigmund. "Humor." Trans. Joan Rivière. *International Journal of Psychoanalysis* 9 (1928).

———. *Jokes and Their Relation to the Unconscious.* Trans. and ed. James Strachey. Harmondsworth: Penguin, 1976.

Friend, Tad. "What's So Funny?" *New Yorker* 11 Nov. 2002: 78–93.

Hutcheson, Francis. *Reflections upon Laughter.* Glasgow, 1750.

Kant, Immanuel. *Critique of Judgment.* Trans. J. H. Bernard. London: Macmillan, 1892.

Lefcourt, Herbert. *Humor: The Psychology of Living Buoyantly.* New York: Kluwer Academic-Plenum, 2001.

Morreall, John. *The Philosophy of Laughter and Humor.* Albany: State U of New York P, 1987.

———. "The Rejection of Humor in Western Thought." *Philosophy East and West* 39 (1989): 243–65.

———. *Taking Laughter Seriously.* Albany: State U of New York P, 1983.

Ostrower, Chaya. "Humor as a Defense Mechanism in the Holocaust." Ph.D. diss., Tel Aviv University, 2000.

Pirandello, Luigi. *On Humor.* Trans. Antonio Illiano and Daniel Testa. Chapel Hill: U of North Carolina P, 1960.

Ramachandran, V. S., and Sandra Blakeslee. *Phantoms in the Brain.* New York: William Morrow, 1998.

Roeckelein, Jon. *The Psychology of Humor: A Reference Guide and Annotated Bibliography.* Westport, CT: Greenwood, 2002.

Schopenhauer, Arthur. *The World as Will and Idea.* 6th ed. Trans R. B. Haldane and John Kemp. London: Routledge and Kegan Paul, 1909.

31

Queer Comedy

Ken Feil

Humor is not resigned, it is rebellious. It signifies the triumph of the pleasure principle, which is strong enough to assert itself here in the face of adverse real circumstances.... Its meaning is: "Look here! This is all that this seemingly dangerous world amounts to. Child's play—the very thing to jest about!"
—Sigmund Freud, "Humor"

[Camp] is however always, and at whatever cost, a cry against conformity, a shriek against boredom, a testament to the potential uniqueness of each of us and our rights to that uniqueness.

It should not be forgotten . . . that when, in Greenwich Village, for the first time and without precedent, a group of effeminate little queens refused to accept the police's casual invasion of one of their bars, they repelled them, not with knuckledusters or karate blows, but with hand-bags!
—George Melly, discussing camp and its relation to the 1969 Stonewall riots that sparked the Gay Liberation Movement

Queer comedy is inextricable from the practice of camp sensibility. Through camp humor, queers have constructed a cultural identity using the very objects and forms that ostensibly efface our presence. As Jack Babuscio puts it in his now classic essay, "Camp and the Gay Sensibility," "Humor constitutes the strategy of camp: a means of dealing with a hostile environment and, in the process, of defining a positive identity" (47). Camp humor arises when queer audience members or artists realize that the manifest culture and its texts render them deviant (in the form of a stereotype) or invisible. Appropriating the power of meaning-making, queer camp humor rejects the finality of content and makes the text signify "queerness" through an ironic interpretation of mainstream conventions. Thus, camp humor renders mass culture and other elements of mainstream life contrived, constructed, theatrical. If, in camp, "the line separating being and role-playing becomes blurred," this occurs self-consciously, as a means for criticizing and remaking the "theatre" of social roles that ostensibly oppress us (Babuscio 43). As a creative aesthetic, camp has informed drag performance (e.g., the work of Divine, RuPaul, and Madonna), the graphic arts (e.g., Andy Warhol's pop art), queer satires and parodies (e.g., Oscar Wilde's *The Importance of Being Earnest* and Paul Rudnick's *Addams Family Values*), as well as political activism (e.g., the political art and theatricals of ACT UP/the Aids Coalition to Unleash Power and Queer Nation).

Queer camp strategies have been in practice in the United States since at least the early 1900s, when drag balls were a regular, popular event in New York City (Chauncey 291–99). In the late 1940s, the reorganization of cities due to urban migration and the post–World War II economic boom led to the development of lesbian and gay urban enclaves or ghettos (d'Emilio 225–35; Faderman 118–38). There, camp sensibilities and practices could proliferate. In the late 1960s, lesbians and gay men formed liberation movements. As the epigraph from George Melly shows, camp flamboyance played a vital role in the assertion of queer independence from oppressive laws and moral beliefs. While some queers who sought to assimilate into the norm have felt that "camping" in public seemed too confrontational, nonetheless, camp has remained a common queer cultural practice, in terms of personal pleasure, artistic production, and as an activist strategy.

CAMP STYLE

All deliberately camp works use irony toward largely comedic ends. Camp irony informs four other conventions of camp style: (1) pastiche, (2) trash, (3) masquerade, and (4) displeasure. The execution and meaning of each category can be related to various forms of camp reading and performance.

Pastiche is camp's primary activity. It involves the use of objects, personalities, and references that bear cultural significance outside of the work at hand. This poses a tension between the dominant or accepted meanings of these pastiche objects or references and the new contexts formed by using them within the camp work of art (Ross 151). That tension yields camp pleasure by exploiting the object for ironic effect and remaking the object's meaning. Both Andrew Ross and Mark Booth stress that camp's pastiche project functions by placing objects or texts whose styles have been historically or socially marginalized within the current cultural context (Ross 146–47; Booth 18). *Trash*, the second camp convention, refers to the cultural value given to a particular pastiche object or activity. In *Women on the Verge of a Nervous Breakdown* (1989), written and directed by the openly gay Spanish filmmaker Pedro Almodóvar, the pastiche of 1960s fashion comprises the trash leitmotif for the character Lucía.

Lucía wears large bouffant wigs, miniskirts, go-go boots, lampshade hats, and heavy eyeliner. Having just returned from a mental hospital after twenty years' confinement, she dons the same clothes and accessories she wore before her breakdown. Her mother remarks that she should have thrown them away. Lucía replies, "I like wearing them. It's as if time stood still." She is perfectly aware that time has not stood still, and that these fashions are absurdly out of date. Yet the associations that she makes between this look and the lover whose flight predicated her breakdown transform the value of this retro fashion. She lives in the past by embodying it, resembling Charles Dickens' Miss Havisham, from *Great Expectations*, who wears her wedding gown and preserves the wedding table and cake from the day her fiancé jilted her. Lucía is a Miss Havisham for the camp generation, whose pathos is fundamentally ironic. Her adherence to this trashy fashion, coupled with her lack of self-pity and aggressive undertakings for revenge (she hijacks a motorcycle and attempts to assassinate her selfish ex-lover), discourage a reading of her as simply a victim of masculine abuse, or fashion abuse. Thus, the use of trash in this film bears ambiguous connotations for the character's status within the narrative.

The autobiographical video work of Sadie Benning, a young dyke from Milwaukee who began making her video art at age fifteen, in her bedroom, with a Fisher-Price Pixelvision camera, offers many examples of camp pastiche and trash. Benning's video work exults in extended pastiches of the fragments and detritus of mass culture: domestic objects, Hollywood "woman's films" and horror films, TV news, B movies, antiquated science books, old newspapers, popular and underground music. As film critic B. Ruby Rich states, "With an absolute economy of means, Benning constructed a *Portrait of the Artist as a Young Dyke* such as we've never seen before" (34).

In her video *It Wasn't Love* (1992), Benning continues her exploration of lesbian identity in the story of a young girl's erotic adventures with a fugitive butch dyke (both of whom are "played" by Benning). Benning inserts a series of scenes from the Hollywood film *The Bad Seed* (1956), the story of a "perfect" little girl named Rhoda: blond, sweet, smart, and homicidal. Benning intercuts the clips from *The Bad Seed* with her own footage, a personal narrative (or fantasy) of erotic and illegal doings. By juxtaposing such incongruous scenes of illicit behavior, Benning parodies demonizing stereotypes of lesbian identity as well as normative stereotypes of "ideal" femininity. Campy elements of incongruity and irony arise at the very beginning of the clip from *The Bad Seed*, when Rhoda's hysterically emphatic admission of murder cuts to a smiling, fatherly white man saying, "Now there's a little ray of sunshine, that one." In another clip from *The Bad Seed* in *It Wasn't Love*, prepubescent Rhoda seductively caresses her mother's face and says, "I wanna play the way we used to, mommy. Please play with me." This gesture of nostalgic intimacy cannot conceal Rhoda's hidden or latent "evil." Benning shows how Rhoda is a prepubescent variant of the "killer-lesbian" stereotype. The normative horrors inspired by the killer-lesbian stereotype (especially in a film such as *Basic Instinct*) relate to the killer's masquerade behind an image of "normal" femininity. Here, lesbian desire translates into a hidden desire that is indistinguishable from evil. However, in the context of Benning's transgressive fantasy about a bored teenage girl fleeing suburbia with a fugitive dyke, she besmirches the stereotype of "the sweet little white girl" (as Benning calls it) and eroticizes the horrific elements of the lesbian killer stereotype. Through a pastiche of trash culture, the filmmaker transforms the elements of "normality" and "horror" into an in-your-face posture of dyke pride, pleasure, and fantasy.

Benning's autobiographical fantasies correspond to what Susan Sontag calls, in "Notes on Camp," "the theatricalization of experience embodied in the Camp sensibility" (286). This pertains to the camp convention of the *masquerade*, when characters or personalities portray a role *as a role*. The narrative can present this opportunity, as in *La Cage aux Folles* (1979), where the drag queen Albin, in dire circumstances, masquerades as a housewife for the conservative commissioner of moral order. Or the masquerade might be something that informs an individual's entire performance (e.g., Benning playing both the girl and her fugitive lover in *It Wasn't Love*, or rock star Madonna's play with masculine and feminine fetishes, styles, and postures).

A drag act, for instance, can be considered campy masquerade wherein a performer impersonates a famous person or popular type of the opposite gender, a person or type defined in large part by her/his gender and sexuality (e.g., Bette Davis, Mae West, or Elvis Presley). By choosing to imitate a celebrity whose gender contrasts with that of the performer, the performer can systematically call attention to the very *performance of gender itself*. Based upon interviews with a number of drag queens in the late 1960s and early 1970s, anthropologist Esther Newton observes, "By focusing on the outward appearance of role, drag implies that sex role and, by extension, role in general is something superficial, which can be manipulated, put on and off again at will" (49). For queers, the questioning of assumed-to-be-natural gender roles is paramount, particularly because queer desires do not correspond to traditional gender categories. Lesbian comic Lily Tomlin's extra-cool crooner with a pompadour comes to mind. Here, Tomlin *performs* the gestures and appearance of a figure whose reputation in mass culture derives from its particular embodiment of raw, masculine sex appeal, such as Elvis, and calls comic attention to the very surface characteristics of that figure.

Before the gay and lesbian liberation movements of the late 1960s and 1970s, the camp masquerade served a strategic purpose: to conceal one's forbidden desires as well as transmit them to other queers. Andrea Weiss observes how, in the 1930s, the star images of Greta Garbo and Marlene Dietrich initially developed in part through lesbian codes of dress and bearing that might not have been legible to mainstream audiences. While either star's sexual ambiguity might have titillated many a viewer, filmgoers abreast of lesbian urban culture could have concluded that Dietrich's tuxedo drag in *Morocco* (1930) or Garbo's butch queen (as in royalty) in *Queen Christina* (1933) signified lesbianism. Gossip networks among lesbian filmgoers spread the word about the meanings of these cultural codes, along with stories about the stars' homosexual love lives that were, needless to say, never included in press coverage and publicity materials. Weiss also suggests that Garbo and Dietrich knew that they were "flaunting it" in public for the pleasurable recognition of certain viewers (286–98).

The masquerade can also apply to an entire work. For instance, the naively camp quality of a rigidly moralistic propaganda film such as *Red Nightmare* (1962) stems from its failed masquerade, its obvious constructedness: the unilateral seriousness of the subject matter, the self-consciously didactic and dogmatic script, and the wooden acting styles. These elements combine to expose the film's masquerade, the failed attempt to fool the viewer into suspending disbelief and believing the propagandistic message. Intentionally camp films such as *Moulin Rouge* (2001) are conceived on the level of pure style and theatricality, making no attempt to mask their artifice.

The category *displeasure* specifically concerns the relationship between form and feeling. Booth indicates that tedium provides both a motivation for camp, as well as a strategy (67). Melly also characterizes camp as "a cry against conformity, a shriek against boredom" (6). As a motivation, painful boredom with status quo culture inspires the camp imagination, the activity of reading or creating cultural texts and objects against the intentions of the dominant. These "intentions" correspond to the sanctioned rules for both making art and engaging with it. Thus tedium inspires the creation of nontraditional pleasures that might be perceived by the dominant as unpleasurable or, as Sontag puts it, "excruciating" (287). John Waters' queer camp aesthetic of absurdly excessive violence and "gross" behavior qualifies as an example. Consider Waters' *Female Trouble* (1974), in which the late, great drag queen Divine plays Dawn Davenport, whose ascension to stardom consists of gleefully gunning down the spectators of her performance art show. The film concludes with an excessive coda, showing Dawn's execution in the electric chair. More recently, Waters' *Cecil B. Demented* (2000) concerns the title character's utter frustration with mainstream movies, to the point that he forms a prototerrorist, guerrilla film crew, highjacks a Hollywood premier, and kidnaps a movie star.

Both films confuse the notions of comedy and pathology in their portrayals of alternative pleasures. Whereas Bertolt Brecht's *Threepenny Opera* strategically compares the character Macheath's "sexual obsessiveness" with the obsession for money and power, Waters offers no psychosocial reasons for his characters' outrageousness, nor a clear moral to rationalize these shocking performances. Thus, his films challenge spectators to redefine their notions of pleasure, or to remain entrenched in dominant definitions and be shocked by the excess, or both.

Camp always involves the comedic convention of surprise, moments when the work dissolves the continuity between what is expected and what is delivered (see Neale and Krutnick). Camp works of art that self-consciously play with particular cultural categories, such as man/woman or gay/straight, rend the apparent naturalness of these categories (Babuscio, 41). Pastiche collects and juxtaposes objects, personalities, and textual references. The masquerade enlivens these objects by actively playing with them. Trash and tedium reevaluate the value and pleasure of the pastiche collection.

QUEER CAMP AND COMEDY

In her germinal "Notes on Camp," Sontag articulates the relation between camp and comedy quite directly:

The whole point of Camp is to dethrone the serious. Camp is playful, anti-serious. More precisely, Camp involves a new, more complex relation to "the serious." One can be serious about the frivolous, frivolous about the serious. . . . Camp proposes a comic vision of the world. But not a bitter or polemical comedy. If tragedy is an experience of hyperinvolvement, comedy is an experience of underinvolvement, of detachment. (288)

Sontag's emphasis here on comic detachment should not conceal the serious elements of camp that, as Sontag puts it, are treated with frivolity. The seriousness of camp relates to, in part, the experience of being queer in a society that normalizes bourgeois heterosexuality and punishes differences from that norm. Thus camp incites a process of calling into question many related sociocultural hierarchies: high versus low, serious versus frivolous, masculine versus feminine, heterosexual versus queer. According to Jonathan Dollimore, camp "negotiates some of the lived contradictions of subordination, simultaneously refashioning as a weapon of attack an oppressive identity inherited *as* subordination" (311). Because camp is as much a confrontation of cultural politics as of the social, it negotiates queer marginalization through the lens of high/low value. Indeed, camp transforms the meanings of "low" cultural taste as a strategy to redefine the "low" social identity of queerness. The pleasures of this transformation solidify both the comedy of queer camp and its sincere social motivations.

Freud's model of humor opens up the radical pleasures of queer camp, based upon the "triumph of narcissism [against] the arrows of reality" (265). The party responsible for shooting those arrows is none other than the superego, the agency that represents the internalization of the dominant culture's value systems. The superego "often holds the ego in strict subordination, and still actually treats it as the parents (or the father) treated the child in his early years" (266). Freud differentiates wit from humor by indicating that wit involves the assumption of the paternal function in order to subordinate someone else through mockery (266). This gratifies the joker as "an outlet for aggressive tendencies" (265). Humor, on the other hand, involves the subject's internalization of both parental and infantile roles, mocking her/himself through this process (266). While this may involve self-denigration, Freud focuses upon the phenomenon of altering the function of the superego so that it "is in fact repudiating reality and serving an illusion" (268). Thus humor, according to Freud, incites a remaking of the function of the superego, becoming an agency of pleasure and pride, allowing the ego to gratify itself through self-irony. Camp self-irony acts as, in Sontag's words, "a solvent of morality. It neutralizes moral indignation, sponsors playfulness" (290).

This need not remain within the individual struggle between the ego and superego but can also apply to the social manifestations of these agencies. Queer camp both encourages the mockery of dominant culture and the spectator's identification with the camp object. By identifying with the object, the camp spectator redefines its meaning, making it signify queerness. The pleasure of this process derives, in part, from the irony involved: This low object represents me, and because of that it is no longer low. But everyone else thinks that it is, so I am going to expose the value and power of this object and me, confounding everyone! As Freud observes, "Humor is not resigned; it is rebellious. It signifies the triumph not only of the ego, but also the pleasure principle, which is strong enough to assert itself here in the face of adverse real circumstances" (265). By redefining the superego so that it serves as an agency of pleasure and not policing, a means of gratifying the ego rather than deflating it, the humorist rebels against the societal rules and codes that constructed the dichotomy between pleasure and morality in the first place.

In implicit compliance with Freud's terms, Booth accounts for the general conditions that motivate camp humor when he says, *"To be camp is to present oneself as being committed to the marginal with a commitment greater than the marginal merits"* (18; emphasis in original). He goes on to explain:

The primary type of the marginal in society is the traditionally feminine, which camp parodies in an exhibition of stylized effeminacy. In the extent of its commitment, such parody informs the camp person's whole personality, throwing an ironical light not only on the abstract concept of the sexual stereotype, but also on the parodist him or herself. (18)

Here Booth distills some of the fundamental issues of camp: the identification with the cultural and social margins, the emphasis on androgyny, the parodic attack on sexist stereotypes, and the self-parodic playfulness that underpins the camper's whole attitude.

Camp can be divided into two forms: spectatorship (watching movies, plays, television, etc.) and artistic production. Both forms of camp articulate estrangement within the status quo culture and a corresponding desire to remake the assumptions and representations of mainstream culture. As art critic Jonathan Weinberg articulates the question, "why is one thing money and the other thing shit, why is one kind of work art and another just production?" (51). David Bergman's comment that camp "is not trivial, but a reaction to trivialization" (118) implies how identifying with cultural "shit"

tion of homophobic laws, medical theories, and social conventions. The shift in queer relations with dominant culture, the transition from out of the oppressive closet to open resistance, and the formation of liberated queer communities altered ideas about homosexuality in the post-Stonewall era (d'Emilio 226–38).

In the late 1980s and into the 1990s, queer activist groups thoroughly appropriated camp as an activist strategy. For ACT UP (the AIDS Coalition to Unleash Power), the use of puns to alter cliché phrases (e.g., "Curb your dogma!") and the use of old photographs and popular commercial graphics combined in their AIDS protests (see Crimp and Rolston). ACT UP's activist art used commercial graphics and nostalgia photos as well as the formal language of advertising, constituting a form of camp. For instance, Gran Fury (one of ACT UP's art collectives) imitated a Benetton advertisement but using predominantly same-sex couples in passionate embraces. The caption reads "Kissing Doesn't Kill: Greed and Indifference Do" (Crimp and Rolston 19). In two announcements for a kiss-in protest rally, antique photographs of two male sailors in a passionate embrace and two flapper women staring ardently at each other provide pastiche backgrounds. Queer spectators of this art witness the literal remaking of dominant culture as well as the invocation for acting as participants in undoing and remaking an oppressive social condition. In a new variation on camp irony, the liberating and rebellious humor of "queering" mainstream culture combines with a serious call for political awareness and action. Thus while contemporary queer camp is still predicated upon a sense of cultural distance and invisibility, the presence of real queer communities and manifest political struggles and victories radically alters its meanings. Unlike preliberation gay and lesbian culture, contemporary queer culture contains material that queers can *openly identify with*.

As discussed through Freud's theory of humor, camp involves a queer parody of dominant culture's deficiencies. This project amounts to a rebellious type of pleasure because it stresses the triumph of queerness against the limitations of the social world. Queer camp involves a send-up of the dominant culture's value systems and definitions by ironically juxtaposing the mainstream to post-Stonewall queer culture. This dynamic reaffirms the reality of pride, liberation, and autonomy.

SNAP! Time

Marlon Riggs' documentary video *Tongues Untied* (1990) is an alternately funny and serious, autobiographical and broadly sociocultural documentary about black gay life in the United States in the era of AIDS and Reaganism (see Mercer, Nero, Riggs, and Smith). The video produces both the humor and the confrontation of queer camp while also addressing some of the deficiencies of the camp tradition. Camp is normative to the extent that its parodic meanings are seemingly only explicable in the context of sexuality. This results in a frustrating hierarchical ordering of sexuality first and then: (2) race, (3) ethnicity, (4) nationhood, (5) class, and (6) all of the above. Not all forms of queer camp receive satisfactory significance as explained through the category of sexuality. And not all contexts of queer identities can be divorced from the interpenetrations of race, ethnicity, nationhood, and class (Feil, "From Queer to Hybridity" 97–100; Robertson, "Mae West's Maids" 394–95).

In the "SNAP! diva" sequence of *Tongues Untied*, several African American men recall stories of white gay racism and openly queer expression, as well as instances of spectacular visibility for black gay men. The SNAP!, a rhythmic configuration of fin-

potentially problematizes the derivation of cultural values and need not simply reproduce the same oppressive hierarchies.

As camp humor treats the invisibility or demonization of queers in mainstream culture as a matter of high versus low value, camp attacks the very structures of representation that dictate how texts reflect mainstream realities. Thus Sue-Ellen Case states, "Camp both articulates the lives of homosexuals through the obtuse tone of irony and inscribes their oppression with the same device. Likewise, it eradicates the ruling powers of heterosexist realist modes" (298). Case talks about the "Butch-Femme aesthetic" in lesbian camp performance, "both on or off the stage," as a historical strategy for challenging assumptions about "realistic" depictions of women and men, homosexuals and heterosexuals (295). Case cites the "realisms" of Western constructions of female subjectivity. Two related stereotypes of "woman" emerge from the mythology of female castration: hyperfemininity is related to "normal" heterosexual women, whereas hypermasculinity applies to "deviant" lesbians. Lesbian butch-femme performance problematizes these dualistic stereotypes by "inhabit[ing] the subject position together—'you can't have one without the other,' as the song says." Thus,

> the butch is the lesbian woman who proudly displays the possession of the penis, while the femme takes on the compensatory masquerade of womanliness. The femme, however, foregrounds her masquerade by playing to a butch, another woman in a role; likewise, the butch exhibits her penis to a woman who is playing the role of compensatory castration. This raises the question of "penis, penis, who's got the penis," because there is no referent in sight; rather, the fictions of penis and castration become ironized and "camped up." (300)

According to Case, mythologies of "woman" dissolve when "the butch-femme couple inhabit the subject position together." Lesbian butch-femme performance uses camp to illustrate the absurd play between normality and deviance, sameness and difference. Butch-femme camp plays with and strives to undermine the conventional signs of female difference as well as queer difference while also celebrating these differences. Deflating the very concepts of difference and deviance, butch-femme camp reveals them as either impoverished or infinitely—and so, absurdly and humorously—reproducible (295).

GET IN ON THE ACT(IVISM): FOUR EXAMPLES OF QUEER CAMP HUMOR

All four of the artworks discussed in this section represent examples of what might be called "post-Stonewall" queer camp humor: the documentary *Tongues Untied* (1990), the independent film *Cry Baby* (1990), the photographic series *Dream Girls*, and the mainstream Hollywood parodies *The Brady Bunch Movie* (1995) and *A Very Brady Sequel* (1996). Before discussing these works, it is worth defining what "post-Stonewall" means. It is also vital to address the more recent role of camp humor in queer political activism, as some of these efforts inform the content and style of the works above.

The 1969 Stonewall riots in New York's Greenwich Village involved, as Melly's quote suggested, a number of drag queens and butch dykes who fought back against the police during a routine raid of the drag queen bar Stonewall. This event triggered queer activism throughout the United States and Europe and resulted in the liberaliza-

through the body, the most elemental symbol of identity and ownership. The SNAP! does not involve an exchange any more pricey than the movement of one finger against another. It renders "reality" as a textual site, even when most of us do not think of "reality" as a text, but as "simple" reality. Both of the SNAP! testimonials recall instances in everyday life: outside a gay club and on a city bus. While the instance at the club involves consumerism, the SNAP! that punctuates the story combats the racism that would deny black gay men the right to access (white) gay clubs. This diverges from the camp practice of calling attention to how works of art silence queerness, in that the camp practitioner is at least "permitted" to experience the work of art even though it does not address him/her.

Whereas camp can be used to ironize works without necessarily explicating its identity as a queer practice, the SNAP! is essentially public, *out*. Like camp, the SNAP! contains elements of humor by virtue of its play with high and low value, authority and resistance. The SNAP! is a banal gesture yet it halts events and instances a momentary seizure of authority. On the level of everyday performance, SNAP!ping provides a means for reversing power relations and reinscribing them from the point of view of someone who knows that she/he is being othered or otherwise marginalized. The SNAP! is an ironic, often sarcastic, seizure of power in the often debilitating spaces of everyday life.

Cry Babies and Butch Clones

John Waters' film *Cry Baby* (1990) celebrates the free expression of sexuality, although it also illustrates how difficult this expression is within a repressive society as well as repressive film genres. As Matthew Tinkcom observes of Waters' oeuvre:

Linked to the camp dimensions of films such as *Polyester* (1981) and *Cry Baby* (1990) is the fact that Waters's films have demonstrated a fascination with the Hollywood genre film, most notably the melodrama or "woman's picture," and his movies offer a commentary and accompanying revision of the ideological functions of the melodrama. (157)

Toying with the usual polarities of the 1950s juvenile delinquent film, *Cry Baby* illustrates a full camp community of rejects (the Drapes) whose social marginalization is primarily an issue of their sexuality and class.

The film illustrates in many instances how the marginalized Drape community expresses sexuality through its "vulgar" tastes (fast cars, leather jackets, rock 'n' roll music). This expression and liberation of the self through objects and tastes indicates the extent to which identity is socially constructed and thoroughly theatrical. For instance, Cry Baby (Johnny Depp) tells Alison, the upper-middle-class, Square ingenue, "You just look Square. Underneath, I think you're really hep." When Alison dons Drape clothes, she joins Cry Baby in a rock 'n' roll duet, changing her voice from thin and high pitched to a lower, gravelly, seductive tone. The film also illustrates how the Square (or straight) community views the Drapes as trash owing to their tastes and behaviors. In reference to Cry Baby's singing, Baldwin (Alison's Square boyfriend) states, "His kind of music isn't even on the *Hit Parade*." Alison's grandmother, Mrs. Vernon-Williams (Polly Bergen), condemns the Drape women for wearing tight "hysterectomy pants" and the Drape men for having long hair and tattoos. When Mrs. Vernon-Williams joins the cause of the Drapes, she pins on a skull-and-crossbones

ger snapping, closes each recollection as a sign of resistance or jubilation. The video then cuts to a circle of men, Riggs included, SNAP!ping. The title "Institute of SNAP!thology" is superimposed over the scene, and, as each man produces a particular configuration of SNAP!s, a new title designating the "genre" SNAP! appears.

In this sequence, *Tongues Untied* surfaces one performative device in the lexicon of African American gay culture, the SNAP!, as a mode of ironic and resistant interruption within the taken-for-granted flow of meanings in everyday life. The SNAP! shatters the transparency of representation and strengthens the practitioner whom such transparent or naturalized representation threatens to render marginalized, othered, and/or invisible. Besides conveying the meanings and varieties of the SNAP!, this sequence combats a range of naturalized representational figures, from the meanings of "gay" (read: white) identity, to the problematic power relations of documentary. One of the testimonials accounts for racism within white gay culture, when an Anglo doorman at a club bars entrance to a group of African American men. The defiant SNAP! that ends the man's story renders this testimonial not just another victim narrative, but a story of resistance: "Never mess with a SNAP! diva," challenges the man. The SNAP! signifies an appropriation of language; it is a means of transforming the taken-for-granted oppressiveness of the status quo.

The "Institute of SNAP!thology" sequence directly parodies the ethnographic documentary film genre that, in Bill Nichols' words, constructs "an 'ethnotopia' of limitless observation.... The fascination of the Other is stressed; it avails itself for knowledge. It is a world in which We *know* Them, a world of wisdom triumphant" (218). If Riggs risks the reproduction of an ethnographic mode by making a documentary about the familiar-yet-exotic moments of everyday black gay life, he incorporates the camp humor of the SNAP! into his representational practice. He SNAP!s the ethnographic documentary and its audience that desires a bit of the other by ironizing the whole documentary project of delivering "truth" to the viewer in an objective and distanced manner. Through camp humor, Riggs *does* inform us about the SNAP! without diminishing the vitality of SNAP! practices or the larger context of black gay life in the United States. As Riggs shows how SNAP!ping has a history in black gay culture, the use of titles reflexively calls attention to traditional ethnographic documentaries that would attempt to scientifically study or capture this phenomenon through the authoritative styles of documentary film and the social sciences. Scientizing the SNAP!, subjecting it to the "objectively" curious gaze of the camera lens much the way "exotic" cultures are studied by the ethnographic documentarian, would remove SNAP!ping from its origins and imprison it, concretize it, within an exploration by "experts." Thus Riggs represents the phenomenon of SNAP!ping and maintains its authority by cinematically SNAP!ping traditional forms of ethnographic documentary. At the same time, such parody also encourages thought about the virtual mainstream invisibility of black gay life.

If the SNAP! diva's mark indicates black gay dissent toward white gay racism and African American homophobia, the SNAP! also heralds black gay visibility, identity, and humor. While SNAP! practices are campy in their strategies of irony, resistance, and reinvention, they differ from traditional camp. If traditional camp attempts to halt the production of an oppressive reality through texts, it also maintains an element of conspicuous consumption: seeing movies, collecting bric-a-brac, buying clothing and furniture, and so forth. In this respect, camp retains an aura of bourgeois privilege that connotes wide cultural exposure, mobility, and ownership. The SNAP! articulates

medallion given her by Cry Baby's grandmother, Ramona. Mrs. Vernon-Williams then proceeds to seduce the Judge, another character whose oppressiveness dissolves when he begins to dance to "dirty" rock 'n' roll and experience his sexual feelings. Mrs. Vernon-Williams also joins Ramona and the Cry Baby gang women in a dance number involving any number of sexual connotations. The sexual repression and liberation of the film's characters applies directly to their use or rejection of trash taste in fashion and music.

Furthermore, the film presents a camp spectacle of masculinity that appeals to the post-Stonewall redefinition of gender categories. The men are infantilized, as the title character's name explicates. The film opens on a school vaccination scene, the initial image of a boy with large ears and short hair crying out hysterically as a doctor plunges a needle into his arm. It introduces Belvedere (Iggy Pop), Cry Baby's young grandfather, as he bathes himself in a washtub. His long legs hang over the side of the tiny tub as he gleefully scrubs his crotch. When the Squares start a rumble with the Drapes, Belvedere fights back by giving the Square boys noogies. Thus his boyish behavior undercuts the classic masculine authority figure. Later in the film, when the initially patriarchal Judge falls in love, he too indulges in liberating, childish behavior (unabashed grinning, dancing about in his robe, setting prisoners free). Even the leering Photographer, who pays young girls to pose nude for him, appears as a big baby. With his Falstaffian shape, baggy Bermuda shorts, and by rhyming all of his words, his potential threat diminishes in infantile lasciviousness and sartorial vulgarity.

The film's masculine discourse provides a complex of associations between sexual desire and infantilism. Cry Baby represents the attractiveness of an *emotional* masculinity. As a performer, his overwrought songs reinstate his emotionality with their high-pitched octaves and titles like "Cry Baby," "King Cry Baby," "Tear Drops Are Falling," and "Doin' Time for Being Young." Like a little boy, his passions rule his behavior, to the extent that he tattoos a teardrop on his face in order to prove his genuine love for Allison. The film further infantilizes him when, during his attempted escape from prison, he ends up crawling through sewer tunnels wearing only briefs. This sequence thoroughly connects visually infantile behavior (crawling, the briefs resembling diapers) with sexual desire (the actor Depp's physique and "butch" attributes), providing queer male spectators with a libidinal fantasy object who is also an emotional subject.

In terms of masculine and feminine sexual types, the Drape men (all of whom are primarily emotional rather than aggressively masculine) appear as gay butch clones in their boots, denim, and black leather jackets. The powerful female Drapes embody a dyke image with their dominant attitude, tight jeans, and motorcycle jackets. Thus the film's spectacle of gender, while certainly not radical, opportunes the reading of many mainstream queer references as part of its camp project. The self-conscious artifice and spectacle of masculine roles involves the incongruous pairing of infantile emotion with a butch fashion exterior. However, the film represents this irony as all the more attractive (the Square men dress in conservative, preppie attire and behave with aggressive violence). For queer men after Stonewall, this coupling of macho style with emotionality and ironic humor indicates a significant behavioral change from the stereotypical effeminacy of gay men before Stonewall. Likewise, queer women can luxuriate in female characters who embody a "masculine" image of power and take eager pleasure in their erotic desires. For post-Stonewall queer camp, gender is a masquerade to participate in, in order to remake its traditional definitions. The comedy of this queer masquerade stems not from mistaken identities but from the newfound range of gender roles to choose from, play with, parody, and eroticize.

Bright's Horizons

In her photography series *Dream Girls*, Deborah Bright reproduces a series of film stills from famous Hollywood movies that emphasize a heterosexual norm: Julie Andrews and Christopher Plummer in *The Sound of Music*, Katherine Hepburn and Spencer Tracy in *Adam's Rib*, George Segal and Glenda Jackson in *A Touch of Class*, among others. However, Bright makes one vital alteration. She inserts herself in these stills, bedecked in many of them in butch dyke garb: closely cropped hair, leather jacket, and motorcycle boots. Bright is gleefully and sensuously engaging in butch-femme camp, disrupting the straight hegemony of masculine versus feminine by including an image, that of herself, that combines both polarities. Further, Bright contrasts her own image to the femme female stars who provide an object for her erotic gaze. Not only does Bright undermine the hetero-male gaze by foregrounding her own desirous gaze, but she provides what Case describes as a campy forum between women where "butch" and "femme" are interchangeable, theatrical *roles*. Indeed, Bright's photographs provide both a witty parody of Hollywood's (and society's) conservative gender norms and an eroticized replay of classic Hollywood romance for a lesbian audience.

In an essay accompanying her photographs, Bright attests to how her work represents "what many young, middle-class proto-dykes 'saw' in these films in the early 1960s . . . concrete (if attenuated) suggestions of erotic possibilities that they could not name and that their own lived experience did not provide" (152). Bright seizes on the queer camp pleasures of transforming a work by identifying with it in an ironic way, enjoying what is already there but also remaking it in order to articulate, rather than silence, queerness. By implanting images of herself dressed as a butch dyke, she is making fun *out of* these Hollywood movies instead of merely making fun *of* them; she both attacks their absences as well as celebrates their content, especially the female stars who populate them.

Bright's affection for the movies and pride in her own self-image takes over where her mockery leaves off. Parodying the stereotypes of Hollywood gender roles and lesbian imagery, Bright also appropriates them for her own identification, as well as for other lesbian viewers. Her comic inversion of Hollywood gender norms leaves space for more serious musings on queer pride and power and, no less important, cultural taste and erotic fantasies.

Bright's photo series plays out the comedy of queer camp irony, incongruity, and inversion. As Bright puts it:

My pleasure in these montages is with the power relations among the characters they depict; with the sabotage of the heterosexual Hollywood set-up by a supplementary or substitute character of ambiguous gender who upsets the heterosexual economy of the scene. . . . For example, the lesbian "driver" in Katherine [sic] Hepburn's car makes Spencer Tracy's kiss benign and impotent—little more than a grandfatherly peck on the cheek which Hepburn indulges. . . . Before its alteration, the dinner scene from *A Touch of Class* showed Glenda Jackson staring fixedly off-screen as George Segal held forth over his wine. I gave Jackson something more interesting to look at, leaving Segal firmly locked out of the visual loop. . . . To the lesbian friends who've seen them, these *Dream Girls* have provoked a whoop of recognition and pleasure, and that is satisfaction enough. (152–54)

Bright's description of both the pictures and her mates' reactions to them expresses the "rebellious" pleasures of humor, as Freud calls it. She mocks the spectacle of Hollywood heterosexuality as well as the absurd presence of a butch lesbian in them. One can only imagine the whoops Bright alludes to in her friends' responses to her pictures. However, the distinctly queer camp pose of frivolity taken by Bright and evident in her work gives a good indication that laughter was a significant part of their "recognition and pleasure."

Out with *The Brady Bunch*

As we drift away from the off-mainstream realms of documentary, independent cinema, and art photography, explicit examples of queer camp become harder to find. However, "mass camp" occasionally signifies its subcultural ties (Klinger 132–156). Network television has provided *Will and Grace*, in which one of the two gay male leads, Jack, camps it up in terms of unabashed effeminacy and a devotion to low popular culture (especially Cher). Two feature films of the 1990s also appeared to illuminate queer camp on mall movie screens. *The Brady Bunch Movie* (1995, directed by Betty Thomas) and *A Very Brady Sequel* (1996, directed by Arlene Sanford) eagerly align the so-normal-they're-queer Brady Bunch with lesbians and gays. The Brady family's TV-perfect normality, dated as it is, renders them queer within a 1990s Los Angeles where, among other things, drag queen RuPaul is the school guidance counselor advising Jan Brady about how to fit in with her peers. If a butch dyke or screaming queen announces her queerness publicly through behavior and dress, so do the Brady Bunch. Besides wearing double-knit polyester and never going to the bathroom, the Brady Bunch also sing chipper songs whenever they venture in public. Being themselves, they are continually gawked at, derided, or told to stop behaving that way. But the Bunch is too benign to yell, "Get used to it," as in the queer activist dictum, "We're here! We're queer! Get used to it!" Their "very Brady" visibility is not intentionally subversive.

The Brady Bunch Movie offers a direct and affectionate acknowledgement of queer desire in the character of the young butch teen Noreen. She lusts after Marcia Brady, her best friend, and even punches a man in defense of Marcia's honor. While Noreen's flirtation eludes Marcia altogether, Noreen ends up with another gorgeous blond girl, someone also harassed by the boy that Noreen slugged on Marcia's behalf. While *A Very Brady Sequel* is less expressive about lesbian desire, it is unmistakably brimming with queerness. Carol and Mike's marriage and the existence of the Bunch are threatened when Carol's first husband returns after all these years to reunite. The story line about marriage and the meaning of family combined with the double entendres and kitsch of the Brady Bunch make this film a contender for mainstream queer camp. As director Sanford observes in the promotional material for the film:

There is a serious theme to this movie, which is that you make your own family. Even if it's not the one you were born into. . . . [Mike Brady] says something like, "The family you make is the family you have and is the only family you need." . . . The basic idea is that this is a family that wasn't born together, but got married and became a family. And it's true for people who've been married a lot. It's true for gay people who make their own families. And, that's really what I think this is about at its core.

While I have no idea if Sanford is a lesbian, she observes one of the film's themes that speaks to queers. Sanford also describes the classically camp strategy of the work's masquerading as "normal" yet containing a queer subtext, practiced by numerous Hollywood directors and writers of yore.

In both Brady movies, the queer subtexts and double entendres are accentuated and meant to be noticed, from Marcia and Noreen snuggled in the same single bed during a sleepover, to Marcia (in the sequel) thinking that a phone-sex caller's request for a ménage à trois means that he thinks Marcia's "the most." When RuPaul, as school guidance counselor Mrs. Cummings, advises Jan, "You better work," this directly refers to RuPaul's drag act, in which her catch-phrase is, "You better work, bitch." Carol also has a brush with queerness when she sneaks to a salon called Taboo and requests a contemporary hairdo from a queeny leather boy and his heavily body-pierced assistant. The most spirited example of queer camp in *A Very Brady Sequel* occurs at the end of the film when a kidnapper absconds with Carol Brady to Hawaii. When Mike tells Alice that Carol is "tied up in Hawaii," Alice replies that the kidnapper probably took her there because of the state's "liberal policies." In Hawaii, the wistful Carol remarks to a tourism official, "I wish I could be gay again, with Marcia, Jan, Cindy and Alice." Later, when the same tourism official warns Mike that his wife wants to be "gay again," Mike responds, "Sure she does. We all do." The tourism official's face drops for a second time.

Clearly, the camp effects of the Brady flicks differ significantly from those of Riggs' *Tongues Untied*, Waters' *Cry Baby*, and Bright's *Dream Girls*. It might even be a stretch to call either of the Brady pics queer camp. However, the Brady Bunch movies surpass simple nostalgia in their extended parodies of normality, depicting the Bunch as so hypernormal and dated that they are indeed queer in the eyes of everyone else. In queer camp, the love of outdated popular culture translates into an affectionate critique where the joke is, finally, on anyone who can't or won't notice how queer normality can be.

REFERENCES AND FURTHER READINGS

Babuscio, Jack. "Camp and the Gay Sensibility." *Gays and Film*. Ed. Richard Dyer. New York: Zoetrope, 1984.

Bergman, David. "Strategic Camp: The Art of Gay Rhetoric." *Gaiety Transfigured: Gay Self-Representation in American Literature*. Madison: U of Wisconsin P, 1991.

Booth, Mark. *Camp*. New York: Quartet, 1983.

The Brady Bunch Movie. Dir. Betty Thomas. Paramount Pictures, 1995.

Bright, Deborah. *Dream Girls. Stolen Glances: Lesbians Take Photographs*. Ed. Tessa Boffin and Jean Fraser. London: Pandora, 1991.

Bronski, Michael. *Culture Clash: The Making of Gay Sensibility*. Boston: South End, 1984.

Case, Sue-Ellen. "Towards a Butch-Femme Aesthetic." *The Lesbian and Gay Studies Reader*. Ed. Henry Abelove, Michèlle Aina Barale, and David M. Halperin. New York: Routledge, 1993.

Chauncey, George. *Gay New York*. New York: BasicBooks, 1994.

Core, Philip. *Camp: The Lie That Tells the Truth*. New York: Delilah, 1984.

Crimp, Douglas, and Adam Rolston. *AIDS Demo Graphics*. Seattle, WA: Bay, 1990.

Cry Baby. Dir. John Waters. Universal Pictures, 1990.

d'Emilio, John. *Sexual Politics, Sexual Communities: The Making of a Homosexual Minority in the United States, 1940–1970*. Chicago: U of Chicago P, 1983.

Dollimore, Jonathan. *Sexual Dissidence: Augustine to Wilde, Freud to Foucault*. Oxford, UK: Clarendon, 1991.

Dyer, Richard. "Judy Garland and Gay Men." *Heavenly Bodies: Film Stars and Society*. New York: St. Martin's, 1986. 156–68.

Evans, Sarah. "Madonna Wannabe." *CineAction* 24/25 (1991): 16–24.

Faderman, Lillian. *Odd Girls and Twilight Lovers*. New York: Penguin, 1992.

Feil, Ken. "Ambiguous Sirk-Camp-Stances: Gay Camp and the 1950s Melodramas of Douglas Sirk." *Spectator* 15.1 (1994): 31–49.

———. *Dying for a Laugh: Disaster Movies and the Camp Imagination*. Wesleyan UP, forthcoming. Fall 2005.

———. *"From Queer to Hybridity: Questions of Cultural Difference in Contemporary Queer Film and Video."* Ph.D. diss., University of Texas at Austin, 1995.

———. "Male Sexuality in A(d)dress: Post-Stonewall Gay Camp in Mainstream Film and Television." Masters thesis, Emerson College, 1991.

Freud, Sigmund. "Humour." *Character and Culture*. Ed. Philip Rieff. New York: Collier, 1963. 263–69.

Harries, Dan. *Film Parody*. London: BFI, 2000.

Jackson, Isaac. "Reading Madonna." *Gay Community News* 18.43 (26 May–1 June, 1991): 15–20.

Klinger, Barbara. *Melodrama and Meaning: History, Culture and the Films of Douglas Sirk*. Bloomington: Indiana UP, 1994.

Melly, George. Preface. *Camp: The Lie That Tells the Truth*. By Philip Core. New York: Delilah, 1984.

Mercer, Kobena. "Dark and Lovely Too: Black Gay Men in Independent Film." *Queer Looks: Perspectives on Lesbian and Gay Film and Video*. Ed. Martha Gever, John Greyson, and Pratibha Parmar. New York: Routledge, 1993. 238–56.

Musto, Michael. "Old Camp, New Camp," *Out* April/May, 1993. 32–39.

Neale, Steve, and Frank Krutnik. *Popular Film and Television Comedy*. New York: Routledge, 1990.

Nero, Charles I. "Toward a Black Gay Aesthetic." *Brother to Brother*. Ed. Essex Hemphill. Conceived by Joseph Beam. Boston: Alyson, 1991. 229–52.

Newton, Esther. "Role Models." *Camp Grounds: Style and Homosexuality*. Ed. David Bergman. Amherst: U of Massachusetts P, 1993. 39–52.

Nichols, Bill. *Representing Reality*. Bloomington: Indiana UP, 1991.

Rich, B. Ruby. "New Queer Cinema." *Sight and Sound* 5 (Fall 1992): 30–34.

Riggs, Marlon. "Black Macho Revisited: Reflections of a SNAP! Queen." *Brother to Brother*. Ed. Essex Hemphill. Conceived by Joseph Beam. Boston: Alyson, 1991. 253–57.

Robertson, Pamela. " 'The Kinda Comedy That Imitates Me': Mae West's Identification with the Feminist Camp." *Camp Grounds: Style and Homosexuality*. Ed. David Bergman. Amherst: U of Massachusetts P, 1993. 156–72.

———. "Mae West's Maids: Race, 'Authenticity,' and the Discourse of Camp." *Camp: Queer Aesthetics and the Performing Subject*. Ed. Fabio Cleto. Ann Arbor: U of Michigan P, 1999. 393–408.

Román, David. " 'It's My Party and I'll Die If I Want To!' Gay Men, AIDS, and the Circulation of Camp in U.S. Theatre." *Camp Grounds: Style and Homosexuality*. Ed. David Bergman. Amherst: U of Massachusetts P, 1993. 206–33.

Ross, Andrew. *No Respect: Intellectuals and Popular Culture*. New York: Routledge, 1989.

Sadie Benning Videoworks. Dir. Sadie Benning. Vols. 1 and 2, 1989–1992. Distrib. by Video Data Bank.

Smith, Paul Julian. *Desire Unlimited: The Cinema of Pedro Almodóvar*. New York: Verso, 1994.

Smith, Valerie. "The Documentary Impulse in Contemporary U.S. African-American Film." *Black Popular Culture*. Ed. Michèlle Wallace and Gina Dent. Seattle: Bay, 1992. 61–63.

Sontag, Susan. "Notes on Camp." *Against Interpretation and Other Essays*. New York: Farrar, Straus and Giroux, 1966. 275–92.

Tinkcom, Matthew. *Working Like a Homosexual: Camp, Capital, Cinema*. Durham, NC: Duke UP, 2002.

Tongues United. Dir. Marlon Riggs. Frameline, 1989.

A Very Brady Sequel. Dir. Arlene Sanford. Paramount Pictures, 1996.

Viegner, Matias. "Decontrolled Boundaries: The Body as Artifact." *Documents* (1993): 69–70.

Weinberg, Jonathan. "It's in the Can: Jasper Johns and the Anal Society." *Genders* 1 (Spring 1988): 40–56.

Weiss, Andrea. " 'A Queer Feeling When I Look at You': Hollywood Stars and Lesbian Spectatorship in the 1930s." *Stardom: Industry of Desire*. Ed. Christine Gledhill. New York: Routledge, 1991. 283–99.

Wilde, Oscar. "The Decay of Lying." *De Profundis and Other Writings*. New York: Penguin Classics, 1987.

Women on the Verge of a Nervous Breakdown. Dir. Pedro Almodóvar. Orion Classics, 1988.

32

Roman Comedy

Maurice Charney

From the rich subject of Roman comedy we have selected a few characteristic Latin writers: Plautus, Terence, and Juvenal. All of these had an enormous influence on English and Western European literature because they were studied in school by students learning Latin. Horace, the genial satirist, has also been very influential, especially on English literature. Roman comic dramatists generally use Greek originals for their plays, but they are radically transformed. The Roman sensibility in comedy is quite different from the Greek.

The Roman dramatist Titus Maccius Plautus was born in Umbria in 254 B.C.E. and died in 184 B.C.E. Twenty-one of his comedies survive, all modeled on Greek new comedy originals. What makes Plautus so important for the history of comedy is that he provides models for farce and situation comedy that were extremely influential on such later writers as Niccolò Machiavelli, William Shakespeare, Ben Jonson, and Molière. Most of our current television sitcoms are indebted to the example set by Plautus. He was not a sophisticated, intellectual dramatist like Aristophanes, who dealt with political and ethical issues. His plots derive from situations of daily life and he uses stock characters freely. Before he began writing plays, he worked as a stage carpenter and a baker. He is not at all subtle but appeals to the vagaries of daily life.

Plautus is a great believer in the role of chance and fortune. A good deal happens in his plays by coincidence. For example, mistaken identity was one of his favorite themes. He uses twins and twinning often as a plot device, most obviously in *The Menaechmus Twins*, but also in *Amphitryon*, where the gods Jupiter and Mercury stand in for Amphitryon and his slave Sosia, and also in *The Braggart Soldier*, in which Philocomasium also plays her imaginary twin sister. Plautus' plays are very self-conscious. The characters appeal directly to the audience, and the prologue usually tells the audience explicitly all the details of the plot. Plautus often breaks the illusion of his comedies, and the actors speak knowingly to the audience about their assigned roles.

Let us take a characteristic play, *The Braggart Soldier*, to examine some of the assumptions of Plautine farce. The Latin title is *Miles Gloriosus*, which refers to the stock character of Pyrgopolynices ("terrific tower taker"). There are many other examples of the *miles gloriosus* type in Plautus, for example, Stratophanes in *The Savage Slave*. Later we have Shakespeare's Falstaff and Jonson's Captain Bobadil (in *Everyman in His Humor*) and many others. *Braggart* is not quite the right word to describe the "glorified" (or grandiloquent) military man, whose grandeur is all in his uniform and his language and who is actually a coward at heart. Pyrgopolynices only figures at the beginning and end of the play, but he is the one on whom various clever tricks are played. They serve as a comeuppance for his unlimited and foolish vanity. We are not sorry to see him deflated.

In the opening action we see the soldier with his parasite, Artotrogus. The parasite is a standard figure of Roman comedy. He is the yes-man, the freeloader, the flattering sidekick, who is constantly talking about the good meals he is having at his host's expense—*parasite* is Greek for "by the food." The soldier and his parasite are the classic pair described in Aristotle's *Nicomachean Ethics* (4.7) as the *alazon*, or boaster, and the *eiron*, the ironic, sly, and understated man. They often appear in American film comedy as the fat man and the thin man (for example, Laurel and Hardy). Pyrgopolynices is an exaggerated, hyperbolic braggart, as everything in farce tends to be overstated and overwrought. He enters with several minions carrying his monstrous shield. In his first speech, he is "*[p]osing pompously, declaiming in heroic fashion:*"

> Look lively—shine a shimmer on that shield of mine
> Surpassing sunbeams—where there are no clouds, of course.
> Thus, when it's needed, with the battle joined, its gleam
> Shall strike opposing eyeballs in the bloodshed—bloodshot!
>
> (1: 73)

Artotrogus, the parasite, flatters his master to his face and makes fun of him to the audience:

> (*To the audience, as he hides behind the soldier's shield*)
> If any of you knows a man more full of bull
> Or empty boastings, you can have me—free of tax.
> But I'll say this: I'm crazy for his olive salad!
>
> (1: 74)

Or further: "It's only for my stomach that I stomach him" (1: 74).

The prologue proper does not begin until Pyrgopolynices and Artotrogus have left the stage. This is spoken by Palaestrio, the comic slave of Pyrgopolynices (formerly of Pleusicles). The comic slave who manipulates the plot is the most important of Plautus' stock figures. He is witty, ingenious, impudent, and independent, not at all slavish in our sense of the word (Roman slaves were often Greek prisoners of war). Palaestrio has a long address to the audience, in which he speaks to them confidentially about the plot and about any other matters that occur to him. As is usual in Plautus' comedies, the play is very much driven by a complicated and improbable plot. This is one feature of Plautus that has survived into television situation comedy: although the setting may be ordinary domestic life, the events of the plot are extraordinary, if not far-fetched. There is a certain farcical wildness or craziness built into the plot.

In *The Braggart Soldier*, for example, it is taken as a matter of course that Palaestrio has tunneled through the wall of the adjoining houses of Pyrgopolynices and his neighbor, Periplectomenus, so that Philocomasium, Pleusicles' old girlfriend from Athens who has been abducted by Pyrgopolynices, can have free access to her lover, who just happens to be Pleusicles. Unfortunately, Sceledrus, a slave of Pyrgopolynices, while on the roof of his neighbor's house chasing a little monkey, saw the lovers kissing. Now Sceledrus has to be persuaded that he didn't see what he is certain that he did see. The first trick is that Philocomasium has an imaginary twin sister who has just arrived in Periplectomenus' house to meet her lover. So the play begins with plenty of complications in the plot, which are present both in the original situation and also in Palaestrio's clever machinations. Many of the characters have prepared roles (with appropriate costumes) to play: Philocomasium acts her supposed twin sister; Acroteleutium, a courtesan, plays a rich and love-sick suitor to Pyrgopolynices; Pleusicles is disguised as a sea captain who has come to take Philocomasium and Palaestrio back to Athens. Coincidence and mistaken identity operate freely, and all of Palaestrio's schemes work out perfectly in the end. Chance operates very freely in this play and in all of Plautus.

Palaestrio's plotting demands skillful acting on everyone's part. *The Braggart Soldier* is very histrionic in the sense that it is always conscious of its own artifice. The audience is appealed to as a silent partner in the deception. Palaestrio plays the role of director, who rehearses everyone in his or her assigned role. For example, he tells the rich and old and fun-loving neighbor, Periplectomenus, how Philocomasium is to act the part of her twin sister and how to confuse Sceledrus about what he actually saw:

> She must force the fellow who found her [Sceledrus] into full forgetfulness.
> Even if he saw her here a hundred times, have her deny it.
> She has cheek, a lot of lip, loquacity, audacity,
> Also perspicacity, tenacity, mendacity.
> If someone accuses her, she'll just outswear the man with oaths.
> She knows every phony phrase, the phony ways, the phony plays.
> Wiles she has, guiles she has, very soothing smiles she has.
>
> (1: 82–83)

You can see from this quotation, very imaginatively translated by Erich Segal, that Plautus is a lively dramatist close to the style of a musical comedy like *Guys and Dolls*.

Palaestrio's second trick is to get a courtesan, pretending to be Periplectomenus' wife, who will make love to Pyrgopolynices. This is Palaestrio's greatest triumph: to persuade the stupid and vain soldier to get rid of his abducted girl, Philocomasium; to send her back to Athens with all her clothing and gifts of jewelry; and to return along with her, a free man in Athens. Again, everything in the plot falls out perfectly. Acroteleutium, the courtesan, with her maid Milphidippa, is a consummate actress who pretends to be not only rich, but dying with love for Pyrgopolynices. She needs no coaching but plays her role like a real professional. While the soldier overhears, she says, probably parodically: "He's near—somewhere—the man I long to see. I smell him!" (1: 161).

In typical Plautine fashion, the young lover, Pleusicles, is represented as a not very bright, not very skillful person who desperately needs the clever slave to accomplish his purposes. He clearly cannot do this himself unaided. Palaestrio takes great pains to lay everything out for Pleusicles (something he didn't have to do with Acroteleutium). For example, when he is to play the ship's captain at the end, Palaestrio is very explicit in his instructions:

> Have a wide-brimmed hat—rust-brown—and on your eye a woolen patch.
> Also have a rush-brown cloak—since that's the color sailors wear.
> Fasten it to your left shoulder; tie it round with one arm bare.
> One way or another, you must seem the master of a ship.
>
> (1: 154)

To these directions, Pleusicles "*nods, having taken great pains to memorize all this.*" At the end, however, he almost spoils everything by being too amorous with Philocomasium.

Periplectomenus, the old man who is the soldier's neighbor and who is extremely fun-loving, is a well-developed character and he is almost in competition with Palaestrio as a plot manipulator. He makes some speeches against the institution of marriage in the middle of the play that fit well with Plautus' misanthropy. But he is almost too insistent on his youth and freedom: "I'll make you admit I'm really just a youngster in my way" (1: 116). This is all said to impress Palaestrio:

> I can show you that I'm even more amusing than you say:
> Never at a party do I screw around with someone's girl,
> Never do I filch the food or take the goblet out of turn.
>
> (1: 116)

Methinks the old bachelor doth protest too much!

Among Plautus' most successful comic slaves is Pseudolus, from the play of the same name, which was first performed in 191 B.C.E. Cicero suggested that it was Plautus' own favorite play, and it has generally been regarded as Plautus' masterpiece. It is self-confidently original and assured in its composition. It is also skillfully constructed, outstanding among comedies that all have complicated, far-fetched, and farcical plots. We even get a physical description of Pseudolus from Harpax, the military messenger: "Let's see now . . . red hair . . . pot belly . . . thick calves . . . swarthy complexion . . . large head . . . sharp eyes . . . ruddy face . . . and, oh yes! tremendous feet!" (4: 305). This may describe the actor who played Pseudolus on the Roman stage. We admire Pseudolus' exuberance, his gruff honesty in telling all of his victims that he is planning to cheat them and warning them to beware of him.

Pseudolus carries the role of comic improviser very far. He makes up the plot as he goes along, and he thinks of himself as a surrogate dramatist:

Here you are without a shred of a plan, cashless and clueless. No idea where to start or finish weaving one's web. Well, after all, that's how a poet works when he takes up his pen in his pursuit of something that doesn't exist—yet somehow finds it and fashions fantasy into fact. I fancy I'll play the poet now; those twenty *minae* are nowhere to be found, and yet, I'll find them! (4: 262)

Plautus ventures far into breaking the illusion of verisimilitude. The audience is constantly appealed to for its help, and it plays an important role in the manipulation of the plot. Plautus always takes the audience into his confidence. This probably goes back to the illusion Plautus wants to create that his plays are unscripted and are improvised by stock characters and stock situations that are well known to the audience. This idea comes to fruition in the Italian comedy of the fifteenth century (and later) called *commedia dell'arte*.

Pseudolus appeals to the audience to support him in his schemes and to applaud his inventiveness. There are quite a few direct addresses to the audience in the course of the play, as at the end of act 1, which Richard Beacham translates in Gilbert and Sullivan anapestics:

> As for what I *shall* do . . .
> well, I haven't a clue!
> Still, I know I'll somehow bring it off!
>
> When an actor's on stage
> it's his job to engage
> in some intrigues both novel and droll.
> If he fails in that task
> let him turn in his mask
> to another more fit for the role!
>
> (4: 270)

There is a lot of talk in all of Plautus about the dire punishments the comic slave will encounter should he fail. But, in fact, he always remains immune from punishment. In an amusing quip, Pseudolus says to his master: "Take me as your slave, if I fail," and Simo makes the obvious answer: "Oh, that's well said! Now it seems you don't already belong to me" (4: 268).

The end of the play is unusual for its comic exaltation. The tables are turned and Pseudolus is triumphantly drunk. The master Simo pays him the twenty *minae* he has won in his wager and actually gets down on his knees and kneels to his slave. The tableau is touching:

> *They stand face to face.* PSEUDOLUS *points to the slave collar and cuffs he wears, which* SIMO *removes one by one, as* PSEUDOLUS *counts out the money to him.* SIMO *hesitates, then gives the money back. They embrace.* (4: 311)

This is proof of the wish-fulfillment quality of Plautus' comedies, which have little to do with the actual conditions of Rome life at the time. In the final stage direction, "*They leave, arm in arm*" (4: 311). Presumably, Pseudolus is manumitted as a reward for his cleverness, and he invites Simo to go drinking with him. So the Liar (which is what the name *Pseudolus* literally means) is now transformed into the comic poet.

Calidorus, the lover, is the stock type of the not-very-smart or inventive young man who can do nothing at all for himself. Plautus seems to be making fun of these assumptions when he shows Calidorus posturing histrionically:

PSEUDOLUS: Get hold of yourself! Don't let your spirits droop when things are hard. Keep your pecker up.
CALIDORUS: But that's absurd! What's the fun of being a lover, if you can't play the fool.
    (*Poses melodramatically*)
PSEUDOLUS: Oh, do can it! (*Grabs him*)
CALIDORUS: Pseudolus, dear, let me indulge myself! (*Weeps extravagantly on him*) (4: 251)

The love affair is all a game, and Plautus doesn't let the girl, Phoenicium, speak a single line. This is unusual. It is assumed that all of the love objects are infinitely beautiful and desirable, but they are much better developed in other plays of Plautus.

The evil and crude pimp, Ballio, is a stock figure. There is great openness about sex for sale, even though the girls are often freeborn women from wealthy families who were abducted as children. The girls have papers and other identifying objects (like toys) that prove their status but which the pimp conceals. All of the pimps, no matter how sleazy, have easy relations with other characters in the play, and there is never any serious moral and ethical condemnation of what they do for a living.

Ballio is immune from insults. When Simia, Charinus' slave, is playing the rehearsed role of Harpax, the military messenger, he says to Ballio: "The man I'm looking for is a real scoundrel: a criminal, deceitful, godless slimebag!" Ballio recognizes himself at once: "Goodness! Sounds like he's after me. I answer to all of those" (4: 292). Later, when Simo is eager to get all the details of the deception, Ballio answers quite frankly:

Oh, more theatrical patter; the usual line of abuse a pimp gets in comedies; stuff schoolboys know. He said I was nasty, and wicked, and a liar.

To Simo's reply, "he didn't exaggerate," Ballio answers with good-natured honesty:

Indeed. Consequently I took no offense. What good is it to insult a man like me, who's beneath reproach and not bothered by abuse? (4: 297)

This clinches the fact that the audience has definite assumptions about stock characters and stock situations. They do not anticipate any surprises.

The Haunted House (*Mostellaria*), one of Plautus' most popular plays, has another brilliant comic slave, Tranio. But in this play all does not work out well in the end. Tranio's schemes prove to be mere fantasy without any possible practical solution. That is the point of the play. Philolaches' friend, Callidamates, agrees to reimburse the father, Theopropides, for all expenses incurred, and, surprisingly, the father pardons his wastrel son:

> Let him follow his heart; make love,
> Enjoy his wine, and count on my friendly indulgence.
> If he's genuinely sorry he's wasted all this money,
> That's punishment enough for me.
>
> (3: 399)

Even Tranio, sitting on the altar that confers immunity in front of the house, is reluctantly pardoned. At the end, all the actors call for "handfuls of applause" (3: 400).

This is an unusual play in its focus on partying and pleasure. It is un-Roman in its hedonistic thrust, and Plautus uses the word *pergraecari*, "to act like a Greek," three times during the play. Tranio is a fantasy surrogate for all youth when he helps his master's son, Philolaches, banquet and carouse with wine, women, and song while his father is away for three years. They are almost at the end of their resources when the master suddenly returns. Tranio has a whole series of inventive lies to conceal what has actually happened: the house is haunted and hasn't been lived in for at least six months, the son has made a wise investment by buying the house next door, and so forth.

Although nothing can be done to ameliorate the situation, Tranio's bravado never falters. He foresees the superhappy ending as if he were a god:

> But the mark of a man of genius is seen
> When he steers the complicated mess
> On through its mischievous confusion
> To a calm and innocent conclusion
> And suffers no punishment, not even deep embarrassment.
>
> (3: 340)

He is enormously self-confident in his good fortune:

> But however it all turns out, I plan to proceed
> To continue to confuse things as chaotically as I can:
> That looks like what they demand.
>
> (3: 343)

We are caught up in Tranio's boundless optimism regardless of how unwarranted it is. And Tranio is, of course, right!

Tranio is grandiose in his conception of himself. He is the maker, the architect (like Pseudolus), the visionary:

> Single-handed, I frame
> These fiendish designs that will live on to future times
> And make me remembered as one who, like Alexander,
> Was Great, or like Agathocles, the noble but late
> King of Sicily.
>
> (3: 366)

It is pure wish-fulfillment, the essence of a comic conception of reality. Action, movement are what is needed even if they have no immediate purpose:

> I got busy immediately getting ready to do
> What any intelligent, strong-minded person would do
> In my situation so fraught with peril and confusion.
> Create even more confusion, surely that's the solution!
> Keep it all moving around and around. I'll be found
> Out, of course. . . .
>
> (3: 390)

Only the ultimate comic hero can take as his motto, "Create even more confusion." It is supremely irrational.

Even at the end, Tranio is unfazed by Theopropides' toughs (the Lorarii) waiting to beat him up. He advises Theopropides to take some profit from the present situation:

> Offer it to the comic poets.
> If you're a friend of the writers Diphilus and Philemon
> Tell them how your slave made a comic character
> Out of you. That's good frustration material for them
> To use in their comedies.
>
> (3: 398)

Diphilus and Philemon were two Greek writers whom Plautus used as sources for his plays.

Shakespeare must have been intrigued by this play because he uses Grumio and Tranio in *The Taming of the Shrew*. There are some additional extravagant details in *The Haunted House* that are worth mentioning, for example, the elaborate drunk scene for Callidamates, the friend of Philolaches (1: 4). He is falling-down drunk as he embraces his mistress, Delphium, "*intricately*" (3: 332), as the stage direction tells us. The play celebrates the irresponsible and irrepressible values of youth versus age, of sons versus fathers, a traditional comic theme.

We should also mention the completely superfluous dog on stage when Tranio takes his master for a look at Simo's house, which he pretends to have bought in the name of Philolaches. Tranio enters vividly into the immediate scene:

> *Sssst! Woof!*
> Get going, you mutt: Go find the nearest tree.
> Come on, lope! Still lying there, you son of a dogma?
> Make tracks! Follow your nose!

And Simo adds:

> She's not dangerous.
> You can walk right up and she won't do a thing but lie there
> Like any other pregnant bitch. Just go on in
> And march right past her.
>
> (3: 372)

Why all this elaborate concern for the dog, who has nothing whatsoever to do with the plot? He is completely gratuitous like much else in this wonderful play, but he is an important part of the audience's awareness of what is happening on stage.

Plautus' best-known play to English-speaking audiences is undoubtedly *The Menaechmus Twins*, on which Shakespeare's *Comedy of Errors* is based (and also on Plautus' *Amphitryon*). *The Menaechmus Twins* is also the source for two very successful Broadway farces: *The Boys from Syracuse* and *A Funny Thing Happened on the Way to the Forum*. That is one of the reasons why I am using Lionel Casson's slangy, musical-comedy translation of this play. The setting, as the prologue tells us, is not "Athensis" but "Sicilyish" (109). It is very substantial: "*A street in Epidamnus. Two houses front on it: stage left Menaechmus', stage right Lovey's. The exit on stage left leads downtown, that on stage right to the waterfront*" (108). This is the typical Plautus setting of two adjoining houses, usually in a city. It is very solid and realistic, no cloud-cuckoo-land as in Aristophanes' *Clouds* or *Birds*. But the absurdity and improbability of the action plays against the seemingly realistic setting. There is a great deal of stupidity built into the play, so that it is virtually impossible for either of the Menaechmus twins—or for anyone else—to figure out the conclusion that is staring them in the face: if everyone is calling the wrong Menaechmus by the right name, then the long-lost twin brothers must have found each other. That is the goal of Menaechmus of Syracuse's long quest.

Plautus' use of twins and twinning is a favorite device to illustrate the role of chance and luck in human affairs (he uses it again in *Amphitryon* and *The Braggart Soldier*).

The reliance on twins tends to distract us from psychological problems of human identity, in which Plautus had little interest—the double is a frequent tragic theme in Western literature. The weight of the dramatic action is placed on identification rather than on identity. The resolution of the entangling action depends upon producing the "marks of recognition," as Aristotle calls them in the *Poetics*. There is no doubt that the twins are mirror images of each other, since everyone takes the one Menaechmus for the other. Plautus, however, goes to some length to distinguish the twins temperamentally from each other: "*Menaechmus of Epidamnus is gay, generous, and fun loving; his brother is shrewd, calculating, and cynical*" (120).

There is a point at which Menaechmus of Syracuse begins to enjoy his new situation, and he is converted from nay-saying to yea-saying. It is not only that he is "*shrewd, calculating, and cynical*," but also that he wants to have some fun in Epidamnus. In the course of the play he seems to change characteristics with his "*gay, generous, and fun loving*" brother. Plautus cleverly has one brother metamorphose into the other. With Lovey, the courtesan, Menaechmus of Syracuse stops struggling to explain himself and decides to yield to her blandishments: "I'm going to say yes to whatever she says: maybe I can get myself some free entertainment" (128). Shakespeare picks this up in *The Comedy of Errors* when Antipholus of Syracuse decides to go along with the beneficent "errors":

> What error drives our eyes and ears amiss?
> Until I know this sure uncertainty,
> I'll entertain the offered fallacy.
>
> (2.2.185–87)

In going along with the game, Menaechmus of Syracuse joins the world of comedy, and he is fittingly wined, dined, and wenched by a perfect stranger—not only that, but gifts are heaped upon him. It is a splendidly dreamlike wish fulfillment.

Once Menaechmus of Syracuse agrees to go along with the mad reality that surrounds him, he also begins to enjoy himself and to indulge in the pleasures of his new status. All the good things that everyone is giving him create a mood of comic euphoria. To the mythical dress and gold bracelet he claims as gifts to Lovey, he adds, "*after a few seconds of highly histrionic deep thought*," a pair of armlets. Lovey's maid catches him short: "You never gave her any armlets" (133), and Menaechmus is forced to forgo the extravagance of fantasy generosity in which he has been indulging himself.

It is easy to understand, therefore, why the recognition scene in act 5 between the two brothers proceeds so slowly and so disappointingly. Neither brother is too eager to welcome the other, and even though they are staring at each other for the entire scene, they demand proofs of identification that even the most scrupulous bank teller would not require of a stranger. It is clear that they have no intention of throwing themselves into each other's arms. The servant Messenio is needed to urge them on in what presents itself as farcical obstinacy. Messenio's enthusiasm is matched by the brothers' reluctance, as in the following exchange:

MESSENIO (*excitedly*): He's your image! He couldn't be more like you.
MENAECHMUS OF SYRACUSE (*following Messenio's gaze*): By god, you know, when I think about what I look like, he *does* resemble me. (162)

Lovey, the courtesan, is like other gold-digging professionals in Plautus, most notably the brilliantly grasping Phronesium in *The Savage Slave* and her maid Astaphium; also the Bacchis sisters in *Two Sisters Named Bacchis*. They are all businesswomen, heavily made-up and perfumed and unsentimental. Plautus definitely has a misogynistic streak, but the women clearly get their revenge in *A Funny Thing Happened on the Way to the Wedding* (*Casina*), as close as Plautus ever comes to writing a feminist play. When Lovey first appears, she is described as "*a good-looking girl in a brassy sort of way, flashily dressed and heavily made up*" (116). In Latin her name is Erotium, or "little love." She is very accomodating to her lover and is responsive to his every wish so long as the gifts keep flowing. There is no trace of tenderness in Plautus' courtesans. They are all consummate actors playing a well-defined role.

The parasite, Sponge, is a standard figure of Plautine comedy. He is like the comic servant, go-between, and manipulator in other plays. He is a factotum, a toady, a flatterer, a scrounger, a freeloader, and a man who lives by his wits. He does odd jobs and is a yea-sayer and messenger boy in return for his meals. Sponge puts a rhapsodic emphasis on food, or at least the anticipation of food—comedy rarely deals in the actual satisfaction of appetites. As a kind of second chorus, the parasite opens the play with visions of Menaechmus' bounty: "This Menaechmus is a man who doesn't just feed a man; he bloats the belly for you, he restores you to life . . . he overloads the tables, he piles up the plates like pyramids; you have to stand on your chair if you want something from on top" (111). Sponge is, of course, doomed to disappointment, since he is so dependent on the good mood of Menaechmus of Epidamnus. He is the one who turns the tables (to use an appropriate pun) by informing on his benefactor, although the affair with Lovey seems almost like a public event.

Madness, too, in farce is enjoyable for its own sake, as are all forms of eccentricity and irrationality. Menaechmus of Syracuse has a wonderful scene impersonating a madman who hears the voices of the gods directing his actions: "That's a big order, Apollo. Now I'm to get a team of fierce wild horses, harness them to a chariot, and mount it so I can trample down this stinking, toothless, broken-down lion, eh?" (152). But his wife's enfeebled and ancient father does more than hold his own as he brandishes his stick menacingly. Madness, or the assumption of madness, is exceedingly common in farce because it offers a seeming explanation for the total inexplicability of the events occurring on stage. It runs parallel to the comic mayhem.

Shakespeare's *Comedy of Errors* is also indebted to Plautus' *Amphitryon*, but the twinning here is different because the gods Jupiter and Mercury take the guise of Amphitryon and his slave Sosia in order that Jupiter may sleep with Alcmena, Amphitryon's wife. The slave Sosia's reaction to having a double is much more interesting dramatically than Amphitryon's general indignation. Sosia tries to make sense of this mysterious situation without being able to figure out that the gods are playing a trick on him. He approaches the matter rationally (as Amphitryon doesn't):

> My guess is, there's another Amphitryon
> Who's taking over the place when you're away
> And doing your job at home while you're with the army.
> It was a shock when I found I had a twin
> But to find that you have a double—that's even worse.

(1: 48)

Why is it even worse? Probably because Sosia is only a slave and Amphitryon is a general and they inhabit different social realities. Notice how delicately Sosia euphemizes the lustful Jupiter's relation to Alcmena; he is only "doing your job at home."

Sosia is an endearing character who tries valiantly to accept whatever fate has in store for him without complaining. He defends himself against the high-handed Mercury, who ventures to beat him. He reflects "*to himself, perplexed*":

> I can't refute evidence. I'll just go and look
> For another name for myself. Somehow or other,
> This character [Mercury] has seen it all.
>
> (1: 24)

He asks Mercury politely: "But look: if I'm not Sosia, who am I?" and the god replies offhandedly: "Oh, you can have the name when I don't want it. / *I'm* Sosia and you're nameless." Like Menaechmus of Syracuse, the slave is willing to go along with the new reality:

> We could be twins.
> My hat, my clothes . . .
> Leg, foot, height, haircut, eyes, nose, even lips—
> Jaws, chin, beard, neck—no difference. I'm speechless.
>
> (1: 25)

Sosia comes to the ludicrous conclusion, "he's more like me than I am." This is generous to a fault.

Sosia can't restrain his master from thinking differently—and hostilely—about this new situation, but he tries to be reasonable: "I'm here and I'm there, and I'm not surprised that you're baffled. / It's no less puzzling to me than it is to you." Again, Sosia patiently explains the truth to his master: "Why, hours ago when you sent me home from the harbor. . . . There I was at home before I got there" (1: 33). Plautus in the prologue calls the play a tragicomedy because gods and slaves are involved, but it's not tragic at all. It's a real mystery, ending in Jupiter's deus ex machina explanation at the end, when he appears on the roof of Amphitryon's house.

Plautus did not write all lighthearted comedies. Toward the end of his career he probably wrote some darker comedies like *The Savage Slave* and *The Captives*. These have never been among his most popular works. *The Savage Slave* (*Truculentus* in Latin) is a tormenting comedy dominated by the courtesan Phronesium and her maid Astaphium. It resembles *Two Sisters Named Bacchis*—both sisters are courtesans who scheme together. *The Savage Slave* is a play about love, not romantic love between peers but sexual love that is bought with money and gifts on the open market. You could call the play cynical because there is no free exchange of love—nothing is free. As Diniarchus realizes about Phronesium, "her name is one I should learn from, but don't. / *Phronesia*, you know, is Greek for 'good sense' " (2: 330). As a suitor, he is completely disillusioned about his mistress, yet he obsessively continues a love affair that is bankrupting and ruining him. We tend to see the action of the play through his eyes.

His soliloquy at the beginning of act 4 is typical of his muddled thinking. He enters "*transported by ecstasy*":

> Pure joy, that's me! I've got the ball now!
> With the soldier jilted, the woman's mine forever.
> I'm saved at last, because I'm lost. . . .
> I'll keep watch from here on my future fortunes.
> I have nothing! She has everything! I'm at her mercy!
>
> (2: 375)

The conclusion is already present in his long opening soliloquy of the play. He appears as "*a dissipated young man with circles under his eyes*" and his first words are:

> A lover can spend his whole life learning
> yet never really learn
> how many ways there are to die for love.
>
> (2: 327)

Both Phronesium and her maid, Astaphium, are attractive, intelligent, and well-spoken women. They don't deliberately intend harm to anyone, yet they are totally mercenary and without any of the sentiments usually connected with love. Neither of the two is hypocritical. They speak their minds directly and unashamedly. Phronesium readily admits that she has borrowed a baby to play upon Stratophanes, the braggart soldier's, generosity. There is a certain built-in absurdity in Phronesium's fervent speech:

> The baby needs food!
> The mother needs it too! He needs a maid to bathe him,
> and he needs a nurse! His nurse needs to drink
> vintage wine by day and night to have enough milk!
> We need wood, we need coal, we need kindling, oil, flour,
> diapers, pillows, a cradle, bed clothes for the cradle!
> *We need indeed the whole day long! Our needs
> are never met in one day! There's always need!*
>
> (2: 390)

This is the kind of extravagant hyperbole that Plautus delights in. Of course, it is all fantasy; vintage wine doesn't produce baby's milk, and the baby itself is only on temporary loan. Astaphium has an even more explicit recital of the courtesan's credo:

> As long as he has it, he can have *it*;
> once he doesn't have it, let him get *it*
> somewhere else. When he doesn't have it,
> he ought to be sensible and make way for one who does.
>
> (2: 340)

The puns on "it" are part of James Tatum's lively translation. All of which is summed up by a witty simile: "A courtesan should be like a cactus: / any man she touches should suffer a sting, or a loss" (2: 340). The logic is impenetrable and neither of the two women are open to discuss their basic principles (or modus vivendi).

It is not possible to go through all of the intricacies of this frustrating play. Once we get past Diniarchus, the other lovers are merely posturing fools, especially the *miles gloriosus* Stratophanes. He enters in elaborate pomp and ceremony, *in triumphal procession. He is preceded by dancing girls, drummers, and slaves bearing spoils and trophies. At a signal from him, the dancing and chanting cease and his scribe takes up his position at the warrior's elbow. Throughout the scene the scribe tries to take down* STRATO-PHANES' *more eloquent lines.* (2: 356)

Fresh from the experience of the Punic Wars with Carthage, Plautus delights in satirizing military rodomontade. Stratophanes is remarkably thick. When he says about the infant, "Has he served in a legion yet? What sort of spoils did he get?" Astaphium reminds him, "He was born only *five* days ago!" (2: 359).

Strabax is even more absurd as a male rival to Diniarchus. He is described as "*a simple country youth whose face shows not the remotest gleam of intelligence*" (2: 371). As he squanders his father's money, he keeps asserting that all he wants to do is "*have some fun.*" Phronesium offers him "*a nice hug, a little kiss,*" to which he answers, "I don't care what you do as long as I *have some fun*" (2: 392). He is oblivious of the "*winces of dismay on all sides*" at his speech and behavior.

At the very end of the play, Phronesium leads both of the arch rivals, Stratophanes and Strabax, into the house together. She addresses the audience, with Astaphium "*beaming*" and "*looking on*":

How cleverly I've netted them, and just the way I meant to! I've managed this *so* nicely! Perhaps I could take care of some of you as well? (*Points to members of the audience*) (2: 395–96)

This is not exactly a happy ending. It is harsh and sardonic, lewd also, because sex is so thoroughly commodified. Love has nothing at all to do with it.

The Captives is also a harsh play, ostensibly about slaves and slavery. It has no women in it and no love action. The beginning is unusual:

SCENE: *Stage in darkness. Spotlight reveals two young men with their wrists chained to the arms of a scaffold so that they can't sit down. The clothing of each is in a sorry state.* (1: 189)

At the end of the play, Tyndarus, who is actually the long-lost son of Hegio, the master, is being punished for his deception. He enters, "*in rags, caked with dirt, hardly able to stand—absurdly so*" (1: 247). He has been forced to labor in the quarries. In the last lines, Stalagmus, Hegio's slave who stole his four-year-old son away and sold him, is going to receive new and harder punishments. Hegio says, "Give *him* new chains!" and Stalagmus answers sardonically, "Since I have nothing now—thank you!" (1: 249).

The most unusual character in the play is Ergasilus, the parasite, the most developed parasite in all of Plautus. He has no connection with the slave action, and critics have speculated about what his function might be in *The Captives*. He is, most obviously, a kind of choral commentator. He is a life-affirmer in a play loaded with cruel details. When he enters he is described as "*a tall man, very fat and flabby*" who "*recoils in disgust*" at the scene with the slaves. Also, "*He is much given to the grand manner*" (1: 192). It's as if he comes out of a completely different play, and the contrast with the other characters is telling. He represents fullness, copiousness, endlessly fulfilling fantasies of eating and drinking in a play that is filled with tightness, narrowness, and the limited vision of Hegio and his panoply of slaves. In act 4 Ergasilus is ecstatic, frenzied, manic, because he comes with news of the return of Hegio's son, Philopolemus, from slavery in Elis:

> Jupiter, serve me and minister unto my plumpness!
> Boundless abundance, abundance unbounded, you bring me.
> Joy, praise, profit; festivity, jollity, pleasure;
> banqueting, pompous with edibles, roaring with goodies.
>
> (1: 232)

Ergasilus the parasite is the only person who speaks so positively in this somber play.

Hegio regards him as mad, although he welcomes his good news. Meanwhile, Ergasilus is in a Bacchic frenzy of anticipation at all the good things he will have to eat. He speaks orgiastically and in mock-military terms of what awaits him:

> Gone! [Hegio has run off] And this whole great house of digestibles open,
> bared to my loving attentions. Immortals of heaven!
> I shall strike smartly, and heads shall fly from their bodies.
> Ham's poor case shall be hopeless and bacon be battered.
> Pork shall be potted and sow's udder udderly done for.
> Lamb-butchers, pig-vendors, all who bring joy to the belly,
> how can I mention you all? To the glorious work, then!
> Hams hung high in suspense are awaiting the judgment.
>
> (1: 241)

The overwrought language is entirely in the style of the *miles gloriosus*. The abundant presence of Ergasilus in *The Captives* offers a contrary perspective of joy and indulgence in this sober slave play.

I have said nothing about Plautus' style, since all the plays are discussed here in translation. But the translators make a valiant effort to imitate in English Plautus' verbal facility, especially his punning, his alliteration, and his linguistic inventiveness. The songs in Plautus are in a great variety of meters, which lend themselves to a musical comedy kind of translation. None of the original music survives. Plautus' exuberance and extravagance extend into the conception of the plays, which were all based on Greek originals. They are essentially adaptations, but loose and very Roman adaptations.

Some of the stage effects and "business" of Plautus' plays are obvious to readers, but he evidently did a great deal to appeal to the audience. The actors are constantly taking the spectators into their confidence. The illusion that the play is being improvised—that there is no script—is important to Plautus. It is no wonder that he proved so important to Shakespeare, Jonson, and Molière, to name just a few of his imitators—and Machiavelli, especially in his wonderfully ingenious play *Il Mandragola* (1518). This is pure Plautus. He has been so influential in the history of comedy because he was so original and inventive. Even with stock characters and stock situations, he manages to drive them forward with a marvelous energy and excess. It's clear that he pushes his hyperbolic action beyond probability and good sense, but that is also the secret of his success as a comic dramatist. He definitely seems to be amusing himself by unexpected turns and a certain personal wildness.

Terence is a very different kind of comic dramatist from Plautus. He had tremendous influence on English and European literature since his plays were a favorite school text. Publius Terentius Afer was born in North Africa around 190 B.C.E., more than fifty years after Plautus. He came as a slave to Rome in the household of a Roman senator,

Terentius Lucanus, whose name he adopted when he was freed. Six of his plays survive, all based on Greek originals, especially Menander. He is supposed to have died in 159 B.C.E. on a journey to Greece. Terence's plays all have a serious if not ethical purpose, especially the relations of sons and fathers. His plots are often double and always complex. He is not a writer of farces like Plautus, although he uses the same kinds of characters but in a more realistic and lifelike way.

The Brothers (*Adelphoe*), translated by Constance Carrier, is a characteristic play by Terence. It is not like Plautus at all because it focuses on serious issues in the relations of fathers and sons (the most Plautine of Terence's plays is *The Eunuch*). *The Brothers* was first presented in 160 B.C.E. and is Terence's last play. The central theme is the relation between two brothers, Demea and Micio, who have very different ideas about how to rear their sons. Aeschinus is not actually Micio's son, but he adopted him at an early age.

The play is really about two different lifestyles. Micio is easygoing, urbane, and wants to enjoy life, whereas his brother Demea is a frugal, work-oriented farmer who lives in the country. So one of the large themes is country versus city. Micio's permissiveness in bringing up Aeschinus is much criticized by his very moral brother, whose own son, Ctesipho, has been brought up much more strictly. Aeschinus is pretty much of a wastrel. Micio supports and indulges him, but he doesn't really approve of his excesses. He chalks this up to sowing his wild oats and having a good time while he is young, in anticipation of all the cares and responsibilities that will be thrust upon him when he is married and has children. The brothers seem fond of each other and spend a good deal of time in arguing their positions.

Micio lays out the contrary points of view in a long speech in the first scene:

> My life's been a good one: all the joys of the city,
> No profession, no wife—how many envy me that!
> He's at the opposite pole: he lives in the country,
> He worships thrift and simplicity, has a wife
> And a couple of sons.
>
> (310)

Micio prides himself on his easy relation with his adopted son:

> I support him, don't often punish, try not to nag,
> And as a result, while others are pulling the wool
> Over their fathers' eyes, he's honest with me.
>
> (310)

Demea's authority is based on force, Micio's on friendship. *The Brothers* is an elaborate rationale for the values of Micio.

Ctesipho, Demea's son, is not what his father thinks him: a model of virtue. Unbeknownst to his father, we see him partying and dallying with his beloved lute-girl. It is only natural for a young person to do what Ctesipho is doing. His brother helps him buy the lute-girl Bacchis from her greedy procurer, Sannio. He lodges Bacchis in Micio's house for fear of how his father, Demea, will react.

The most surprising turn in the action is Demea's conversion to the values of Micio (act 5, sc. 4). This occurs quite spontaneously and unpredictably:

> I've learned
> The hard way that there's nothing really better
> For any man than easy-going kindness.
>
> (345)

Demea envies his brother's fulfilled and happy life:

> He's lived in leisure; loved society;
> Been calm and kind; hurt no one; smiled at all;
> Lived for himself, and spared no luxury—
> Everyone loves him and speaks well of him.
> But I—a farmer rough and mean, hot-headed—
> I married—that was misery. We had sons:
> More worries. So it goes! and in my struggles
> To save for them, I've ground away life.
>
> (345–46)

This leads directly to the superhappy ending, which is based on ideas and values, not just the ingenious trickery of a clever slave as in Plautus.

Quintilian, the Roman rhetorician of the first century, said that satire was a uniquely Roman invention (*satura . . . tota nostra est*). The Latin satirists follow the model of Lucilius, who died at the end of the second century B.C.E. His satires are very personal and autobiographical and attack the follies, vices, and crimes of his time. The language is often coarse and colloquial—not at all literary. The word *satura* means "medley," so that the satirist is free to speak in his own voice on a wide variety of topics. Horace (65–8 B.C.E.) is the best known of the Roman satirists, but his approach is much more gentle and gracious than that of Juvenal (Decimus Iunius Iuvenalis), who was born between A.D. 50 and 65, and who was still writing in the year 127. Juvenal wrote sixteen satires that are a biting and often angry attack on the degeneracy and corruption of his times.

Juvenal's first satire is a manifesto of what he will do in his writing. He feels a compulsion to write satire in these terrible times:

> it is difficult NOT to write satire. What human being
> Has such iron control of himself in this city of evil
> As to hold his tongue. . . .
>
> (*Satires* 18)

In his first satire Juvenal seems bursting to express himself: "Talent perhaps I lack, but anger's an inspiration" (20). Juvenal represents himself as a spokesman for the older values of probity, integrity, and plain speaking who cannot keep silent at the enormity of what he sees:

> When was there ever a time more rich in abundance of vices?
> When did the jaws of greed ever open wider, or gambling
> Have such consummate appeal?
>
> (20)

Juvenal is a self-appointed moralist inveighing against the evils he sees around him and against those in positions of power and influence.

One of Juvenal's large subjects is sexual morality. Satire 2, "Against Hypocritical Queens," is a coarse attack on sodomy and male prostitution, vices that were never so evident in the olden days when Romans were not so egregiously wealthy. The poet is very misogynistic, especially in Satire 6, "Against Women," which is almost twice as long as any of the other satires. The poem is specifically addressed to Postumus and the foolishness of his desire to marry. Juvenal attributes the decline in morals to "Dirty money . . . that first imported among us / Foreign vice" (74). There is a vivid portrait of drunken Venus:

> She can't tell one end of a thing from another,
> Gulping big oysters down at midnight, making the unguents
> Foam in the unmixed wine, and drinking out of a conch-horn
> While the walls spin round, and the table starts in dancing,
> And the glow of the lamps is blurred by double their number.
>
> (75)

Some of the accounts of vice are like those in Gibbon's *Decline and Fall of the Roman Empire* (1776–1788). Thus the wife of Emperor Claudius, "This imperial whore," slips out at night and visits a brothel:

> Reek of old sheets, still warm—her cell was reserved for her, empty,
> Held in the name of Lycisca. There she took off her dress,
> Showed her golden tits, and the parts where Britannicus came from,
> Took the customers on, with gestures more than inviting,
> Asked and received her price and had a wonderful evening.
>
> (67)

Presumably, this could never happen in preimperial Rome.

Juvenal's best-known satire is number 10, "On the Vanity of Human Wishes." This is the title of Samuel Johnson's imitation in 1749, and the Earl of Rochester used it as the basis for his "A Satire against Mankind" in 1675. Satire 10 is more wide-ranging than any of the others. It adopts the guise of the laughing Democritus to consider the falls of great princes and military and civic leaders such as Sejanus, Cicero, Demosthenes, Hannibal, Alexander, and Xerxes. The tone is elegiac because it is vain to hope for undying glory and conquest. Toward the end of the poem there is a bitter, pessimistic denunciation of long life:

> But a long old age is full of continual evils:
> Look, first of all, at the face, unshapely, foul, and disgusting,
> Unlike its former self, a hide, not a skin, and chopfallen;
> Look at the wrinkles too, like those which a mother baboon
> Carves on her face in the dark shade of Numidian jungles.
>
> (128)

This is the essence of Juvenalian *saeve indignatio*, savage indignation.

Juvenal follows the classic pattern of the satirist: return to the solid values of the simple life, especially the life lived in the country. Satire 11, "With an Invitation to Dinner," is a nostalgic appeal to the attractions of a rural existence. There is a special emphasis on food, not the degenerate, wildly expensive banquets of imperial Rome, but the wholesome pleasures that a homegrown meal can provide:

> Now, Persicus, listen.
> Here's what we're going to have, things we can't get in a market.
> From a field I own near Tivoli—this you can count on—
> The fattest kid in the flock, and the tenderest, one who has never
> Learned about grass, nor dared to nibble the twigs of the willow,
> With more milk in him than blood; and mountain asparagus gathered
> By my foreman's wife, after she's finished her weaving.
> Then there will be fresh eggs, great big ones, warm from the nest
> With straw wisps stuck to the shells, and we'll cook the chickens that laid them.
> (137–38)

These simple, natural country dishes offer a romantic counterbalance to the sophisticated and corrupt charms that Rome has to offer.

Plautus, Terence, and Juvenal all represent different aspects of the Roman genius for comedy. Plautus is very down-to-earth, Terence very ethical, and Juvenal very angry and acerbic, yet all three inveigh against the corruption and folly of the contemporary Roman life they see around them. Roman comedy is much less intellectual than the Greek comedies on which it is based. It speaks directly to us about the folly, vices, and crimes that are rampant in society. It is also amusing in its directness and its unpretentiousness.

REFERENCES AND FURTHER READINGS

Anderson, William S. *Barbarian Play: Plautus' Roman Comedy*. Toronto: U of Toronto P, 1942.
Duckworth, George E. *The Nature of Roman Comedy*. Princeton, NJ: Princeton UP, 1952.
Highet, Gilbert. *Juvenal the Satirist*. Oxford, UK: Clarendon, 1954.
Hunter, R. L. *The New Comedy of Greece and Rome*. Cambridge, UK: Cambridge UP, 1985.
Juvenal. *The Satires of Juvenal*. Trans. Rolfe Humphries. Bloomington: Indiana UP, 1958.
McCarthy, Kathleen. *Slaves, Masters, and the Art of Authority in Plautine Comedy*. Princeton, NJ: Princeton UP, 2000.
Miola, Robert S. *Shakespeare and Classical Comedy: The Influence of Plautus and Terence*. Oxford, UK: Oxford UP, 1994.
Moore, Timothy J. *The Theater of Plautus: Playing to the Audience*. Austin: U of Texas P, 1998.
Plautus, Titus Maccius. *The Comedies*. 4 vols. Ed. David R. Slavitt and Palmer Bovie. Baltimore, MD: Johns Hopkins UP, 1995. I have quoted from the following plays: *Amphitryon*, Trans. Constance Carrier (vol. 1); *The Braggart Soldier*, Trans. Erich Segal (vol. 1); *The Captives*, Trans. Richard Moore (vol. 1); *A Funny Thing Happened on the Way to the Wedding*, Trans. Richard Beacham (vol. 1); *The Haunted House*, trans. Palmer Bovie (vol. 3); *Pseudolus*, Trans. Richard Beacham (vol. 4); *The Savage Slave*, Trans. James Tatum (vol. 2).
———. *The Menaechmus Twins*. Trans. Lionel Casson. *Classic Comedies*. Ed. Maurice Charney. New York: New American Library, 1985.

Segal, Erich. *The Death of Comedy*. Cambridge, MA: Harvard UP, 2001.
_____, ed. *Oxford Readings in Menander, Plautus, and Terence*. Oxford, UK: Oxford UP, 2001.
_____. *Roman Laughter: The Comedy of Plautus*. Cambridge, MA: Harvard UP, 1968.
Slater, Niall W. *Plautus in Performance*. Princeton, NJ: Princeton UP, 1985.
Terence: The Comedies. Ed. Palmer Bovie. Baltimore, MD: Johns Hopkins UP, 1992. I have quoted from *The Brothers*, Trans. Constance Carrier.

33

The Romantic Period

William Galperin

In a period not noted for its great comic achievements, Jane Austen (1788–1824) and George Gordon, Lord Byron (1775–1817) are the notable exceptions. Austen's reputation as a comedienne of manners scarcely needs burnishing, and Byron's comparable achievement as a comic writer achieved its most succinct, if ultimately backhanded, confirmation in M. H. Abrams' exclusion of the poet from his great study of British romanticism, *Natural Supernaturalism*. Commenting in the book's preface on his decision to "omit [Byron] altogether," Abrams notes by way of justification that in his "greatest work [Byron] speaks with an ironic counter-voice and deliberately opens a satirical perspective on the vatic stance of his Romantic contemporaries" (13). Austen, needless to say, does not even warrant exclusion from this—or for that matter any—consideration of romanticism in England despite the fact she is perhaps the greatest writer of the period and by far the greatest novelist. Nevertheless, the reasons for her neglect in this regard are quite similar to those that Abrams enlists for Byron. Over and against the visionary strain of romanticism, with its emphasis on individual development and interiority along with its commitment to a better, more ecumenical world, the achievements of Austen and Byron are not just satiric and otherwise opposed to the sublime earnestness of their Romantic contemporaries; their achievements, on the arguments of critics such as Abrams, are also implicitly conservative in the way their satire is perceived as primarily regulatory rather than expansive in its ends.

Lurking in the background of these discriminations is the epochal break, as the Romantics construed it, between the eighteenth, or what Charles Lamb disparaged as the "past," century, and the early nineteenth century, which the Romantics for their parts saw as a moment of irrevocable change rather than a late flowering of the Enlightenment. While this break is primarily political, with romanticism becoming (through its various emphases) an armature of social change, the differences between the Romantics and their predecessors—as Abrams again reminds us—are very much aesthetic as well. Where the eighteenth century was viewed by the Romantics (and subsequently by their admirers) as an age of satire or comedy, embracing a multiplicity of forms, from poetry to drama to the growing institution of the novel, the romantic period is by comparison a moment of high seriousness in which these same genres are not simply turned to different purposes, but turned in such a way that only one of them—poetry—seems consistently to have worked in supporting a romantic ideology. There were, to be sure, many plays produced during this time, including gothic dramas, both native and imported. And virtually all the canonical Romantics, including Byron, tried their hands at drama with varying degrees of acclaim. The novel is a different matter, and while it too took on a romantic or Jacobin form in the late eighteenth century, most famously in William Godwin's *Caleb Williams* (1794), where the gothic conventions of terror and fear are put to uses both psychological and political, the novel that eventually emerged from this period, or that Ian Watt describes as having "risen" at this juncture, was anything but romantic in a conventional sense. It was, in fact, the realistic novel bequeathed to posterity by Jane Austen.

Defined by their deployment of free indirect discourse, an important effect of Austen's realistic comedies, both at the time and as a paradigm for novels afterward, was to make all of the characters, but primarily a central character, subservient to an overarching or omniscient authority. The primary function of this authority would appear to be regulatory or conservative in the tendency to judge a given character as opposed to aligning and otherwise sympathizing with that character, as might happen in a first-person narrative. Novels of the period that we recognize as romantic or radical were ones, then, where aesthetic form was made answerable to an individual protagonist in his or her struggle with society, usually by recourse to narration in the first-person. But the narrative form on which Austen settled, and that she simultaneously helped to codify, remained one in which the heroine or protagonist was necessarily subordinate to a social order whose spokesman was the all-seeing narrator. Such regulation was not simply a matter of making fun of and otherwise criticizing a given character; it depended more specifically—and with inescapable relevance to the sympathetic romanticism it ostensibly opposes—on a privileged access to a character's inner life. This access, in turn, allowed the omniscient narrator (and the reader in her image) the double prerogative of viewing both the world of the novel along with the subjective and perforce limited vantage of the character (or characters) within it. Thus, in perhaps the most well-known example of this procedure in Austen, Elizabeth Bennet's view of the world in *Pride and Prejudice* (1813), and of Mr. Darcy in particular, is blinkered by prejudice in a way that is made clear and a matter of consensus well in advance of Elizabeth's understanding of her limitations.

The allusion earlier to Austen's comedies was a reference primarily to the generic imperatives that the novelist followed in ending her novels with a series of marriages along with a requisite number of scapegoats. As a measure indeed of how studiously Austen avoided any genre apart from comedy (much less anything resembling tragedy), there are no observed deaths in any of her novels and just one reported death, which actually works to comedic purposes in relieving *Emma*'s Frank Churchill of any obligation to his imperious (and now deceased) aunt. But the reference here to Austen as a "comedienne" is more directly linked to the regulatory work of free indirect discourse and to its reliance on a relatively stable irony where, to quote Wayne Booth, readers are encouraged to "join" with Austen's narrator "in looking down on other men's follies" (42–44). An example of such irony, turned to both regulatory *and comic* effect, would be the famous first sentence of *Pride and Prejudice*: "It is a truth universally acknowledged, that a single man in possession of a good fortune, must be in want of wife" (1). The humor in this statement resides primarily in the condescension it invokes not just in miming the wish-fulfilling fantasies of anxious parents and desperate daughters, but in implicitly identifying these behaviors as components of the human comedy. To the extent that this sentence is funny it is also remarkably inured to "things as they are," and to the asymmetry, in particular, currently governing the relations of men and women. And this of course is only the beginning. *Pride and Prejudice* continues in this vein, derogating Elizabeth's mother, Mrs. Bennet, to such an extent that her legitimate worries over having to marry off not one but *four* daughters are all but displaced by her consistently hysterical and embarrassing reactions to that charge.

If comedy and irony are sufficient to describe both the initial statement of *Pride and Prejudice* and much of what ensues in the novel, they also describe *only one* aspect of the novel and its ironic stance. For just as the famous first sentence can be read along an axis of stable and ultimately comic irony, it modulates simultaneously to an unstable irony whose effect is far from either funny or conservative. In this latter configuration, the peculiar alignment with narrative authority, by which reading becomes a matter of "looking down," is interrupted by an incentive to reflection that is more a matter of looking up, or *beyond*, and in which laughter or even self-recrimination are secondary matters. While it may be "universally acknowledged," and by that sanction a truism, that "a single man in possession of a good fortune, must be in want of a wife," this altogether probable, and as such normative, scenario turns out, on another reading, to be *only that* and little else. It marks an imposition of social form, where the coercive weight of public opinion is necessarily synonymous with the wish-fulfilling fantasies of women, whose affirmation of "truth" is also a by-product of their vulnerability—or what is otherwise suppressed in a merely comical reading of this same observation. For the probabilistic scenario to work, that is, there must not only be a plethora of single, independent men and unmarried (and potentially indigent) women available for emplotment in a narrative of eventual and necessary union. There must also exist something on the order of "universal" inequality, since only in this climate is there enough pressure on both men and women to produce a phenomenon so widespread that it wears the mantle of truth.

The fact, then, that "truth" must be "universally acknowledged" in *Pride and Prejudice*, that it cannot stand *without* the continuous prop of opinion, custom, and fantasy, raises another possibility that all the weight of probability and all the force of conventional comedy cannot fully suppress. This possibility would be a world where women no longer need to marry to survive and where men, accordingly, are no longer obligated, much less entitled, to rescue them. Such a view presupposes that conventional marriage, especially in its mystified form as the happy close of either romance or comedic narrative, is also an impediment to women and on a continuum with the subordination that drives them to desire marriage to begin with. However taken in context—in conjunction with an observation that identifies men and women as both the objects *and agents* of cultural imperatives—the *prospect* of things being otherwise, however far from the "truth," is surprisingly close at hand.

In suggesting the potential revisability of truths universally acknowledged, I am drawing in some measure on the theories of Anthony Giddens and other social thinkers who urge that social forms and structures are not simply impositions but testimony paradoxically to the agency of those who both make and abide by them. More immediately, however, I am pointing to the way ironic practice—far from characterizing

Austen's irreducible difference from her romantic contemporaries—allows Austen to fixate on the very horizons of change that more conventional irony (and comedy), as Abrams suggests, tend largely to contravene. The truth of the novel's first sentence may look universal. Yet as the sentence indicates in a longer, less stable view, it is a truth that can theoretically change at any moment. That such change is almost exclusively a matter of abstraction in *Pride and Prejudice* does not diminish either the prospect itself or its power to contest what is presumed, on a more conventionally ironic reading, to be the whole truth and nothing but the truth. Nor does it diminish the fact that even here, in Austen's crowning comedic moment, a more romantic world of possibility shadows the probable and comical world of the novel, which is continually open to a current of revisability that stable irony may contain but never abolish. Thus while Mrs. Bennet goes on to bear the brunt, along with the majority of the female characters, of a seemingly justified misogyny to which stable irony and narrative authority lend constant support, *Pride and Prejudice* does not exactly conceal the fact that misogyny and the hierarchies it presupposes are equally inimical to society in general. We see this most clearly in the case of Mr. Bennet, whose jibes at his wife and at women's worries in general, though amusing in a localized way, redound on him to a degree that he emerges as perhaps the most pathetic and certainly the most isolated figure in the novel. Comedy and irony may have their uses. But these uses, Austen also shows, are potentially abusive and unlikely to work to a productive, much less meliorative, effect.

Pride and Prejudice is not the only text of Austen's where a stable, largely conservative irony is upended by a less stable, more progressive irony or where misogyny, to put the problem directly, shifts between a comic resource and a more progressive and self-reflexive apparatus. *Sense and Sensibility* (1811), which begins with a scathingly ironic portrait of the machinations of Mrs. John Dashwood as she works to deprive her sisters-in-law and their mother of all but a mere subsistence, is awkwardly suspended between practicing misogyny and identifying it as the veritable ether that the novel, like the society it represents, breathes. Much fun, of course, is made of a variety of women in the novel: from the anxious and emotional Mrs. Dashwood (who like Mrs. Bennet is obsessed with marrying her daughters), to the insipid Lady Middleton and her sister, Mrs. Palmer, whose flighty enthusiasm is alternately a counterweight to and a justification for her husband's disaffection, to the meddling Mrs. Jennings, to the overbearing Mrs. Ferrars, not to mention Mrs. John Dashwood herself. Such contempt or condescension works as much to the purposes of comedy as it does to display the social conventions in which women are perforce the butt of almost everything. Thus the very novel that begins on a note of vicious delectation in one woman's selfishness is also careful at that same moment to point up the inheritance practices by which the Dashwood sisters and their mother are, upon the death of the father, suddenly evicted from their proper residence. What serves for the purposes of comedy or satire, in other words, is necessarily continuous on another reading (and by a different irony) with the forces and practices that threaten and bedevil the novel's heroines.

A similar dynamic is evident in *Northanger Abbey* (1818), which is a satire not only on the gothic novel but on the gothic novel as a decidedly female enthusiasm. So determined is the narrator to make fun of both her heroine and that heroine's reading habits that she constantly overplays her hand, failing to control either the materials from which the narrative of *Northanger Abbey* is fashioned or the irony, again, by which comic control is exerted in the novel. The novel's first sentence—"No one who had ever seen Catherine Morland in her infancy, would have supposed her born to be a heroine" (1)—

is plainly a satire on readerly expectation or on the appetite for sensationalistic novels whose heroines are extraordinary in every way. Still, by the time that Catherine is described as "a strange, unaccountable character" (2) or as a character whose apparent lack of interest in normal sexual relations is "strange indeed" (4), the comic irony, which is initially quite stable, attenuates to an instability where the "strange" or "unaccountable" is prevalent and sufficiently readable to complicate the probabilistic—and ironic—attack on fictions of the marvelous. Far from being reducible to the ordinary or translatable (through stable irony) to the quotidian, the "strange" in these initial pages also figures alternatives amid ordinary circumstance to which the narrator is simply inattentive.

Chief among these possibilities is Catherine's boyishness, specifically her "love of dirt" and "hat[red of] confinement and cleanliness," all of which give way, in the narrator's self-confident description, "to an inclination for finery" and to other proclivities and developments:

she began to curl her hair and long for balls; her complexion improved, her features were softened by plumpness and colour, her eyes gained more animation, and her figure more consequence. . . . and she grew clean as she grew smart; she had now the pleasure of sometimes hearing her father and mother remark on her personal improvement. "Catherine grows quite a good-looking girl,—she is almost pretty to day," were words which caught her ears now and then; and how welcome were the sounds! (2–3)

On the face of it, this seems a witty description of the inevitable course of a young woman's growth. Yet with the history of Catherine's initial resistance already in view, her gendering, which the narrator sees as entirely natural and inevitable, opens onto an horizon of possibility that works to denaturalize and to deconstruct Catherine's seemingly typical development. Becoming a woman appears as much a "consequence" of external motivation here—notably the sporadic, even sadistic, praise inherent in the regulatory work of intermittent gratification—as the result of certain innate longings that cannot in any case be divorced from the incentives and rewards by which coercion becomes what Austen later calls "internal persuasion" (*Persuasion* [1818] 207) or conviction. The "inclination" to be a full-fledged woman tends, in the narrator's accounting, to conflate personal improvement and the improvement of the person so that coercive force behind the imperative to gender (a socially assigned identity) is entirely a matter of biology.

It is not that Austen's narrator is preternaturally mindful of the nonequivalence of sex and gender to undertake a knowing and somewhat sinister strategy of obfuscation and containment. It is rather that there is enough slippage between the narrator's claims and the materials from which these claims (and the intended comedy) are fashioned so that narrative authority, or incompetence as the case may be, is marshaled on behalf of certain possibilities that it is the manifest aim of both free indirect discourse and its resultant comedy to discountenance and contain.

Nowhere are the limits to authority, and to comedy as *both* an ironic practice and a genre, more evident than in the narrator's obtuseness to same-sex relations in *Northanger Abbey*, which variously circumscribe Catherine's affective life, including her relation to both men and the male-dominated culture at large. Nor is it a coincidence that the first relationship of this sort in the novel, the short-lived friendship with Isabella Thorpe, is initially cemented by a shared interest in novels, specifically gothic novels, whose function was to represent, if allegorically, the perilous condition of women at the time they were written. This last point will be revisited much later in *Northanger Abbey* when, in his famous correction of Catherine's gothic fantasies regarding his father's ill treatment of his late wife, Henry Tilney effective rewrites the gothic by instructing Catherine in the difference between "the country and age in which we live" (159) and the gothic anterior, whose only referent, in Henry's jingoistic calculus, is a world elsewhere. In the meantime the task of disabusing the gothic—specifically the novels of Ann Radcliffe—of any explanatory function regarding the present is taken up by the narrator, who, without even mentioning the novels that Catherine and Isabella "shut themselves up . . . to read . . . together" (21) uses the occasion of their joint reading to launch a paean to the novel in general that has virtually no bearing on the specific reading habits that have apparently provoked it. If anything it is the effect of the narrator's pointed defense of probabilistic fiction—particularly in conjunction with the disclosure that this is not the kind of fiction that Catherine reads or enjoys—to perform two functions: to situate the narrator still more firmly in the regulatory or satiric camp, and to introduce a protocol of reading that follows the example of *readers in the novel* in opposing the narrator's strictures and aims.

If Austen's early novels gyrate between a stable irony whose function is comic and satiric, and an unstable irony that consistently undermines the regulatory aims of the satiric narrator, Austen's later novels are somewhat more integrated not only in their management of irony but also in the way their comedy is no longer merely regulatory. In fact, in the very way that comedy is initially mobilized to a primarily conservative function in the early novels, it tends, if anything, to work to opposite effect in both *Mansfield Park* and *Emma*. Whether this represents a wholesale change in Austen's outlook is a matter of debate. What is clear is that the contest of ironies (and ideologies) that previously spelled trouble for the comic and satiric stance in Austen has apparently been resolved or reconfigured in such a way that comedy no longer strictly serves either narrative authority or the conservative social work in which that authority has been implicated. In the later novels, by contrast, the comic set-pieces appear more as transcripts of reality shorn of any bias or authority or directed meaning, making comedy a more ambiguous and, by turns, a more progressive engine.

In *Mansfield Park* (1814), there is a splendid scene immediately following Sir Thomas Bertram's surprise return to Mansfield Park and his discovery that his children (including his son Tom) and their friends have been mounting a private theatrical in his absence and, even worse, in a room intended exclusively for Sir Thomas' own use. Sir Thomas, it should be noted, is something of a prig as is his niece, the heroine Fanny Price, who has been adamant in her opposition to the play, claiming over and over that she cannot act. Nevertheless, as the following scene with Sir Thomas makes clear, there is no end to acting, especially for those who, like either Fanny or Sir Thomas, think that they are simply themselves when they are *already* performing as social constructions and (de)formations:

[Sir Thomas] stept to the door [of his room] . . . and opening it, found himself on the stage of a theatre, and opposed to a ranting young man who appeared likely to knock him backwards. At the very moment of Yates perceiving Sir Thomas and giving perhaps the best start he had ever given in the whole course of his rehearsals, Tom Bertram entered at the other end of the room; and he never found greater difficulty in keeping his countenance. His father's looks of solemnity and amazement on this his first appearance on any stage, and the gradual metamorphosis of the impassioned Baron Wildenhaim into the well-bred and easy Mr. Yates, making his bow and apology to Sir Thomas Bertram, was such an exhibition, such a piece of true acting as he would not have lost upon any account. It would be the last—in all probability the last scene on that stage; but he was sure there could not be a finer. (164)

If the meaning of this encounter defies a more precise articulation by either the narrator or Tom, it is not for failure to fathom "what" a "theatre," to quote another character in the novel, "signifies" (111).

Tom's notably cryptic delectation may be traced now to the way the encounter between the "baron" and the baronet makes truth or transparency a condition of the particular text—or the particular social text—in which the subject literally discovers himself. The "true acting" that has an indelible if strangely benign effect on Tom pertains less to Yates' natural good manners than to the way this performance, actually this metamorphosis, highlights the theatricality or insincerity of true being in general. For by passage from Wildenhaim to Yates, the body to which either "Wildenhaim" or "Yates" has been assigned does little more than shift roles, exposing the equally theatrical, equally duplicitous arrangement in which it is obliged as Yates to show deference to the ingenuous Sir Thomas. Beyond the oedipal strife, which might appear to justify Tom's amusement at his father's unease, there is something in this encounter that not only gives Tom pause but also has the more important effect of projecting a position beyond or opposed to the one that Sir Thomas and the performing Yates are compelled, in different ways, to sustain.

If this beyondness has a certain vatic or utopian quality that, as Abrams sees it, is necessarily incongenial to satire or comedy, it is because Austen, though far from reconciled to the world in which she finds herself, has hardly given up hope. And while hope in Austen—or more precisely the vistas it contemplates—maintains a strangely indeterminate character in the novels, it is only because hope, or its object, is necessarily the "other" to what *is* or currently abides. This is particularly evident in Austen's later comic scenes where reading, in the image of Tom's response, becomes the repository of possibilities on which the world continually forecloses but to which *comedy* now increasingly provides steady access. This is especially the case in Austen's greatest novel, *Emma* (1816), where comedy in, say, the treatment of Emma's valetudinarian father becomes a way to meditate on male privilege and on the way its particular tyranny takes on seemingly benign but by no means inconsequential forms. In a novel, indeed a world, where women are routinely susceptible to judgment and blame, not to mention indigence, men, comedy reminds us, get off virtually scot-free. An extended dialogue between two relatively peripheral characters—Mr. Weston and Mrs. Elton—provides just such a reminder.

As readers of *Emma* will recall, Mr. Weston is blessed with particularly good fortune and a good reputation despite a history of chronic irresponsibility, beginning with his marriage and with the subsequent consignment of his son Frank to the care (and nomenclature) of his in-laws upon the death of his wife. Readers will also recall that Mrs. Elton is concomitantly held up to a standard of judgment—chiefly in trying to insinuate herself into a small society that clearly wants no part of her—that is nowhere evident in the treatment of any male character in *Emma*. Nevertheless, in a somewhat extended dialogue toward the end of the second volume some redress is provided by agency of comedy. No matter how much Mrs. Elton contrives to get a foothold in a conversation initiated and dominated by Mr. Weston, who will talk of nothing but the very son he abandoned and who will be arriving soon to pay *his* respects to his father's second and much younger wife, she fails utterly. In every effort indeed to turn the conversation to herself and her family (or to a topic other than Mr. Weston and his progeny) Mrs. Elton is rebuffed. When Mr. Weston admits early on to having opened a letter from Frank addressed to his wife, and is lightheartedly scolded by her for having done so, he responds by reminding Mrs. Elton that "we men are sad fellows" and that she "must take of [her]self" (275) before immediately returning to the topic of his son's arrival. When Mrs. Elton contrives to draw parallels between her family and the in-laws who adopted Frank, they are completely ignored. Only when Mrs. Elton makes it impossible not to notice her, expressing the hope that her own relatively recent arrival had been communicated to Frank by letter, are her entreaties met. But what the dialogue also demonstrates is that Mrs. Elton's "call for a compliment" (278), far from simply endemic to her character, is primarily a reaction to being minimized both as a woman and as a stranger. This tendency reaches something of a crescendo when Mrs. Elton is suddenly "stopped by a slight fit of coughing," which far from eliciting concern or commiseration allows Mr. Weston "instantly" to seize "the opportunity of going on" (278) with his discourse—just as with the arrival of tea, "Mr. Weston, having said all that he wanted, soon [takes] the opportunity of walking away" (280).

This brief summary does scant justice to the hilarity of the encounter, in which Mrs. Elton contrives with absolutely no luck to make herself the center of attention. But where such efforts might have redounded on her in an early Austen novel, they are met in *Emma* with enough circumstantial, if now comic, detail that the specter of blame or more properly reflection—beginning indeed with what to Mr. Weston is a completely unproblematic violation of his wife's privacy—is transferred more directly to things as they are and, more importantly, to things that should change. Where the initial sentence of *Pride and Prejudice* opens tentatively onto this latter—and more progressive—orientation, the comic practice of Austen's later novels, based primarily in the nicely observed but still-cryptic vignette, places far greater weight on readerly response (and reflection) than on any gratification that might come through joining the narrator in always judging people. The more progressive the comedy, in other words, the more democratic the relationship with the reader.

Lord Byron, for his part, suffered significantly less confusion, particularly as a comic writer. And while Abrams and others are right to see this as Byron's distinguishing feature, especially in the company of his romantic contemporaries, they are somewhat less accurate in the tendency to view Byron's politics, and more specifically his position on social change, entirely though the lens of a seemingly conservative aesthetics. Byron, it should be remembered, does have his romantic moments as well, most notably in *Childe Harold's Pilgrimage*, a travelogue-cum-commentary tracing one figure's response to the state and decline of postrevolutionary Europe. This isolated individual in Byron's poetry, or what we have come to identify as the "Byronic hero," is in one sense a somewhat extravagant self-dramatization that both the British and the European public found fascinating. But the Byronic hero is just as much a critique of the solitary or meditative individualism projected in the works of William Wordsworth and others. There is, in short, something futile about the isolation of the solitary subject in Byron—so that what is otherwise put to democratic or progressive purposes in, say, Percy Bysshe Shelley's paeans to subjectivity and to the significance of individual lives and experiences is shown by Byron to be an obstruction to the very solidarity or democracy or conversation that is both the object of and, more importantly, the *means* to social change.

The comic tendency, then, that effectively frames Byron's career, beginning with his first fully mature volume, *English Bards and Scotch Reviewers* (1809), and culminating in *Don Juan*, the great comic epic he was at work on until his death in 1824, is not the retrenchment, particularly on political grounds, that Abrams argues for (and implicitly against). If anything, comedy in Byron is very much a leveling or democratizing apparatus. Like so much else in Byron's writing, including the highly critical theatricalization of individualism in the dramatic poem *Manfred*, comedy is directed less on behalf of an earlier or more conservative orientation than against the newer, more progressive ideals of inherent worth and individual potentiality, which have been insufficient in removing either hierarchy or hegemony from the social and political landscape. Far from presupposing either a traditional or even a stable set of values, comedy in Byron is remarkably open-ended and pitched toward the achievement of a better society that has yet to come into being.

We see this provisional comedy in *English Bards and Scotch Reviewers*, the satirical survey of the (then) current literary and political scene that marks Byron's real entry into the literary public sphere. The poem is roundly satirical and seemingly conservative, both in its imitation and admiration of writers like Alexander Pope and John Dryden and in its concomitant disdain of the "new schools of Poetry" (line 135) that characterize "these degenerate days" (line 103). Here, for example, is Byron on Wordsworth, who is glimpsed, along with his contemporaries Robert Southey and Samuel Taylor Coleridge, in a procession of pompous, pious fools:

> Next comes the dull disciple of [the lake or romantic] school,
> That mild apostate from poetic rule
> The simple Wordsworth, framer of a lay
> As soft as evening in his favourite May,
> Who warns his friend "to shake off toil and trouble,
> And quit his books, for fear of growing double;"
> Who, both by precept and example, shows
> That prose is verse, and verse is merely prose;
> Convincing all, by demonstration plain,
> Poetic souls delight in prose insane;
> And Christmas stories tortured into rhyme
> Contain the essence of the true sublime.
> Thus, when he tells the tale of Betty Foy,
> The idiot mother of an "idiot boy;"
> A moon-struck, silly lad, who lost his way,
> And, like his bard, confounded night with day;
> So close on each pathetic part he dwells,
> And each adventure so sublimely tells,
> That all who view the "idiot in his glory"
> Conceive the bard the hero of the story.
>
> (lines 235–54)

To make fun of Wordsworth's earnest, if unorthodox, interest in rural primitivism, along with his commitment to writing in what he called the language of real men in contrast to more formal poetic diction, was—as Byron surely realized—an easy move and probably too easy. It is noteworthy that Byron concentrates his satire on Wordsworth's "The

Idiot Boy" rather than on, say, "Tintern Abbey," which appeared in the same volume (*Lyrical Ballads*) and whose claims to the "sublime" are incontestable and far harder to lampoon.

Not all of Byron's subjects are treated as harshly in *English Bards*. Some, including Sir Walter Scott, are simply urged to abandon certain contemporary traits, whereas others—Thomas Campbell and Samuel Rogers—are pushed to continue their already good work. Still, it is interesting that where Byron lavishes his praise and encouragement on writers who, in retrospect (and even at the time) are relatively minor (with the exceptions naturally of Scott and Robert Burns), he reserves both his strongest praise and strongest blame for canonical writers, present and past. Wordsworth is the apotheosis of all that is wrong with modern poetry, while the standard-bearers of excellence turn out to be none of Byron's contemporaries but in fact poets long deceased. What all of this means—in conjunction with Byron's decision here to imitate Pope—is that poetry's future, especially as a public and political resource, is very much up for grabs along with Byron's impending and projected career. The recourse to Popean satire may work as a protest to the new, as Byron construes it. But it does precious little in making poetry *relevant* to a society and a culture whose various transformations have given rise to aesthetic forms, like Wordsworth's, that may be attacked but cannot—on the urgency of these attacks—be simply wished away.

Thus even as Byron contrives to assume the pose of a condescending authority on all matters literary and cultural, he ends on a more assailable and provisional note of brashness and ambition:

> And though I hope not hence unscathed to go,
> Who conquers me shall find a stubborn foe. . . .
> But now, so callous grown, so changed since youth,
> I've learned to think, and sternly speak the truth;
> Learn'd to deride the critic's starch decree,
> And break him on the wheel he meant for me;
> To spurn the rod a scribbler bids me kiss,
> Nor care if courts and crowds applaud or hiss:
> Nay more, though all my rival rhymesters frown,
> I too can hunt a poetaster down;
> And, arm'd in proof the gauntlet cast at once
> To Scotch marauder, and to southern dunce.
> Thus much I've dared; if my incondite lay
> Hath wrong'd these righteous times, let others say:
> This, let the world, which knows not how to spare,
> Yet rarely blames unjustly, now declare.
>
> (lines 1050–70)

Byron later wished that he had "[never written] the greater part of this satire"—"not only on account of the injustice of much of the critical, and some of the personal part of it—but the tone and temper are such as I cannot approve" (*Selected Poems* 47).

Nevertheless, as even the satire's seemingly intemperate conclusion makes clear, the poem is primarily an invitation to dialogue rather than a draconian exercise in administering praise and blame to a regulatory and repressive effect. The tone and diction are belligerent and less comical certainly than the attacks on Wordsworth. But they are also exaggerated or performative in functioning as a goad rather than in providing an answer, much less a resolution, to the crisis (as Byron perceives it) of the current literary scene. There is, if anything, a decided and eminently *readable* difference between the "world" or public as it is enlisted in these closing lines and the speaker/provocateur, whose own blame or tendency to judgment is—against this horizon of both arbitration and conversation—implicitly unjust or at least inconclusive. Byron may have had his quarrels with his contemporaries. But his decision to project those quarrels outward and onward in an ongoing conversation suggests that the answer, specifically the generic or aesthetic answer, cannot rest in tradition—or in this case eighteenth-century satiric tradition—but must pursue new forms and means of engagement.

The apotheosis of these forms is Byron's magnum opus *Don Juan*. Begun in exile following Byron's scandalous separation from his wife of merely one year, the poem was, like *Childe Harold*, conceived as a meditation on Europe's moment of revolution from the vantage of its unhappy return to monarchical legitimacy in the wake of Napoleon Bonaparte's defeat. But the point to stress, even if in one plan the poem—indeed epic—was to have ended with Don Juan at the guillotine during the Reign of Terror, is that this rather charged and polemical reflection was accomplished by primarily comical means. The hero, for example (whose name is waggishly pronounced "Don *Joo*-an" in accordance with the poem's rhyme), is an inversion of the fabled seducer memorialized in many works including those by Molière and Mozart. Where Don Juan (or in Mozart's case Don Giovanni) is invariably portrayed as an amoral figure, controlling and overpowering women according to his desires, Byron's hero—whom the narrator seizes upon only after lamenting that the present age offers no suitable rivals or alternatives—is for much of the poem a virtually epicene figure at the disposal of older or more powerful women.

Exactly how this jibes with the poem's geopolitical focus, beyond the narrator's tendency to digress to matters that include the current state of Europe and the world, is not immediately clear. Nor is it clear for that matter—apart from the narrator's early dismissal of any number of "modern" heroes on whom an epic might be based—that the poem is about anything apart from the human comedy as projected in, among other places, the famous first sentence of Austen's *Pride and Prejudice*. That sentence, we recall, modulates from a comical, if resigned, view of the marriage market, particularly as it shapes and distorts female desire, to a more visionary recognition of the capacity of both men and women to change things. This turns out, then, to be the case with Byron's poem as well, especially in its preoccupation with change in the aftermath of failed revolution. Focusing (like Austen) on gender, marriage, and the relation between the sexes, *Don Juan* is indeed about the human comedy but to the degree that comedy and social change may be linked, once again, along an axis of hope. In other words, *Don Juan* is about change—albeit change by other means. Beginning indeed with the poem's subject matter, which is primarily local or domestic, these other means extend to the way that the local as such comes to characterize the experience or more specifically the *yield* of the poem as a political and social text. For if *Don Juan* can be said to resemble the world on which it dilates, both as an object of scrutiny and a site of possibility, it is due primarily to the poem's narrator, whose intimacy and humorous sociability are reminders that textuality, like solidarity, is more properly interactive or a matter of conversation rather than a matter of mere authority.

Among the many inversions of epic convention in *Don Juan*, then, is the narrator's decision to begin his poem not in *in medias res* (in the middle of things) but with, as he puts it, the "beginning." It is only appropriate that we do the same. Attached to the manuscript of the poem's first canto is a single stanza in ottava rima (the poem's rhyme scheme) that gives an excellent sense of what both Byron and his comedy are ultimately all about:

> I would to Heaven that I were so much clay,
>   As I am blood, bone, marrow, passion feeling—
> Because at least the past were passed away,
>   And for the future—(but I write this reeling,
> Having got drunk exceedingly to-day,
>   So that I seem to stand upon the ceiling)
> I say—the future is a serious matter—
> And so—for God's sake—hock and soda-water!
>
> (5)

The primary features of *Don Juan*, from the narrator's wit and intimacy to the poem's necessary juxtaposition of comedy and a progressive or at least projective seriousness, are gathered in this one stanza. The stanza begins with a typically Byronic—indeed romantic—claim for human primacy over other modes of being, or what Byron in numerous places refers to as our antithetical mixture of divinity and dust. But it quickly turns—with the past or history as a goad—to something at once comic and (dare we say it) more visionary. In falling back somewhat drunkenly on the cliché of seriousness in addressing the future before calling for even more to drink, Byron's speaker is certainly adopting the comical pose of an improviser who, despite inebriation, is able somehow to follow the imperatives of versification. But in the very way, again, that stable irony—in for example Austen—can morph into something less stable and contained, so it is the case here that futurity, far from being something that the speaker can hardly confront much less comprehend, is very much the point. Shadowed by a past that may be as much a matter of personal history for Byron as a matter of convention, tradition, and culture, both the future and the related efforts at its mitigation, whether by drink or laughter, are ultimately circumscribed, or at least inflected, by a seriousness unmoored from cliché but not necessarily from comedy. For the future, after all, is not only something from which the speaker is in flight; it is also another term for the poem that will ensue in which self-irony, comedy, and sociability are the stylistic complements to a world whose transformation, particularly in the postrevolutionary era, bespeaks the conviction now that all politics, and certainly the politics of social change, are necessarily local.

It bears repeating, then, that, in addition to seizing on gender and domestic relations, not simply as objects of ridicule but as the site of a futurity as yet unrealized, *Don Juan* was produced serially over six years—so that "the future" and the poem's future are in many ways equivalent. While the future in general can be said to open onto a horizon of change (if only as the obverse of things as they are), the other future in *Don Juan*—the poem itself—is palpably the means of effecting or realizing the former. And what better way to change domestic life than through a discourse of domesticity—or more properly a conversation—where the narrator's self-irony, particularly as someone who is effectively one of us, remains paramount?

It is frequently remarked that the real hero of *Don Juan* is not the eponymous character (whose primary action is reaction) but rather the narrator himself, whose digressions on a variety of matters threaten to usurp the narrative of young Juan's various encounters. Indeed even when the poem is about Juan, particularly in the first canto, where we trace his development into a sexual being, it is more properly about gender relations and their discontents. If Juan's mother, Donna Inez, is something of moral tyrant, particularly in her management of Juan's education, it is due mostly to a doctrine of separate spheres where men are permitted to transgress and where marriage, accordingly, is a site of conflict rather than improvement or melioration:

> Don Jose and Donna Inez led
>   For some time an unhappy sort of life,
> Wishing each other, not divorced, but dead;
>   They lived respectably as man and wife,
> Their conduct was exceedingly well-bred,
>   And gave no outward signs of inward strife,
> Until at length the smothered fire broke out,
> And put the business past all kind of doubt.
>
> For Inez called some druggists and physicians,
>   And tried to prove her loving lord was *mad*,
> But as he had some lucid intermissions,
>   She next decided he was only *bad*;
> Yet when they asked her for depositions,
>   No sort of explanation could be had,
> Save that her duty both to man and God
> Required this conduct—which seemed very odd.
>
> She kept a journal, where his faults were noted,
>   And opened certain trunks of books and letters,
> All which might, if occasion served, be quoted;
>   And then she had all Seville for abettors,
> Besides her good old grandmother (who doted);
>   The hearers of her case became repeaters,
> Then advocates, inquisitors, and judges,
> Some for amusement, others for old grudges.
>
>   (canto 1, st. 26–28)

If this seems a decidedly satiric account of the deformity to which modern marriage reduces its participants, with particular attention to women, it is not because Byron either is misogynist or has given up hope. It is because the problems that currently afflict humans are largely structural and matters of social form and convention rather than inherent and unalterable. If Donna Inez appears deformed here it is a deformation linked to the imbalance of power and to the prerogatives that devolve upon men—with the notable exception here of Juan himself. An exception, rather, who thereby proves the rule, Juan moves quickly and parodically from the charge of his mother to the plaything of a variety of women whose power over him, to the degree they can exert it, is plainly a reaction to their being disempowered or subordinate in some other way. There is Dona Julia, for example, a family friend married to the much older and possessive (and by no means faithful) Don Alphonse. She is succeeded by Haidee, on whose island Juan washes up following a shipwreck, and whose power over Juan is conditional upon the absence of her father, the pirate Lambro, who eventually returns, sending Juan away. Both of these encounters end tragically or with a return to normalcy that spells trouble for female agency. Julia's infidelity is discovered and she is sent to a convent, and Haidee dies from an aneurysm suffered upon her father's return. There is also the Sultana Gulbeyaz, who picks Juan out from a group of slaves into which he has been captured and sold (following his removal from Haidee's island) and ultimately secretes him in her husband's harem. Needless to say, the comic dimension to the harem, with Juan as a proto-Tootsie, is fully exploited by Byron, but only as a prelude to the seriousness that inevitably ensues. For upon Juan's resistance to her advances, the sultana breaks down in tears, reminding us not only that she is incapable of imitating her husband's example of polygamous (or extramarital) indulgence, but also that gender necessarily trumps power (as it did in Byron's time, when women, no matter their background, could neither vote nor generally hold property).

A defining feature of comedy, prevalent in the works of Shakespeare and others, is its inversion of power relations between the sexes. While Byron's poem clearly recapitulates this tendency, it does so less to provide a respite from things as they are normally than as an incentive to change. The comic if still "serious" apparatus of female agency may be invoked by Byron but almost always as a prelude to a more normative reversal that is far from amusing or comforting. Save in one crucial instance: the mock-gothic episode of the Black Friar on which *Don Juan* effectively ends and which enlarges upon its precedents (in, say, either Haidee or Gulbayez) in making comedy and the "serious matter" of futurity coterminous.

By this point in the poem, Juan has traveled to England in a diplomatic capacity where he is soon ensconced in the very world—the "great world" of aristocrats and gentry but also the world of women and domesticity—that Byron inhabited in his "years of fame" and which he was obliged to depart following his separation from Lady Byron. In returning to this world, then, or in taking his poem there, Byron is returning not simply to the site of his marriage, but also to a site that—given everything else in the poem—is very palpably one of missed opportunity. Lady Byron, it must be stressed, is everywhere on *Don Juan*, beginning with Donna Inez and continuing on to the later cantos, where she is figured in a number of different characters, including Lady Adeline Amundeville, Aurora Raby, and the Duchess Fitz-Fulke. These characters, needless to say, are far from unambiguous, either as characterizations in their own right or as signifiers for a marriage gone awry. But what they represent in aggregate, far more than their male counterparts (including Juan), is a futurity that, as the fragment attached to canto 1 indicates, is palpably linked to a past that simply will not go away. Just because Byron was dispositionally unsuited for marriage does not also mean that he did not recognize its virtues, especially as a companionate union of equals. And what better way to mark that equality than by acknowledging female desire as being equal to male desire, which is where the Don Juan tradition (as opposed to its inversion here) normally proceeds?

In the poem's crowning comic moment, a sleep-deprived Juan is aggressively pursued by a spectral figure who, tradition has it, is the ghost of a friar who actively resisted the appropriation of church lands during the reign of Henry VIII. What Juan discovers of course is that the figure haunting him is not that fabled ghost but the very married Duchess Fitz-Fulke, a guest of Lord and Lady Amundeville, at whose reconverted abbey/country house Juan is staying. After catching glimpses of the ghost for several evenings Juan finally encounters the specter in his room and discovers furthermore that it is quite reluctant to leave him:

> But still the Shade remained: the blue eyes glared,
>   And rather variably for stony death;
> Yet one thing rather good the grave had spared,
>   The ghost had a remarkably sweet breath:
> A straggling curl showed he had been fairhaired;
>   A red lip, with two rows of pearl beneath,
> Gleamed forth, as through the casement's ivy shroud
> The Moon peeped, just escaped from a grey cloud.
>
> And Juan puzzled, but still curious, thrust
>   His other arm forth—Wonder upon wonder!
> It pressed upon a hard but glowing bust,
>   Which beat as if there was a warm heart under.
> He found, as people on most trials must,
>   That he had made at first a silly blunder,
> And that in his confusion he had caught
> Only the wall, instead of what he sought.
>
> The Ghost, if Ghost it were, seemed a sweet soul
>   As ever lurked beneath a holy hood:
> A dimpled chin, a neck of ivory, stole
>   Forth into something much like flesh and blood;
> Back fell the sable frock and dreary cowl,
>   And they revealed—alas! that e'er they should!
> In full voluptuous, but *not o'ergrown* bulk,
> The phantom of her frolic Grace—Fitz-Fulke!
>
> (16.121–23)

Among the conventions being mocked here are not just the gothic, which was a popular subgenre in poetry, fiction and drama in the decades preceding *Don Juan*, but more specifically the gothic associated with the novelist Ann Radcliffe, whose popularity, we recall, was a central feature in Austen's *Northanger Abbey* and the source of its ostensible satire. Unlike many of her contemporaries, notably Matthew "Monk" Lewis, whose gothic representations had recourse to supernatural elements, Radcliffe's novels, including *The Italian* and *The Mysteries of Udolpho*, were notable in providing rational explanations for seemingly supernatural phenomena. Regardless then of any political allegory or subtext embedded in them, Radcliffe's writings were typically viewed as less subversive and less radical than other gothic productions since they did not, on balance, undermine the metaphysical or divine sanctions of conventional, indeed Christian, morality.

The Radcliffean gothic, then, especially as a genre intended to give comfort, is very much an issue at the conclusion of canto 16. But the point, indeed the comic point of Fitz-Fulke's disclosure, is that female desire—or worse, the assumption of male prerogative by a woman in this instance—may well be more frightening and more threatening to the dominant order than an actual ghost. The "supernatural" has undoubtedly been explained. But its explanation proceeds in both a way and along an axis of change that makes this explanation (and the society it projects) more terrifying, again, than ordinary gothic machinery, which is merely supernatural rather than natural (or social) in its reach. There is no question that the irruption/disclosure of "Fitz-Fulke" operates primarily as a punchline whose efficacy resides (despite the precedents of Gulbayez and others) in the unlikelihood and unseemliness of female aggressiveness. But it is a punchline that ultimately founders on surprise or on a perplexity instilled by desire regardless of its bearer. Far from looking down on or askance at the grotesque spectacle of the ravenous duchess, Byron's poem mobilizes that condescension, and the comic/satiric conventions it evokes, to redound on any reader who is unwilling or unable to look beyond to a better world where gender is no longer a pretext for creating differences and constructing hierarchies. The scene with Fitz-Fulke is surely funny. But, as Sigmund Freud among others would claim, it is necessarily more than that and completely in keeping with a comic spirit that is progressive and, with all due to respect to Abrams, remarkably, even poignantly, visionary.

REFERENCES AND FURTHER READINGS

Abrams, M. H. *Natural Supernaturalism: Tradition and Revolution in Romantic Literature*. New York: Norton, 1971.

Austen, Jane. *Emma*. 1816. Ed. James Kinsley. Oxford, UK: Oxford UP, 1971.

———. *Mansfield Park*. 1814. Ed. James Kinsley. Oxford, UK: Oxford UP, 1970.

———. *Northanger Abbey*. 1818. Ed. John Davie. Oxford, UK: Oxford UP, 1971.

———. *Persuasion*. 1818. Ed. John Davie. Oxford, UK: Oxford UP, 1971.

———. *Pride and Prejudice*. 1813. Ed. James Kinsley. Oxford, UK: Oxford UP, 1970.

———. *Sense and Sensibility*. 1811. Ed. James Kinsley. Oxford, UK: Oxford UP, 1970.

Booth, Wayne. *A Rhetoric of Irony*. Chicago: U of Chicago P, 1971.

Byron, Lord George Gordon. *Don Juan*. 1819–1826. Ed. Leslie Marchand. Boston: Houghton Mifflin, 1958.

———. *English Bards and Scotch Reviewers*. 1809. *Selected Poems*. Ed. Susan J. Wolfson and Peter J. Manning. Harmondsworth, UK: Penguin, 1996.

Freud, Sigmund. *Jokes and Their Relation to the Unconscious*. Trans. and ed. James Strachey. New York: Norton, 1963.

Giddens, Anthony. *The Constitution of Society: Outline of the Theory of Structuration*. Berkeley: U of California P, 1984.

Lewis, Matthew. *The Monk*. Ed. Howard Anderson. Oxford, UK: Oxford UP, 1973.

Radcliffe, Ann. *The Italian*. Ed. Frederick Garber. Oxford, UK: Oxford UP, 1968.

———. *The Mysteries of Udolpho*. Ed. Bonamy Dobree. Oxford, UK: Oxford UP, 1967.

Watt, Ian. *The Rise of the Novel*. Berkeley: U of California P, 1957.

Wordsworth, William, and Samuel Taylor Coleridge. *Lyrical Ballads 1798*. Ed. W.J.B. Owen. Oxford, UK: Oxford UP, 1969.

34

Satire

Harry Keyishian

A satire is a work of literature or graphic art that uses humor for the purpose of censure or ridicule. Describing, dissecting, and discrediting behavior of which the satirist disapproves, satire can be expressed in many tones, from harsh and bitter to mild and gentle. Harsh satirists are angry about serious crimes or offenses and want to punish the people they attack. Gentle satirists, on the other hand, aim at human shortcomings, quirks, and eccentricities (sometimes ones they admit to themselves) and hope to reform those they describe. In form, satire can be direct, with the satirist speaking to the audience in his or her own voice or the voice of some definite persona, or it can be indirect, expressing its criticism through a story or fable.

Writers of harsh satire include the Roman writer Juvenal (60–140 C.E.) and the English author Jonathan Swift (1667–1745). Addressing his audience directly, Juvenal portrays himself as a moral vigilante, punishing evildoers who are beyond the reach of law or conscience. Swift, who makes equally fierce criticisms of human evils, instead uses the form of a travel narrative, *Gulliver's Travels* (1726). Both are more interested in denunciation than they are in reform, because they take a generally negative view of their fellow humans. Other satirists follow the gentler example of the Roman author Horace (65–8 B.C.) and the English poet Alexander Pope (1688–1744), who more temperately criticize human foibles and eccentricities and hope that those they criticize will mend their ways.

Whatever its tone or form, satire tries to invoke the authority of common sense, basing its criticism on universally valid standards of morality and behavior. The truth is, however, that satire can also be deeply subjective, reflecting the personal indignation, contempt, or even prejudice felt by the satirist. As a result, satirists often have to dispute the accusation that their criticisms are just nasty personal attacks aimed at specific individuals. They usually defend themselves by claiming that they aim at negative qualities in general, not specific persons, and that they serve the general good rather than expressing private grudges.

Satire is not restricted to any specific morality or political position. Satirists may attack individuals who deviate from social norms, or they may attack the norms themselves on the basis of a higher morality. Satire can be used by social and economic elites to suppress criticism through ridicule as Juvenal, a conservative, condemned social innovation and class mobility and John Dryden (1631–1700) used *Absalom and Achitophel* to ridicule the opponents of Charles II. However, satire has also served the disenfranchised, for whom language may be the only available means of redress. Lucian (c. 120–c. 180 C.E.) was famed as a mocker of establishment values and reputations; Voltaire (1694–1778) suffered imprisonment for his writings, and Swift lived in constant danger of arrest, had his authorship of certain satires been revealed.

Satire is closely allied to irony, which deals with discrepancies between what is and what should be. Satirists especially like to attack unwarranted pride, particularly when someone demands more respect than he or she should. They will pursue the pompous and the parvenu, the hypocrite and the fool, and even tyrants—if they dare—but off limits are the cripple and the victim, who did not choose their circumstances or create their misfortune. A satirist will certainly attack the fake warrior who claims more honors than he is entitled to, but not the military hero who earned the medals he wears—that is, unless he tries to exploit them in inappropriate ways.

While we have come to expect satire to be funny, it lies, as a form, between "pure" comedy, which aims only to amuse and has no moral intention, and pure denunciation, which has only a moral or didactic purpose and need not make us laugh. Humor is not necessary to jeremiads, harangues, and diatribes, which simply express indignation, and invective relies on abuse and insult. However, lampoons, which are broad and abusive satires in prose or graphic form, feature gross forms of humor. The pasquinade—named for a perhaps apocryphal fifteenth-century Italian cobbler, Pasquino, noted for his sharp tongue—has a similar function, in verse. Caricatures, whether graphic or literary, exaggerate some distinguishing feature of a person for purposes of ridicule. Parodies focus closely on the manner or style of some well-known work in order to mock its seriousness, as Henry Fielding (1707–1754) wrote *Shamela* (1741) as a spoof of Samuel Richardson's popular but morally counterfeit *Pamela* (1740). (Travesties do the same, but in more exaggerated ways.) Burlesques begin, as parodies do, by mocking forms of "high art," but they are not truly satirical as they quickly go off in ridiculous directions, using distortion or exaggeration. The Marx Brothers send up serious music in *A Night at the Opera* (1935), but only as an excuse for developing ludicrous comic situations. (In recent years, the term *burlesque* has come to refer to variety entertainments featuring farcical humor and nudity.)

The word *satirical* is also used to describe a tone, attitude, or turn of phrase that might appear in any context, from a sermon to a popular song. Isaiah's denunciation of the Daughters of Zion (3.16–26) and Job's reply to his comforters (12.1–25) are both satirical in tone. Jesus turned to satire to expose and mock the scribes, "who like to walk around in long robes, and to be greeted with respect," but who, at the same time, "devour widows' houses" (Mark 12.38–40), and the Pharisees, who follow all proper rituals but inside "are full of greed and wickedness" (Luke 12.39), and both Scribes and Pharisees at once, who "do not practice what they teach" and are "like whitewashed tombs, which on the outside look beautiful but inside . . . are full of the bones of the dead" (Matt. 23.3, 27). The wandering goliards of the Middle Ages mocked scholastic education and religious morality in their songs. The theological works of Martin Luther (1483–1546) are suffused with satiric rants larded with obscenities. Using popular folk music, English dramatist John Gay (1685–1732) exposed social and legal hypocrisy in *The Beggar's Opera*. William S. Gilbert (1836–1919) and Arthur Sullivan (1842–1900) composed a series of popular operettas that poked fun at British social mores and prevailing literary conventions. Playwright Bertolt Brecht (1898–1956) and composer Kurt Weill (1900–1950) updated Gay's opera and adapted it to conditions in Nazi Germany in *The Threepenny Opera*. Country Joe MacDonald's "Fixin' to Die Rag" of 1965 was a raucous attack on the Vietnam War; Carly Simon's "You're So Vain" of 1975 deftly exposed narcissism.

The term *satire* derives from Latin *satura*, a mixture of fruit—and, by extension, a medley or olio. The term implied that satire was exempt from the formal characteristics of other genres. Petronius Arbiter's fragmentary *Satyricon* (first century C.E.), using a mixture of poetry and prose, is a lively series of adventures introducing, in often crude detail, the activities of a variety of Roman characters worthy of the writer's scorn. François Rabelais (c. 1490–1553), in *Gargantua and Pantagruel* (1534), uses a picaresque structure to range freely among targets of satire. Many humanists working in many styles composed the *Satyre Menippée* (1593), a loosely structured work full of incidents and oddities that protested the presence of foreign powers and papal forces in France at that time. Stanley Kubrick's (1928–1999) film *Dr. Strangelove; or, How I Learned to Stop Worrying and Love the Bomb* (1964) is a bizarre collection of incidents that demonstrate the ways our hubristic faith in technology might doom the human species.

During the Renaissance, *satire* was connected etymologically to *satyr*, based partly on the similarity of sound and partly on seeming connections to the satyr plays of classical Greece, which often mocked the protagonists of the tragedies they followed. Satyrs, woodland creatures noted for sensuality, were also, according to Renaissance literary theorist George Puttenham (1529–1591), close observers of human affairs "and spiers out of all their secret faults" (25)—thus natural, unregulated commentators on human follies. Although this false etymology had been discredited by scholars of the day, it was often invoked anyway to emphasize that satire could be rough, raw, and dangerous.

Our modern understanding of satire is shaped by the distinctions the poet and critic Dryden drew in his "Discourse concerning the Original and Progress of Satire" (1693). It was he who differentiated between bitter and genial satire and associated the forms with Juvenal and Horace. He stressed the distinction between formal or "direct" satire, in which a single speaker addresses an audience (or an imagined friend who "stands in" for the audience), and "indirect" satire, which works through some form of narrative or "fable." Dryden suggests that the satirist seems most at home expressing an aristocratic viewpoint, though most satirists favor aristocracies of character and values, not birth status.

The indirect form has come to be known as Menippean satire, after the Greek Cynic philosopher Menippus (c. 225 B.C.E.). As it tends to work through narrative, it uses many voices and situations to produce its critique. Menippus' works do not survive, but his influence is acknowledged by such successors as Lucian, who wrote satirical dialogues mocking human credulity—for example, in which Zeus is portrayed as a self-indulgent lecher and Menippus himself is confounded by a wily and duplicitous Tiresias. This form is also called Varronian satire, after Marcus Terentius Varro (116–27 B.C.E.), who adopted the Menippean mode in earthy, loosely structured commentaries on social follies, sectarianism, and modern fashions he thought silly, like the craze for Greek philosophy.

Menippean satire, in terms of sheer bulk in influence the most dominant form, has also taken the form of the fable, as with Aesop's tales; of ironical philosophy, as in Erasmus' *Praise of Folly* (1511); of social commentary achieved through mock utopias, as in Samuel Butler's *Erehwon* (1872); or of dystopias like Aldous Huxley's *Brave New World* (1932). Because such satires include a variety of voices and introduce the possibility of self-parody, the Menippean form has attracted the attention of such theorists as Mikhail Bakhtin, whose interest lies in "dialogic" texts that are neither stable nor easily resolved and that lack the voice of a "central authority." (Following Bakhtin, Joel C. Relihan identifies an inherent ambiguity in such works as Petronius' *Satyricon*, which places readers in such a complex relation to the narrative that the supposed satirist might himself be the object of derision.)

While the formal satirist overtly claims the high moral ground, the voice of the satirist using the Menippean form may never surface. Rather, the satiric effect is gained through dialogue, narrative, and description. Bakhtin diminishes the moral element of satire by tying it to the notion of carnival. For Bakhtin, the defining quality of the "menippea" is a philosophical and narrative freedom—fantasy, fantastic voyages, extraordinary situations—that embodies a search for or testing of truth, absent the self-proclaimed seeker of truth present in formal satire. The search for truth takes place not in the pure space of the philosopher's mind, but "on highroads, in brothels, dens of thieves, taverns, market places, prisons, and at secret cults' erotic orgies" (Bakhtin 94). Hence the wild settings of Petronius and Apuleius are not accidental but organic to Bakhtin's conception of satire; the picaresque adventures of Lazarillo de Tormes in the eponymous novel (1554) give plenty of opportunity for satirizing both the many fraudulent masters to whom he attaches himself in his adventures and the many foolish victims of their opportunism. This carnival element is characterized by the breaking down of hierarchies and a "jolly relativity." Its symbols "always include within themselves the perspective of negation (death), or its opposite. Birth is fraught with death, and death with new birth" (Bakhtin 102) and "in the act of carnival laughter death and rebirth . . . are combined" (104). In "killing" its target, satire simultaneously engenders a new birth.

Indeed, though the aims of satire may seem purely negative—to discredit or destroy—they are, necessarily, joined to positive ones. In mounting their attacks, satirists implicitly invoke ethical, moral, or aesthetic standards of which they approve, standards that have been violated by the target of their attack. When Petronius holds the vulgar freedman Tremalchio up to ridicule, it is for ostentation that offends norms of modesty and class position. When Michel de Montaigne (1533–1592) mocks the assumptions that Europeans make about the superiority of their morality, he does so in the name of simple and transparent virtues that he sees practiced by "primitive" peoples who have remained close to nature. This double aspect of satire reflects the rites out of which Greek comedy developed. In the preclassical era, phallic songs were elements of rituals practiced widely in Asia Minor that, on the one hand, expelled bad spirits through abuse and invective and, on the other, promoted fertility by invoking good spirits. Only the most pessimistic of satirists will give up on humanity entirely. Most hope, if only implicitly, that their work will reform or better the world, if only a little, or only for a while. Otherwise, why bother?

The targets of satire may be specific individuals (like the romantic poet Robert Southey [1774–1843], lampooned by Lord Byron [1788–1824]) or general types (like the overfed priests and sneering judges in the political cartoons of Honoré Daumier

[1808–1879]). Gender satire, bent against women by male authors, has a long tradition, including Juvenal's Satire 6 and a host of misogynistic works of the Middle Ages and Renaissance, among them the popular genre of *fabliaux*, ribald tales in verse that mocked women and priests, and Shakespeare's *The Taming of the Shrew*. Class satire was practiced widely during the French Revolution, when pornographic images of Marie Antoinette were widely circulated; satire of the lower classes was also produced in England by such apologists for aristocracy as Dryden. Religious satire appeared during the Reformation, when the papacy came in for sustained ridicule in northern Europe; Christian doctrine and behavior were satirized in the work of Jewish writers like Jonah Rapa (*Haggadah*, c. 1380), and Benjamin of Genezzano (fifteenth century); in the mid–nineteenth century, Isaac Erter turned a satirical eye on Hasidic Jews.

The entire human race was condemned by John Wilmot, Earl of Rochester (1647–1680), who, in his "Satire against Mankind" condemns "that vain animal / Who is so proud of being rational" (lines 6–7) but instead displays vanity, hypocrisy, pointless violence, and greed. The Duc de la Rochefoucauld (1613–1680) satirizes human virtue by wittily exposing the underside of altruism in his remark, "The refusal to accept praise is a desire to be praised twice." Most famously, he mocked optimistic suppositions about the strength and value of empathy by noting, "In the misfortune of our best friends, we always find something not altogether displeasing." Observations like this take satire to the furthest verge of irony.

While the class-conscious Juvenal was offended by upstarts who behaved as though they were the equals of their social superiors, satirists like the anonymous author of the fifteenth-century *Piers Plowman* aimed at the materially privileged who demanded a respect to which they were not morally entitled. Other satirists (Horace, Dryden, and Byron, for example) ridiculed bad poets who claimed the respect due to good ones; Voltaire, in *Candide* (1759), and Samuel Johnson, in *Rasselas* (also 1759), mocked foolish philosophers who claimed wisdom they did not possess. Shakespeare condemned satirists whose gibes turn out to be motivated by personal bile rather than moral concern or aesthetic taste with such characters as Jacques in *As You Like It* (1599–1600) and Thersites in *Troilus and Cressida* (1601–1602).

At one extreme, as straight invective, satire uses language as a magical weapon, in the manner of the curse. For Robert C. Elliott, satire derives historically from magic rituals: "Satire was believed to be magically efficacious because the original ritualistic formula was efficacious; the belief remained attached to the satiric content of the formula long after the rite had been forgotten" (58). Although we tend to associate satire with the descriptive element of the curse, satire gets its killing force—its "venom"—from the component of magic inherent in words. The first satirist of name, Archilochus (fl. seventh century B.C.E.), was widely celebrated for an act of verbal vengeance. When his engagement to a member of a noble family was broken by his fiancée's father, he attacked them in verses so powerful that (the story goes) both hanged themselves. Elliott connects such curses to those uttered in tragedy—for example, Thyestes' curse on the house of Atreus—not least because they share the mission of righting a wrong. In one extant fragment, Archilochus wishes a terrible calamity on an enemy, envisioning him freezing in a storm at sea, tangled in seaweed: "This 'tis my wish to see him suffer, who has trodden his oaths under foot, him who was once my friend" (11).

Reflecting a similar personal indignation, Juvenal famously declared, "It is hard *not* to write satire. For who can be so tolerant of this monstrous city, who so iron of soul, as to contain himself when the brand-new litter of lawyer Matho comes along, filled with his huge self; after him one who has informed against his noble patron and will soon sweep away the remnant of our nobility already gnawed to the bone?" (7). He lambasts pretentious married women who flaunt their low-born lovers, arrogant men "who earn legacies by nightly performances" (8). He attacks the gambler who can "lose a hundred thousand sesterces, and not have a shirt to give to a shivering slave" (8) and assaults bad poets and all the other uppity scum who offend his sense of decorum.

Like Archilocus before him, Juvenal has an eye for punishment, which he sees coming from two quarters. First, bad behavior punishes itself, as the gluttonous man will soon discover: "You will soon pay for it, my friend, when you take off your clothes, and with distended stomach carry your peacock into the bath undigested! Hence a sudden death, and an intestate old age; the new and merry tale runs the round of every dinner-table, and the corpse is carried forth to burial amid the cheers of enraged friends!" (6). The other source of punishment is the conscience, aroused by the biting words of satirists like himself and by his great predecessor, the founder of Roman satire: "When Lucilius roars and rages as if with sword in hand, the hearer, whose soul is cold with crime, grows red; he sweats with the secret consciousness of sin. Hence wrath and tears. So turn these things over in your mind before the trumpet sounds; the helmet once donned, it is too late to repent you of the battle." But Juvenal holds forth no promise of broader reform, for "our grandchildren will do the same things, and desire the same things, that we do" (Satire 1, 9). Though perhaps awakened by the scorching energies of the satirist's indignation, unredeemable humanity faces bleak prospects. As a positive ideal, Juvenal gives us his friend Umbricius, who, finding that he can do none of the things necessary to make a living in Rome (lying, becoming a soothsayer, hiring out as an assassin), turns his back on the city and exiles himself to a pastoral existence.

Horace took a different path. He acknowledges the virtues of such caustic predecessors as Lucilius, but characterizing himself as slower-witted and not driven by righteous indignation, does not presume to speak with their moral authority. Rather, he hopes to improve the world by gentle suasion, just as his father had improved his character by presenting him with examples of good and bad behavior: "Thanks to his training I am free of those disastrous vices and faults only in those little things which you can easily forgive. Perhaps even those faults will go with the years and with honest friends and self-criticism" (Satire 4, bk. 1). In a fable, "The Town Mouse and the Country Mouse," Horace gently reminds the reader that the simple life might have virtues lacking in the great world of affairs.

The implied audiences of satire vary. Horatian satirists may directly address the targets of their wit because they acknowledge fellow feeling with them and rarely claim great moral superiority. They seek to rouse a smile of recognition in a fellow sinner and to encourage reformed behavior. The Juvenalian satirist, on the other hand, draws a firm line between behavior that is moral and behavior that is sinful or criminal and excludes the objects of satire, seeking to rally a community of indignation. Pope addressed an audience of enlightened rationalists amused by the pretensions and intellectual laziness of others; Voltaire rallied those for whom the practice of superstition (and religion) seemed criminal.

In the broadest sense, satire has been part of human history from its beginnings. Early graphic satire manifests itself in an Egyptian bas reliefs. Greek and Roman vase paintings were likewise sites for burlesques and satirical portraits. Homeric myths are satirized in vase paintings of the fifth century B.C.E., especially the amorous activities of the gods. Krishna's lusts are portrayed in Hindu art: one illustration has him riding an elephant-shaped creature whose bodily parts are all women.

In the sixth or seventh century B.C.E., the anonymous Greek poet known as the Pseudo-Homer produced an astonishingly deft parody of the *Iliad* (with meticulously described war scenes, set forth in Homeric similes and mythical allusions), now known as "The Battle of the Frogs and Mice." Human pretentiousness is mocked in the boasts of the King of Mice, his subsequent accidental drowning when the frog who is bearing him across the water accidentally dumps him in, and his call for vengeance upon the race of frogs by the armies of the mouse kingdom. The smallness of it all—by implication, the smallness of all human endeavors—is underscored by the narrator's final observation that the great war was over in a day.

The great Greek comic dramatist Aristophanes (448–385 B.C.E.) turned a satiric eye upon the demagogue Cleon in *The Knights*, the philosopher Socrates in *The Clouds*, and the playwright Euripides in *The Frogs*. In *The Wasps* he commented on the general decline of Athens and, most famously, the follies of wasteful war in *Lysistrata*. He was followed, in Greek literature, by the skeptic philosopher Timon (fl. 279 B.C.E.), who composed popular satires called *silli*—some in the form of direct satire, some in the form of dialogue—in which he ridiculed the tenets of other philosophers.

Among pre-Islamic Arabs, satiric poets rode into battle alongside warriors, armed only with words insulting the foe. In pre-Christian Ireland, poets (*filid*), assigned the function of praise and blame, inflicted terror among all classes through the threat of satire. The "beast epic" popular in the Middle Ages accomplished social satire by portraying animals in human situations, calling up traits associated with animals—the shrewdness of Reynard the Fox, the vanity of Chanticler, the rooster—to comment on human folly.

In *Gargantua and Pantagruel*, Rabelais uses a crowded carnival scene, mock-epic adventures, and low scatology for purposes of satire. The giant Gargantua (so named for the large throat required to satisfy his huge appetite), his companion Panurge, and his son Pantagruel appear in a loose narrative that is the occasion for commentary on a range of human foibles, mainly pedantry and Puritanism. Gargantua suffers from both these afflictions in his early education, being forced to carry a large writing desk around and to read dull treatises in Latin and commentaries by such intellectual impostors as Broken Biscuithead, Talktoomuch, and Cuntprober. After eighteen years of this education, his dissatisfied father observed that his son had grown to be lazy and rather stupid. He is put on the right track by a teacher in Paris, Powerbrain, who introduces a disciplined but more varied curriculum, mixing learning with games, music, physical exercise, hunting, jousting, a good diet, and monthly excursions for pleasure—the wide range of experiences that constituted a humanist education.

Taking a lesson from his own experience and carrying the experiment a step further, Gargantua founds and finances a utopian coed abbey—"Thélème, Abbey of Desire," overlooking the River Loire and dedicated to gracious living. Banned from entry were all hypocrites, bigots, hairshirts, cynics, lawyers, and moneylenders, but warmly welcomed were "noble knights and gentlemen," "ladies of noble birth," and those who knew the holy word and preached it correctly. No laws governed Thélème, where people lived by their free will, following the Abbey's one-sentence constitution: DO WHAT YOU WILL. For Rabelais, Thélème represents the ideal society, in which well-taught men and women following their reason express the inherent goodness that is within them. Through this ideal commonwealth, he satirizes repression and moral pretentiousness and restrictions that would thwart the natural human drive toward self-actualization.

Thomas More's *Utopia* (1516), describing an ideal society, adroitly blends the serious and the satirical by putting a stinging critique of many social injustices practiced in England into the mouth of Raphael Hythloday, an imaginary traveler who has visited a land in which those faults have been remedied by better institutions and the abolition of all private property. The utopian practice whereby grooms and brides were required to appear naked before each other before the wedding ceremony—as a person purchasing a horse would want the opportunity to examine the animal for defects—mocks customs that require people to bind themselves for life in matrimony without having the opportunity to fully know each other. In *The Praise of Folly*, More's friend Desiderius Erasmus condemns the pride of worldly-wise philosophers, theologians, and princes by exalting the wisdom of the Goddess Folly, in the light of St. Paul's observation that the purest Christians are nothing but fools, in the eyes of humankind.

The tradition of aggressive formal satire was consciously revived around 1600 in England by writers like Joseph Hall (1574–1656) and John Marston (1576–1634). Hall sees the writing of satire as a hazardous activity requiring a warrior's courage:

> I first adventure, with foolhardy might,
> To tread the steps of perilous despight;
> I first adventure; follow me who list,
> And be the second Engish satirist.
>
> (*Virgidemiarum*, Prologue 1–4)

Acknowledging (and perhaps boasting) that his first effort at satire "doth somewhat resemble the sour and crabbed face of Juvenal," he portrays himself as one beleaguered by envy but allied with truth in his effort to discredit the "meal-mouthed," parasitic poets of the "smoothing age," who not only shroud vice from shame, but crown it "with Virtue's mead, immortal fame." Urging his "daring muse" to unmask "the ugly face of Vice," he does not neglect to give his discerning reader a conspiratorial wink: "It is not for everyone to relish a true and natural satire, being of itself, besides the native and inbred bitterness and tartness of the particulars, both hard of concept and harsh of style, and therefore cannot but be unpleasing both to the unskillful and unmusical ear" (*Virgidemiarum*, bk. 1). A year later, John Marston followed with *The Scourge of Villainy* (1599), the title of which suggests the militancy of its spirit. Calling on the power of melancholy to aid him—the satirist's companion and ally, evidently—Marston vows to plow up

> The hidden entrails of rank villainy,
> Tearing the veil from damn'd impiety.
>
> (*Proemium In* 17–18)

He speaks in a sort of ecstasy of indignation:

> My rage must freely run.
> Preach not the stoic's patience to me!
> I hate no man but man's impiety.
> My soul is vex'd. What power will'th desist

> Or dares to stop a sharp-fang'd satirist?
> Who'll cool my rage? Who'll stay my itching fist,
> But I will plague and torture whom I list?
>
> *(Satyre II 4–10)*

When formal satire was banned in England in 1599 (as an act of political censorship) many practitioners of the art shifted their venue to the theater where, especially in the arena of the "private" theaters composed of child actors, they practiced their art and thereby introduced new vibrancy to Jacobean comedy. The playwright Ben Jonson well expresses the anxiety of the dramatic satirist in an authoritarian state in his induction to *Bartholemew Fair* (1614), which asks the audience to apply the play's critique of human behavior generally, rather than maliciously trying to search out "who was meant by the Ginger-bread-women, who by the Hobby-horse-man, who by the Costermonger . . . what great lady by the Pig-woman, what conceal'd statesman by the Seller of Mouse-traps, and so of the rest." At the play's end, the author's anxiety is further expressed by Jonson's direct request to King James I to assure the author that he has not gone beyond "the scope of writers" and indulged in "license" (Epilogue, lines 3–5).

Shakespeare did not proclaim himself a satirist as Jonson did, but he expressed the tone and spirit of satire through a variety of characters—the embittered Shylock, the witty Rosalind (who easily outperforms Jacques, the "designated" satirist of *As You Like It*), the embittered Hamlet, the scheming Iago (who falsely appropriates the satirist's pose of personal integrity), King Lear's Fool, and a number of clowns, like Feste and Touchstone. Speaking of Feste in *Twelfth Night*, Viola plays tribute to the social usefulness of the fool-as-satirist in the following terms:

> This fellow is wise enough to play the fool,
> And to do that well craves a kind of wit.
> He must observe their mood on whom he jests,
> The quality of persons, and the time,
> And, like the haggard, check at every feather
> That comes before his eye. This is a practice
> As full of labor as a wise man's art;
> For folly that he wisely shows is fit,
> But wise men, folly-fall'n, quite taint their wit.
>
> (3.1.60–68)

The satirist's skills, which include wisdom, keenness of observation, and courage, are meant to serve the ends of philosophy when philosophers falter.

Molière (Jean-Baptiste Poquelin, 1622–1673) was an undistinguished player of tragedy until he discovered his gift for writing stage satire and was launched by his audience into huge success. He was fortunate both in the time he lived, which was attuned to his methods and, with exceptions, sympathetic to his targets, and in the monarch whom he served. Louis XIV provided significant cover for Molière from attacks by religious groups and others offended by his choice of topics; Molière's other targets include social pretentiousness, in *The Pretentious Ladies* (1659); rival actors, in *The Impromptu at Versailles* (1663); and religious exhibitionism, in *Tartuffe* (first performed in public in 1667). Louis at times enlisted Molière as an ally, as in the composition and performance of *The Bourgeois Gentleman* (1671), commissioned by the king as retaliation for a perceived slight at the hands of a Turkish ambassador the year before.

With royal support (within the limits of royal power), Molière could stand his own before his enemies, but took care to justify his practice when he could. In *The Critique of the School for Wives*, a companion piece to *The School for Wives* composed after the original play had succeeded with the public but elicited attack, he created characters who critiqued his creation. Climène, speaking as a moralist, asks how any virtuous person could "find any charm in a play which forever keeps modesty in a state of alarm, and constantly befouls the imagination" (102). Uranie, in response, calls ridiculous a "delicacy of honor which takes everything amiss, and gives criminal meaning to the most innocent words, and takes offense at mere shadows" (103). Later, she vows never to take satire personally, even satire directed at women, as it "hits at manners and customs, and only indirectly at individuals" (113). Speaking as the ideal audience for the Horatian satirist, she suggests that the wisest response to satire is to profit from the lessons it teaches.

Voltaire's *Candide* takes aim not at wicked behavior but at something perhaps as dangerous: stupid assumptions about the world made and taught by smug philosophers who should know better—in particular Enlightenment thinkers like Leibniz, who displayed an unwarranted optimism about human existence. The topic could have been handled with a light and witty touch, but Voltaire's satire, while embedded in an adventure yarn, is vivid, violent, and irate. Priests are lecherous; the Inquisition is cruel; the military are violent, greedy, and heedless of human life; ordinary people are selfish and ignorant. The work is full of accounts of rape, slaughter, rank ingratitude, and greed, but the sharpest satire is directed at the teleological thinking of the pedagogue Pangloss, with his fatuously naive assumptions about this being "the best of all possible worlds" in which disastrous events—violence and exploitation and even the spread of venereal disease—serve the benign ends of a kind deity. The philosopher who ignores the evidence of reality in favor of stubborn abstractions receives the most sustained scorn of all. The compassionate Anabapist James, who provides a positive model of charitable behavior, suffers for his goodness; the other affirmative image, the garden to which Candide, Cunegunde, and Pangloss retire at the end, represents a capitulation to reality, a realization that satire, though it can affirm some virtues and propose havens from the incorrigible world, solves nothing.

Among English satirists, formal honors go to Alexander Pope, whose polished style was ideal for dissecting manners. He produced a masterpiece of genial satire in *The Rape of the Lock*, whose aim was, through wit, to defuse a potentially deadly feud that had arisen over an act of social mischief. He also planned a systematic Horatian satire on the grand scale, of which only fragments survive. His *Epistle 4: To Richard Boyle, Earl of Burlington* starts off this way:

> 'Tis strange, the miser should his cares employ,
> To gain those riches he can ne'er enjoy:
> Is it less strange, the prodigal should waste
> His wealth, to purchase what he ne'er can taste?
>
> (1–4)

Pope could also adopt a Juvenalian tone, as when he boasted of the power of satire to punish those offenders who have evaded the law.

> Yes, I am proud; I must be proud to see
> Men not afraid of God, afraid of me:
> Safe from the Bar, the Pulpit, and the Throne,
> Yet touch'd and sham'd by Ridicule alone.
> O sacred Weapon! left for Truth's defence,
> Sole Dread of Folly, Vice, and Insolence!
>
> ("Epilogue to the Satires" 208–213)

At the same time, he—like other satirists—projects an air of anxiety about being misunderstood, fearing that the wish to condemn sin or to reform behavior will be taken as mere personal hostility. Hitting at malicious readers who saw meanings in his work that he did not intend, Pope complains in "An Epistle from Mr. Pope to Dr. Arbuthnot" (1741) of the false friend

> Who reads but with a lust to misapply,
> Make satire a lampoon, and fiction lie.
> A lash like mine no honest man shall dread,
> But all such babbling blockheads in his stead

The satirist cannot always count on the approval of the society he believes he is serving.

The prize for satire in the Juvenalian mode, however, goes to Jonathan Swift, whose *Gulliver's Travels* is itself a journey from the mockery of court manners in book 1, set among the Lilliputians, to the devastating condemnation of humanity itself in book 2. When Gulliver, created by Swift as an *eiron*, a well-meaning soul who undertakes to be spokesman for European civilization, describes the institutions and practices of his culture (including the court, the military, the justice system, and the legislature), the astonished King of Brobdingnag, unimpressed by his account, declares humanity to be "the most pernicious race of little odious vermin that nature ever suffered to crawl upon the surface of the earth" (132). On hearing this, Gulliver experiences indignation; we, and Swift, enjoy a grim laugh because the king has it right: the elements of our society that he views with disgust are the very ones that trouble us as well, but he is a king (in a book) and can speak from a position of both moral and political authority. What turns *Gulliver's Travels* from a fine satire to a work of transcendent genius, however, is the final turn, in book 4, toward the universal, morally ambiguous satire of the Houyhnhnms, whose rationalism both critiques delusions nourished by the Enlightenment and, at the same time, drives humanity mad—as mad as the escapee from Plato's cave who, having apprehended the truth, found it useless, as it forever alienated him from human society. In this instance, the satirist is neither moral authority nor benign commentator. Rather, he is deeply implicated in a universal folly.

Swift's most startling satire, however, remains his pamphlet of 1829, "A Modest Proposal for Preventing the Children of Poor People in Ireland from Being a Burden to Their Parents or Country, and for Making Them Beneficial to the Public," a work aimed not at humanity in general but at a specific social ill, the exploitation of the Irish peasantry by absentee English landlords. Using the voice of a sincere individual who believes that he has found a humane solution to a vexing social problem, the pamphlet addresses the problem of starvation among the Irish. The solution proposed, in disingenuous logic of a high order, is for them to raise their babies as farm produce, as they do hogs or cattle, to be sold to wealthy people for food when they reach the age of one year. Though frequently reprinted, the essay retains its power to stun readers who are lulled by its earnest rhetorical tone and then confronted with its utterly logical and utterly hideous solution.

The romantic age was not noted for satire, but, in *English Bards and Scotch Reviewers*, his dazzling reply to the critics who savaged his initial book of verse, Lord Byron claims for satire the role of unacknowledged judiciary. Vice and folly are "by satire kept in awe, / And shrink from ridicule, though not from law" (36–37).

The American satirist Ambrose Bierce (1842–1914?) expresses the frustration of a Juvenalian who finds his method unappreciated. Defining satire as "an obsolete kind of literary composition," he complains that in America, "satire never had more than a sickly and uncertain existence, for the soul of it is wit, wherein we are dolefully deficient, the humor we mistake for it, like all humor, being tolerant and sympathetic" (355–56). He finds the situation deplorable because "although Americans are 'endowed by their creator' with abundant vice and folly, it is not generally known that these are reprehensible qualities, wherefore the satirist is regarded as a sour spirited knave, and his every victim's cry for co-defendants evokes a national assent" (*The Devil's Dictionary*, 356). His view represents a consensus among social critics of all periods who are stymied in their efforts to reform intolerable behavior.

In his most blistering satires, Mark Twain uses the form of the mock encomium, pretending sympathy with the target of his fury. In *King Leopold's Soliloquy* (1905), Twain lets the Belgian monarch expose his criminality through his complaints about the way he has been portrayed in the public press and from the pulpits:

Yes, they go on telling everything, these chatterers! They tell how I levy incredibly burdensome taxes upon the natives—taxes which are a pure theft; taxes which they must satisfy by gathering rubber under hard and constantly harder conditions. . . . They tell it all: how I am wiping a nation of friendless creatures out of existence by every form of murder, for my private pocket's sake. But they never say, although they know it, that I have labored in the cause of religion at the same time. . . . They tell only what is against me, they will not tell what is in my favor. (184–85)

Leopold's self-exculpation barely contains the rage of the satirist behind the scenes, who makes the king fully aware of his deeds and their effects.

The twentieth century offered a full range of satirical targets and forms in a variety of tones. George Orwell's *Animal Farm* (1946) uses the form of the beast fable to mount a vivid and devastating critique of utopian schemes for perfecting humanity. Using thinly disguised allusions to historical figures, this anticommunist allegory portrays a rebellion of oppressed farm animals against their owner that begins with high hopes and noble slogans when an idealistic pig (representing Karl Marx) proposes the establishment of a humane social order. When put into practice after his death, however, the revolution of the animals—led by pigs—degenerates quickly into a series of struggles that suggests the deadly rivalry of Joseph Stalin and Leon Trotsky, the devastating social and economic experiments of the USSR, and the development of terror trials, secret police, a propaganda network, and other elements of the modern totalitarian state.

The fate of satirists under totalitarian regimes is full of danger, as exemplified in the career of the Russian writer Michail Bulgakov (1891–1940). Although he found temporary refuge in the whimsy of Joseph Stalin, his skeptical view eventually caught up with him. Bulgakov's most celebrated work, *The Master and the Margarita*, in which he lampoons the head of the writer's union that denounced him for his deviations from orthodoxy, was banned from publication in 1973. The power of satire is sometimes underrated by those who practice it, but not by those who fear it.

Satire has been the subject of considerable theoretical examination in recent years. In *Anatomy of Criticism*, his influential study of genres and mythic structures, Northrop Frye characterizes satire as "militant irony" as "its moral norms are relatively clear, and it assumes standards against which the grotesque and the absurd are measured" (223). Identifying two elements that he calls "essential" to satire—"wit or humor founded on fantasy or a sense of the grotesque or absurd" and "an object of attack" (224)—Frye places satire within a spectrum that has at one extreme pure denunciation, "attack without humor," and at the other extreme romance "the humor of pure fantasy" (224–25).

Leonard Feinberg invites us to be skeptical of the moral claims of satire, remarking that the wish to deride can be easily detached from the urge to reform. While ethical satisfaction may be one of the pleasures of the satiric experience, "there are many, many others" (7). Sigmund Freud acknowledged the existence of the kind of joke that "is an end in itself and serves no particular aim" (90), but he also recognized the sort that is "tendentious" or "obscene," the former "serving the purpose of aggressiveness, satire, or defense" (97) and the latter serving the purpose of "exposure." In fact, both can be said to serve the aims of satire, which cannot aggress or ridicule until it exposes (and thereby diminishes).

As with all great literature, a work of satire may escape authorial control. Dustin Griffin suggests that "unless it is closely harnessed, the energy released in satire tends to run away with the satirist" (69). Just as villains, often being more interesting than heroes, tend to dominate works of drama and fiction, so the object of satire might gain allure. But while Griffin rightly remarks the limits of authorial control, it may also be that satires that fall in love with their putative targets may in fact simply have shifted genres. Jonson's Volpone can be said to function as a satirist—self-interested, to be sure, since he uses his awareness of the weaknesses of his victims for his own gain rather than as an occasion of reproach—so long as he accurately appraises his grotesque dupes. When his personal confidence turns to self-indulgent arrogance, however, he becomes himself a mark as, in turn, does the servant Mosca who has tried to outdo him. The satire remains valid; it simply grows baroque.

Griffin helpfully reviews the debate over which social conditions provide the best environment for satire (133–41). Some scholars have held, with Juvenal, that egregious social wrongs naturally elicit criticism from honest and observant people who, transcending the moral fashions of the day, speak out for justice (or good taste or better standards of behavior). Others have argued that satire flourishes as a reaction to a period of upheaval, as in early-eighteenth-century England (that "golden age" of satire), recovering from the political upheavals of the previous era. One train of thought suggests that satire arises "at a time when moral norms are so firmly fixed that the satirist can freely and confidently appeal to them" (Griffin 134); another, that "it arises at a time when moral norms are being called into question and must therefore be reaffirmed with some force to prevent a further breakdown of moral order" (134); yet another, that it comes into being when there is no public consensus about morality or taste. Finally, there is a more limited literary explanation: that satirists are seeking to reinvigorate poetic forms by adopting harsher tones and more critical language, as many English poets did around 1600 to rebel against the honeyed tones of their contemporaries.

While it has a complex literary and graphic history, it should be stressed that the satiric impulse derives from basic and essential human traits. One is the critical capacity, which allows us to observe and analyze social phenomena. Another is a desire for equity and a capacity for indignation in the face of evil or inappropriate behavior. Yet another is the capacity to be amused as well as angered by bad behavior, and to express our feelings through artistic forms. Finally, humans have a healthy desire for self-assertion that satire serves by providing effective channels for expressing social and personal values. The impulse for satire may be considered part of our equipment for living.

REFERENCES AND FURTHER READINGS

Bakhtin, Mikhail. *Problems of Dostoevsky's Poetics*. Trans. R. W. Rotsel. N.p.: Ardis, 1973.

Bierce, Ambrose. *The Collected Writings of Ambrose Bierce*. New York: Citadel, 1966.

Dryden, John. *The Works of John Dryden*. Ed. Edward Niles Hooker and H. T. Swedenberg, Jr. Berkeley: U of California P, 1956–1978.

Elliott, Robert C. *The Power of Satire: Magic, Ritual, and Art*. Princeton, NJ: Princeton UP, 1960.

Feinberg, Leonard. *Introduction to Satire*. Ames: Iowa State UP, 1967.

Freud, Sigmund. *Jokes and Their Relation to the Unconscious*. Trans. James Strachey. New York: Norton, 1960.

Frye, Northrop. *Anatomy of Criticism: Four Essays*. Princeton, NJ: Princeton UP, 1957.

Griffin, Dustin. *Satire: A Critical Reintroduction*. Lexington: UP of Kentucky, 1994.

Hall, Joseph. *Collected Poems*. Ed. A. Davenport. Liverpool: Liverpool UP, 1949.

Horace. *Satires, Epistles, and Ars Poetica*. Trans. H. Rushton Fairclough. Cambridge, MA: Harvard UP, 1966.

Jonson, Ben. *Ben Jonson*. 11 vols. Ed. C. H. Herford and Percy Simpson. Oxford, UK: Clarendon P, 1954–1962.

Juvenal. *Juvenal's Satires*. Trans. William Gifford. London: Dent, 1954.

Kermode, Frank. *The Plot of Satire*. New Haven: Yale UP, 1965.

Marston, John. *The Scourge of Villanie*. Ed. G. B. Harrison. New York: Barnes and Noble, 1966.

Molière. *Eight Plays by Molière*. Ed. Morris Bishop. New York: Modern Library, 1957.

More, Thomas. *Utopia*. Trans. Edward Surtz. New Haven, CT: Yale UP, 1964.

Pope, Alexander. *Collected Poems of Alexander Pope*. Ed. Bonamy Dobree. New York: Dutton, 1956.

Puttenham, George. *Art of English Poesie*. Ed. Gladys Wilcock and Alice Walker. Cambridge, UK: Cambridge UP, 1936.

Rabelais, François. *The Histories of Gargantua and Pantagruel*. Trans. J. M. Cohen. New York: Penguin, 1955.

Relihan, Joel C. *Ancient Menippean Satire*. Baltimore, MD: Johns Hopkins UP, 1993.

Shakespeare, William. *The Riverside Shakespeare*. Ed. G. Blakemore Evans and J. J. Tobin. 2nd ed. Boston: Houghton Mifflin, 1997.

Swift, Jonathan. *Gulliver's Travels*. Ed. Herbert Davis. Oxford, UK: Basil Blackwell, 1959.

Twain, Mark. *On the Damned Human Race*. Ed. Janet Smith. New York: Hill and Wang, 1962.

Wilmot, John. *The Works of John Wilmot, Earl of Rochester*. Ed. Harold Love. Oxford, UK: Oxford UP, 1999.

35

Shakespeare's Comedies and Romances

Margaret Mikesell

"Jack shall have Jill" (3.2.461)

So says Puck at a particularly confusing juncture in the lives of the four lovers in *A Midsummer Night's Dream*. Puck terms this certainty a "country proverb," and indeed it is a truism in William Shakespeare's comedies and romances, which almost without exception avert death, the province of tragedy, and end in marriage. Close to half of Shakespeare's plays fall into this category. Scholars group them by date and dramatic technique. The early comedies (*The Comedy of Errors*, *The Taming of the Shrew*, *The Two Gentlemen of Verona*, *Love's Labor's Lost*, and *Dream*) date from the early to mid-1590s and are thus largely contemporaneous with the early histories. Though the dialogue is witty and complex, the plays are plot-driven, for the most part—characterization may be sharply etched but not deep. The middle comedies (*The Merchant of Venice*, *The Merry Wives of Windsor*, *Much Ado about Nothing*, *As You Like It*, and *Twelfth Night*), dating from the last half of the 1590s through the early 1600s, are contemporaneous with the later history plays and early tragedies, with *As You Like It* and *Twelfth Night* framing *Hamlet*. Though equally reliant on plot contrivances, these plays offer the characters somewhat more interiority, or inner life. The later "problem" comedies (*All's Well That Ends Well* and *Measure for Measure*), written during the early 1600s, after *Hamlet* but likely before the other major tragedies, are so designated because though they too end in marriage, both the process of courtship itself and the pairings at plays' end are riven with tension and, at times, an overtly moralistic edge. The joy characterizing earlier comedies has largely disappeared. Finally, the romances (*Pericles*, *Cymbeline*, *The Winter's Tale*, and *The Tempest*) were written after most of the tragedies, from about 1607 to 1611. While retaining comic structure, these plays often include political themes and a focus on royal fathers, more serious sexual threats to the heroines, and a greater reliance on the "marvelous"—exotic journeys, prophetic dreams, apparent deaths—all conventions found in the earlier comedies, but with an intensity here that gives them a distinctive timbre.

Following the custom of the time, Shakespeare wrote many of these plays by combining original material with a complicated pastiche of refashioned sources that vary widely from Roman New Comedy, to popular ballads and folk tales, to earlier sixteenth-century plays and novellas. The diversity of these sources creates textured and heterogeneous playtexts. Structurally, the comedies are very busy. Plots interrupt and intersect each other, with the main plots tracking the fortunes of, generally, two heroines, some sharing adventures and others making their independent way toward marriage in only tangentially related narrative lines. These stories are interspersed with subplots populated by characters whose interests and events diverge quite dramatically from those of the romantic protagonists. The interwoven, multiple plots comment on one another, creating connections that are not devised for the largely oblivious characters but rather for the entertainment and edification of the audience, privileged witnesses of all the action. Within all this busyness, Shakespeare employed familiar comic conventions of plot and character to shape the stories of his protagonists.

A young man loves a young woman and vice versa—or, an unattached young man and woman are available to love one another. Thus runs the stock opening of any romantic comedy of the last 2,000 years, most all of which are anchored firmly in the courtship stage of love and marriage. In Shakespeare's plays, sometimes the couples who are to be wedded at play's end have rather complicated past histories. In *Dream*, for instance, Hermia and Lysander are defiantly in love as the play opens. Helena and Demetrius were once committed to each other, although currently Demetrius loves Hermia. In *Much Ado*, Beatrice and Benedick refer to an unspecified past entanglement, while Hero and Claudio bring to the opening scene an unexplored interest in each other that began before Claudio went off to war. Perdita and Florizel, the second-generation protagonists in *Winter's Tale*, announce their plight-troth in their first scene together. In other plays—for instance, *Taming of the Shrew*, *Love's Labor's Lost*, *As You Like It*, and *Twelfth Night*—the couples meet onstage. This meeting triggers love at first sight, with perhaps the most amusing instance being Lucentio's outburst to his servant after he first sees Bianca, "Whose sudden sight hath thrall'd [captured] my wounded eye": "Tranio, I burn, I pine, I perish, Tranio, / If I achieve not this young modest girl" (*Shrew* 1.1.220, 155–56). While this state of instant lovestruck is not uncommon, being repeated surreptitiously by the English king and his retinue when they meet the French princess and her retinue in *Love's Labor's Lost* and rapturously by Miranda and Ferdinand in *Tempest*, sometimes there is *un*love at first sight, most notably Katherine's vocal aversion to Petruchio when they meet in *Shrew*.

"Jack shall have Jill; / Nought shall go ill" (3.2.461–62)

Actually, much must go ill. This is what theater is all about. However involved or not the characters are at the opening of the comedy, the trick for the playwright is to delay the inevitable weddings for five acts. Following the dictum articulated by Lysander in *Dream*, "The course of true love never did run smooth" (1.1.134), Shakespeare employs a great variety of tactics to protract the courtship. Some problems are clear from the characters' situation at the outset. The triangles—and rectangles—of lovers have to be sorted out, for instance. In *Dream*, Demetrius needs to transfer his love back to Helena so as to end his hostile competition with Lysander for Hermia's love. In *Twelfth Night*, Viola is in love with Orsino who is in love with Olivia who has vowed to renounce all men for a period of seven years following the death of her brother.

Often, however, the impediments are more complex than the messes the lovers have gotten themselves into; they are familial or even societal. Northrop Frye, who is interested in genre, or how the form of a literary work dictates its features, terms this sort of impediment the "irrational law" (166): "law" as in hardened custom or legal decree, and "irrational" because it blocks passion, preventing Jack from having Jill. In *Dream*, an Athenian law compels Hermia either to marry the man chosen for her by her father, to whom she is a "form in wax, / By him imprinted," or "to die the death, or to abjure / For ever the society of men" (1.1.49–50, 65–66), as the duke states it. In *Merchant of Venice*, Portia's successful suitor must choose correctly among three ornate boxes (termed *caskets*) according to her father's bequest. As Portia says of this arrangement, "I may neither choose who I would, nor refuse who I dislike; so is the will of a living daughter curb'd by the will of a dead father" (1.2.23–25). The irrational law is most often imposed on the hapless lovers by an authority figure, termed "a blocking figure" by Frye (166). The blocking figures are generally fathers, dukes, or kings and the unhappy or defiant lovers, generally daughters or nieces. The dramatic conflicts that open comedy thus involve a gendered confrontation between the most and least powerful members of the domestic and political hierarchies.

Finances, a crucial issue in the preponderance of real-life marriages contracted during the early modern period, also figure in many of Shakespeare's comedies, invariably in those with merchant characters. In *Shrew*, Baptista bargains with the play's suitors over the financial settlements (called a dower) they are willing to guarantee his daughters. The finances of marriage are also crucial in *Merry Wives of Windsor*, where the one marriageable woman in the play, the lower-gentry Anne Page, is often mentioned in conjunction with her father's wealth. In *Merchant*, Shylock's emotional investment in his daughter is enmeshed with his love of his ducats.

Sometimes the obstacles are not an external irrational law or blocking figure but internal, that is, located within the lovers themselves. One or both are afflicted by an attitude that keeps them from being able to acknowledge their love for the other. Katherine's shrewishness makes her unmarriageable, as we are told more than once: "Think'st thou . . . though her father be very rich, any man is so very a fool to be married to hell?" (*Shrew* 1.1.123–25). Other examples include stubborn, disloyal Demetrius in *Dream*, callow Bertram in *All's Well*, and Beatrice and Benedick in *Much Ado*, where Leonato refers to the "merry war" and "skirmish of wit" that characterize their relationship (1.1.62, 63). Both *Shrew* and *Much Ado* juxtapose a plotline with exterior impediments (Bianca-Lucentio in *Shrew* and Hero-Claudio in *Much Ado*) with an interior one (Kate-Petruchio and Beatrice-Benedick), creating a complex comic structure with the external plot focused on the social dynamics among parents, children, and rulers, and the internal one on the psyches of the lovers. In them, an inchoate, early modern interiority is apparent.

The removal of the impediments separating the lovers, the heart of the dramatic action, is also conventional, again following precedents from New Comedy and the novellas. In virtually all the comedies, the heroes and heroines travel. While some arrive from someplace else as the play opens, as in *Comedy of Errors*, *Much Ado*, *Twelfth Night*, and *Tempest*, typically the travel takes place during the course of the play, which is often trisected; a frame setting, often in court or city, begins and concludes the action of the play, while its crucial center takes place elsewhere. In some of the plays, the characters travel from city or court to an isolated manor (*Shrew*, *Merchant*), or occasionally to a foreign city, such as Helen's and Bertram's separate trips from France to Florence in *All's Well*. The romance protagonists in *Pericles*, *Cymbeline*, *Winter's Tale*, and *Tempest* all travel from one exotic country to another. Occasionally the trip itself is important. Grumio recounts with relish Katherine's torturous journey from Padua to Verona, which his master Petruchio uses to begin his "taming" of his wife; on the return trip we witness Kate's capitulation to her husband in the sun/moon episode. Sometimes Shakespeare plays against this pattern; in the claustrophobic *Measure*, the Duke of Vienna leaves for a trip but then surreptitiously circles back to watch and manipulate his subjects.

The major comic action and successful pairing of the lovers, then, happens "elsewhere." Shakespeare's most memorable and constant choice for elsewhere is a forest setting, termed by Frye the "green world" (182–83). In *Two Gentlemen*, *Dream*, and *As You Like It*, the green world is the refuge for characters fleeing ducal or parental decree back in court or city; thus an unregulated, fertile, and natural setting functions as a social and theatrical free space where the various impediments separating the lovers are removed.

Conventionally, a problem solver masterminds this dismantling process. Generally lacking the social and political status of the blocking figures, the problem solvers have a different kind of power, one wielded in the elsewhere world of the play. Such figures are readily identifiable—Oberon (and Puck) in *Dream*, Petruchio for the Kate plot and Tranio for the Bianca plot in *Shrew*, Portia in *Merchant*, Rosalind in *As You Like It*, Don Pedro in *Much Ado* (with his bevy of coconspirators), Helen in *All's Well*, the Duke in *Measure*, and Prospero in *Tempest*. Notably, only four of these characters have titular power in the play. And while only two—Tranio and Puck—are actually servants, this problem-solving character has been termed a "tricky slave" (Frye 173–74), because in the plays' New Comedy ancestors, the lovers are conventionally somewhat dim and helpless and so require the aid of a shrewd and resourceful household slave. Often Shakespeare's tricky servant is also the play's heroine, a strategy that makes her parallel to New Comedy's tricky servant, also a socially powerless character empowered by the playwright. It likewise reflects an enhancement of the role of women seen elsewhere in early modern literature.

The tricky servant figures control—in fact, create—the plot at the middle of the play, removing the impediments to marriage (whether social or "psychological") by instigating a kind of joyous mayhem whose ingredients are disguise, trickery, concealment, and sometimes magic. Frequently, before the world is reordered into pairs, the wrong people have fallen in love (social classes are mixed, heterosexuality eschewed, plight-troths and friendships fractured) and the characters' personal identity itself has been challenged, beginning with the disguises commonly adopted by the lovers. The confusion that temporarily reigns often distresses and enrages the characters but delights and entertains the audience.

A brief look at this process in an early and middle comedy, both with memorable green world settings, will demonstrate the patterns—and the great flexibility and variety—of these comic conventions. The woodlands of *Dream* and the later *As You Like It* are essentially political as well as botanical settings that rival the act 1 courts. The green world of the earlier play is both natural and magic; fairies (Peaseblossom, Cobweb, Mustardseed) are denizens of a kingdom governed dictatorially by Oberon, who rules with the aid of a magic flower. Both groups of humans, the craftsmen and lovers, are accidental and temporary visitors. The Forest of Arden in *As You Like It*, in contrast, is wholly human, being the site for the alternative court of the exiled duke. Although Duke Senior touts the merits of being so distant from the "painted pomp" of the "envious court" (2.1.3, 4), in fact all the personages of this green world are carefully stratified; duke, attendants, and fool coexist with pastoral herders and village priest. The four aristocrats of *Dream* are all lovers on the lam in one way or another, while three of the parallel four in *As You Like It* are fleeing political tyranny.

The tricky servants—Oberon, the reigning power in the green world, and Rosalind, arguably the aristocratic character with the least power—cause havoc by accident and design. For Oberon, the lovers are incidentals straying across the sight lines of his struggle with Titania over the Indian boy. He and Puck view their miseries with bemused detachment—"Lord, what fools these mortals be!" (3.2.115)—and Puck especially is as delighted as the audience by the misprisions that initially deepen rather than resolve their misalliances. The chaos that they engineer mismatches the fairy queen Titania with the human craftsman-ass Bottom; switches Demetrius' and Lysander's hostile competition from Hermia to Helena; and seemingly destroys, as Helena complains, the longtime friendship between the two women. In *As You Like It*, Rosalind decides equally casually to "prove the busy actor" in the "play" between the disdainful shepherdess Phebe and her lovesick suitor Silvius (3.4.60). In the muddle that results, Phebe rejects Silvius for Ganymede/Rosalind, the female she believes to be male, and Orlando woos a male pretending to be a female (Rosalind/Ganymede) who is in fact the young woman she is pretending to be.

At the end of the green world sections both tricky servants have sorted out the mismatches. Puck wields his magic to pair up the rightful lovers and detach Titania and Bottom, while Rosalind, in one of the busily administrative speeches often allotted to the tricky servant at this juncture, promises that Silvius, Phebe, Orlando, and she herself will be properly coupled and wedded on the morrow (5.2.109–21). Unusually in *As You Like It*, Shakespeare creates two more pairs who manage without the ministrations of the tricky servant, Touchstone the court fool, who deftly extricates the goatkeeper Audrey from her swain William, and Celia and Oliver, who meet, fall in love, and plight troth offstage in record time, to the surprise of Rosalind and audience alike.

The pattern, then, shows the conflicts of act 1 deepening to multiple mismatches and misunderstandings, an erotic maelstrom enacted in the free space of the elsewhere. Tricks and contrivances fuel the comic plot. This dynamic even governs the "internal" comic plots, which involve a change in one or both lovers. The changes are psychological, if it is not anachronistic to term them thus, but the process is not; rather, the tricky servants—Petruchio, Don Pedro, and Helen, for instance—employ the same sort of intrigue that we have seen in the plots with external impediments. In *Much Ado*, the opposition of Benedick and Beatrice to each other and to marriage in general is removed by two hilarious parallel episodes contrived by Don Pedro, where each resistant lover "overhears" the conspirators speak about the unrequited passion of the other. Bertram, the reluctant husband in *All's Well*, is forced to accept his marriage to Helen once she employs the bed trick to accomplish the seemingly impossible set of conditions he imposed on the day of their marriage. However, while these processes involve character change and the marriages go forward, character development is embryonic. We watch a "before," then some tricks, followed by an "after," with the psychological complexity, such as it is, controlled by plot and the change itself invisible. The sun/moon game precisely locates Katherine's transformation in *Shrew*, but its nature is so undefined that literary scholars and directors can—and do—read it several ways. Is Katherine really a subservient wife, or has she merely learned to act like one? The hegemony of plot over character is largely a generic phenomenon; as a rule, comedy privileges (presents as most important) social interaction while tragedy offers more space for interiority.

The final stage in comedy invariably begins with what Frye terms the "cognitio," or recognition scene (163), the point where everything that was concealed is revealed, misunderstandings cleared up, the lovers acknowledged, and weddings anticipated. It may be as simple as in the plot-driven *Comedy of Errors*, when the two sets of twins finally run into each other. Adriana, wife of one of the twins, says, "I see two husbands, or mine eyes deceive me" (5.1.332). This happens more complexly in the later *Twelfth Night*; when Viola's twin Sebastian suddenly shows up, Orsino exclaims, "One face, one voice, one habit, and two persons, / A natural perspective, that is and is not!" (5.1.216–17). Again, the understanding is often superficial, with necessary bits of plot falling rapidly into place; Sebastian's resuscitation allows him to wed Olivia, who has fallen in love with Cesario/Viola. In a few lines, Orsino, long besotted with Olivia, switches his attachment to Viola, who has loved him from the outset. And the characters in *Dream* have no comprehension of the confusions of the preceding night. Demetrius says with bewildered certainty, "I wot not by what power / (But by some power it is) my love to Hermia / Melted as the snow" (4.1.164–66); in the delicious soliloquy closing act 4, Bottom converts his vestigial memory of Titania's love into a dream.

The plays close with a banquet or dance that gathers together all the key characters, often to celebrate the multiple offstage weddings. (Shakespeare is uninterested in the ceremony itself, including it only when something goes wrong, for instance Petruchio's deliberate, comic bungling of his wedding with Katherine, or the havoc created by Claudio's brutal interruption of his wedding in *Much Ado*.) This being comedy, an attempt is made to draw in even the agents of disorder, the best example being Master Page's kindly words to the mortified Falstaff in *Merry Wives*: "Yet be cheerful, knight. Thou shalt eat a posset to-night at my house, where I will desire thee to laugh at my wife, that now laughs at thee" (5.5.170–72). This being Shakespeare, the offer is sometimes refused, as in Malvolio's exiting lines in *Twelfth Night*, "I'll be reveng'd on the whole pack of you" (5.1.378), or the celebration sometimes interrupted, as in *Love's Labor's Lost*, which closes with the death of the princess's father, the dispersal of the celebrants, and the delay of four weddings.

Shakespeare's construction of his comic plots features diversity within conventional conformity, a dramaturgic pattern that also appears in his portrayals of the protagonists. Gender is perhaps the single most important defining characteristic of his lovers. The fact that at least four of Shakespeare's female lovers are tricky servants manipulating the other characters suggests how radically they have changed from their minimal, often nonspeaking ancestors in Roman new comedy and how indebted they are to their more recent romance and novella progenitors. Within the world of comedy they have agency (i.e., autonomy) and power, a de facto domestic power rather than the sanctioned power of the kings, dukes, and fathers who preside over their worlds. Moreover, these comic heroines defy behavioral ideals for women widely touted in sermons, in the numerous family conduct books published during the period, and even in laws enacted by Parliament—prescriptions that were of course regularly breached not only on the stage but also by women of all classes. These prescriptions for women enjoined them to be "chaste, silent, and obedient," subservient first to fathers and then husbands (see Hull 47–60, 142–43).

Shakespeare's characters refer approvingly to these injunctions. However, the plays themselves interrogate (closely examine) them with complexity and subtlety. Look, for instance, at the way that Shakespeare brings *Shrew* to closure. Petruchio wins the banquet wager through Katherine's loving submission. Katherine then makes a final speech that articulates, and justifies, a wife's obedience to her husband, unquestionably the single most often-repeated injunction of the conduct books. Yet in this very speech, the obedient wife Katherine is simultaneously dictating behavior, albeit submissive behavior, albeit to women. And her dramatic agency is unparalleled; she delivers her speech—at close to forty-five lines the longest single speech by any character in the play—to twelve utterly silent men and women gathered in the comedy's all-important closing cluster. This mixture of subservience and agency shaping the final moments of *Shrew* is representative of Shakespeare's construction of his comic female protagonists.

Silence

In *Merry Wives of Windsor*, Slender lists the assets of Mistress Anne Page, the woman he wants to wed. Second after her brown hair, he mentions that she "speaks small like a woman" (1.1.48), that is, gently, docilely. Similarly, Imogen apologizes for an outburst by saying, "I am much sorry, sir, / You put me to forget a lady's manners / By being so verbal" (*Cymbeline* 2.3.104–6). However, Katherine is only one of Shakespeare's many talkative heroines. Think of Viola's brash address to Olivia on Orsino's behalf, a courtship that to her amused alarm wins Olivia for herself (*Twelfth Night*), Rosalind's loquacious control of her courtship with the obliging Orlando (*As You Like It*), Katherine's and Beatrice's battles of wit with their wooers (*Shrew*, *Much Ado*), Portia's learned, assured defense that preserves Antonio's pound of flesh (*Merchant*), Hermione's spirited and eloquent speech of self-defense at her trial in *Winter's Tale*, and other important speeches of persuasion, including Helen's to the widow in *All's Well* and Marina's hortatory speeches in the brothel—"divinity preach'd there"—whose power we hear about secondhand (*Pericles* 4.5.4).

Obedience

While Petruchio methodically battles Katherine's frowardness (assertive disobedience) into submission, her "mild" and "modest" (1.1.71, 156) sister Bianca is slyly choosing her own husband even as her father is negotiating with her suitors. When these same suitors scrap among themselves over access to her, she says, "Why, gentlemen, you do me double wrong / To strive for that which resteth in my choice" (3.1.16–17); she selects the disguised Lucentio and elopes, aided by the tricky servant Tranio. At the wager banquet she then disobeys her husband, losing him, as he tells her bitterly in this cost-conscious play, a "hundred crowns since supper-time"—to which she replies, "The more fool you for laying on my duty [i.e., wifely obedience]" (5.2.128). Of course, filial disobedience is one of the most common strategies that Shakespeare deploys to propel his comedies forward. Besides Bianca, examples include Sylvia (*Two Gentlemen*), Hermia (*Dream*), Celia (*As You Like It*), and Imogen (*Cymbeline*).

More than this open defiance, however, are the autonomy and independence of these comic heroines, who go forth (Julia and Sylvia in *Two Gentlemen*, Helena and Hermia in *Dream*, Portia and Nerissa in *Merchant*, Rosalind and Celia in *As You Like It*, Viola in *Twelfth Night*, Helen in *All's Well*, and Imogen in *Cymbeline*), shaping their own plot to attain their romantic desire. Of these characters, Portia is undoubtedly the heroine with the most agency. Although her life is initially bound by patriarchal restrictions (the caskets), Shakespeare consistently empowers her, first by making her, as he does Olivia in *Twelfth Night*, the assertive head of a luxurious country manor. But Portia's project extends far beyond the domestic goals of similarly placed female characters. In her betrothal speech to Bassanio, echoing the sentiment and even the words of Kate in *Shrew*, she speaks of herself as "an unlesson'd girl," who offers herself "to be directed / As from her lord, her governor, her king" (3.2.159, 164–65). However, she explodes her self-enclosure as submissive wife in her next scene with Bassanio, Antonio's trial scene. Disguised as a lawyer's assistant, Portia is iconoclastic in her use of formal rhetoric and "professional" knowledge in the public sphere of the ducal courtroom. Her speech is strikingly assertive, not only in articulating the "quality of mercy" that sets up an ethos countering the contractual justice demanded by Shylock (4.1.184–205), but also in her control of the twists of the complex proceedings: "You, merchant, have you anything to say?" (263), "Tarry, Jew, / The law hath yet another hold on you" (346–47), and so on.

Chastity

(Non)silence and (dis)obedience are fairly straightforward components of Shakespeare's construction of his comic heroines, particularly in the comedic free space away from court. Chastity, with its early modern meaning of premarital virginity and marital fidelity, is treated much more complexly. Virtually all of the comic heroines are chaste maidens or wives. Miranda refers to her chastity as "my modesty / (The jewel in my dower [dowry])" (*Tempest* 3.1.53–54), evoking its dynastic importance. Isabella terms unchastity "abhorr'd pollution," and threatened with Claudio's death should she not capitulate to Angelo, instructs herself, "Then, Isabel, live chaste, and, brother, die; / More than our brother is our chastity" (*Measure* 2.4.183–85). Such valuations of chastity are characteristic. Even Hermia asks her betrothed, Lysander, to lie further off as they settle to sleep in the forest, for "humane modesty; / Such separation as may well be said / Becomes a virtuous bachelor and a maid" (*Dream* 2.2.57–59).

Chastity for many heroines, moreover, is the physical sign of their invariable, unwavering loyalty to the man Shakespeare has picked for them to love. The most extreme of the steadfast comic heroines is undoubtedly Mariana in *Measure*. Angelo broke off their formal betrothal when her dowry was lost in a shipwreck, accusing her of infidelity, and then had sex with Isabella, or so he believed. When the Duke forces Angelo to marry Mariana in order to protect her honor and then announces plans to execute him, Mariana cries out, "O my dear lord, / I crave no other, nor no better man" (5.1.425–26). This is characteristic. The Demetriuses, the Bertrams, once loved, are loved unconditionally.

In contrast, the comic heroes demonstrate an equivocal engagement with chastity that reveals much about Shakespeare's construction of male character. This is apparent in *Measure* in Claudio's response to his sister's preference for her virginity over his life. His initial horror matches hers; however, his fear of death, which he starkly evokes, soon turns him into a relativist: "What sin you do to save a brother's life, / Nature dispenses with the deed so far / That it becomes a virtue" (3.1.133–35). Many of the male characters have a similarly flexible view of chastity. Most amusingly, in *Merry Wives* Falstaff determines, like his heroic predecessor Bassanio (*Merchant*), to pursue an erotic solution for his financial woes, only in this upside-down comedy it is women, not woman, and adultery (a quick financial fix) rather than marriage (a lifetime revenue).

More complexly rendered is the disregard for chastity by the comic heroes themselves, such as Proteus (*Two Gentlemen*), who tries to rape his best friend's betrothed, Sylvia. The wronged friend Valentine undergoes rapid, freeze-frame changes: before watching the attempted rape he had pined, "Repair me with thy presence, Sylvia" (5.4.11); upon witnessing his friend's perfidy he cried out, in a startling series of metonymies, "Who should be trusted, when one's right hand / Is perjured to the bosom?" (67–68); but on listening to Proteus' most perfunctory of apologies he generously forgives him by offering, "that my love may appear plain and free, / All that was mine in Sylvia I give thee" (82–83).

One aspect of Shakespeare's examination of chastity to receive repeated attention in the comedies (*Merry Wives*, *Much Ado*) and romances (*Cymbeline* and *Winter's Tale*), along with *Othello* in the middle of this comic cluster, is men's deep anxiety about cuckoldry (the situation resulting for the man when his wife or beloved is unchaste). There are, for instance, references in many plays to "horns" and "forehead," words that instantly evoke cuckoldry. Touchstone says, "As horns are odious, they are necessary [inevitable]" (*As You Like It* 3.3.51–52). This motif, generally lodged in casual badinage among the men, does more focused work in *Much Ado*, controlling character (Benedick's) and plot (Claudio's).

In the case of Benedick, the jokes accumulate and deepen to offer a revealing basis for his aversion to marriage, one factor preventing an act 1 pairing with Beatrice. This anxiety emerges when he hears of his friend Claudio's intention to marry Hero: "Is 't come to this? In faith, hath not the world one man but he will wear his cap with suspicion?" (1.1.197–99). Interestingly, his anxieties about sexual fidelity are generalized, never once focusing on Beatrice. As he says of women, "Because I will not do them the wrong to mistrust any, I will do myself the right to trust none" (242–44). Although Beatrice and Benedick become one of Shakespeare's most committed and admirably loving of couples, he is still making cuckoldry jokes in his closing lines: "There is no staff more reverent than one tipp'd with horn" (5.4.123–24), he says of marriage.

Benedick's anxiety does not affect the course of his true love. Rather, cuckoldry anxiety is "performed" in the Claudio plot, in the sexual slander of Hero. The interrupted wedding, with its displays of wrath by lover, father, and prince, is one of the most wrenching scenes in the comedies, matched only by the parallel scene in *Winter's Tale*, and provides Shakespeare's most thoughtful problematizing of men's view of chastity. We witness how deeply invested the male characters are in the chastity of "their" women, which for them works as a synecdoche for female character as a whole: Hero's father Leonato cries out that she was "mine so much / That I myself was to myself not mine, / Valuing of her—why she, O she, is fall'n / Into a pit of ink" (4.1.137–40). The passage also shows how the discourse of unchastity is permeated with the men's polarization of women, as in Claudio's charge to Hero: "You seem to me as Dian in her orb . . . But you are more intemperate in your blood / Than Venus" (57, 59–60). The accusers also vastly exaggerate the offense, as in Don Pedro's reference to the "vile encounters they have had / A thousand times in secret" (93–94). What is perhaps most striking, finally, is how irrelevant the actual character of the accused is to her accusers.

All of these dynamics appear forcefully in this painful scene. However, Shakespeare has carefully constructed it to interrogate the intemperance of Hero's accusers. "By noting of the lady" (instead of listening to Don John), the Friar sees in her eyes "a fire / To burn the errors that these princes hold / Against her maiden truth" (158, 162–64). Shakespeare supports this alternative perspective in the responses of Beatrice and Benedick, who also immediately discount the slander; in Leonato's anguish in his later encounters with his brother and with Claudio and Don Pedro, "Scambling, outfacing, fashion-monging boys" (5.1.94); and finally, following the sorrowful confession of Borachio, in the shocked dialogue between the Prince ("Runs not this speech like iron through your blood?") and Claudio ("I have drunk poison whiles he utter'd it" [245–46]). With this rich medley of voices, and with the advantage of being privy to the hoax from its inception, the audience is able to take stock of Claudio's shockingly shallow rebound: "Sweet Hero, now thy image doth appear / In the rare semblance that I lov'd it first" (251–52).

Shakespeare's romances deepen his scrutiny of the suspicious hero. In *Cymbeline* Iachimo's double slander, of both husband and wife, allows a juxtaposition of Imogen's dismissive exclamation to Iachimo, "Thou wrong'st a gentleman who is as far / From thy report as thou from honor" (1.6.145–46), with Posthumus' quick capitulation to the slanderer. Interestingly, however, Posthumus comes to rue his condemnation and (as he thinks) murder of his wife in a manner that dismantles the rigid prioritizing of women's sexual fidelity voiced by Shakespeare's other anxious heroes; speaking to all husbands, he warns, "how many / Must murther wives much better than themselves / For wrying [erring] but a little!" (5.1.3–5). Imogen's (apparent) infidelity is thus remitted in his larger admiration for her. In his raw scrutiny of Leontes in *Winter's Tale*, Shakespeare homes in on the irrational nature of jealousy rather than its cause or aftermath. At her "trial," Hermione cuts to the center of the issue: "My life stands in the level of your dreams, / Which I'll lay down" (3.2.81–82), and indeed it is Leontes' fantasies that interest Shakespeare. Again, an assertive, articulate heroine is both loyal partner and victim of a flawed comic hero.

Moreover, although morbidly preoccupied by the unchastity of the women they love, the heroes are careless of other women's and of their own. A number of them break betrothal or nuptial vows; guilty of this infidelity are Demetrius and Lysander (*Dream*), Proteus (*Two Gentlemen*), Bertram (*All's Well*), and Angelo (*Measure*). Commonly these fickle lovers are extravagantly, unthinkingly infatuated with their new beloved and, when Shakespeare allows them the opportunity, aggressively dismissive of the old. Proteus, for instance, discards his betrothed and attaches himself to his friend's in a compact twenty-five line speech (2.4.192–214). In *Dream*, Demetrius says to the doggedly persistent Helena, "Tempt not too much the hatred of my spirit, / For I am sick when I do look on thee" (2.1.211–12), while Lysander, under the influence of the magic flower, exclaims to his betrothed, "Hang off, thou cat, thou burr! Vile thing, let loose" (3.2.260). The elaborately courteous language that is one marker for the comic heroes is replaced, hyperbolically, by language of abuse, reflecting the extremity of the betrayal.

Of course, Shakespeare puts it right in the end. Generally the unfaithful lovers are subjected to public exposure in recognition scenes, with their repentance and recuperation following swiftly, given their protected status as comic heroes. Bertram, confronted in the recognition scene of *All's Well* with Diana, whom he believes he bedded, lies to her face, telling the king that she is merely a woman with whom he has flirted: "Let your Highness / Lay a more noble thought upon mine honor / Than for to think that I would sink it here" (5.3.179–81). As his deception unravels he acknowledges that he in fact "boarded her i' th' wanton way of youth" (211). However, upon his wife Helen's sudden appearance, he cries out, "Both, both. O pardon!" and, of Helen, "I'll love her dearly, ever, ever dearly" (308, 316). Angelo's contrition in *Measure* is equally rapid, with perhaps more reason since he capitulated to his desires so reluctantly. Faithful wives are invariably the reward for perfidy.

Another convention in Shakespeare's construction of his comic heroes is their attention to class and wealth. Petruchio states bluntly that "wealth is burthen of my wooing dance" (*Shrew* 1.2.68). Bassanio in *Merchant* speaks equally frankly about the necessity of gaining immediate access to Portia's fortune to relieve himself of the huge debt he has accumulated by living "something too prodigal [lavishly]" (1.1.129). And Bertram's aversion to Helen's middle-class status, which underlies his rejection of her, launches the comic plot. Similarly, the governor Lysimachus, who visited Marina in the brothel, states his interest in marriage "were I well assur'd" that she came "of a gentle kind [well-born family] and noble stock" (*Pericles* 5.1.67–68). Equally telling are the casual references to material advantage uttered by the male lovers, for instance Claudio's question to Don Pedro about Hero, "Hath Leonato any son, my lord?" and the prince's reassuring reply, "No child but Hero, she's his only heir" (*Much Ado* 1.1.294–95). The heroines are free of such material and class interest, with Imogen's elopement with the "poor but worthy gentleman" Posthumus—a defiance excoriated by father, stepmother, and step-brother—being the most notable example (*Cymbeline* 1.1.7).

Shakespeare does not punish his heroes for introducing crass materialism into the romantic equation; invariably they win their wealthy beloveds. Rather, it is part of a larger pattern. The complexity and texture of the heroines are created from wholly admirable qualities crafted out of their defiance of female ideals of silence and obedience, generally as acts of loyalty to their beloved. The complexity and texture of the heroes, in contrast, are grounded in their "flaws," their anxieties about chastity, class, and wealth, destabilizing qualities that suggest their potential for becoming blocking figures a generation hence. Writing from within a deeply patriarchal and (hence) hierarchical society, Shakespeare uses the freedoms offered by comic form to query early modern values from different directions in his male and female protagonists. Discussing the fragile understandings achieved by lovers forced to submit to fifth-act comic closure, Catherine Belsey finds evidence of a "structural anxiety at the heart of the early modern celebration of conjugal love," an anxiety that also surfaces in didactic texts and artifacts of the period (*Shakespeare* 81).

"Jack shall have Jill; / Nought shall go ill; / The man shall have his mare again" (3.2.461–63)

The inexplicable presence of a "mare" in a limerick about marriage evokes a notable aspect of Shakespeare's comedies—how many parts of the plays have no immediately apparent function in the inexorable process toward matrimony. Analysis of some of these disparate elements will reveal the breadth of issues covered in the plays and how such "mares" connect with the construction of marriage in Shakespeare's comic paradigm.

Many of the plays feature what recent critics have termed "homosocial," or same-sex bonds that pull against the heterosexual pairings of the heroes and heroines. These forces vary in kind and intensity, from youthful friendship to much stronger ties with homoerotic overtones, to complicated metatheatrical elements. Childhood friendships, such as those between Hermia and Helena (*Dream*), Rosalind and Celia (*As You Like It*), and Beatrice and Hero (*Much Ado*) are depicted as powerful, even passionate. Helena, for instance, speaks of how as children she and Hermia sewed and sang together, growing "Like to a double cherry . . . / So with two seeming bodies but one heart" (3.2.209, 212). Celia similarly says to Rosalind that their love teaches "that thou and I are one" (1.3.97), a well-known Pauline concept (Ephesians 1.31) commonly applied to husband and wife. Scholars have seen the rupture of Helena and Hermia's friendship as emblematic of the passage from childhood homosocial to adult heterosexual relationships. In general, such references cluster in the early acts of the plays, exerting no lasting competitive tension with the developing romances.

Male characters similarly utilize what might be called the discourse of friendship, with Polixenes in *Winter's Tale* saying of his childhood closeness with Leontes, "We were as twinn'd lambs" (1.2.67). However, the homosocial dynamics among men in plays such as *Much Ado*, *Merchant*, and *Twelfth Night* are far more complicated, following the general pattern of Shakespeare's construction of male character. For example, Shakespeare depicts the Antonios in both *Merchant* and *Twelfth Night*, like Don Pedro in *Much Ado*, as solitary bachelors deeply invested in the romantic crises of the heroes (even risking their lives, for instance the *Merchant* Antonio offering his pound of flesh and the *Twelfth Night* Antonio entering Illyria, where he is wanted for piracy). However, they are excluded from the nuptial closure. They have no "Jill." Benedick's cry at the end, "Prince, thou art sad, get thee a wife, get thee a wife" (*Much Ado* 5.4.122), emphasizes this exclusion and draws attention to the melancholy (a symptom of unrequited love) common to the portrayal of these passionate friends (see also *Merchant* 1.1.1).

The complexity of these friendships is illustrated in *Merchant*, where a shadow triangle—Antonio/Bassanio/Portia—emerges, appearing for instance in Shakespeare's use of the ring device, long a love token in romance, to draw attention to the competition between Bassanio's friend and wife. When Balthazar/Portia demands her husband's wedding ring as payment for saving Antonio's life, Bassanio, initially aghast, hands it over at Antonio's urging: "Let [Balthazar's] deservings and my love withal / Be valued 'gainst your wive's commandement" (4.1.450–51). The *Twelfth Night* Antonio, Sebastian's rescuer, is no more necessary to the plot than Viola's captain, who makes a perfunctory appearance early in the play. Yet Shakespeare devotes some attention to his portrayal; at its center is his love for Sebastian—"I do adore thee so" (2.1.47)—whose power he defines as "witchcraft" (5.1.76), a quality generally applied to seductive women (see, e.g., *Winter's Tale* 4.4.423). The representation of friendship, particularly of the two Antonios, is passionate, even erotic; however, the plays leave such friendships inchoate and suspended (see Sinfield).

Yet another manifestation of these homosocial entanglements is metatheatrical, a consequence of the English custom of using boys to play female parts on the stage. Sometimes the boy actors play heroines disguised as boys (*Two Gentlemen*, *Merchant*, *As You Like It*, *Twelfth Night*, and *Cymbeline*). Shakespeare emphasizes the humor in these multiple levels of "play-acting," for instance when Sylvia asks Julia, acting the part of Sebastian, "Dost thou know her [i.e., Julia]?" and Julia/Sebastian replies, "Almost as well as I do know myself" (*Two Gentlemen* 4.4.142–43) and so on, for another forty lines, a joke repeated in *Merchant*, *Twelfth Night*, and *All's Well*. But the dramatic effects of this cross-dressing, or "transvestism" as critics term it (Rackin 33–37; Crewe for instance) go beyond humor; in the comedic free space, females woo females (Rosalind/Ganymede and Phebe, Viola/Cesario, and Olivia) and males woo males (Ganymede/Rosalind and Orlando, Cesario/Viola, and Orsino). Valerie Traub points to the homoerotic language sometimes marking this same-sex courtship, for instance when Phebe, listing the attributes of her newly found beloved, focuses increasingly on the explicitly feminine qualities of Ganymede (Rosalind) such as the "pretty redness in his lip, / A little riper and more lusty red / Than that mix'd in his cheek" (*As You Like It* 3.5.120–22). Traub argues that at such times, "the characters temporarily inhabit a homoerotic position of desire" (128), one that ultimately dissolves when women are "securely repositioned as objects of exchange in a patriarchal economy" based on heterosexual marriage, a containment shaped not only by comic closure but also by the anxiety that accompanies such displays of nonsanctioned desires (119).

Rosalind's epilogue in *As You Like It* makes fun of these gender acrobatics. She dallies with both male and female members of the audience, with the boy actor venturing halfway out of character into his own gender while still flirting with the men: "If I were a woman, I would kiss as many of you as had beards that pleas'd me" (1–23, passim; Belsey, "Disrupting" 180–181). It is a coup de théâtre that perfectly captures the equivocal balance achieved by the boy actors playing female characters, and the use Shakespeare makes of these gender ambiguities.

Now, the subplots: the comedies are populated by clusters of mostly lower-class characters who are largely indifferent to the play's main task of marrying off two or four wealthy young men and women. Shakespeare creates these peripheral characters as vibrant, engaged personages with their own concerns and values, then draws them into the crises of the lovers and thereby into the central issues of the play. Some characters are allotted flashy but fleeting stage time, a few among many examples being Petruchio's household servants (*Shrew* 4.1), the fishermen who find Pericles (2.1), and Posthumus' jailer (*Cymbeline* 5.4). Others receive elaborate plots of their own, such as the craftsmen in *Dream* and the denizens of Olivia's household in *Twelfth Night*. These subplots often have a thematic, generally counterpointal, relation to the main plot.

Love's Labor's Lost has two sets of subplot characters that interrogate both halves of the king's pronouncement opening the play—to plunge the court into study and to forgo all contact with women. The commitment to study is countered by the vapid rhetoric of the pedant Holofernes and his friend the curate Nathaniel, all learned words sans wisdom. The aristocrats' intention to eschew women, and their extravagant language and behavior once they fall in love, are juxtaposed to the lush sensuality of Jaquenetta, desired both by the phlegmatic underclass Costard ("I suffer for the truth, sir; for true it is, I was taken with Jaquenetta, and Jaquenetta is a true girl" [1.1.311–12])—notice, in the reference to "truth," the hit at the study program as well—and the courtly braggart Armado ("Adieu, valor, rust, rapier, be still, drum, for your manager is in love; yea, he loveth. Assist me, some extemporal god of rhyme, for I am sure I shall turn sonnet" [1.2.181–84]—notice the hit at the sonnet, the courtship discourse favored by the four lovers). Jaquenetta's pregnancy, hilariously announced in the midst of the Pageant of the Nine Worthies by Pompey (the rejected swain Costard) to the father-to-be Hector (Armado), provides a speaking picture of the heroic/antiheroic perspectives with which Shakespeare infuses the play and offers a blunt reminder of the material consequence of the romantic crises that permeate the action for the courtly characters.

The low-life characters of *Measure* are similarly, but much more bitterly and pedantically, deployed by Shakespeare to complicate the debate about law and justice raised in this problem play. They offer the concerned Escalus, the impervious Angelo, and of course the audience all the human messiness that renders Vienna's laws so hard to adjudicate.

Escalus: How would you live, Pompey? By being a bawd? What do you think of the trade, Pompey? Is it a lawful trade?
Pompey: If the law would allow it, sir.
Escalus: But the law will not allow it, Pompey; nor it shall not be allow'd in Vienna.
Pompey: Does your Worship mean to geld and splay [castrate] all the youth of the city? (2.1.224–31)

A similar message is more sharply etched in the earnest, didactic Angelo main plot.

Sometimes a main-plot character is exposed by his interaction with subplot characters, with one of the most complex examples being the Prospero/Ariel/Caliban nexus in *Tempest*. Here the wronged (ex-duke) Prospero, pursuing justice against the brother who usurped him, is triangulated with the funny, bitterly angry, vengeful slave Caliban, proprietary owner of the island before Prospero's arrival, and with the impatiently compliant Ariel, liberated by Prospero from Caliban and his mother into renewed slavery to him. The move toward order and justice driving Prospero in his two-generational effort to regain his dukedom is disturbingly destabilized for the modern audience by his colonial tyranny.

Shakespeare never offers a single view of the matters that concern him in the comedies. Rather, his plays are prismatic, with the subplot characters in the busy world surrounding his protagonists providing a commentary on their activities, concerns, and discourses.

And finally, the humor: these plays are comedies not only because of their trajectory from familial and sometimes political disorder to nuptial order, but because they are deeply funny. Shakespeare uses many strategies to solicit grins, chortles, and guffaws from his audiences.

The malapropism is one of many examples of humor generated by the language of Shakespeare's comedies. A prolixity of language styles individuates characters by class, ethnicity, profession, and attitude (Magnussen 160). The malapropism (misuse of a word by an oblivious speaker) functions as a humorous class marker, invariably among underclass (hence subplot) characters. Malapropisms generally appear in clusters, for instance in the speeches of the mechanicals in *Dream*, the constabulary in *Much Ado*, and the brothel characters in *Measure*. Most often the speaker uses a word that is comically the opposite of the meaning he intends, as when Gobbo and his son Launcelot plead for Launcelot's transfer in service from Shylock to Bassanio; their speeches are clotted with malapropisms and ruptures as the two tumble over each other to ensure the change: "He hath a great infection, sir, as one would say, to serve—," "In very brief, the suit is impertinent to myself, as your worship shall know," and "That is the very defect of the matter, sir" (*Merchant* 2.2.125–26, 137–38, 142). In Launcelot's long ruminative speech on fortune that follows, offering quiet chuckles for the audience, there is nary a malapropism. The device emerges, then, as a kind of class stutter, comically marking the efforts of lower-class characters to speak like their betters. Another example is the dialogue in *Measure* between the judge Escalus and village constable Elbow, whose rage toward Pompey is expressed in a cascade of malapropisms. At one point Elbow sputters to Pompey, "Prove it before these varlots here [Angelo and Escalus], thou honorable man [Pompey], prove it," about which Escalus remarks to Angelo, "Do you hear how he misplaces?" (2.1.86–88), a patronizing aside that emphasizes the denigration of under-class characters propelling this form of humor. While these malapropisms are played for laughs, occasionally they affect events, as at the end of act 3 of *Much Ado*, when Dogberry's digressions and malapropisms cause the impatient Leonato to rush off to his daughter's wedding without waiting to hear what the "two aspicious persons" "comprehended" by the constables might have to confess. This "excommunication" (3.5.46, 63–64) is delayed until act 5, with the intervening act filled with the misery caused by the misunderstanding.

Other times the actions of the characters more than their words release laughter. One common form of plot humor is the situational joke. In *Comedy of Errors*, Shakespeare keeps two pairs of twins, all four separated from birth and unaware of their sibling, revolving on and off the stage in various combinations, confounding companions, family, and one another. Many such instances occur in *Tempest*; in one, Caliban and Trinculo, hiding under a cloak, become an English-speaking "monster of the isle with four legs" for the drunken Stephano (2.2.65). Commonly one character plays a joke on others, as, for instance, when Ariel uses ventriloquism to kindle the rage of these same three characters toward one another (3.2). In constructing this kind of humor, Shakespeare relies on dramatic irony (a situation where the audience knows more than the characters) to create a community of knowing people (the audience) laughing at oblivious targets (the characters); as in the Ariel example, sometimes there is an alliance between the audience and some characters at the expense of others.

Shakespeare often enriches these situational jokes by loading them with additional dramatic functions, as when they also serve as the play's recognition scene. One by one, the four lovers in *Love's Labor's Lost* lament that they have broken their ascetic compact by falling in love. Berowne, the first on the scene, watches as each confessor becomes an eavesdropper to those following him, his comments heightening the humor of the situation: "Shot, by heaven! Proceed, sweet Cupid, thou has thump'd him with thy bird-bolt under the left pap" (4.3.22–24). His smug (and hypocritical) superiority quickly collapses when Jaquenetta brings in his sonnet to Rosaline, which had been misdelivered to her. Marking the play's turn, Berowne ruefully concludes, "Let us once lose our oaths to find ourselves" (4.3.358). In *Much Ado* the elaborate double eavesdropping hoax plotted by Don Pedro offers, besides the guffaws, the recognition scene for the Beatrice/Benedick plot and a structural parallel to the dastardly scheme perpetrated in the Hero plot (also overheard), with the one uniting lovers and the other driving them apart.

Finally, Shakespeare often relies on familiar stock characters, with the audience spotting the character type, knowing the plot, and anticipating the laughs. One such stock character, the braggart, can be traced back to ancient Greek and Roman comedy; in early modern comedy he (always a he) is a particularly fruitful comic target due to his social pretensions, a sure-fire source of humor during this time of rapid socioeconomic change. The braggart's portrayal evolves in three stages. Early scenes display the character to the audience; Falstaff (*Merry Wives*), Malvolio (*Twelfth Night*), Parolles (*All's Well*), and, in a smaller role, Lucio (*Measure*) share a lofty superiority, a certainty that they control the plot, and often an overweening social ambition that appear early on and prepare the audience to enjoy their inevitable downfall. Falstaff's comic vulnerability is his sexual vanity; convinced of Mrs. Ford's and Mrs. Page's desire for him, he remarks complacently of the latter that "sometimes the beam of her view gilded my foot, sometimes my portly belly" (*Merry Wives* 1.3.61–62), with "gilded" indicating his stratagem to use her (supposed) lust to relieve his penury. A second set of scenes focuses on the elaborate planning that will bring about the braggart's downfall. In *All's Well* the repeated line, "O, for the love of laughter" (3.6.34, 41), suggests the glee of the plotters and the chortles for the audience in this part. The social exposure and humiliation of the braggart follow. As with other aspects of these comedies, psychological and social complexity is depicted by trickery, with the containment and isolation of the braggart represented dramatically by convoluted scenes of physical capture, (mock) torture, and imprisonment: Falstaff first in the dirty clothes basket, then forced into disguise as a woman, then prone, pinched and burned by "fairies" in the forest; Malvolio imprisoned as a madman; Parolles captured by "enemy" soldiers, interrogated, and threatened with torture.

While all of these scenes are played for audience guffaws, Shakespeare does not neglect their didactic function for main-plot characters and audience alike; as a chastened Parolles warns, "Who knows himself a braggart, / Let him fear this, for it will come to pass / That every braggart shall be found an ass" (*All's Well* 4.3.334–36). The Falstaff plot exposes and disciplines the uxorious Ford; the Parolles plot is explicitly designed by the plotters for the edification of Bertram; and Malvolio joins *Twelfth Night*'s roster of hopeless lovers (Orsino, Viola, Olivia, and Aguecheek), providing an explicit social dimension that is only intimated elsewhere.

The humor of humiliation is a delicate business; it is threatened by its proximity to meanness, which elicits sympathy, not laughter. Shakespeare explores this conjunction in the elaborate entrapment of Malvolio in *Twelfth Night*, a braggart's plot incorporating all the conventional devices, including an early display of Malvolio's ambition and puritanical rigidity, followed by the concoction of the humiliation plot by Maria and her coconspirators (witnessed, of course, by the appreciative audience in a nonspeaking role). This arrangement remains stable as Malvolio decodes the false love letter and preens over its promises, and in the later scene as he presents himself, smiling and cross-gartered, to Olivia and then point by point misinterprets her appalled response. However, in the last stage of the hoax, Malvolio's imprisonment as a madman transforms our laughter, which distances us from him, to an appalled sympathy, a turn that Olivia succinctly captures in her assessment: "He hath been most notoriously abus'd" (5.1.379). While the structure of Shylock's ruin is similar to those in other braggart episodes, audience discomfiture is at wide variance with the glee of Portia the plotter and her Christian community.

"Jack shall have Jill; / Nought shall go ill; / The man shall have his mare again, and all shall be well" (3.2.461–64)

Note that a happy ending is promised twice in this short jingle—an anxious reassurance, and perhaps a necessary one, given the narrowly averted tragedies, dubious last-minute conversions, and happy coincidences often required to produce the closing celebrations. The compulsion of comedy to transform problems into solutions adumbrates its larger social task, which is to explore and then contain fraught social issues of the time within a lithesome, frequently funny, and ultimately orderly performance narrative. Shakespearean comedy illustrates this transformative process, addressing as it does the ongoing reformulation of marriage ideology. A product of the Reformation and of a larger movement from feudal to early capitalistic structures, changes in the institution of marriage involved a rejection of Catholic dogmas that privileged celibacy over marriage and of aristocratic practices that used marriage for family empowerment and financial aggrandizement. A middle-class, Protestant vision of marriage was evolving to replace these older structures, one founded on the love of husband and wife within the domestic hierarchies of the time (Belsey, *Shakespeare* 59–83; Rose 1–42). The comedies speak to these changes, in their rejection of celibacy (*Dream*, *Love's Labor's Lost*, and *Measure*); in the successful efforts of upstart young lovers to choose their mates instead of submitting to their domestically and politically entrenched elders (*Shrew*, *Dream*, *Merchant*, *Merry Wives*, *Cymbeline*, *Winter's Tale*); and, most problematically, in the efforts of the couples to effect a loving, conjugal commitment (*Shrew*, *Two Gentlemen*, *Dream*, *Love's Labor's Lost*, *As You Like It*, *Much Ado*, *Twelfth Night*, *All's Well*, *Cymbeline*). The comic paradigm is a remarkably fertile and elastic one, offering opportunities not only for exploring marriage but also for challenging gender and class hierarchies (Howard 93–128). Shakespeare's plays, profoundly but conventionally literary and theatrical, engaged urgent social issues in a time of social instability and change.

REFERENCES AND FURTHER READINGS

Belsey, Catherine. "Disrupting Sexual Difference: Meaning and Gender in the Comedies." *Alternative Shakespeares*. Ed. Terence Hawkes. New York: Methuen, 1985. 166–90.

———. *Shakespeare and the Loss of Eden: The Construction of Family Values in Early Modern Culture*. New Brunswick, NJ: Rutgers UP, 1999.

Charney, Maurice. *Shakespeare on Love and Lust*. New York: Columbia UP, 2000.

Crewe, Jonathan. "In the Field of Dreams: Transvestism in *Twelfth Night* and *Crying Game*." *Shakespeare and Gender*. Ed. Stephen Orgel and Sean Keilen. New York: Garland, 1999. 183–203.

Frye, Northrop. *Anatomy of Criticism: Four Essays*. 1957. New York: Atheneum, 1966.

Howard, Jean E. *The Stage and Social Struggle in Early Modern England*. New York: Routledge, 1994.

Hull, Suzanne W. *Chaste, Silent and Obedient: English Books for Women, 1475–1640*. San Marino, CA: Huntington Library, 1982.

Leggatt, Alexander, ed. *The Cambridge Companion to Shakespearean Comedy*. Cambridge, UK: Cambridge UP, 2002.

Magnussen, Lynne. "Language and Comedy." *The Cambridge Companion to Shakespearean Comedy*. Ed. Alexander Legatt. Cambridge, UK: Cambridge UP, 2002. 156–78.

Rose, Mary Beth. *The Expense of Spirit: Love and Sexuality in English Renaissance Drama*. Ithaca, NY: Cornell UP, 1988.

Rackin, Phyllis. "Androgyny, Mimesis, and the Marriage of the Boy Heroine on the English Renaissance Stage." *PMLA* 102 (1987): 29–41.

Salinger, Leo. *Shakespeare and the Traditions of Comedy*. Cambridge, UK: Cambridge UP, 1974.

Shakespeare, William. *The Riverside Shakespeare*. Ed. G. Blakemore Evans and J. J. Tobin. 2nd ed. Boston: Houghton Mifflin, 1997. All dating of the plays and all textual citations are taken from this edition.

Sinfield, Alan. "How to Read *The Merchant of Venice* without Being Heterosexist." *Alternative Shakespeares*, Vol. 2. Ed. Terence Hawkes. New York: Routledge, 1996. 122–39.

Traub, Valerie. *Desire and Anxiety: Circulations of Sexuality in Shakespearean Drama*. New York: Routledge, 1992.

36

Spanish Comedy

Nina Gerassi-Navarro and Raquel Medina-Bañón

From its earliest literary expressions to its most recent forms of cultural production, humor has had a major role in Spanish culture. Through the centuries, Spanish humor has stood out for its satirical and parodic traits with its distinct burlesque and grotesque style. In fact, one could even say that the use of humor as a weapon to deal with the innumerable "bad times" is the best way to define Spanish idiosyncrasy. Spain's history is full of social, political, and economic injustices, religious persecutions, civil wars, and foreign invasions; yet throughout all of it, Spaniards have tried to respond in a critical and cathartic way using humor.

The troubadour lyrics of the eleventh and twelfth centuries, written in Provençal and Limousin, are perhaps the earliest humorist expressions in a Romance language. At the time, Spain was divided into autonomous kingdoms that had united in 718 to reconquer the Iberian Peninsula occupied by the Arabs in 711. Given its geographical location, Cataluña was closer to the south of France than to the rest of the Iberian Peninsula not only in terms of its lyrical production or linguistic characteristics, but even politically.

The Catalan troubadours, who belonged to the upper classes, composed their songs against the vices and customs of the kings, noblemen, and clergy above them. These men were taunted and ridiculed through a variety of insults. Among the troubadours, Guillem de Berguedá is one of the best known for his songs that illustrate how social critique was articulated in medieval Spain through sexual allusions.

During the twelfth and thirteenth centuries the Galaico Portuguese lyrics appeared in full force with their famous songs of insults and slander (*cantigas de escarnio*). Strongly influenced by the Provençals, these troubadours like the Provençals and Catalans before them dedicated their insults to critique the sexual, economic, political, and social vices of all those in power in the different kingdoms. The majority of these compositions attack one individual who is named in the poem with the purpose of being ridiculed, although sometimes the critique can address collective defects. These kinds of compositions, written by some of the best-known writers in Spain, such as Martín

Codax, Nuno Fernandes, Airas Nunes, Xohan Zorro, and King Don Denís, are found in specific collections such as *Ajuda*, *Vaticana*, and that of the *Biblioteca Nacional* or *Colocci-Brancuti*. Even the well-known king Alfonso X, "the knowledgeable one," in addition to his famous collections of sacred *Cantigas of Santa María* (*Songs of Saint Mary*), also composed these songs of insults where he showed the same level of obscenity as many of his contemporaries. The following is one of his examples against traitors:

> Let him be damned!
> He who handed out his money
> Without attracting any good knights—
> Is it because he wasn't first in the fight
> That he's bragging now?
> Since he came at us with his rear,
> Let him be damned!
> ....
> He who filled up his bags
> With a bit of gold and a lot of rubbish,
> And never quite entered the town of Vega,
> Is he bragging now?
> Since he's more like fat than butter,
> Let him be damned!
>
> (Alfonso X 299–300, our translation)

El cantar del mio Cid (The Song of the Cid), one of the best-known poems written in mid-twelfth century about the Castilian hero Rodrigo Díaz de Vivar, also has many comical traits. But it is the fourteenth-century *Libro de Buen Amor* by Juan Ruiz, Archpriest of Hita, that stands as the banner of Spanish medieval comedy. In addition to the way the author parodies sermons and other established genres of this period, the richness of the book is its ambiguity that stems from its double theme: the love of God and sexual love. *The Book of Good Love* inaugurates a trend of carnival humor in Spain through the battle between Carnival (don Carnal) and Lent (doña Cuaresma). It is not only a parody of epic poetry, but more importantly a dramatic antiecclesiastical satire in which soldiers appear as dishes of meat and fish. When the Archpriest focuses on women the carnival spectacle becomes grotesque. This is exemplified in his portrait of one *serrana*:

> Her mouth was like a mastiff dog's, with a huge, thick snout,
> And big, long teeth, such horsy teeth, projecting from between.
> Her eyebrows draped across her forehead, blacker than two thrushes.
> You men who die to marry, don't turn deaf ears to this queen!
>
> (Arcipreste de Hita 157, our translation)

This particular portrait, as well as many other examples, reflects the misogyny that characterized and would continue to characterize Spanish culture for many years.

During the fifteenth century, the reigning political instability gave rise to many satires. *Coplas del Provincial* (Ballads of the Provincial) speaks against the vices of the courtesans; *Coplas de ¡Ay Panadera!* (Ballads of Oh Miss Baker!) belittles the cowardly noblemen of the Battle of Olmedo (April 14, 1445); *Coplas de Mingo Revulgo* (Ballads of Mingo Revulgo) lampoons Henry IV. In 1492, the siege of Granada, the last Arab outpost, marked the end of the Reconquest, and ushered in several centuries of religious and political persecutions that accompanied the colonial expansion of the new Spanish Empire. Jews and Arabs foremost, followed by Protestants (who were considered another kind of heretic), were the center of a large part of the literary production in subsequent years. Although this persecution had begun earlier, it was heightened with the forced conversion that was imposed in 1391 until the complete expulsion of Jews and Arabs in 1492. It is no wonder that the *Cancionero de Baena* (The Songbook of Baena, 1445) would compile numerous poetic compositions against the converts:

> He defiantly flaunts like
> a palatine;
> the poor devil, trying to look Christian
> as he travels down the road
> eats a cabbage cooked with lard.
>
> He sticks his hand into his mouth
> to clean his head and stomach
> of any guilt.
> He travels through Ubeda and Baeça,
> And stumbles
> On the flat road.
> Let's get him, he's a dirty Jew!
>
> (Scholberg 308, our translation)

The word used in the original for "dirty Jew" is *marrano*, an offensive term referring to converted Jews whose religion prohibited them from eating pork. In this case, to prove his conversion the man eats the pork but then forces himself to vomit to cleanse his soul, thus revealing his true religious beliefs.

In 1554, the simultaneous publication of the anonymous *El Lazarillo de Tormes* in three cities—Burgos, Alcalá de Henares, and Amberes—marks the beginning of the picaresque genre that would comically portray the vices of society through satire and the grotesque. Although the book was banned five years later by the Inquisition, it became such a best seller that King Phillip II was forced to order a purged version entitled *Lazarillo Castigado* (Lazarillo Punished, 1573). These are the years during which the Spanish Empire began to collapse: In 1557 it declared bankruptcy after King Charles V abdicated, thus splitting the largest empire in history between the Spanish and Austrian line of the Habsburg family; wars with France, the Netherlands, and England were devastating and culminated with the disastrous defeat of the "Invincible Armada" in 1588. The situation in Spain can be seen through the satire and the grotesque of this anonymous text in which the irresponsible vagabond Lázaro takes the reader through many adventures and misfortunes. The story begins when Lázaro's mother hands her son over to a sinister blind man as his guide; from then on his life is a continuous succession of masters, all of the same caliber: an avaricious priest, a poor and starving nobleman, and so forth. Eventually Lázaro marries a maid who is his own master's concubine. Thanks to the sexual favors his wife offers his master, Lázaro is allowed to climb the social ladder and become proclaimer of the town of Toledo. Once again, just as medieval literature had done before, literature in the sixteenth century would focus its criticisms on state properties and present a grotesque picture of Spanish society that was becoming bleaker and bleaker.

Another well-known satirical text in which the critique becomes much sharper as the solutions seem more implausible for the picaro's problems, as well as for society in general, is *Guzmán de Alfarache* (1599). The attacks in this book are aimed at government representatives who cannot impart justice in their rulings, for they are all corrupt, inept, ignorant, and stupid. By 1623, when Francisco Quevedo published his picaresque novel *El buscón* (The Swindler), the character of the picaro has been so ridiculed that he has become a caricature, just like the rest of the characters who surround him. While Quevedo is well known for his sarcastic ridicules, by far his most corrosive satire is *Gracias y desgracias del ojo del culo dirigidas a Doña Juana Mucha, Montón de Carne, Mujer gorda por arrobas* (*Graces and Disgraces of the Asshole Directed to Doña Juana Much, a Lot of Flesh, Fat Woman in Great Quantities*, 1626). In this text, Quevedo describes a specific sexual body part in a detailed nonsexual manner to enhance the parodical aspect of his satire:

That the ass is so unfortunate shall not surprise those of you who know that all profitable things in nobility and virtue run the misfortune of being disgraced, especially the ass for having a larger empire and higher veneration than the rest of the body. Looking at it carefully, it is the most perfect and well placed part of the body, and the most favored by Nature. Its shape is round just like the circle, and it is divided in a diameter or zodiac. Its place is in the middle like the sun, its touch is soft, and it has only one hole, like an eye, and some for that reason call it one-eyed. But if we look at it carefully it must be praised for this reason, as it reminds us of the Cyclops who had only one eye and was said to descend from the gods of sight. Not to have more than one eye shows lack of a powerful love, because the grave and authoritative asshole does not consent, my dear. If you look at it carefully, there's more to see than the eyes of the face, even if it is not so apparent it has much more stitching. If you don't believe me just look at the faces, without sculpting, so simple, without any grace like the hole of the ass, full of creases and moldings, with hems and cuffs, and a brow that could be the tail of an old horse, or the beard of a man of letters or doctor. Thus, such a necessary and precious beauty we keep tucked away in the most secure part of the body, greased between two walls of thighs, shrouded in a shirt.... (Quevedo)

The seventeenth century also marks the rise of the great European comic novel: *Don Quijote* by Miguel de Cervantes, the most recognized Spanish author outside the Spanish-speaking world. Published in two parts, in 1605 and 1615, *Don Quijote*, categorized by many critics as the first great novel of world literature, is a novel based on parody. The author himself—that is, if we can trust his own words—declares at the beginning of his novel that his intention is to criticize the books of chivalry. In order to achieve his goal, Cervantes creates a parodic scheme of chivalric literature set in motion through his protagonist's craziness.

In a word, Don Quijote so buried himself in his books that he read all night from sundown to dawn, and all day from sunup to dusk, until with virtually no sleep and so much reading he dried out his brain and lost his sanity. He filled his imagination full to bursting with everything he read in his books, from witchcraft to duels, battles, challenges, wounds, flirtations, love affairs, anguish, and impossible foolishness, packing it all so firmly into his head that these sensational schemes and dreams became the literal truth and, as far as he was concerned, there were no more certain histories anywhere on earth. (10)

Don Quijote's madness is based on a series of Renaissance European treatises such as *In Praise of Folly* (1510) by Desiderius Erasmus, *Orlando Furioso* (1532) by Ludovico Ariosto, and *The Examination of Men's Wits* (1575) by John Huarte de San Juan. Alonso Quijano, the main character, also known as Don Quijote de la Mancha, becomes delusional from reading books of chivalry, those best-selling fictions of the Renaissance where knights and squires, dwarfs and giants, as well as phantoms and enchanters, fill the pages with fascinating journeys that take the heroes through exotic lands of adventures where they always seem to encounter a damsel in distress. Don Quijote not only believes the absurd things he reads, but he takes it upon himself to bring back the lifestyle and values of the errant knight. Cervantes' irony highlights the break with realism that occurred within the feudal world vision at the beginning of the seventeenth century, where nothing is what it seems. Quijote will confuse reality with fiction, as will Sancho—his potbellied, sarcastic squire—and the readers, thus transforming the narrative itself into a series of deceptions that question the limits between reality and imagination. Cervantes' use of irony will become a determining trait of Spanish culture, influencing all types of cultural expressions still evident today.

Baroque poetry shares a similar burlesque trait with this new genre. While most topics during the seventeenth century address the vices of the courts, the power of money, the heroic ideals of the ailing empire, military defeats, and the conquest of America, not all critiques are serious social ones. There are innumerable poems on drunkards, cuckolds, fatsos, and big-nosed people, adding a lighter perspective to the surrounding reality.

Continuing the satirical vein that characterized his essays, Quevedo takes the topic of the nose and gives it a significance in his poems that goes well beyond the physical characteristics that were previously used to identify Jewish ancestry. The following poem illustrates how Quevedo inscribes the topic of the nose, transforming it into a recurrent theme in Spanish literature while simultaeously opening it up to hold a variety of references:

To a man with a big nose
Once there was a man stuck to a nose,
it was a nose more marvellous than weird,
it was a nearly living web of tubes,
it was a swordfish with an awful beard,

it was a sundial doomed to face the shade,
an elephant that looked up to the sky,
it was a nose of hangman and of scribe,
Ovidius Naso nostrilled all awry,
it was the bowsprit of a mighty ship,
like Egypt's pyramid it pierced the sky,
it was of noses all of the twelve tribes;

it was in noseness truly infinite,
an archnose shudder, and a frightening mask,
a monstrous chilblain, purpley and fried.

(Quevedo 2: 5)

Rather than focusing on different parts of the individual's anatomy, the poem targets one single feature from a variety of angles. The juxtaposition of these unrelated images (a living web, a sundial, an elephant, etc.) not only reinforces the critique but, more importantly, creates a grotesque portrait.

Although Quevedo will expand the references of the nose to a general level, he will also use it as a poignant tool of ideological criticism. In another poem, entitled "Sonnet to Góngora," he uses the topic of the nose to directly attack another great poet of his time, Luis de Góngora, with whom he had an ongoing poetic battle. In this case Quevedo transforms his intellectual animosity into a clear and simple insult with a reference to Góngora's nose that highlights the poet's Jewish ancestry: "Why censor the Greek language, / being only a rabbi of the Jews, / something your nose does not hide?" (Quevedo 3: 238). Through humor, poets, essayists, playwrights, and novelists alike portrayed their surrounding reality. It was a form of making sense of a fast-paced, changing world that at times surpassed any form of rationalization, and humor seemed the best way to grasp that instability.

The sixteenth and seventeenth centuries, known as the Golden Age, are without a doubt one of richest literary periods in Spanish culture. It is a period during which everything was questioned, twisted, and complicated. To discuss Spanish comedy, for example, during this period means talking about drama, because the term *comedy* referred to both tragic and tragicomic pieces. During these years the government sponsored a series of theatrical representations for public entertainment and built a number of open-air theaters for this purpose. The major national figure of these representations was Félix Lope de Vega Carpio, the creator of the "new comedy" (*comedia nueva*), a genre that mixes tragic and comic elements, and the founder of modern drama. Lope was one of the most prolific playwrights in history. He is said to have written 1,500 plays, though we know of only 426. He wrote several kinds of comedies, all of which were very successful: comedies of deceit; cloak-and-sword comedies, characterized by the fool who stood out for his truths and sharp-witted criticisms; and comedies of manners that depicted contemporary manners and intrigue, such as *The Dog in the Manger* (1618) and *The Foolish Lady* (1613). Lope's incisive and comical portrayals, full of idiomatic and proverbial expressions, render his dialogue with a lively colloquial flavor that still resonates today, as Pilar Miró's popular 1995 cinematographic version of *The Dog in the Manger* attests. Despite Lope's success with the *comedia nueva*, his most famous work is his historical play *Fuenteovejuna* (1611–1618), the name of the town and the main character. The play recounts a peasant uprising in which the common people oppose corrupt feudal nobility. In part, Lope's success was predicated on being in touch with public sentiment, and he knew, like no other author at the time, how to portray those feelings with style. History and comedy seemed to be intertwined in these years as the Spanish sorted through difficult times of crisis.

By the eighteenth century, poverty had become rampant. The country, devastated by so many wars and religious persecutions, was overrun with debt, while its fervent and entrenched Catholicism and monarchical absolutism continued to resist new ideas brought about with the Enlightenment that were becoming more prominent in the rest of Europe. Despite its precarious economic situation, Spain, however, refused to give up its imperial quest and thus went to war with England to recover Portugal. The seriousness of the times demanded artists to be serious, forcing comedy to adopt a more moralizing tone. A new theatrical piece was born called the *sainete*, a short play similar to the Golden Age interlude (*entremés*) that reproduced life in the streets, especially those of Madrid. Basically, the sainete portrayed a bourgeois society much more concerned with appearances than anything else. In the streets of Madrid, everything French, from clothes to manners to linguisitic jargon, had acquired a new status. If it was French it was seen as stylish and worth imitating. New social types, like the dandy, appeared, emulating French culture. This development gave way to a new kind of debate, one that focused on defining the national culture. The purpose was to position the Spanish as superior to the French, who, because they were so concerned with looks, were seen as effeminate and corrupt. Subsequently, this categorization would extend to everything foreign, creating a dividing line between the true Spanish character and those who believed that Spain needed to become more modern and European, and therefore looked beyond its borders for models of modernity.

While humor was no longer as popular in the theatrical realm, the Spanish satirical vein truly came alive in a number of journals and periodicals. *El Duende* (The Dwarf, 1735), *Caxón de Sastre* (The Box of the Taylor, 1760), *La Tertulia de Aldea* (The Town's Literary Salon, 1775), and *Semanario Erudito* (The Weekly Erudite, 1787) are a few of these journals that burst onto the literary scene. *Caxón de Sastre* presents itself as offering its public "a whole bunch of good things, better, so-so, useful, funny and modest ones too, to scare off idleness without imposing the rigidity of work, but rather in tune with the caresses of pleasure" (López Ruiz 10). *La Tertulia de Aldea* enjoyed publishing "entertaining adventures and funny jokes as pastimes during winter evenings and summer" (11). The appearance of these first comic publications marks a change of course in Spanish satire, which becomes tainted with dark humor that will ultimately remain a distinctly Spanish trait. The political events under the reign of King Fernando VII, the great absolutist monarch who would lose almost all of the crown's colonies in America, and the Napoleonic invasions undoubtedly helped catapult the satirical press—often subversive and clandestine—as the vehicle of critical analysis. Humor thus became a form of sharp political and social critique. When Napoleon Bonaparte invaded Spain in 1808, he replaced the Spanish monarch Fernando VII, whom he forced into exile, with his brother Joseph Bonaparte (José I). This change was seen by the people of Spain as an insult and rapidly increased the latent anti-French sentiment. The Spanish would ridicule José I, whom they considered a mere puppet, dubbing him *Pepe el botella*, or "Pepe the bottle" (Pepe is the nickname for José) because of his well-known drinking; and as a counter partner to Pepe el botella they would nickname the constitution, written in the Cádiz Cortes by the exiled government, "la Pepa."

The Spanish resistance, first to the French invasion and then to the return of Fernando VII, who installed a reign of terror and persecution, augmented the satirical representations inciting all sorts of humorist critiques of Spanish society. Francisco de Goya, the famous painter, best represents this new kind of black humor during times of crisis. Goya's *Los caprichos* (*The Whims*), a series of etchings satirizing human folly and weakness, would become the emblem of this Hispanic humor considered dark and grotesque that is closely connected to Quevedo's style. Goya was the consummate Spanish painter who believed that the artist's vision was the most important element of his painting. Thus, he painted his portraits and scenes of everyday life the way he saw them, in a manner that evolved into a bold, free new style close to caricature.

In *Burial of the Sardine*, one of the most famous paintings in this series, Goya presents a caricature of Spanish Catholicism through his portrayal of the religious tradition. The burial symbolizes the end of Lent, the period during which all good Catholics are prohibited from eating meat, and marks the beginning of Carnival. Continuing the tradition of *The Book of Good Love*, Goya highlights the hypocrisy of Spanish society by portraying everyone, masked and unmasked, dancing and drinking in the streets together as equals. Goya, however, questions this circumstantial "happy union" of all classes through the sharp contrasts of colors and a banner of an eerie smile positioned center stage. In his grotesque exaggeration of this tradition, Goya exposes the theatricality of the event and its illusionary state.

In 1820 a number of satirical publications began to appear in Spain, where humor has played an important role in both the written and the graphic world. In Madrid alone, in just three years eight magazines were published, among them *Diario Burlesco* (The Burlesque Newspaper) and *Periodicomanía* (Newspapermania) in 1820, *El Garrotazo* (The Big Blow) and *La Manopla* (The Gauntlet) in 1821, and *El Amoldador* (The Sharpener) in 1822. Satirical journalism became one of the bastions of social and political critique during the nineteenth century, as developed by Mariano José de Larra, a sort of literary Goya figure, considered the first humorist journalist of Spain. Founder of satirical magazines such as *El duende satírico del día* (The Satirical Goblin of the Day, 1828) and *Pobre Hablador* (Poor Speaker, 1832), Larra populated his articles with ironic caricatures, many of which are grotesque and cruel. He had a very clear idea of the humorist's role: "The satirical writer is he who destroys errors with his writings and chases the worries that fall upon society" (qtd. in López Ruiz 11). He clearly shows this in his article "The Day of the Dead in 1836" (published in *El Español* on November 2, 1836), exemplifying how satire and irony together project a grotesque reality that is none other than reality itself. In this article he focuses on the Spanish custom of visiting cemeteries on the day of the dead. Larra moves beyond the superficial facts of this tradition to critique the institutions that govern the country:

Let's make it clear, I said to myself, where is this cemetery? Outside or inside? A sudden terrifying vertigo hit me, and it all became clear. The cemetery is in Madrid, Madrid is the cemetery. A vast cemetery where each house is a family vault, each street the tomb of an event, each heart the cinerary urn of hope or desire.

So, while those who believed to be living went to the mansion they presumed to belong to the dead, I began to stroll down the streets of the great ossuary with all the devotion and spiritual absorption that I was capable of.

—What monument is this? I exclaimed as I began my walk through the vast cemetery—. Is it an immense skeleton of past centuries or the tomb of other skeletons? *A Palace!* On the one hand it looks towards Madrid, meaning towards the other tombs; on the other hand, it looks towards Extremadura, that virgin province . . . as it has been called. (Larra 549)

Larra goes on to describe the frontispieces of several tombs and mausoleums in the cemetery. In doing so he reviews Spain's history, deriding the role of different institutions, such as the Ministries of Justice and Education, as well as criticizing the legitimacy of the throne.

Larra wrote at a time when Spain was submerged in poverty as a result of wars, the loss of its American colonies, and its backwardness. The government had sold off the crown's land to finance its survival. In fact, the government was so concerned with its economic survival that the Spanish people had been left to fend for themselves and the political institutions had become obsolete. Larra underscores this disarray as he comes upon the Mausoleum of Justice and Freedom, which he compares to the prison Spain has become:

What's this? *The Prison! Here lies the freedom to think.* Dear God, in Spain, in the country that has already been educated for free institutions! Then I remembered that famous epitaph and added, by accident: Here lies thinking. It did something else in life.

Two reporters from *El Mundo* were the teary-eyed figures of this great urn. You could see a chain, a gag and a feather on the relief. I asked myself if this feather belonged to the writers or to the notaries. In prison everything is possible. (Larra 549–50)

The general state of disorder, lawlessness, and economic turmoil gave birth to a new class of landowning oligarchs who would ultimately take charge and run the country, displacing the monarchy. The power of the Church and the aristocracy was reduced to the rural zones, where illiteracy was rampant. In the cities, the lack of industry dramatized the split between the deprived lower classes and the upper classes, who sought only to benefit themselves. A number of popular uprisings led to the 1868 revolution, *La Gloriosa* (The Glorious One), which sent the Bourbon monarchy into exile and installed the Republic of 1873. Yet the power of the upper classes and the Church was so strong that by 1875 the monarchy was restored and the Bourbons returned with Alfonso XII. During the restoration, journalistic humor lost its edge, giving way to a more benevolent, less critical and harsh humor. One exception that renewed violent political criticism was the weekly satirical magazine *Gedeón*, which appeared in 1895, in the midst of the war with Cuba. This in turn would spur a revival of journalistic magazines that used humor to articulate their political critiques. *Mundo Cómico* (Comic World, 1872), *Madrid Cómico* (Comical Madrid, 1880), *La Broma* (The Joke, 1881), *La Avispa* (The Wasp, 1883), and *La Caricatura* (The Caricature, 1892) are a few of the 125 comic magazines that appeared in Madrid in the following twenty-five years. It is evident that in times of crisis, while humor may not be as satirical or political as at other times, it becomes a sort of refuge for the Spanish. A good example is the eight magazines that appeared during the "Disaster of 98." As the United States entered the war with Cuba as a "disinterested" party, the Spanish did not believe the United States for one moment and sought to expose American hypocrisy. The Spanish knew exactly what "disinterested" meant and made a point of stating it clearly through cartoons and caricatures.

While politics and social criticism were generally an integral part of Spanish humor, sexual innuendos were present as well. In 1920 a new magazine, *¡Ahí vá!* (There It Goes!), appeared in which the treatment of sex became more graphic and risqué. In previous years, references to adultery, extramarital relations, prostitution, and the strayings of both men and women could be found in Spain's great literary works such as *La Regenta* (*The Governor's Wife*, 1884–1885) by Leopoldo Alas, alias "Clarín," and *Fortunata y Jacinta* (1887) by Benito Pérez Galdós. With the appearance of *¡Ahí vá!* and the *cuplé*—a musical composition with picaresque characters full of sexual allusions—sexuality became much more prominent and was incorporated into everyday culture as part of Spanish national humor. Magazines like *La Hoja de Parra* (The Vine Leaf), *El Gato Negro* (The Black Cat), and *El Viejo Verde* (The Dirty Old Man) followed the model proposed by *¡Ahí vá!*, and began including illustrations to expose this kind of humor more openly.

World War I ushered in a period during which Spain was torn between pro-Germans and anti-Germans. The publication of magazines that had become popular in previous years, developing a wide readership, echoed this split. However, the volatile political circumstances watered down for a short period of time the kind of humor that was published. Once the war ended a general optimism invaded Spanish society, and a new magazine, *Buen humor* (Good Humor), appeared in 1921. *Buen humor* is emblematic of the Belle Epoque, a period overwhelmed by a fascination with new technological inventions like the airplane, the automobile, the radio, and film. A sense of future permeated cultural life. Artistic vanguards began experimenting, and this also influenced the conceptualization of humor.

Ramón Gómez de la Serna, Enrique Jardiel Poncela, Miguel Mihura, and Edgar Neville are a few of the ingenious humorists who began experimenting with humor. Based on the unlikely, the playful, and the absurd, their humor was directed to a wide audience with the hope of providing simple entertainment. Simultaneously, another, more complex and critical humor emerged with the work of Ramón Valle-Inclán, the well-known writer of the "Generation of 98," creator of the *esperpento*. According to Valle-Inclán, *esperpento* occurs when the writer looks at his characters from above. From this perspective they become ridiculous little puppets, nincompoops, or midgets playing a tragedy. The principle behind the aesthetic of the esperpento is distortion; everything is deformed to show the true state of reality, which is for the most part skewed and hidden from our eyes. Thus, characters in Valle-Inclán's novels are degraded and acquire a double-sided trait of buffoon and tragic clown. We see them gesticulating in a vacuum that makes them look utterly ridiculous. Through the juxtaposition of opposites like the comic and the painful, black and white, parody and acerbic black humor, Valle-Inclán achieves his aesthetic. While esperpento is distinctly Spanish, strongly influenced by the legacy of both Quevedo and Goya, it is also a European product that distances itself from the Belle Epoque. One can trace elements of European expressionism, the parodies and grotesque of the Italian futurists like Luigi Pirandello, as well as elements from Franz Kafka's novels. *Light of Bohemia* (1920), an unconventional play, initiates the *esperpento* series. The following dialogue between Max Estrella ("Star"), the poor, blind poet who physically resembles Homer, and Don Latino de Hispalis, his friend who takes advantage of him, reflects Valle-Inclán's use of the absurd in distorting his characters:

MAX. Don Latino of Hispalis, grotesque persona par excellence! I shall immortalize you in a novella!
DON LATINO. In a tragedy, Max.
MAX. Our tragedy is no longer a tragedy.
DON LATINO. But it has to be something!
MAX. An Esperpento.
DON LATINO. Stop twitching me, Max!
. . . .

MAX. Now you have been transformed into an ox, I can't recognize you. Breathe hard on me, illustrious ox from Bethlehem's stable. Bellow, Latino! You are the bell-ox and if you bellow hard enough Buey Apis, the Sacred Bull will appear. We shall fight with him in the bullring.

DON LATINO. You're beginning to frighten me. This joke isn't funny anymore.

....

MAX. Classical heroes reflected in concave mirrors give us the Grotesque or Esperpento. The tragic sense of Spanish life can only be rendered through an aesthetic that is systematically deformed. (Valle-Inclán 160)

In April 1931 a sense of hope erupted in Spain as the Second Republic, known as "the beautiful girl," was restored, ending the Bourbon monarchy. There was an exhilarating feeling of joy and freedom. The military and the Church were stripped of their long-held powers and there was hope that Spain would finally be free to imagine its future. But political, social, and economic problems undermined the reigning happiness, which ended with Francisco Franco's military coup in 1936, thus initiating the Spanish Civil War. During the short-lived Republic there were two different humorist venues: one was political satire, the other was pornography and excess. The Church was the center of a great many satires during this time, particulalry in the magazine *Fray Lazo* (Friar Lazo, 1931).

During the Civil War (1936-1939) a combative kind of humor dominated the scene. There was in fact little room for humor, and very few humorous magazines were published. The end of the war coincided with the beginning of World War II, and the national panorama was terribly demoralizing. Poverty, hunger, thousands of Spaniards jailed without trials (even more were exiled), censorship, betrayals, fear—all this left little room for humor. Only political jokes circulated, and mainly orally, for everything became clandestine. Censorship was rampant. But in 1941 a new periodical, *La codorniz* (The Partridge), was founded. During its first few years, it was directed by Miguel Mihura, who had been involved with Jardiel Poncela and Edgar Neville in making abstract and absurd humor.

In 1944 Alvaro Laiglesia replaced Mihura at *La codorniz* and a more critical kind of humor made its way into the magazine. Its anticonformist take provoked the government, which banned several issues. In 1968 *La codorniz* dared to print a caricature of each and every one of Franco's ministers, although there was not one of the *generalísimo* himself. Most of the cultural production during the postwar era using humor would follow the style of the initial years of *La codorniz*, creating a lighter and evasive kind of entertainment. This set the standard for the kind of humor that would dominate the postwar era. Mihura was particularly successful with plays like *Un marido de ida y vuelta* (A Husband Back and Forth, 1939) and especially *Tres sombreros de copa* (Three Top Hats, 1932). The latter in particular was a big hit, anticipating the theater of the absurd emblematic of Eugène Ionesco. It is a play that rebels against the bourgeois lifestyle and values. Ionesco, upon seeing the production in Paris in 1958, said, "It has the advantage of associating tragic humor, a profound truth, the ridiculous that, as all caricature, sublimates and highlights the truth of things" (qtd. in Ruiz Ramón 324). Whole passages from this play would become part of the collective memory for many of the postwar generation. One such sentence remembered by many is delivered when Paula, the female protagonist, asks Dionysius if he is married and he responds "yes, but just a bit" (Mihura 117). Another example is the dialogue between Dionysius and Bubby Barton, a black music-hall director:

Dionysius: (to gallantly break the stifling silence) Have you been black for many years?
Bubby: I don't know. I have always seen myself like this in the moon of the mirrors.
Dionysius: God Bless! When a tragedy happens it never comes alone, and what made you stay like that? A fall? (Mihura 77)

During the postwar era, Franco's government took advantage of the power of the media to propagate its own ideals and impose a cultural brainwashing. CIFESA (the Spanish film industry) was created to encourage and control national ideologies of the Franco regime. During these years the film industry was governed by an extremely conservative Catholic ethos; thus the primary kinds of films produced were historical, religious, or folkloric. Nevertheless, there were a few low-key comic films, known as *frac* comedies. *Ella, él y Sus millones* (She, He and Their Millions, 1944) by Juan de Orduña stands out among the "white telephone" comedy films, in which the signature white telephone always appeared as a symbol of progress and a general state of well-being that supposedly reigned in Spain.

Despite harsh censorship from the government, which dubbed all foreign films to make sure the dialogue was "appropriate" and cut out certain kisses and overt sexual displays, a small group of directors was successful at challenging the status quo precisely through humor. Luis García Berlanga was one of them. His film *Bienvenido Mr. Marshall* (Welcome Mr. Marshall, 1952) parodies Spanish nationalism and folklore under the guise of ridiculing "the American friend" who never quite makes it to Spain with the Marshall Plan but shows up with military bases instead.

During the 1960s, Spain opened up to tourism and consumerism, bringing in a huge wave of foreign influences. This quickly exposed Spain's backwardness. For example, while Swedish, German, English, and American women flocked to Spain's beaches showing a lot of skin, Spanish women had to cover their bodies from head to toe. Before films were able to portray these ridiculous contradictions, a group of comic films pushed the supposed well-being of Spanish society to the extreme. The best-known example of these kinds of films is Pedro Lazaga's *Sor Citroën* (Sister Citroën, 1967). The film portrays a group of nuns who run an orphanage and who desperately need a car to fulfill their duties. After great efforts they are able to buy one, a Citroën of course, and Sister Teresa is named the designated driver. Soon after, she becomes the terror of all drivers in Madrid, racing through the city following her own rules and creating great havoc wherever she goes.

Also popular are the "sexy Celtiberian" comedies, otherwise known as "Landism films," named after the well-known actor Alfredo Landa. These films present the libertine female foreigner desperately in search of the irresistible short, bald, and boorish Iberian Man (*Macho ibérico*). Opposing these frivolous and perverse foreigners stand the respectable Spanish women, pure and chaste. *Turistas y bribones* (Tourists and Rogues, 1968), *El turismo es un gran invento* (Tourism Is a Great Invention, 1968), *Verano del 70* (Summer of 1970, 1969), *Objetivo bi-ki-ni* (Bi-ki-ni Objective, 1969), and *No desearás al vecino del quinto* (Thou Shall Not Desire Thy Neighbor from the Fifth Floor, 1970) are a few of these parodic films in which other well-known actors, such as José Sacristán and José Luis Vázquez, also appear. Because of censorship and limited resources, many Spaniards were leaving the country to seek work elsewhere. Rather than focus on Spain's current issues, these films sought to ridicule foreigners to highlight Spanish decency over outside influences.

Television also played an important role in affirming Spain's national image under Franco. Again, the government held tight control over programs and scheduling. And once again, despite censorship, humor too made its way into the public arena. Many of the creative humorists who worked in television had worked on *La codorniz* earlier, and they left an indelible imprint in the media as they worked in radio, television, and the theater. Their humor focused on the absurd, tapping into the grotesque, the esperpento and surrealist tradition the Spanish had developed. Tip and Coll and Miguel Gila are a few of the comedians that emerged. One comedian in particular, Miguel Gila, a republican who had survived his execution during the Civil War as well as several years in jail, stands out among the rest for his famous telephone skits. He would make a phone call announcing war to show the absurdity of wars and armed confrontations.

In the early 1970s, Spain entered a new era known as the Spanish transition. Some cultural critics claim it began with the assassination of Carrero Blanco, Franco's second in command, by the Basque revolutionary group ETA; other critics mark the beginning with Franco's death in 1975. In any case, the Spanish transition is the moment when Spain ceased to be governed by a dictatorship and opened up to democracy. Chumy Chumez, a well-known humorist of *La codorniz*, began to collaborate on *Hermano lobo* (Brother Wolf, 1972), the most important comic magazine of the transition, in which political commentaries and social and political book reviews abound. Although Spain was slowly opening up, censorship continued, and a few issues of *Hermano lobo* were banned. One humorist was particularly censored: Antonio Fraguas ("Forges"), who voiced his criticism of the government in the newspaper *El país* (1977).

Throughout most of the twentieth century there had been a number of comic-strip magazines geared at younger audiences. Some sought to create national heroes, others were simple adventure comics, others targeted women's education, while others, geared for an even younger audience, focused on well-known children's stories like Tom Thumb, Mortadelo and Filemón, Zipi and Zape, and so forth. But during the transition a split occurred between adult comics and those written for adult entertainment. The first kind are short vignettes accompanied by a series of complaints on social instability, the need for political reforms, and cultural critiques. A particularly strong sociopolitical critique that was voiced during these years was against the Church. Most of these adult comics advocated the need to separate the Church from the state and to address issues such as divorce and abortion. The other kind of comic directed toward adults blended satire, terror, and eroticism, attracting voyeurlike readers avid for a little skin. In 1976 a new magazine emerged that brought together both kinds of humor: *El Jueves* (Thursday). Shortly after, another magazine, *El víbora* (The Snake), appeared, presenting an alternative culture that rejected traditional values, vindicating instead sex, drugs, night life, alcohol, and violence. A new kind of language, full of idiomatic expressions and slang, accompanied these magazines in which older generations were criticized for not understanding anything. Unlike the generations before them, the younger generations preferred to ignore politics; they looked for adventure and entertainment. This is the kind of spirit that motivated the well-known *movida madrileña*, a cultural movement that invigorated Spanish cultural life.

The culture of the movida madrileña is best articulated in Pedro Almodóvar's earlier films: *Pepi, Luci, Bom and Other Girls on the Heap* (1980), *Labyrinth of Passions* (1980), and *Dark Habits* (1983). These films represent the new hedonistic spirit of Spanish youth, submerged in an underground life of drugs and sexual freedom. Everything is celebrated and explored. Censorship is nowhere to be found. The irreverence toward institutions and all things sacred permeates the scene, provoking the audience's violent reaction or greatest laugh. Thus, we find references to Islamic terrorism in *Labyrinth of Passions* with the lead song: "Gan, Gan, Gan, Gan, Gan, Gan, they are from Teheran" or the "improper" behavior of nuns as found in *Entre tinieblas* (Dark Habits), where the main character, a nun, is a drug addict obsessed with cleanliness who has fantastic visions thanks to her use of LSD. Almodóvar brings to film what Larra articulated in his incisive articles and Goya depicted in his canvases before him: the reinscription of the religious dichotomy between sacrifice and redemption. The Spanish title *Entre tinieblas* (literally, "In Darkness") plays with the Catholic ritual that takes place the day before Good Friday: the extinguishing of candles in church.

Even in his most impressive worldwide box office hit, *Women on the Verge of a Nervous Breakdown* (1988), Almodóvar explores a world of marginal characters intertwined with humor, parody, and a certain tragic sense of life. The film is a frenetic comedy that portrays the world and characters of Spain during the 1980s in the midst of Spain's economic boom. Almodóvar's brilliant use of pastiche, camp, parody, and dark humor incites multiple laughs. At the same time, while some laughs might be superficial, others, more acid, are charged with critical insight geared at breaking down Spanish stereotypes and myths of economic, social, and political changes. Almodóvar has made great use of satire and mass forms of communication to dehumanize modern technology. His films present the undermining of the cannibalistic urban setting of the postmodern city.

More recently, globalized forms of communications and mass media have originated a humor that has little to do with the dark, acid, and satirical humor of the past. It is an insignificant kind of humor that circulates widely on television, like the *Cruz and Raya* programs, as well as in the theater. But as Spain entered into a new political crisis with the 1996 election of the Popular Party, a more ingenious form of humor began to emerge. The political satires of the Canal Plus TV channel, resembling the "Grand Guignol," or the now defunct satire of Channel 5, *Caiga quien Caiga* (May Whoever Falls Fall) by Gran Wyoming, are a few of the successful and highly creative programs. And in literary circles the novels of Juan José Millás and Carmen Rico Godoy also echo this political satire. Lastly, the somewhat raunchy films of Santiago Segura, *Torrente: El brazo tonto de la ley* (Torrente: The Silly Man of Law, 1995) and *Torrente 2: Misión Marbella* (Torrente 2: Marbella Mission, 2001), bring back a more scatological humor, taking us all the way back to the picaresque.

As Spain continues to navigate through different crises, it will undoubtedly be humor, in its very different forms and genres, that will echo the nation's mores and values, helping to heal and overcome its painful times. This is the way it has been since the earliest of times, and it will most likely continue to be this way for years to come.

REFERENCES AND FURTHER READINGS

Alfonso X (el Sabio). *Cantigas*. Ed. Jesús Montoya. Madrid: Cátedra, 1988.
Arcipreste de Hita. *Libro de Buen Amor*. Madrid: Castalia, 1978.
Arribas, Inés. *La literatura de humor en la España democrática*. Madrid: Editorial Pliegos, 1997.

Cervantes, Miguel de. *Don Quijote*. Trans. Burton Raffel. New York: Norton, 1995.
La codorniz: Antología 1941–44. Madrid: Arneo, 1987.
Larra, Mariano José de. *Artículos varios*. Madrid: Castalia, 1990.
López Cruces, Antonio J. *La risa en la literatura española: Antología de textos*. Alicante, Spain: Editorial Aguaclara, 1993.
López Ruiz, José María. *La vida alegre*. Madrid: Compañía Literaria, 1995.
Mihura, Miguel. *Tres sombreros de copa*. Madrid: Castalia, 1989.
Quevedo, Francisco de. *Gracias y desgracias del ojo del culo*. <http://cervantesvirtual.com/servlet/SirveObras/12815395888903289860513/p0000001.htm#I_1_>.
———. *Obra Poética*. Ed. José Manuel Blecua. 3 vols. Madrid: Castalia, 1969–1971.
Rebes, María Dolores, and Francisco García Pavón. *España en sus humoristas (1885–1936)*. Madrid: Taurus, 1966.
Rodríguez Puértolas, Julio, ed. *Poesía crítica y satírica del siglo XV*. Madrid: Castalia, 1981.
Ruiz Ramón, Francisco. *Historia del teatro español: Siglo XX*. Madrid: Cátedra, 1977.
Scholberg, Kenneth R. *Sátira e invectiva en la España medieval*. Madrid: Gredos, 1971.
Smith, Paul Julian. *Desire Unlimited: The Cinema of Pedro Almodóvar*. New York: Verso, 1994.
Valle-Inclán, Ramón del. *Plays: One. Divine Words. Bohemian Lights. Silver Face*. Trans. María Delgado. London: Methuen, 1993.

37

Stand-Up Comedy

Lawrence E. Mintz

Stand-up is surely the oldest, the most basic, and the universal form of comedy. Its roots are in the shaman, the fool, the jester, and the clown. Stand-up comedy is a part of the ancient Greek theater, Native American tribal rites, Balinese clowning, carnival activities, court entertainment, and traveling performance throughout the world, past and present.

Essentially, stand-up comedy is live performance in which a comedian tells jokes and/or behaves in a manner designed to generate laughter, often ridicule, either directed *at* the comic persona or directed *by* the persona at others or at social issues and topics familiar to the audience. In a 1985 article entitled "Standup Comedy as Social and Cultural Mediation," I provided a somewhat loose definition of the genre that included a single comedian working without costumes or props, appearing as himself or herself, telling jokes and anecdotes, but also included two acts—often a comedian and a straight man—and extended to circus clowns; medicine showmen; minstrel end men; variety theater performers from burlesque, vaudeville, and other popular theatrical entertainments; comic magicians, jugglers, musicians, and other such performers; improvisational comedy groups; and an assortment of other entertainers who used humor to amuse and enlighten their audience.

David Marc, in his 1989 book *Comic Visions: Television Comedy and American Culture*, agonizes over such a broad definition of the term *stand-up comedy*. Marc argues that such a loose, generous, inclusive definition of stand-up used by the present writer is too vague and that with it the term is somehow in danger of losing its meaning. Marc's strict definition limits the use of the term to a comedian telling jokes or anecdotes in live performance in a club or concert environment. It excludes the more theatrical aspects of variety entertainment, and it is particularly uncomfortable with the more "anthropological" parallels that reference clowning, the work of jesters and shaman, and quasidramatic, group comedy. Marc worries over the failure to locate a Neanderthal stand-up comedian, and about documenting the roll call of costume and prop comedians, for instance, those working in drag. Even so, in passing, Marc goes back to the same performance roots for stand-up comedy, roots that are hardly as narrow or limited as a strict definition would imply.

There is something of a continuum from the single performer working without costume or props to a theatrical comedy with sets, script, and the other accoutrements of a "play." Along this continuum there are blurrings and crossings of the boundaries that might define stand-up comedy as different from theatrical comedy. Performance comedy, discussed here, is often marketed as theater, and in a vehicle such as Lily Tomlin's *The Search for Signs of Intelligent Light in the Universe* (1985), written largely by Jane Wagner, is such a definition-busting case. It is a one-woman show, largely verbal, relying only slightly on costume and prop. But it is marketed as a "Broadway Show," Lily is always one or another character, it is entirely scripted, and it has little of the audience interaction or awareness that characterizes stand-up. The show can be considered to be a comedy play, but it is surely related to stand-up comedy performance.

I prefer the broader, more inclusive definition, appreciating that "pure stand-up comedy" is at the part of the continuum where a comic talks directly to the audience. Along that continuum comedians develop personae, utilize props and costumes, develop acts of two or even more comedians, mix in juggling, music, magic, singing, and other entertainment genres, flirt with improvisational theater, and engage in a complex performance art as well as telling jokes, sharing anecdotes, and just being funny folks. Complicating the definition even further is the mixing of stand-up comedy with other genres including circus, variety entertainment vehicles of all sorts, including of course the minstrel theater, vaudeville and burlesque, and film and broadcast comedy, both radio and television. At *Carnival Knowledge* (a 2003 off-Broadway theatrical performance), for instance, Todd Robbins recreates traditional sideshow stunts such as walking on glass, sword swallowing, fire breathing, and staged oddities, punctuated by constant humorous patter, the art of the "outside talker" who lured customers into the show and served as a master of ceremonies guiding the audience through the experience. This comedy routine, complete with puns and all sorts of jokes, is an important part of the show. It is also stand-up comedy.

This account of the history of American stand-up comedy must necessarily deal with the full range of humorous live performance, stopping if at all as close to the comedy play as possible, without trying to cover that large and separate genre. But before that, it will be helpful to consider some of the basic roles of the stand-up comedian. One role is that of the negative example. Drawing on the universal and time-honored role of the Fool, the comedian directs laughter at himself or herself, allowing the audience to feel superior but also delineating models of improper, inappropriate, reprehensible, or at least ridiculous belief and/or behavior. Some of the character traits we laugh at have been a source of comic ridicule since at least the *commedia dell'arte*—stinginess, pomposity, vanity, intemperance, anger, lecherousness, and of course the old standby, stupidity. We laugh at the fool, the grotesque, the loser, but also at the arrogant, the overly educated pedant, the bully, and the narcissist. The humor assures that we recognize these human failings as a part of the reality of life to be accepted and dealt with without undue rancor. It also helps soothe us when we recognize some of these traits in ourselves and those we love.

But we do not always laugh *at* the comedian. The comedian is often a comic spokesperson orchestrating our laughter directed at others, and occasionally a daring performer can even turn it on ourselves. To do this the comedian adopts other stances including that of the naïf, innocently observing phenomena, seemingly without analytic purpose, exposing the target of the humor "accidentally." This is of course just another stage of the wise fool persona. The naïf also can be traced back to the fools of the medieval court and ancient theater, the mental defective, or "God's Fool," who is the progenitor of the professional jester. The naïf is a fool just like the negative fool cousin, but one whose basic goodness, simplicity, and honesty lead him or her to expose the folly of others rather than his or her own failings. A naïf who is too clever in his observations to be credibly stupid or ignorant gravitates toward yet another stage, that of the commonsense philosopher. This persona uses experiential wisdom to trump "book-learning" or other profundity, using a crude realism to puncture pretension or error. To borrow an example from a literary source, when someone tells Langston Hughes' brilliant character Jesse B. Semple, or "Simple," that he sees in the newspapers that things are getting better for "black folks," Simple replies that he sees out of his Harlem window that they are not.

Stephanie Koziski instructively uses the term *anthropologist* to describe how the stand-up comedian examines our everyday life, but the comedian is not just observing how we live, what we say and do; she is exposing it to a cynical, humorous light. Louis Rubin Jr.'s invaluable concept of "the Great American Joke" explains how our humor relentlessly uses what we know of reality to expose the failure of our idealism, and the ideals we believe in and accept, to make us aware of the inadequacy of our reality. Stand-up comedians such as Jerry Seinfeld, for example, are famous for building a comedy routine about "nothing" (in Seinfeld's case that was the rap on his eponymous television situation comedy, but it fits his stand-up work as well). His nothing is, of course, everything in terms of daily life, the actual personal reality of most of us. Seinfeld comments on the ordinary, and we notice that it is not so ordinary, or that the fact that it is ordinary is worthy of our attention and understanding. Stephen Wright does the same thing with language, pointing out the odd aspects of language; its ambiguities, inadequacies, and power. Wright wants to know "if you ate pasta and antipasta, would you still be hungry?" The stand-up comedians of everyday life call attention to our frustration with convenience store clerks whose poor command of English leaves us frustrated and confused, or our battles with the bureaucracy and, of course, the telephone programming and procedures that seem designed to drive us off the deep end. They also take on more serious, significant matters such as dating mores, parenting, divorce (and divorce settlements), and the doings of celebrities and others in the public eye.

Comedians can be more than casual observers, of course. Another role that they can and do assume is that of a comic spokesperson; social, political, and cultural critic; or satirist. It is often assumed that the comedian in this role is somehow courageous, bravely risking social disapproval by attacking the accepted norms. This is not usually the case, however. First, the comedian is almost always establishing agreement, consensus within his or her specific audience. This is done by developing rapport and understanding between the comedian and the audience, but also by keeping the comments within the frame of acceptability for the particular group. Occasionally a comedian will misjudge the views or position of the audience and have to handle boos or other expressions of disagreement with various forms of saving remarks such as "just kidding!" or other reminders that this is a comedy performance, and unpopular sentiments are traditionally licensed by the comedic frame. Comedians such as Lenny Bruce (late in his career when he was highly critical of the establishment), George Carlin, Jon Stewart, or Chris Rock first firmly establish their personas as social critics, link themselves as best they can to the points of view of their audience, shield themselves with reminders of comic license, and then engage in social and cultural commentary. Their work is no less valuable for its protective frame, but it is surely less brave than it is often thought to be.

In all of these roles—the negative example to be laughed at or ridiculed, the innocent observer, and the social critic—the comedian constructs audience consensus. Perhaps the most important role of the stand-up comedian is to orchestrate a sense of homogeneity, community, and shared values and perspectives. We laugh together, and we feel less alone. Comic observation may possibly instruct or change views, but far more often it allows for public expression of what we already believe, sanctioned by the consensus of audience laughter and permitted by the frame of comedy, the claim that by being "not serious" we can safely consider the most serious things in our lives—race; religion; politics; sex; gender; marriage and family; social class and regional differences; and stereotypes of profession (e.g., lawyer jokes), of hobby (golfer jokes), or of just about any identifiable trait, issue, or circumstance.

American stand-up comedy can be traced back to our earliest cultural experiences. Early traveling medicine shows employed various forms of entertainment including magic, juggling, song and dance, historical dioramas, and comic patter. Circus clowns, in the days before the rings got too large to permit it, often performed verbal as well as physical comedy. John H. Towsen's valuable account of American clowns connects the acts of such talking clowns as Dan Rice, among many others less famous, to the tent and minstrel theaters as well as to the circus venue. Early theatrical performances in traveling tent repertory and in the newly established urban theaters also featured comedy and other variety entertainment to extend the bill of fare and to keep audiences amused between acts.

Another important early influence on the development of stand-up comedy was the comic lecture. In the nineteenth century, as the serious lecturer circuits such as the outgrowth of the Chautauqua gatherings became more popular, comic lecturers took to the circuits as well. The most famous of them were Artemus Ward and Mark Twain (with the former having an acknowledged influence on the latter), but there were dozens of others as well, offering mock lectures on all sorts of subjects including religion (e.g., Ward's mockery of the Mormon faith), Native Americans, exotic travels, politics, and so forth. Twain pioneered the relationship between live performance and public appearance and the promotion of books, similar to the radio and television talk show tour today. Twain would come out on stage, light up a cigar or his pipe, and observe, as though he was thinking about it for the first time, how it must be easy to stop smoking since "I've done it dozens of times."

Perhaps the most important influences on the development of stand-up are the minstrel theater, vaudeville, burlesque, and the variety theater from the early nineteenth century through the first half of the twentieth. These theaters were not exclusively about comedy, of course, much less primarily venues for stand-up comedy per se. They featured song and dance, exotic costumes and sets, beautiful women, and just about any kind of professional entertainment imaginable that might bring in and delight a paying audience. But comedy was just about always a part of the bill—often a very central part of it, and sometimes a dominant feature. In the minstrel show, for instance, the interplay between the two end men, Tambo and Bones, and the interlocutor was virtually indispensable. Tambo and Bones, wearing blackface makeup, and the interlocutor, portrayed as an upper-class snob, engaged in joking discourse that covered all sorts of topics from cultural mores to political and topical events. Tambo and Bones were the objects of the humor in that they were portrayed as stereotypically lazy, irresponsible, ignorant (naïf), and worse, but they were also wise fools, mocking the unrealistic, experientially ignorant stance of the interlocutor and championing a more fun-loving, popular if not socially approved, spirit. If they were portrayed as sexually irresponsible or overly indulgent in their use of alcohol, for instance, their behavior was likely to be applauded by audiences as well as repudiated. It could be acknowledged that such behavior was "wrong" at the same time as it was familiar, common, and not entirely rejected by the members of the audience despite more public avowals of morality. This type of comedy is familiar today in nightclub acts that celebrate drinking, drug use, and liberal sexuality, while at the same time connecting them with the comedian as a sort of scapegoat, taking pressure off the audience.

The early years of vaudeville and burlesque featured ethnic humor as well as jokes about sex, gender differences, marriage, and other social mores. The ethnic humor is sometimes thought to be aggressive, hostile, or insulting joking, as it might be when it is engaged in by individuals making fun of members of another ethnic community. Surely in the theater, as well, it could serve the purpose of allowing people to laugh at stereotyped, caricatured portrayals of various ethnic characters, ridiculing accents and alleged traits of belief and behavior. But it may have served another purpose as well. Members of the audience were all "off the same boat" so to speak, all a little "green." They could feel superior, first, to the comically portrayed failures, stupidities, and misunderstandings of the even greener characters on stage, and second, they could feel less singled out, more accepted in a community made up of equally disparaged ethnic people. Ethnic humor was eventually banned from vaudeville, and it diminished in importance in the burlesque and variety theaters as well. It served a purpose for a particular period in our cultural history, and then it faded. It did not disappear, however. Stand-up comedians such as Jackie Mason, Don Rickles, and many others carried it into more modern stand-up comedy, and racial and ethnic joking is far from banished in the world of stand-up performance today.

Similarly, jokes about sex, gender, and relationships had a particular purpose when they flourished in the days of vaudeville, burlesque, and the variety theater. They can be seen as part of a national trend in humor that was very prominent in other genres including literature, comic strips, theater, and film—misogynist humor, he-she conflict joking, and comedy that turned marital to martial in the blink of an eye. As women became more politically and socially visible and as the "little man" humor reflected a sense of a loss of confidence, a sense of vulnerability in men, sex, gender, and relationship humor has allowed for commentary and expression on this most sensitive of topics. Stand-up comedians in burlesque and vaudeville theaters and in Broadway variety entertainment shows exaggerate for comic effect the aggressive, brassy, dominant female; the dizzy, dumb blonde; the unfaithful husband; the cuckold; and all of the issues associated with them. This humor too became a part of the staple repertory of modern stand up-comedians. Sexually related topics are by far the single most common subjects in American stand-up comedy.

It is sometimes said that the death of vaudeville, burlesque, and variety theater nearly killed stand-up comedy. These theaters were surely the training grounds for the comedians who flocked to radio and motion picture work, and, later, television as opportunities became available. But stand-up did not die for two reasons. First, the lure of the dollars associated with radio and film comedy careers encouraged comedians to hone their acts and generate attention through live performance, so theaters held on to comedy acts well into the era of electronic media, even as the sizes of the audience shrank and profits shriveled. Second, nightclubs and resort venues began to feature comedy along with some variety entertainment, mostly musical. The Catskill mountain resorts, the so-called Borscht Belt, are often celebrated as the savior of stand-up comedy, and to be sure contributed to the careers of some notables who populated the genre's later venues. Red Buttons, Jan Murray, Joey Adams, Buddy Hackett, Danny Kaye, Phil Foster, and dozens of other prominent stand-ups broke into the profession as "tummelers," or comic masters of ceremony, at the Borscht Belt resorts and as feature comedians in club acts that grew out of the resort entertainment format. The Catskills did not have the only hotel clubs, of course, and there was work in the emerging Las Vegas scene eventually, and in urban clubs in most major U.S. cities. Clearly, though, the money in stand-up was to be found in radio, film, and television success. This remains the case, of course, despite developments over the past few decades that have given live performance stand-up more respect if still not the top financial rewards. Most of the few histories of stand-up comedy pay little attention to the club scene before the emergence of the "new wave" of stand-up comedy in the 1960s and the "improv" comedy clubs later on, but Phil Berger's *The Last Laugh* does offer a few useful pages setting up the later developments.

We might term the comedians who came out of the nightclub and resort circuits "traditional" stand-ups in the sense that they offered a pure comedy of jokes strung together without much of a unifying premise or theme. The comedian established a persona of sorts, perhaps as a brash or aggressive type (e.g., Bob Hope, Milton Berle), or a self-effacing, self-deprecating chronicler (Myron Cohen), but the jokes themselves were the key feature of the act, and the delivery was more a matter of timing and projection than any sort of structuring of the routine or connecting it with the development of the persona. A comedian who stuck around long enough to become prominent would eventually utilize the persona more fully, so that Jack Benny's trademark stinginess or Berle's abrasive obnoxiousness would generate laughter almost independently of the specific jokes. But there was still little if any theme or topical structure to the traditional stand-up routine. The comedian came out, told jokes, and, hopefully, exited to applause and laughter.

It is acknowledged that this began to change, or at least was supplemented by a new kind of stand-up comedy, sometime in the late 1950s or in the 1960s (depending upon how much prominence one gives a few of the early manifestations). The "new wave" stand up, as it is sometimes termed, was of course not entirely new. In its informal, anecdotal, lecturelike style, it resembled the comic lectures of Ward and Twain. In its accommodation of physical, prop, costume, and skit comedy it resembled the humor of variety theater. There are plenty of parallels between the radio comedy of Fred Allen and his repertory company and much of the new wave fare. But the new stand-up comedy was clearly different from the traditional rapid-fire joke telling of the traditional stand-up comedians described above.

While Lenny Bruce was capable of coming out and doing five minutes of jokes, as a couple of early television appearances attest, such performance hardly describes what his comedy was about. New wave comedians were about the development of themes through storytelling, punctuated by comic observations that served as jokes or punch lines of a sort. Bruce is often credited with developing the new style, but actually he was but one of several important figures working in nightclubs, coffeehouses, and tiny theaters; and rather than there being one narrowly defined new wave style, the movement, such as it was, incorporated several different characteristics. Bruce, for instance, is thought of as a topical satirist, largely based on a few observations about racism and social hypocrisy and his later struggles with the authorities over obscenity and drug busts. But political satire was not characteristic of most of the comedians of the new wave, and indeed only Mort Sahl, who does perhaps deserve credit for being the first and most important figure in the new stand-up comedy (if any one person has to be so identified), was consistently political and topical. More of the new wave observed social mores and everyday life than deep or controversial issues.

This is not to diminish the sense of cutting edge or counterculture purpose implied in a lot of the new wave performance. Much of it was aimed at a young, hip audience, and indeed "hipster" comics like Richard "Lord" Buckley referenced marijuana, jazz, the forthcoming sexual revolution, and an antiauthority, antibourgeois, anti-suburban-white-middleclass-Eisenhower America attitude that parallels but is not a part of the beat movement or later counterculture expressions. New wave comics like Shelley Berman, Bob Newhart, Mike Nichols and Elaine May, Woody Allen, Bill Cosby, and Robert Klein were not revolutionary or radical. They came out and talked about what was happening around them with a kind of sardonic disdain rather than anger. Even Dick Gregory, a pioneer in dealing with racial themes, was more likely to find racism ironic or foolish than anything to get upset about, much less up in arms over. Later African American comedians, notably Richard Pryor, for instance, might take a harder, more cutting look at race than Gregory did (in his early days, when he was still essentially a comedian rather than a social critic), but others such as Cosby and Eddie Murphy were able to develop other themes. New wave comedians revolutionized stand-up, not America. They established that theme was at least as important as joking, doing "shtick" (engaging in funny behavior), or establishing persona. Their anecdotal, informal style was most conducive to the longer sets they could do in small clubs, and while it was not easily translatable to the tighter time demands of electronic media or later comedy club schedules, it pretty much eclipsed the traditional joke telling, one-liner, quipster comedians of the earlier generation. These did not disappear, of course, and in the persons of Hope, Johnny Carson, Berle, Henny Youngman, and even younger performers like Jay Leno, the traditional format survives.

New wave comedy was not strictly stand-up per se. It also embraced the improvisational comedy troupes such as Chicago's Second City, the Ace Trucking Company, Upstairs and the Downstairs, and others. It also spawned an important market for comedy on LP records, the first really wide-selling comedy albums, though there had been important recorded comedy for decades. New wave has to include the antics of Jonathan Winters along with the monologues of Rodney Dangerfield and Woody Allen, and the calm appraisal of everyday life of the brilliant Cosby as well as the more engaged commentary of Sahl, the later Bruce, or the contemporary holdover of new wave style, George Carlin.

A most important development in the history of the genre of stand-up comedy is the advent of the comedy clubs. The clubs are an outgrowth of the coffeehouses, bars, and nightclubs that were the venue for most of the live new wave stand-up, and as such it is hard to cite definitively which was the first, the archetypal club, but it is probably best to award the title and credit to Budd Friedman's New York Improv, from the early 1960s. While performers like Cosby had headlined at Greenwich Village coffeehouses years earlier, and clubs like the Hungry I in San Francisco were a vitally important venue for stand-up also well before Friedman's club, the New York Improv was the first of a huge wave of comedy clubs devoted exclusively to comedy and utilizing a unique format of open mikes, unknown and beginning comedians, and emerging stars sharing time and space according to a carefully constructed pecking order administered by the club owner as czar of comedy. Betsy Borns has written a fascinating account of the history and development of the "improv clubs" as they have come to be called generically, including Friedman's Improv chain and such franchise-worthy venues as the Comedy Store, the Comic Strip, and dozens of imitators.

Dozens of important stand-up comedians come out of the Improv clubs. David Brenner, Leno, Gabe Kaplan, Freddie Prinze, Andy Kaufman, Robin Williams, Allen, Seinfeld, Judy Tenuta, Paul Rodriguez, Wright, and literally hundreds of other comics familiar to today's audiences are (or were) all veterans of the comedy-club circuit. Here they started as amateurs working for the opportunity to develop an act in front of a live (if sometimes barely) audience, and they honed their professionalism on a circuit where they could barely earn a decent living if they were willing to endure a hard life of traveling and hanging around clubs while working on their material.

Since they were rarely given sufficient time to develop their themes early in their career, they had to tighten their acts, but still rather than resemble traditional stand-ups in a joke-telling barrage, they would construct two or three minithemes each with a few punch lines clustered around a concept, so for instance if the theme was fast food restaurants or dating or the travails of their life on the road, they could do five minutes or so on each and have an act of ten to fifteen minutes. To expand the act, they needed only to add more themes as they became prominent enough to command more time. A good description of the evolution of such an act is Seinfeld's interesting film *The Comedian* (2002), an account of his rehabilitation as a live stand-up comic after his tremendous success in television situation comedy and retirement. The goal for these club comics was television exposure that could lead to sitcom stardom, a movie career, concert-level stand-up, and other more lucrative gigs. The clubs, however, prospered, multiplied rapidly, and established themselves as an important part of the entertainment scene in just about every city and resort in the United States. Comedy-club centrality has waned somewhat since its peak in the 1980s and particularly post 2000, but it is still so firmly established that it shows no sign of disappearing. Comedy clubs are still the place for the would-be comic to break in, develop an act, and with luck take it to one of the next levels.

These next levels include television, first as a stand-up guest on a talk show, then a position on a comedy show such as *Saturday Night Live* or a sitcom berth. This in turn may lead to a film career, and if you are very good or very lucky, you become a Robin Williams, a Whoopie Goldberg, a Billy Crystal, or a Jerry Seinfeld and you can do it all: club comedy for your amusement and to keep your edge; concert stand-up before a huge live audience at venues such as the Cowpalace or the Met, with taping for HBO or Showtime, videotape and CD sales; and just about any other form of comic expression that might strike your fancy. The superstars of stand-up comedy today are rarely exclusively stand-up comics, yet they rarely abandon stand-up entirely. Even a supersuccessful film comedian like Williams is drawn to concert comedy, and as we see in Seinfeld's film, the challenge of developing a great stand-up act can lure a multimillionaire star back into the clubs to work up material for the concert stage.

Another level at which stand-up comedy (at least by the broader definition of the genre suggested here) flourishes today might be called "performance comedy." Performance comedy, as it is usually self-described, would be by definition at the border of stand-up comedy and theatrical comedy. It embraces the work of monologists such as the late Spaulding Gray, Eric Begosian, John Leguizamo, and Danny Hoch, who are essentially stand-up performers who work in a theater environment with more unified, fully developed, personal themes, and it extends to artists like Stephen Wade, whose *Banjo Dancing*, which ran for more than a decade at the Old Vat Room of the Arena Stage in Washington, D.C., as well as in road performances, to the dramatic art of the Tomlin/Wagner play *The Search for Signs of Intelligent Life in the Universe*. In *Extreme Exposure: An Anthology of Solo Performance Texts from the Twentieth Century*, Jo Bonney has identified more than three dozen such performance artists whose work is at least worth mentioning in the context of contemporary stand-up comedy. These artists work in live performance, though their work is sometimes taped for television viewing, and engage their audience in ways that closely parallel the stand-up comedian's art. Because of the high artistic seriousness of their presentations, it may be necessary to emphasize their roles as performance artists and actors as much as comedians, but their work is often hilariously funny, brilliantly insightful, and analytic of society and culture in the same ways that the best stand-up comedy can function.

So our continuum runs from progenitors such as Rice, the nineteenth-century talking clown who brought to life the dialect humor and social observation that was sweeping American journalism and local color, "literary" comedy, to the reinvention of medicine show and carnival patter, comic magic acts, and juggling such as that provided by Penn and Teller and the Flying Karamazov Brothers. Along the way we honor Twain and other anecdotal comic lecturers who told funny stories and interpreted the interesting and the mundane phenomenon of a nation developing an identity and an interest in itself as an entity. The minstrel theater, vaudeville, burlesque, and the variety theater entertainments led us through encounters with race and ethnicity, regional and social class differences, urban and rural lifestyles, and changing sexual mores. Traditional stand-up comedians coming out of this training ground were able to develop comic personae that were widely recognized. We laughed at Benny's trademark vanity and stinginess, George Burns and Gracie Allen's celebration of illogic and the frustrations of male-female communication. Hope went from simple patter and jokes aimed at his comic persona to political jokes, entertaining troops by poking fun at the military bureaucracy and delineating the comedian as a representative of a loyal opposition, a friend of government and mainstream society, who was licensed to point out some of its errors and weaknesses. Comedians like Bert Williams, Moms Mabley, Redd Foxx, Gregory, and Pryor entertained their audience of fellow African Americans, but they also introduced a larger, more racially diverse audience to a comic perspective on race that was not always positive or politically correct by today's standards, but which demonstrates the value of comedy as a means of mediating what may fester if kept hidden from the lights of theater and comedy.

A lot of stand-up comedy was and is pretty mundane. We laugh at very simple comic images, the puns and one-liners of a comedian such as Henny Youngman, or the over-the-top physical comedy of Red Skelton or Jackie Gleason, and we vent with comedians such as Alan King when they complain about airline food or long waits in the doctor's office. But stand-up comedy can also produce cutting social observation such as Bruce's account of an uncomfortable liberal trying to be friendly to a black person at a party without knowing how to avoid stereotyping and demeaning comments, or his account of "Religions, Incorporated," a cynical look at contemporary religion, a topic he shared with others such as "Lord" Buckley and the duo Wayne and Schuster, to name but a few of many.

Performance comedy is sometimes called "new vaudeville" or "new burlesque" or "new performance stand-up," but it is not new in its basic structure, format, or audience appeal. In fact, it keeps alive old, even ancient, forms of comedy communication. Its value, in an era of electronic media, is its generation of wonder and creativity. Stephen Wade walks out among his audience in "Banjo Dancing." He establishes a rapport that is almost mystical before even saying a word. Moving up to the stage, in the small venues where he usually performs, Wade tells a story about how he learned to play the banjo, following a tradition of urban popular theater entertainers he encountered in his native Chicago. His entry into a traditional banjo contest in the South forces him to realize he needs to do more to, as he puts it, "practice." That practice includes more amazing musical virtuosity, but it also employs a mélange of traditional stories including Twain's famous fence whitewashing scene from *Tom Sawyer*, Works Progress Administration–sponsored literature, folklore, salesmen's spiels, and much more. Its value is in its creative tour de force, perhaps, but also in its underscoring of cultural traditions that are not simple and linear, and, ultimately, in its use of humor to show us who and what we are.

A performance comedian like Danny Hoch, in vehicles such as "Some People" and "Jails, Hospitals, and Hip Hop," introduces his audience to people they might never meet but need to know. His incarcerated misfits, physically and psychically wounded victims of social oppression, indifference, and hard reality, and others such as his Cuban souvenir hustler; his white wannabe rapper; his anxious Jewish mother refusing to face her own prejudices; and his self-created cast of blacks, Hispanics, and whites, male and female, are all funny, artistically admirable, but ultimately much more than that. They are people we need to know, and they are us.

So stand-up is at its essence the work of comedians who behave in funny ways and who say funny things, allowing us to laugh *at* them and *with* them as they represent and present things about themselves and ourselves that we need and desire to view through the lens of humor. It is a part of an ancient and universal human social tendency to explore, to mediate, and to express ourselves about all of the things that matter to us. It is entertainment, surely, and it brings pleasure and release to its audiences. It is also a vitally important social ritual, at the center of the ways in which art informs us about life.

REFERENCES AND FURTHER READINGS

Berger, Phil. *The Last Laugh: The World of the Stand-Up Comics.* New York: William Morrow, 1975. Rev. ed. San Francisco: Limelight, 1985.

Bonney, Jo. *Extreme Exposure: An Anthology of Solo Performance Texts from the Twentieth Century.* New York: Theater Communications Group, 2000.

Borns, Betsy. *Comic Lives: Inside the World of American Stand-Up Comedy.* New York: Simon and Schuster, 1987.

Franklin, Joe. *Joe Franklin's Encyclopedia of Comedians.* Secaucus, NJ: Citadel, 1979.

Jenkins, Ron. *Acrobats of the Soul: Comedy and Virtuosity in Contemporary American Theatre.* New York: Theater Communications Group, 1988.

Koziski, Stephanie. "The Standup Comedian as Anthropologist: Intentional Culture Critic." *Journal of Popular Culture* 18.2 (Fall 1984): 57–76.

Marc, David. *Comic Visions: Television Comedy and American Culture*. Boston: Unwin Hyman, 1989.

Mintz, Lawrence E. "Standup Comedy as Social and Cultural Mediation." *American Quarterly* 37.1 (1985): 71–80.

Peterson, Michael. *Straight White Male: Performance Art Monologues*. Jackson: UP of Mississippi, 1997.

Smith, Ronald Lande. *The Stars of Stand-Up Comedy: A Bibliographical Encyclopedia*. New York: Garland, 1986.

Stone, Laurie. *Laughing in the Dark: A Decade of Subversive Comedy*. Hopewell, NJ: Ecco, 1997.

Towsen, John H. *Clowns*. New York: Hawthorne, 1976.

38

Television Sitcoms

Leo Charney

Four young, neurotic New Yorkers sit around and talk to each other in a coffee shop. Six young, neurotic New Yorkers sit around and talk to each other in a coffee shop. Four young, female New Yorkers sit around and talk to each other in a coffee shop. Four elderly, female Floridians sit around and talk to each other at a kitchen table. Six middle-aged Bostonians sit around and talk to each other at a bar.

Like Greek myths and Elizabethan sonnets, TV situation comedies are a highly ritualized form. From their origins to the present, they have operated within strict formal guidelines: a half-hour time frame; a setting in a home and/or workplace; a set of four to eight recurring characters, each defined by fixed character traits that generate predictable reactions and ritualized conflicts; and three genres: family comedy, friends-as-family comedy, and workplace comedy.

SITCOM FORMS

Family Sitcoms

Both literally and metaphorically, the family has been the mainstay of the situation comedy. Literally, the nuclear and extended family has formed the core of most long-running sitcoms, be they families as diverse as those of *The Goldbergs*, *The Beverly Hillbillies*, *Good Times*, *Roseanne*, *Married with Children*, and *Everybody Loves Raymond*. Metaphorically, the sitcom has extended "family" to include friends, co-workers, and neighbors, a form of "friends-as-family" sitcom that includes such classic examples as *The Mary Tyler Moore Show*, *Seinfeld*, *Cheers*, *Friends*, *Sex and the City*, *The Golden Girls*, and *Will & Grace*.

The family sitcom template has remained essentially unchanged from the early 1950s. The father's status as nominal head of household is constantly under siege, whether from his wife, his children, or his parents and in-laws. He is almost always a figure of self-delusion, who believes himself wiser, more respected, and more in control of the family than everyone else, including the audience, knows him to be. His wife rarely works outside the home but clearly runs the household. She treats her husband as another child, with an affectionate yet acerbic manner that always makes clear that, while he believes himself to be in charge, she and we both know that she is. (This dynamic was made explicit in a 2004 episode of *Everybody Loves Raymond* in which Ray discovers that his wife and daughters make bets behind his back about his foolish behavior.) The children are generally rebellious and flippant, eager for independence yet still wanting the safety and warmth of their family. They initiate quarrels and misbehavior that reflect their need to separate themselves, yet those conflicts are always resolved with the family intact and lessons learned—whether children from parents, parents from children, or both.

Friends-as-Family Sitcoms

The theme song of the classic friends-as-family sitcom *Cheers*—which stresses the titular bar as a safe haven where your friends know who you are and are always happy to see you—encapsulates the promise of the friends-as-family sitcom on which friends, more than literal family, provide comfort, support, and affection in the face of life's tribulations. Friendship forms the sitcom's secret heart, anchoring the form from *I Love Lucy*'s Lucy and Ethel through *Sex and the City*'s Carrie, Miranda, Samantha, and Charlotte. While sitcoms are often scabrous and negative about families and workplaces, they rarely look askance at friendship. Even the nervous neurotics of *Seinfeld*, no matter how churlish and cynical they might be about the world around them, find in one another a bond of friendship as sustaining as that of the four elderly women of the same era's *Golden Girls*, whose theme song thanks them for being friends.

Because it is closely based on its characters, rather than on a repetitive storyline or gimmick, the friends-as-family sitcom illustrates especially well the centrality to the sitcom of fixed character traits. David Bordwell has written that many classical Hollywood films, drawing on traditions of the novel and nineteenth-century melodrama, featured characters defined by a pre-determined set of three to five traits, which then became spurs for action (Bordwell, Staiger, and Thompson 13–18). This device is exemplified in the sitcom, in which each character's familiarity allows the format to perpetuate itself from week to week. When we watch *The Golden Girls*, we know that, no matter what new situation arises, Rose will be ditzy, Blanche will be sexual, Dorothy will be blunt, and Sophia will be outrageous. Fixed traits often define a show's supporting players more sharply than its star: for example, in *Sex and the City*, Miranda is the tense workaholic, Charlotte is the preppy prude, and Samantha is the uninhibited siren, but protagonist Carrie, the romance-seeking writer, is defined less rigidly by set characteristics. So too on the classic friends-as-family sitcoms *Cheers* and *Seinfeld*, on which leads Sam and Jerry, respectively, have a wider range of possible responses than the eccentrics who surround them—but also a corresponding vagueness of character definition. The emblematic *Friends* followed *The Golden Girls* in having no central character and, therefore, a full complement of interacting traits, which repeat themselves so consistently that they become fodder for the characters' teasing one another, as if they were their own home viewers.

Friendships were already central to *I Love Lucy*, one of the earliest sitcoms, on which the bond between Lucy and Ethel grounded much of the show's action. But the friends-as-family subgenre came into its own in the 1970s, when it responded to rising numbers of divorces and urban, sexually liberated singles. For example, *M*A*S*H* and *The Mary Tyler Moore Show*, two of the decade's most popular shows, both focused on a single person in the middle of a workplace, surrounded by friends and co-workers. The two shows fit remarkably similar patterns: a single working person (Hawkeye, Mary) with a same-sex best friend (Trapper John/BJ, Rhoda) working for a gruff but lovable boss (Henry/Colonel Potter, Lou Grant) in a workplace with a designated nincompoop (Frank, Ted) who nevertheless has a woman who loves and admires him (Margaret, Georgette), a female co-worker with a reputation for loose sexuality ("Hot Lips," Sue Ann), and a saner male co-worker who provides some stability among the hijinks (Radar, Murray), as well as an additional figure of wackiness and eccentricity (Klinger, Phyllis).

Workplace Sitcoms

The workplace sitcom often overlaps the friends-as-family sitcom, as in such classic dual examples as *M*A*S*H*, *Cheers*, *Taxi*, *Murphy Brown*, and *The Mary Tyler Moore Show*. It is probably the most ritualized sitcom format, as it relies on the repetition of a setting, of each character's traits, and of each set of conflicts and alliances. *Cheers*, one of the most successful sitcoms in TV history, provides a succinct example of the workplace sitcom's attributes. It transpired in a single setting: a Boston bar and its adjacent office. (In the show's later years, when it started delving into its characters' home lives, this geographic focus no longer held true.) It presented a set of highly ritualized characters, whose personality traits were extremely fixed, and who interacted with one another in the same ways each week:

1. Bartenders Sam Malone (Ted Danson), defined as a vain ladies' man yet with the broader character definition common to sitcom leads; Coach (Nicholas Colasanto), defined as gruff yet lovable; and then, after Coach's death, Woody Boyd (Woody Harrelson), defined as a sweet, gullible, none-too-bright country hick.
2. Waitress Diane Chambers (Shelley Long), defined as prissy, uptight, and overeducated, who regularly clashes with waitress Carla Tortelli (Rhea Perlman), defined as Diane's opposite: crude, brash, and street-smart.
3. Patrons Cliff Clavin (John Ratzenberger), defined as a buffoonishly know-it-all mailman; Norm Peterson (George Wendt), defined as an overweight, probably alcoholic barfly who will do anything to avoid going home to his unseen wife Vera; and eventually Frasier Crane (Kelsey Grammer), Diane's boyfriend, defined as a pompous, overeducated psychiatrist; and his eventual wife Lilith (Bebe Neuwirth), defined as an icy, monotonal, overeducated psychiatrist.

Cheers never focused on more than eight regular characters at a time, the standard limit for the genre's twenty-two-minute form. The show's predictability for its viewers came to mirror the comforting regularity of its setting for its characters, the neighborhood safe haven where everyone knows who you are.

The workplace sitcom generally divides into two varieties: casts composed exclusively of co-workers (e.g., *M*A*S*H*, *Taxi*, *Barney Miller*, *WKRP in Cincinnati*, *NewsRadio*, *Just Shoot Me*) and shows on which a central character interacts primarily with work colleagues but also with neighbors and friends at home (e.g., *Murphy Brown*, *The Mary Tyler Moore Show*, *The Bob Newhart Show*). Usually, in the latter subgenre, the character has one principal "wacky neighbor": Eldin the painter on *Murphy Brown*, Rhoda (and later Phyllis) on *The Mary Tyler Moore Show*, Howard on *The Bob Newhart Show*. A variation of the workplace sitcom may reverse this formula by emphasizing the main character's home life while subordinating the workplace and work colleagues: for example, the classic sitcoms *The Dick Van Dyke Show* and *Frasier*, separated by thirty years, both combined in roughly equal proportions the protagonist's home life and workplace.

The Andy Griffith Show, originally aired in the 1960s and enduringly popular in syndication, provides the best example of a sitcom that combined the family, workplace, and friends-as-family genres into a successful whole—perhaps because all three aspects were unified by a central town (Mayberry, North Carolina) and a central protagonist, Sheriff Andy Taylor (Griffith). The life of widower Andy spanned his home, with his son Opie (Ron Howard) and Aunt Bee (Frances Bavier), who functioned as a housekeeper and surrogate mother/grandmother for the two males; workplace, which included canonical sitcom character Barney Fife (Don Knotts), Andy's hapless deputy; and town, which featured such colorful eccentrics as Andy's friends Howard Sprague (Jack Dodson), Goober Pyle (George Lindsey), and his cousin Gomer Pyle (Jim Nabors), who after one season spun off into his own series, the military comedy *Gomer Pyle, U.S.M.C.* Like the same decade's *Green Acres* and its spinoff *Petticoat Junction*, the show focused as much on the life of the town as on developing a governing situation or a character's psychology. Andy remained a basically static figure, as did his family and friends, so that the show's central character almost became the town itself, which was also its setting and its governing situation. This quietly novel structure allowed the show to bring together the family, workplace, and friends-as-family strands with a seamlessness that few, if any, other sitcoms have been able to imitate successfully.

SITCOM HISTORY

The Early Years

Most of the earliest sitcoms focused on families, and they established the pattern of mischievous children, wise moms, and addled dads that would mark the family sitcom's lifespan. Such 1950s and early 1960s classics as *The Adventures of Ozzie and Harriet* (1952–1966), *Leave It to Beaver* (1957–1963), *Dennis the Menace* (1959–1963), and *Father Knows Best* (1954–1960) featured conventionally white, suburban families, with patriarchs nominally in charge, adhering to the 1950s stereotypes of a businessman dad, stay-at-home mom, and children who are good-hearted and law-abiding, if straining for independence. This conventionality did not set in immediately. The family at the center of *The Goldbergs* (1949–1954), for example, which migrated from a popular radio show, was both heavily ethnic and dominated by the show's star, Gertrude Berg, as matriarch Molly Goldberg. And, in any case, these shows' seeming conformity (perhaps encouraged by *Father Knows Best*'s easy-to-mock title) is somewhat misleading, since sitcom tradition, begun in these early examples, holds that father does not always—or perhaps ever—know best. The title is a patronizing pat on the back more than a literal description: father, even when he clearly does not know best, is always led to believe that he does by the wife and family (especially daughters) who humor and coddle him.

The Dick Van Dyke Show (1961–1966) broke new ground by rejecting the model of an older, clueless dad with several children leaving each day for a mystery job in favor of a younger, hipper, urbane father with an attractive wife and a single child working in an exciting TV job that was as integrated into the show as the protagonist's family life. Like the previous decade's *I Love Lucy* (1951–1957), *Dick Van Dyke* included, and thereby helped to initiate, all six of the sitcom's defining themes: marriage, family, workplace, friends-as-family, women/mothers, and men/fathers. We saw not only the home life of Rob Petrie (Van Dyke) with wife Laura (sitcom icon Mary Tyler Moore) and son Richie (Larry Mathews), but also his work life, as a writer on the fictitious *Alan Brady Show* with cut-up colleagues Sally (Rose Marie) and Buddy (Morey Amsterdam), whose raspy one-liners anchored the show in the earlier entertainments of vaudeville and burlesque. Rob and Laura were a young, attractive, and stylish couple for their time, especially compared to *I Love Lucy*'s more traditional central couple, and their relationship felt more equal, affectionate, and up-to-date than that of other sitcoms' traditionally older couples and parents.

The classic *I Love Lucy* centered on the antics of Lucy Ricardo (Lucille Ball), her husband Ricky (Desi Arnaz), a nightclub performer, and their neighbors and landlords Fred (William Frawley) and Ethel Mertz (Vivian Vance). Lucy and Ricky's union began the double-edged balance of power that has been the constant of sitcom marriages through such contemporary examples as *Everybody Loves Raymond* and *Curb Your Enthusiasm*. The wife/mother does not work outside the home and is portrayed as subservient to her husband in money and ostensible status. Yet, as if to compensate for this public discrepancy, she is the real power of the household—the wise, commonsensical mainstay who keeps the family and the marriage on track behind a husband/father almost invariably portrayed as a bumbler or fool. The storylines of *I Love Lucy* consistently played out one of the eternal themes of farce: the "Emperor's New Clothes" (or *Wizard of Oz* or *Marriage of Figaro*) story of unmasking, of a seemingly foolish figure who sees behind the facade of social pretension, strips it away, and comes out ahead of those with greater status, money, and power, either by bumbling into triumph or by using native shrewdness to undermine social follies. (This pattern also often characterizes detective stories, including popular TV detectives Jessica Fletcher of *Murder, She Wrote* and Peter Falk's perennially rumpled *Columbo*.) Sitcoms frequently make this theme gendered, as wives/mothers are put-upon yet sagacious and triumphant in the face of trials inflicted on them by insensitive and oblivious husbands. This pattern received an especially paradoxical twist on *The George Burns and Gracie Allen Show* (1950–1958), transferred from radio like many of its early TV counterparts, on which Gracie was represented as simultaneously a ditzy airhead and a fount of common sense.

This kind of relationship reached an early apex in the brutal marriage at the center of *The Honeymooners* (1955–1956) between volatile, frustrated bus driver Ralph Kramden (Jackie Gleason) and his long-suffering wife Alice (Audrey Meadows). While the marriage of Lucy and Ricky seemed rooted in some core of affection, admiration, and attraction, the union of the Kramdens saw only fleeting fondness (often unconvincingly pasted on) amidst an overwhelming mood of bitterness, unhappiness, and working-class disaffection. The show seemed related more to the gritty "kitchen sink" dramas of the period, which tried to reflect the realities of urban blue-collar life (exemplified by the Oscar-winning film *Marty* [1955], about a lonely New York butcher, which began as a 1953 TV drama), than to *I Love Lucy*, for which it functioned as a kind of dark mirror image, if not an outright parody. Full of failed dreams and schemes for escaping the confines of his life, Ralph was not shy about taking out his frustrations on his acerbic, sharp-tongued wife, who could return as much fire as she received. When Ralph says to Alice, "One of these days, Alice—Pow! Right in the kisser!" their marriage seems based as much on verbal and possibly physical abuse as on the putative humor of a situation comedy.

The Honeymooners' unusual bitterness probably arose from both its earliness, before sitcom conventions fully took hold, and its strange place as an offshoot of Jackie Gleason's variety show. Its level of acrimony has never been matched, except perhaps by its truest heir, *Everybody Loves Raymond* (1996–2005), another saga of middle-class bitterness in the outer boroughs of New York. *Raymond* focuses on two (eventually three) couples in the same family. Sportswriter Ray Barone (Ray Romano) and his homemaker wife Debra (Patricia Heaton) exemplify the sitcom pattern of bumbling husband/covertly powerful wife, a dynamic explicitly addressed in countless episodes that focus on the day-to-day frustrations of a suburban family with three children. The Barones live next door to Ray's parents, two of the most scathingly negative characters ever witnessed in a nominal comedy: Marie (Doris Roberts), whose manipulation and vindictiveness extend primarily to her husband and beleaguered daughter-in-law, and Frank (Peter Boyle), a seething cauldron of insults and negativity. Were it not for the laugh track, *Raymond* might be barely recognizable as a comedy, as filled as it is with reprisals, recriminations, and regrets. Add the resentment of Ray's brother Robert (Brad Garrett)—whose fierce sibling rivalry informs the show's sarcastic title—as well as Robert's own new marriage and dysfunctional in-laws (Fred Willard and Georgia Engel), and the show provides perhaps the most complete catalogue of family strife and individual unease ever seen in a TV sitcom.

After the Early Years

It was no accident that *The Dick Van Dyke Show*'s perfect distillation of sitcom form arrived in 1961. By the early 1960s, the sitcom genre had established the themes, structures, and conventions that remain remarkably unchanged today. Although periodizing sitcoms risks oversimplifying trends, some clear generational patterns emerge in the genre's programming history: the 1960s can be seen as the era of the gimmick; the 1970s was the decade of social relevance; the 1980s saw the post-1950s heyday of the family sitcom; and the 1990s became the age of alternative families.

The 1960s

Situation comedies of the 1960s seemed to take "situation" literally, as show after show placed its characters in an artificial—even surrealistic—framework. At the most magical extreme, *Bewitched* (1964–1972) featured a witch (Elizabeth Montgomery) as a suburban housewife who indulges in a little magic now and then, despite her ordinary surroundings, ad executive husband (Dick York, then Dick Sargent), meddling mother (Agnes Moorehead), and host of wacky neighbors and relatives. *I Dream of Jeannie* (1965–1970) similarly placed a genie (Barbara Eden) in the household of astronaut Tony Nelson (Larry Hagman), whom she pledges to "serve" in whatever ways he desires. These two shows used magic as an allegory of female difference, creating a surreal spin on the sitcom's wife-as-power-behind-the-man theme while evoking the potential isolation of the suburban housewife, the difficulty of fitting in and defining normality amidst nosy neighbors, noisy relatives, and rapid world change. In the years after the publication of Betty Friedan's *The Feminine Mystique* (1963), the manifesto of suburban housewife liberation, these shows asked: What does it mean to be "normal" as a suburban American housewife? What beleaguered housewife wouldn't like a little magic to spice up her life, solve her daily problems, divert herself from her daily routine, and, when necessary, supply a little vehicle of revenge?

The 1960s also furthered a trend toward unmarried working women as sitcom protagonists. Begun by Eve Arden's single schoolteacher in *Our Miss Brooks* (1952–1956), this subgenre continued with *Hazel* (1961–1966), a suburban housekeeper (played by Oscar and Tony winner Shirley Booth in what was at the time a daring move into series television) who runs the Baxter household with cheerful efficiency. Hazel's bossy yet maternal nature made her more like a traditional sitcom wife than an employee, even though George Baxter (Don De Fore) already had a (fairly icy) wife. *Petticoat Junction* (1963–1970) similarly featured maternal widow Kate Bradley (Bea Benaderet) and her three sexy single daughters running a rural hotel with Kate's lazy brother Joe (Edgar Buchanan). The decade's swinging single girl emerged more fully in *That Girl* (1966–1971), starring Marlo Thomas as Ann Marie, an aspiring New York City actress and model who seemed to step right out of the pages of *Cosmopolitan* magazine or its editor Helen Gurley Brown's *Sex and the Single Girl* (1962). Although much of Ann's life revolved around her boyfriend and parents, her neurotic yet charming personality, urban sensibility, and work worries paved the way for such later figures as Murphy Brown, Rachel and Monica on *Friends*, and TV's most canonical single working woman, who first appeared in 1970: Mary Tyler Moore as Mary Richards in *The Mary Tyler Moore Show*.

All of these shows reflected the changes going on in American society of the time. It was no coincidence that Jeannie's mate was an astronaut and NASA the show's workplace. What is stranger, *I Dream of Jeannie* asked, men walking on the moon or a genie walking on earth? This same question echoed in *My Favorite Martian* (1963–1966), on which a space alien (Ray Walston) poses as a reporter's "Uncle Martin" after he is stranded on earth by a near miss between his spaceship and a NASA rocket. A similar theme grounded the parodies of nuclear, suburban families in *The Munsters* (1964–1966) and *The Addams Family* (1964–1966), which ran in the same seasons and offered satirical yet affectionate evocations of "normal" American family life. Herman Munster (Fred Gwynne), who looks like Frankenstein's monster, cannot understand why his neighbors don't treat him and his ghoulish family like average people, since they share the same family cohesion and affection as everyone else. The Addams family, however, revels in its eccentricity and zest for life, which husband Gomez (John Astin) and wife Morticia (Carolyn Jones) feel make them superior to the dully ordinary folk around them. From their different perspectives, both shows encapsulated the normative values of an American way of life that was, at the same time, being subverted from within—a development that both shows also allegorized. In this way, they moved one step beyond the animated Stone Age family of *The Flintstones* (1960–1966) and the animated futuristic family of *The Jetsons* (1962–1963), both of which transported suburban-style nuclear families into the doubly defamiliarizing realms of cartoons and the extreme past/extreme future.

The Munsters and *The Addams Family*, like *I Dream of Jeannie*, also formed part of the 1960s' most common sitcom theme: the fish out of water. This story line encompassed a wide range of different situations, including the New York City couple relocated to rural Hooterville in *Green Acres* (1965–1971); the Ozark hillbillies become West Coast millionaires in *The Beverly Hillbillies* (1962–1971); the alien on Earth in *My Favorite Martian*; the disparate, roguish inmates of a World War II prisoner-of-war camp rebelling against oppressive military authority in *Hogan's Heroes* (1965–1971); the disparate, roguish crew of a World War II PT boat rebelling against oppressive military authority in *McHale's Navy* (1962–1966); the seven castaways marooned on a tropical island in *Gilligan's Island* (1964–1967); and the decade's closest thing to a literal fish out of water, *Mister Ed* (1961–1966), a horse who talked—but only to his owner. At a time of rapid social change, these shows offered the balm of silly escapism while dramatizing a cultural mood of dislocation and uncertainty. Ostensibly playing for laughs, they could draw on the cultural currency of change and upheaval, while using their jokey formats to assuage the anxieties that accompanied those states.

The 1970s

The 1970s were the sitcom's high-water mark of groundbreaking content and cultural relevance. These innovations were largely associated with producer Norman Lear, who dominated the era with such controversial, socially conscious shows as *All in the Family* (1971–1979), which rewrote the rules of sitcom content by focusing on the wrongheaded beliefs and outrageous statements of working-class New York City bigot Archie Bunker; its spin-offs *Maude* (1972–1978), which pushed the envelope even further by featuring an outspoken, uncompromising left-wing woman as its lead character, and *The Jeffersons* (1975–1985), which featured an upwardly mobile African American couple on New York's wealthy Upper East Side and their neighbors, a mixed-race couple; *Maude* spin-off *Good Times* (1974–1979), which presented the life of a poor African American family in a Chicago housing project; as well as *Sanford & Son* (1972–1977), about a cantankerous African American junkman, his son, and their eccentric friends and relatives; and *One Day at a Time* (1975–1984), about a recently divorced single mother struggling to raise two teenage daughters.

Lear's shows reflected the upheavals and advancements of their era by spotlighting social issues and characters very different from the sitcom's usual focus on white, middle-class protagonists. At the same time, the shows retained the sitcom's traditional forms and structures, concentrating on conflicts both within families (even if they sometimes had a single mother or father) and faced by families banding together against outside oppression or injustice, a frequent theme of *Good Times* and even the more traditionally comic *Jeffersons*. Archie Bunker (Carroll O'Connor), spouting racist invective and railing at his left-wing "Meathead" son-in-law (Rob Reiner), was a traditional comic fool, a patriarch predictably proven misguided and self-deluded. Archie's wife Edith (Jean Stapleton), regularly derided by him as a "dingbat," showed herself to be, like all sitcom wives, the wiser and more level-headed partner; and Archie, like Ralph Kramden, was even known to openly (if occasionally) express his love and devotion to her. This pattern repeated itself in *The Jeffersons*, which presented patriarch George (Sherman Hemsley) as a self-aggrandizing reverse racist who alienates everyone around him—except his loyal wife Louise (Isabel Sanford), who stands by him even as she stands up to him, and who invariably comes across as sensible and patient compared to her buffoonish mate.

Maude, *Good Times*, and *One Day at a Time* broke this mold by focusing on strong women as heads of households. Maude Findlay (Beatrice Arthur) remains the most forceful (and definitely the most left-wing) woman ever to anchor a sitcom—or, possibly, a TV series of any genre; deep-voiced and blunt, she wore the pants (often literally) in her marriage to relatively meek Walter (Bill Macy). The show attained its greatest moment of controversy by tackling the issue of abortion, when Maude found herself with a midlife pregnancy and struggled to decide what to do about it. *One Day at a Time*'s Ann Romano (Bonnie Franklin) was a more conventional sitcom protagonist, modeled on the era's sitcom sweetheart Mary Tyler Moore. The challenges of a divorced single mother provided relatively new fodder for a television series, even if the situations that arose, especially in relation to her two teenage daughters (Mackenzie Phillips and Valerie Bertinelli), were often fairly conventional.

Good Times broke more significant new ground in recasting the sitcom's traditional two-parents-and-three-children nuclear family as struggling African Americans in a small Chicago housing-project apartment. After John Amos, who played father James Evans, left the show, it officially became the story of a struggling single mother—but Florida Evans (Esther Rolle), originally the housekeeper on *Maude*, had been the show's focus from the start, and Amos had publicly complained about not getting enough airtime. And yet the show's popularity depended from day one on the breakout success of son J.J. (Jimmie Walker) and his catchphrase, "Dyn-o-mite!" What began as an effort to present a different kind of African American family devolved into what many critics derided as a modern-day minstrel show, with Walker wringing laughs from his stick-thin body and syncopated inflections. The public complaints of nominal stars Amos and Rolle—she too quit the show, only to return later—about what they perceived as the show's demeaning direction only intensified the public nature of this conflict. Similar complaints dogged *The Jeffersons*, on which self-inflated George seemed to some observers a caricature worthy of *Amos 'n' Andy*, and *Sanford & Son*, which featured a cast of African Americans drawn in part from old burlesque and "chitlin circuit" performers, including star Redd Foxx and LaWanda Page, who played his cartoonish Aunt Esther.

Lear's shows were by no means the only action in the 1970s sitcom arena. *The Mary Tyler Moore Show* (1970–1977), *Laverne and Shirley* (1976–1983), and *Alice* (1976–1985) all featured unmarried working women as their protagonists; *Rhoda* (1974–1978), the spin-off of *Mary Tyler Moore*'s best friend and neighbor, eventually got divorced, another TV first; *Three's Company* (1977–1984) played off the era's sexual liberation by featuring a young man (pretending, for the landlord's benefit, to be gay) living with two young women, all of them preoccupied with sex and relationships; *The Bob Newhart Show* (1972–1978) featured a childless professional couple living in a big-city high-rise apartment (though still surrounded by eccentric co-workers and wacky neighbors); and *Chico and the Man* (1974–1978), tragically cut short by the 1977 suicide of star Freddie Prinze, contrasted the worldviews of a cantankerous, elderly white garage owner (Jack Albertson) and the young Chicano who comes to work for him and live in his garage. Like *Good Times*' Walker, Prinze was part of a generation of young, male, often ethnic stars who shot to prominence in the 1970s, as emblems of a youthful, countercultural sensibility. This group included John Travolta in *Welcome Back, Kotter* (1975–1979), who became a movie star in *Saturday Night Fever* (1977), and Henry Winkler, whose Fonzie character in *Happy Days* (1974–1984) emerged as an unexpected cultural icon, like *The Simpsons*' Bart Simpson almost twenty years later.

Kotter and *Happy Days*, both featuring and to some extent aimed at teenagers, articulated two sides of the TV industry's response to the era's social contexts. *Kotter* featured an inner-city high school teacher who has returned to his alma mater to teach the "sweathogs," misfits and delinquents who conveniently include a Puerto Rican, a Jew, an Italian American, and an African American. While their antics and catchphrases ("Up your nose with a rubber hose!") were often played for laughs, the show's dingy setting and disadvantaged protagonists kept its social framework front and center. *Happy Days* responded to its period from the opposite direction: loosely modeled on George Lucas' nostalgia movie *American Graffiti* (1973), the show evoked an idealized suburban family of the 1950s, as teenager Richie Cunningham (former *Andy Griffith Show* child actor Ron Howard) interacted with his wholesome family and friends, chased girls, hung out at the local diner, and tried to emulate the coolness of greaser Fonzie. *Happy Days* offered a counter-countercultural vision of the stability and harmony of the decade before the Vietnam War, the civil rights movement, and assassinations. In the process, it deliberately highlighted the gap between the 1950s and the show's present—a discrepancy bluntly encoded in its title.

While *Happy Days* gave the family sitcom a nostalgic spin, *The Brady Bunch* (1969–1974) and *The Partridge Family* (1970–1974) updated it for the era's new social contexts. Both shows presented traditional family conflicts in the framework of untraditional, socially relevant families: on *The Brady Bunch*, a blended family of three girls and three boys trying to live together when their parents marry; and, on *The Partridge Family*, a single mother raising five children who also comprise a singing group. The children in both families have standard clashes with one another and their parents, even as their situations—not to mention their clothes, attitudes, and language—reflect the hipper standards of the late 1960s and early 1970s.

The 1970s also saw the beginning of the heyday of the friends-as-family sitcom, which drew from increasing numbers of urban singles and decreasing numbers of conventional nuclear families. Moore, as single Minneapolis news producer Mary Richards on the classic *Mary Tyler Moore Show* (1970–1977), became the emblem of this new direction, even if the show's network rejected the producers' original intention to make Mary a divorcée. While Mary Richards was far from a sexual revolutionary, it was her average midwesternness—together with Moore's familiarity as the stay-at-home wife and mother from *The Dick Van Dyke Show*—that made her an ideal proxy for the values of a new era. In her unsubversive way, Mary struggled daily with the balance between assertiveness and subservience that characterized many women's uncertain social roles in this era of women's liberation—a conflict encapsulated in the show's first episode, in which, despite Mary's nervousness and hesitation in a job interview, gruff Lou Grant (Edward Asner) tells her, "You've got spunk. I like spunk." The show successfully sidled up to its social contexts, combining familiar sitcom elements with diversity and sexual liberation. Eccentric Phyllis Lindstrom (Cloris Leachman), who would eventually spin off into *Phyllis* (1975–1977), was a traditional sitcom "wacky neighbor" yet also a post–*Feminine Mystique* free spirit full of newfangled ideas about her marriage and her child; Mary's Ethel Mertz, Rhoda Morgenstern (Valerie Harper), was overweight and ethnic, complete with a stereotypical Jewish mother (Nancy Walker); and cooking-show host Sue Ann Nivens was a vindictive, promiscuous narcissist played radically against type by TV veteran Betty White.

In similar fashion, *M*A*S*H* (1972–1983) fused the workplace and friends-as-family sitcoms into a portrait of ordinary Americans serving in a military hospital during the Korean War. Based on a freewheeling 1970 movie directed by Robert Altman, the show combined comic and dramatic elements in an allegory of the ongoing Vietnam War, complete with a level of recreational and adulterous sex, copious alchohol consumption, and crude language and behavior that might have been unimaginable in a situation comedy only a few years earlier. In the tradition of *Hogan's Heroes*, *McHale's Navy*, and *The Phil Silvers Show* (1955–1959), military authority was represented as not just oppressive but also foolish and bumbling, while the show's protagonists were represented as crafty and subversive yet sympathetic. Unlike its antecendents, *M*A*S*H* incorporated noncomic elements about war's absurdities, tragedies, and strange bedfellows, especially in the show's later years, when it was increasingly influenced by star Alan Alda. Even more than *Mary Tyler Moore*, it incorporated socially conscious material into traditional comic frameworks, especially in the sparring between prim Frank Burns (Larry Linville)—later replaced by patrician Charles Emerson Winchester (David Ogden Stiers)—and more liberated Hawkeye (Alda) and roommates Trapper John (Wayne Rogers) and B.J. (Mike Farrell). These conflicts gave the series a running comic engine and two traditional comic prigs, as it encapsulated the divide between a younger antiwar generation and an uptight older generation, here identified with support of the war and military authority.

The 1980s and the 1990s

If the sitcoms of the 1970s often responded to the era's tumultuous social contexts, the most popular shows of the 1980s seemed to react against that impulse, returning to visions of more traditional nuclear families. *Family Ties* (1982–1989) began as a story of generational division, as two former 1960s hippies (Michael Gross and Meredith Baxter) raise a son (Michael J. Fox) who is a Reagan Republican. But this theme quickly gave way to Fox's breakout popularity and the generic (in both senses) demands of the family sitcom, which require "family ties" to endure in the face of all temporary challenges. *The Cosby Show* (1984–1992), the decade's dominant sitcom, similarly traced the generation gaps among a cranky doctor father (Bill Cosby), his regally elegant lawyer wife (Phylicia Rashad), and their five very independent children. Cosby mastered the art of seeming put-upon by his childrens' behavior and attitudes, finding numerous new twists and facial expressions to augment the stock character of the besieged-by-his-family sitcom dad.

The trifecta of popular family sitcoms was completed in the 1990s by *Home Improvement* (1991–1999), featuring stand-up comic Tim Allen as a suburban father who hosts a TV home improvement show. Paired with acerbic Patricia Richardson as his wife, Allen exemplified the clueless sitcom husband and father, looked upon by both wife and sons as a bumbling incompetent. In this case, the patriarch was not even given the power outside the home accorded earlier breadwinners, as Allen's Tim Taylor was as consistently over his head at work as at home. The show also included a playful gloss on sitcom tradition: a wacky neighbor who was literally disembodied, appearing as only a head and voice above a backyard fence. This family emphasis of the 1980s extended as well to less traditional, nonnuclear families. *Diff'rent Strokes* (1978–1986) featured a wealthy older gentleman who adopts two African American children, a theme repeated in *Webster* (1983–1987), about a childless white couple who adopts an African American orphan. Along similar lines, *The Facts of Life* (1979–1988) centered on a nontraditional substitute family, with matronly Edna Garrett (Charlotte Rae) serving as housemother to a group of boarding-school girls.

The late years of the 1980s saw an increasing backlash against the family harmonies of *Cosby* and *Family Ties*, with the advent of the rude, crude, blue-collar families of *Married with Children* (1987–1997), *Roseanne* (1988–1997), and *The Simpsons* (1989–). Roseanne Barr's landmark sitcom was a rebuke to the suave, upper-class family of *The Cosby Show*. Working mother Roseanne Conner (Barr) was not wise and poised but loud and struggling, sometimes unemployed, short on patience and wise solutions. Her husband Dan (John Goodman) was less patriarchal than baffled, often a pale shadow of his domineering wife, despite his physical bulk. Their children were snide, oversexed, and maladjusted, and they did not necessarily improve or learn lessons as the show went along. Roseanne's demanding, self-centered mother (Estelle Parsons), touchy father-in-law (Ned Beatty), and boisterously inappropriate grandmother (Shelley Winters) deliberately counterpointed the wise, twinkling elders of the Cosby brood, as well as the general TV tradition of warm, loving grandparents. On *Roseanne*, parenting and grandparenting conferred no special qualities of understanding or affection on otherwise troubled and troublesome adults. Squalling conflicts simply expanded to include children, even if the show did provide more conventional moments of family solidarity and affection. In *Roseanne*'s highly class-sensitive universe, family always triumphed over class; no matter how much the family might battle each other, its members always united against the insults and humiliations inflicted on the working class by the outer world.

Married with Children and *The Simpsons*, both of which defined the fledgling Fox network as an alternative to the established networks' tasteful, time-honored pieties, featured families even coarser and more fractious than the Conners. *Married*'s patriarch was aggrieved, carping shoe salesman Al Bundy (Ed O'Neill), an indifferent husband and father whose primary goal was to get his wife and children to stop pestering him for money, attention, and sex. As on other sitcoms, his wife and children treat him as an ignorant fool. The difference here: he *is* an ignorant fool. The show played as an overt burlesque of the American nuclear family and the heartwarming traditions of the family sitcom, with a lower quotient of redemptive family bonding and affection than any TV show before it. (It in turn spawned such later nonredemptive family sitcoms as *Everybody Loves Raymond* and *Malcolm in the Middle* [2000–].) Somewhat more lovable was reprobate Homer Simpson, the father of the animated *Simpsons*, which included bratty Bart, brainy Lisa, baby Maggie, and matriarch Marge. An alcoholic and binge eater, incompetent both at work and at home, cartoon character Homer, sympathetically voiced by Dan Castellaneta, avoided seeming as malevolent as he might if he were embodied by a human actor. Despite its animated format, the show has sustained and sharpened many of the family sitcom's most familiar tenets, including the two parents/three children structure, the wise wife/bumbling husband dichotomy, and the children who are rebellious yet ultimately tied to their family. After all, Bart, who became and remains a popular icon of childhood misbehavior, was just a contemporary update of his mischievous ancestor Dennis the Menace.

As cartoon characters, the Simpsons have a sitcom advantage over their live-action counterparts: they never have to change or age. Their show becomes a pure instance of sitcom form, since its governing traits, relations, and situations can stay resolutely the same, no matter how many years they continue. *Seinfeld* (1990–1998), which showed a similar lack of advancement, was in that sense more like a live-action cartoon than like its sitcom cousins. Frequently if inaccurately characterized as "about nothing" (a description that actually came from a self-parody episode), *Seinfeld* infused a cynical, even nihilistic sensibility into the friends-as-family format of four single urbanites whose primary life connections are to one another. Jerry (Jerry Seinfeld), George (Jason Alexander), Elaine (Julia Louis-Dreyfus), and Kramer (Michael Richards) meet often in Jerry's living room or around a diner table (a similar setting to such other friends-as-family classics as *Cheers*, *Friends*, and *Sex and the City*), though Kramer does double duty as Jerry's wacky neighbor. The show's innovations arose primarily from its adult content and ingenious story structures. Cocreator Larry David constructed a storytelling format—which he later used in his improvisational cable sitcom *Curb Your Enthusiasm* (2000–)—that relied on seemingly random story lines that eventually coincide by the end of the episode, often in cleverly far-fetched ways.

While the show's intricate situations still involved the characters' workplaces, relationships, love lives, parents, and friends, its tone and content upped the level of urban cynicism, political incorrectness, and sexual references beyond where most sitcoms had gone before. Classic episodes included such subject matter as a contest to see which friend could refrain from masturbating the longest; a girlfriend whose name Jerry cannot remember but which rhymes with "a female body part"; a make-out session during Holocaust drama *Schindler's List*, duly reported to Jerry's Jewish parents; and the death of George's fiancée from licking poisonous glue on their wedding-invitation envelopes. Yet underlying the show's nihilism, like a safety net, was the unbreakable bond of the four friends, who stayed together even to the extent of occupying a communal jail cell in the controversial final episode, on which they were finally brought to justice (literally) for their callousness and inhumanity.

Many of the 1990s' most popular sitcoms also centered on alternative families. *Cheers'* spinoff *Frasier* (1993–2004), which won the Emmy Award as Best Comedy Series five years in a row, played like a catalogue of family dysfunction transfigured as French farce. Frasier Crane (Kelsey Grammer), a middle-aged divorced psychiatrist, lives with his elderly widowed father (John Mahoney) and the father's physical therapist (Jane Leeves). His brother Niles (David Hyde Pierce) is trapped in a loveless marriage to an unseen, anorexic wife whom he eventually divorces to marry the physical therapist. The retired policeman father, who raised his two sons alone after the death of his wife, has nothing in common with his wealthy, prissy, overeducated sons, so that the show manages to include class conflict within the bounds of the family itself. For good measure, Frasier's radio station workplace includes a promiscuous, persistently unhappy-in-love producer (Peri Gilpin), as well as a succession of foolish bosses and obnoxious co-workers. Even more explicitly, *3rd Rock from the Sun* (1996–2001) presented a broad burlesque of the nuclear family in which a group of space aliens came to earth and posed as an American family. As on *The Munsters* and *The Addams Family*, the sitcom's very premise embodied a defamiliarizing perspective on the rituals of American suburban life and the interactions of a "normal" American family.

Other shows of the era embraced not so much alternative families as alternatives *to* families. *Mad about You* (1992–1999) starred Paul Reiser and Helen Hunt as urban, brittle Paul and Jamie Buchman, a New York couple whose daily lives and interactions included lots of wacky relatives and sarcastic repartee but emphatically not children—until the show inexplicably sabotaged its premise in its last season by giving the Buchmans a newborn child. An equally cynical, urban sensibility infused comedian Garry Shandling's two cable sitcoms, *It's Garry Shandling's Show* (1986–1990) and *The Larry Sanders Show* (1992–1998). Both shows pitted a neurotic, phobic, self-obsessed protagonist against the neighbors, co-workers, and romantic partners who struggle to put up with him—a theme that placed Shandling in a comic line of misanthropes stretching from seventeenth-century Molière plays through such twentieth-century figures as Jack Benny, George Burns, and Groucho Marx to TV ubercranks Shandling, Seinfeld, and Larry David of *Curb Your Enthusiasm*, whose chilly marriage and self-obsession also left no visible room for children.

The 1980s and 1990s also consolidated the friends-as-family surge of the 1970s, as several hit shows celebrated friendship, often in an urban setting, as an alternative to families and relationships. *Friends* (1994–2004), the ultimate friends-as-family series, capped this trend, which began with *The Golden Girls* (1985–1992) and *Murphy Brown* (1988–1998) and also included the cable hit *Sex and the City* (1998–2004). *Will & Grace* (1998–) expanded the alternative family to alternative sexuality, centering on the closer-than-lovers friendship of gay man Will Truman (Eric McCormack) and best friend Grace Adler (Debra Messing), together with Jack's flamboyantly gay friend Jack (Sean Hayes) and Grace's flamboyantly medicated co-worker Karen (Megan Mullaly). With the character of Jack, gayness became a comic character trait like any other, reinforced from week to week in all interactions. *Sex and the City*, about four women whose bonds with one another surpassed their bonds with anyone else, often played like a raunchy, urban update of *The Golden Girls*, about four women whose bonds with each other surpassed their bonds with anyone else. Both shows subordinated family to friendship, represented as a more lasting connection than the vagaries of romance. The shows' differences worked themselves out around tone and content: four women who find solace in one another near the end of their lives versus four women who find solace in one another in the whirlwind of city life, disappointing boyfriends, and unexpected life events.

Friends presented a similar point of view, limning the lives of six young, single New Yorkers who over ten years become each other's confidants, roommates, lovers, and even spouses. Although the characters eventually moved toward the domestic staples of marriage and children, their interactions in the show's earlier years focused on personal and professional entanglements with lovers, parents, bosses, co-workers, and one another. The show confirmed for a new generation the importance of fixed character traits to the friends-as-family sitcom, featuring Monica, the anxious, neat-freak chef (Courteney Cox Arquette); Rachel, the spoiled fashion victim (Jennifer Aniston); and Phoebe, the ditzy, new-agey massage therapist (Lisa Kudrow), paired off against Chandler, the sarcastic joker (Matthew Perry); Joey, the dumb, good-looking actor (Matt LeBlanc); and Ross (David Schwimmer), the dorky paleontologist who cannot sustain a relationship.

In the end (literally), *Seinfeld* and *Friends* demonstrate the two poles of the sitcom's development: the show on which no one changes versus the show on which everyone changes. The static sitcom, resolutely sticking to its generative characters and themes, resembles a classic cartoon, as exemplified by the dual-citizen *Simpsons*. Jerry, Elaine, George, Kramer, and, above all, Jerry's nemesis Newman have more in common with such never-changing cartoon icons as Bugs Bunny and Road Runner, ceaselessly bringing the same traits to the same situations, than they do with their more dimensional sitcom brethren. *Friends*, *Sex and the City*, and *Mad about You*, with their long arcs of character evolution and carefully worked-out resolutions, seem more like hybrids of the sitcom and the soap opera, in which we follow characters who age, change, and grow as they would in real life. Between a model of dimensional change and a model of rigid repetition lies the mutability of the sitcom form, which, like other classic genres, has remained predictable enough to be recognizable across generations and flexible enough to adapt to new styles and social contexts.

REFERENCES AND FURTHER READINGS

Allen, Robert C. *Channels of Discourse, Reassembled: Television and Contemporary Criticism.* Chapel Hill: U of North Carolina P, 1992.

Bogle, Donald. *Primetime Blues: African Americans on Network Television.* New York: Farrar, Straus and Giroux, 2002.

Bordwell, David, Janet Staiger, and Kristin Thompson. *The Classical Hollywood Cinema: Film Style and Mode of Production to 1960.* New York: Columbia UP, 1985.

Brook, Vincent. *Something Ain't Kosher Here: The Rise of the "Jewish" Sitcom.* New Brunswick, NJ: Rutgers UP, 2003.

Coleman, Robin R. Means. *African American Viewers and the Black Situation Comedy: Situating Racial Humor.* New York: Garland, 1998.

Hamamoto, Darrell Y. *Nervous Laughter: Television Situation Comedy and Liberal Democratic Ideology.* New York: Praeger, 1989.

Jones, Gerard. *Honey, I'm Home! Sitcoms, Selling the American Dream.* New York: Grove Weidenfeld, 1992.

Leibman, Nina C. *Living Room Lectures: The Fifties Family in Film and Television.* Austin: U of Texas P, 1995.

Marc, David. *Comic Visions: Television Comedy and American Culture.* 2nd ed. Malden, MA: Blackwell, 1997.

———. *Demographic Vistas: Television in American Culture.* Philadelphia: U of Pennsylvania P, 1984.

Morreale, Joanne, ed. *Critiquing the Sitcom: A Reader.* Syracuse, NY: Syracuse UP, 2003.

Smith-Shomade, Beretta E. *Shaded Lives: African-American Women and Television.* New Brunswick, NJ: Rutgers UP, 2002.

Spigel, Lynn. *Make Room for TV: Television and the Family Ideal in Postwar America.* Chicago: U of Chicago P, 1992.

Staiger, Janet. *Blockbuster TV: Must-See Sitcoms in the Network Era.* New York: New York UP, 2000.

Taylor, Ella. *Prime-Time Families: Television Culture in Postwar America.* Berkeley: U of California P, 1989.

Glossary

Absurdism. Dramatic technique, attitude, and movement associated with Martin Esslin's term *Theatre of the Absurd*. Absurdist playwrights such as Eugène Ionesco (1912–1994), Samuel Beckett (1906–1989), Harold Pinter (1930–), and Edward Albee (1928–) match themes of alienation and irrationality with grotesque, repetitive language and gestures, and wacky and often circular plots to create comic and terrifyingly bizarre dramatic worlds.

ACT UP and Queer Nation. Queer activist groups of the late 1980s and 1990s targeting AIDS discrimination and homophobia. Each group used artwork that cleverly appropriated and punned on popular culture forms, constituting a sort of retooled, militant camp humor.

Addison, Joseph (1672–1719). Poet, dramatist, and prose writer, now chiefly known as coauthor with Richard Steele of *The Spectator* (1711–1714), the first English periodical essay series, which featured gentle satire of rural gentry and urban mores.

Aesthetic irony (sick irony). A kind of dramatic irony in which the intentions that are satirized (by showing how men and women are unable to realize them) are not misguided notions or fads but universal norms such as justice or peace.

Airplane! **(1980).** Classic movie parody written and directed by Jerry Zucker, David Zucker, and Jim Abrahams that used the outline of the disaster movie, especially *Airport* (1970), as the framework for literate, rapid-fire jokes and parodies of the genre's situations and character types.

All in the Family **(1971–1979).** Landmark TV comedy series from producer Norman Lear that rewrote the rules of sitcom content by focusing on the wrong-headed beliefs and outrageous statements of working-class New York City bigot Archie Bunker. The show reflected its volatile social contexts even as it retained the sitcom's conventional forms, presenting Archie as a traditional comic fool and wife Edith as wise and levelheaded.

Allais, Alphonse (1854–1905). French humorist and author of several collections of humorous anecdotes, aphorisms, dialogues, and stories. Works include the humorous anthology *A Se tordre* (1891) and novels such as *L'Affaire blaireau* (The Skunk Affair, 1899), and *Le Boomerang, ou Rien n'est mal qui finit bien* (The Boomerang, or Nothing Is Bad That Ends Well, 1902).

Allen, Woody (1935–). Writer, director, and star of dialogue-driven comedies often centering on his neurotic, urban, Jewish persona. Films range from such early comedies as *Bananas*

(1971) and *Sleeper* (1973) to the Oscar-winning romantic comedy *Annie Hall* (1975) to such later, more bittersweet comedy/dramas as *Manhattan* (1979), *Stardust Memories* (1980), and *Crimes and Misdemeanors* (1989).

Almodóvar, Pedro (1949–). One of Spain's most celebrated directors; also a screenwriter, composer, singer, and actor. His films emblematize the young urban culture of Madrid in its marginality and resistance to mainstream lifestyle. From kitsch to punk, Almodóvar's smart satirical movies have seduced national and international audiences alike. Among his most important films are: *Pepi, Luci, Bom* (1980); *Matador* (1986); *The Law of Desire* (1987); *Women on the Verge of a Nervous Breakdown* (1989), the most successful Spanish film ever. In 2000 his *All about My Mother* won an Oscar for best foreign film, and in 2003 he was awarded his second Oscar for best screenplay for *Talk to Her*.

Ambivalence. Simultaneous and diametric emotional responses to a single stimulus. Dark comedy is powered by the emotional and textual turbulence caused by themes and events that simultaneously foment positive and negative emotions. This can be contrasted with the presence of dark passages in more traditional comedies because in traditional comedy the "dark" and "light" material are not simultaneously present from the same source.

Ameipsias (fl. 423–c. 395 B.C.E.). Premiered a few years after Eupolis and Aristophanes. Although few of his plays survive even in fragments, at least two of his comedies defeated Aristophanes' masterpieces. His *Connus* placed second at the City Dionysia of 423, where Cratinus' *Wine Flask* won and Aristophanes' *Clouds* lost. Connus was Socrates' music teacher; Socrates himself had a role; and the chorus featured a band of sophists. In 414 his *Comastae* robbed Aristophanes' *Birds* of a victory at the City Dionysia.

Amis, Kingsley (1912–1995). English novelist, poet, and critic noted for his antiheroic characters, many of whom came from lower-middle-class or working-class backgrounds. These individuals often discover that despite hard work and effort, they still remain far behind the privileged, who continue to occupy positions of power and influence. Amis is best known for *Lucky Jim* (1953), about a young university lecturer; his many other books include *That Uncertain Feeling* (1955), also about an antihero; *I Like It Here* (1958); *One Fat Englishman* (1960); *Take a Girl Like You* (1960); and *The Anti-Death League* (1966).

***The Andy Griffith Show* (1960–1968).** Classic American TV comedy series that combined the sitcom's three genres of family sitcom, workplace sitcom, and friends-as-family sitcom into one successful whole, unified by a central town (Mayberry, North Carolina) and a central protagonist, Sheriff Andy Taylor (Griffith).

Animal comedy. A style of modern movie comedy, initiated and typified by *Animal House* (1978) and *Porky's* (1981), that emphasizes the sexual and social liberation of groups of young, rowdy men.

Aragon, Louis (1897–1982). Dadaist, surrealist, social realist, poet, essayist, and novelist. Co-founder, with André Breton, of the journal *Littérature* in 1919, and author of *Le paysan de Paris* (1926), *Traité du style* (*Treatise on Style*) (1928), and *Les yeux d'Elsa* (1942), among others. *Traité du style* contains long passages on humor, including what it is and is not.

Aristophanes (c. 440s–c. 338 B.C.E.). Perhaps the most influential Greek comic dramatist of the genre known as old comedy. He belonged to the city deme of Cydathenaeum. Little else is known about Aristophanes' personal life aside from his work in the theater. Although he wrote over forty-four comedies, only eleven of them survive intact: *Acharnians* (Lenaea 425), *Knights* (Lenaea 424), *Clouds* (City Dionysia 423), *Wasps* (Lenaea 422), *Peace* (City Dionysia 421), *Birds* (City Dionysia 414), *Lysistrata* (Lenaea 411), *Thesmophoriazusae* (City Dionysia 411), *Frogs* (Lenaea 405), *Ecclesiazusae* (c. 391), and *Wealth* (388).

Aristotle (384–322 B.C.E.). Greek philosopher and student of Plato. There exist written versions of his lectures on a wide variety of subjects, including logic, metaphysics, natural science, ethics, politics, and the dramatic arts. His influence on medieval European thought was enormous, particularly because of his influence on major theologians of that period. His work is the foundation of much of modern philosophy. Aristotle had a negative view of most humor and comedy, and was a proponent of the Superiority Theory of humor. Works relevant to his philosophy of humor include *Nichomachean Ethics* and *Poetics*.

Austen, Jane (1775–1817). Austen is arguably the most important and most beloved British novelist of all time and certainly the most important novelist of her age. Her six completed novels are: *Sense and Sensibility* (1811), *Pride and Prejudice* (1813), *Mansfield Park* (1814), *Emma* (1816), and *Northanger Abbey* and *Persuasion* (published together and posthumously in 1818). Known primarily for their practice of free and indirect discourse—or more specifically for their omniscient narrator who ranges into the minds of characters while allowing readers to view the same world on more capacious or objective terms—Austen's narratives are also marked by keen and often witty observations of the habits, manners, and materials of country life among the gentry or middle class in the early nineteenth century. Her essentially realistic novels center on domestic life and always involve the progress (or regress) of a heroine (or heroines) toward matrimony.

Auteurism. In the French film journal *Cahiers du Cinéma* in the 1940s and 1950s, French film critics labeled movie directors the *auteurs* ("authors") of their films. A film auteur not only conveyed a personal style, but also had a recognizable mise-en-scène, design, and message. Auteurist cinema is sometimes considered inaccessible to popular audiences, representing art cinema rather than popular entertainment, but this was not the original meaning of the term. The term is evoked in African cinema to demonstrate a cultural link between the stylistic storytelling of the *griot* and the film director as auteur.

Avery, Fred "Tex" (1908–1980). Animator at Warner Bros., MGM, and other studios; creator of Woolfy and the Showgirl, Droopy Dog, Screwball Squirrel, and an important early contributor to Bugs Bunny's personality.

Babcock, Barbara (1943–). Professor of anthropology at the University of Arizona, Babcock has been concerned with the history and ethnography of the Southwest, as well as with a feminist perspective on the history of anthropology (e.g., her book edited with Nancy Parezo called *Daughters of the Desert: Women Anthropologists and the Native American Southwest, 1880–1980*). Her 1975 essay on the trickster gathered together the major scholarship to that time and offered a variety of important perspectives on the subject. Her interest in trickster and related topics is also apparent in the 1978 volume she edited, *The Reversible World: Symbolic Inversion in Art and Society.*

Babuscio, Jack. Prolific writer for the London periodical *Gay News*. Babuscio's "Camp and the Gay Sensibility" (1977) ranks as one of the earliest discussions that takes a close look at camp humor's role in gay male culture.

Bain, Alexander (1818–1903). Scottish psychologist and philosopher who sought physiological explanations for behavior over cognitive or metaphysical ones. He was an opponent of the incongruity theory of humor, most versions of which find that humor is an intellectual recognition of absurdity. He located humor in a physiological release of the stress of everyday life, thus making him a proponent of the relief theory of humor. Works relevant to his philosophy of humor include *The Emotions and the Will* (1859).

Barbour, Douglas (1940–). With Stephen Scobie (1943–), Barbour edited the second significant anthology of Canadian comic verse (following *The Blasted Pine* of 1957), *The Maple Laugh Forever: An Anthology of Canadian Comic Poetry* (1981).

Baroque. A literary and artistic style especially prevalent in France during the first half of the seventeenth century and characterized by movement, instability, and surprise. The fifth act of Pierre Corneille's *Illusion comique* (1636) offers a particularly fine example of the baroque, where Clindor's father and the audience witness Clindor's murder only to be happily disabused on learning *subsequently* that it was only the climax of a tragedy in which Clindor was performing.

Basoche, La. A theatrical troupe in Paris dating from the early fourteenth century; originally a fraternity of lawyers and other legal functionaries. The Clercs de la Basoche (or Bazoche) were of considerable importance in the development of the medieval French comic theater, often pushing their satire on current events to farcical extremes and not infrequently incurring the ire of king and nobles.

Beaumont, Francis (c. 1584–1616). Educated at Oxford and at the Inner Temple, where he was introduced to the law, the theater, and a coterie of sophisticated and witty and satirical young gentlemen. A member of Shakespeare's acting company, the Lord Chamberlain's Men (later, the King's Men), he was noted primarily for his collaborations with John Fletcher and, later, Shakespeare. His solo Jacobean comic masterpiece is *The Knight of the Burning Pestle* (pr. 1613), an exuberant City comedy that can stand as the equal to anything by Ben Jonson. Unlike Fletcher and Shakespeare, Beaumont quit the theater after 1613, having married a wealthy heiress.

Bechdel, Alison (1960–). Comic-strip cartoonist who has drawn *Dykes to Watch Out For* since 1983, presenting issues vital to the lesbian community. The strip combines witty narrative with social satire and stances critical of government policies. *Dykes* appears in mainstream humor journals as well as gay publications. There are ten published collections of her weekly strips.

Beckett, Samuel (1906–1989). Ireland and the world's great absurdist writer. Began as a disciple of James Joyce, but then devoted his career to writing increasingly opposite to Joyce's. Outdid the European Joyce by actually writing many of his major works in French and by winning the Nobel Prize in 1969. Author of such great works as the trilogy of novels *Molloy* (1951), *Malone meurt* (*Malone Dies*, 1951), and *L'innomable* (*The Unnamable*, 1963), and such plays as *En attendant Godot* (*Waiting for Godot*, 1953), and *Fin de partie* (*Endgame*, 1957).

Bedroom farce. A term often used to describe the broadly suggestive farce, especially in mid- and late-nineteenth-century Paris, that originally flourished in the non-government-subsidized theaters of the so-called Boulevard, and that eventually gained official acceptance when crafted by such comic masters as Georges Feydeau. For all their suggestions of naughty physicality, these comedies never went beyond the bounds of acceptable taste and would be considered quaintly tame in comparison with the often no-holds-barred theater of the late twentieth century and today.

Bekolo, Jean-Pierre (1966–). Cameroonian filmmaker whose sardonic humor and avant-garde techniques have made him popular with festival audiences. His first full-length comedy, *Quartier Mozart* (1992), won him an award from the British Film Institute, which then invited him to make a film commemorating cinema's centennial. He wrote and directed *Le Complot d'Aristote* (Aristotle's Plot; Cameroon, 1996), which parodies Aristotle's rhetoric and tells an engaging and satirical tale of filmmaking woes in West Africa.

Bellew, Frank (1823–1888). Did political cartoons for *Harper's Weekly* from 1861 to 1865, thereafter creating nonpolitical illustrations for humor magazines. During the American Civil War he pioneered signed cartoons and an individualistic style, reshaping cartooning aesthetics with simpler and less cluttered images.

Bengough, J. W. (1851–1923). Publisher and editor of *Grip* (1873–1894), nineteenth-century Canada's most important comic magazine. Bengough was also its chief contributor of editorial cartoons.

Bergson, Henri (1859–1941). French philosopher and winner of the 1927 Nobel Prize for literature. Bergson wrote a number of works describing sets of conflicting dualities: the duality of an essential "life force" in all of us and the materiality of the world, and the duality of intuition and intellect. He was especially concerned about the way modernity contributes to a kind of "mechanization" of human life. He was a proponent of an updated version of the superiority theory of humor: laughter is an expression of ridicule of overly mechanized and inflexible attitudes toward life. Works relevant to his philosophy of humor include *Laughter: An Essay on the Meaning of the Comic* (1901).

Bernhard, Sandra (1955–). Comic and actress Bernhard's concert film, *Without You, I'm Nothing* (1990), is a contemporary camp masterpiece. Bernhard sifts through the stuff of popular culture, from music to gender roles, and deconstructs them with heavy streaks of irony.

Bierce, Ambrose (1842–1914?). American journalist and fiction writer whose experiences in the American Civil War shaped his mordant view of life. His most famous work, *The Devil's Dictionary* (1911), is a bitterly satirical lexicon based on journalistic items he had written over his lifetime.

Black humor. Literary genre generally dating from the 1950s in which comic or farcical elements are juxtaposed with absurd or bizarre touches to produce a shocking, incongruous effect. Though the genre's progenitors can be said to include such varied figures as Rabelais, Jonathan Swift, Voltaire, and Eugène Ionesco, among others, writers since the 1960s such as Vladimir Nabokov, Joseph Heller, Kurt Vonnegut, and Thomas Pynchon and entertainers such as Lenny Bruce, are often mentioned as writers of black humor because of their ability to combine morbid, obscene, or absurd elements with comic or farcical ones to produce shocking, disturbing, or especially incongruous effects.

Blackout Gags; also called Spot or Sight Gags. A visual image that serves to punctuate a gag, often in the form of a literal pun or metaphor. These often parodied live-action shorts like newsreels and travelogues.

Boas, Franz (1858–1942). Generally regarded as the founder of professional, university-based anthropology in the United States. His publications are voluminous and include a considerable number of collections of folktales and myths of indigenous peoples of the United States and Canada and many studies of indigenous languages. It seems most likely today that Boas was the first to use the term *trickster*, in his 1898 introduction to a collection of Thompson River Indian tales collected and published by James Teit, a Native intellectual trained by Boas.

Bookooing. The practice of loud talking, bullying, or woofing in African American vernacular culture (as defined by Zora Neale Hurston).

Boucicault, Dion (1820–1890). Most celebrated Irish playwright of the mid-nineteenth century. Born in Dublin, he achieved his greatest successes in London and New York and is best remembered today for his "stage-Irish" trilogy *The Colleen Bawn* (1860), *Arrah-na-Pogue* (1864), and *The Shaughraun* (1875).

Boughedir, Ferid (1950–). Tunisian critic and filmmaker whose first feature, *Halfouine* (1990), was a humorous coming-of-age story about twelve-year-old Noura, at the threshold of manhood, who must decide if he will remain in the protective women's world of his childhood or engage in the tough environment of adolescent males. It was a popular success, breaking all previous box office records in Tunisia. Boughedir has been writing criticism since the early 1980s, is the author of numerous books on the history of African cinema, including *Le Cinéma Africain de A à Z* (1987), and is a professor of cinema studies at the University of Tunis.

Bradbury, Malcolm (1932–2000). English novelist, critic, and playwright whose books probe wittily and satirically into problems of moral responsibility and the clash between basic humanistic decency and goodwill, on the one hand, and the frequent indifference to these values and desires on the other. Bradbury's characters, often in a university setting, try to change their worlds and lives in one absurdly exaggerated situation after another. These cameo situations add up to suggest major lacks of understanding or communication or competence, whether in personal relations, academic governance, political or governmental squabbles, or any other venal or meretricious conflict with moral overtones. Bradbury's many novels include *Eating People Is Wrong* (1959), *Stepping Westward* (1965), *The History Man* (1975), and *Rates of Exchange* (1983); his nonfiction includes *The Social Context of Modern English Literature* (1971), *Possibilities: Essays on the State of the Novel* (1973), and *The Modern American Novel* (1983).

Breathed, Berke (1957–). Created outrage over the surreal social and political satire in his comic strips *Bloom County* (1980–1989) and *Outland* (1990–1994), especially when he won the Pulitzer Prize for political cartooning in 1987. His defense against his editorial cartoonist critics appeared in *The Comics Journal* 125 (October 1988).

Breton, André (1896–1966). Poet, essayist, critic, author of the first *Surrealist Manifesto*

(1924), *Nadja* (1928), and *L'amour fou* (1937), and editor of *L'anthologie d'humour noir* (*Anthology of Black Humor*) (1947).

Bright, Deborah (1950–). Art photographer and scholar. Bright's photography series *Dream Girls* commits the high camp gesture of appropriating Hollywood movie stills and ironizing them. She implants a lesbian gaze into the photos, humorously disrupting the heterosexist assumptions of classic films.

Brooks, Mel (1926–). Writer/director of comic movies, especially such genre parodies as *Blazing Saddles* (1974), a western parody; followed by *Young Frankenstein* (1974), a monster movie parody; *Silent Movie* (1976), a silent comedy parody; *High Anxiety* (1978), a Hitchcock parody; and *Spaceballs* (1987), a *Star Wars* parody.

Bruce, Lenny (1925–1966). Born Leonard Schneider, a stand-up comic and author arrested repeatedly for the obscenity of his nightclub act. Many artists, performers, and critics consider Bruce a martyr for enabling his many successors to explore sex and ethnicity more candidly than had been allowed before the 1960s.

Burlesque. A broad but generally unfocused form of satire. Burlesques are similar to parodies in that they mock forms of "high art," but they do not sustain that connection and tend instead to develop in ludicrous directions, using distortion or exaggeration.

Butler, Samuel (1612–1680). Poet and satirist known for his mock-heroic poem *Hudibras* (1663; part 2, 1664, part 3, 1678) attacking the Puritan Party in the English Civil War.

Byron, George Gordon, Lord (1788–1824). The most flamboyant and popular of the British romantic poets (William Blake, Samuel Taylor Coleridge, John Keats, Percy Shelley, and William Wordsworth), Byron was also the most notorious. Shortly after the publication of his wildly popular *Childe Harold's Pilgrimage 1–2* (1812) and "Eastern Tales" (1813–1814), he was separated from his wife (the former Annabella Milbanke) of only one year and left England for good under the cloud of scandal in 1816. He wrote copiously while in exile in Italy, completing the final cantos of *Childe Harold's Pilgrimage* (1816–1818) in addition to other important works, including the dramas *Manfred* (1817), *Sardanapalus* (1821), and *Cain* (1821). His most important work during this interval was the comical/satirical epic *Don Juan*, which he began in 1819, published in installments over the next five years, and was at work on at the time of his death. Byron died in Greece at Missolonghi, where he was assembling an army to help the Greeks in their fight for independence from the Turks.

Caldecott Medal. A medal named in honor of nineteenth-century English illustrator Randolph Caldecott. It is awarded annually by the Association for Library Service to Children, a division of the American Library Association, to the artist of the most distinguished American picture book for children.

Camp humor. Revolving around a humorous approach to serious matters. Camp humor allows serious ideas to slip by hostile eyes in the form of frivolity. Camp humor combines self-parody with an ironic, often biting take on matters. Camp humor served queers before Stonewall (1969) as a shield against a hostile world while also commenting critically on that world.

Capp, Al (1909–1979). Created *Li'l Abner* from 1934 to 1977. At one time it was the most read and respected comic strip in America, entering national folklore and making both Capp and his creations larger than life. A witty populist spokesman, he appeared on radio and television and was treated as a pundit. His political and social stances made him at first the darling of liberals and later of conservatives.

Caricature. A work of art or literature that humorously ridicules a person or type through exaggeration and distortion. Polemical political cartoons often caricature opposition figures by placing them in ludicrous situations and portraying them in a recognizable but unflattering light.

Carrey, Jim (1962–). Leading physical comic since his debut in *Ace Ventura: Pet Detective* in 1994, whose rubber face and pretzel body have expressed a string of outsiders and misfits, from *Ace Ventura*, *Ace Ventura: When Nature Calls* (1995), and *Dumb and Dumber* (1994) to such seriocomic turns as the asocial, embittered *Cable Guy* (1996) and the real-life misfit comic Andy Kaufman in *Man on the Moon* (1999).

Carroll, Lewis (1832–1898). The pen name of Oxford mathematician Charles Lutwidge Dodgson. His best known works, *Alice's Adventures in Wonderland* (1865) and *Through the Looking-Glass* (1872), are dream visions intended for children. Both works are rich in fantasy and nonsense, with elaborate wordplay and plays on logical reasoning. Carroll also parodies didactic Victorian poetry. He wrote humorous verse, such as *The Hunting of the Snark* (1876), and other books for children, notably *Sylvie and Bruno* (1889) and *Sylvie and Bruno Concluded* (1893). He was an important photographer, especially of children.

Catch-22. From Joseph Heller's *Catch-22* (1963), in which the protagonist, Yossarian, discovers that an official order, Catch-22, dictates that a pilot has to be crazy to be grounded. Yossarian reasons that he must be crazy to keep risking his life by flying bombing missions. But if a pilot asks to be grounded, that shows he is *not* crazy, so he must continue flying. The phrase has entered the lexicon, meaning (a) a situation in which a desired outcome or solution is impossible to attain because of a set of inherently illogical rules or conditions, or (b) rules or conditions that create such a situation:

Cels. Transparent celluloid sheets that replaced transparent paper as the principal material for animation. These enable different sheets, with different parts of the character, props or background, to be laid over each other, and then photographed frame by frame. Invented by Earl Hurd as a time-saving device.

Cervantes Saavedra, Miguel de (1547–1616). Spain's most famous and accomplished author, who wrote *Don Quijote* and numerous plays, exemplary and picaresque novellas, and poems. Cervantes had a life of adversity: escaping poverty, he joined the military, only to lose his left hand while fighting against the Turks in the battle of Lepanto (1571). On his way home, he was accosted by Barbary pirates and then held captive in Algiers for five years. Cervantes was never able to escape this life of privation and poverty even when he achieved fame with the first part of the *Quijote*. Considered the first modern novel, the influence *Don Quijote* has had in literature can be traced through the centuries until today. In this text, Cervantes demystifies both authorship and authority through his playful narration, structured by the recovery of lost manuscripts, hearsay, and imagination.

Chaplin, Charlie (1889–1977). One of the great movie icons, Charlie Chaplin mixed physical comedy, social commentary, and poignant storytelling in films that often spotlighted conflict between a callous upper class and a noble, striving lower class of workers, immigrants, and tramps. Chaplin's great films ranged from the early masterpiece *The Gold Rush* (1925) to the sentimental dramas *City Lights* (1931) and *Limelight* (1952) to the social satires *Modern Times* (1936), *The Great Dictator* (1940), and *Monsieur Verdoux* (1947).

Chappelle, Dave (1973–). Creator and star of the eponymous sketch show who is carrying the baton of Richard Pryor and Chris Rock. Chappelle, an African American, pushes all the buttons smartly, without resorting to wall-to-wall obscenities. The political commentary on his half-hour Comedy Central show pulls no punches. The sketches pick at everyone from accused R&B singer R. Kelly to former U.S. secretary of state Colin Powell, while turning conventional ideas about race relations upside down.

Chaucer, Geoffrey (c. 1340–1400). English poet, author of lyrics, dream-visions, *Troilus and Criseyde*, and *The Canterbury Tales* (unfinished at his death). Chaucer was a courtier and administrator who served the royal court and who traveled to France, Italy, Spain, and Flanders on official duties. From those journeys he brought back with him to England an awareness and often texts of the new writers, forms, and literary ideas flowering on the Continent. The poets of fifteenth-century England thought of him as the father of English poetry.

***Cheers* (1982–1993).** Classic American TV comedy about the workers and patrons of a Boston bar that exemplified both workplace and friends-as-family sitcom genres.

Chekhov, Anton (1860–1904). Russian playwright, short-story writer, and doctor. The son of a former serf, Chekhov was born in the Crimea, on the Black Sea, studied medicine in Moscow, and eventually became associated with the Moscow Art Theater. He started writing humorous sketches early but also experimented with theater. His full-length plays—notably *The Seagull* (1898), *Uncle Vanya* (1899), *Three Sisters* (1901), and *The Cherry Orchard* (1904)—innovatively combine tragic and sentimental issues with realistically comic and farcical elements. Chekhov's techniques have greatly influenced mid- and late-twentieth-century drama. David Mamet's adaptation of *Uncle Vanya* (1988) is the text used by director Louis Malle in his film *Uncle Vanya on 42nd Street*.

Chesnutt, Charles W. (1858–1932). Teacher, lawyer, businessman, and writer, Chesnutt was born in Cleveland as the son of free black parents and came of age in Fayetteville, North Carolina. After a teaching career in the Carolinas, he moved to New York City in 1883 and worked as a Wall Street stenographer and reporter. He returned to Cleveland in 1884 and began writing. He passed the Ohio bar in 1887 and built a court-reporting business. *The Conjure Woman* stories (1899) are humorously ironic, while the stories collected in *The Wife of His Youth, and Other Stories of the Color Line* (1899) explore many of the painful ironies in the lives of American mulattoes. His two novels, *The House behind the Cedars* (1900) and *The Marrow of Tradition* (1901), were controversial for their realistic treatments of racism in America. Nonfiction works include the biography *Frederick Douglass* (1899), "What Is a White Man?" (1889, for the New York *Independent*), "The Disfranchisement of the Negro" (1903), "Peonage; or, The New Slavery" (1904, *Voice of the Negro*), and "Post-Bellum—Pre-Harlem" (1931, for *Colophon* and *Crisis*).

Chrétien de Troyes (c. 1140–c. 1200). French poet active in the late twelfth century, presumably at Troyes, the court of Champagne. His patron was the countess Marie de Champagne, daughter of Eleanor of Aquitaine, with her first husband, Louis VII of France. Chrétien is considered the father of Arthurian romance on the basis of his five surviving works in that genre: *Erec and Enide* (written ca. 1170), *Cliges* (written in the mid-1170s), *The Knight of the Cart* (now known as *Lancelot*, written in the late 1170s), *The Knight with the Lion* (or *Yvain*, early 1180s), and *The Story of the Grail* (or *Perceval*, from the late 1180s or early 1190s). He established the form of Arthurian romance by involving the stories and legends of Arthur with the ideals of chivalry and courtesy, the narrative pattern of the development of the hero, the psychology of love, the relationship of love and chivalry, and, in his unfinished final work, the mysteries of the Grail.

Chutzpah. Yiddish word now popular among English speakers denoting offensive boldness, especially verbal effrontery. A famous example is the child who kills his parents and then demands sympathy for being an orphan.

Cibber, Colley (1671–1757). Foremost comic actor of his day, dramatist, and poet laureate of England. Originated the character of Sir Novelty Fashion in his plays *Love's Last Shift* (1696) and *The Careless Husband* (1704), and played him in Sir John Vanbrugh's sequel, *The Relapse* (1616), as Lord Foppington.

City comedy. A type of comedy identified by Brian Gibbons (*Jacobean City Comedy*, 1968), focusing on plays whose setting and subject both were the City of London. It is characteristically concerned with the darker or satirical face of comedy, attending to a social, economic, and political discontent that would lead ultimately to the English Civil War. Its principal dramatists were John Marston, Thomas Middleton, Francis Beaumont, and, most of all, Ben Jonson.

City Dionysia. The most important dramatic festival in Athens in the fifth and fourth centuries B.C.E., a five-day event held sometime during March or April in the Theater of Dionysus, an open-air structure located on the south slope of the Acropolis. It attracted a national audience and provided Athens with the opportunity to showcase to non-Athenians the performances of its best producers, playwrights, actors, choral singers, and dancers.

Claymation. Short for *clay animation*, a form of 3-D animation made from plasticine, not clay. Used by Art Clokey for his TV character Gumby (1956) as well as by Nick Park and Peter Lord (*Chicken Run*, 2000) and other animators. Claymation is a process patented by animator Will Vinton, who with Bill Gardiner made the Academy Award–winning short *Closed Mondays* (1974).

Clemens, Samuel Langhorne. *See* Twain, Mark.
CODCO. A satirical, outlandish Newfoundland comedy theater troupe originally composed (1973) of Paul Sametz, Robert Joy, Diane Olsen, Cathy Jones, Andy Jones, Mary Walsh, Greg Malone, and Tommy Sexton. CODCO (Cod Company) was subsequently a TV show until 1993.
Cohen, Ted (1939). A professor of philosophy at the University of Chicago, Cohen is a specialist in aesthetics and author of *Jokes* and the chapter on humor in *The Routledge Companion to Aesthetics*. Cohen is a proponent of the incongruity theory of humor. He argues that incongruity can have either of two effects on us: to inspire a feeling of freedom or a feeling of willing acceptance of powerlessness. Either of these can give rise to pleasure associated with humor.
Cohl, Emile (1857–1938). Creator of *Fantasmagorie* (1908), arguably the first animated cartoon, and an important pioneer French animator who created 250 animated films between 1908 and 1921.
Comedia nueva. A new kind of theatrical genre characteristic of the Spanish golden age introduced by Félix Lope de Vega Carpio.
Comedy of humors. Principally developed by Ben Jonson, this type of comedy was based on the ancient and medieval physiological theory of four cardinal humors or bodily fluids (blood, phlegm, black bile, and yellow bile) whose imbalance in the body determined both physical condition and behavior. An excess of one fluid produced the particular personality trait associated with it: thus too much blood made one "sanguine" (from the Latin *sanguis*, "blood"), excessively cheerful or optimistic; too much phlegm made one sluggish or apathetic ("phlegmatic"); black bile produced melancholy, and yellow bile produced choler, or bad temper. Jonson exploited this popular notion throughout his comedies and outlined its application in the "Induction" to *Every Man in His Humour*. It is interesting to note that the use of the word *humor* to mean something that produces laughter is not found until the 1680s (*OED*, def. #7).
Comedy of manners. Plays, poems, or novels that depict social mores and morals peculiar to a particular period, often in a critical or satirical way. Some examples from the Restoration are William Wycherley's *The Plain Dealer* (1677) and William Congreve's *The Way of the World* (1700).
Comenius, John Amos (1592–1670). Born Jan Komensky in Moravia, Comenius developed a system of education that he hoped would help achieve universal peace by unlocking the confusing aspects of language and creating better interpersonal communication. Important to comedy is *Orbis sensualium pictus* (*The World around Us in Pictures*, 1659), also the first illustrated book written and published for children.
Commedia dell'arte. Developed around the middle of the sixteenth century in Italy, where actors, unlike their English counterparts, had formed their own guild and were thus the earliest Renaissance professionals in the craft. Their plays were based on stock characters and basic scenarios, with improvised dialogue. Its stock types and plots frequently included a pair of young lovers, aided by a clever servant (*arlecchino*, or harlequin), whose union was resisted by a rich and foolish old father (*pantalone*, or pantaloon). Itinerant *commedia* troupes were extremely popular throughout Europe and had an important influence upon William Shakespeare, Ben Jonson, and their contemporaries in England.
Congreve, William (1670–1729). Preeminent comic dramatist of the late Restoration whose first play, *The Old Batchelor* (1692), was called by John Dryden the best first play he had ever read. His later plays such as *Love for Love* (1694) and *The Way of the World* (1700) are considered the high point of Restoration comic wit.
Cooper, James Fenimore (1789–1851). The first successful American novelist, Cooper grew up on Otsego Lake, New York, the son of a wealthy Quaker landholder. In 1806 he became a sailor after expulsion from Yale, and in 1808, a midshipman in the U.S. Navy. *The Spy* (1821), a historical romance set during the American Revolution, opened up new sociopolit-

ical materials for American fiction that he continued to mine in the five Natty Bumppo or *Leatherstocking Tales*, published between 1823 (*The Pioneers*) and 1841 (*The Deerslayer*). Of these, *The Last of the Mohicans* (1826) was most popular at home and abroad. *The Pilot* (1824) and *The Red Rover* (1828) established the subgenre of American sea fiction. He also wrote two historical novels set in seventeenth-century New England and a trilogy set in Europe: *The Bravo* (Italy), *The Heidenmauer* (Switzerland), and *The Headsman* (Rhine Valley). His nonfiction prose includes a history of the U.S. Navy, a travel book that humorously mocks European accounts of American society (*Notions of the Americans* 1828), and a discussion of the American political system, *The American Democrat* (1838).

Cooper, Mary (?–1761). Mary Cooper collected and published *Tommy Thumb's Pretty Song Book* (1744), the earliest extant book of nursery rhymes. The collection, intended for children, includes a number of truly bawdy rhymes and is important because it is one of the earliest texts that makes this humor available to children.

Corneille, Pierre (1606–1684). A long-standing French tradition (one that found expression by the late seventeenth century) makes Corneille and Jean Racine (1639–1699) the two uncontested creators and unequaled exemplars of national tragedy: Corneille stressing a rational, self-controlled, heroic vision, Racine one of all-consuming, catastrophic passion. However valid this perspective may be, like all sweeping generalizations, it paints with a broad stroke that obscures the finer distinctions. Thus, in Corneille's case, it ignores his plays that cannot be classified as tragic: the youthful tragicomedy *Clitandre* (1630), the spectacle-oriented "machine" plays, and, above all, his eight early love comedies, instrumental in adapting the pastoral structure to contemporary expectations. This same critical tradition neglects, furthermore, the clear baroque tendency in the Cornelian worldview, particularly strong in the period before Louis XIV's long reign (1643–1715).

Cosby Show, The **(1984–1992).** The dominant American TV comedy series of the 1980s traced the generation gaps among a cranky doctor father (Bill Cosby), his regally elegant lawyer wife (Phylicia Rashad), and their five very independent children. Cosby mastered the art of seeming put-upon by his childrens' behavior and attitudes, finding numerous new twists and facial expressions to augment the stock character of the besieged-by-his-family sitcom dad.

Court masque. Like the *commedia dell'arte*, the masque originated in Renaissance Italy and flourished at the English court throughout the Elizabethan, Jacobean, and Caroline periods. Based on thin plots loosely constructed around mythological or allegorical figures, its real "mythology" was the glory of the monarch and his or her court. Masques were extravagant, expensive productions combining music, poetry, dance, elaborate costumes, and spectacle; performers were often amateur actors, sometimes courtiers, wearing masks. In England, the undisputed master of the masque was Ben Jonson, whose scripts were supported by the elaborate and, for their time, mechanically and technologically sophisticated set designs of the architect Inigo Jones. Notable examples of their collaboration include *The Masque of Blackness* (1605), *The Masque of Beauty* (1608), and *The Masque of Queens* (1609).

Coyote. Coyote is probably the character who appears most frequently in trickster stories in those parts of the United States where coyotes live. He can change shape and sex or make himself invisible, and, like other tricksters, he is amoral, bawdy, and lustful, and usually indifferent to the consequences of his actions. Nonetheless—another quality he shares with other tricksters—he has extraordinary, even godlike powers, and is responsible for much of what we know today as *culture*.

Crates (fl. c. 450–430 B.C.E.). Composed comedies that featured banquets and symposia instead of references to contemporary individuals. Celebratory scenes of this sort certainly became stock features of old comedy at the end of the fifth century and contributed to the tradition of featuring a cook or mad chef in middle comedy and new comedy. Crates was also credited with creating more universal plots and moving the genre away from *ad hominem* attacks. His *Animals*, for example, imagined what would happen if humans were forced to stop consuming animals as food.

Cratinus (fl. c. 453–423 B.C.E.). Aristophanes' most formidable predecessor and the fiercest competitor of his early career. In 430 B.C.E. Cratinus staged his *Dionysalexandros*, one of our most complete fragmentary comedies. It draws its plot from the mythological tale of the Judgment of Paris. However, Cratinus' most interesting play was not this mythological burlesque but the semiautobiographical comedy *Wine Flask*, which won the comic competition at the City Dionysia of 423 B.C.E., the same festival where Aristophanes' *Clouds* finished last.

Cuckold. A man whose wife has committed adultery. Early modern plays refer repeatedly to cuckoldry; Shakespeare's comedies focusing on this issue include *Much Ado about Nothing*, *Merry Wives of Windsor*, *Cymbeline*, and *Winter's Tale*. The term refers to the cuckoo, a tufted bird that lays eggs in other birds' nests (connecting to the dynastic worries of men with unfaithful wives). Words associated with cuckoldry are *horns*, *forehead*, and the like (from the cuckoo's tufts). Cuckoldry is a gendered term that has meaning for anxious men in a strongly patriarchal society. If a man commits adultery, his wife is not cuckolded.

Dadaism. Movement in art and literature that established itself in several European capitals and in New York after World War I. Works of the Dadaists were published in several reviews including *Dada*, *391*, *Littérature*, and *Proverbe*. Dadaists, with their destructive and provocative humor, include Louis Aragon, Marcel Duchamp, Tristan Tzara, Francis Picabia, and Hans Arp. The movement began to die in the early 1920s, and many members became affiliated with André Breton's surrealists.

Dancourade. A one-act French comedy, so called for its master exponent Florent Carton, sieur Dancourt (1661–1725). Rather casual and slapdash, the *dancourade* has only the flimsiest, most intermittent of plots, often based on current events. These little plays do offer, nevertheless, a lively dialogue and illustrate the cynicism so prevalent in the second half of Louis XIV's reign (1680–1715).

Dark comedy. John L. Styan's term for modern tragicomedy, a type of play that flirts with both tragedy and comedy but refuses to be either one. Dark comedy is by turns (and at once) comic and serious, incongruous and moving. Mixed moods and techniques, such as absurdities undermining naturalistic elements, tend to distinguish modern dark comedy from traditional tragicomedy, a drama that moves toward tragic conflict but averts catastrophe.

Dard, Frédéric (San Antonio; 1921–2000). A writer of humorous detective fiction, Dard was the undisputed king of the pun and word games in French fiction. Over 20,000 neologisms have been found in his work, which includes some 300 titles, 175 of which were signed San Antonio.

Darling, Jay "Ding" (1876–1962). A genial conservative who worked for the *Des Moines Register* from 1906 to 1949, anecdotal about politics and nostalgic about small-town America but becoming a League of Nations crusader and an avid conservationist who founded the National Wildlife Federation. He helped continue a lighter approach to political cartooning into the twentieth century.

Davies, Robertson (1913–1995). One of Canada's premier men of letters through the middle of the twentieth century, Davies was born in Thamesville, Ontario. He began as a journalist, and his columns collected in *The Diaries of Samuel Marchbanks* (1947) and *The Table Talk of Samuel Marchbanks* (1949) are a trove of satire of middle-Canadian (Ontario) society. He conceived of most of his major novels in groups of three, and the first of these, the so-called Salterton trilogy—*Tempest-Tost* (1951), *Leaven of Malice* (1954), and *A Mixture of Frailties* (1958)—remains his greatest purely comic achievement.

Dead baby jokes. A large (nearly inexhaustible) category of simple (some would say puerile, some would say horridly vulgar) jokes in which some graphic and mortal harm comes to an infant in the form of a punch line. While they are not, even in the most liberal atmospheres, generally considered to be of scholarly interest, they nevertheless potently and concisely foment the important issues related to dark comedy. Essentially, they are sick jokes, the simplest form of ambivalence-producing comedy in that the same joke simultaneously conjures disgust from tragedy and laughter from comedy.

Debate Poem. A literary form in which two or more speakers take opposing sides and dispute a particular subject or range of subjects. In the Middle English poem *The Owl and the Nightingale* the disputants are birds who are emblematic of their respective positions; in the Middle English poem *Winner and Waster* they are allegorical human knights.

Débrouillardise. Otherwise known in French as *Système-D*, the art of being resourceful or hustling to survive. In popular comedies, it defines the comic hero's quality of knowing how to get by, extricating him- or herself from uncomfortable situations, and reaching goals through manipulation and street smarts.

Deconstruction. A subversive rhetorical device described by Jacques Derrida and others that questions prior belief systems. Instead of offering a single, "correct" vision of truth, deconstruction holds that truth is many-faceted, and that for the many facets of truth to be understood or constructed, the single version of truth needs to be deconstructed. Rather than being interested in preserving and empowering the canon, deconstructionists are interested in expanding the canon to include the perspectives of people of different genders, ethnicities, ages, social strata, geographies, times, and so forth.

Dekker, Thomas (1572?–1632?). In contrast to many of his fellow Elizabethan/Jacobean playwrights, not much is known about Dekker's life, his family, or his education; our sense of him must come from his plays. Some of his more successful contemporaries thought he was no better than a hack, collaborating on or contributing to more than sixty plays in his lifetime. Caught up in a nasty professional rivalry known as the War of the Theaters (to which Dekker contributed, probably in collaboration with John Marston, a play called *Satiromastix*, primarily a retaliatory attack on Ben Jonson for his satirically competitive *Poetaster* [1601]), Dekker was a prolific writer who never seemed to make enough money to keep him out of debtors' prison, where he spent nearly seven years from 1612 onward. His best-known plays are *The Shoemaker's Holiday* (1599), which owes a great deal to Greene's *Friar Bacon and Friar Bungay* (c. 1589), and a late Jacobean play, *The Witch of Edmonton* (c. 1621).

DeMille, James (1833–1880). Late nineteenth-century Canada's most prolific comic novelist, DeMille is best known for the fantastical *A Strange Manuscript Found in a Copper Cylinder* (1888), which is set in a lost Antarctic world where the values of Judeo-Christian civilization are inverted to splendid satiric effect.

Deus ex machina. In the theater of classical antiquity, a divinity (*deus*) descending to the stage in a movable "prop" (*machina*), such as a cloud or chariot, for the purpose of resolving an irreconcilable conflict created by the plot. This Latin expression has come to mean any contrived expedient, in particular an authority figure, introduced at the last moment to provide a convenient though improbable way out of the dramatic impasse. Louis XIV's divinelike intervention at the end of Molière's *Tartuffe* (1664–1669) is an example.

Dick Van Dyke Show, The **(1961–1966).** American TV comedy series that broke new ground by rejecting the model of an older, clueless dad with several children leaving each day for a mystery job in favor of a younger, hipper, urbane father with an attractive wife and a single child working in an exciting TV job that was as integrated into the show as the protagonist's family life. Like the previous decade's *I Love Lucy* (1951–1957), it included, and thereby helped to initiate, all six of the TV sitcom's defining themes: marriage, family, workplace, friends-as-family, women/mothers, and men/fathers.

Diegetic/nondiegetic. The term is derived from *diegesis*, "story." In films, diegetic sound is sound derived from the world of the story (e.g., footsteps, dialogue), whereas nondiegetic sound is the soundtrack.

Dietrich, Marlene (1901–1992). A movie star in the 1930s and 1940s who held a secret appeal for lesbian audiences reading between the lines of her characters, who often dressed in men's clothes and appeared to be bisexual. Dietrich's ironic attitude has kept her in the unofficial camp pantheon. See the film *The Meeting of Two Queens* (1992) for a fond, campy remembrance of both Dietrich and Greta Garbo as lesbian camp icons.

Disney, Walt (1901–1966). Influential pioneer and founder with his brother Roy Disney of Walt

Disney studios. Pioneered personality animation, animated realism, the multiplane camera, and the development of feature animation beginning with *Snow White and the Seven Dwarfs* (1937).

Displeasure. One of the fundamental motives for engaging in camp humor and one of the common aesthetic strategies undertaken by deliberately camp works of art.

Divine (1945–1988). Born Harris Glenn Milstead in Baltimore, Maryland, a drag queen best known for her breakthrough performances in John Waters' movies *Pink Flamingos* (1972), *Female Trouble* (1974), *Polyester* (1981), and *Hairspray* (1988). A preeminent camp ironist, Divine played characters based upon Hollywood genre film-types: the femme fatale, the troubled teenager, and the bored middle-class housewife.

Doppelganger. A rhetorical device whereby a single character is duplicated. This duplicated character can be a mirror image of itself, as with Tweedledum and Tweedledee or Rosencrantz and Guildenstern. This duplicated character can also be an alter ego of itself, as with Dr. Jekyl and Mr. Hyde or Dorian Gray and the picture of Dorian Gray.

Double Exposure. A long-running Canadian radio and TV show focusing on political satire and performed by impressionists Bob Robertson and Linda Cullen.

Double registre. A literary technique identified and fully explored by the late Swiss critic Jean Rousset (1910–2002). Most frequently utilized in love comedies by Pierre Marivaux (1688–1763), the *double registre* depicts alternately the growing affection felt by both masters and servants—with humorous differences in refinement (but *not* sincerity) reflecting class distinctions. An embryonic *double registre* is already at work in Pierre Corneille's *Suite du Menteur* (1643), where subalternate Cliton and Lyse begin to experience an attraction similar to that of their employers Dorante and Mélisse.

DOUBLE TAKE. The act of taking a second look at something or someone, usually with a marked physical reaction—surprise, rage, and so forth, often with eyes popping, face turning red, and (in animated works) smoke coming from the head. It is often used in cartoons.

Doyle, Roddy (1958–). A Dublin schoolteacher turned novelist. Doyle worte the popular and critically acclaimed novels *The Commitments* (1987), *The Snapper* (1990), *The Van* (1991), and *Paddy Clarke Ha Ha Ha* (1993). The first two were turned into very successful movies.

Dr. Seuss (1904–1991). Born Theodore Seuss Geisel, Seuss was an author and illustrator of unusual nonsense books for children. His books broke records on the *New York Times* adult bestseller list and were translated into as many as twenty languages. Seuss is famous for rejecting the primers of the 1950s, substituting for them easy readers of his own, the first of which was his famous *The Cat in the Hat* (1967). Seuss thought that reading could be humorous and educational at the same time and broke the ground so that other writers could produce creative texts. In *The Cat in the Hat*, two children left alone for the day are encouraged by a mysterious visitor to break all the household rules. Other important works are *Green Eggs and Ham* (1960), *Horton Hatches the Egg* (1940), and *How the Grinch Stole Christmas* (1957).

Dr. Strangelove; or, How I Learned to Stop Worrying and Love the Bomb **(1964).** Classic political satire directed and cowritten by Stanley Kubrick, in which an ill-motivated attack on the Soviet Union threatens to end all human life. The film turned the anxieties of the nuclear age into farce and black comedy, exaggerating cold war fears by taking them to their logical, if terrifying, conclusion, at which nuclear "deterrence" winds up eradicating all the life it is designed to protect.

Dramatic irony. A series of events in a work in which the actions of the characters brings about a resolution that is opposite to their intention. There is a preponderance of confusion between dramatic irony and things such as poetic justice, circumstance, and tragedy. For example, if a used-car salesman is hit by a car crossing the street, this is simply unfortunate. If the car salesman is hit by a car he himself has sold, this is circumstance. If the car salesman is hit because it is has faulty brakes, much like the junkers he sells at his business, this is poetic justice. Even if one of the cars he has sold hits him, it is still most likely not irony. However, if the car salesman is on foot deliberately to avoid the dangers of driving when he is struck and killed by the car, that is authentic dramatic irony.

Dream-vision. A favorite literary form of the Middle Ages. The narrator falls asleep and dreams that he is in an allegorical landscape peopled with allegorical figures with whom he converses. The dreamer awakens from the dream with a changed outlook on something troubling. The form has its roots in Latin literature, and though it was known in Old English literature (e.g., *The Dream of the Rood*), the thirteenth-century French *Romance of the Rose* was the important influence on Middle English literature, especially on Geoffrey Chaucer, whose early works were dream-visions (e.g., *The Parlement of Foules*).

Dryden, John (1631–1700). The greatest English poet, satirist, translator, and dramatist of the Restoration, and poet laureate from 1668 to 1688. *Macflecknoe* (1676) and *Absalom and Achitophel* (1681) are the two best verse satires of the period.

Duncan, Sarah Jeannette (1861–1922). Prolific journalist Duncan was humorous in everything she wrote; her main contributions to the continuum of Canadian comedy were her "Saunterings" columns for *The Week* (1883–1896) and her novel *The Imperialist* (1904), which gently satirizes the social and political doings of a small Ontario city at the turn of the last century.

Durang, Christopher (1949–). American playwright and actor raised in suburban New Jersey and educated at Harvard University and the Yale Drama School. His plays satirize, often savagely, church power and hypocrisy (*The Nature and Purpose of the Universe*, 1971; *Sister Mary Ignatius Explains It All to You*, 1979), middle-class American family life (*The Vietnamization of New Jersey*, 1977; *The Marriage of Bette and Boo*, 1985), and psychotherapy and dating (*Beyond Therapy*, 1982). *Betty's Summer Vacation* (1999) tests theories of savage farce and the limits of sensibility. Durang's introductions to his plays explain the careful balance he means to strike between preposterous violence and poignant sympathy.

Dylan, Bob (1941–). Born Robert Zimmerman. Founding father of folk-rock and a leading figure in the upsurge of protest songs in the 1960s, considered by many the voice of his generation, Dylan wrote many songs characterized by wordplay, sarcasm, and comically incongruous juxtaposition.

Edgeworth, Maria (1767–1849). The first great Irish novelist. Although she could not vote, being a woman, she changed the course of literature and history. Her father was Richard Lovell Edgeworth, an influential Anglo-Irish educator who moved with his family to an estate in County Longford in 1782 that he and Maria turned into an unusually progressive place. Maria collaborated with him on *Essays on Practical Education* (1797) and *Essays on Irish Bulls* (1803). She is best known for her novella *Castle Rackrent* (1800) and its longer though less compelling Irish sequels, *Ennui* (1809), *The Absentee* (1812), and *Ormond* (1817).

Entremés. The Spanish term for a comic, usually farcical, interlude in the medieval religious *autos sacramentales*. Like the French (and, subsequently, English) term *farce* ("stuffing"), its meaning ("side dish") stems from a culinary metaphor, suggesting that such comic interludes were "stuffed" into more serious dramatic offerings, usually of a biblical or hagiographic nature.

Esperpento. Colloquially meaning ugly or ridiculous, as well as absurd or nonsensical, the term was coined by Ramón del Valle-Inclán to represent reality with all its grotesque and tragic contradictions. The *esperpento* is not only an aesthetic position but also an ethical one that insists on exposing the degraded contemporary reality in its authentic grotesque dimensions. Valle-Inclán does so by portraying his characters from "above," making them appear like absurd little puppets. This desire to deform reality to underscore its brutal essence can also be found in art, particularly in Francisco Goya's paintings, and in the work of the European expressionists.

Etherege, George, Sir (1635?–1691). English diplomat, courtier, and amateur writer considered the originator of the Restoration comedy of manners. He wrote only three plays—*The Comical Revenge; or, Love in a Tub* (1664), *She Wou'd If She Cou'd* (1667), and *The Man of Mode; or, Sir Fopling Flutter* (1676)—but is among the two or three best comic dramatists of the time.

Eupolis (fl. 429–412 B.C.E.). One of Aristophanes' fiercest rivals. He won seven first-place victories from his seventeen entries at the festivals. At the Lenaea of 421 B.C.E., he staged in his *Maricas* a satire of the demagogue Hyperbolus that resembled Aristophanes' caricature of Cleon in *Knights*. Two of Eupolis' other plays were clear forerunners of Aristophanes' *Frogs*. His *Demes*, performed somewhere between 418 and 406, featured illustrious Athenians of the past who were summoned from Hades to offer advice. In *Taxiarchs*, Eupolis depicted Dionysus aboard a boat in a scene where Phormion instructed the god of theater on military and naval training just as Charon taught Dionysus to row in *Frogs*.

Everybody Loves Raymond **(1996–2005).** American TV comedy series that focuses on the middle-class disaffection of sportswriter Ray Barone (Ray Romano) and his homemaker wife Debra (Patricia Heaton), who exemplify the sitcom pattern of bumbling husband/covertly powerful wife, as well as Ray's resentful brother and caustic parents, three of the most scathingly negative characters ever witnessed in a nominal comedy. Like its ancestor, *The Honeymooners*, Raymond illustrates the sitcom's ability to represent bitterness and unhappiness in its nominally joking format.

Extreme take. In animation, a more pronounced version of the double take, particularly developed by Tex Avery: eyes pop out of the head, limbs detach from the body, the figure elongates in an exclamation point.

Fable. Strictly speaking, an animal tale illustrating a specific lesson, or moral (e.g., "When the fox preaches, beware your geese"). More generally, the fable is a tale in which some or all of the characters may be animals and that may simply illustrate the cleverness of one character, the gullibility of another, or the foolishness of both. The Middle English *The Fox and the Wolf*, Geoffrey Chaucer's *Nun's Priest's Tale*, and the Uncle Remus stories of Joel Chandler Harris are all fables in this more general sense.

Fabliaux. Old French verse narratives of varying lengths and often bawdy taste, usually in octosyllabic couplets and popular from the late twelfth through the mid-fourteenth centuries, of which some 150 remain extant. There is a lot of academic controversy as to the origins of the *fabliaux,* their often antiaristocratic and antichurch satire leading to the conclusion, on the one hand, that they were of bourgeois inspiration, and, on the other, that they stemmed from tongue-in-cheek upper-class self-ridicule. Many of their subjects were later developed in the poetry of Geoffrey Chaucer and the prose of Giovanni Boccaccio and other storytellers. Often dramatized, their plots became the subject of numerous medieval farces.

Family sitcom. Subgenre of the television sitcom that focuses on family interactions, with the father/husband generally a benign fool; the mother/wife wise, reliable, and commonsensical; and the children rebellious and flippant, eager for independence yet still wanting the safety of their family. Primary examples include *Father Knows Best, Leave It to Beaver, The Cosby Show, Home Improvement*, and *Everybody Loves Raymond*.

Farce de Maître Pathelin, La. An anonymous work dating from about 1470 in traditional octosyllabic couplets and generally considered the masterpiece of the medieval comic theatre in France. Farcical in its portrayal of the trickster-victim hoist by his own petard, it puts onstage several social types of the period, all motivated by self-interest, and who—all else being equal—would not be out of place in the modern theater.

FESPACO. The acronym for *Festival Panafricain du Cinéma et de la Télévision de Ouagadougou*, the largest film festival on the African continent, meeting semiannually in Ougadougou, Burkina Faso. An international jury awards the *Etalon d'Or* (Golden Stallion) to the best film of the festival.

Festive comedy. Identified by C. L. Barber in his landmark study *Shakespeare's Festive Comedy* (1959). Though Barber's discussion is limited to Shakespeare's plays and the poetry of his contemporaries, no study of Renaissance drama is complete without reference to this work. Festive comedy is associated, either by calendar or by content, with native English customs and holidays, in celebration of the natural rhythms of the rural year. Some of these holidays are as old as pagan Britain (e.g., May Day, Harvest Home, Midsummer Eve, winter and summer solstices) while others are attached to Christian festivals such as Christmas (a favorite time for school plays, often called "comedies"), Twelfth Night (Epiphany), and All Souls' Day (preceded, of course, by Halloween, retained from pagan times). The "festive" for Barber is the trajectory of comedy achieving (social) clarification through the release of natural energies; thus comedy imitates the rhythms of life at its most productive and celebrates renewal.

Feydeau, Georges (1863–1921). Generally considered the leading French comic author after Molière, and most successful of the many farce writers of the late nineteenth and early twentieth century. His works are taken as models of the genre. Feydeau began his career with numerous modest salon monologues and playlets. After studying the technique of three predecessors—Labiche, Meilhac, and Alfred Hennequin (father of one of his later collaborators)—he became one of the most widely performed comic playwrights of his own and future generations. "Rediscovered" in France in the 1950s, his name has become virtually synonymous with masterfully crafted, often nightmarelike constructions peppered with observation of both social and individual shortcomings, linguistic drollery, and a general madcap lunacy that offers a foretaste of the latterday "absurd." Among his best-known plays are *Le Dindon* (*The Sucker*, 1896), *La Dame de Chez Maxim* (*The Lady from Maxim's*, 1899), and *On purge Bébé* (*Going to Pot*, 1910).

Feynman, Richard (1918–1988). A physicist born in New York City, Feynman was cowinner of the 1965 Nobel Prize in physics for work in quantum electrodynamics, especially theories of interacting particles. A professor at the California Institute of Technology from 1950 to 1988, he made comedy out of scientific inquiry in *Surely You're Joking, Mr. Feynman!* (1984).

Fielding, Henry (1707–1754). Preeminent comic and satiric dramatist and novelist. His plays were topical and farcical satires, although as a comic dramatist he is most remembered today for his parody of Restoration heroic plays, *The Tragedy of Tragedies; Or, The Life and Death of Tom Thumb the Great* (1731). Considered by many, then and now, to be the best comic novelist of the period, especially for *Joseph Andrews* (1742) and for his masterpiece, *Tom Jones* (1749).

Fields, W. C. (1880–1946). Comic actor, primarily of the 1930s, whose sour, misanthropic, often drunk and cruel characters violated most conventions of both polite society and mainstream movie-making. From the classic *It's a Gift* (1934) through *My Little Chickadee* (1940), *The Bank Dick* (1940), and *Never Give a Sucker an Even Break* (1941), Fields' best films relentlessly undermine not only American ideals of hard work, success, generosity, and family values but also the rosy stories that convey them.

Fish-out-of-water sitcom. Subgenre of the TV sitcom, primarily of the 1960s, whose stories arose from characters in an unfamiliar place or situation, such as a New York City couple relocated to rural Hooterville in *Green Acres* (1965–1971), Ozark hillbillies become Beverly Hills millionaires in *The Beverly Hillbillies* (1962–1971), or seven castaways marooned on a tropical island in *Gilligan's Island* (1964–1967). At a time of rapid social change, these shows offered the balm of silly escapism while dramatizing a culture of dislocation and uncertainty.

Fleischer Brothers (Max, Dave, Charles, Joe and Lou). Studio (1915–1942) headed by producer/inventor Max and animator Dave. It pioneered many early technical devices and advances in sound and created Betty Boop, the Out of the Inkwell Series, and the animated adaptations of Popeye and Superman.

Folktale. A story circulated orally that is anonymous, contains elements or motifs found within other storytelling traditions, and whose form is often similar from culture to culture. Folktales can be ancient or current; they can be centuries old or created in modern society. In its entry for *folktale*, the *Columbia Encyclopedia*, 6th edition, claims that storytelling "appears to be a cultural universal, common to primitive and complex societies alike." *The Story of Grandmother* (recorded 1885) is believed to be a French folk version of the Little Red Riding Hood tale. Folktales are the earliest form of comedy available for children.

Frame-tale. A story that establishes a storytelling situation in which the characters of the story tell other stories, "inner" tales within the "outer" frame-tale. In practice, the frame-tale is a useful way of organizing collections of stories. The form may derive from India, where *The Panchatantra* is a well-known early collection of fables. The Arabic *Thousand and One Nights*, Govanni Boccaccio's *Decameron*, the Spanish *Book of Good Love*, and Geoffrey Chaucer's *Canterbury Tales* are major medieval examples of the form.

Freleng, Friz (1906–1995). Animator at Disney, Warner Bros., and MGM; important contributor to Sylvester and Tweety and Bugs Bunny, and creator of Yosemite Sam and the Pink Panther.

Freud, Sigmund (1856–1939). Austrian physician and founder of psychoanalysis, a theory that he developed while studying the relation between arrested sexual development and psychosomatic illnesses later in life. His psychoanalytic theories, which initially met with hostility, profoundly influenced twentieth-century thought in and beyond the field of psychology. With regard to humor, Freud's theory addresses society's collective superego, the social norms. These norms frustrate psychological mechanisms attempting to gain catharsis in order to relieve the stress of life. According to Freud, wit is a socially viable way to trigger the anxiety people feel about certain things and allow them (under the right conditions) to experience catharsis. Freud differentiated wit into four tendencies: aggression, exhibition, cynicism (skepticism), and absurdity.

Friends-as-family sitcom. Subgenre of the TV sitcom, primarily since the 1970s, on which friends, more than literal family, provide comfort, support, and affection in the face of each character's tribulations. Primary examples include *Friends*, *Cheers*, *Seinfeld*, *Sex and the City*, *The Golden Girls*, and *Will & Grace*.

Frye, Northrop (1912–1991). Influential literary scholar of the twentieth century, Canadian critic Frye is especially revered for his 1957 *Anatomy of Criticism*, as well as for *The Educated Imagination* (1964) and *The Critical Path* (1971). He divided literature into four categories: romance, comedy, irony, and tragedy.

Garbo, Greta (1905–1990). Like Marlene Dietrich, classical Hollywood star Garbo appealed to lesbian audiences who interpreted her strong, often masculine characters (especially *Queen Christina*) as secret clues to her being lesbian. As a camp icon, Garbo's appeal not only stems from her array of dominant female characters, but also her mannered and consistent acting style: the low voice, slow speech with a Swedish accent, and, oftentimes, monotone delivery of dialogue.

Garçon et l'aveugle, Le. The earliest extant medieval French farce. The 265 lines of "The Boy and the Blind Man," an anonymous thirteenth-century trifle, dramatize, in the artistically unsophisticated octosyllabic couplets typical of much medieval French literature, the victimization of a crafty pseudopauper by an even craftier boy—first in a long line of unscrupulous lackeys—employed to aid him in his begging. Unlike most of his descendants, who would long people the comic theater, however, this prototypical servant who succeeds in humbling his master is motivated not by greed and self-interest but by a desire to share his bounty with his peers.

The *Gawain*-poet. Also known as "the *Pearl*-poet," after his other major poem. Both terms refer to the author of *Sir Gawain and the Green Knight*, the finest Middle English Arthurian romance, which was written sometime in the period 1360–1390. Three other poems occurring with the romance in a single manuscript are assumed to be works by the same author: *Pearl*, *Purity*, and *Patience*. The dialect of the manuscript suggests a poet from the northwest Midlands of England, and the poem itself richly suggests a courtly provenance.

Geisel, Theodore Seuss. *See* Dr. Seuss

Goldsmith, Oliver (1730–1774). Anglo-Irish essayist, historian, poet, and comic dramatist, part of the literary circle surrounding Samuel Johnson in the 1750s and 1760s. His play *She Stoops to Conquer* (1773) was seen as a break with the prevailing sentimental comedy, and he wrote about the superiority of "laughing" stage comedy to sentimental plays in his brief but influential "Essay on the Theatre; or, A Comparison between Sentimental and Laughing Comedy" (1773).

Gothic. A genre that emphasizes medieval, primitive, and wild forces of nature. Supernatural, mysterious, and horrific elements are expected in gothic novels, which are often set in medieval castles or haunted houses with underground passages, trap doors, dark stairways, mysterious rooms, and unexpected sounds and shadows. The weather is dark and stormy and the stories so exaggerated that they often become ironically amusing or comic and lend themselves to parody.

Gottfried von Strassburg (fl. 1210). A German poet known primarily as the author of the best surviving version of the romance of Tristan and Isolt, which he composed at the beginning of the thirteenth century. Later writers give him the title *meister*, which suggests someone who has completed a period of advanced study at one or more of the humanist cathedral schools that had developed in the twelfth century. Gottfried was thoroughly educated in German, French, and Latin literature, and was well trained in theology, law, and rhetoric. We know from *Tristan* that he was a skilled poet and virtuoso stylist, was well versed in the forms of courtly behavior (though he himself probably belonged not to the nobility but to the upper bourgeois class of Strassburg), and was familiar enough with Christian mysticism to adapt its language and ways of thinking to express the highest reaches of the experience of love.

Goya, Francisco José de (1746–1828). Acclaimed painter of the Spanish Enlightenment. From 1775 to 1792 Goya was the designer for the Royal Tapestry Factory in Madrid. During those years he also became the portrait painter of the Spanish aristocracy. In 1792 a serious illness left him permanently deaf, forcing him into a deep isolation that reflected his new style of the *Caprichos* (*Whim*, 1799), a series of etchings satirizing human folly and weakness. During the Napoleonic invasions and the Spanish War of Independence (1808–1814), Goya was the French court painter. *The Disasters of War* belong to this period. After the restoration of the Spanish monarchy under Ferdinand VII, Goya was pardoned for serving the French. Nevertheless, the Inquisition persecuted him for his painting *The Naked Maja*, which was considered irreligious and obscene.

Greene, Robert (1558–1592). One of the "University Wits," a rowdy group of well-educated graduates of Oxford or Cambridge who arrived in London during the late 1570s and early 1580s determined to succeed as professional writers. Greene is best known for *Friar Bacon and Friar Bungay* (c. 1589), an immensely popular comedy whose comparison to Marlowe's famous tragedy *Doctor Faustus* (c. 1592), probably written and performed around the same time, has been discussed and debated a great deal; it is impossible to determine which influenced which. Other comedies attributed to him are *George a Greene, the Pinner of Wakefield* (c. 1590) and *Orlando Furioso* (c. 1591), based on Ariosto's well-known epic poem. He is also known for his collaboration with Thomas Lodge on *A Looking Glass for London and England* (c. 1590) and the prose romance *Pandosto*, widely accepted as the source of Shakespeare's *The Winter's Tale*. He died young, from (as legend has it) an overindulgence in Rhenish wine and pickled herring.

Gregory, Lady Augusta (1859–1932). Cofounder with Yeats of the Irish dramatic movement that led to the Abbey Theatre and many of the greatest plays of the twentieth century, mostly comedies; also a great popularizer of Irish mythology and creator of Irish-English styles of writing. Married Sir William Gregory in 1880 and widowed in 1892, after which she turned her Coole Park estate in County Galway into an important retreat and meeting place for other major authors. Today her house is gone, but there remains a tree with the autographs of William Butler Yeats, Sean O'Casey, John Millington Synge, and Bernard Shaw (among others). Yeats called her *Cuchulain of Muirthemne* (1902) "the greatest book to come out of Ireland in my time." She helped perfect the one-act peasant play, key to the Abbey's success, with such works as *Spreading the News* (1904), *The Gaol Gate* (1906), and *The Rising of the Moon* (1907).

Griot. The *griot* in West African societies was a hereditary position that involved "praise singing" at feasts and rituals. If individuals did not contribute to the griot's fee, he might signify on them publically. Griots were thus feared, and they were buried apart from other citizens in baobob trees. Griots are better known for their alternate function, historians who memorized the stories of the people. Humor was the key tool in the griot's arsenal in terms of entertaining, instructing, shocking, or persecuting members of his audience. Griot traditions have much to do with oral and vernacular roles and patterns in African American culture.

Grotesque. In literature, the grotesque includes elements of exaggeration, deformity, and freakishness along with subject matter of a work or a style of expression categorized by humorous exaggeration, deformity, and freakishness.

Grotesque Comedy. A kind of harsh comedy derived from the early-twentieth-century theater of the grotesque, perfected by Luigi Pirandello. Reacting against naturalism and realism, grotesque comedy uses irony, farce, bizarre plots, and the like to criticize modern society and to depict deep discrepancies between illusion and reality.

Haliburton, Thomas Chandler (1796–1865). Born in Nova Scotia, Haliburton authored Canada's—and, indeed, North America's—first great work of comic literature, *The Clockmaker; or, The Sayings and Doings of Samuel Slick of Slickville* (1837). Begun as a newspaper serial in 1835, the original twenty-one sketches had numerous sequels. The shrewd dialect-speaking Yankee peddler, Sam Slick, had a wide influence on North American comic writings. He died in England.

Hand of the artist. In animation, a convention in which the animator (in live action) interacts with his artwork, typified by Max Fleischer, interacting with Koko the Clown and Fitz in the *Out of the Inkwell* series.

Hart, Moss (1904–1961), and George S. Kaufman (1869–1961). A duo of stage and cinema immortals, authors of some of the best-known comic plays and films of the American theater. Their collaboration began in 1930 when Kaufman, the already legendary wit of the Algonquin Roundtable, doctored up a Hart script that eventually became the wildly successful *Once in a Lifetime.* The story, which deals with the theatrical revolution caused by the talkies, catapulted Hart to a celebrity that lasted well beyond the pair's amicable breakup ten years later. Many of their individual and collaborative comedies are highly farcical in nature. Perhaps the most characteristic example is *The Man Who Came to Dinner* (1939), the film version of which, in 1941, with the acerbically droll Monty Woolley, is considered by many as the funniest American film farce ever made.

Heller, Joseph (1923–1999). Author of *Catch-22* (1961) and in many ways an innovator in the field of dark comic literature. Heller flew sixty missions as a B-25 bombardier out of Corsica during World War II. The experience percolated for nearly two decades before he wrote his first novel while working at an advertising agency. His later novels, although well written, failed to live up to the success of his first work. Those works include *Something Happened* (1974), *Good as Gold* (1979), *God Knows* (1984), and *Closing Time* (1994), a "companion" to *Catch-22* that continues to follow Yossarian as its protagonist.

Henley, Beth (1952–). American playwright and screen writer. Born in Jackson, Mississippi, Henley studied drama at Southern Methodist University and the University of Illinois. *Crimes of the Heart*, her first produced play (1979), won the Pulitzer Prize in 1981. Her early plays—including *The Miss Firecracker Contest* (1984) and *The Debutante Ball* (1988)—are set in the American South and are written in the dark comic, southern gothic mode of *Crimes of the Heart*. Since *Abundance* (1989), Henley has experimented more widely with comic grotesque. *Control Freaks* (1992) seems almost Euripidean in its violence and odd sense of transcendence. *Impossible Marriage* (1998), on the other hand, has been called Henley's version of *A Midsummer Night's Dream*.

Hennequin, Alfred (1842–1887). One of the most prominent practitioners of late-nineteenth-century French farce and light operetta. Hennequin, born in Belgium, spent most of his life writing for the French stage with a variety of collaborators and composers. Among his most popular works were *Le Procès Vauradieux* (1875), *Niniche* (1878), and *Lili* (1882). His style was characterized by the profusion of ever-opening and closing doors that was to become a staple of the farce, and by a rigorously tight plot construction, evidence perhaps of his early years as an engineer. This technique, inherited from the "well-made play" of Augustin Eugène Scribe and developed to perfection by Georges Feydeau, caused such comedies to be dubbed *hennequinades*, and gained for him the reputation of "father of the farce." His son Charles-Maurice Hennequin was one of Feydeau's collaborators and a successful *farceur* in his own right.

Hepburn, Katharine (1907–2003). A central romantic comedy protagonist whose independent, outspoken professional woman characters want to find love without compromising their own identity and integrity. Major romantic comedies include, with Cary Grant, *Bringing Up Baby* (1938) and *The Philadelphia Story* (1940), and with Spencer Tracy, *Woman of the Year* (1942), *Adam's Rib* (1949), *Pat and Mike* (1952), and *Desk Set* (1957).

Hiebert, Paul (1892–1987). Authored *Sarah Binks* (1947), the mock biography of the "sweet songstress of Saskatchewan," Sarah Binks, whose poetry, if hilariously bad already, is worsened by her silly fictitious literary critics.

Hobbes, Thomas (1588–1679). English philosopher best known for his political philosophy, which was based on his views of the close relationship between human nature and social and political life. His greatest work, *Leviathan* (1651), describes an ideal society in which a collection of essentially selfish individuals could live in peace by being united under an absolute monarch. Despite the nondemocratic nature of the society he recommended, his work introduced notions of rights and a social contract that later formed the basis for European Enlightenment theories of democratic government. His view of human beings was that they are essentially selfish and individualistic, and that human interaction tends to be competitive. His support for the superiority theory of humor derives from this position: laughter for Hobbes is the result of a feeling of dominance over other human beings, who tend to be viewed as potential competitors. Works relevant to his philosophy of humor include *Human Nature* (1650).

Hoffman, Abbie (1936–1989). Political agitator, writer, cofounder of the Yippies, a movement that pioneered comically anarchic protest performance during the 1960s in opposition to war and domestic oppression. Books include *Steal This Book*, *Revolution for the Hell of It*, and *Woodstock Nation*. Novelist E. L. Doctorow observed in his eulogy for Hoffman that, for Hoffman to have been "very funny, with the precision, the insight, of a great political cartoonist," he had to seem "insufferable because he held up the mirror so that we saw ourselves."

Hogg-Reave, Ursula. Hogg-Reave is the fictitious editor of *Piggy* (1996), "A Snorton Critical Edition," whose contributors were pseudonymous Canadian writers. *Piggy* continues the satiric-critical tradition of *Sarah Binks* and *The Incomparable Atuk*, with sights set on a range of deconstructive approaches to Canadian literature and its winking postmodern stars.

***The Honeymooners* (1955–1956).** Classic American TV comedy series about the brutal marriage of volatile, frustrated bus driver Ralph Kramden (Jackie Gleason) and his long-suffering wife Alice (Audrey Meadows). The show's mood of bitterness, unhappiness, and working-class disaffection made it seem less like a comedy than like the gritty "kitchen-sink" dramas of the period, which tried to reflect the realities of urban working-class life.

Horace (65–8 B.C.E.). Quintus Horatius Flaccus, known as Horace, was a Roman poet and critic who wrote satires in hexameter verse. Horace's name is attached to gentler forms of satire that focus on human failings rather than their crimes. Horatian satire is often contrasted to the harsher kind written by the angry moralist Juvenal.

Hôtel de Bourgogne, L'. A Paris theater, originally home of religious dramas performed by the Confrérie de la Passion. In 1599 it was leased by the troupe of Valleran-Lecomte and, for several decades, was the venue for the production of robust and often indelicate farces performed by the Troupe Royale. The latter, merging in 1680 with a pair of other troupes, including that of Molière, formed the basis of the Théâtre Français—or Comédie Française—at which time the old Hôtel de Bourgogne became home to the Comédie Italienne, whose troupe remained there, with varying degrees of political disfavor, until the construction of the Opéra-Comique in 1783.

Hroswitha of Gandesheim (c. 930–c. 1002). A nun, the first known German poetess, and author of six Latin comedies. The manuscript of her work, found at the end of the fifteenth century, also contains a number of nondramatic works of religious inspiration. Her plays are thought to owe their inspiration and a certain technical debt to Terence, with whose comedies, as well as those of Plautus, the erudite nun was clearly acquainted. One assumes, in fact, that she penned her comedies to divert admiration away from the secular Latin writers and toward plots of sacred devotion. Where Terence emphasizes easy female virtue, Hroswitha counters with a defense of chastity; and while her comedies are not uproariously comical, there are moments of broad farce, as in the second of her plays, *Dulcitius*.

Hudibrastics. Verse form so called after Samuel Butler's *Hudibras*—eight-syllable comic poetry with deliberately awkward rhymes.

Hughes, Langston (1902–1967). Born in Joplin, Missouri, and raised in Kansas, Hughes attended Columbia University and graduated from Lincoln University. He was a major player in the Harlem Renaissance, when he published much of his best work, including two major collections of poetry, *The Weary Blues* (1926) and *Fine Clothes to the Jew* (1927); an autobiographical novel, *Not without Laughter* (1930); and a short-story collection, *The Ways of White Folks* (1934). He collaborated with Zora Neale Hurston on a comic folk play that was not produced during their lifetime, *Mulebone*. Hughes went on to write many fine plays, including the drama *Mulatto*, which was produced on Broadway (1935), and rollicking comedies such as the Harlem romp *Little Ham* (1936). His comic masterpiece was the creation of Jesse B. Semple, a Harlem raconteur whose comic conversations with his intellectual friend Boyd were first published in African American newspapers, and then in edited volumes. During a long and distinguished career, Hughes published anthologies of African American humor, folklore, and poetry, and kept writing, out of his Harlem apartment, in virtually all genres.

Humor of the Old Southwest (1830s–1860s). Beginning with Augustus Baldwin Longstreet's *Georgia Scenes* (published as a collection in 1835), southwestern humorists drew on the plain folk and tall tale traditions of oral storytelling, treating the lifeways and speechways of men and women in semi-isolated frontier settings and middling-to-low life circumstances. Southwest tales and sketches appeared regularly in *The Spirit of the Times* (New York), the *New Orleans Picayune*, and the *St. Louis Reveille* and were the precursors of post–Civil War local color writing. Works in this tradition include William Thompson's *Major Jones's Courtship* (1843), Johnson Jones Hooper's *Some Adventures of Simon Suggs* (1845), George Washington Harris's *Sut Lovingood's Yarns* (1867), and Joseph Baldwin's *The Flush Times of Alabama and Mississippi* (1853).

Hurston, Zora Neale (1891–1960). Born in Notasulga, Alabama, and raised in all-black Eatonville, Florida, Hurston, a minister's daughter, was spared many of the worst aspects of southern racism and developed a talent for tale-telling from the rich folklore she heard all around her. After attending Morgan State College and Howard University, she studied folklore and did field research in Florida as part of her education at Barnard and Columbia. Concurrently, she had an active social life in Harlem, where she began her writing career, which led to four novels, two books of folklore, an autobiography and much more. Her infectious, sly sense of humor included all the conventions of both African American oral culture and white literature. Her subversive deconstruction of white racism has few peers. She also wrote plays and dreamed of a Negro theater where comedy would both entertain and instruct.

Hutcheson, Francis (1694–1746). Philosopher of Scottish descent and education who taught philosophy and worked as a Presbyterian minister in Scotland and Ireland. He believed that humankind has an innate moral sense. He opposed Thomas Hobbes on the subject of human nature and the nature of humor: Hobbes thought that human beings were essentially selfish and violent, while Hutcheson thought that they are innately moral and benevolent. He thus opposed Hobbes' superiority theory of humor, which locates humor in a competitive feeling of domination over others. He observed instead that we find humor in absurd incongruities, which distract us from negative emotions. He was thus a proponent of the incongruity theory of humor. Hutcheson is best known for his theory of beauty, which employs the notion of an innate aesthetic sense like the innate moral sense he also believed we possess. Works relevant to his philosophy of humor include *Reflections upon Laughter* (1750).

I Love Lucy (1951–1957). One of the most popular TV comedy series, this production of comic actress Lucille Ball and her husband, producer and bandleader Desi Arnaz, focused on Ball's slapstick antics, as well as on her interactions with Arnaz and their neighbors Fred and Ethel Mertz (William Frawley and Vivian Vance). *Lucy* exemplified the sitcom's representation of wives as covertly powerful yet overtly subservient as it also played out one of the eternal themes of farce: the seemingly foolish figure who sees behind the facade of social pretension, strips it away, and comes out ahead of those with greater status, money, and power.

Incongruity theory. A philosophical theory of humor, espoused in different forms by Francis Hutcheson, Immanuel Kant, Arthur Schopenhauer, Søren Kierkegaard, and John Morreall. According to this theory, humor is primarily found in an intellectual recognition of an absurd incongruity between conflicting ideas or experiences.

Intertextuality. A concept first proposed by Julia Kristeva, who said that every text is an absorption and transformation of earlier texts. In a way this is related to Carl Jung's collective unconscious whereby the symbols, allusions, and epiphanies of more modern texts are based on earlier concepts and words that have been passed along from each generation to the next.

Ionesco, Eugène (1912–1994). Romanian-born French playwright of absurd plays. Best-known plays include *The Bald Soprano* (1956), *La leçon* (1951), *Les chaises* (1952), and *Rhinoceros* (1959).

Irish Gaelic. Ireland's native language, one of the Celtic family of languages along with Scottish Gaelic and (in this family's other branch) Welsh, Manx, and Breton. Today only about 3 percent of Irish people speak Irish every day, mostly in the three Gaeltacht regions (and dialects) of counties Donegal; Galway and Clare (including the Aran Islands); and Kerry and western Cork. A much higher percentage of the population has proficiency or familiarity with the language through school. Irish Gaelic tremendously influenced the English language as it is spoken and written throughout the country.

Irony. The property a statement has when its literal meaning is the opposite of its actual meaning.

Irving, Washington (1783–1859). American writer, lawyer, businessman, and diplomat. His first major publication was a pseudonomous comic epic, *A History of New York from the Beginning of the World to the End of the Dutch Dynasty* by Diedrich Knickerbocker (1809). Lived in Europe between 1815 and 1832 where he composed *The Sketch Book* (1820), which gained him an international reputation. As attaché to the American Legation in Madrid (1826), he produced a history of Christopher Columbus and a Spanish sketchbook, *The Alhambra* (1832). He served as secretary to the American legation in London from 1829 to 1831, returned to America in 1832, settled in the Hudson River Valley, and published three studies of the American West: *A Tour on the Prairies* (1835), *Astoria* (a history of John Jacob Astor's fur-trading colony, 1836), and *The Adventures of Captain Bonneville, U.S.A.* (an account of western exploration, 1837). Served as minister to Spain from 1842 to 1846. During the 1850s he published two biographies: *Mahomet* (1850) and a five-volume life of George Washington (1855–1859).

Jacobs, Melville (1902–1969). A student of Franz Boas, Jacobs specialized in the Native American cultures of the Northwest, recording—at times on an enormous and unwieldy field recorder—a great many stories, trickster stories among them. He was especially attentive to the way in which Native people referred to their stories and the titles that they gave them. Jacobs provided many more or less Freudian interpretations of the stories he collected, attending to them in great and particular detail.

Jarry, Alfred (1873–1907). Creator of the series known as the Ubu Plays, Jarry's theater can be seen as a forerunner of the Theater of the Absurd. *Ubu Rex*, a parody of Shakespeare's *Macbeth*, premiered in 1896 to mixed reviews.

Je ne sais quoi, le. An elusive concept loosely translated as "I can't explain it" or "that certain something." Current in seventeenth-century France, the idea derives from the neo-Platonic theories of the fifteenth-century Italian humanist Marsilio Ficino (1433–1499) and is used to describe the mysterious attraction drawing two people irresistibly to each other. It is a kind of metaphysical "sympathetic vibration" that explains why Pierre Corneille's heroes and heroines fall in love. Or, as a popular American song of 1929 would have it: "You were meant for me; I was meant for you."

Jit. *Jiti* or jit-jive, from Zimbabwe, sometimes known as the "Harare beat," is a highly danceable popular music characterized by fast guitar playing, rapid drumming, and a blend of Tanzanian guitar and a bass line of Congolese rhumba. Jit gained international exposure during the 1980s through such bands as the Bhundu Boys and the Four Brothers.

Jones, Chuck (1912–2002). Famed animator at Warner Bros. and MGM, creator of Pepé Le Pew, Roadrunner, and Wile E. Coyote, Michigan J. Frog, the Tasmanian Devil, and important contributor to Daffy Duck, Bugs Bunny, and many others.

Jonson, Ben (c. 1572–1637). Next to Shakespeare, Jonson was arguably the most important playwright of Elizabethan and Jacobean comedy. Born a month after his father, a clergyman, died, his earliest work was as an apprentice to his stepfather, a bricklayer. He married young and served in the military in Flanders. By the time he was twenty-five, he had joined a company of strolling players, and soon thereafter was writing plays for the professional London companies. From about 1605 (after King James took the throne), Jonson began to write court masques to celebrate festive occasions at court and inaugurated his famous collaboration with Inigo Jones. His best-known plays are *Volpone* (1606), *Epicene* (1609), *The Alchemist* (1610), and *Bartholomew Fair* (1614).

Joyce, James (1882–1941). The most influential, innovative novelist of the twentieth century. Published four books of fiction—*Dubliners* (1914), *A Portrait of the Artist as a Young Man* (1916), *Ulysses* (1922), and *Finnegans Wake* (1939)—and in each one Joyce invented an entirely new style and changed the course of world literature. Lived almost entirely out of Ireland after 1904—mostly in Trieste, Paris, and Zurich—but wrote obsessively about his native Dublin during his entire life.

Juegos de escarnio. A medieval Spanish term for "plays of mockery," or farces. Referring to comedies more specifically suggestive—even lewd—than the more general *entreméses*, these dramatic interludes were the subject of official condemnation as early as the mid-thirteenth century. Nor were they enjoyed only by the populace. An edict promulgated by the king of León and Castile in 1252 forbade the clergy to watch such playlets or to act in them. Apparently they continued to be performed, however, with or without clerical approval. In 1765 Carlos III, king of Spain (1759–1788), put a belated end to the performance of religious *autos sacramentales*, no doubt because of the farcical interludes that accompanied them.

Juvenal (55-60–c. 127). Decimus Junius Juvenalis was a Roman satirical poet who flourished in the first century A.D. Though little is known of his life, Juvenal produced harsh and bitter satires aimed at serious human crimes and sins and established what has come to be known as Juvenalian satire. He is often contrasted with Horace, who was more genial in his criticism of the behavior of others. His main targets are the self-indulgence, tyranny, and immorality that he saw as rampant in Rome. He is praised for his epigrammatic style.

Kafka, Franz (1883–1924). Czech fiction writer whose German-language masterpieces include "Metamorphosis," "A Hunger Artist," and three incomplete novels: *The Castle*, *The Trial*, and *Amerika*. His deadpan literalism makes him a leading practitioner of existential, grotesque, and absurd black comedy.

Kant, Immanuel (1724–1804). Prussian philosopher who wrote important works on ethics, political philosophy, epistemology, and metaphysics. His theory of knowledge derives from an attempt to reconcile the key discoveries of the rationalist and empiricist schools of thought. His theory of ethics, in which he develops an objectivist notion of moral duty based on reason, is regarded as the foundation of the modern study of ethics. Kant was a proponent of the incongruity theory of humor. He identified laughter as a pleasant physiological response to intellectual confusion. Works relevant to his philosophy of humor include his *Critique of Judgment* (1790).

Kaufman, George S. *See* Hart, Moss, and George S. Kaufman

Keaton, Buster (1895–1966). Classic physical comic of silent movies whose films typically staged a conflict between an impassive, stone-faced protagonist and some kind of unmanageable machine or object, be it a train, cannon, steamboat, or movie projector. Major films include *Our Hospitality* (1923), *Sherlock Jr.* (1924), *The Navigator* (1924), *Seven Chances* (1925), and *The General* (1927).

Kelly, Walt (1913–1973). Creator of the comic strip *Pogo* from 1949 to 1972. *Pogo* was an inimitable combination of "funny animal" humor and sharp, courageous political commentary. Kelly often lampooned the political process but directly took on Senator Joseph McCarthy and Nixon administration leaders. Like Jay "Ding" Darling, he championed ecological causes.

Keppler, Joseph (1838–1894). Political cartoonist who created the illustrated humor magazine *Puck* in 1876. Unlike Thomas Nast, Keppler trained artists who were entertaining as well as partisan and created an influential new style of political cartooning. Keppler pioneered sustained series of cartoons on controversial issues rather than candidates and was the first cartoonist to publish book-length collections of topical commentary.

Kesselring, Joseph (1902–1967). An American playwright, author of some dozen plays. His inauspicious prior career gave no indication of the incredible success of his best-known work, the macabre farce *Arsenic and Old Lace*. Originally entitled *Bodies in Our Cellars*, this tale of two sweet old ladies who charitably put old gents out of their lonely misery with poisoned elderberry wine, then bury them in their cellar, opened on Broadway in 1941. Thanks, no doubt, to the judicious doctorings of producers Harold Lindsay and Russell Crouse, it ran in New York for over three years and was equally successful in London. It has had numerous revivals and continues to be a staple in both professional and amateur theater. The film version of 1944 starring Cary Grant was equally successful.

Kids in the Hall. The name of both the innovative Canadian TV show that ran from 1989 to 1995 and the troupe: Scott Thompson, Kevin McDonald, Dave Foley, Mark McKinney, and Bruce McCulloch.

Kierkegaard, Søren (1813–1855). Danish philosopher of religion who wrote a large number of works dealing with the relationship between religion and human existence. He separated the stages of individual development into three phases: the aesthetic, the ethical, and the religious. As individuals move through these stages and become more aware of God, their awareness of the conflict between their finite existence and eternal truth becomes more pronounced. Kierkegaard was a proponent of the incongruity theory of humor, in that he thought the essence of the comic was found in the incongruity between the finite and the infinite. In several of his works he expressively described the existential struggle within the individual that takes place in relation to this awareness of incongruity. Works relevant to his philosophy of humor include *Concluding Unscientific Postscript* (1846).

Kirby, Rollin (1875–1952). The first three-time Pulitzer Prize winner, dominating the 1920s and creating the anti-Prohibition icon "Mr. Dry" for the *New York World*. His style of angry or sardonic humor inspired other prize-winning crusaders like Herbert Block ("Herblock," 1909–2000), a liberal cartoonist for over seventy years; Edmund Duffy (1899–1962), dominant during the 1930s; and Bill Mauldin (1921–2003), beloved World War II G.I. cartoonist and staff artist for the *St. Louis Post-Dispatch* and the *Chicago Sun-Times* from 1958 to 1992.

Kroetsch, Robert (1927–). Poet and novelist born in Heisler, Alberta, Canada. Kroetsch's self-titled "Out West Trilogy"—*The Words of My Roaring* (1966), *The Studhorse Man* (1969), and *Gone Indian* (1973)—employs a boisterous comic technique to demythologize false, mainly Hollywood, versions of the Canadian West.

Labiche, Eugène (1815–1888). Usually thought to be the most important French comic author between Molière and Georges Feydeau. Most of Labiche's more than 170 comedies were written with a group of collaborators, and it is probably thanks to them that, during his heyday (1845–1865), it was a rare Paris theatrical season that saw fewer than a half-dozen of his comedies on the boards, even as many as nine in a single year. Most of these were so-called *vaudevilles*—comedies with accompanying ditties set to popular contemporary tunes. Among his sprightly comedies depicting the concerns and affectations of the bourgeoisie, a number of farces stand out, the best-known being *Un Chapeau de paille d'Italie* (An Italian Straw Hat, 1851), typical of the wit and craftsmanship—the technique of the inexorable chain of farcical events—that Feydeau would study and bring to perfection. Labiche was elected to the Académie Française in 1880.

Language play. The flexible and creative use of language. Because language play allows the map (language) to fit the territory (the real world), children with small vocabularies and scientists with large vocabularies can both talk about a total range of human experiences. Language play allows speculation, invention, and imagination, for it can adapt to all worlds, both real and fancied. On another level, language play (metaphors, puns, riddles, rhymes, etc.) stretches and exercises the mind much as regular play stretches and exercises the body.

Larra, José Mariano de (1809–1837). Novelist, playwright, and journalist of Spanish romanticism. His critical outlook of Spanish society and politics led him to be an incisive social critic. He exemplifies the torment of the modern writer in a capitalist society who must sell his work to live yet resents having to write what sells. His most important journalistic writings include "The Day of the Dead of 1836," "Christmas Eve of 1836," and "Who Is the Public and Where Is It?" His turbulent love life and disillusionment with Spanish society led him to commit suicide at age twenty-eight.

Laurel and Hardy. The comic team of Stan Laurel (1890–1965) and Oliver Hardy (1892–1957) shaped a universe in which their own childish incompetence was matched only by the spitefulness and malevolence of the "adults" around them. In such films as *Two Tars* (1928), *You're Darn Tootin'* (1928), *Brats* (1932), and *The Music Box* (1932), Laurel and Hardy, like anarchic children, created a cascading series of errors, invoking chaos all around them and shattering polite veneers of civil behavior and proper procedure.

Lawrence, D. H. (1885–1930). English novelist, short-story writer, poet, painter, and essayist who was a major shaper and influence on modern fiction. Lawrence believed that the industrialized West had become dehumanized because of its emphasis on intellectual rather than instinctual influences and that only humanity's renewed sense of its oneness with nature, with blood consciousness (including the depths of sexual relationships) rather than brain consciousness, could alter the dehumanization. Lawrence emphasized the depths of sexual relationships as a necessary balance between these influences, with his mystical doctrines of sex and power sometimes reaching messianic levels as he sought a healing relationship between men and women. His major works include *Sons and Lovers* (1913), *The Rainbow* (1915), *Women in Love* (1920), and *Lady Chatterley's Lover* (1928), all of which focus on the results of denying human oneness with nature.

Leacock, Stephen (1869–1944). Canada's greatest humorist, Leacock published some sixty books in political science, economics, history, literary criticism, and biography, including a book of humor a year from 1910 until his death. His two masterpieces of humorous satire, neatly showing the range of his concerns and techniques, are *Sunshine Sketches of a Little Town* (1912) and *Arcadian Adventures with the Idle Rich* (1914). *Sunshine Sketches* tells of the goings-on in the small Canadian town of Mariposa at the turn of the twentieth century. *Arcadian Adventures*, a companion volume to the *Sketches*, satirizes the wealthy plutocrats who come to dominate an anonymous American city at about the same time.

Lear, Edward (1812–1888). Lear, the youngest of twenty children, had a difficult early life.

He did not have any formal artistic training, but was already known by age twenty for his clever drawings and limericks. Though he tried to work as a landscape artist, it was the publication under the pseudonym of Derry Down Derry of his first book, *A Book of Nonsense* (1846), that brought him success. Before it very little humorous material had been published, especially for children.

Lear, Norman (1922–). Landmark producer of television sitcoms, primarily of the 1970s, whose shows reflected the era's upheavals and advancements by spotlighting social issues and untraditional characters, even as they retained the sitcom's conventional forms and structures. Lear's shows included *All in the Family* (1971–1979), *Maude* (1972–1978), *The Jeffersons* (1975–1985), *Good Times* (1974–1979), *Sanford & Son* (1972–1977), and *One Day at a Time* (1975–1984).

Lee, Spike (1957–). Shelton Jackson "Spike" Lee was raised in Brooklyn and earned degrees at Morehouse and New York University prior to his spectacular career as a filmmaker. He has created historical films (*Malcolm X*, 1992; *Four Little Girls*, 1994) and others focused on serious social problems (especially race), such as *Do the Right Thing* (1989), *Mo' Better Blues* (1990), *Jungle Fever* (1991), and *Clockers* (1995). He has also created hilarious comedies, such as *She's Gotta Have It* (1986), *School Daze* (1988), and the controversial minstrelsy film *Bamboozled* (2000).

Lenaea. A local dramatic festival started by the Athenians in the 440s B.C.E. for the residents of the city. It was celebrated in January or February. At first, the Lenaea was probably held in a different theater than the one that housed the City Dionysia, but by the fourth century the performances were definitely transferred to the Theater of Dionysus. Comedy, a genre that in Athens openly debated political and civic issues of crucial concern to the citizenry, dominated this festival where few foreign visitors were in the audience. Perhaps Athens was reluctant to air its greatest concerns before the delegates from the subject states and chose rather to promote the civic dialogue that comedy generated at a festival that was organized primarily for the home community.

Lesage, Alain-René (1668–1747). Novelist and playwright, author of some hundred plays—frequently in collaboration—in the repertory of the popular *Théâtre de la foire* ("Theater of the Fair"). This usually comic, often outdoor genre was characterized by plays of slim literary merit but great public appeal. Lesage's reputation rests on two important comedies of social significance, reflective of the early years of eighteenth-century France: *Crispin rival de son maître* (1707) and, especially, *Turcaret* (1709). The former gives a twist to the *commedia dell'arte* and Molièresque tradition of the merely mischievous but faithful servant, making of him a rival for the affections of his master's inamorata. The second, far more pessimistic, paints the conniving—and successful—ruses of an unscrupulous lackey who causes the downfall of an equally unscrupulous but bunglingly bourgeois tax-collector, let loose in the venality of post–Louis XIV Paris.

Lévi-Strauss, Claude (1908–). Lévi-Strauss is the most important founding figure of structural anthropology, a method of analysis based, first, upon treating cultural phenomena as though they were a kind of "language," and then analyzing that language as a system of binary oppositions, after the method innovated by Ferdinand de Saussure, regarded as initiating the method of structural *linguistics*. If, for example, one starts with the smallest language units, a "p" and a "b," for instance, in English, resemble each other but differ in that the first is unvoiced and the second is voiced, differences English speakers recognize and take as significant. In much the same way, a "woman" and a "lady" both have meaning not inherently or referentially, but, rather, as a function of their relation to one another—a certain similarity and a certain difference as well—within a system of meaning, or *semiotics*. In much the same way, myths or folktales could be interpreted by discovering the abstract oppositional elements underlying them. Lévi-Strauss' many publications include *Structural Anthropology* (1958), *The Raw and the Cooked* (1969), and the more nearly autobiographical volume, *The View from Afar* (1985).

Lewis, Jerry (1926–). Wild physical comic who set the terms for anarchic slapstick in such films as *The Bellboy* (1960), *The Nutty Professor* (1963), *The Patsy* (1964), and *The Disorderly Orderly* (1964), in which his characters' infantile antics destroy everything they touch. For some curious reason he is much more admired in France than in the United States.

Lightning sketch. Derived from vaudeville and traveling fairs, the lightning sketch was a quick improvisational sketch, often featured in early silent animation.

Limited animation. Pioneered by William Hanna and Joe Barbera, limited animation was the reduction and simplification of the number of animated drawings in animation, necessitated by television production. Typified by *The Flintstones, Yogi Bear, Huckleberry Hound*, and other series. Replaced full animation, which predominated before the fifties in the work of Walt Disney and other studios.

Linguistic irony (also called verbal irony). A figure of speech in which the meanings or the intent of the words is opposite to the literal meanings. Good examples include Jonathan Swift's "A Modest Proposal," Mark Twain's "A War Prayer," and the line in Shakespeare's *Julius Caesar* when Marc Antony insists that he has come to bury Caesar, not to praise him.

Literal pun. The visualization of a pun, proverb, cliché, or metaphoric term, for example, electric eel, banana boat, "raining cats and dogs," and so on.

Lodge, David (1935–). Lodge, a British novelist, literary theorist, and critic, is a university professor who deftly combines juicy satire with a sensitive sympathy for his characters. He demonstrates a deep intimacy and sympathy with the academic world and its habitués, and he is open to literary experiment, though he finds the English "realistic" tradition continually appealing. He writes out of a lifelong identity as a Roman Catholic from a lower-middle-class urban background, and he knows the comic complications that necessarily result from these religious, economic, social, and professional worlds. More than most contemporary novelists, he is concerned with the theory of fiction, with those characters from the academic world (as in *Changing Places* [1975]) serving both as fictional foils and as case studies of various ideologies. His novels are broadly funny, with parodies, puns, satiric thrusts, and absurd situations in abundance. They include *The Picturegoers* (1960), *Ginger, You're Barmy* (1962), *The British Museum Is Falling Down* (1965), *Out of the Shelter* (1970), *How Far Can You Go?* (1980), and *Small World* (1984); his nonfiction includes *Language of Fiction* (1966), *The Novelist at the Crossroad* (1971), *The Modes of Modern Writing* (1977), and *Working with Structuralism* (1981).

Lubitsch, Ernst (1892–1947). German émigré filmmaker known for romantic comedies with a European aura of charming talk, titillating sexuality, and frivolous romantic entanglements, often centered on obstacles and misunderstandings in the path of romantic soulmates. Major films include *Trouble in Paradise* (1932), *To Be or Not to Be* (1942), *The Shop around the Corner* (1940), and *Ninotchka* (1939).

Lyly, John (1554–1606). Came to London straight from Oxford University in 1576, just as the first public playing house, the Theater, was built. Lyly was only interested in court-sponsored performances, where he could best demonstrate his classical learning and wit and thereby gain patronage. His earliest plays, *Campaspe* and *Sappho and Phao*, were presented at court during the Christmas festivities of 1583–1584, followed during the next decade by a half dozen plays, notably *Gallathea* (1585), written for the boys of the choir of St. Paul's. His most popular play was *Endymion* (1588), an homage to Queen Elizabeth; the title character loves Cynthia, the moon, who stands for purity, the ideal, the imaginary, and of course, for the queen, and is hindered by his former lover Tellus, the earth, representing the desires of his senses. His prose narratives *Euphues: The Anatomy of Wit* (1578) and *Euphues and His England* (1580), extremely mannered and balanced compilations of virtually every rhetorical device known to an Elizabethan educated elite, gave a name to his writing style (found also in his plays), known forever after as euphuism.

Mac, Bernie (1958–). Star of eponymous sitcom and known as the anti-Cosby. On his eponymous show about old-school ideas of discipline and parenting on the Fox network, Bernie

Mac has taken in the three children of his sister (on a "state-sponsored vacation"—she has been convicted of a drug crime). After the oldest, a glowering and deadpan teen named Vanessa, will not open her door, Uncle Bernie spews his bark. "I'm gonna bust your head till the white meat shows!" Audiences wriggle and laugh. He looks straight at the cameras and says, "That's right. I said I'm gonna bust her head till the white meat shows. And I ain't ashamed of it, and ain't nobody gonna make me take it back." But do not fidget too much for Mac has little bite, except comically; he is a Ralph Cramden (*The Honeymooners*) or Archie Bunker (*All in the Family*) for the new millennium, racially tinged and affected.

Machiavellian. Emulating the subject or principles of behavior described in *The Prince* (1512) by Niccolò Machiavelli (1469–1527), characterized by indifference to morality, deceit, cunning, and ruthlessness in attempting to get and keep power. These principles consider that any means serve to justify an end, no matter how unscrupulous, deceitful, expedient, or evil these means are in order to achieve political power. This perspective denies any role of morality in politics since craft and deceit justify the seeking and wielding of political power.

MacNelly, Jeff. *See* Oliphant, Pat, and Jeff MacNelly

Mad. Monthly magazine started in 1955 by William Gaines and edited in its years as America's most influential magazine by Harvey Kurtzman and later Al Feldstein. *Mad*, along with TV comics such as Milton Berle and Phil Silvers, diffused Jewish humor into the American mainstream during the fifties by lampooning American mass culture, mores, and politics.

Magnes (fl. 470s–460s B.C.E.). The most prominent playwright in the fifth century B.C.E. He earned a total of eleven victories at the City Dionysia, a record that was not surpassed in the history of old comedy. Aristophanes implied that the quality of Magnes' comedy was not very high.

Magritte, René (1898–1967). Belgian surrealist painter who used humor and the absurd to show the mechanisms behind representation and linguistic description, as in his perhaps most famous painting, *Ceci n'est pas une pipe*.

Malory, Sir Thomas (c. 1416–1471). Author of *Le Morte Darthur*, the influential fifteenth-century cycle of Arthurian romance. Although the identification is not certain, he is probably Thomas Malory of Newbold Revel in Warwickshire, who was a knight and from about 1450 on was imprisoned for short and long periods during the turbulent years of the Wars of the Roses. In colophons within the one surviving manuscript copy of *Le Morte Darthur*, the author tells us his name ("Syr Thomas Maleoré, Knyght"), identifies himself as a "knyght presoner," and asks the reader to pray for his "good delyveraunce." He was still a prisoner when he finished the book, which he tells us was in "the ninth yere of the reygne of Kyng Edward the Fourth" (March 4, 1469–March 3, 1470).

Mamet, David (1947–). American playwright, fiction and screenwriter, essayist, and stage and film director. Born in Chicago, Mamet learned some of his comic trade at Second City listening to the likes of Mike Nichols and Elaine May. He studied at Goddard College in Vermont and at the Neighborhood Playhouse School of Theater. *Sexual Perversity in Chicago* (1972) and *American Buffalo* (1975) established Mamet's reputation as a serious but very funny dramatist of social criticism; *Glengarry Glen Ross* won the Pulitzer Prize in 1984. *Boston Marriage* (1999) demonstrates Mamet's ability to write in (and parody) a traditional comedy of manners mode. His essays on the theater—appearing in *Writing in Restaurants* (1986) and *Three Uses of the Knife* (1998)—illuminate contemporary drama and Mamet's own dramaturgy.

Man of words, the. In African American society, the man of words has a creative gift with language, and uses it to establish his power, to entertain, and to instruct. He can use his "mother wit" to signify on opponents, to charm and dazzle women, and to make his reputation in the world of men through verbal dueling. He seeks to adorn his speech and to use it to dramatic effect. In all these aspects, his humorous and often irreverent use of language leads to power.

Mandelazation. A term coined by French film critic Olivier Barlet in his review of *Chikin Biznis* (by Michael Raeburn, South Africa, 1998) that refers to South African films set in the townships outside Johannesburg, which tell the stories of the working classes in postapartheid townships, emphasizing local dialect and situations, and in which white South Africans are not present.

Marivaux, Pierre Carlet de Chamblain de (1688–1763). Novelist and essayist Marivaux is perhaps best known for his subtly dialogued, delicate comedies that renew the internalized emotional tensions of the early Italian pastoral. No longer held in check, for example, by a vow of chastity to the goddess Diana (e.g., Tasso's *Aminta*), the Marivaldian *prima amorosa* is reluctant to avow her growing affection for more down-to-earth reasons: the fear of marriage in a young, inexperienced girl (*Le Jeu de l'amour et du hasard* [*The Game of Love and Chance*], 1730), the unpleasant taste left by an apparently far-from-unforgettable first marriage in a young widow (*Les Fausses Confidences* [*Untrue Secrets*], 1737). There is, more often than not, a gentle *double registre* to add further charm to the plot.

Marx Brothers. Quartet of Groucho (1890–1977), Chico (1887–1961), Harpo (1888–1964), and Zeppo Marx (1901–1979), whose films of the 1930s and 1940s manifested a consistently anarchic, antiestablishment, antiauthoritarian point of view, whether through Groucho's sarcastic remarks, Chico's faux-Italian mangling of logic and language, or Harpo's childish behavior and refusal ever to speak. Zeppo, a straight actor, dropped out after 1933. Major films include *Animal Crackers* (1930), *Horse Feathers* (1932), *Duck Soup* (1933), and *A Night at the Opera* (1935).

Mary Tyler Moore Show, The **(1970–1977).** Popular American TV comedy series in which star Moore, as Minneapolis news producer Mary Richards, became the emblem of the era's young, single working woman. The show combined familiar elements of the TV sitcom with diversity and sexual liberation germane to its social context. In her unsubversive way, Mary struggled daily with the balance between the assertiveness and subservience that characterized many women's uncertain social roles in this era of women's liberation.

*M*A*S*H* **(1972–1983).** Long-running American TV comedy series. It fused the situation comedy subgenres of workplace sitcom and friends-as-family sitcom into a portrait of ordinary Americans serving in a military hospital during the Korean War. Based on a freewheeling 1970 movie by Robert Altman, the show combined comic and dramatic elements in an allegory of the ongoing Vietnam War, complete with recreational and adulterous sex, copious alchohol consumption, and crude language and behavior that might have been unimaginable in a sitcom only a few years earlier.

Masquerade. Literally "putting on masks," the masquerade applies to camp's penchant for theatricality, irony, and parody. The masquerade could apply to a single performer's style (e.g., Madonna, Greta Garbo, and Bette Davis), a plot-motivated moment in a narrative, or an entire work of art. The masquerade calls concrete truth into question and opens up spaces for dual, opposing meanings, often making fun of the conventional meaning of a person, gender role, or cultural object.

Matière de Bretagne. The "matter of Britain," Arthurian stories and others from Celtic Britain (including Brittany), which formed the basis for the development of Arthurian romance in France. The term comes from the French poet Jean Bodel in the late twelfth century, who divided the material of narrative poetry into three groups: the "matter of Britain," the "matter of Greece and Rome" (romances of antiquity, based on stories of the Trojan War, Aeneas, and Alexander the Great), and the "matter of France" (epics, or *chansons de geste*, such as the *Song of Roland*). The three "matters" are a familiar and convenient set of categories, though even in the Middle Ages they were soon inadequate or misleading, unable to accommodate, for example, a "matter of England" (Middle English romances such as *King Horn* and *Havelok*, both from the thirteenth century).

McCarthy, Mary (1912–1989). American writer McCarthy, best known for her highly intellectual short fiction but also adept with novels, travel and political analyses, and criticism, is the author of sometimes ruthlessly analytical portrayals of contemporary educated men and women in their battles with each other and with larger societal forces. She carefully, wittily dissects her characters' accumulated social pretense and hypocrisy as a way of determining why certain patterns of behavior occur, sometimes basing her plots and characters on autobiographical models. Her fiction has sometimes been criticized for its occasional lack of careful plotting and endings, but her characterizations are particularly rich and vivid, and at its best her fiction is richly satiric and pointed. Her books include *The Company She Keeps* (1942), *The Oasis* (1949), *The Groves of Academe* (1952), *A Charmed Life* (1955), *Memories of a Catholic Girlhood* (1957), *The Group* (1963), *Birds of America* (1971), and *Cannibals and Missionaries* (1979).

McCulloch, Thomas (1776–1843). Author of Canada's first sustained comic work, *The Letters of Mephibosheth Stepsure* (ser. 1821–1823; in book form 1862). McCulloch's satiric mouthpiece, the overly prudent Stepsure, tells comically instructive stories of his loutish neighbors. The success of *Stepsure* inspired Thomas Chandler Haliburton to write *The Clockmaker* (1837), North America's first great work of dialect fiction.

McGruder, Aaron (1974–). Creator, writer, and illustrator of African American political satire daily comic strip, *The Boondocks*, which debuted in newspapers April 19, 1999, from the Universal Press Syndicate. It was the largest debut for a new strip, with a record 160 papers printing it. It centers on two African American prepubescent brothers uprooted from the inner city of South Chicago to suburban Woodcrest. Race, politics, music, and much more are explored by Afro-wearing, self-proclaimed anarchist Huey Freeman and his unapologetic wanksta (gangsta wannabe) younger brother Riley.

Menander (b. 343–341–292 B.C.E). He composed over 108 comedies, many of which were probably produced outside Athens. Although he was not a popular playwright during his own lifetime, he was considered the most noteworthy poet of new comedy in later generations. Menander's success developed from his ability to mold the stock characters of middle comedy into more individualized and compelling figures with sympathetic and distinctive traits. A student of both the comic playwright Alexis and the philosopher Theophrastus, Menander took care to bring his characters to life and to carry Greek comedy one step further toward realism.

Menippus (third century B.C.). Greek cynic philosopher who founded the literary genre known as Menippean satire, in which social and personal criticism is expressed in a rambling and loosely structured fable. Menippus influenced the development of Roman satire and his influence stretches beyond that to all who have used narrative to criticize the behavior of others.

Mercier, Vivian (1919–1989). Author of the single most influential book about Irish comedy, *The Irish Comic Tradition* (1962). Mercier argued for a continuity linking comic writing in both English and Irish and from ancient to modern times. He had a special affinity for Samuel Beckett as a fellow Anglo-Irishman who attended the same northern boarding school and Trinity College, Dublin, loved French literature, and even died in the same year. Taught most of his career in New York, Colorado, and California, but came back to Ireland to study Irish and later retire.

Mérite, le. The concept of *le mérite* ("merit," "intrinsic worth"), frequently employed in the French seventeenth century, refers either to an accomplishment that raises you above your normal social station or to an aura, an intimation of future accomplishment about the person. In the latter sense, *le mérite* has much in common with *le je ne sais quoi*—except that the former must result in performance. Witness Pierre Corneille's first serious masterpiece, *Le Cid* (1636), where Don Rodrigue's untested *mérite*, felt by both Chimène and the Infanta of Castile, is proven by *three combats* in twenty-four hours.

Metamorphosis. In animation, a transformation or change achieved fluidly by a series of drawings that change one creature/object into another, for example, a mirror turning into a frying pan with 2 fried eggs in *Snow White* (Fleischer Bros., 1933).

Mickey-Mousing. The use of music as an auditory analogue to a physical action, for example, a character falling down stairs accompanied by a glissando on a xylophone.

Middle comedy. A phase in the history of Greek comedy that began at the death or retirement of Aristophanes (c. 385 B.C.E.) and lasted until the premier of Menander's first comedies (c. 321 B.C.E.), although most scholars agree that these dates are an artificial construct generated to facilitate discussion of Greek comedy's evolution. Unfortunately, the fragments of middle comedy do not allow scholars to construct detailed portraits of the playwrights who thrived during this period. Comic poets such as Anaxandrides (fl. c. 385–348), Antiphanes (fl. c. 387–306), Eubulus (fl. c. 375–c. 335), and Alexis (fl. c. 350–c.275) composed plays that featured banquet scenes and the preparations for such feasts; that provided comic commentary on social institutions such as marriage or on workaday experiences such as encounters with marketplace personalities; and that offered philosophical yet lighthearted observations about life in general.

Middle English. The name given to the English language from about A.D. 1100 to 1450. Middle English existed in various dialects, which did not begin to become standardized until the introduction of printing into England near the end of the fifteenth century. At the beginning of the Middle English period, French and Latin were more likely to be used by the aristocratic and educated classes for both speaking and writing, with English being the spoken language of the people. That gradually changed and by the end of the fourteenth century the greatest poet of medieval England, Geoffrey Chaucer, wrote his works in Middle English.

***Miles gloriosus*, or braggart soldier.** Traditional comic character derived from Roman comedy. Shakespeare's Falstaff is a version of this character, just as Laurence Sterne's Uncle Toby is a drastic, sentimental rejection of this comic type.

Milne, A. A. (1882–1956). Born in London and trained as a mathematician, Alan Alexander Milne started his career as a freelance writer. Milne is best known for his stories featuring a bear named Winnie-the-Pooh that he created through collaboration with his young son Christopher. Milne created Pooh with adult wisdom and childlike humor, making him a figure that adults and children embraced easily. *Winnie-the-Pooh* (1926), *The House at Pooh Corner* (1928), *When We Were Very Young* (1924), and *Now We Are Six* (1927) are Milne's important children's texts.

Mise-en-scène. French for "putting in the scene": placing all the elements in front of the camera: settings, costume, performance, props, and lighting.

M-Net. South African media giant that broadcasts satellite television throughout Africa. Similar to such Western cable channels as Arte and Canal+ in Europe and Sundance Channel in the United States, it funds and coproduces televison and film comedies. It is also a major sponsor of Sithengi (Southern African International Film and Televison Market), an international market of the film and video industry. Some critics believe that M-Net monopolizes production and distribution and therefore has a negative influence on the development of new films in Africa.

Mock-heroic. Using the language and frame of reference of classical epic to write about trivial or common modern events to create a sense of false and comic elevation. Alexander Pope's *The Rape of the Lock* (1712) is the most notable eighteenth-century poem in this mode.

Mockumentary. A genre of film that either makes fun of the conventions of documentary films or uses the fictional premise of a documentary to present comic characters. Albert Brooks' *Real Life* (1979) and Woody Allen's *Zelig* (1983) were the progenitors of mockumentary. Another kind of mockumentary originated with Rob Reiner's *This Is Spinal Tap* (1984), a parody of a heavy metal rock group, and has continued with *Waiting for Guffman* (1996), about a small-town theatrical pageant; *Best in Show* (2000), about competitive dog shows; and *A Mighty Wind* (2003), about folk music, all of them directed by Christopher Guest and cowritten with Eugene Levy.

Molière (1622–1673). The stage name, to date unexplained, of Jean-Baptiste Poquelin, an actor, director, and playwright who in his all-too-brief, meteoric Parisian career (1658–1673) made comedy the equal of tragedy in the literary hierarchy of the French classical age. For later generations, he accomplished this feat through the approximately eight grand social comedies that hold up to ridicule (as well as pity, more often than not) certain morally flawed characters Molière noted in the world about him. These same generations sometimes overlook the remainder—in effect, most—of the Moliéresque canon (some thirty-two or thirty-four plays in all) running the gamut from slapstick farce to fast-paced comedy of error and/or social satire, not to mention the numerous royally commanded court entertainments that flatter his majesty, mock the less fortunate, or waft the audience to some distant pastoral land.

Monty Python's Flying Circus. A British comedy team that achieved huge success between 1969 and the early 1980s. Its members included Graham Chapman, John Cleese, Terry Gilliam, Eric Idle, Terry Jones, and Michael Palin. They started with thirteen TV shows for the BBC including *Monty Python's Flying Circus* (1969–1974), and went on to do several ironic movies, including *Monty Python and the Holy Grail* (1975), *Life of Brian* (1979), and *Monty Python's The Meaning of Life* (1983). They chose their name to communicate something both slimy (a python) and powerful (the commanding military name Monty).

Mooney, Paul (1948?–). Richard Pryor writer and cult legend of contemporary African American comedy. Mooney is a favorite but he may never be widely known and may remain in the shadow of his friend and rival Pryor. Witty and clever, giving civics lessons through the comedy of social issues, this droll performer was established by Pryor as his right-hand writer. Over time his contribution has begun to be more appreciated. He pushes all kinds of buttons and then grins a smirky, evil grin—constantly mixing the absurdity of incongruity theory, the release of panicky ferment strain of relief theory, and amusingly demeaning things deemed inferior in superiority theory.

Morreall, John (1947–). Contemporary philosopher of humor and proponent of the incongruity theory of humor. He argued that incongruity is amusing when it triggers a pleasant cognitive shift, thereby spurring the development of cognitive flexibility. He wrote *Taking Laughter Seriously* (1983) and was the editor of *The Philosophy of Laughter and Humor*.

Movida, la **("the movement").** A popular cultural and creative urban movement in the early 1980s in Madrid. It encompassed music, film, the comic magazine industry, and an attitude that broke with the religious and traditional Franco-era lifestyle. A new satirical language originated with this young urban attitude that soon became part of the new democratic Spain. The most relevant figure of *la movida* is Pedro Almodóvar.

Myers, Mike (1963–). Born in Scarborough, Ontario, Myers is an alumnus of the long-running American TV comedy *Saturday Night Live*. He went on to star in many movies, including *Wayne's World* (1992) and *Shrek* (2001), and is best known for his Austin Powers movies (1997, 1999, 2002).

Nast, Thomas (1840–1902). Best known for his successful attack on Boss Tweed of Tammany Hall in *Harper's Weekly*. From 1862 to 1887 he employed a heavily crosshatched style for somber, emotive, dogmatic attacks that riveted reader attention in their appeal for action. Nast helped create the belief that cartoonists could mobilize public opinion and affect politics.

National Film Board of Canada. Pioneering government-sponsored animation studio. From 1941 headed by Norman McLaren, who in turn nurtured George Dunning, Grant Monroe, René Jodoin, Evelyn Lambert, and other animators.

Netfunny.com. One of the largest online electronic humor magazines, which claims that over 500,000 people worldwide read its jokes daily.

New comedy. Technically begins with the production of Menander's first comedy circa 321 B.C.E. The playwrights of this period, including Straton (fl. 302), Diphilus (fl. c. 320–c. 285), and Philemon (fl. 327–c. 263), based the humor and richness of their scripts on the intricacies of their narratives and their creative portrayals of the stock characters of middle comedy. The Roman playwrights of the third and second centuries B.C.E. championed new comedy and closely modeled their productions on the scripts of Menander and his contemporaries. Later generations of dramatists, from Shakespeare to the creators of modern sitcoms, used the comic misunderstandings and thwarted love affairs of these narratives as source material for their romantic comedies and domestic farces.

Ngangura, Mweze (1950–). Congolese filmmaker who trained at Belgium's Institut des Arts de Diffusion in Brussels. In addition to the full-length feature comedies *La Vie est belle* (1989) and *Pièces d'identités* (1998), he has made two short fiction films and several documentaries that deal with everyday life in urban and village settings and the history of colonial encounters with Africa. He is the greatest proponent of developing an African popular cinema for worldwide distribution.

Nonsense. Also nonsense poetry, nonsense verse. Language that has been inverted from the usual authority-driven rules of order and logic. Situations and happenings that could never take place are enacted as though they are logical. Nonsense is characterized by playful, inexact language that closely approximates standard usage but has been altered. Nonsense was made famous by Edward Lear and Lewis Carroll but was also used by other writers like Jonathan Swift, Dennis Lee, Roald Dahl, and Dr. Seuss.

O'Brien, Flann (1911–1966). Leading Irish satirist of the twentieth century, a worthy successor to Jonathan Swift though from a very different, Gaelic, Catholic background. Born Brian O'Nolan in County Tyrone, O'Brien earned a B.A. and an M.A. in Irish at University College, Dublin—James Joyce's University—and became the most Joycean writer after Joyce. Invented Flann O'Brien as his pseudonym as author of the novels *At Swim-Two-Birds* (1939), *The Hard Life* (1961), *The Dalkey Archive* (1964), and *The Third Policeman* (1967, but written much earlier). Beloved as "Myles na gCopaleen," author of the Gaelic novel *An Béal Bocht* (*The Poor Mouth*, 1941) and the long-running satiric column in the *Irish Times*, "Cruiskeen Lawn" ("little full jug").

O'Casey, Sean (1880–1964). One of the two or three best Irish playwrights, O'Casey was born in Dublin as John Casey, self-educated, and the son of working-class or lower-middle-class Protestants. Worked as a laborer and as secretary to James Connolly's Irish Citizen Army. He burst onto the Abbey stage with his great Dublin trilogy *The Shadow of a Gunman* (1923), *Juno and the Paycock* (1924), and *The Plough and the Stars* (1926). William Butler Yeats championed those plays but then rejected *The Silver Tassie* (1928), an experimental play about English soldiers in World War I, and O'Casey moved permanently to County Devon in England, where he lived for decades writing more innovative and socialist plays as well as six volumes of autobiography.

Old comedy. The first major phase in the history of Greek comedy. Although plays of this type were introduced into the comic competition at the City Dionysia in 486 B.C.E. and at Lenaea in the 440s B.C.E., our knowledge of this genre is shaped largely by the comedies of Aristophanes, the only old comic playwright whose scripts survive intact. However, Aristophanes' extant comedies represent only a fraction of the work produced during this period. From 486 to 388 B.C.E., over 600 comedies, written by approximately fifty playwrights, were performed in Athens. Old comedy focused on the social and political questions most germane to contemporary Athenian life; however, by combining this type of critical civic analysis with comic spectacle and slapstick humor, the playwrights allowed the audience members to purge themselves of the problems they confronted on a daily basis and to use the performance as a springboard for further reflection and debate.

Oliphant, Pat (1935–), and Jeff MacNelly (1947–2000). Acknowledged as the greatest influences upon the recent generation of editorial cartoonists, combining ribald humor, naturalism, and slashing caricature in the same drawing and irreverently belittling even the most powerful political leaders. They were celebrated for never presenting their beliefs cautiously.

Opper, Frederick B. (1857–1937). Combined a long and successful career as both a political and a comic strip cartoonist and created the symbolic "Common Man" for *Puck* and, later, the *New York Evening Journal*. A master of sly caricature and slapstick humor, he made political and business leaders behave and look ridiculous in such series about Progressive Era politics as *Willie and His Papa*.

Orwell, George (1903–1950). Pen name of Eric Arthur Blair, the English novelist whose satiric beast-fable *Animal Farm* (1945) mounts a shrewd and memorable attack on supposedly egalitarian dictatorships.

OULIPO. The *Ouvroir de Littérature Potentielle*, or Workshop of Potential Literature, was founded in France in the 1960s by mathematician François le Lionnais and writer Raymond Queneau. Writers and poets use a series of literary constratints, which they invent or take from mathematics, to create new works. Central to OULIPO is the idea of the importance of play in literature. Members include Queneau, Jacques Roubaud, Georges Perec, and Marcel Bénabou.

Parody. In literature, what a caricature or a cartoon is in art. In all three cases, the salient features are isolated and exaggerated. A parody is more than an objective imitation because the parodist starts out with an attitude. But ironically, in the process of ridiculing the original, the parodist is also making it more famous. Parodies sometimes focus on the work of individual authors whose style is distinct, such as Ernest Hemingway or William Faulkner. Jonathan Swift's *Gulliver's Travels* (1726) is a parody of travel literature, and Henry Fielding's *Shamela* (1741) is a parody of Samuel Richardson's realistic domestic novel *Pamela* (1740).

Pastoral. As a dramatic genre, the pastoral originated in sixteenth-century Italy with works such as Torquato Tasso's *Aminta* (1573) and Giovanni Battista Guarini's *Faithful Shepherd* (1589). Set in a happier, simpler world of shepherds and shepherdesses, the pastoral follows the progress of a love that depends solely on the consent of the young people involved, especially the women. With playwrights like Pierre Corneille (1606–1684), the setting changed to contemporary society, but to the extent possible, the subject remains love unfettered by the traditional, external obstacles created by old or otherwise grotesque blocking characters.

Pastoral comedy. A comedy whose setting is primarily or entirely the countryside and whose main characters are shepherds and shepherdesses. The fiction behind this type is the idea that country life, though often requiring hard work under difficult conditions, offers simple pleasures and a purer morality not available to city dwellers.

Personality Animation. Animation pioneered by Winsor McCay and Walt Disney Studios, which emphasized nuances of personality and movement over the gag structure in narrative animation. Evident in most feature animation since *Snow White and the Seven Dwarfs*.

Personality comedy. A style of comedy that spotlights one central comic, who has generally established a persona outside movies and who therefore can operate both inside and outside the story, both playing a part in a fiction and commenting on it as if from the outside. Prominent examples include Groucho Marx, Bob Hope, Jack Benny, Woody Allen, and Eddie Murphy.

Pherecrates (fl. 437–after 415 B.C.E.). Generated "courtesan comedies" in which prostitutes starred as the leading characters. He was considered an obvious forerunner of later Greek playwrights who favored love themes as opposed to political satire. He also staged such utopian comedies as *Wild Men* (*Agrioi*), where men leave "civilized" urban life to live a more "primitive" existence, and *Miners* (*Metalles*), which portrayed the Underworld as full of luxuries and abundance.

Picaresque. A prose autobiography of a real or fictitious character who describes his or her experiences as a social parasite and satirizes the society in which he or she is exploited. The first picaresque novel is the *Life of Lazarillo de Tormes and of His Fortunes and Misfortunes* (1554). The authorship of this book and circumstances of its publication are not clear, but it was a best seller by 1559.

Pinero, Arthur Wing (1855–1934). Prominent late Victorian playwright known especially for his farces. Pinero, much to his mother's chagrin, abandoned his study of the law to join the dramatic company of the famous actor Sir Henry Irving for a five-year apprenticeship. He eventually turned from acting to writing, scoring an early major hit with *The Magistrate* (1885), a satirical farce reflecting, no doubt, his early legal training. Despite considerable success as a writer of farce, his ambitions to write socially relevant theater were something of a failure, though the controversial *The Second Mrs. Tanqueray* (1893), the first of his social dramas, was sufficiently well received to encourage him to continue. His most widely performed play was, and continues to be, the semiserious comedy *Trelawney of the Wells* (1898).

Pirandello, Luigi (1867–1936). Italian playwright, novelist, and poet. The son of a wealthy Sicilian mine owner, Pirandello was educated in Rome and Bonn, where he wrote a doctoral dissertation on Sicilian dialect. He settled on a career as a writer, eventually becoming Italy's most important twentieth-century dramatist. He is particularly well known for his grotesque comedies dramatizing madness, illusion, and the relativity of truth, identity, and reality. His best-known plays—including *It Is So! (If You Think So)* (1917), *Six Characters in Search of an Author* (1921), and *Henry IV* (1922)—are collected in *Naked Masks* (1952), edited by Eric Bentley. Pirandello won the Nobel Prize for Literature in 1934.

Plato (427?–347 B.C.E.). Greek philosopher, student of Socrates, and founder of the Academy at Athens. He wrote a large number of dialogues that were foundational to the modern study of topics like epistemology, metaphysics, ethics, and politics. His main concern throughout these works was the relationship between virtue and the good life. Plato had a negative view of humor and comedy, and was a proponent of the superiority theory of humor. Aristotle was his student. Works relevant to his philosophy of humor include *Philebus* and *Republic*.

Plato Comicus (fl. 422–c. 380 B.C.E.). Secured his first victory at the City Dionysia around 410. Throughout his career, he composed both political satires and mythological burlesques.

Plautus, Titus Maccius (fl. c. 205–184 B.C.E.). Author (or, more accurately, adapter) of the Greek new comedy of Menander, with plots focusing primarily on mistaken or confused identities, romantic intrigues, and exaggerated types such as the *miles gloriosus*, the clever or scheming servant, and the *senex* (foolish old man) that survived and developed into the Renaissance forms of the *commedia dell'arte*, the early Tudor interlude, and school comedies such as *Ralph Roister Doister* and *Gammer Gurton's Needle*.

Playing the dozens. Verbal dueling, usually by African American male teenagers, begun by a sexual insult hurled against the mother or other female relative of the opponent, who in turn must reply with an even more outrageous taunt. To respond violently is uncool; the winner succeeds by "capping" the exchange, that is, uttering something that can't be topped. In recent years young girls have begun to play the dozens too. Humor is a crucial and dominant element of the exchanges, most often employed through outrageous hyperbole such as "Yo mama does it with the Turkish army." The dozens is an important element in black male identity construction and is basic training for the man of words. In northern U.S. inner cities, the practice is sometimes called "sounding."

Plight-troth. Spousals, or an early modern version of our wedding engagement. Under certain circumstances, betrothal was legally binding in a way that modern engagement is not, so that children born after spousals but before the wedding were often considered legitimate. Nevertheless, because the legality of betrothal was subject to different interpretations in various places and times—and sometimes by a man and woman involved with each other—it occasioned matrimonial litigation in the church courts, which handled such cases. The fact that a couple could plight troth without parental consent or witnesses made it a useful device for authors of early modern romantic comedies.

Pope, Alexander (1688–1744). The greatest eighteenth-century English poet. Pope became wealthy through his translations of the Homeric epics and famous and feared for his satiric poems, notably *The Rape of the Lock* (1712) and *The Dunciad* (1728–1744). *The Rape of the Lock* is mock-heroic and *The Dunciad* is a merciless attack on contemporary authors.

Poquelin, Jean-Baptiste. *See* Molière

Praxinoscopes, Thaumatropes, and Zoescopes. Optical toys, many of which were invented in the nineteenth century and which use persistence of vision to create the illusion of motion. The zoetrope, for example, was a circular disk with a series of images, not unlike a filmstrip, on the inside. The disk had slits in a drum through which the viewer would look at the images; when the disk was rotated, the images appeared to move.

Prima amorosa. In Italian *commedia dell'arte* troupes, the first feminine love lead, who is promised to the handsome young suitor at the happy ending. The Mélite of Pierre Corneille's homonymous comedy (1629) is a French *prima amorosa*, as is Molière's Célimène, the latter in a negative sense, however, since she is rejected finally by leading man Alceste.

Producers, the **(1968 movie, 2001 Broadway musical).** Written and directed by Mel Brooks. Crooked theater producer Max cons rich old ladies and plots with an accountant to make a fortune by producing a tax-write-off flop, a musical comedy about Nazis entitled *Springtime for Hitler*.

Pryor, Richard (1940–). Pryor was born in Peoria, Illinois, where his grandparents ran a brothel and pool hall. He acted in local productions, dropped out of high school, joined the army, and performed in amateur shows. After his discharge he began to work the comedy-club circuit, which led to engagements on TV. Soon he was performing on the Ed Sullivan Show and in Las Vegas. He became famous as a movie star, first working alongside Sid Caesar in *The Busy Body* (1967), and then going on to make over forty films, most memorably a series in which he costarred with Gene Wilder (especially *Silver Streak*, 1976).

Queneau, Raymond (1903–1976). Poet, novelist, and founding member of the OULIPO (1960). Author of *Zazie dans le métro* (1959), *Les Exercices de style* (1947), and *Cent mille milliards de poèmes* (1961).

Quevedo y Villegas, Francisco de (1580–1645). Author best known for his burlesque and incisive critique of the collapse of the Spanish empire. Quevedo was the main representative of the literary *conceptista* movement, characterized by a sharp and ingenious form of expression that opposed the complex formalism of *culteranismo*, represented by Luis de Góngora. His style is compressed, elusive, and elliptical, embracing the obtrusively learned and the vividly colloquial with equal ease. He mastered poetry, essays, and novels that include *The Scavenger* (1604) and *Dreams* (1622).

Radcliffe, Ann (1764–1823). The most popular and influential writer of gothic romance in the late eighteenth century, Radcliffe produced four fictions in remarkably short order, on which her fame is based. They are *A Sicilian Romance* (1790), *Romance of the Forest* (1791), *The Mysteries of Udolpho* (1794), and *The Italian* (1797). Unlike other gothic practitioners who had recourse to supernatural machinery, Radcliffe ultimately provided rational explanations for the elements of terror in her novels that appear supernatural. As such, her novels are concerned more in the end with the character, sensibility, and resourcefulness of their various heroines and are more properly about the condition of women in the (then) present time than they are incentives to religious doubt or institutional change.

Radin, Paul (1883–1959). Radin was the first student to receive a Ph.D in anthropology in the United States as a student of Franz Boas. At Boas' suggestion, Radin did fieldwork among the Winnebago tribe in 1912, and it was around that time that he collected, through a Native consultant, the cycle of trickster tales that was not published in book form until 1956 in *The Trickster*. Radin was also interested in the cultures of Africa and South America, and, with a decided psychological orientation, he also studied Native American religion and philosophy.

***Raisonneur* (m.), *Raisonneuse* (f.).** A type of Moliéresque character who resembles the chorus of classical antiquity in that they are both moderately involved in the play's action at best but spend considerable effort to enunciate the social lessons to be gleaned from the spectacle—in Molière's case, the importance of nature unhampered and of the "golden mean." Though primarily *raisonneurs* (e.g., Philinte in *Le Misanthrope* [1666]), there are occasional *raisonneuses*, too (e.g., Eliante of the same play).

Rall, Ted (1963–). One of the most outspoken of the younger political satirists. Since 1992 he has published eight collections of cartoons for different syndicates taking radical positions on social and political topics, is often deliberately outrageous and confrontational, and has introduced readers to cartoonists outside the mainstream through his anthology *Attitude* (2002). He is as much an essayist as a cartoonist.

Raven. Raven or Crow is probably the foremost Native American trickster after Coyote, most prevalent in northern areas. A great many stories from many indigenous peoples have been published about his adventures. That Raven lives in the imaginations of indigenous storytellers today is wonderfully demonstrated by the publication in 1999 of Tommy McGinty's Northern Tutchone (Athapaskan Indians of the Yukon) *Story of Crow*.

Recognition scene. To extricate himself at the denouement from a self-made impasse, the seventeenth-century comic playwright could resort (none more than Molière) to a conventional expedient other than the deus ex machina; to wit, the well used, highly improbable recognition scene. By this device, a minor, generally late-arriving character reveals a principal role's unsuspected true identity that will miraculously permit the happy ending. Thus, in Molière's *Ecole des femmes* (1662) does Arnolphe learn that Agnès is not the penniless girl he had raised to be his future wife but, rather, the daughter of wealthy Enrique, just returned from abroad, who had betrothed this his only child to Horace, the young man she truly loved.

Reed, Ishmael (1938–). The major comic African American novelist of the twentieth century, a noted poet, essayist, and cultural activist, Reed was born in Chattanooga, Tennessee, and grew up in Buffalo, New York. He attended the University of Buffalo before moving to New York City, where he edited a newspaper and helped establish the *East Village Other*. Over a long career, he has published many major satirical novels such as *The Freelance Pallbearers* (1967), *Mumbo Jumbo* (1972), *Yellow Back Radio Broke-Down* (1969), and *Flight to Canada* (1976). *Mumbo Jumbo* inaugurated Reed's interest in "neohoodooism," an aesthetic and often comic approach to key issues in African American culture. He has satirized the slave narrative, the western, and, recently, the East-West economic system. His controversial views on virtually every subject may be found in his lively collections of essays, which demonstrate a ferocious wit.

Relief theory. A philosophical and psychological theory of humor, espoused in different forms by Alexander Bain, Herbert Spencer, and Sigmund Freud. The relief theory is the view that laughter is a manifestation of the release of nervous excitement or emotional tension. It is associated with a larger theory of humor or comedy stating that our enjoyment of the comic is a result of some release of negative feeling, or redirection of emotion or nervous energy.

Remarque, Erich Maria (1898–1970). German-born writer best known for *All Quiet on the Western Front* (1929), a novel based on his experiences in World War I in which Remarque stripped the romantic sheen from warfare to show its pointless brutality. While other novels of the period had shown the same brutality Remarque depicted, most continued to glorify the abstract concepts of nobility and patriotism in the context of combat.

Richardson, Samuel (1689–1761). Author of the innovative realistic epistolary novel *Pamela* (1740), parodied by Henry Fielding in *Shamela* (1741) and in *Joseph Andrews* (1742).

Richler, Mordecai (1931–2001). Novelist, essayist, and screenwriter born in Montreal, which Richler most famously made his fictional territory in *The Apprenticeship of Duddy Kravitz* (1959). Canada's leading comic novelist of the second half of the twentieth century, his *The Incomparable Atuk* (1963) and *Cocksure* (1968) satirize Canadian cultural nationalism and the movie industry respectively. His other major comic novels are *St. Urbain's Horseman* (1971), *Joshua Then and Now* (1980), *Solomon Gursky Was Here* (1989), and *Barney's Version* (1997).

Riggs, Marlon (1957–1994). Award-winning documentarian whose work largely focuses on African American and gay cultures. Despite the seriousness of his subjects and the social problems dealt with in his work, Riggs consistently employs camp humor in order to experiment with documentary form and open up questions about complex subjects such as racism and homophobia.

Rock, Chris (1965–). Chief Richard Pryor/Bill Cosby humor descendant and popular African American comedian. In the post-Pryor generation, the crown and baton have been passed to Rock, a comedian who spent three seasons on *Saturday Night Live* (1990–1993) after being discovered by Eddie Murphy. In early 2004, he was voted the Funniest Person in America by *Entertainment Weekly*, adding to honors already bestowed by *Time* and *Vanity Fair*. This Emmy-award winner became internationally known through his eponymous HBO series

(1997–2000) and three comedy specials that showcased his brand of humor: *Chris Rock: Bring the Pain* (1996), *Chris Rock: Bigger & Blacker* (1999), and *Chris Rock: Never Scared* (2004).

Romance. A form of narrative in prose or verse typically dealing with the themes of adventure, chivalry, courtesy, love, and the marvelous. The narrative emphasis on individual quests, the settings remote in time and place, and the idealized content are all characteristics of the form. Romance developed in France and became the major literary form of the High Middle Ages (the twelfth through the fifteenth centuries). It has antecedents in the Hellenistic romances of antiquity and descendants in the fantasy novels of today, but it is especially associated with the medieval period in western Europe.

Roseanne **(1988–1997).** American TV comedy series that provided a working-class alternative to the upper-class family harmonies of the leading 1980s TV comedy, *The Cosby Show.* Working mother Roseanne Conner (Roseanne Barr) was not wise and regal but loud and struggling, sometimes unemployed, short on patience and wise solutions. Squalling conflicts expanded to include children, family always triumphed over class, and parenting or grandparenting conferred no special qualities of understanding or affection onto otherwise troubled and troublesome adults.

Rosten, Leo (1908–1997). Under the pen name Leonard Q. Ross, Rosten wrote *The Education of H*y*m*a*n K*a*p*l*a*n* (1937), a comic novel about an immigrant night-school student's reinvention of both himself and the English language.

Roth, Philip (1933–). With its mordant depiction of the suburban mass migration of American Jews, Roth's breakthrough novella *Goodbye Columbus* (1959) inaugurated a career that produced more than twenty novels. With comic explicitness in treating masturbation, oral sex, and impotence, *Portnoy's Complaint* (1969) breaks new ground in American sex comedy, just as *The Ghost Writer* (1979) treats the Holocaust with unprecedented comic candor. His novel, *The Plot Against America* (2004), is also focused on Jewish themes.

Royal Canadian Air Farce, The. The name of a troupe and its long-running radio and TV series satirizing all things Canadian, composed variously of Roger Abbot, Dave Broadfoot, Don Ferguson, Luba Goy, and John Morgan.

Rubberhosing. An animation style used predominantly in the 1910s, 1920s, and early 1930s featuring balloonlike bodies and rubber-hose limbs. Animated rubber-hose characters were not consistent in terms of body weight or size but could expand and contract at will.

Rube Goldberg device. A deliberately complicated mechanical device or series of interconnected devices that perform a simple task; named after the American cartoonist and, briefly, animator (of *Boob Weekly*, Pathé) who made the devices famous in his comic strips of the mid-twentieth century.

Rudnick, Paul (1957–). An openly gay writer whose screenplays consistently employ camp strategies of parody, irony, and masquerade. The title alone of *Addams Family Values* (1993) ironizes the right-wing, fundamentalist campaign against queer rights based upon "family values," here reinterpreted through the protoqueer Addams family. His *In and Out* (1997) tells the story of a closeted schoolteacher who is outed on national television by one of his students.

RuPaul (1960–). Drag queen RuPaul was first known by queers for her hilarious concert performances. She crossed over into mainstream popular culture in the early 1990s with campy appearances on MTV's *Spring Break*, two Brady Bunch movies, and a short-lived chat show on VH1. She is best known for her sweet but domineering attitude and quick wit.

Sarcasm. From the Greek *sarkazein*, "to bite lips in rage." Sarcasm is similar to irony in that the literal meaning differs from the actual meaning. However, the meanings need not be directly opposite, and sarcasm is delivered in a distinctive tone of voice. Sarcastic remarks are usually cutting, derisive, and contemptuous.

Satire. A genre that uses humor and wit to ridicule humans or human behavior. Without humor and wit, satire would be invective. If the attack becomes too personal, the satire becomes sarcasm. Literary satire does not deal with criminals and truly despicable people because its creators are hoping to bring positive changes to fools, knaves, ninnies, oafs, codgers, pedants, and frauds. Horatian satire is gentle, urbane, and amusing as it uses broad laughter as a corrective force; Juvenalian satire is biting, bitter, and angry, as it reveals the corruptness of human beings and human institutions; and Menippean satire expresses itself indirectly, through a story or fable.

Schopenhauer, Arthur (1788–1860). German philosopher who theorized that the "will" is the inner force that drives human beings and the inner force underlying all reality. The will is also the cause of our suffering; aesthetic experience temporarily relieves us of this drive and so relieves us of this suffering. Release from all desire is an ideal goal. Schopenhauer was a proponent of the incongruity theory of humor: our response to humorous situations derives from our resentment of our higher cognitive faculties; the experience of incongruity represents the triumph of perception over those higher faculties that impose control over desire. Works relevant to his philosophy of humor include *The World as Will and Idea* (1818).

Schuyler, George (1895–1977). Born in Providence, Rhode Island, to middle-class parents, Schuyler grew up in Syracuse, New York. He spent seven years in the army before joining the editorial staff of the *Messenger*, where he edited a satirical column from 1923 to 1928. Later he wrote for the *Pittsburgh Courier*, contributing a weekly "Views and Reviews." He was a force in the Harlem Renaissance and specialized in racial satire, particularly in his 1931 novel *Black No More, Being an Account of the Strange and Wonderful Workings of Science in the Land of the Free*, a wild tale about Dr. Crookman, who invents a machine that makes blacks white. He went on to write several other novels and a 1966 autobiography, *Black and Conservative*.

Scott, F. R. (1899–1985). Canada's best satiric poet of the modern period, Scott's work is typified by "The Canadian Authors Meet," satirizing his poet predecessors and their readers, and "W.L.M.K.," flailing Canada's longest-serving prime minister, William Lyon Mackenzie King. With A.J.M. Smith (1902–1980) he edited *The Blasted Pine: An Anthology of Satire, Invective and Disrespectful Verse* (1957), Canada's first significant anthology of comic poetry. An updated edition was published in 1967.

Screwball. A zany, wiseacre character with unpredictable, crazy behavior.

SCTV. Canada's popular TV comedy series of the 1970s and 1980s, *Second City TV* created a wealth of recurring characters and sketches and launched such talents as John Candy, Joe Flaherty, Eugene Levy, Andrea Martin, Rick Moranis, Catherine O'Hara, Harold Ramis, Martin Short, and Dave Thomas.

Seconda amorosa. In Italian *commedia dell'arte* (and French) troupes, the second female love lead, who must, in almost every case, accept willy-nilly any marriage furthering the *prima amorosa*'s ultimate happiness. Such is the lot of the male protagonist's "sacrificed" sister in Cornelian comedies. Occasionally, however, in an original twist, the French playwright may disappoint the conjugal aspirations of the *prima amorosa* but gratify the *seconda*'s. Witness Pierre Corneille's *Place Royale* (1634), where the wrong woman marries while principal Angélique enters a convent, and Molière's *Misanthrope* (1666), in which the *raisonneuse* Eliante, a secondary part, has alone hopes to wed as the curtain falls.

Seinfeld, Jerry (1954–). A stand-up comic who became the creator of the eponymous TV series that ran from 1989 to 1998. Though it skirts its characters' seemingly Jewish ethnicity, *Seinfeld* became the culmination and epitome of modern Jewish humor in America due largely to its relentlessly deadpan reduction of commonplace profundities to banalities and its corresponding inflation of apparent quotidian trivia to metaphysical quandaries.

Sembene, Ousmane (1923–). Senegalese writer and director of numerous comedies and dramas that represent events from everyday life and satirically shed light on many of the problems that plague African progress, such as corruption, abuse of power, tribal and religious conflict, and the tension between the old and the new. After studying film at the Sorky Studio in Moscow, he made *Borom Sarret* (The Wagon Driver, 1963), the first professional film by an African in Africa. The father of African film, Sembene depicts not only the disenfranchised and marginalized, but also the wealthy and government elite. He has been making films since 1963 and is sometimes called the cinematic griot of Africa.

Sendak, Maurice (1928–). One of the early picture book writers and illustrators who moved beyond straightforward directly representational images when articulating his text in art. As such, he paved the way for the modern market of sophisticated and complex children's picture books. Sendak is important to the development of comedy in children's literature because his controversial illustrated picture books depict children in humorous ways while giving voice to their fantasies. Important works are *Where the Wild Things Are* (1963), *The Sign on Rosie's Door* (1960), *In the Night Kitchen* (1970), *The Nutshell Library* (1962), and *Outside over There* (1981).

Sennett, Mack (1880–1960). Sennett's Keystone Film Company, founded in late 1912, popularized physical, slapstick comedy in the crucial early years of cinema, primarily through the Keystone Kops, the bumbling police force whose acrobatic antics epitomized the anarchic physical universe of Sennett shorts.

Sententia **(sing.),** *sententiae* **(pl.).** Latin for maxim, aphorism. In his stated goal to improve (*corriger*) the audience, Molière sprinkles his socially oriented comedies with *sententiae* via the *raisonneur*. Employed since classical antiquity, this procedure is evident in Pierre Corneille, too, who, for example, has contented Mélite exclaim: "*en fait d'amour la fraude est légitime*" ("in matters of love deception is legitimate"—*Mélite* [1629]), a proverb surprisingly close to the English "All's fair in love and war."

Sentimental comedy. The tendency in eighteenth-century comic writing to value good feeling and charity in characters over satire and wit and to present dramatic situations for their good humor and pathos rather than their comedy or absurdity. Richard Steele's "The Conscious Lovers" (1722) may be said to initiate this tendency. Uncle Toby in Laurence Sterne's *Tristram Shandy* (1759–1766) is a comic sentimental hero.

Shakespeare, William (1564–1616). Shakespeare wrote romantic comedies throughout his career, experimenting with the conventions of the form. As was the custom, he refashioned plots and characters from Plautus and other ancient authors, medieval romance, sixteenth-century novellas and plays, and popular literature. He not only adapted but parodied earlier genres and discourses, most notably Petrarchan and courtly love conventions. While most of the comedies focus on aristocratic or wealthy merchant characters, subplots bring in a great variety of underclass characters; while most are set, with varying degrees of early modern specificity, in European kingdoms, several are placed in the ancient world and some in English settings. All the plays have complex dramatic structures with intersecting double or multiple plots. Their socially varied casts of characters and their focus on courtship and marriage allow them, in spite of the distancing effect of comic artifice, to engage important early modern issues, particularly those concerning courtship and marriage, and the autonomy of the individual in a strongly hierarchical society.

Shaw, George Bernard (1856–1950). Irish playwright whose career was the longest and most successful of any modern dramatist. Born in Dublin, he moved to London at age twenty, thereafter writing acerbically about English society from the perspective, like Oscar Wilde, of an nonconformist, Anglo-Irish outsider. His sole Irish play, *John Bull's Other Island*, was turned down by the Abbey Theatre, the principal literary theater in Ireland, but staged in London in 1905.

Shelton, Gilbert (1940–). The most consistently political of the 1960s "underground comix" artists. The Fabulously Furry Freak Brothers wreaked havoc on the forces of law and respectability in their never-ending search for drugs and the superhero parody, Wonder Warthog, satirized American society as fascistic. Shelton still produces cartoons and comic books in Europe.

Shephard, Sam (1943–). American playwright, fiction writer, essayist, screenwriter, actor, and film director. Born in Illinois, Shepard (né Samuel Shepard Rogers) grew up in southern California. Rather than go to college, he headed east to New York, where he became active in the avant-garde East Village theater scene. In London in the early 1970s he experimented with full-length plays parodying Elizabethan tragedy (e.g., *The Tooth of Crime*, 1972) and wrote in the Samuel Beckett mode (e.g., *Action*, 1974). Back in the United States in the late 1970s, he started writing his trademark family plays parodying American culture and western myth and subverting tragedy with farce. These plays include *Curse of the Starving Class* (1977), *Buried Child* (1978; Pulitzer Prize, 1979), *True West* (1980), *Fool for Love* (1983), and *A Lie of the Mind* (1985). Shepard reprises family tensions using dreamlike realism in *The Late Henry Moss* (2000).

Sheridan, Richard Brinsley (1751–1816). Prominent comic dramatist, theatrical manager, and politician whose *The Rivals* (1775) and *The School for Scandal* (1777) are by common consent the two best English comedies after William Congreve's.

Sick humor. Humor that derives its comic value by violating norms of social and culture values. Sick humor is not ambivalent; instead, it artificially imposes comic connotations on an event which is solely tragic. The result of this is a sense of cavalier amorality that can prevent investment in characters. Perhaps for these reason, sick humor is highly effective as a joke because in a joke's succinct format investment in characters is not necessary.

Signifying. The general practice of comic critique in African American culture. The practitioner may or may not intend harm, as one often signifies for the fun of it. Characteristics of the practice include indirection, or circumlocution; use of metaphorical-imagistic language rooted in daily life; humor and irony; rhythmic fluidity and sound; teaching but not preaching; direction toward someone present; punning; and use of the unexpected.

***Simpsons, The* (1989–).** Classic American animated television comedy featuring the family of reprobate Homer Simpson, bratty Bart, brainy Lisa, baby Maggie, and matriarch Marge. Together with *Married with Children* (1987–1997), the show defined the fledgling Fox network as the home of untraditional situation comedy families that were crude, fractious, and working class. *The Simpsons* is noted for its intelligent and well-written commentary on political and moral issues.

Slapstick comedy. The term usually applied to the boisterously physical type of farce characterized by pie-in-the-face clowning and similar unsubtle devices. It takes its name from the flat, double-paneled stick, joined at one end and free at the other, that makes a sharp clacking noise far worse than the minor discomfort suffered by the victim when whacked with it. This brand of farce, particularly prevalent in the early silent film comedy virtually from its beginnings, is associated with the work of such artists as Max Linder (pseudonym of Gabriel-Maximilien Leuvielle) in France, and the likes of Buster Keaton, Laurel and Hardy, the Keystone Kops, and numerous others in America; even, at times, in the intellectually more subtle artistry of Charlie Chaplin. It reached its peak in the offerings of the Three Stooges.

Slow Burn. A term in animation. A dim character slowly conceives that he or she has been duped, and becomes enraged (face turns red, grits teeth, etc.). Characteristic reactions of cartoon characters Elmer Fudd and Yosemite Sam.

Somerville and Ross. The joint pen name of Edith Somerville (1858–1949) and her cousin "Martin Ross" (Violet Martin, 1862–1915), forming one of the most successful coauthorships in modern literature. In 1898 Martin suffered a riding accident that shortened her life, but Somerville cosigned even the books that she wrote solo after Martin's death, convinced that she was still writing in joint inspiration. Of their many books, among the best are the novel *The Real Charlotte* (1894) and the great comic stories collected in *The Experiences of an Irish R. M.* (1899), *Further Experiences of an Irish R. M.* (1908), and *In Mr. Knox's Country* (1915).

Sotie (or sottie). A fifteenth- and sixteenth-century offshoot of French farce, and not to be confused with a fixed, light poetic form of the same name. The dramatic *sotie* was so called because its principal characters were portrayed as *sots* ("fools"), whose folly, however, was a thin disguise for contemporary social and political satire. Guilds—*confréries* like Les Enfants Sans Souci (The Carefree Lads) in Paris, and similar ones in other French cities—performed their fare with the double aim of entertainment and propaganda. Of the several dozen extant soties, the best known is *La Sotie du Prince des Sots* (The Sotie of the Prince of Fools) of Pierre Gringoire (c. 1480–1539), that prestigious title having been conferred upon him as leader of Les Enfants Sans Souci. Performed in Paris in 1512, it is a defense of Louis XII, threatened with excommunication in his rift with Pope Julius II.

Specifying. A more intense form of comic signifying within African American vernacular culture, wherein the critique is more pointed and insulting. It frequently involves comparisons with animals and negative comments about appearance.

Spencer, Herbert (1820–1903). English philosopher, social reformer, and biological theorist. Spencer was the primary originator of the relief theory of humor. He argued that laughter represents a release of nervous energy that has nowhere to go after an unexpected event distracts from an emotionally tense mood, or after an expectation of a need for emotional energy is frustrated. Works relevant to his philosophy of humor include *The Physiology of Laughter* (1910).

Stable irony. A type of irony that is intentional, well thought through, and well presented by an author or speaker. The name comes from the stable relationship between what the creator intends and what the reader or listener perceives. Stable irony contrasts with observed or accidental irony, which is not intended or planned and is interpreted in different ways by different observers.

Stage Irishman. Comic stock character who is generally drunk yet clever and endowed with the verbal "gift of the gab." Shakespeare's MacMorris in *Henry V* (1600) is an early example from outside Ireland; Dion Boucicault's tricksters in his nineteenth-century Irish plays helped solidify this type for Irish dramatists. Sean O'Casey created great stage Irishmen such as Seumas Shields in *The Shadow of a Gunman* (1923), Captain Boyle in *Juno and the Paycock* (1924), and Fluther Good in *The Plough and the Stars* (1926). Stage Irishmen were not limited to the stage: Handy Andy in Samuel Lover's 1842 novel of that title was another one.

Steele, Richard (1672–1729). Essayist (author with Joseph Addison of periodical essays in *The Tatler* [1709–1711] and *The Spectator* [1711–1714]), playwright, and politician. *The Conscious Lovers* (1722) began a vogue for sentimental comedy.

Stein, Gertrude (1874–1946). Novelist, poet, critic, librettist, widely celebrated as founder of the so-called Lost Generation of American writers because of her mentoring of Ernest Hemingway and Sherwood Anderson as well as her patronage of Paris artists such Pablo Picasso, Georges Braque, and Henri Matisse. Stein's humor often prompts readers to look at American English and American ethnicity from a paradoxically illuminating distance. Her most influential books include *Three Lives* (1909), *The Making of Americans* (1925), and *The Autobiography of Alice B. Toklas* (1933).

Sterne, Laurence (1713–1768). Clergyman turned novelist who took the literary world by storm with his zanily witty *Tristram Shandy* (1759–1766), which parodied conventional narrative and offered readers a collection of memorable comic characters, including the sentimental hero, Uncle Toby.

Sturges, Preston (1898–1959). Writer and director of classic movie satires, most notably a string of eight films between 1940 to 1944 that included spoofs of American politics (*The Great McGinty*, 1940), small-town values (*The Miracle of Morgan's Creek*, 1944), Hollywood self-absorption (*Sullivan's Travels*, 1941), and mindless militarism (*Hail the Conquering Hero*, 1944).

Superiority theory. The oldest Western philosophical theory of humor, espoused in different forms by Plato, Aristotle, Thomas Hobbes, and Henri Bergson. The superiority theory holds that the amusement we find in comedy and in comical situations is essentially a form of ridicule, through which we regard the object of amusement as inferior and/or ourselves as superior.

Surrealism. International literary and artistic movement founded circa 1919, primarily by André Breton. Using a variety of techniques and ideas, from automatic writing to psychoanalysis, surrealists sought to explore every aspect of rational and irrational thought and their relation to inspiration and creativity. French surrealists include Louis Aragon, André Breton, Robert Desnos, Paul Eluard, and Philippe Soupault.

Swift, Jonathan (1667–1745). Clergyman and political writer, the greatest English satirist. His masterpiece is *Gulliver's Travels* (1726), although some of his shorter political satires such as "A Modest Proposal" (1729), and "An Argument to prove that the Abolishing of Christianity in England, may as things now stand be attended with some Inconveniences, and perhaps not produce those many good Effects proposed thereby" (1708), and the early *A Tale of a Tub* (1704) are among the most powerful satiric works of the period.

Synge, John Millington (1871–1909). The outstanding playwright of the first years of the Abbey Theatre, a Protestant Anglo-Irishman educated in Dublin and exiled to Paris. After spending the summers of 1898–1902 on the Aran Islands off Galway, he wrote unforgettably about peasant life in such comedies as *In the Shadow of the Glen* (1903) and his masterly tragicomedy *The Playboy of the Western World* (1907). He died young of Hodgkin's disease.

Tabarin (?–1626). Pseudonym of Antoine Girard, the best known of the Parisian street performers. These mountebanks flourished at the end of the sixteenth century and into the seventeenth, hawking their various miraculous elixirs, to the displeasure of the medical establishment, and gave the Hôtel de Bourgogne considerable and not always cordial dramatic competition. Though the name—from the Italian *tabarinno* ("little coat")—had been used by a number of his predecessors in the trade, this Tabarin was by far the most successful, with his comic and frequently indelicate skits (*farces tabariniques*) and gibes at the public, usually accompanied by music, presented on the Pont Neuf and the neighboring Place Dauphine. Tabarin was abetted in his offerings by his wife and his brother Philippe, known under the name of Mondor, who usually played the role of the pompous master to Tabarin's roguish valet, inherited from the *commedia dell'arte*.

Tati, Jacques (1908–1982). French actor and filmmaker, born Jacques Tatischeff, best known for his comic films starring himself as Monsieur Hulot. Tati's films use a minimum of dialogue and a maximum of physical comedy and sound effects. They include *Les Vacances de Monsieur Hulot* (1953), *Mon oncle* (1958), Playtime (1967), and *Trafic* (1971).

Terence (fl. 160s B.C.E.). Publius Terentius Afer, Roman playwright of highly successful comedies, notably *Phormio, Adelphoe* (*The Brothers*), and *Eunuchus* (*The Eunuch*). Terence was a standard inclusion in the early modern English school curriculum (as well as throughout Europe). His work had a major influence on the comedies of Shakespeare and his contemporaries. His plots were often adapted from those of Plautus, with additions or alterations that softened the presentations of family relations, and generally offered a sympathetic if still laugh-producing presentation of ordinary human foibles and common predicaments based on situation rather than on character.

Théâtre du Marais. So called for the section of Paris (Le Marais) in which the theater was located. The building, a handball court, appears to have been first used in 1634 by a rival troupe to the Hôtel de Bourgogne's and continued to be occupied by its successors until 1673, when they were merged by royal decree with the remnants of Molière's troupe after the latter's sudden death in that year. Many of Pierre Corneille's plays were first performed at the Théâtre du Marais.

Third Cinema. A term commonly credited to Argentine filmmakers Fernando Solanas and Octavio Getino. After completing their film *La Hora de los Hornos* (Hour of the Furnaces, 1968), they wrote a manifesto categorizing three kinds of cinema: First Cinema conveys messages of dominant ideology through its content and mode of production (e.g., Hollywood, Bollywood); Second Cinema includes auteurist and art cinemas, which they considered as institutionalized as First Cinema; and Third Cinema expresses a new way of representing the world outside genre categories, with political content and practice, telling antiracist stories of the people's will to decolonize and liberate.

This Hour Has 22 Minutes. Canadian TV show, first broadcast in 1994, that parodies the nightly news; cast members have included Cathy Jones, Rick Mercer, Colin Mochrie, Greg Thomey, and Mary Walsh, most of whom started with Newfoundland's comedy troupe CODCO.

Thorpe, Thomas Bangs (1815–1878). American author, journalist, and landscape and portrait painter. Thorpe came of age in New York and Connecticut. He lived in Louisiana between 1837 and 1854 and is best known for his 1839 sketch of a Louisiana bee hunter and 1860 view of Niagara Falls. In 1841 he published "The Big Bear of Arkansas" in *Spirit of the Times*, a story that lent its name to Southwest tall-tale writing ("the Big Bear school of literature"). In 1845 he published *Mysteries of the Backwoods; or, Sketches of the Southwest*, and he wrote and illustrated *Our Army on the Rio Grande* (1846), about the Mexican War, before returning to New York in 1854 to write for *Harper's*. Thorpe also wrote for *Knickerbocker Magazine*, *Frank Leslie's Illustrated Newspaper*, and *Appleton's*. In 1862 he served in Union-occupied New Orleans to distribute food and restore sanitation. From 1869 on Thorpe was a New York City Custom House officer.

Tomlin, Lily (1939–). Comedian and actress whose work in one-woman shows such as *The Search for Signs of Intelligent Life in the Universe* (written by her longtime partner Jane Wagner) shows incredible comic versatility. Her camp humor generates from performing as both men and women as well as a consistent sympathy for low culture (street people, lounge singers, children, workers).

Townley, James (1714–1778). British dramatist, referred to by several sources as "Rev. James Townley," though perhaps through confusion with another of the same name. This theatrical Townley was a colleague of celebrated Shakespearean actor, comic author, and Drury Lane impresario David Garrick (1717–1779), and is reputed to have had a prominent hand in many of the latter's productions, though, with a self-effacing modesty rare among theater people, never taking credit. His farce *High Life below Stairs* (1759) is a good case in point. Running for seventeen seasons at Drury Lane and considered the prototypical British farce of its time, it was long attributed to Garrick. A portrait of the servant class, it contained a lyric that was especially popular in Colonial America: "Come here, fellow Servant, and listen to me, / I'll show you how those of superior degree / Are only dependents, no better than we. / Both high and low in this do agree."

Township comedy. A term used to define postapartheid South African comedies whose mise-en-scène, actors, and plot focus on life in black working-class and working poor townships.

Tragic Farce. A sardonic, often violent form of farce applied to the themes, techniques, and situations of tragedy. Tragic farce differs from traditional exuberant farce by seeming to be more insistently grotesque, metaphysical, and lethal. European and some American dramatists have found tragic farce to be a particularly viable form for depicting an irrational universe and disturbingly contradictory social and domestic situations.

Trailer Park Boys. An original Canadian TV show of the twenty-first century that satirically documents life among a cast of losers in New Brunswick's Sunnyvale Trailer Park, and manages it with an abiding affection that would have been familiar to Stephen Leacock. Writers and cast members include Mike Clattenburg, Barrie Dunn, Mike Smith, Jean Paul Tremblay, and Robb Wells.

Trenet, Charles (1913–2001). French singer/songwriter whose songs truly represent the spirit of French *chanson* of the post–World War II era, with their lyric playfulness spanning the full range of wordplay from the pun to onomatopoeia.

Trickster. Although the first use of the term *trickster* has often been assigned to Daniel G. Brinton, in the last third of the nineteenth-century, it presently seems that the claim to first usage should be that of Franz Boas, who used it in his introduction to the 1898 publication of Thompson River Indian tales collected by James Teit. Trickster may appear in many forms—animal for the most part (e.g., coyote, raven, rabbit, jay, wolverine, and so on) but also indeterminate (e.g., as Gluskap or Napi or Tusasas)—and he also has the ability to change form or sex too. He is, as Paul Radin, an important student of trickster tales put it, both benefactor and buffoon, posing great danger to order and propriety and yet also having the power to establish many of the cultural conventions necessary to order and propriety.

Tudor interlude. One of the more popular (and hilarious) forms of comedy in the years immediately before Queen Elizabeth I took the throne. Modeled on the medieval form of the *débat*, or debate, the interlude was essentially a discussion delivered in dialogue form, designed partly to instruct and primarily to entertain in the private halls of wealthy aristocrats. Its best-known author was John Heywood (c. 1497–1578), grandfather of the poet John Donne, whose *Play Called the Four P's* (c. 1520) along with *The Play of the Weather* (c. 1528) and *John John, Tib, and Sir John* (c. 1520) still entertain students of early drama. The form is important for its enduring influence on later plays.

Twain, Mark (1835–1910). Born Samuel Langhorne Clemens; preeminent nineteenth-century American humorist, lecturer, and writer. He grew up in Hannibal, Missouri, where he apprenticed as a printer and later trained and worked as a Mississippi riverboat pilot from 1858 to 1861. He traveled to the American West (1861) and the Mediterranean (1867) producing the newspaper letters and sketches that were reworked in his humorous travel books *Roughing It* (1872) and *Innocents Abroad* (1869). His most successful work was published between 1865 and 1885: another travel book, *Life on the Mississippi* (1883), and the novels *The Adventures of Tom Sawyer* (1876) and *Adventures of Huckleberry Finn* (1885). A humor of despair and cynicism informs writings published after 1890: *The Tragedy of Pudd'nhead Wilson* (1894), *What Is Man?* (1906), and *The Mysterious Stranger* (1916, published posthumously).

Udall (or Uvedale), Nicholas (1504?–1556). British dramatist, ecclesiastic, translator, and teacher, author of what is recognized as the first English-language comedy. *Ralph Roister Doister* (1535?), performed while Udall was headmaster of Eton, was presented by his students, for whom he had already prepared a Latin handbook based on passages from Terence. Dismissed in 1541 for undisclosed "improprieties," incurring a brief imprisonment, he returned to academe as headmaster of Westminster School in 1553 or 1554. Despite his somewhat Lutheran leanings, his dramatic talents ingratiated him with the Catholic queen Mary Tudor—"Bloody Mary"—for whom he organized various dramatic productions. Udall is known to have written several other plays, but only the five-act, colloquially English *Ralph Roister Doister*, based loosely on the *miles gloriosus* of Plautus, has survived.

Unstable irony. Irony in which the literal meaning is clearly intended to oppose an actual meaning; however, the actual meaning is obscured by the fact that it may itself be ironic, that is, a statement with multiple levels of irony in which the intention is ambiguous. Unstable irony is at work, often subtly, in many works of absurdism.

Valle-Inclán, Ramón María del (1866–1936). A novelist, playwright, and poet, Valle-Inclán initially participated in the Hispanic *modernista* movement, publishing his famous ballads of the four seasons (*sonatas*). However, he is most recognized as the creator of the *esperpento*, a literary form of portraying reality that mixes the tragic and the grotesque. His unconventional play *Luces de Bohemia* (*Lights of Bohemia*, 1920–1924) is the emblem of this new aesthetic.

Vanbrugh, John (1664–1726). Architect and comic dramatist, two of whose comedies, *The Relapse* (1696) and *The Provok'd Wife* (1697) strike a comic balance between the rough satire of earlier Restoration comedy and the pure wit associated with William Congreve's comedies.

Vaudeville. A light comic genre originating in France, usually farcical in nature. Not to be confused with its nineteenth-century American namesake—the variety show imported from England and lasting until its television-caused demise—the *vaudeville* grew out of the repertory of the Théâtre de la Foire and the performances of its street actors and their companies, usually including popular songs, or *ariettes*. Forerunner of the operetta, this comic form supposedly took its name from the town of Vau (or Val) de Vire, in Normandy, known as early as the fifteenth century for the satirical ditties that apparently abounded there. (Another etymology suggests the phrase *voix de ville* ["voices of the city," i.e., street cries] as the origin.) Shedding its music by the end of the nineteenth century, the term was eventually applied to any light comedy or farce, especially those characterized by the tightly knit construction of the "well-made play." Many of Eugène Labiche's and Georges Feydeau's works are so designated.

Vega Carpio, Félix Lope de (1562–1635). Spain's most prolific playwright, Lope de Vega wrote hundreds of plays, epic and lyrical poetry, and a variety of novellas. His *Arte nuevo de hacer comedias* (*New Art of Writing Plays*, 1609) is a poetical essay in which the principal characteristics for *comedia nueva* were defined as a violation of the Aristotelian unities (of action, time, and place), division of the play in three acts, and the use of a variety of metrical forms in each play. Lope de Vega mixes the tragic and the comical to cause delight, while trying to imitate nature. His plays cover a wide range of subjects that include mythology, religion, national and foreign history, and folkloric traditions.

Vian, Boris (1920–1959). French writer, poet, and musician whose novels, poems, and songs are filled with word games, puns, neologisms, parodies, and pastiches. His most famous novels include *L'écume des jours* (1947), a parody of existentialism, among other things; *L'herbe rouge* (1950); and *L'arrache-coeur* (1953). Vian was also a superb jazz musician.

Video film. An inexpensive and popular form of video-making that is transferred to film for theatrical release or copied to VHS or DVD for rental. While it has made the art of visual storytelling accessible to just about anyone, its major drawbacks are poor production values of image, sound, and editing. The promotion of video production in Anglophone Africa, in particular, has led recently to a burgeoning indigenous film/video culture and industry.

Visual irony. Commercial artists, especially cartoonists, rely heavily on visual irony, and so do serious artists, sculptors, and architects. Nature also creates visual irony, as shown by the way different cultures acknowledge the phenomenon of a sunshiny shower or give such descriptive names to plants as "Jack in the Pulpit" and "Teddy Bear Cholla."

Vizenor, Gerald (1934–). An extraordinarily prolific author of mixed Anishinaabe (Chippewa) and French ancestry, Vizenor has been a journalist, a poet, a writer of screenplays and critical essays, and, perhaps foremost, a brilliant and innovative novelist. For a quarter of a century he has meditated upon the trickster as the most important character of traditional oral narrative, which he has presented and reinvented as an ironic, subversive, revolutionary, and liberatory figure essential to the *survivance* (a word he coined) of Native peoples.

Waters, John (1946–). Self-proclaimed "trash" filmmaker Waters began his career making no-budget independent films with a cast composed of drag queens, hippies, and other underground figures. Best known for his collaborations with drag queen Divine (among them, *Pink Flamingos* [1972], *Female Trouble* [1974], *Polyester* [1981], and *Hairspray* [1988]), Waters continues to ply his version of camp in more mainstream independent features: *Serial Mom* (1994), *Pecker* (1998), and *Cecil B. Demented* (2000).

Wayne and Shuster. Canada's most popular mid-twentieth-century comic duo, Johnny Wayne (1918–1990) and Frank Shuster (1916–) admirably represented their country's quietly quirky take on the world while establishing the record (sixty-seven) for most appearances on that staple of American TV, *The Ed Sullivan Show*.

West, Mae (1893–1980). 1930s and 1940s Hollywood movie star who is said to have developed her style from the example of male drag queens with whom she worked in vaudeville. Since then, West's stylized demeanor and outrageous sexual double entendres have been imitated endlessly by drag performers. Her first play, *Sex*, which she wrote, produced, and directed on Broadway in 1926, created a scandal, and she was imprisoned for obscenity. She played in many movies, beginning with *Night after Night* in 1932. With W. C. Fields, she played in *My Little Chickadee* in 1940. She made her reputation as a provocative sexual goddess, specializing in innuendo and double entendre.

West, Nathanael (1903–1940). Born Nathan Weinstein; novelist whose books include *The Dream Life of Balso Snell* (1931), *A Cool Million* (1934), and two classics: West's mordant exposé of yellow journalism entitled *Miss Lonelyhearts* (1933) and *The Day of the Locust* (1939), an astringent depiction of Hollywood hype. Twentieth-century America's most influential man of letters, Edmund Wilson, singled out West for coloring his treatment of such distinctly American milieus as Puritan New England and Hollywood with an eastern European Jew's appreciation of suffering and a European's sense of the grotesque, reminiscent of writer Nikolai Gogol and painter Marc Chagall.

Wiesner David (1956–). Through innovative drawings, Wiesner, both as writer and picture book illustrator, has created a body of work that contains sophisticated humor that is funny to children as well as adults. In his Caldecott Award–winning book *The Three Pigs* (2001), Wiesner creates humor by coordinating his artistic vision to a complete retelling of the story, turning it upside down. Other books include *Tuesday* (1991), also a Caldecott winner, *Hurricane* (1990), and *Sector 7* (1999).

Wilde, Oscar (1854–1900). Perhaps the funniest Irish playwright ever, though he moved to London, became more English than the English themselves, and wrote only about English society in his most famous plays, such as his masterpiece *The Importance of Being Earnest* (1895). Wilde was an Anglo-Irishman born and educated in Dublin before proceeding from Trinity College, Dublin, to England's Oxford University. Like Shaw, he was able to explode English society so hilariously and effectively because he examined it from the outside. He had the reputation of a great wit and "dandy," believing in art for art's sake. In 1891 he was accused of having a homosexual relation with Lord Douglas and sent to prison for two years.

Wilder, Billy (1906–2002). Writer and director of caustic, cynical comedies, dramas, and comedy/dramas, primarily in the 1940s–1960s, that reflected acidic attitudes toward such targets as the movie industry (*Sunset Boulevard*, 1950), the news media (*Ace in the Hole*, 1951), marriage (*The Seven Year Itch*, 1955), gender roles (*Some Like It Hot*, 1959), corporate life (*The Apartment*, 1960), lawyers (*The Fortune Cookie*, 1966), and the cold war (*One, Two, Three*, 1961). His efforts in both comedy and serious drama were recognized by twenty Academy Award nominations and five Oscars, and by a variety of tributes throughout his long life.

Williams, Bert (1875–1922). Born in Jamaica, Egbert Williams was raised in California, where he began performing comic routines and dances in bars and road shows. He met George Walker in San Francisco in 1893; they formed an act and soon played Dahomeyans in an exposition at Golden Gate Park, where they observed real Africans dancing and singing. Later, they adapted the usually demeaning "Coon Song" minstrel stereotype, billing themselves as "Two Real Coons." Walker played the dandy jokester and Williams, the straight man, usually in burnt-cork makeup. They became cakewalk and vaudeville stars and eventually performed in their own show, *In Dahomey* (1902), on Broadway. Two other plays, *In Abyssinia* (1908) and *In Bandana Land* (1919), were also successful. Walker succumbed to syphilis in 1911. Williams went on to the Ziegfield Follies, but his last personal success was in his show *Under the Bamboo Tree* (1922), which inspired much of the comic writing of the Harlem Renaissance.

Wilmot, John (1647–1680). Earl of Rochester and libertine Restoration courtier. He was a brilliant and subversive satiric poet noted even in his own day for the shocking sexuality and brutal humor of his verses.

Woofing. In African American culture, talking around a subject by the use of humor, or simply aimless and humorous talking. It may also be known as bookooing, but that term has several other definitions.

Workplace sitcom. Subgenre of the TV sitcom on which co-workers interact in a fixed workplace setting (e.g., newsroom, bar, radio station, hospital), sometimes with the addition of the main character's family, friends, and neighbors in an additional home location. Primary examples include *M*A*S*H*, *Taxi*, *The Mary Tyler Moore Show*, *Barney Miller*, *Murphy Brown*, and *Cheers*.

Wycherley, William (1640–1716). Comic playwright whose *The Country Wife* (1675) and *The Plain Dealer* (1677) are masterpieces of comic misanthropy and social satire.

Zagreb School of Animation. Famed Yugoslavian animation studio in Zagreb, Croatia, with an avant-garde aesthetic, including collage and assemblage. Known for two major chronological periods: (1) 1957–1964, characterized by the work of Vukotic, Mimica, and Kristl; and (2) 1965–1980s, with Dragic, Grgic, Dovnikovic, and others.

Index

Abbot and Costello, 112
Abrahams, Jim, 85–86
Abrams, M. H., 512, 519–20
Absa, Moussa Sene, 54
absurdism, 2, 4, 14, 19, 24, 63, 167–68, 172–73, 175, 177, 187, 307, 320–22, 358, 412
academic humor, 2, 9–23
Addison, Joseph. *See* Steele, Richard
Adorno, Theodor, 257
Aesop, 220, 531
African American comedy, 4, 24–33, 34–47, 118–19, 132, 141, 383, 484–86, 581, 583, 593–94
African film, 4, 48–61
Albee, Edward, 9, 63, 407
Alexakis, Vassilis, 323
Ali G., 194–95
Allais, Alphonse, 316–17
Allen, Fred, 580
Allen, Woody, 8, 83–85, 88–89, 94, 96, 103, 205, 397, 581–82
Almodóvar, Pedro, 478, 572–73
Altman, Robert, 86, 596

American drama since, 1975, 62–77
American film comedy, 4, 78–92
American literature in the nineteenth century, 106–20
Amis, Kingsley, 13–15, 17
animation, 3, 135–52, 189
Aragon, Louis, 314–15
Arbuckle, Fatty, 80
Ariosto, Ludovico, 332, 564
Aristophanes, 3, 154, 170, 172, 174–75, 177, 248, 298–99, 347, 353, 367–77, 464, 493, 500, 534
Aristotle, 1, 199, 211, 257, 351, 374, 463–65, 471, 494, 501
Arthurian romance, 3, 153–66, 444
Ascham, Roger, 219
Atwood, Margaret, 208
Audé, Françoise, 55
Auden, W. H., 381
Austen, Jane, 10, 16, 396, 512–19

Babcock, Barbara, 454
Babuscio, Jack, 477–78
Bain, Alexander, 467–69, 471

Bakhtin, Mikhail, 32, 190, 199, 206, 212, 531
Banks, J. R., 16, 19, 21
Barlet, Olivier, 59
Barnet, Sylvan, 173
Bates, Kathy, 400
beast fable, 34–35, 40, 126, 141, 208, 429, 431, 443, 448–51, 534
Beaumont, Francis, 255–57
Beckett, Samuel, 1, 63–64, 190, 205, 307–8, 318, 320–22, 391–92, 407–8
Bekolo, Jean-Pierre, 53–54
Bellow, Saul, 11, 84, 397
Benchley, Robert, 205
Benigni, Roberto, 427
Benjamin, Walter, 458
Benning, Sadie, 479
Benny, Jack, 85, 94–95, 103, 205, 310, 580, 583, 599
Bergman, David, 482–83
Bergson, Henri, 93, 100, 172–74, 184, 212, 311–12, 314, 411, 470–71, 474
Berle, Milton, 580–81
Bernbach, Bill, 96
Bierce, Ambrose, 539
Bigsby, Christopher, 18
Bird, Louis, 458–59

black comedy, 1–5, 18, 62, 72, 87, 167–84, 212, 405, 412, 427, 569
Bloom, Harold, 96, 100
blues, 24, 36, 39–41
Boas, Franz, 447
Boccaccio, Giovanni, 298, 440
Bonney, Jo, 583
Booth, Mark, 482
Booth, Wayne, 172, 398, 405–6
Bordwell, David, 587
Borscht Belt (the Catskills), 93, 99, 580
Boucicault, Dion, 385–86
Boughedir, Ferid, 48, 52
Bradbury, Malcolm, 15–19, 20–21
Brassens, Georges, 325
Breathed, Berkeley, 121, 130–31, 133
Brecht, Bertolt, 189, 355–56, 358, 481, 530
Brel, Jacques, 325–26
Breton, André, 315–17, 319
Bright, Deborah, 488–89
Bristol, Michael D., 258
British contemporary comedy, 4, 185–98
Brockmann, Stephen M., 361
Brodkin, Karen, 96–97
Brooks, Albert, 87–88
Brooks, Mel, 44, 85–86, 97
Brown, Sterling, 42
Bruce, Lenny, 94, 103, 186, 577, 580–81
Büchner, Georg, 353
Bulgakov, Michail, 339–40
burlesque, 63, 85, 114, 116, 141, 155, 164, 166, 174, 346, 529, 578–79, 584
Burns, George, and Gracie Allen, 94–95, 102, 583, 590, 599
Bushmiller, Ernie, 127
Butler, Samuel, 266–67
Byron, George Gordon, Lord, 202–3, 512, 519–27, 531–32, 539

cabaret and nightclub, 3, 85, 186, 188, 193, 355–57, 359–60, 579–81

Caesar, Sid, 85, 302
camp sensibility, 2, 86, 91, 196–97, 477–92
Canadian comedy, 199–213
Capellanus, Andreas, 156
Capp, Al, 125–26
caricature, 21, 122–23, 149, 195, 197, 292, 529
Carlin, George, 577, 581
Carrey, Jim, 80–81, 85, 150
Carroll, Lewis (Charles Lutwidge Dodgson), 3, 222–24, 226, 282–85, 316–17, 319, 396–97, 407
Carroll, Michael, 455–56
cartoons, 1, 3, 78, 80, 90–91, 102, 135–52, 174, 195, 283, 389, 392, 400–401, 408, 597, 599; political, 121–34, 203
Case, Sue-Ellen, 483, 488
Casson, Lionel, 500
Cedric the Entertainer, 28
Cervantes, Miguel de, 166, 266, 563–64
Chaplin, Charlie, 79, 82, 84, 86–87, 141, 184, 205, 233, 305, 404
Chappelle, Dave, 4, 25–26, 29–30
Charney, Maurice, 11, 173
Charon, Jacques, 304
Chaucer, Geoffrey, 10, 12, 166, 298, 429, 431, 435, 437–45
Chekhov, Anton, 1, 63, 65, 170
Chesnutt, Charles W., 40, 45, 118–19
Chesterton, G. K., 174, 177
Chevillard, Eric, 322–23
children's comedy, 2, 35, 83, 131, 138, 214–32, 283–84, 287, 400–404, 471
Childress, Alice, 43
Chrétien de Troyes, 155–59
Cibber, Colly, 272
circus, 80, 578
Cismaru, Alfred, 319
city comedy, 252–57
civic pageantry, 257–61
Clyne, Robert M., 32
Cohen, Myron, 580

Cohen, Ted, 474–75
Coleman, Robin R. Means, 25
comedy clubs, 581–82
comedy of manners, 71, 251, 289
Comenius, John Amos, 219
comic strips and books, 31–32, 54, 121, 125–28, 131–32, 137, 142, 194, 400, 572
commedia dell'arte, 3, 150, 244–47, 299–300, 333, 410, 419–20, 496, 576
confusionism, 112–13, 115–16
Congreve, William, 273–74, 303, 385
Cook, David, 79–80
Cook, Peter, 187–88
Cooper, James Fenimore, 106, 108–11
Cormier, Robert, 403–4
Corneille, Pierre, 334–40
Cosby, Bill, 26, 31, 581, 596
court masque, 257–61
Crates, 375
Cratinus, 374–75
Crosby, Bing, 202
Crumb, R., 127–28

dada. See surrealism
Dahl, Roald, 227
Dame Sirith, 432–33, 441
Dartmouth, Thomas, 37–38
Darwin, Charles, 469
Daumier, Honoré, 531–32
David, Larry, 599
Davies, Robertson, 21, 204, 208
Davis, Bette, 480
De Filippo, Eduardo, 417–18
de Man, Paul, 18
Defoe, Daniel, 220
Dekker, Thomas, 252–56, 259–60
Devos, Raymond, 316
dialect humor, 41
Diawara, Manthia, 50
Dickens, Charles, 18, 200, 204, 281, 292, 406, 478–79
Dietrich, Marlene, 480
Disney, Walt, 141–43
Dixon, Thomas, 40

Doctorow, E. L., 102
documentary and mockumentary, 87–88, 195–96
Dorson, Richard M., 106
Douglas, Ann, 97
Douglas, Mary, 251
Doukouré, Cheick, 55
Doyle, Roddy, 381
dozens, the, 25, 37, 43
Dr. Seuss (Theodor Geisel), 121, 125, 140, 227–28, 402–3
Dryden, John, 206, 264–66, 520, 529–30, 532
DuBois, W.E.B., 41–43
Duchamp, Marcel, 317
Dumont, Margaret, 82
Dunbar, Paul Laurence, 39, 41
Duncan, Isadora, 402
Durang, Christopher, 62–63, 69
Dürrenmatt, Friedrich, 358–59
Dylan, Bob, 97–98, 101

Edgeworth, Maria, 387–88
Eliot, T. S., 185, 228, 401
Elliott, Robert C., 532
Ellison, Ralph, 43, 45
Englander, Nathan, 101
English comedy, Elizabethan and Jacobean, 248–62
English comedy, Restoration and Augustan, 263–79
English comedy, Victorian, 280–95
English Romantic comedy, 512–27
Erasmus, Desiderius, 535, 564
Escher, M. C., 397
Esslin, Martin, 320
Etherege, George, 272
ethnic humor, 4, 25, 36–38, 579
Eupolis, 375
Euripides, 174

fabliaux, 161, 298–99, 432, 441, 532
farce, 1–2, 18, 21, 24, 63, 65, 74, 87, 174, 296–313, 320, 494, 500, 529

Farquhar, George, 385
Farrelly brothers (Peter and Bobby), 90
Fauset, Jessie, 36, 42
Favre, Robert, 315
Feibleman, James K., 9
Feiffer, Jules, 94, 126
Feinberg, Leonard, 540
Fellini, Federico, 412, 415, 420, 425–26
feminist (anti-feminist) and gender, 52–53, 128, 164, 196, 445, 502, 547–51, 579, 591–93
Fersen, Thomas, 326
Feydeau, Georges, 296, 302, 304–9, 312
Feynman, Richard, 97–99
Fielding, Henry, 10, 14, 16, 275–76, 529
Fields, W. C., 81–82, 436
film, 1, 3–4, 9, 11–12, 15, 21, 39, 404–5, 587; German, 360–61; Italian, 411–12, 420–27; Queer, 477–92; Spanish, 571–73
Fisher, Rudolph, 42
Fo, Dario, 233, 238, 299, 412, 419–20, 425
folk humor and folktale, 36–37, 42, 106, 119, 154–55, 214, 216–17, 382–83, 420, 441
Fox and the Wolf, The, 431–32, 443
Foxx, Redd, 44, 583, 594
Franklin, Benjamin, 122, 201
Fratti, Mario, 418–19
French contemporary comedy, 314–329
French drama in the seventeenth century, 331–49
Freud, Sigmund, 1–2, 80–81, 170–73, 183, 212, 361–62, 411, 452, 468–69, 481–82, 484, 489, 527, 540
Frisch, Max, 359
Frye, Northrop, 199, 202, 394, 403, 540, 547

Gaines, Ernest, 45
Gainsbourg, Serge, 326

Gamarra, Edward A., 360, 362
Garbo, Greta, 480
Gardner, Martin, 223
Garrick, David, 303
Gay, John, 529–30
gay and lesbian. *See* queer comedy
gender. *See* feminist (anti-feminist) and gender
German comedy, 350–62
Germi, Pietro, 424–25
Gervais, Ricky, 195
Gibbon, Edward, 509
Gilbert, W. S., and Arthur Sullivan, 287–89, 303, 407, 497, 530
Gilman, Richard, 321
Gilman, Sander, 95
Gladwell, Malcom, 94
Gleason, Jackie, 302, 583, 590–91
Gleick, James, 97–98
Godwin, William, 513
Gold, Mike, 102–3
Goldberg, Whoopi, 25, 44, 97, 582
Goldoni, Carlo, 237–38, 299, 410, 412, 414, 419
Goldsmith, Oliver, 273
Gomes, Flora, 57
Gopnik, Adam, 95
Gottsched, Christoph, 351
Gower, John, 429, 440
Goya, Francisco de, 566–67, 569
Gozzi, Carlo, 237–38
Graham, Judy, 99
Grant, Cary, 310
Greek comedy, 363–79
Greene, Robert, 252
Gregory, Dick, 27, 43, 581
Gregory, Lady Augusta, 383–84, 388
Griffin, Dustin, 540
griots, 35, 39, 50
gross-out or animal comedy, 90–91
grotesque, 63, 72, 164, 323, 425, 569
Gruner, C. R., 464
Guest, Christopher, 88
Gunning, Tom, 136

Haley, Alex, 35
Haliburton, Thomas Chandler, 201–2
Hall, Joseph, 535
Hardy, Willene, 12
Harlem Renaissance, 41–43
Harris, Joel Chandler, 39–40, 118, 431
Harvey, R. C., 130
Harvey, Steve, 28
Hauptmann, Gerhart, 354
Hayman, Ronald, 95
Hazlitt, William, 211
Hegel, Georg, 169, 174–75
Heller, Joseph, 1, 167, 172, 177–84, 208, 400
Hemingway, Ernest, 200
Henkes, Kevin, 229–30
Henley, Beth, 72–76
Hennebelle, Guy, 52
Hepburn, Katharine, 89, 142, 149
Herblock (Herbert Block), 124–26
Hill, Benny, 188, 191, 193, 195
Himes, Chester, 44
hip-hop, 45, 327
Hitchcock, Alfred, 107, 400
Hitler, Adolf, 13, 83, 87–88, 96–97, 100, 127, 144, 151, 172, 181–82, 197, 206, 351, 356, 358
Hobbes, Thomas, 5, 170–72, 176–77, 182, 464–65, 471–72, 475
Hoch, Danny, 583–84
Hoffman, Abbie, 102
Hofmannsthal, Hugo von, 355
Homs, Brice, 326
Hope, Bob, 81, 84–85, 94, 202, 580–81, 583
Horace, 265, 351, 493, 508, 528, 530, 532–33
Hroswitha, 298, 352
Hughes, Langston, 35, 42–43, 45, 577
Hughes, Thomas, 10
Hughley, D. L., 28
Hurston, Zora Neale, 37, 41–42, 45

Hutcheson, Francis, 465–66
Hyde, Lewis, 447, 454

Ionesco, Eugène, 1, 63, 168, 173, 307–8, 321–22
Irish comedy, 4, 380–93
irony, 2–3, 12, 18, 34, 161, 163, 169, 172, 174, 191, 193, 197, 200, 268, 394–409, 486, 529
Irving, Washington, 106–8
Italian comedy, 410–28
Ives, David, 70

Jacobs, Melville, 452–53
James, Henry, 17–18
Jarrell, Randall, 13
Jarry, Alfred, 317
Jewish humor, 4, 35–36, 44, 84, 89, 93–105, 143, 475
Johnson, James Weldon, 41–42
Johnson, Samuel, 509, 532
jokes, 1–5, 25, 34, 36, 44, 72, 79, 85, 97, 103–4, 135, 146–47, 171, 190, 437, 466, 540, 575–85; sick jokes, 4–5, 167–69, 180, 183
Jones, Inigo, 252, 258, 260
Jonson, Ben, 190, 241–43, 249–50, 252–55, 258–60, 263, 303, 493–94, 506, 536, 540
Joyce, James, 13, 206, 282, 380, 384–85, 387–91
Jung, Carl, 452
Juvenal, 186, 189, 206, 275, 412, 508–10, 528–30, 532–33, 535, 538–40

Kafka, Franz, 94–95, 208, 317, 569
Kahn, Madeline, 93
Kant, Immanuel, 465–66
Keaton, Buster, 9, 80–82, 84, 141, 305, 404
Kehr, Dave, 90
Keillor, Garrison, 399–400
Kelly, Walt, 125–26
Kermode, Frank, 101
Kerr, Jean, 399

Kesselring, Joseph, 309–10
Kierkegaard, Søren, 2, 465
King, Thomas, 209
Kingsley, Charles, 10
Kinnel, Margaret, 220
Kinney, Arthur, 256, 259–60
Kleist, Heinrich von, 100–101, 353
Klera, A. M., 206–7
Knoepflmacher, U. C., 293
Koestler, Arthur, 199, 454, 457
Kristol, Irving, 103
Kubrick, Stanley, 87, 405, 530
Kushner, Tony, 96

Labiche, Eugène, 303–4
Lahr, John, 94
Lamb, Charles, 512
Langdon, Harry, 80, 404
Laplace, Marquis Pierre Simon de, 175
Lapointe, Boby, 325
Larson, Gary, 400–401
Lasseter, John, 142, 151
Laurel, Stan, and Oliver Hardy, 82–83, 165, 404, 494
Lawrence, D. H., 16–17
Lawrence, Martin, 44–45
Lazarillo de Tormes, *El*, 300, 449, 531, 562–63
Leacock, Stephen, 200, 204–6, 209, 211–12
Lear, Edward, 222, 284–87
Lear, Norman, 593–94
lecturers, 4, 205, 578, 580, 583
Lederer, Richard, 399
Lee, Spike, 4, 26, 44–45
Leigh, Mike, 288
Lessing, Gotthold Ephraim, 351–52
Levenson, Jill L., 252
Lever, Charles, 386, 388
Levin, Harry, 24
Lévi-Strauss, Claude, 454–55
Lewis, C. S., 406
Lewis, Jerry, 80–81, 93, 309
Lloyd, Harold, 9, 80–82, 305, 404

Locke, John, 219
Lockhart, John Gibson, 10
Lodge, David, 15–16, 19–21
Looseley, David, 327
Lover, Samuel, 385–86
Lubitsch, Ernst, 83, 426
Lucian, 529–30
Lucilius, 508, 533
Lyons, John O., 10, 21

Mabley, Moms, 44, 583
Mac, Bernie, 25, 30–31
Machiavelli, Niccolò, 332, 412–14, 493, 506
Maddock, Brent, 322
magazines and newspapers, 39–42, 84, 127, 130, 188–89, 203–4, 284–85, 292, 356–57, 566–72
Magritte, René, 317, 324, 397
Makarius, Laura, 453
Malamud, Bernard, 11
malapropism, 555–56
Malory, Sir Thomas, 159, 165–66
Mamet, David, 9, 63, 67–72
Marc, David, 575–76
Marston, John, 252, 254, 535–36
Martial, 186
Martin, Steve, 80–81
Marx brothers, 4, 80–82, 84–85, 94–95, 99, 102, 174, 233, 309, 404–5, 407, 529, 599
Maslow, Abraham, 179
Mason, Jackie, 25, 96, 579
Mast, Gerald, 82–84
Mauldin, Bill, 126
McCarthy, Mary, 11–13
McCulloch, Thomas, 201
McGruder, Aaron, 31–32, 131
McKay, Claude, 36, 42
McLuhan, Marshall, 211
Melly, George, 477–78, 480
melodrama, 65, 587
Menander, 374, 376–79, 508
Mercier, Vivian, 383–85
Meredith, George, 281, 292
Michaux, Henri, 322

Middle English comedy, 429–46
Middleton, Thomas, 252, 255, 260
Miller, Arthur, 63–64, 68–70
Miller, Jonathan, 187
Milligan, Spike, 187
Milne, A. A., 226–27
minstrel shows, 4, 36–39, 41, 44–45, 115, 578–79
Mintz, Lawrence E., 575
Mitchell, Elvis, 30
mock-heroic, 154, 270, 275
mockumentary. *See* documentary and mockumentary
Molière (Jean-Baptiste Poquelin), 2, 83, 237, 241, 281, 300, 339–45, 347–48, 355, 414, 470, 493, 506, 522, 536–37, 599
Monicelli, Mario, 411–12
Montaigne, Michel de, 531
Monty Python, 174, 188–90, 192, 302, 405
Mooney, Paul, 25–28
Moore, George, 10
Moore, Harry T., 10
Moore, Michael, 31
Morace, Robert A., 17
More, Thomas, 535
Morreall, John, 35, 463–64, 471–75
Morrison, Toni, 40, 45
Moseley, Merritt, 14–15
Moses, Gabriel, 58
Motte, Warren F., 318
Munro, Alice, 208–9
Murphy, Eddie, 28, 44, 91, 581
music hall and variety show, 186, 189, 578–79
musical comedies, 41, 57–58, 80, 495, 500
Mussolini, Benito, 4, 181, 425
Myers, Mike, 200, 210–12
mysteries and moralities, 445–46

Nast, Thomas, 124
national characteristics, 2–4, 199–201, 263, 314, 350–51, 411–12
Native American, 141, 575
Native American trickster tales, 2, 447–61
Neale, Steve, and Frank Krutnik, 85
newspapers. *See* magazines and newspapers
Newton, Esther, 480
Ngabo, Léonce, 54
Ngangura, Mweze, 49, 53, 55–57, 60
Nicholson, Jack, 400
Nietzsche, Friedrich, 32, 317, 355
nightclubs. *See* cabaret and nightclubs
Nilsen, Don L. F., 386
nonsense, 3–4, 205, 216–17, 220, 222, 281–89

Obrdlik, Anton, 475
O'Brien, Flann, 384–87, 391
O'Casey, Sean, 386
O'Connor, Flannery, 407
O'Connor, Frank, 384
O'Connor, Theresa, 386
Oldenburg, Claes, 398
Oliphant, Patrick, 126
O'Neill, Eugene, 63–64, 381
oral tradition, 34–35, 48, 113, 155, 214, 216–19, 390, 441, 447–61
Orel, Harold, 284
Orton, Joe, 168
Orwell, George, 539
Osborne, John, 354
Owl and the Nightingale, The, 429–31, 438, 441
Ozick, Cynthia, 93, 102

Page, Thomas Nelson, 40
paradox, 178, 183, 185, 395, 400
parody and travesty, 16–18, 21, 35, 45, 62–65, 67–69, 70–71, 75–76, 78, 84–86, 88, 95, 115, 127, 143, 145, 147, 149, 154, 166, 186, 189, 192–95, 197, 275–76, 284, 286, 319,

346, 385, 387, 395–97, 407–8, 412, 419, 435, 446, 483–84, 488, 529, 531, 534, 569
Partridge, Alan, 194
Paster, Gail Kern, 258, 260–61
pastoral, 246–47
Paul, William, 90
Pesci, Joe, 91
Petronius, 530–31
Phelan, Shane, 456
philosophy of humor. *See* theory of comedy
photography, 488–89
Picasso, Pablo, 185
Piccolo Teatro di Milano, 238
Pinero, Arthur Wing, 303
Pinter, Harold, 1, 63, 307
Pirandello, Luigi, 63, 410–12, 415–17, 425, 465, 569
Plato, 9, 369, 456, 462–65, 470–71
Plautus, 3, 101, 248, 253, 298–99, 334, 378, 410–11, 415, 493–507, 510
Poe, Edgar Allan, 406–7
Poore, Charles, 13
Pope, Alexander, 202, 206, 270–72, 275, 294, 520, 528, 537–38
Porter, W. S. (O. Henry), 407
Pound, Ezra, 99–100
Pratt, E. J., 206
Presley, Elvis, 64, 88, 480
Proctor, Mortimer F., 10
Pryor, Richard, 26, 28–29, 44, 106, 581, 583
puns, 37, 127, 148, 160, 215–16, 324, 384
puppetry, 100, 147, 419
Puttenham, George, 530
Pye, Gillian, 358–59
Pynchon, Thomas, 173

queer comedy, 2, 4, 25, 71, 128–29, 192, 196–97, 456, 477–92, 552–54
Queneau, Raymond, 317–19, 326

Quevedo, Francisco, 563–65, 569
Quintilian, 398, 508

Rabelais, François, 206, 449, 530, 534–35
Racine, Jean, 347
Radcliffe, Ann, 526
Radin, Paul, 448, 452, 458
radio comedy, 1, 41, 187, 579–80, 590
Ramachandran, V. S., 466–67
Rame, Franca. *See* Fo, Dario
Randolph, Vance, 217–18
rap. *See* hip-hop
Redfern, Walter, 318
Reed, Ishmael, 40, 45
Reik, Theodor, 103–4
Reiner, Rob, 88
Remarque, Erich Maria, 178, 180
Renaud (Renaud Séchan), 327
Riber, John, 54
Richardson, Samuel, 529
Richler, Mordecai, 200, 202, 204–5, 208, 212
Rickles, Don, 579
Riggs, Marlon, 484–86
Rochefoucauld, Duc de la, 532
Rock, Chris, 28–29, 44–45, 578
rock music, 64, 88, 185, 192
Roman comedy, 493–511
romance, 153–54, 542, 551–52
romantic comedy, 83, 88–90
Rosenbaum, Ron, 100
Rosten, Leo, 100
Roth, Philip, 44, 84, 93–94, 100
Rousseau, Jean-Jacques, 222
Rowling, J. K., 403
Rudnick, Paul, 478
Ruiz, Juan, 561
Russell, Willy, 9

Sadowitz, Gerry, 193
Sahl, Mort, 212, 581
Saintsbury, George, 10
Sales, Grover, 178

Salinger, J. D., 15, 404
Saltman, Judith, 220, 222
Salwak, Dale, 14–15
San Antonio (Frederic Dard), 323–24
Sanders, Carol, 320
Sandler, Adam, 81
Sanford, Arlene, 489–90
Sanou, Daniel Kallo, 51–52
Santayana, George, 467
satire, 2–4, 10, 12–13, 17, 20–21, 29, 31, 35, 48–52, 63, 73, 78, 82, 86–88, 118, 127, 135, 145, 174–75, 182, 186–89, 264–78, 289–92, 385, 394–95, 405, 408, 412, 419, 508–10, 512–13, 520–22, 528–41, 581; Menippean, 530–31
Scarron, Paul, 346
scatology, 214–16, 221, 268, 270, 314–15
Schlueter, Paul, 11
Schnitzler, Arthur, 354–55
Schoenberg, Arnold, 185
Schopenhauer, Arthur, 465–67, 474
Schuyler, George, 42
Scieszka, Jon, 228–29
Scudéry, Georges de, 301
Seidman, Steve, 85
Seinfeld, 29, 95, 97–98, 233, 577, 582, 587, 597–99
Sellers, Peter, 187
Sembene, Ousmane, 49–50
Sendak, Maurice, 228
Seneca, 298
Sennett, Mack, 79–80
Service, Robert, 206
Shakespeare, William, 2–3, 160, 170–71, 174, 177–78, 190, 233, 236, 240–43, 247, 249–50, 254–55, 263, 298, 302–3, 378–79, 380–81, 385–86, 406–8, 412–15, 419, 436, 464, 493–94, 500, 502, 506, 525, 532, 536, 542–59
Shandling, Garry, 598–99
Shapiro, Norman, 300, 306
Shaw, George Bernard, 303, 385, 417

Shepard, Sam, 63–67
Sheridan, Richard Brinsley, 385
Shohat, Ella, 48
Sir Gawain and the Green Knight, 163–65
Skelton, Red, 143, 583
slapstick, 24, 54, 78–80, 129, 135, 141, 150, 174–75, 184, 191, 221, 296, 298, 374
Smitherman, Geneva, 37
Smollett, Tobias, 10, 276–77
Snow, C. P., 11
Solaar, MC (Claude M'Barali), 328
Somerville and Ross (Edith Somerville and Violet Martin), 388
Sontag, Susan, 397, 479, 481
Sophocles, 170, 406
sotie, 297
Southern, Terry, 405
Southwest humor, 111–19
Spanish comedy, 560–74
Spaulding, Henry D., 41
Spencer, Herbert, 468–69, 471
Spiegelman, Art, 128
stand-up comedy, 4, 39, 45, 85, 95, 98, 138, 185, 190–91, 196, 205, 575–85
Steele, Richard, 273–74
Stein, Gertrude, 99–100
Steinbeck, John, 65, 165, 170
Sterne, Laurence, 18, 277–78
Sternheim, Carl, 355
Stewart, Jon, 577–78
stock characters, 2–3, 11, 238–44, 249, 278, 299, 306, 493–94, 497, 502, 545, 547, 556–67, 586–600
Stoppard, Tom, 407–8
Strassburg, Gottfried von, 159–63
Sturges, Preston, 87, 426
Styan, J. L., 62
Sullivan, Arthur. *See* Gilbert, W. S.
Sullivan, Lawrence, 456

surrealism and dada, 139, 181, 189, 197, 317–20, 357
Swift, Jonathan, 132, 208, 220, 267–70, 275–76, 294, 317, 380–81, 384, 387, 528–29, 538–39
Sykes, Wanda, 25
Synge, John Millington, 383–84, 386
Sypher, Wylie, 174

tall tale, 4, 111–15, 204
Talmudic stories, 101, 103
Tarantino, Quentin, 397, 405
Tati, Jacques, 321–22
Taviani brothers (Paolo and Vittorio), 420–23
television and video, 4, 29–31, 41, 44, 84–85, 90, 138, 145, 207, 209–11, 420, 479, 484–86, 489, 579–80, 582; "reality" TV, 195–96
television sitcoms, 4, 44, 302, 363, 493–94, 586–600; British, 185, 190–93, 302; German, 360; Spanish, 572–73
Tennyson, Alfred Lord, 165, 285–86
Teno, Jean-Marie, 52
Terence, 101, 248, 298–99, 332, 378, 410, 506–8, 510
Testaments, Old and New, 9–10, 449, 529
Thackery, William Makepeace, 10, 284, 292–94
theater of the absurd. *See* absurdism
theory of comedy, 2–3, 93–94, 139, 167–77, 199–200, 211–13, 307–9, 311–12, 411, 415, 454, 462–76
Thomas, Brandon, 309–10
Thorpe, Thomas Bangs, 111–13
Three Stooges, The, 80–83, 174, 309, 464
Thurman, Wallace, 42
Tinkcom, Matthew, 486
Tison, Jean-Pierre, 323

toasts, 36–37
Toelken, Barre, 457–60
Tolkien, J.R.R., 406
Tomlin, Lily, 399, 480, 576, 583
Townley, James, 303
tragedy, 1, 3, 5, 24, 63–64, 70, 168–70, 174, 176–77, 179–80, 183–84, 190, 246, 254, 350–51, 363, 427, 542
tragic farce. *See* black comedy
tragicomedy, 49, 67, 72
Traub, Valerie, 554
Travers, P. L., 225–26
travesty. *See* parody
Trenet, Charles, 324–25
trickster, 35, 45, 56, 60, 118, 141, 413, 424. *See also* Native American trickster tales
Trudeau, Garry, 121
Turpin, Ben, 404
Twain, Mark (Samuel Langhorne Clemens), 4, 113–18, 200–202, 204, 224–25, 387, 396, 539, 578, 580, 583–84
Tynan, Kenneth, 187

Udall, Nicholas, 248–49, 298–99
Ukadike, N. Frank, 52

Valentin, Karl, 355–56
Valle-Inclán, Ramón, 569–70
Vanbrugh, John, 272
vaudeville, 40, 78–80, 85, 94, 137–38, 141–43, 302, 304, 320, 578–79, 584
Vega Carpio, Felix Lopa de, 565
Vian, Boris, 319
video. *See* television and video
Villon, François, 180
Vizenor, Gerald, 457
Voltaire (François Marie Arouet), 529, 532, 537

Wade, Stephen, 584
Wakefield Master, 250

Walker, Alice, 45
Wallace, David Foster, 94
Ward, Artemus, 202, 578, 580
Waters, John, 480–81, 486–88
Waters, Maureen, 385
Watt, Ian, 513
Waugh, Evelyn, 11, 405
Wayans brothers, 25
Weaver, Jace, 449
Weinberg, Jonathan, 482
Weiss, Andrea, 480
Wertmuller, Lina, 412
West, Mae, 480
West, Nathanael, 101–2
White, E. B., 226
White, Felix, Sr., 458–59
Wiesner, David, 231
Wilde, Oscar, 71, 289–92, 303, 385, 478
Wilder, Billy, 83–84
William of Occam, 171
Williams, Robin, 582
Williams, Tennessee, 63
Wilmot, John, Earl of Rochester, 264–65, 509, 532
Wilson, August, 46
Wilson, Flip, 44
Winner and Waster, 433–34
Winston, Mathew, 169, 176
Wiseman, Richard, 466
Wisse, Ruth, 99
wit, 24, 170–72, 264
Wolfe, Tom, 397–98
Wordsworth, William, 520–21
Wright, Richard, 43
Wycherley, William, 272, 303

Yeats, William Butler, 381, 384, 388
Youngman, Henny, 581, 583

Zuckmayer, Carl, 357–58
Zucker, David, 85–86
Zucker, Jerry, 85–86

About the Editor and Contributors

Maurice Charney is distinguished professor of English at Rutgers University in New Brunswick, New Jersey. He has written widely on Shakespeare, including the following books: *Shakespeare's Roman Plays*, *Style in* Hamlet, *All of Shakespeare*, and *Shakespeare on Love and Lust*. He has also written *Comedy High and Low*. He is past president of the Shakespeare Association of America and the Academy of Literary Studies and the recipient of the medal of the city of Tours, France.

Frances K. Barasch is professor emerita at the Baruch College, the City University of New York. She is author and editor of studies in art and literature, including the Grotesque, Norwich Cathedral sculptures, and Renaissance theatrical prints. Recent essays on Shakespeare and *commedia dell'arte* have appeared in *Shakespeare Yearbook: On Page and Stage . . . World Culture*; *Intertestualità Shakespeariane*; and *English Literary Renaissance*, among others.

Adrian Bardon is assistant professor of philosophy at Wake Forest University. He has published articles on the early modern history of philosophy in *Ratio, Kantian Review*, *Philosophy and Theology*, and *Idealistic Studies*. He has also published articles on epistemology, ethics, and social philosophy. He is a member of the North American Kant Society, the Hume Society, the Philosophy of Time Society, and the American Philosophical Association.

James D. Bloom is professor of English and American Studies at Muhlenberg College, where he chairs the English Department and oversees the Self-Directed Inquiry program. He is the author of four books: *Gravity Fails* (2003), *The Literary Bent* (1997), *Left Letters* (1992), and *The Stock of Available Reality* (1984). His shorter works have appeared in *American Literary History, American Studies, Contemporary Literature, Style*, the *New York Times*, the *Philadelphia Inquirer*, and other publications.

Bettina Brandt taught at M.I.T. and Columbia University and is currently assistant professor of German at Montclair State University. She has published articles and book chapters on eighteenth-century German culture, on the historical avant-garde, and, most recently, on German contemporary transnational literature.

Heather L. Braun currently teaches English at Boston College. Her primary interests include nineteenth-century medievalism, the interplay between poetic motifs and Gothic novels, and the specific overlaps between Romantic and Victorian poems and novels. She has published book reviews in *The British Journal of Aesthetics* and *Women Studies Journal* and helped to edit the expanded edition of *An Encyclopedia of British Women Writers*. Her chapter "Mamet in the 1990s" appears in *The Cambridge Companion to David Mamet*, and her article on Sydney Owenson's *The Wild Irish Girl* will appear in the upcoming issue of *Irish Studies Review*.

Richard Brucher teaches English at the University of Maine, Orono. He has published articles on nostalgia and parody in plays by David Mamet, Arthur Miller, and Eugene O'Neill, as well as on revenge and violence in plays by Shakespeare and his contemporaries. At present he is working on cold war plays by Lillian Hellman and Miller. He is also the production review editor for the *David Mamet Review*.

James M. Cahalan is professor of English at Indiana University of Pennsylvania, where he is a past recipient of the Distinguished Faculty Award for Research. His five books on Irish literature include *The Irish Novel: A Critical History* (1988) and *Double Visions: Women and Men in Modern and Contemporary Irish Fiction* (1999). Most recently he has collected a set of essays as a Backward Glance, an occasional feature in the *New Hibernia Review*, on Vivian Mercier's classic book *The Irish Comic Tradition* (1962). He wrote the introductory essay for that collection after giving presentations on Mercier in 2004 at the American Conference for Irish Studies in Liverpool and the International Association for the Study of Irish Literature in Galway.

Leo Charney is associate director of publications at the Wharton School of the University of Pennsylvania. He is the author of *Empty Moments: Cinema, Modernity, and Drift* (1998) and coeditor with Vanessa R. Schwartz of *Cinema and the Invention of Modern Life* (1995). He has taught film studies at New York University, Northwestern University, and the University of Iowa.

Kathryn Douglas has taught Milton and Adolescent and Children's Literature for the past eighteen years and was director of the Children's Studies Minor at Fairleigh Dickinson University. In 2003–2004 she was a visiting scholar at Rutgers' Center for Children and Childhood Studies in Camden, New Jersey. She now teaches Cisneros to freshmen and Beowulf to seniors at Madison High School in Madison, New Jersey.

Mary C. English is currently an assistant professor of classics and general humanities at Montclair State University, where she serves as coordinator of classical languages and academic advisor to students seeking teaching certification in Latin. She is now working on a translation of Aristophanes' *Wasps*, a student commentary for Aristophanes' *Acharnians*, and a book that explores Aristophanes' influence on American playwrights of the 1920s.

Ken Feil teaches courses in media arts at Emerson College. He received his doctorate from the Department of Radio-TV-Film at the University of Texas at Austin in 1995. Since then, he has written for the *Boston Phoenix* and *Bay Windows* and performed for the comedy group Chuckle Bucket. His book *Dying for a Laugh: Disaster Movies and the Camp Imagination* is due out in 2005.

William Galperin is professor of English at Rutgers University and the author of three books: *Revision and Authority in Wordsworth: The Interpretation of a Career* (1989), *The Return of the Visible in British Romanticism* (1993), and *The Historical Austen* (2003). He has held fellowships from the Howard Foundation and the American Council of Learned Societies and was the recipient in 2004 of the Rutgers University Board of Trustees Award for Excellence in Research.

Nina Gerassi-Navarro is associate professor at Mount Holyoke College, where she teaches Latin American literature. Her primary fields are colonial and nineteenth-century literatures. She also teaches Latin American film. She is the author of *Pirate Novels: Fictions of Nation Building in Spanish America* (1999) and has published articles on pirate films, popular culture, and women and nation building. She has coedited a volume on space and subjectivity in early America and is currently working on a book-length manuscript on marginality and displacement in Latin America.

Kalman Goldstein is emeritus professor of history at Fairleigh Dickinson University and has served on the editorial board of Fairleigh Dickinson University Press since 1978. Initially specializing in pre–Civil War U.S. politics, he was redirected by an National Endowment for the Humanities fellowship toward political humor and cartoons. He has published essays on Finley Peter Dunne, George Ade, Walt Kelly, Al Capp, and World War II–era G.I. cartoonists in various journals and scholarly encyclopedias. In 1998 he cowrote and edited *Graphic Opinions: Editorial Cartoonists and Their Art*. Currently he is studying alternative comics of the 1980s and 1990s and contemporary graphic novels.

David Hawkes is associate professor of English at Lehigh University. He is the author of *Idols of the Marketplace* (2001) and *Ideology* (2nd edition, 2003), and has edited John Milton's *Paradise Lost* (2004) and John Bunyan's *The Pilgrim's Progress* (2005). His work has appeared in such journals as *The Nation*, the *Times Literary Supplement*, the *Journal of the History of Ideas*, *Milton Studies*, and the *Huntington Library Quarterly*. Professor Hawkes recently received a long-term fellowship from the National Endowment for the Humanities to work on a book-length history and analysis of the Faust myth.

Harry Keyishian is professor of English at Fairleigh Dickinson University. His published books are *Michael Arlen* (1976), *Critical Essays on William Saroyan* (1996), *The Shapes of Revenge: Victimization, Vengeance, and Vindictiveness in Shakespeare* (1996), and *Screening Politics* (2003). He is director of Fairleigh Dickinson University Press. He has published essays in a variety of journals and essay collections, including *Studies in English Literature, On-State Studies, Ararat, Shakespeare Bulletin, Modern Language Notes, The American Journal of Psychoanalysis, Shakespeare in Performance*, and *The Cambridge Companion to Shakespeare on Film*.

Philip Koch is professor emeritus of French and Italian at the University of Pittsburgh. Formerly chair of the department, he also held various administrative positions in the French seventeenth-century section of the Modern Language Association and in the American Society for eighteenth-century Studies. Dealing primarily with Franco-Italian theatrical questions of those two centuries, his publications include articles in American, British, French, and Italian journals as well as critical editions of Ferdinando Galiani's *Dialogues* and, in the *Oeuvres complètes de Denis Diderot* (Hermann edition), of the latter's *Apologie de l'abbé Galiani*.

Arnold Krupat teaches literature in the Global Studies Department of Sarah Lawrence College. His most recent books are *Red Matters: Native American Studies* (2002) and *The Turn to the Native: Studies in Criticism and Culture* (1996). He has coedited (with Brian Swann) *Here First: Autobiographical Essays by Native American Writers* (2000) and, with Michael Elliott, contributed the section on Native American fiction to *The Columbia History of Native American Literature since 1945* (2005). He is completing a new book, *All That Remains: Studies in Native American Literature*.

Naomi Conn Liebler is professor of English and University Distinguished Scholar at Montclair State University. She has been awarded several grants by the Folger Institute in support of her research at the Folger Shakespeare Library, most recently in the summer of 1998, as well as three National Endowment for the Humanities Summer Seminar stipends, and is completing a three-year term as trustee of the Shakespeare Association of America. She is the author of *Shakespeare's Festive Tragedy: The Ritual Foundations of Genre* (1995); coeditor of *Tragedy* (a critical anthology, 1998), and editor of *The Female Tragic Hero in English Renaissance Drama* (2002). Her current projects include editing a collection of essays on early modern prose fiction and a critical edition of Richard Johnson's *Seven Champions of Christendom*.

John W. Lowe is professor of English and comparative literature and director of the program in Louisiana and Caribbean Studies at Louisiana State University, where he teaches African American, southern, and ethnic literature and theory. He is author of *Jump at the Sun: Zora Neale Hurston's Cosmic Comedy* (1994), editor of *Conversations with Ernest Gaines* (1995), and *Bridging Southern Cultures* (2005), and coeditor of *The Future of Southern Letters* (1996). He is currently completing *The Americanization of Ethnic Humor*, a cross-cultural, multidisciplinary examination of changing patterns in American comic literature.

Gerald Lynch is professor of English specializing in Canadian literature at the University of Ottawa. His books include *Stephen Leacock: Humour and Humanity* (1998), *The One and the Many: English-Canadian Short Story Cycles* (2001), and the compilation *Leacock on Life* (2002). He is also the author of four books of fiction, including the novels *Troutstream* (1995) and *Exotic Dancers* (2001).

Raquel Medina-Bañón is associate professor of modern Spanish literature at the University of Massachusetts-Amherst. She has published widely on contemporary Spanish poetry, modern Spanish women writers, and contemporary Spanish culture. She is the author of the book *Surrealismo en la poesía española de posguerra* (1997) and the coeditor of and contributor to a collection of essays on Spanish women studies entitled *Sexualidad y escritura* (1850–2000) (2002).

Margaret Mikesell is professor of English at John Jay College, the City University of New York. She coedited *Othello: An Annotated Bibliography* (1990); *The Instruction of a Christen Woman* by Juan Luis Vives (2002); and a book of essays, *Culture and Change: Attending to Early Modern Women* (2003). She has published articles on Vives, Shakespearean comedy, and Jacobean tragedy. She is active in both local and national groups on early modern women (since its inception serving on the planning committee of the Attending to Early Modern Women conferences, University of Maryland). She is currently working on a study of gender in Hamlet.

Frank J. Miles is a master's candidate in the Institute for Research in African American Studies at Columbia University. He graduated with honors from Rutgers College and copyedited at the Philadelphia *Inquirer*.

Lawrence E. Mintz is associate professor of American Studies and director of the Art Gliner Center for Humor Studies at the University of Maryland. His publications include *Humor in America* (1988) and numerous book chapters, reviews, and conference papers, nearly all of which deal with humor or popular culture. Most recently he has been working on tourism and themed environments.

Nina daVinci Nichols is professor of English at Rutgers University, where she teaches Shakespearean and other drama. Since receiving her Ph.D. from New York University, she has written, adapted, developed, and translated plays, ancient and modern, and served as dramaturg the past four years for the Pulse Ensemble Theater. Her work as drama critic appears regularly in the distinguished journal *Shakespeare Newsletter*, and as a feature in *CultureVulture.net*. Her recent essay, "Dreams, Sprites, and the Recognition Game" (on *The Tempest*), will appear in *Shakespeare and Italy*, edited by M. Marrapodi for Cambridge University Press. Nichols has published five books including *Pirandello and Film* (1996), which surveys modern Italian stage and screen comedy.

Don L. F. Nilsen and Alleen Pace Nilsen have been on the faculty in the English Department at Arizona State University, Tempe since the mid-1970s. Don teaches linguistics and Alleen teaches English education. Between 1982 and 1987, they organized annual conferences on academic approaches to humor held on April Fool's Day weekends. They are founding members of the International Society for Humor Studies. Don served as its executive secretary between 1988 and 2004. Alleen edited the "Humor in the News" column for the organization's quarterly journal between 1993 and 2003. They are coauthors of the *Encyclopedia of 20th-Century American Humor* (2000), which was chosen as one of the 20 Outstanding Reference Books by the American Library Association and an Outstanding Academic Book by *Choice* magazine.

John Richetti is A. M. Rosenthal Professor of English at the University of Pennsylvania. Among his books are *Popular Fiction before Richardson: Narrative Patterns 1700–1739* (1969), *Defoe's Narratives: Situations and Structures* (1975),

Philosophical Writing: Locke, Berkeley, Hume (1983), *The English Novel in History, 1700–1780* (1999), and the forthcoming *The Life of Daniel Defoe* (2005). He is also the editor of *The Cambridge History of English Literature: 1660–1789* (2004).

Benjamin Nathan Schachtman is a former editor of the *Medium*, the Rutgers entertainment magazine. He is currently living in Wilmington, North Carolina, where he is active in the arts community and is a founding member and codirector of the WiMPP (Wilmington Motion Picture Project), an independent, nonprofit production company.

Paul Schlueter has published widely on modern literature and other subjects. His books include *The Novels of Doris Lessing* (1973) and *Shirley Ann Grau* (1981), and his edited works include *A Small Personal Voice: Essays, Reviews, Interviews by Doris Lessing* (1974) and, with June Schlueter, *The English Novel: Twentieth Century Criticism*, Vol. 2: *Twentieth-Century Authors* (1982), *Modern American Literature* (supplement 2, 1983), and *An Encyclopedia of British Women Writers* (1988, 1999). He has published many essays on modern literature in scholarly journals and collections, as well as in such reference works as the *Encyclopaedia Britannica* and various volumes in the Dictionary of Literary Biography series. He has also published extensively as a reviewer of books, film, drama, and classical music. He taught English at Southern Illinois University and other universities for many years before turning to research and writing.

Norman R. Shapiro is professor of romance languages and literatures at Wesleyan University and a translator of French poetry, prose, and theater. His many published volumes span centuries, genres, and styles, from Anne Hébert's Canadian thriller *Kamouraska* (1973) and Jean Raspail's controversial *The Camp of the Saints* (1975) to the farces of Feydeau (*Four Farces of Georges Feydeau*, 1970; *Feydeau, First to Last*, 1982; *A Flea in Her Rear, and Other Vintage French Farces*, 1994); from the largely political and social poems of black Africa and the Caribbean (*Negritude*, 1971) to a nine-century array of French fables (*The Fabulists French*, 1992); from the lyrics of Marot, Du Bellay, and Ronsard (*French Renaissance Lyrics*, 2002) to the very different lyrics of Baudelaire (*Selected Poems from "Les Fleurs du mal,"* 1998) and Verlaine (*A Hundred and One Poems of Paul Verlaine*, 1999). His most recent translations are two plays by New Orleans mulatto Victor Séjour (*The Jew of Seville* and *The Fortune-Teller*, 2002) and *Creole Echoes: Francophone Poems of 19th-Century Louisiana*, 2003). His *Complete Fables of La Fontaine* and *The Distaff and the Pen: Nine Centuries of French Women Poets* will appear in 2006.

Kirsten Thompson is an assistant professor of film studies in the English Department at Wayne State University. She specializes in animation and contemporary American, German, and New Zealand cinema. She is coeditor with Terri Ginsberg of *Perspectives on German Cinema* (1996) and is the author of several articles, including "Fear and Trembling: Adaptations of *Cape Fear*" in *Film and Literature: The Reader* (2004); "Once Were Warriors: New Zealand's First Indigenous Blockbuster" in *Blockbusters* (2003), and "Ah Love! Zee Grand Illusion! Pepé Le Pew, Narcissism and Cats in the Casbah" in *Reading the Rabbit: Explorations in Warner Bros. Animation* (1998).

Andrew Welsh is an associate professor, recently retired, of English and comparative literature at Rutgers University, where he taught poetry, folklore, and medieval literature and language. He is the author of *Roots of Lyric* (1978, 1987), which was awarded both the James Russell Lowell Prize of the Modern Language Association of America and the Melville Cane Award of the Poetry Society of America. His articles on romance and on Old English, Middle English, and Middle Welsh literature have appeared in the journals *Cambridge Medieval Celtic Studies, Philological Quarterly, Speculum, Viator*, and elsewhere. Other encyclopedia articles of his are published in *The New Princeton Encyclopedia of Poetry and Poetics* (1993), the *Dictionary of Literary Biography: Old and Middle English Literature* (1994), and *Medieval Folklore: An Encyclopedia of Myths, Legends, Tales, Beliefs, and Customs* (2000, 2002).

Alyson Waters teaches in the French Department at Yale University, edits the journal *Yale French Studies*, and is a translator. In 2004, she was awarded a National Endowment for the Arts translation grant to translate Vassilis Alexakis's 2002 novel *Les mots étrangers*. She lives in Brooklyn, New York, with her husband and daughter. She likes to quote Alphonse Allais in her spare time.

Susan Welsh is associate professor of English and director of the Writing Program at Indiana University of Pennsylvania, where she teaches introductory and advanced writing courses. Her articles on American literature and on composition have appeared in *Modern Language Studies, Poe Studies*, and *College Composition and Communication*. She has also published a biographical essay in *Past and Promise: Lives of New Jersey Women* (1990).

Carina Yervasi is assistant professor of French at Swarthmore College. She specializes in francophone film and contemporary French literature. She has published articles on film in *SITES: The Journal of 20th-Century/Contemporary French Studies, Film and History*, and *Film/Literature Quarterly*. She is completing a manuscript on francophone West African film.

Ref PN 6147 .C565 2005 v.2

Comedy